THE BUDAPEST MODEL

A liberal urban policy experiment

Edited by

Katalin Pallai

Consultants

János Atkári, László Láng, Sándor Tóth

Cover photos

Gábor Demszky

Budapest, 2003

First edition published by

Open Society Institute – Budapest /
Local Government and Public Service Reform Initiative (OSI/LGI)

Nádor utca 11., 1051. Budapest, Hungary;
Telephone: (+36 1) 327 3104

The publication was sponsored by

World Bank, World Bank Institute, DEXIA
Open Society Institute – Budapest /
Local Government and Public Service Reform Initiative (OSI/LGI)

Copy editor

Martin Tisne

Translators

Iván Sellei, Tibor Szendrei

Individual papers © World Bank, World Bank Institute
The whole book © Open Society Institute – Budapest

ISBN 963 9419 49 4

CONTENTS

INTRODUCTION

Running a city is an extremely complex affair. Day in, day out, the politician who undertakes this task has to make difficult choices between options that do not lend themselves to comparison. He or she has to decide whether to give priority to sewage treatment, traffic regulation, educational development or welfare provision. The politician might consider all these tasks to be important, yet is constrained by limited resources that are not sufficient to address them simultaneously. The city's leader has to weigh the various goals against each other and devise strategies whereby noble objectives can be transformed from dreams into reality.

Budapest is a multi-dimensional and exciting city rich in traditions and values, that at the same time displays serious deficiencies and causes for concern. It is a major challenge to manage it effectively. This was especially true in the years immediately following the Socialist era when the city and its local government, discarding its old way of functioning, had to devise a strategy to meet the demands of an emerging democracy and free market economy.

The city's leaders had to replace the Socialist-type approach to local politics (which maximized central subsidies and depended heavily on the will of the central authorities) with a new approach that aimed to adapt to the new political context by optimizing the resource allocations of the autonomous local governments. Simultaneously, they had to restructure and streamline the executive organs and decision procedures on the local level. All these they had to accomplish in the wake of the change of the political system, when the public sphere still lacked a clear set of democratic principles and the economic resources of the developed market economies were not yet present in Hungary.

The term 'Budapest model' is used to comprehensively identify the approach and the set of urban management methods and solutions which the key figures of the municipal leadership have devised over the past twelve years.

The 'Budapest model' is the product of the period when the Municipality of Budapest adapted to post-Socialist conditions. In those years the transformation of the city's financial management was inevitable. It served to enable the benefits and potentials of the local governments' new-found independence to arise, and ensured responsible management and balanced operation. The course of Budapest's urban management policies was based on the careful assessment of the potential for change of the economic, financial and political contexts, rather than being pronouncedly vision-driven. The adaptation process was centered around financial reform, and within that, on the reform of planning.

The present volume focuses on the city's financial management. The studies all refer to the financial context when discussing the transformation of the general urban management policies and practices of the city. The same applies to the articles on strategic planning. We do obviously not consider financial management to be a technical issue. Instead, we prefer to define it as an activity that enables the city's leaders to translate their principles and objectives into practice and to implement their most important political decisions.

The decision of whether Budapest has been managed effectively or poorly during the past dozen years falls beyond the competence of those who have been actively involved in the shaping of the city's urban policies. Despite all the tensions, conflicts and grievances, since the change of the political system the citizens of Budapest have cast their votes for practically the same group of people to lead the city. It is no exaggeration to say that the majority of Budapest's inhabitants approve of the city's leaders' performance. If only for this, it is worthwhile to take a closer look at their approach. The history of the past twelve years, complete with the city leaders' actions, successes and failures, deserves a comprehensive analysis. This is what the present volume attempts to do.

We introduce the reforms in their immediate context. The first study focuses on the broader political environment, while the second offers a detailed analysis of the local government's operating conditions and its comprehensive policies during the transition period. These two studies lay the foundations for the ensuing discussion of the financial management reform process. The reform of the budget management processes is discussed separately from the public utility policies pursued by independent, extra-budgetary companies. The individual reforms and decisions are tackled following the logic of political decision making: first we look at the starting conditions and assess the potential approaches based on the city leaders' liberal thinking, and then we provide an analysis of the actual steps taken and results achieved.

This volume assesses the reform of Budapest's urban management policies over the past twelve years. The chapters of this study look into the individual areas and aspects of the process. In order for us to provide our readers with the appropriate contextual background, we had at certain points to reiterate the guiding values of the city's leaders, the key elements of the broader political environment or the fundamental tools of urban management. We hope that this redundancy will enable readers to consult the chapters and studies herein independently from one other.

The studies were written by experts who were directly and actively involved in the reform process. They rely on facts and evidence in their accounts, and describe the way the city's leaders assess their own achievements and failures. The authors draw on first-hand experience, and seek to present the reality that lay behind the documents and the motives behind the decisions that were made. They shed light on facts and considerations often unknown to the external observer, and thus contribute greatly to future research.

Although the authors were actively involved in the reform process, all authors have done their best to provide objective, critical and – wherever possible – neutral accounts of the developments. The last study of the volume is an exception: the concluding analysis of the broader context of the reform process and of the 12-year history of Hungary's local governments was written by experts who had no direct involvement in the municipality's reform process.

During the past 12 years, Budapest has been led by liberal politicians. The liberal Mayor was in minority in the first four-year term, and since then has been working in coalition with the reformed Communist party. It is also important to note that the national political scene went through quite radical changes over the period at issue (with liberalism playing a key role only during the change of the political system). In their analyses of the 'Budapest model', the authors evaluate the policies of the Budapest Municipal Government against the constantly changing (and often contradictory) national political context. The track record of the leaders of Budapest provides an example for the practical implementation of liberal principles, and reveals the potentials these principles have to adjust to a fundamentally non-liberal broader environment.

It is an uplifting and invigorating experience to be in charge of a large city. In the case of Budapest – a city so very rich in traditions, controversies and problems – the challenge is particularly great. The achievements and failures of Budapest's leaders will certainly be of interest to those who follow the transition process in Eastern Europe or have a vested professional interest in this sphere. The studies in the present volume may also provide lessons to the mayors and citizens of other post-Socialist countries who tread the same thorny path.

LECTORI SALUTEM!

Katalin Pallai

CONTRIBUTORS

ATKÁRI, JÁNOS – politician. Before the political changes he was an editor of a monthly review, then the deputy editor- in - chief of an economic daily. He translated several books and studies on economy and economic philosophy into Hungarian. He has been working for the Municipality of Budapest since 1991, first as press secretary, later as the head of the Cabinet of the Mayor. He was elected a member of the General Assembly with the support of the liberal Alliance of Free Democrats in 1994 and has been the deputy mayor responsible for financial matters since then.

DEMSZKY, GÁBOR – politician, the Mayor of Budapest since 1990. By education he is a lawyer and sociologist. Before the political changes he was an editor of a monthly review of social sciences and took part in research programs of sociology. He was one of the leading figures of the opposition movement in Hungary and the founder of the AB underground publishing house. He is also one of the founders of the liberal Alliance of Free Democrats and a member of the party's leading body. All reforms and policies constituting the so called Budapest Model and included in this book have been drafted and implemented during his terms in office.

GYŐRI, PÉTER – economist, sociologist. He is a Ph.D. in sociology and a university lecturer. He conducted research projects in urban sociology, focusing on the status of the poor in Budapest and published studies on the housing situation, lifestyle and indebtedness of the low income families in the 1980s and 1990s. He was a member of the General Assembly between 1990 and 2002, and the chairman of the Welfare Policy and Housing Committee. He played a leading role in drafting and implementing the Budapest homeless aid system, the system of public utility allowances and also the program for the rehabilitation of the capital city's backward districts.

HORVÁTH, TAMÁS M. – specialist in public administration. He is a professor at the Faculty of Political and Legal Sciences of the University of Debrecen, deputy general director of the Hungarian Institute of Public Administration, has a Ph.D. and a post-doctoral degree in political and legal sciences. He published books and papers on public administration, on local government affairs and on public service management. Policy proposals on local government legislation have been done in different countries.

LÁNG, LÁSZLÓ – specialist in local government administration and finance. He has been a member of the expert team of the Mayor in his Secretariat since 1992 in different positions; at present chief co-ordinator of planning. He has been a participant in the drafting and implementation of the economic and urban policy reforms in Budapest. Before the political changes he was a teacher, translator, later editor of books and economic reviews, editor of an economic daily.

PALLAI, KATALIN – specialist in urban policies and finance. Since 1991, as a freelance expert, she has been working directly for the Mayor and for his expert team. She was a participant in the drafting and implementation of the economic and urban policy reforms in Budapest. Several times she led expert teams drafting various comprehensive urban policy documents. She is also involved in training activities and consulting in various countries of the post socialist region on the commissions of major international institutions and firms.

PÉTERI, GÁBOR – Economist, PhD, research director of the Local Government and Public Service Reform Initiative (LGI), affiliated with Open Society Institute-Budapest. Consultant for local governments. After a decade at the Hungarian Institute of Public Administration he worked as a freelance consultant on several projects in Hungary with the British Know How Fund, US AID and the World Bank. In 1996/97 he was actively involved in launching the Council of Local Government Associations, an umbrella organization of municipal associations. Published extensively in local finance, financial management, municipal policy formulation, finances of public education.

SZŰCS, FERENC – economist. At Finance Research Co., he is the executive responsible for businesses, directing the business activity and consulting branch of the company since 1989. Since 1991, he has been doing consulting for local governments (Budapest and other big cities) in reorganizing their public utility companies and preparing them for privatization, in organizing privatization transactions, in working out investment constructions and other special accounting constructions.

TÓTH, SÁNDOR – specialist in local government administration and finance. Following the political changes he was a representative in a district local government and a deputy district mayor. He worked for the municipal Expo-office between 1992-1994. He has been the head of the financial deputy mayor's office since 1994. He is a participant in the drafting and implementation of the economic and urban policy reforms in Budapest.

VALENTINY, PÁL – economist. A Ph.D., senior research fellow in the Research Institute of Economics at the Hungarian Accademy of Sciences. His main fields of research are the theory of regulated markets and questions related to the regulation and privatization of networked infrastructure. As an expert, he took part in the creation of the conditions for the privatization process in Hungary. Between 1994-1998, he was a member of the Board of Directors of the Hungarian Electric Works. Requested by the Municipality of Budapest he has made analyses on the privatization and deregulation of public utilities in Western Europe. He was a member of the Advisory Board on Privatization of the Municipality of Budapest and of the team working out the privatization concept for the Budapest Water Works. Since 1993 he has been a member of the Board of Directors of the Budapest Gas Works.

VINCE, PÉTER – economist. He is a senior research fellow at the Research Institute of Economics at the Hungarian Academy of Sciences. His main fields of research are behavior of firms, different organizational and adjustment patterns of firms; innovation and entrepreneurship; transformation and decentralization of monopolized industrial organizational structure; energy policy; privatization and regulation of public utilities; corporate governance in transforming economies. Between 1993 and 2003 he was a member of the Board of Directors of the Budapest District Heating Company and since 2003 he has been a member of the Financial Control Committee of the Assembly of the Municipality of Budapest.

VOSZKA, ÉVA – economist, working at the Finance Research Co. During the last years she has published several books and articles on the transformation and privatization of large en-

URBAN POLITICS AND POLICY

LIBERALISM IN PRACTICE

GÁBOR DEMSZKY

I assume that our readers – and especially those who live outside Hungary – are interested in our efforts and achievements for fundamentally different reasons, depending on whether they are more used to living in a Western or an Eastern economic culture.

The success of Budapest's municipal leaders in keeping this Eastern European city afloat during transition to a market economy and multi-party democracy may interest Western readers wishing to learn more about the city's financial management system (also known as the "Budapest model"). Budapest is capable of holding its own ground, and for all the difficulties it has encountered, the city is able to manage its own life. The question is: How does it succeed in doing that?

Our readers from the East, who most likely include local government officials and municipal leaders, may have first-hand experience of what it means to have scarce resources. They see Budapest as a creditworthy city that duly services its debts. Again: How does it succeed in this? (To quote Iago in Shakespeare's Othello, "Go, make money!" – But how?) This book will analyze the "how."

When I sat down to write this introduction, I felt a strong urge to delve deep into some of the most interesting professional aspects of this problem. However, I decided instead to let the authors of the studies below describe and evaluate the city's recent history and current status. I would rather not take the bread out of their mouths.

Nevertheless, I shall attempt to very briefly summarize basic issues relating to the capital city's economic and financial management, but first of all, I shall give an account of my personal experience as Mayor of Budapest. Being a liberal politician, I shall give a subjective assessment of the significance of the local government system and related economic and financial problems, and I shall also highlight those phenomena and lessons that I believe our readers should pay attention to.

None of Hungary's new political parties had any experience in 1990 of how to apply the rules of the game called Democracy in everyday political practice. The new political leaders of Budapest, who came to office after the political system turned democratic, also lacked prior experience in public administration. While the political parties already had a brief – 18-month – "practice period" covering the direct transition process, local government leaders had to take the plunge immediately.

There was perhaps one thing only that was clear to us all: we were aware of our own scale of values. In a short length of time we drafted a document based on these values: this became the policy platform of the mayor of Budapest. In a single volume it summarized the liberal mayor's approach to, and goals for, the city.

It goes without saying that these approaches and goals have since been modified in several respects. For the most part, they have become more complex and comprehensive, while the basic principles have remained unchanged. I would say that the 1990s were the start of a learning process for all of us.

The concepts mentioned or referred to in this volume form part of a system, which we – rightly or wrongly – identify as the "Budapest model." These concepts are all products of this learning process. Some of them had been around for ages, while others we created on the fly. Through these concepts we attempted to find answers to the questions that were posed by reality and experience.

CREDO I

"We have never made it all the way to civil society. This task is still ahead of us. We must consult the theoreticians of the 17th century. The British thinkers of the 17th century are of utmost relevance today. […] At issue here is lawfulness, which also entails the rehabilitation of civil virtues. This is our only hope." The above statements come from two unidentified activists of the democratic opposition in Budapest. Hans Magnus Enzensberger quoted them in his 1985 essay entitled Hungarian Confusions. The essay was published as a samizdat on mimeographed sheets. I am holding a copy in my hand: the pages are foxed and hardly legible. It fills me with pride that the works of Enzensberger, along with those of such classics of Hungarian liberal thought as István Bibó and Oszkár Jászi, reached many a reader in Budapest thanks to the activists of the underground press.

Having read through this outstanding political travelogue again, I am inclined to conclude that those "confusions" were not so confusing. True enough, in those years we in Budapest (along with our colleagues in Prague and Warsaw) applied ourselves to the works of the classical theoreticians of liberal thought. I recall a seminar on the works of J.S. Mill, which was held by the democratic opposition in a private apartment. Of course, at the time none of those present would have reasonably expected the theories we read about ever to be translated into reality by a change in the political system.

In retrospect, we must admit that reality has far exceeded our political anticipations. In other words, I would say that liberalism scored an exceptionally fast (although far from complete) victory in those countries where the period of transition to democracy ran consistently. However, right upon its victory, liberalism was confronted with the question of whether its triumph had eliminated the reasons for its own existence. The question is whether liberalism's popular elements (such as constitutional democracy or the market economy) have become "common property," shared by other schools of political philosophy as well, while the elements that *have* remained exclusively within the domain of liberalism (such as the protection of minorities) are utterly unpopular.

I do not share this view. However, the election records of the liberal parties appear to buttress the above argument. In the Czech Republic, the Civil Forum lost its seats in Parliament in the previous elections, and in Hungary the Alliance of Free Democrats (SZDSZ) could barely qualify for the legislature in the past two election rounds. The SZDSZ's only consolation was that it could retain support in Budapest and in a few large cities.

The liberals' loss of popularity on the Hungarian national scene is partly overwritten by their three consecutive victories in the capital city's municipal elections. And this comes despite the fact that Hungarian liberals have constantly been looked down upon, practically since the first day of the democratic turn of the system, by those who have a hard time accepting freedom – if at all. They argue that liberalism had its day with the change of the system, and that since then the pendulum has swung way too much toward freedom. They think the time is ripe to rehabilitate the rule of "order," to revive the traditions of servility, and to restore the public's trust in the caring goodwill of "our party and government." They believe that liberalism is a thing of the past in the West as well, and this is how they explain the relatively small size and weight of the liberal parties there.

I think they are wrong. First: the freedom of liberalism is also a kind of order: the order of exercising the fundamental human rights. Those oppose the strictly regulated enforcement of these rights and cry for "order" instead, who are unable to tolerate the articulation and representation of interests other than theirs, and strive for the exclusive dominance of the "order" of their own interest groups. Liberalism has always supported the establishment of a social order based on the principle of human integrity and individual rights, and effective for each member of the society, Second: there is no denying that in certain countries of Western Europe liberal parties are small, but this does not mean that liberalism carries no weight there. Quite the contrary: liberalism is alive and well, and to an extent all the important parties have become liberals themselves. In Western Europe all the large center-right and center-left parties have identified with the most important tenets of liberalism. If and where they fail to do so, they tend to be kept away from power by the voters.

This is what the electorate did to the Social Democrats in Germany and the Labour Party in Britain, and this is why the Democrats in the United States could not come to power for twelve straight years. Their opposition status ended when they adopted the most important liberal principles in their platforms. US President Bill Clinton, UK Prime Minister Tony Blair, and German Chancellor Gerhard Schroeder entered the scene. They revived their parties by offering a new ideology, which political analysts call the "Third Way." By adopting this new ideology, left-wing parties also admit that there is no alternative to the market economy, and that canceling the reforms introduced by former UK Prime Minister Margaret Thatcher and US President Ronald Reagan in the 1980s would amount to political suicide. Let us add that these were liberal reforms, even though they are associated with the names of conservative politicians. Today, the social democratic parties proclaim essentially liberal principles: they want the state to withdraw and yield more ground to the private sector. In fact, these parties do more than just proclaim these principles: in France, the Socialist government went on with privatization much faster than its right-wing successor.

In the West, nobody thinks of nationalization any more. Privatization is the call of the day, and the parties in power strive to curtail the state's bureaucratic activities and broaden economic freedom. In the wake of the experiments of the 20th century it became clear that the less involved the state is in a country's economy the freer the people become. The state's withdrawal results in more rational economic policy decisions, less squandering, and more efficient work, and thus the public's relative welfare will increase.

In the early 1960s South Korea and the Sudan had a rather similar development status. Today, South Korea counts among the richest countries of the world, while the Sudanese still have to rely on humanitarian assistance. It falls upon us, liberals, to dispel the myth that more freedom entails a higher level of inequality. Inequality is most marked in those countries of the Third World where economic freedom is restricted by detailed regulations and widespread corruption.

Of course, Enzensberger could find further anti-liberal "Hungarian confusions" in today's domestic political scene. For example, he could analyze the political evolution of the former Hungarian Prime Minister and his party, the Alliance of Young Democrats (Fidesz). The dissolution of their liberal principles and program in exchange for a chance to become the leader of the conservative national right is clearly shown by using the liberal-led capital city as a scorecard – even by violation of the law. A grave example of this is the Fidesz-government's unilateral cancellation of the agreement between the State and the Municipality on co-financing the construction of a new Metro line. According to the court of justice this was a breach of contract.

An established and civilized market economy is not compatible with fraud, contract violations, and bullying. Instead, it is based on co-operation, credibility, constitutionality, and a permanent quest for mutual benefits. It was on this basis that the capital city decided to protect its rights by going to court against the government. In four instances, the court ruled in Budapest's favor. We, Hungarian liberals, would like to live in a country where nobody, not even the government, can cancel contracts without consequences, and where nobody, and especially not the government, can be superior to law. Let us just recall Enzensberger's words: "At issue here is lawfulness, which also entails the rehabilitation of civil virtues."

A contract is worth less than the sheet on which it was written if there is no efficient and unbiased constitutionality behind it and unless the appropriate tools to make the potential violators observe their commitments and pay for the losses they have caused are in place. The citizens of those countries where the holders of power and influence regularly ignore contracts, live in gangster capitalism and not in a free market. Furthermore, they live in destitution. We could cite examples by the plenty from developing or post-communist countries. The rule of law is a prerequisite to the welfare of the people. In a market economy, keeping one's word is considered a cardinal virtue.

What is ahead for Hungary? Of course, I know that liberalism has not a strong tradition in Eastern Europe, thus neither in Hungary. Liberal politics has never enjoyed mass support. But the trend-line of the economic-political turn that has taken place in the Eastern-European countries coincides with the liberal efforts, and the drive of transformation provides a historic opportunity for establishing Hungary as the society of free and responsible citizens. I believe that the country will have a better chance to join the European path under the new government elected in 2002.

FOR A CIVIL BUDAPEST

Twelve years ago, the only development in Budapest that could be described as "modern" was the fast ghettoization of some of its formerly upstanding neighborhoods. This happened in a city which ranks among the most scenic in the world, and which has always been considered one of the region's foremost economic and cultural centers. Budapest has always attracted more than just capital (at least when it was allowed to do so). This is the only city in the region where the locals simultaneously know and appreciate the origins and works of Eminescu, Caragiale, Musil, Andrić, Mrožek, Gombrowicz, and Hrabal.

The sad state of Budapest was a true reflection of the fiasco of forty years of dictatorship. Behind the perceptible decay you could find an empty treasury and senseless squandering. At stake in the municipal elections of 1990, which brought the liberals - who have been at the helm ever since - to power, was the so-called democratic opposition's ability to introduce and implement its liberal modernization program. We had to prove that we knew how to steer the city out of its crisis in a functional and morally acceptable manner.

Ever since the liberals' victory in 1990, the moderate members of the political opposition have been recounting their argument that liberalism may have its merits but has nothing to do with Hungary. That it may be appropriate in the "developed" West but is not applicable in the backward and historically tormented Central-Eastern European region. They argue that liberalism places intolerable burdens on the socially handicapped, and only helps to broaden the gaps within society.

I have always been irritated by this half-hearted and disparaging attitude. I firmly believe that the past twelve years have furnished convincing proofs against the arguments of those who would rather reject freedom than live with it. The liberals' modernization program is successful, and Budapest has caught up with other major European cities. Today, in terms of quality of life or professional career development Budapest is on par with Vienna, London, or Paris.

The demise of socialism has made it clear that history will not repeat itself in this part of the world. The former regime's modernization concepts were based on central planning and central distribution, and culminated in wastefulness and the exhaustion of economic reserves. Even if we had wanted to, we could not have practiced the same policies, simply because all the resources were gone. We chose to follow another path. We, politicians and urban development experts, were determined to enable citizens to become masters of their own life. Politics should not aim for more, but cannot aim for less either.

In a constitutional democracy, the citizen commands respect and defends his or her own rights. The citizen is never at the mercy of "benefactors." The citizen does not allow the state to fob him off with the leftovers of redistribution. Quite the contrary: the citizen expects politicians and public servants to spend his tax money on honest and decent work for the benefit of all, and to promote the welfare of both the individuals and their freely formed communities. The citizen does not court the favor of the mighty. Quite the contrary: the party politicians curry favors with him and the public servants serve him. The citizen assumes responsibility for himself and feels responsible for the community. Should the state grow out of proportions in peacetime, the citizens of Budapest will react with their invincible sense of humor. In this city it is not appreciated if the state prescribes what or whom to love and how to live. Budapest is a city of free citizens.

In Budapest it is natural to hear all kinds of music in the bars, that people from all over the world stroll the streets downtown, or that there should be churches for all religions and denominations. This is a city where knowing what is on in terms of plays, concerts, movies, or parties takes time, for there is simply so much on offer.

The liberals respect and love this diversity, as they themselves are different. They have been serving this free city for twelve years, and have learned a lot from its citizens.

The checks and balances inherent in local government have on many occasions proved an insurmountable obstacle to authoritarian ambitions.

In our opinion, the state should be strong whenever and wherever it has constitutional tasks. The state does not have a direct role to play in the life of the citizens' self-organized groups, and should not meddle with legitimate local governments, except for those cases when it has constitutionally prescribed servicing or legal controlling responsibilities.

It is our task to protect the distinctive spirit of Budapest, which includes its citizens' stubborn sense of independence, of humor, of solidarity, the diversity of their cultures and their right to lead a free life. It is our task to restrict the state's powers, and to keep its influence within the bounds of constitutionality.

SCALE OF VALUES

Let us now recount the values that we considered crucial to the success of our work.

First, we thought we should take democratic institutions seriously: Institutions we have always supported and accepted. In a multi-party system there are several powers shaping politics, and we are but one of them. Accordingly, we believe we should strive to enforce our interests in this context – to the extent that we can do so.

We believe we should also respect the fact that a capitalist system is based on private property and the free market. We do not consider this merely as an external factor, this is something we wholeheartedly support. The previous forty years have provided us with first-hand experience in the dysfunctional nature of the voluntaristic socialist system. The inefficiency of the system was such that it simply could not generate the resources required for providing long-term welfare to the citizens, for regenerating itself, or for becoming competitive on international markets. That system was doomed to lag behind and fail.

If this country aims to remain competitive, it must give preference to an efficient economic system based on private property and the free market. Consequently, its local governments must operate amid these considerations and conditions. In other words, we believe that things should be construed as they are, within their context. When we talk about services, we should consider prevailing market conditions. Similarly, social issues (which are also tied to market conditions) should also be considered within their own, in part market-defined, context. Failure to follow these rules would lead us towards a less transparent and less efficient economic system.

This is especially true in post-socialist societies, where the switch to market-based prices and wages caught people unprepared. (This was made worse by the fact that wage increases always come second to price increases. The reasons for which I will not discuss here.)

A transition of this magnitude represents a serious economic challenge for any country and society. The transition from state socialism to market-based capitalism is a costly undertaking, and thus results in a predictable economic downturn. Transition also creates significant social differences.

Hungary was no exception to this rule. By the mid-1990s the country found itself in a serious economic crisis (at least partly due to regrettable political procrastination at the time with regards to the necessary economic reforms). This crisis then prompted the government to introduce the so-called Bokros package.[1] The package consisted of a rather incomplete set of budgetary reform measures. Without the measures entailed in this package the country could not have retained its competitive position among transition countries.

Local governments also had to adapt their activities to an economy based on market conditions. On the one hand they had to recognize the rules and workings of the market, while on the other they had to find the most economical ways to manage public funds. Local governments had to rid their public expenditures from wasteful elements in order to maintain or even improve the quality of public services. This way they could also pay more attention to the needs of socially handicapped people living under their authority.

THE POLITICAL CONTEXT

We have always known that urban policy decisions hail from political contexts. However, it was interesting and new for us to experience first-hand (i.e. on an empirical and not merely theoretical level) how the economic context also strongly influences these decisions. In other words, economic possibilities tend to determine the scope for political activity. We had to realize that decisions aimed at promoting the common good (which, at least in principle, can be the goal of any political leadership irrespective of its political-ideological identity) are reached within an extremely tight political scope. There is always some room for decisions that extend beyond providing basic services, but this tends to be very small. The scope of the decisions we make is limited by insufficient development potentials and by the tasks that local governments are bound by law to fulfill.

---

[1] Finance Minister Lajos Bokros introduced his stabilization program on March 12, 1995.

Furthermore, we had to realize that these decisions tend to have very strong political overtones. Political parties tend to interpret even the most obvious issues as if they and they alone know the answer. The parties want to show the public that they are different, and go out of their way to capitalize on this. We have experienced this quite often with our coalition partner as well. All in all, this phenomenon has been increasingly characteristic of the decade following our transition to democracy.

In Budapest, the city's peculiar public administration system has led to a very strong overpoliticization of decisions. When the local government system was established, the districts of the city received a status equal to that of the Municipality of Budapest. Each district has an elected mayor, a body of representatives, an independent budget, and local legislative powers. The local governments of the districts are not subjected in any form to the municipality. The municipality is responsible for the services that affect the city as a whole (e.g., public transportation, waste management, clean drinking water supply, etc.), and has the power to approve "umbrella" legislation (e.g., by setting general construction rules, identifying development zones, or setting general rules for pay parking) under the relevant higher-level laws. The only restriction that applies here is that the districts' detailed regulations must not contradict the capital city's "umbrella" legislation. In certain areas the city and the districts divide up the tasks through special agreements (e.g., in the fields of education or health care).

This is why the political battlefield is much larger in Budapest than elsewhere in the country. The city's and the districts' particular interests tend to clash rather dramatically, and professional issues often assume marked political overtones. In other words, the compulsion to be politically different often takes over.

Seen from the mayor's chair, all this may be described (with a touch of self-irony) as uncomfortable. I believe that there is room for reform in this field. Of course, these reforms should be well considered and democratic, and should not result in over-centralization or the violation of legitimate and equitable forms of interest representation.

Although independent experts have worked out several models during the past decade, we have not yet seen a satisfactory solution that would command consensus-based support. Pending that, we are bound to stick with the current municipal system, which is overheated, overpoliticized, and lacking in rationality. However, in principle it is still better than centralized absolutism.

The situation described above has also had some positive results in that we were forced to learn the rules of democracy. I do not believe to be exaggerating when I state that the leaders of the Municipality of Budapest have had to take more "classes in democracy" than the leaders of the Hungarian state.

We had to learn to co-operate, to seek compromises, but never for a moment did we withdraw from our principles, whether in the fields of economy, welfare or cultural policy. We had to approach public life in a principled manner, and occasionally confront other people's less principled positions. We had to learn to recognize the fact that those democratic forces that are different from us also have a right to – and, in fact, must – exist. We had to learn to stay in contact with them, co-operate with them, clash with them, and even to suffer defeat from them. In short, we had to (and still have to) learn to "behave" in our new democracy.

In discussing the political field I aimed to make it clear that the city's liberal leaders have had to wage permanent wars and strike a series of compromises in order to enforce their will, which, after all, is quite normal.

Particularity and Totality

The following phenomenon I know from experience to be universal: a minister or the leaders of a sector are judged by the public, the press or the political sphere on the basis of the extra resources or discounts they have secured for their own fields – at the expense of other fields. I shall call this phenomenon sectoral blindness.

Of course, these ministers or leaders would never admit wishing to gain ground for their sector at the expense of other sectors. However, in a country or settlement with limited revenues, an increase (justified or not) in one sector's expenditure is necessarily to the detriment of the other sectors.

In some instances the extra (increased) expenditures may be justified, because the tasks at issue are important and require more urgent solutions. However, these examples tend to be used as justification for policies that lead to direct political gain and regretfully reinforce sectoral blindness.

True leaders who feel responsibility towards their country or local community must be able to establish when such policies should be justifiably enforced. Good leaders know how to fine-tune the diverse demands of various sectors, taking into account actual demands and shortages (including the projected shortages in preparation for the future), and yet also enforce their own value choices. They know which demands to push back and which ones to highlight. A minister is not worse than the others if he or she chooses to grant fewer priorities to his or her sector for the benefit of the country as a whole.

The accomplishments of the leaders of Budapest (or, specifically, those of a small group within that leadership), which were born out of arguments with different interest groups, both within and beyond their own party, should be understood within this context and spirit.

We have had to choose a strategy and tactics that could force the interest groups to pay heed to the development of the city as a whole.

A Fundamental Principle and a Technique

One crucial lesson that should be drawn from the city's management during the past decade is the importance of establishing and agreeing on the fundamental principles, goals, and rules of the game which the city's leadership will follow (i.e., the procedural rules pertaining to the specification of the goals). Once these goals and rules are set and approved, it becomes more difficult for politics to enforce particular interests on a day-to-day basis.

In case of disagreement on policy (e.g., by arguing over the scarceness of resources for a given task), politicians' agendas tend to muddy financial issues by couching contrary policy arguments in made-to-measure political and economic theory. This generally leads to demagogical arguments with little substance. In Hungary, the general level of political culture and economic knowledge is fairly low, and the problems at issue are complex even for professionals. Consequently, it is fairly easy to fish in troubled waters. However, by applying the principle detailed above, the chances for arbitrary and case-by-case decision-making can be significantly reduced.

Of course, in practice it is never possible to completely eliminate such practices. Moreover, in today's national and municipal political culture – due to historic and political reasons not to be analyzed here – policy of strength is gaining ground and as a consequence, it has become increasingly marked by lax discipline in reasoning and a general lack of credibility. In such circumstances it is difficult to stand by our aforementioned principle. And yet, I must say that since a liberal municipal leadership is bound to observe and honor the rules of democracy, this principle remains its most salient distinctive feature.

Administration

At the beginnings of the new regime, we politicians, did not know much of the city hall administration; only we had our doubts that the administration would be friendly to the new setup. To an extent this proved to be a political prejudice borne by those who were dissenters under the previous regime. From the beginning, the administration has been characterized by sectoral rather than political or ideological biases. It did not take long before we realized that – apart from a few exceptions – there was no need to introduce radical reforms of political nature within the administration. (In retrospect I would add that we could not have done that anyhow. Public services must never be interrupted, and a radical overhaul of the mayor's office would have required the active involvement of the administrative staff.) I believe it would be fair to state that the administrative staff at the Municipality of Budapest has been stable, notwithstanding a few recurrent organizational and personnel changes.

We have established a unified city hall administration. Having sized up our resources, we could not but realize that the previous system, under which the major sectors belonged to their respective departments and had independent budgets, resulted in the multiplication of a basis-approach financial management system and was thus especially inflexible. There were a number of independent "empires," which made it very difficult to enforce the city's overall interests. We had to eliminate this internal power-based structure in order to enable us to contrast, evaluate, and balance the tasks faced by the city as a whole.

RESTORATION ATTEMPTS

During the initial period we did not really feel just how narrow the scope really was for managing the city's finances. We did not have the experience that would have forced us to consider the long-term consequences of the prevailing financial conditions and decisions.

Our financial limitations themselves did not appear to be as tight as they were. For example, in the first year after the approval of the law on local governments the central budget's revenues from personal income taxes (PIT) were transferred to the local governments in their entirety. However, it did not take long for the state to withhold a portion of these revenues. First the transfers were reduced to 50 percent, and later to a yet smaller figure. As a result, the municipality found itself in a precarious financial situation. How could the city be expected to draft its more than HUF 100 billion annual budget? How could it earmark funds both for current tasks and for long-term investments, if tasks imposed on local governments change and increase year by year, and regulations on resource allocation change annually and adversely and in a non-systemic way?

THE GREATEST CLASH OF LOCAL DEMOCRACY

In the fall of 1993, a group of people showed up in the corridors of the Hungarian Parliament. They handed out origami-folded sheets to the representatives. On those sheets, they called on the MPs to vote against a motion by the finance minister who sought to reduce the local governments' share in the central budget's PIT revenues from 50 to 30 percent. Their counter-proposal was reasonable, considering the national burdens associated with economic transition. They sought to set this share at 35 percent.

And they nearly made it! Opposition MPs of the time all voted in favor of the 35 percent share and about a dozen representatives of the governing coalition also supported this option. However, since certain liberal MPs were regrettably absent from the vote, this constructive counter-proposal eventually got turned down.

The characters with the sheets were untiringly lobbying local government activists. Many of them were mayors themselves and many came from small towns and villages. They were fully aware that the reduction of the local governments' share from 50 percent to 30 percent was a matter of principle, as it threatened to seriously curtail local governments' financial freedom. No wonder their bitterness over the result of the vote. They knew that with each cut in the freely utilizable parts of central transfers the state further violated the principle of "local governance."

A year after the change of the system, when the PIT revenues were still transferred to the local governments in their entirety, there was a direct relationship between the local societies' income-generating potential, the settlements' budgets, and the quality of the local public utility services. The subsequently introduced balancing mechanisms managed to correct (justifiably but not properly) the disproportion between local governments' developmental possibilities.[2] However, though the balancing effort itself is justifiable, it is unacceptable

---

[2] This correction system was rather complicated. Suffice it to mention here that after 1995 the local governments' share from the PIT (Personal Income Tax) was also divided into two parts: one part was re-channeled on derivation basis to the local governments, while the other became a decisive element on the resource side of the balancing mechanism. The latter part has been constantly growing since then, and thus by now the former part has shrunk to a mere 5 percent.

that the balancing mechanism does not take into consideration the dynamism of resources both on the state and on the local government side, and equalizing is carried out exclusively within the circle of local government allocations. Thus the system brought about marked the beginning of the restoration of the system of central distribution. Since then, the Hungarian state has been sticking to this line that unfortunately leads to a well-known model.

According to the ideology of the former party-state, the state is the entity best able to assess society's needs and the related tasks it should handle. The theory assumes that it is reasonable to expect central financing to be operable and even efficient. The stealthy revival of this ideology lays the foundations for the nationalization of local governments' uncomfortable powers.

Of course, the model also entails concealing mechanisms. The state extends subsidies to certain services in the form of per-capita quotas (so-called norms[3]). These norms are specified under the state's annual budgetary laws. The state then employs the following technique: by raising these norms ("naturally" at a rate below inflation) it counters the effects of the local governments' reduced share in the PIT revenues. Eventually, the central resources channeled under two titles will even have a higher nominal value. However, it is also true that in 2000 the real value of these central resources amounted to only 62 percent of that measured in 1991. Within this, the value of the Municipality of Budapest's share dropped to 41.4 percent.

In 1989, we witnessed the fall of a social system that based its economic practices on central redistribution. It fell because it did not encourage the reinvestment of revenues, because it leveled off differences by pushing the standards downwards, and because it fettered the economy. It comes as no surprise that the liberal local government should use every legitimate tool at its disposal to counter the proponents of this restoration.

CREDO II

Looking back on the debates within the SZDSZ over the 35 percent proposal we must admit to the failure of our successive efforts to increase this figure. One reason for this was that the party's national leaders were ambiguous and half-hearted about our efforts. Hereafter I shall discuss the evolution of this fracture within the party from my viewpoint as mayor of Budapest.

In my capacity as a liberal mayor, I believe in a few simple truths.

First, that freedom, which we link with individual responsibility, serves the people better than constraints on freedom that may lead to unintended, counter-productive consequences.

---

[3] Norms: the amount of per capita quota associated with a specific type of task.

Second, that an overly centralized state has always caused more problems than it could resolve.

Third, that the people can exercise their freedom to choose on the local level as well as the central level, and that they will not misuse this right.

From all this it follows that we are deeply convinced that the citizens, through their elected representatives, are fully able to manage their own local affairs without the fatherly care of the central powers.

It was thanks to these truths that the SZDSZ became a strong or even a key player in the country's local governments.

And yet, the SZDSZ's national bodies have been less satisfied with local Free Democrats than the citizens of the towns and villages of Hungary who have supported their Free Democrat mayors. Since 1990, this strong and influential group of liberal mayors has permanently been seeking the attention and support of the party's leading bodies and parliamentary representatives. Saying that this conflict is a natural side effect of the coexistence of the central and the local political levels would amount to an oversimplification.

It is worth noting that these internal clashes always occurred during the annual negotiations on central budgets. The mayors tried to prove with their performance that the local governments' demands were worthy of the party's support. Meanwhile, the party's economic policy experts failed to expressly identify with the sums associated with these demands. These experts thought that the successful and therefore "conflict-ready" mayors posed a threat to the results of the stabilization policy. According to their misinterpretation the support of local government interests would mean the support of particular interests as confronted to the national ones. They disregarded that local governments did not expect unfair preference, only proportionate burdening. And their demands went along with efforts for structural changes and for task revisions aiming at the establishment of a rational and reasonable resource allocation system. A self-conscious liberal approach has emerged in the local government sector and collided with a non-liberal approach – within a liberal party. This conflict has always come to a head with the debates on the PIT proportion to be directly re-channeled to local governments and regrettably has reduced the question of principle into a quantitative problem of central redistribution, while the system of resource allocation continued to be distorted. The national leaders of the SZDSZ have remained silent on this fundamental issue.

One reason for this silence was that between 1994 and 1998 the balance of power within the coalition did not allow for an increase of this figure without the Socialist Party's consent.

Another reason was that the economic policy experts of both the Finance Ministry and the SZDSZ felt threatened by the "local governments' lobbyists."

To a certain extent, the part of politicians and experts may be justified who really feared the dilution of the otherwise indispensable strict financial policy line, and resisted all other forms of pressure for increasing the expenditures. At the same time, it was regrettable and unacceptable because they failed to realize that the existence of locally governed settlements is a foundation pillar of a democratic system. The local governments require the same treatment as that of the central government. Both spheres must be granted the same conditions for operation and development, in proportion to the country's load-bearing capacities.

How did this come to be seen as a threat? Well, if we take these arguments seriously, it becomes impossible to refloat the state budget on the local governments' account. Furthermore, we are talking about an exceptionally large professional challenge, and to date no state government has been able to come up to these requirements.

> *"The main problem with the current setup is that it corners both sides,"* I wrote in an analysis dating from that period. *"The local governments may be able to secure a few billion forints' worth of discounts for themselves, but they are unable to win the* [central government's] *sympathy. They deal with each other as enemies and not as partners. Meanwhile, the financial state administration is unable to define in clear and positive terms its stance on structural reforms in this sector, and thus remains unable to go beyond the mere negation of the supplementary claims."*

In this situation, it fell on the mayors and the local government bodies to internally reform the local government system and to execute the required institutional reforms.

RENEWAL

COMPULSION ON THE LOCAL GOVERNMENTS TO INNOVATE

It is my conviction that political forces must work together to accomplish the internal renewal of the local government system and to implement associated institutional reforms. The mayors and the bodies of the local governments found themselves in a fix during the past decade when they had to face these tasks on their own.

The continuous postponing of the rational, incentive but reasonable revision of state regulations do not exempt local governments from the obligation to try to increase their own scope of activity, and to renew their budgetary subsystem through innovative solutions. Once we are able to implement the pressing reforms within our jurisdiction and can make advances in savings and prove that we strive not merely for central resources, we will certainly win the sympathy and support of the government's liberal-minded economic politicians as well.

All the more so since "through our innovative techniques and cost-saving solutions we and only we can make the local governments' activities inexpensive and friendly. To this end, we must create examples and models for each other and also for the state administration," I argued at a conference of the Free Democrats where we summed up the fundamental principles behind the "Budapest model," and sought to encourage our fellow liberal mayors.

"We must admit that without reducing our operating costs we will prove unable to perform our duties and execute the developments that are expected from us. The central resources get ever tighter, and our only chance for survival is for us to maximize our revenues and reduce our expenditures.

We can prove that in our case innovation is not simply an involuntary and inevitable response to changing circumstances. By rationalizing institutional financial management and by reducing expenditures we shall meet the requirements for a responsible and economical management of the taxpayers' money. The support of the voters that we may win through our development projects will compensate for the short-term drawbacks of our restrictive policies and also for the conflicts entailed. We must change our attitude by translating our liberal principles into practical deeds."

In practice, this means the need to transform public utility companies (which used to belong to the earlier councils) into entities that follow the law of the market. The local governments and the mayors are responsible for creating new and efficient economic ventures. It falls upon us to devise solutions for involving outside capital in the development of these services. This will result in lower costs and better and higher quality services.

Consequently, the main goals of the privatization process are to involve capital in the necessary development projects and to improve efficiency through the direct controlling role of the private owner. The ultimate goal is to provide high quality services to the public in the long run. The rates associated with these services should and will be lower than those charged by the centrally financed non-market-based mammoth companies.

Public infrastructure services have already changed their outlook in order to factor in the market and outside capital. As a result, the previously static public service sector has shifted gears. The result is a spectacular development in infrastructure services. Today, natural gas is available practically everywhere, and the dynamic development of the sewage system as well as the telephone network has brought about significant changes in the quality of life all through the country.

We ought to realize that innovations by local governments lay the foundations for more comprehensive structural reforms. Occasionally, these innovations themselves qualify as structural reforms. And we must also add that this is happening against and under prevailing budgetary restrictions. This kind of attitude should be supported (and not merely tolerated) by the state. This support should manifest itself in new incentives for local governments to continue innovating.

Back in those years, we never stopped calling for structural budgetary reforms:

"If the local governments are expected to respond to the restrictions with structural innovations, then the state itself must also be innovative. This in turn requires a concept. It is not enough to stick with macro-level cardinal figures in the budget. It is not enough to 'brainstorm,' and to urge cuts in the number of local governments. We all know that the saving from this would be nominal at best. It is rather unfair to urge local

governments to increase their income from local taxation (business tax) while keeping up central tax pressures that limits overall tax paying capacities. The government should be fully aware of the actual processes that occur at the level of local public services. It should be familiar with the positive examples set by local governments."

We called for co-operation and urged the two opposing sides to think together:

"On this specific issue the Free Democrat party bodies can find common ground with the Free Democrat mayors and the liberal members of the governing coalition. Our task is to use our remaining time in office to devise a detailed action plan for these converging political approaches to meet, and to make certain to implement this plan during our next term in office.

This requires a new type of consensus between the central and local levels. This consensus should be based on the understanding that the reform of the local governments' financing system means more than simply just cutting back resources as understood by the current budgetary politicians. The state should not attempt to score apparent successes while in practice (not through legislation) limiting the possibilities of local taxation (business tax), or threatening to amalgamate small local governments. The ultimate goal is saving, and this should be primarily subjected to pertinent structural considerations, and not the other way around.

There are foreign and domestic examples galore to prove that only a thorough structural reform can result in long-term savings. Local governments should be encouraged to implement structural reforms within their own scope of authority.

In exchange, local governments can generate support for the social consensus needed for the implementation of this reform.

The success of our liberal policies hinges on the support of the authoritative local elite. Better yet, these elites should be the initiators of innovative reforms. Today we are witnessing dramatic cuts in our state resources. The leaders of cultural, educational, and other local government-owned institutions must live with the uncertainty caused by a lack of resources. Those who hold leading positions within these institutions must decide whether to choose solutions for short-term survival or instead opt to make sacrifices. Several directors of schools, hospitals, and theaters have been forced to choose between continuing their fight for survival at the head of a decaying institution, or launching and implementing strategic programs beneficial to their sector as a whole."

We urged reforms citing the classical liberal parable:

"If we want to be innovative and want to enforce our liberal convictions, we must refrain from making a fetish of the public sphere and the established forms of public supply. The liberal approach starts out from the understanding that these activities and services benefit a specific audience. A service is good if it is accessible to the largest possible number of people and gives them the greatest possible advantage

or benefit, and this at a cost that is acceptable to the given community. Society is but a crowd made up of customers. We together with the professional intellectuals interested in pursuing those reforms must heed the real and genuine demands of the public – and simultaneously reduce public expenditure – in our quest for a way to set up and operate our institutions.

By failing to do so, we fall into the trap of the 'common pasture.' According to the well-known economic metaphor, everybody can drive his or her herd out to the common pasture. Eventually, everyone will want to send more cattle to graze on the same pasture, which is limited in size. The meaning of the parable is that unlimited 'free' use of the common pasture bears the risk of bringing ruin upon all its users.

This explains the need for interference by the community, or sometimes by the state. The aim of this interference is to keep the market up and running.

I believe that we also need this kind of pressure from the budget. This pressure should strive to encourage innovation in order to achieve the desired goals. However, it must never be used to cut to size those who stand out of line."

But what about those who do not have the necessary tools for innovation, many may ask. Well, this is where the state may play a role. It must not, however, continue to level off the inertia. Instead, the state should support the efforts toward innovation in a strictly regulated manner.

Back in those years, we could not foresee that the practice of 'continuing to level off the inertia' was to survive the changes of government. Since 1998, the state's interference has been accompanied not by reforms but by selective dispensation. A year after its accession to power, the Orbán cabinet settled down to dispensing the state's resources on the basis of its political preferences. Between 1998 and 2002, conservative or right wing politicians headed the vast majority of the local governments that had access to the state's addressed grants and targeted subsidies. The liberal-socialist-led capital city did not receive central budgetary subsidies for any of its investment projects. The conservative government punished the liberal city of Budapest, which was labeled as leftist, liberal-bolshevik, and was called a 'sinner.' The policy of restrictions was replaced by open discrimination, which caused unsurpassable damage to the city. At the same time, the ruling right-wing also managed to shoot itself in the foot, as it lost the general elections in 2002 thanks to the votes of the citizens of Budapest.

OUTLINE OF THE FINANCIAL REFORM IN BUDAPEST

In Budapest, the reform of the financing system, the institutions, and the public services was largely completed during the first two election cycles following 1990. The aim of this reform was to maintain the city's operability, to identify the tasks that could be assumed, and to rationalize the execution of these tasks. In other words, the aim was to increase the city's own revenues and to switch over to a transparent and sustainable financial management system.

The bulk of the investment projects that were completed in the capital city during the past decade could only manage to keep abreast with the growing demand. Experience shows that the Municipality of Budapest must spend approximately 20 percent of its revenues on investment projects indispensable to the city's operation. This is the minimum level for investment, and yet year-on-year the city finds it very difficult to satisfy this demand. The explanation for this should, at least in part, be sought in changes in external conditions.

Since the past decade witnessed a gradual reduction in the local governments' economic autonomy, it was especially important to apply financial management principles that still gave a realistic chance for the city to cover its resource requirements and to keep operation and development within controllable limits.

At birth, local governments were allocated assets (primarily real estate indispensable for their services), as well as central – so called normative – subsidies as a contribution to their basic services (which do not cover the actual costs of these services). They also received the legal right to have their own revenues (primarily from taxes and duties, and also from fees and fines).

During past decades, efforts to increase the standards and quality of local government services have been stymied by the rather high level of inflation and the disproportionate withdrawal of resources from the local government sphere. Since it became increasingly difficult to maintain the level and quality of the services on a day-to-day basis, several local governments felt compelled to finance their daily operations not only from their current revenues but also from the sale of their assets. To varying extents, local governments began to exhaust their assets and thus gradually became impoverished.

Having realized this threat in due course, the Municipality of Budapest managed to enforce the principle that the local government assets can only be converted to other local government assets. In other words, the revenues from the sale of assets can be used only for financing development projects. This has become a key principle in the capital city's financial management. It was on the basis of this principle that the city privatized many of its large public utility service provider companies. The revenues from these sales were spent on large infrastructure investments.

At the same time, it was also clear that in the absence of further marketable assets the city would cease to have privatization revenues, and thus would have to finance its development projects from its current revenues. Consequently, the city had to approve a schedule for the reduction of its running operating expenditures in order for its current revenues to become the main source of coverage for its development projects. It goes without saying that the effort to achieve a positive operating result has created quite a few problems for the city's institutions. However, since the city's institutions (similarly to the institutions of other Central-Eastern European cities) were characterized by "prodigal poverty," the restrictions did not bring about the collapse of the servicing systems.

At the same time it is clear that such a process can be sustained for a limited period only despite the Municipality of Budapest's principle by which economically viable operations are achieved both through economic restrictions and through investments improving operating conditions by reducing costs. For this purpose, the capital city's budget regularly allocates money to its institution rationalization fund. Due to the unfavorable changes in the external conditions, the Municipality of Budapest does not expect to have a 20 percent operating result before 2008.

As I have mentioned before, certain theoretical and practical constraints have prompted the city to start planning for a medium-term balance between tasks and resources. The drafting of a seven-year financing projection played a key role in this planning process – the financing model was elaborated with the help of a French expert company (Crédit Local International Conseil). On the basis of this projection it became possible to plan the operating result which will enable future investments.

Simultaneously, the Municipality of Budapest introduced a seven-year rolling planning for its investment projects. This method establishes and schedules priorities in order to make long-term planning possible, but also remains open (at least in principle) to the annual reviews and to reasonable modifications.

The capital city aims to keep the annual proportions of its investments at a stable level. It does not want to subject its development projects to the fluctuations in its revenues. The goal is to be able to plan these projects in advance, and to spread the associated burdens across several years. The city wants to give priority to urgent development projects that would have materialized only decades later under the principle of "advance savings."

To accomplish these goals, the city has been pursuing an active borrowing policy for several years now. Budapest enjoys a strong debtor status, and the loan market has acknowledged this: the large international financial institutions (the World Bank, the EBRD, and the EIB) extend loans to Budapest's development projects under their best credit terms, without mortgage obligations. Another important step was the capital city's entering the international bond market. The primary advantage of this presence is that the funds secured in this market can be used in a more flexible manner, together with resources originating from other sources.

TODAY'S PROBLEM

By the end of 2000, the leaders of Budapest had reached a crossroads partly due to the accumulated shortcomings in the local government financing system, and – more importantly – due to the previous government's measures directed expressly against the city.

Under the previous government, Parliament withdrew HUF 14.6 billion from the capital city's current resources. As a result, the operating result for 2001 that the city could plan with was reduced to HUF 4.4 billion. This amount was too small a portion of the total municipal budget for the city to effectively finance its development projects and to service its debts. Budapest also had funds invested in securities which were earmarked for development. However, ongoing investments, the planned debt service, and certain targeted reserves (e.g., a new metroline, urban rehabilitation fund) had already blocked half of these funds. At the end of 2000, the city's leaders had to reckon with a HUF 40 billion deficit in connection with the planned investments valued at HUF 87 billion.

The above-mentioned loss of HUF 14.6 billion generates an approximately HUF 120 billion deficit (calculated at current prices) over the seven-year plan period. Since this sum is missing from the city's debt servicing potentials, this deficit also deprives the city of a chance to draw a further HUF 120-130 billion in long-term (or refinancable) loans. Accordingly, the withdrawal's total accumulated effect on the seven-year development plan is minus HUF 250 billion.

Simply put, the city's leaders had the following choices: they could opt for a conservative strategy, under which they could have immediately and fully shifted the obvious negative effects of the central measures on to the city's legally prescribed or voluntarily assumed servicing obligations (which, regrettably, could have resulted in cuts even in the city's statutory obligations), or they could choose a dynamic strategy, under which they could have presumed a change of government in 2002 and could have built this assumption openly into their financial plans. The latter option appeared to be rationally and morally justifiable on the following grounds: without a change of government (and an eventual significant change in financing) both strategic choices would have brought Budapest on the brink of collapse.

The Municipality of Budapest opted for the dynamic model. It did not shift the effects of the previous government's discriminative decisions on to the city's inhabitants, and it thus stayed afloat. In general terms this means that while the city's seven-year financing plan does feature the effects of the unfavorable amendments in the revenues columns for fiscal years 2001 and 2002, it calculates with the "pre-amendment" figures and projections for the period after 2003. The city's leaders felt justified to believe that it would be possible to eliminate the negative effects of the previous government's measures by a single (non-base) correction. This scheduled correction was expected to receive support from the new government.

The change of government did take place. At the time of the publication of the present volume the city's leaders are still expecting reactions from the new government.

Predictably the response will fail to be systemic. For the time being the city cannot expect the government to implement a comprehensive reform package that would draw all the conclusions from the experiences of the past few decades.

The new government has managed to settle the accumulated HUF 38 billion debts of the Budapest public transport company – still (which came from the residual funds of the 2002 state budget) as a one-time solution. This one-time subsidy enabled the company to operate in 2003, but left the scheme of public transport financing unchanged. Thus public transport in Budapest will go into the red again in 2003, most likely by more than HUF 20 billion. The following years will see the debt accumulating.

Local governments repeatedly raise this issue and now, in the summer of 2003 we have hopes that the 2004 state budget will allocate standardized resources for public transport financing.

It is also promising that the Parliament passed a new Metro Act in the Spring of 2003, determining a framework of a Government–Municipality agreement for co-financing the new Budapest metro line (which had been blocked by the previous government).

Beyond (or prior to) solving the larger Hungarian cities' public transport problems there is an urgent need – recognized by the new government – to stabilize the local governments' bankrupt financing system. Unfortunately, there is no really promising effort in sight. The problem is dangerously rolling on and slowly gathering momentum. For lack of radical, systemic measures the government will be compelled to provide ever increasing individual financial support for local governments on the verge of bankruptcy. This essentially runs counter to the original efforts made at the change of the political system: the operational basis of the sovereign local government sector is undermined and local communities are at the mercy of the central state government; just like in the good old times.

Of course, neither previous nor existing governments ever declared principles pointing to this direction. Yet, this tendency is inherent in the system – there is no safeguard against it. No central government in Hungary has sufficiently recognized that it is in the very interest of the state to have a stable local government sector able to carry out local tasks smoothly and with full responsibility.

The Municipality of Budapest – just like other local governments and their associations – is busily trying to influence government policy on local governments. Referring to the "Budapest model" in particular, and local government policy in general only makes sense as long as we have hopes to influence government policy in this direction.

STRATEGIC PLANNING AND MANAGEMENT REFORM

KATALIN PALLAI

The change of political systems markedly decentralized the previously centralized system of state administration in Hungary. On the settlements' level, local governments were established with broad responsibilities and independent budgets and the state allocated appropriate assets and resources for these local governments to fulfill their role. The newly changed political system, quickly transforming country economy and emerging strong local governments provided a great opportunity to pursue autonomous policies on the local level. These new sets of conditions led to new challenges and to the drafting and implementation of new local strategies.

The local responses to these challenges were always determined by the local political leaders' value choices. The local politicians' credo and affinities played a key role in defining the thrust of the local governments' policies, i.e., the long-term goals and methods applied. At the same time, external conditions[1] limited their possibilities and determined the paths along which their goals could be realistically identified and achieved.

In the 1990s, the long-term goal of the liberal politicians who led the city of Budapest was to create the "essential conditions" for a flourishing metropolis. They wanted to turn Budapest into a livable and competitive city that would satisfy the needs of its population and its economy alike. These politicians' liberal principles emphasized the need for a lean public sector concentrating on basic public tasks, and relying on market techniques and processes in order to increase efficiency. They wanted their own activities to become transparent and accountable, thereby creating the predictable conditions necessary for the improvement of the city's operation and for the successful development of other progressive forces' strategies.

In Budapest, it was already clear in the early 1990s that external conditions limited the city leaders' realistic goals down to the maintenance of the settlement's operability (in a broad sense). To accomplish this goal, the city had to undertake significant capital investment projects and radically restructure the operation of the municipal government. Medium-term strategy had to be built upon these two pillars.

Urban development was to focus on infrastructure investments improving environmental conditions and the quality of life. Among the infrastructure branches transport – primarily

---

[1] The term "conditions" refers to both the context and the actors. It refers to the political, social and cultural context which the country, city and government are in, as well as the political and attitudinal environment in which the reforms occurred.

public transport – investments were prioritized. The rehabilitation of the downtown areas was an inevitable and omnipresent task, but the city could not undertake this on its own due to the project's substantial resource requirements. Nevertheless, the city has completed a number of capital investment projects that contributed to Budapest's rehabilitation (again, in a broad sense).

The operation of the city government, the scope of its activities, the way of fulfilling, financing and coordinating tasks all had to be reviewed and restructured.

Analyzing the past twelve years following the change of the political system, this chapter aims to review the Municipality of Budapest's attempts to create a strategy for implementing these diverse tasks. The chapter also aims to assess its accomplishments.

In order for us to be able to interpret and analyze the reforms that have been implemented in Budapest, we must first get acquainted with the views and credo of the politicians who launched these reforms, and describe the conditions that defined their possible scope of action. The municipality's goals and policies can only be measured and judged in relation to these factors. Accordingly, we shall begin this chapter with a brief summary of the city leaders' stances and the prevailing conditions they were working in. Drawing on these we shall describe the process by which Budapest's long-term goals were selected and the evolution of the strategy to implement them.

The study that forms the core of this chapter focuses on strategic planning and management in Budapest. It provides a detailed analysis of the changes in the city's urban policies during the past three municipal cycles. The analysis will shed light on the evolution of comprehensive strategic planning and management in Budapest, and will also identify the limitations of the process. Both in the literature and in practice, the concept of strategic planning is used with various meanings. In order to decipher these meanings, we shall first provide a brief summary of ways to manage professional planning and political processes. We will then describe Budapest municipal leaders' approach to strategic planning.

Urban policy entails multi-faceted and complex processes. The present chapter aims to provide a comprehensive overview of the chronological and conceptual development of urban policies in Budapest. It seeks to contextualize the volume's central subject, the reform of Budapest's financial management system and to facilitate the understanding of the reform processes in specific fields.

VALUES AND GOALS

VALUES

Individual freedom is the paramount goal in liberal philosophy. In accordance with the tenets of liberalism, the protection of individuals' personal rights and possibilities has priority in the policies envisioned by the municipal leaders of Budapest. For liberals the main role of government is to protect the rights of individuals to pursue their diverse interests without interference from others and to ensure that individuals are able to exercise their rights. Liberalism aims to enforce legal principles, and prefers legal procedures to authoritative case-by-case decisions. Liberals believe that the state is bound by constitutional democratic rules, and that it must guarantee the rule of law and enforce respect for regulations. In this way, public authorities become predictable in their deeds and actions.

According to the liberal political view, the market mechanism promotes efficiency for its participants (within the framework of honest competition) and, ultimately, spontaneously aggregates selfish, individual decisions and orients them towards the public good. For this reason, the liberals aim to eliminate excess regulations that paralyze the market and strive to curtail the state's redistributive role.

The public sector must also serve the public good. A competitive market secures the efficient use of scarce resources and as a result contributes to better social outcomes. This is why the liberals aim to introduce market type mechanisms for public services.

In practice, the acceptance of market mechanisms entails the realization of the importance of privatization. Privatization is a process that shifts the burdens of directly providing public services from the public sector onto the private sector. Eventually, the role of the public sector is limited to creating the required conditions for the efficient functioning of the services, to act as a monitor and to implement the necessary corrections that may arise as a result of the monitoring. This leads to competition between service providers on the supply side, while on the demand side it promotes transparency and the emergence of a citizenry that has access to information and the opportunity to decide and to choose their service providers. In other words, this process transforms the citizen from a passive "recipient" of services into an active "consumer."

By principle, the liberals favor subsidiarity. On the one hand, they want to bring the decision-making process closer to the citizens, because they believe that this will result in more transparent and accountable decisions being made. On the other hand, the liberals believe that decentralization – since local politicians are closer to the people and have a more intricate picture and more detailed, direct and reliable information on their constituents – can increase the efficiency of service provision and can be conducive to better conditions for implementing integrated policies on the local level. A decentralized system can become efficient if local policies are coordinated by stable, predictable rules and if local autonomy – based on legal and financial independence – can result in strategies and decisions reflecting local interests.

The liberals consider that the municipal governments' role is to provide local public goods and services, and to introduce and enforce a predictable system of regulations. To this end, it is the responsibility of the municipal governments to employ optimal resource management techniques. The efficiency of resource management on the one hand hinges on the presence of successfully integrated strategic planning mechanisms that direct activities towards the targeted goals; on the other hand it hinges on the municipal governments' internal operation that determines the efficiency of resource management. Here the rationalization of activities can increase their efficiency, and by reviewing and refocusing the scope of activities, the municipal governments can guarantee that public funds are spent only on projects where the public sector is demonstrably more efficient than the private sector.

GOALS AND METHODS

In the 1990s, the Municipality of Budapest aimed to create the conditions for the emergence of a metropolis that would be open to the world, livable and competitive. In other words, a 'home" for the citizens and the economy alike. Openness to the "outside world" means ease of travel, of telecommunication access and the facilitation of personal contacts. The quality of urban life is an important factor for individuals and the economy alike, as it is a key factor in the attraction of domestic and foreign investment.

It was already clear when the political system had only just changed that Budapest would have to reform itself if it wanted to become a successful city on the European scene. Parts of the city would have to unite into an organic urban texture with improved public services for its residents, and an appropriate regulatory framework for potential investors would have to be set up. From the very beginnings, the Municipality's primary goal was to improve these conditions. This was the way for the city to become integrated within Europe and the world, to become a major regional center, and to offer a high-quality urban experience that would make the city competitive in relation to other major European cities.

Drawing on the advantages inherent in the local government system, the city's leaders' aim was to use their independence in planning and financial management to create an integrated local policy framework and to operate a responsible, transparent, and plannable municipal system, that in turn would create predictable conditions for the welfare of the citizens and the development of the local economy.

THE CONTEXT

POLITICAL AND FINANCIAL CONDITIONS IN THE WAKE OF TRANSITION

Up until the 1980s, Hungary in several respects shared other socialist countries' problems. The "paternalistic state" extended a series of services to all its citizens. To finance these services, the state redistributed around 60 per cent of the country's GDP. The oversized state apparatus operated in a centralized manner, and through its unregulated decision-making mechanism and case-by-case bargaining it exercised heavy control over the local units of government. The last decade of socialism witnessed a slow but steady elimination of the restrictions on the market, and the 1980s introduced a number of important changes in Hungary. In consequence, the political system went through faster changes in Hungary than in neighboring states.

By the late 1980s, the country's deteriorating macroeconomic condition had clearly signaled the end of the previous system. Reform ideas were in the air, and the harbingers of the new institutional system had already appeared, prior to the "official" change in the political system. Although the long-needed comprehensive public finance reform could not get on the agenda, a few important measures were implemented. Among others, the state introduced personal income taxes and general turnover taxes to buttress the revenues' side of the central budget. The subsidies granted to the municipal governments became a separate entry in the budget. Simultaneously, initial measures were introduced towards the normative financing of the municipal governments.[2]

The change in the Hungarian political system was very strongly influenced by liberal thought, as the establishment of democracy and the market economy – the necessary initial steps of this transition – very much coincided with the liberal drive. The country had to create a legal system for its emerging constitutional democracy, and thus had to redefine individual and property rights. Hungary had to eliminate the excess regulations that hampered the emergence of a free market, it had to reduce state redistribution and redefine social solidarity. Thanks to the political maturity of reform-minded intellectuals, and also to the cardinal agreements reached at the Opposition Roundtable[3] (which prepared the country for a peaceful political transition), Hungary succeeded to put itself en route towards a functioning democratic market economy.

In the early 1990s, Hungary made a number of bold steps towards the inevitable replacement of the previous political and economic system. The country established the institutions of a multi-party parliamentary democracy. Independent and responsible local governments were created in accordance with the stipulations of the European Charter of Local Self-government. The new act on public finance introduced a series of important regulations and prescribed a more transparent, detailed budget. The early 1990s witnessed a marked reduction in the role of central price regulation and price subsidies. New acts were passed on accounting and on bankruptcy, and the country's banks were consolidated. On the basis of all these, the country could start work on the transformation of its economic system. A great beneficiary of all these changes was the country's capital city and only genuine metropolis – Budapest.

The fast change of the system was inevitably accompanied by a deep transformation crisis. The natural side-effects of the transition period included the disappearance of certain companies and economic activities, an increasing rate of unemployment, the destruction

---

[2] This process and the associated reforms are discussed in detail in the study on 'Financial Management Reform'.

[3] Against the backdrop of the Soviet Union's rapid decline and the dissolution of its alliance with the Eastern bloc countries, Hungary's new or reemerging democratic forces launched the Opposition Roundtable in the spring of 1989. Under the auspices of the Independent Lawyers' Forum, six opposition parties and two other organizations pooled their talents in an effort to ensure a peaceful political transition by entering into negotiations with the ruling Hungarian Socialist Workers' Party (MSZMP), which already identified itself as a socialist party.

of the welfare net, and a decline in real wages. Despite its relative economic strength, Budapest was also adversely affected by social problems. Although average wages in the city remained substantially above the national level (at 180 per cent), Budapest also witnessed the negative effects of the economic and social decline of lower social layers and the strengthening of social polarization. Among other things, Budapest became a major hub for the country's homeless.

But for all the problems, the bold first steps resulted in a series of positive changes. The private sector picked up speed rather quickly. While in 1992 it contributed 50 per cent of GDP, by 1997 this figure had increased to 70 per cent. The structure of production was also renewed. The process was most dynamic in Budapest. By the second half of the 1990s, the service sector had already become responsible for 77 per cent of GDP produced in the city. Foreign capital started appearing in Hungary as investors started taking interest in the country and city. During the first decade following political transition, about half of the total foreign investment capital that appeared in the region ended up in Hungary (USD 22.5 billion). This gave a significant boost to the restructuring of the economy, and greatly promoted subsequent moves towards stable economic growth. About 50 per cent of the investments made by foreigners in Hungary materialized in Budapest, which significantly strengthened the capital city's role as the country's economic center. It was amid such conditions that the city's leaders had to manage the reforms to be outlined below.

Hungary can clearly be described as successful in implementing a new political system and creating the conditions necessary for a free market economy. However, much less has happened with regard to public sector reform. Although public sector reform has permanently been on the agenda over the past 12 years, the inertia of the large redistributive systems and the political risks entailed in their restructuring hampered reformist efforts.

The political leaders of the first government cycle did not venture to introduce all the comprehensive measures required for restructuring, and chose only to re-regulate the budgetary process. By the beginning of the second government cycle, redistribution had affected 61 per cent of GDP, the deficit of the central budget reached 8.5 per cent, and the state's debts amounted to 85 per cent of GDP. International financial circles put Hungary in the same bracket as Mexico. By 1995 it became inevitable to reduce the deficit and curtail redistribution. The country's second, socialist-liberal governing coalition attacked the problems with what has become known as the "Bokros package" (named after Finance Minister Lajos Bokros). This stabilization program undertook to address a number of imperative economic policy issues: among others it launched the process of economic liberalization, extended the privatization process, and curtailed private consumption. It also ventured to launch some public finance reforms. As a result, the country's economy returned to a sustainable path. Within two years, the program reduced redistribution to 50 per cent, slashed the budgetary deficit to 3.2 per cent and the state's debts to 65 per cent of GDP. However, for all its successes, the program did not include reforms of the largest redistributive systems (health care, welfare policy, and education). Consequently, the "Bokros package" fell short of reforming the public sector as a whole. While it managed to put the country on the path leading to stable economic growth, Hungary's public sector still retains structural problems.

The third government, which was in power between 1998 and 2002, employed a peculiar mix of conservative nationalism together with old-style left-wing subsidization. The right-wing Fidesz government used the benefits of the country's stable economic growth to finance the reintroduction of universal family subsidies and welfare-type subsidization for the middle classes. It also made efforts to directly influence the economic process. By the end of this government's term it had already become clear that the new economic policy – which strove to achieve short-term successes through wage increases beyond productivity growth and through the excessive and unfounded expansion of domestic consumption – had slowed down the country's economic growth and was detrimental to Hungary's competitive position on the international markets. In addition, it also reduced foreign investors' trust in Hungary.

The third government cycle brought negative changes for municipal governments as well. This markedly statist cabinet – as it did not intend to reduce the role of the central government– shifted the burdens of the central budget's structural deficit on to municipal governments to an extent never previously experienced. By the end of the third government's term it was clear that central financial policy and the local government financing were unsustainable. The signs were unmistakable. An increasing number of municipal governments found themselves in financial straits, which compelled them to significantly curtail their investments. Several municipalities even found it difficult to finance their daily operations.

The country's local governments – and especially the municipality of the capital city, which was on the receiving end of the government's anti-Budapest policies – expect the fourth government to reverse these unfavorable trends. As we write in early 2003, it appears that the new government is inclined both to renegotiate the state's involvement in a few key investment projects in Budapest and to correct the inadequacies of the local government system.

THE SYSTEM OF LOCAL GOVERNMENTS IN HUNGARY

The marked decentralization process of the Hungarian governmental system was a salient feature of the change of the political system, and one which determined subsequent developments. As a result, the country's local governments were established according to the principles laid down in the European Charter of Local Self-government. Hungary's Act on the Local Governments *(ALG – Acts and Decrees, 1)* vests local governments with broad rights and responsibilities. This changed the public administration system and the political life of the country and resulted in the emergence of another strong pole alongside the central government.

In Hungary, the independence of the local governments is guaranteed by the Constitution and the ALG. Local government decisions can only be challenged on the basis that they do not comply with the law. Local governments are obliged to provide public services both in the physical - (roads, sewage etc.) and the human infrastructure (education, healthcare etc.) fields and to institute local regulations (cf. the summary table below). They are free to choose the way they perform these services, i.e., they can cooperate with other local governments, or they can subcontract or privatize services. Furthermore, the local governments are entitled to undertake other activities as well, provided that these do not interfere with their mandatory services.

The local governments' mandatory services are specified in the ALG. It also falls on the legislators to allocate appropriate resources for the accomplishment of the specified tasks. Under the so called Act on Assets (Acts and Decrees, 4)), local governments were given the property rights for the assets needed to perform mandatory. They also received the property rights for plots on their respective territories that were not private property. Furthermore, local governments were authorized to generate their own revenues and to receive transfers from the state such as shared taxes, normative subsidies and investment grants. During the past few years, these resources have totaled 17-11 per cent of GDP. Municipal governments have been authorized to complete their investment resources by drawing loans independently (the limits of which were regulated in 1995).

TASKS AND RIGHTS OF THE MUNICIPALITY OF BUDAPEST

TASKS OF THE MUNICIPALITY OF BUDAPEST	RIGHTS OF THE MUNICIPALITY OF BUDAPEST

• Regulation, urban development planning
• Protection of natural and built environment
• Regulation of transport infrastructure, public transportation, and parking
• Provision of public utility services, such as gas, drinking water, flood protection, sewage, district heating, waste management, urban cleaning, funerals, public lighting, fire protection
• Housing management
• Education (high schools and vocational training institutions, dormitories)
• Provision of social services
• Provision of health care
• Tasks related to arts, public collections, and public education
	• Legal and political independence
	• Property rights over assets and associated rights
	• Access to annual state transfers
	  o Shared taxes
	  o Normative subsidies
	  o Targeted and addressed investment grants
	• Own revenues
	  o Local taxes
	  o User charges
	  o Stamp duties and fines
	  o Revenues from asset management and sale
	• Right to borrow
	• Right to approve regulatory frameworks for urban development and for the protection of natural and of built environment

The local governments received regulatory rights, ample independence, and access to resources – at least initially – commensurate with the broadly defined tasks that were assigned to them. Based on all these, they had the potential to act in local politics and to launch comprehensive reform processes with the aim of adjusting the methods of task fulfillment and financial management they had inherited from the previous (council) system to the requirements of the new era.

While acknowledging the achievements of Hungarian decentralization, we must recognize that it was realistically impossible to create a European-style system of local governments overnight. The main goal of the system that was set up in 1990 was democratization through decentralization. This meant that local governments with general obligations were created on the settlement level, even at the expense of the fragmentation of the system. Under the ALG, in Budapest, the local governments were set up both on the settlement level and on the level of the districts. The Municipality of Budapest and district local governments are equal in rank and legal status. They share tasks according to relevant legal stipulations and share associated resources according to the tasks performed. It falls on the Municipality of Budapest to fulfill the tasks pertaining to the settlement as a whole and to the general functioning of the city, while district local governments are charged with the provision of local services. Local governments' equal status to that of municipal government and their independence has given rise to a series of anomalies and lasting conflicts. This situation has made it extremely difficult to implement coherent urban policies and to draft strategies in an integrated manner.[4]

Another weakness of the Act on Local Governments is that it assigned most of the regional tasks to larger settlements (e.g. Budapest), but without sufficient authority and the necessary financial resources. At the same time, the previous system's tools for regional coordination were transformed – or, in most of the cases, eliminated. As a result, conflicts between the capital city and neighboring small settlements have become an everyday occurrence. As coordination became voluntary, small settlements started displaying the classic free rider behavior[5] which rendered the situation practically unmanageable.

The establishment of local governments in Hungary has produced two structures within public administration: central government and local governments. These two major hubs of authority occasionally – and naturally – find themselves at odds with each other. The Constitution and the ALG guarantee the legal stability of the system of local governments. The ALG was approved by Parliament by a two-thirds majority vote.[6] At the same time,

---

[4] The discussion of the way the municipality cooperated with the districts falls beyond the scope of the present volume. While this issue is complex and riddled with peculiarities, and would certainly deserve to be treated in a separate volume, its lessons would hardly be of interest to the broader public. In addition, it would divert our attention from the matter at hand.

[5] The expression is used here in an economic sense. It refers to those who exploit the common goods but fail to contribute to the costs. In this specific case the term refers to local public services provided by a municipality which are used by the inhabitants and businesses of the neighboring settlements without contributing to the former's expenditures.

[6] "Two-thirds majority vote" requires the approval of two-thirds of the representatives present at voting.

local government financing is regulated by laws which are passed by a simple majority.[7] This makes it possible to influence the system from the resources side, or in a worst-case scenario, to destabilize it. Consequently, the stability and predictability of conditions needed for the development of local plans and strategies may fall victim to political conflicts and clashes on the national level.

Conflicts of interest between central and local government were accompanied by competition between political parties. The emerging local governments created a new political turf for the parties, who readily grasped this opportunity for publicity. In Hungary's fledgling democratic political culture, these conflicts often lead to situations where local political maneuverings (especially on the urban level) take the upper hand over efforts to enforce the interest of the population.

Budapest's local politicians had to perform their tasks amidst such conditions. In principle, decentralized spheres of authority and resources and independence in decision making should have enabled the municipality to establish real local planning processes and to draft and implement strategies adapted to local conditions. At the same time, the coordination of various actors' interests obviously takes time in a fragmented system and strategic opportunities risk being lost. The overly politicized nature of the system on both the national and local levels often diverted decisions from paths deemed rational from an economic or a servicing point of view.

THE POSITION AND STATUS OF BUDAPEST

Budapest, this venerable city with outstanding geopolitical status, was given a unique opportunity when the political system changed. With nearly two million inhabitants, it is the largest city in the region and the capital of Hungary, a leader among transition countries. Budapest functions as the country's political as well as economic and cultural center. The city generates 34 per cent of the country's GDP and over half of its tax revenues. Around 80 per cent of the country's businesses are headquartered in Budapest and the city houses most of the country's high added value ventures (such as telecommunications, financial and economic services etc.). In the wake of the change of the political system, Hungary became the number one destination for foreign investors interested in the post-socialist region. In the 1990s, the country brought in a total of USD 22.5 billion in foreign investment, 54 per cent of which ended up in Budapest (of the registered investment capital). By 1996, half of Budapest's investment projects were under the control of foreign-owned companies. These favorable conditions sparked off a series of positive developments in the city. By 1997, practically all international ventures with an interest in the region had opened an office or regional representation in Budapest. In those years, the service sector was already responsible for 77 per cent of the city's total economic output. The last decade of the 20th century witnessed the construction of one million square meters of new office and

---

7 "Simple majority vote" means a vote requiring more than half of the total votes of representatives present and voting.

business space in Budapest. The city's rate of unemployment was constantly less than half the national average, while the local income level was 1.5 times higher than elsewhere in the country. Budapest has always played a key role in Hungary's economy and always attracted considerable international interest. All in all, the leaders of Budapest had excellent opportunities and a fundamentally dynamic development potential at their disposal.

It goes without saying that the change of the system manifested itself much faster in the political and economic spheres than in the city's physical and infrastructure conditions. While the so-called "soft infrastructure," which supports the city's economy, developed rather dynamically, changes in Budapest's urban structure and "hard infrastructure" were considerably slower (due primarily to the latter's marked inertia). [8]

The heritage of the "socialist" system was most perceptible in the city's low quality road network and its run-down building stock. In the last quarter of the 19th century Budapest developed into a leading European city with a homogeneous and eclectic architectural style, but with areas of varying density and quality. Unfortunately, during the forty years of socialist rule, the city's building stock and public areas fell into disrepair and practically the whole area of downtown Budapest became miserably forlorn.

At the turn of the 19th and 20th centuries, the city's road network and public utility services qualified as outstanding. These covered only the so-called "Little Budapest" area[9] however, which equals today's downtown area. This road network predated the "automobile era." The Communist regime kept it functional only by restricting the public's access to cars and by promoting the use of mass transportation. The turn-of-the-century industrial and servicing zone around the eclectic downtown areas was largely taken over by socialist industries during the previous regime. This area eventually collapsed when the political system changed. As a result, the structure of the city today includes huge enclaves of deserted industrial zones in valuable locations, only a few kilometers from the center.

The 1990s brought about significant changes in the city's ownership, economic and land use structure, as well as in the level of motorization. The state spared no time to transfer its neglected stock of rental apartments to the local governments' ownership, but naturally failed to allocate funds for their rehabilitation. Local governments would have had to introduce astronomical rent hikes in order to finance their inevitable renovation, and this at their own political risk. This situation pitted anxious tenants against the anxious local governments. Finally, the law on rental apartments' privatization offered a practical, albeit rather irresponsible escape route. The law obliged the local governments to sell the apartments to their tenants at symbolic prices. In a few years, 90 per cent of the apartments were transferred to (in essence, forced) private owners. As a result, the bulk of Budapest's apartment stock became the property of mostly old and poor people, thereby fragmenting

---

[8] The policies associated with "hard infrastructure" are discussed in detail in the final chapter of the volume entitled 'Extra-budgetary Utilities.'

[9] The area of the capital city in the pre-war period, which was approximately 60 per cent smaller than today's Budapest.

the ownership pattern of the city's apartment stock, resulting in most buildings being owned by multiple tenants.

While the apartment privatization process gave a boost to mobility, and promoted a certain differentiation between urban areas, it also hampered urban rehabilitation due to co-ownership structures and the owners' lack of capital.

The economic restructuring process improved the quality of certain public services, and also resulted in the structural and territorial reorganization of economic activities. The newly established ventures and foreign companies set up their offices and plants in areas according to the emerging real estate market prices. Privatized companies marketed their real estate accordingly.[10] This rearrangement paved the way for a more efficient urban structure in as much as the activities of high prestige and added value gravitated towards the city center, while others gravitated towards less expensive sites. This rearrangement did not only take place within city limits; it led to both suburbanization and green-field investments. The benefits of these last two trends on urban structure and social cost-efficiency are already questionable, as urban-like quality of life can only be provided at much higher social costs in the suburbs than in the inner, already equipped zones. Nevertheless, moving out of the city is a rational step to take for individual actors, as only a fragment of the social costs are directly paid by the new settlers.

These developments rearranged the residential and business zones in and around the city, which in turn redefined the character of and demand for transportation. The boom in motorization resulted in a steep increase in the number of privately owned cars. The city's modal split (share of public transportation versus individual transportation) changed from 85 per cent versus 15 per cent in 1984 to 67 per cent versus 33 per cent today (if we include commuters, the former figure drops way below 50 per cent). This drastic increase in traffic manifests itself in regular congestion's costing travelers time and causing burdens on the environment.

The 1990s also altered city-dwellers' expectations. The quality of the local environment (physical structure, services, air, noise, atmosphere, security etc.) has come to play an increasingly important role in the choice of business location, in addition to accessibility and geographic position. Similarly, residents have also become more conscious of the environment in which they live in: those who can afford it move to better neighborhoods, even if this means a longer commute. Mobility is greatly facilitated by the fact that the apartment market is now practically completely private. In consequence, we can expect to see a more marked differentiation and segregation of areas within Budapest in the long term.

---

[10] In the Socialist era, the non-existent real estate market and the practice of planning that failed to take the real costs into consideration distorted the city's structure in that the businesses were not allocated real estate on the basis of economic rationality. As a result of the revival of the real estate market and increasing cost sensitivity, businesses with higher prestige and value moved toward the center of the city, while those ventures which required more space or generated less value tended to move to the suburbs.

Since the 1990s, there is a competition among the city's districts, and also between Budapest and its suburbs. The city must strive to keep its wealthy inhabitants and flourishing businesses, since it is their taxes and duties that generate the bulk of Budapest's revenues. For this it is crucial to upgrade the environment and services. Meanwhile, businesses located right outside city limits also rely heavily on Budapest's infrastructure, and the daily traffic of the commuters places serious environmental burdens on the city. Regrettably, the competition between districts and settlements occurs against the backdrop of a dangerously fragmented system of public administration, and relevant regulations are far from ideal. Districts (and suburbs) have the ability to enforce their particular local interests thanks to their independence, and can relatively easily capitalize on their local advantage. The Municipality of Budapest, however, has only limited licenses and resources for the city's general strategic management. In this set-up the weaknesses of regional coordination and the existing system of regulations often hinder the implementation of mutually advantageous solutions.[11]

If we contrast these circumstances with the goals outlined above, we can understand that the municipality's leaders have had to confront a set of rather serious challenges. In order for Budapest to become an organic and livable metropolis again, it has to provide reliable and high-quality services, and must remain competitive against its surrounding suburban neighborhoods. Budapest must become a city where quality of life and of urban services can compensate inhabitants and businesses for the higher costs and other disadvantages of a metropolitan location. The Municipality of Budapest had to devise a strategy that, by utilizing its limited resources and spheres of authority, could establish the conditions for the development of the city.

TRADITIONAL APPROACHES

Under the socialist system the public sector was supposed to implement the ideals of a paternalistic state. To this end, some 60 per cent of the country's GDP was redistributed in the years preceding political transition. The redistribution process was managed by a monolithic and hierarchical public administration system. Central economic planning meant that important strategic decisions were made by the Central Committee of the Communist Party, and strategic management by the ministries. These strategies were rooted in the state's normative goals, and planning was based on a markedly supply-orientated approach. Artificially set prices and wages (extensive price and product subsidies, symbolic public utility rates, and a largely dysfunctional market) meant that decision-makers did not have the necessary information on changes in demand. There were thus no incentives for reconsidering the conditions brought about by supply-oriented thinking.

In this situation the local councils that functioned as deconcentrated state organs could play only a limited role in working out local policies. Case-by-case decision making and soft

---

[11] Although regional coordination also counts as a very important element of urban policy, considerations of space prevent us from elaborating more on this topic.

constraints on their financing reinforced the councils' dependent status. The fate of local capital investment projects often depended on individual decisions made by state leaders, which in turn were influenced by lobbying by local officials. Once the interest representation campaign proved successful and investment resources became accessible, the state budget automatically took over the subsequent operation of the capital investment project at issue. Since it was very difficult to predict if and when a capital investment project would receive the go-ahead from the state government, this vertical system put limits on local and inter-sectoral coordination. In this situation the logical choice for local strategists was to strive to maximize subsidies. They had to draft local capital investment plans with numerous entries in order to stand a chance. The lobbyists had to keep several projects on the table simultaneously, and also had to rely heavily on political contacts. Meanwhile, soft financial regulations did not threaten to paralyze the plans once accepted, and it was thus also possible to avoid matching the investment and financial planning.

This system favored "vision-based" urban planning which translated the visions of the "architects-cum-urban planners"[12] into physical plans, but did not bother to ascertain whether these plans were indeed realistic, and offered no indication of strategies, schedules, or tools necessary to accomplish them.

Following the period of political transition, local governments' independence enabled them to introduce local planning and to coordinate resources, sectoral policies and investments. The simultaneous introduction of hard financing constraints and responsibilities for adequate performance prompted local governments to optimize their resources.

In the new context the old councils' "subsidy-maximizing" strategy, which rested on mo-numental "futuristic" visions, became obsolete. It was replaced by "resource optimization," which required integrated strategic planning. In strategic planning the "visions" and the gener-al strategic goals only serve as a starting point. A consensus must be reached at this general level to guide the subsequent strategic process. Nevertheless, the strategy – with its specifi-cation of tools, timeframes and costs – represents the key element of this approach, together with the bargaining process and agreements that determine the way of accomplishment.

"Resource optimization" required a new approach, the creation of new urban policies and a new strategic process that adjusted professional and political activities to new conditions. The present chapter aims to describe this transformation process through the analysis of the reforms (along with the related urban policy documents) that were introduced in Budapest during the past three government cycles.

---

[12] In Hungary, similarly to other Socialist states, urban planners received their degree from the Technical University's faculty of architecture. Their curriculum was restricted to physical planning, and practically no mention was made of the field's economic, social, and political implications. Consequently, it was up to the students to study these issues on their own initiative.

STRATEGIC PLANNING

Strategic planning can be interpreted in different ways in municipal planning. For this reason, different approaches will be summed up and the Budapest approach to strategic planning and the municipal leaders' expectations towards the strategic process will be presented before entering into a detailed analysis of Budapest's urban policy[13] and development conceptions in the post-socialist period.

THE CONCEPT OF STRATEGIC PLANNING

In municipal planning, strategic planning is generally defined as a comprehensive and goal-oriented process with the aim to coordinate the various professional and political ideas conducive to the efficient realization of targeted goals. This broad definition allows for a range of different approaches that can be situated between two extremes: one centered on professional choices, the other on the political process.

At one end of the spectrum, strategic planning is defined as a planning process breaking down the visions and general goals of the leadership into programs and detailed action plans following a compact and logical system. This interpretation rests on the assumption that, based solely on professional rational thinking,[14] it is possible to deduce the policies to be pursued and ideal solutions to be found from the values and general goals of the leadership. A number of engineers and "architect-urbanists" identify with this interpretation even in the case of complex urban policy issues involving intricate value choices and affected by changing external conditions. The project's managers fix the targeted end state according to their visions and deduct the "inevitable" solutions (based on the professional principles of their choice) in an apparently axiomatic process. In its extreme form, this approach tends to omit the extent to which value choices affect decisions, as well as changing external conditions. The given context and the political process are thus relegated simply to the rank of disturbing factors.

Interpretations on the other extreme see strategic planning in the public sector as meaning the reconciliation of interests and coordination of diverse opinions. Those who identify with this approach also start out from an agreed set of goals and principles which they believe may guide subsequent processes. However, this approach tends to keep the political process in focus throughout the whole strategic process. Adherents of this approach believe that the political process should provide for decisions and choices among different proposals and policy alternatives, and this in a manner that squares with the fundamental principles of

---

[13] Urban policy entails all the policies pursued by a municipal government in connection with all its activities. Urban policy is thus broader than the operation, investment, or sectoral policies (which cover only specific areas), and is also more comprehensive than the broad and often overlapping areas identified by the terms rehabilitation or urban development.

[14] The terms "rational" and "rationality" are used here strictly in relation to means and goals. Accordingly, a decision is considered rational if it attaches optimal means to a given goal.

both the political process and the targeted goals. Simply put, this approach believes that the coordination of policies occurs through successive interest coordination and bargaining.

We must emphasize here that these two extremes are abstractions. Their role here is to highlight the differences between the underlying professional and political logic. In practice, every single municipal planning and policy process mixes elements from these two extremes and relies simultaneously on professional and political considerations and values. Although professional approaches also tend to change with time, one may safely say that deliberations based on professional considerations tend to be more coherent and perspicuous than choices made in the eternally changing external conditions and controversy-ridden political turf. (We must also add here that while professional proposals are expected to be buttressed by clear and logical arguments, the validity of political decisions mostly depends on the authority vested in politicians by the voters). From all this it logically follows that in the public sphere the creation and implementation of strategies tend to be a step-by-step process. Strategies evolve through iterations of the professional and political arguments and are concluded on the basis of successive agreements.

Based on the above arguments, we can define strategic planning as a process (involving professional and political activities) that produces agreements with longer-term validity on values, goals and procedural principles, and that coordinates decisions from a potential pool of policy alternatives in order to implement set goals.

THE PROCESS OF STRATEGIC PLANNING

The process of strategic planning must begin with the identification and approval of the general strategic goals. These strategic goals mostly depend on the value choices of the political group(s) in power. The next step is to identify objectives.[15] This requires assessing prevailing and projected conditions. A politician is expected to spell out his or her value choices and main (strategic) goals during the election campaign. Ideally, the election program also provides elements of the objectives, including some indication of how the main goals could and should be accomplished. If so, the politician's eventual election can be expected to guarantee political legitimacy for the subsequent moves towards the specified goals.[16]

In essence, the aim of strategic planning is to elaborate and coordinate policies falling in line with the already identified strategic goals, and to have them eventually approved. The

---

[15] In the process of strategic planning, the term "strategic goal" is meant to identify those comprehensive goals which are not bound to concrete temporal or accomplishment dimensions. These govern the general direction of the evolving process from its beginning on the basis of the initial vision and choice of values. Concretizing the goals is a subsequent step in the strategic process, where the strategy is broken down into objectives, that are temporally definable, measurable, and controllable and that refer to the method of fulfillment.

[16] The references to political authorization and legitimacy apply to the model of representative democracy that prevails in Central Europe. The direct democracy concepts often promoted by the donor community and technical aid programs propose other forms for participation.

process evolves in the wake of the professional and political efforts of the elected politicians their staff and experts. The process is strategic because it is objective-oriented; i.e., each step relies on the identified goal(s) and tries to find the means conducive to the accomplishment of these goals. The strategic nature of the process is also manifest in the fact that it seeks to build on a sequence of political agreements which form an integral part of public policy making. In this sphere, the process is determined by subsequent comparison between the various conditions and proposals, the permanent iteration of professional and political values, and the quest for the political coalitions required for decision-making.

In an ideal case, coordination between the professional staff and the politician takes place in a structured manner that integrates professional rationality and political value choices in final decisions. In practical terms this means that the professional expert outlines and ranks the problems that he or she considers most relevant, and then the politician reorders these problems according to his or her value choices and offers guidelines for solutions (logically this process is also iterated). Based on these indications, professional experts come up with policy papers that offer alternatives (for the solution of the problem as a whole or for its elements). These policy papers describe the specific alternatives' pros and cons and call attention to the elements of the proposals where decisions can be made on a professional basis and to those elements where decision depends on the value choices of politicians Finally, it falls on the elected politician to accept the proposals and to choose between alternatives.

As we have seen, the direction of the strategic planning process is clearly determined by the initially identified goals that guarantee that the process stays on course. On the other hand the management of the strategic process leans on the appropriately structured policy analysis and decision-making process that channels diverse professional and political considerations towards rational outcomes.

After this short review of the interpretations of strategic planning we will concentrate first on the expectations of the Budapest leadership regarding the strategic process, since these views – together with the liberals' values – are the Budapest model's supporting pillars. The approach to be revealed will help us both to understand the history of the first three election cycles and to evaluate it.

ELEMENTS OF THE BUDAPEST MODEL IN STRATEGIC PLANNING

The Budapest model describes the municipality's liberal leadership's efforts to elaborate and accomplish an independent and responsible urban policy. A policy based on liberal principles is the decisive factor in the model. These principles refer both to the choice of values and methods applied in policy. Among the methods that are employed, process regulation is of special importance as it determines the elements of the strategic process as well as the strategy building process of different fields. It is also worth reviewing "strategic real planning" as a feature of the Budapest model and outlining the cabinet system that is central to the course of accomplishment.

CONSISTENT POLICY AND PROCESS REGULATION

As a starting point in the description and evaluation of the Budapest process of strategic planning and management, we must analyze how the leaders of the municipality interpreted the logic of consistent decision-making. As an example of consistent policy-making logic, we quote from a short paper by the deputy mayor responsible for the financial management of the Municipality, who has always been the most influential Budapest politician besides the Mayor. The paper was sketched in relation to a question of party politics, its temporal scope is thus shorter than that of strategic planning. We do not refer to the political question itself, and quote only the statements that characteristically reveal consistent policy-making logic:

1. *"... principles, values, essential goals that are and can be identified independent of [changing external conditions],"* and are relatively stable, and to be enforced permanently, serve as a starting point in policy-making.

2. *"If we do not classify the goals as variables, we can afford deliberations and ranking only concerning the efficiency of the ways of accomplishment in reaching the goals."*[17]

3. *"Up to the point where we do not wish to reconsider our goals, we must deliberate all the logically possible options for their realization, and set up their priority scheme exclusively according to efficiency."*

4. *"... enforcing the [criterion of efficiency] in political practice means constrained choices from options depending on external factors that can not be directly influenced at the time of decision-making."*

5. *"With regard to the external factors, the elementary rules of logical thinking induce (or should induce) us to take the fact into consideration that theoretically – i.e., when we only contemplate a possible future situation – options may vary depending also on changes in the external factors."*

6. *"Thus, if someone wishes to fix (i.e., to make it accepted as the only possible option) today, what decision will come (what decision will be the most rational) a year later, he or she wishes to thrust his or her own will on reality in a purely voluntary manner."*[18]

Considering this logic, it is easy to find a place for the Budapest standpoint between the two extreme interpretation poles of strategic planning that were previously mentioned. The

---

[17] "To be clear: this consideration refers merely to the 'clean-cut' type of thinking, and has nothing to do with 'the end justifies the means' type of thinking" (Atkári, 2000: 2)

[18] Atkári, 2000: 1-2

ideas above clearly do not follow the approach that focuses on future interventions deduced with professional-minded rationality from an end-vision.[19] Instead, they put emphasis on principles and goals, and press for making decisions with full knowledge of the actual conditions in order to efficiently advance towards those goals.

The Budapest municipal leaders' rational, goal-oriented approach requires a gradual decision-making process. Strategic planning and management as a long-term process must avoid an inflexible implementation of goals, since urban policies must be implemented in a constantly changing environment. Strategic planning in urban policy must pursue a dynamic model always allowing for flexible adjustment to the prevailing conditions while always keeping to the policy's main thrust.

Appropriate process regulations are necessary to guarantee this dynamism in the strategic process. Fixed long-term principles and a principled and exact definition of the necessary conditions for reaching the goals provide stability to the model. This strategic level within the model determines the long-term process. Medium- and long-term conceptual planning must reach this level of definition in formulation. Subsequent steps and actual decisions are to be defined on the basis of the goals and depend on actual conditions i.e., they must be adjusted to the dynamic of current events. This level of tactics is where decisions are adjusted to changing conditions within the limits defined by the strategic direction.

Within this conceptual framework comprehensive planning requires not only strategy-creation, but also the unraveling of the process leading to decision making while guaranteeing both flexibility and steadfastness in keeping to the course. Decision-making must be properly structured to offer the diverse participants – expert, recipient and decision-maker – the possibility to argue for their views at every stage concerning the questions that fall within their competence, in accordance with the preceding agreements. Essentially, this is settled by the "casting" outlined in the subchapter entitled "The Process of Strategic Planning." In practice, this casting is fine-tuned by the exact identification of the professional planning tasks and by the content of the policy papers.[20]

In this approach strategic planning and management is essentially a goal-oriented process regulation. The art of making urban policy means a specific formulation of goals and a constant strategy that – after approval and within the frame of the given decision making process – is able to govern the actual steps of the process and to guarantee the realization of the given goals.

---

[19] 'The urban development conception (1997–2002)' subchapter of this study provides further remarks to this approach. A more detailed discussion and criticism on this approach can be found in the study on infrastructure development.

[20] Ultimately, the details of these identifications and papers define which participant of the decision-making process will, at a given phase, give an answer and to what question. This is of crucial importance for the efficiency of the strategic process.

As we shall see in subsequent chapters, the importance of the logic of this process regulation goes beyond the field of strategic planning.[21] Earlier we called it a supporting pillar of the Budapest model because it is a basic method in formulating urban policy. It exerts itself almost in every field that is constrained to take uncertainties into account.[22] We shall see later that in Budapest, besides general policy, this logic governs the structuring of financial management reforms, the transformation incentives, price formulae, privatization contracts, etc.

STRATEGIC REAL PLANNING

The specificity of the strategic planning process in Budapest may be captured by looking at the importance attached to financing. As we shall see in the next chapter, it became clear to the Municipality of Budapest as early as the early 1990s that the toughest limits to their urban policy plans would come from financing restrictions. Throughout the period at issue, scarce resources bound the municipality's hands. Effects on the strategic planning process were twofold: on the one hand, the reform of the financial management system became (and has remained) the main thrust of the restructuring process, and on the other hand the iteration of the sectoral and financing conceptions became a key element in the strategic process.

The term "strategic real planning" is meant to highlight the importance of the iteration of the sectoral and financing conceptions for reaching realistic solutions. As applied in Budapest during the period at issue, strategic real planning starts from the understanding that capital investment and operation conceptions of the sectoral and functional areas must be based on professional considerations. However, urban planning experts must always heed the prevailing possibilities. This means that the professional staff must as a rule base their work both on actual financial possibilities and must constantly check the viability of their conceptions and strategies against prevailing financial conditions. It now goes without saying that strategic real planning is based on the conviction that the only way towards a potentially realizable strategy, which also holds out the prospect of the involvement of additional resources (EU, IFI, etc.), is through the iteration of the relevant professional and financial considerations.

In the presentation of the history of Budapest's urban policies over the past 12 years, the emphasis will be put on the evolution (introduction) of the method of strategic real planning. Our description focuses on the progress that financial management reform made in working

---

[21] The determination of the long-term direction of the political process by the exact formulation of the goals, principles and main directions, as well as the demand for adjustment within the main thrust permeates the whole volume.

[22] Uncertainties can be found practically in every part of urban and financial management policy: they are brought about either by changing external conditions, by conditions that do not fully surrender to model-making, or simply by mistakes made by the contracting partners. Hence the Budapest leadership's attempt to include the possibility for revision, adjustment or amendment in a regulated, strictly defined form in all strategic means, agreements and contracts, as we shall see later.

out and signaling the realistic space of maneuvering for urban policy, and its effects on professional planning. The story of Budapest is a good case study for understanding the extent to which political and financial considerations and requirements can guide professional planning towards the creation of a realistic and integrated urban policy strategy.

THE CABINET-SYSTEM

The cabinet-system must be mentioned as another valuable tool applied in the Budapest strategic process. The Cabinet of the Mayor – and later the cabinets of the deputy mayors – played an important role in working out and implementing several elements of the Budapest reform.

The cabinet is an organizational unit working for the elected decision-maker with an expert staff who – supporting the work of the decision-maker – conceives and manages innovative ideas and conceptions and follows their adaptation and evolution. The staff prepares them for decision and makes organization proposals for implementing the new activities in everyday operations.

The cabinet members are counselors who keep track of cardinal matters from their inception through the elaboration of the (often alternative) solutions, until their implementation and later monitoring. Their role is far more that of a traditional advisor who provides general information for the leaders on specific problems. Beyond expertise, the cabinet counselors must have the faculty and skills to come up with new ideas and the know-how necessary to understand and bypass potential bottlenecks in their implementation, which implies an acute understanding of bureaucratic structures and how organizations work. This is crucial to the elaboration of new strategies that have a chance of being carried through.

This type of cabinet-system played an important role in the elaboration and accomplishment of the Budapest strategic reforms. In the first election period the staff working directly for the mayor was officially called the Cabinet – now it is called the Bureau of the Mayor. From 1994, the "Cabinet" is not used any more, as the name of the organizational unit. Still, the cabinet-system survived and has been successfully working for the mayor and his deputies, providing essential contribution to the formation of strategic thinking, to the preparatory work for new means and institutions, and to the accomplishment of the municipal reform.

URBAN POLICY IN BUDAPEST
THE FIRST STEPS: CHOICE OF VALUES AND GOALS – 1990–1991

We should begin our description of Budapest's urban policies in the wake of the change of the political system by introducing the city mayor's program for the first election campaign. As we have said already, in an ideal case an election program defines the politician's fundamental value choices and main goals (perhaps coupled with comprehensive programs and definitions of some objectives). Once elected, these allow the politician to begin his or her work as mayor on projects that have already been legitimized by the voters.

However, the change of the political system occurred rather quickly, and the whole process was in a transition phase. The law on municipal governments had to be drafted and approved in a rush, parties picked their candidates for the post of mayor in a matter of weeks, and municipal elections were called in a similarly hurried manner. It was understandably difficult to assess the conditions and challenges the urban policy of Budapest was about to face, and it was likewise not easy to size up the future scope of activity. The candidates did not even have sufficient time to draft substantiated and detailed election programs, and thus could only promise to apply their ideological credo to their urban policies.

Gábor Demszky, the politician who was eventually elected as mayor of Budapest entered the race on his party's liberal platform.[23] The program offered a plain and easily comprehensible summary of the way liberal values could and should be applied in local politics. In this credo basic environmental and strong social responsibilities were also markedly declared. The program described the candidate's guiding values in general terms, but also summed up the liberals' commitments in each sector, and defined the general goals (only a few of which were specific to Budapest), as well as the ways of deliberation concerning the selection of possible future measures. The program perfectly fulfilled its role as a guide for choice, but, due to the rapidly changing conditions in which it was adopted, offered only principles and general statements as regards possible objectives. Nevertheless, this document was coherent, consistent, and comprehensible in its choice of values and in its political direction. It was important because it provided principled foundations and legitimacy for the mayor's subsequent activities.

In addition to all these, the program was also important in that it had a decisive influence on general political culture. The program had the potential to improve the city's political culture, the level of which was rather low at the time of the change of the political system. It managed to communicate the set of liberal values indispensable for the change of the political system. In style and spirit, the program signaled the dawn of a new era.

In the first election cycle, the Free Democrat mayor – who had to lead the municipality by a minority – appointed four Free Democrat deputies. Since it was obviously difficult to reach comprehensive and fundamental urban policy deals in this situation, after the election the mayor focused on drafting his own, more detailed program.

The next logical step in the strategic process was the first confrontation between ideas and prevailing conditions. In the spring and summer of 1991, this could mean only the assessment of the municipality's general status and evaluation of the situation of the various sectors, since the local governments' scope of maneuver – owing primarily to the immature political context – was still too unclear to assess. As there was no awareness of clear, rigid limitations, new conceptions and ideas abounded. This was an extremely exciting moment

---

[23] Alliance of Free Democrats (SZDSZ), 1990

in the municipality's history. Several experts came to the fore who had never been asked to draft official conceptions before, but who felt that the time was ripe to present their ideas. They expected their previously rejected visions to be picked up by the city's new leaders. Since the municipality's financial and political turf was uncharted territory, and there was no time to assess and comprehend its nature, it was a huge challenge for the city's newly elected and inexperienced politicians to filter out the extremes and to decide which of the many and often contradictory expert proposals they should identify with.

The mayor's program of 1991[24] represented the first major attempt at drafting a comprehensive policy document for the city. In the wake of the change of the system, the city's leaders made their first concerted attempt at summarizing the various tasks, problems, and conceptions pertinent to the city's future urban policy, and prepared them for debate.

This urban policy document markedly differed from the mayor's election program in that it went far beyond principles and value choices. It focused on Budapest's potentials and problems, and attempted to give specific answers by identifying alternative solutions. This document represented the first attempt at identifying the municipality's strategic goals and the tools conducive to make them happen.

Naturally, the analysis of the tools and methods of intervention was bound to remain rather vague and the depth of elaboration of the individual programs rather uneven. Nevertheless, this fully satisfied the requirements of the day, as the related laws and regulations were also incomplete, and thus it was not possible to specify the municipality's realistic potentials.

Although this first attempt did not and could not qualify as a coherent urban policy document, it still succeeded in:

- making the first steps towards redefining public roles;
- creating an inventory of the tasks and problems in each sector;
- identifying the most important projects and activities (e.g., the construction of the third "ring road" within the city, the development of the city's public transportation system, or the tasks related to urban rehabilitation) and making proposals regarding associated institutional and material needs;
- assembling the proposals of various policy fields in one document and thereby making them more transparent and comparable;
- promoting further reflection and planning.

Last but not least this document also helped the freshly elected politicians to reconsider the municipal government's roles and responsibilities. At the same time, in retrospect, we cannot but admit that it proved to be completely unfit for influencing the ingrained standpoints and convictions of the professional staff. The document was clear-cut in its choice of values, and it defined the goals and paths that would lead to their accomplishment. Yet it could not provide such a definite framework for professional planning that could make the sectoral experts change their attitude and reconsider their earlier plans.

---

[24] Foundation for a European Hungary, Local Government Experts' Office, 1991

PLANNING DURING THE FIRST ELECTION CYCLE – 1990–1994

The new political era in Hungary naturally opened the way for the Municipality to officially start reviewing the previous regime's sectoral conceptions and plans. The situation had changed completely. The independence of the local governments should have induced a change in the planning approach. The adjustment process between local requirements and capacities should have been the focus, rather than the maximization of central subsidies. Yet the sectoral plans were still written following the old, ingrained principles that had driven the previous regime's urban policy. Planners used a markedly supply-oriented approach to plan the implementation of their dreams about an "ideal network," "complete services," and the "optimal urban structure." They projected astronomical capital investment requirements and instinctively amassed countless project proposals based on the long-standing assumption that some might this way materialize through "hanging on the plan"[25] i.e., on a budgetary item line.

At the time, amidst permanently changing conditions, the city's financial leaders were not yet prepared to think beyond the fiscal year and to project financial frameworks for longer periods of time. Consequently, politicians were likewise unable to see the long term effect of their decisions. Similarly, the value choices and soft goals laid down in the programs dating from 1990 and 1991 did not yet have the potential to provide guidelines to override the ingrained habit of accumulating project proposals. It could not either reconcile the prevailing Babel-like chaotic environment where people spoke different professional languages and communication was difficult.

THE FIRST FILTERING PROCESS – 1992–1993

In the first few years, coherent strategic planning could not reach the stage where accepted goals could be broken down into concrete projects and generic concepts translated into concrete steps. However, by 1992 it had become clear that the proposals needed serious filtering. (The chapter on financial reform will explain how this need for planning was reinforced by the preparations for the World Exposition – scheduled for 1994, postponed to 1996 and ultimately canceled.)

A large number of project proposals were inherited from the socialist period or raised on the basis of the comprehensive conceptual work of 1990 and 1991. The municipality's priority

---

[25] "Hanging on the plan" was a lobbying strategy favored by the sectors during the socialist era. The sectoral leaders strove to keep as many proposals as possible on the table, often by consciously under-planning the costs. Their aim was to make any initial phase of their projects accepted by the government and entered into the budget. Once even a small part of an investment project was launched, the conclusion of the whole could practically be taken for granted.

medium-term development projects document, which was approved in February 1992,[26] was the first attempt to filter those projects. The document's aim was to identify those projects in the field of physical infrastructure that could be realistically completed in the medium term (3-5 years):

> *"In its present state, the urban development conception cannot aim for complexity [...] In its current form, [the document] makes an attempt to identify those 12-14 prominent capital investment programs (projects) on which it seems worthwhile to concentrate the municipality's limited resources – in order to accomplish goals that fit into the longer-term objectives."*[27]

The aim of this document was to enhance the iteration process between long-term visions and prevailing conditions. The document tied the vast majority of the prominent projects to a specific medium-term goal: the city's planned hosting of the World Exposition in 1994, and thus may be seen as a success.[28] As for adjusting programs to available resources, its achievement was far less. The deputy mayor responsible for the conception had to rely on information from the office departments and was not in a position to apply stricter filtering, which would have necessitated political deliberations. Even the political weight of the mayor – governing by a minority – would have been insufficient to press for a more severe approach through the Assembly. Cooperation among the political parties of the Assembly was necessary for any real progress to occur.

In order to have a realistic urban policy, the minority leadership had to establish an agreement with other political parties concerning the importance of this goal and initiate cooperation in creating the conditions necessary for the iteration process between programs and resources. Finally, the parties of the Assembly concluded their agreement on the main items of cooperation in "The Program of Joining Forces, 1992."[29] The document prescribed cooperation in three cardinal fields in order to work out the new urban policy: strategic goals, assessment of the scope of maneuvering, and an investment program to be devised within the limits of this scope. The intention was to direct decision-making towards strategic real planning.

In the background of "The Program of Joining Forces," the working out of a second, more radical filtering of projects was drawn in the two-year capital investment program, which was completed in late 1992 and approved in 1993.[30] Rooted in the previously described set of values, this document defined investment priorities in a more coherent and concrete manner. On this basis it aimed to generate a consensus on the projects that the municipality

---

[26]　The Office of the Mayor of Budapest, 1992b

[27]　The Office of the Mayor of Budapest, 1992b: 1

[28]　The story of the planned Budapest World Exposition is discussed in detail in the chapter on 'Budgetary Policy'.

[29]　Inter-party document of municipal party factions, 1992

[30]　The Office of the Mayor of Budapest, 1993. The two-year capital investment program is also discussed in the study on 'Financial Management Reform'. However, the focus there is on the program's role in the reform of the financing process and not on its general urban policy implications.

should eventually implement.[31] To facilitate agreement on the list of the projects to be accomplished, the document introduced two new elements into the process of iteration: the adjustment of projectable resources and required interventions, and the coordination between professional conceptions and political intentions. This marked the birth of two key elements in Budapest's subsequent strategic planning process: strategic real planning, and the articulation of the professional and political processes.

Although the municipal government still found it difficult to size up its sphere of activity (as the context continued to be in a state of flux), it became inevitable to assess projectable resources in order to be able to make a selection from among acceptable proposals. As filtering reached the Capital Investment Program stage, project proposals were in part judged on the basis of financing possibilities.

> *"[...] in defining the program we must start out from the possibilities of financing. In spite of – or in certain cases because of – the scarcity and unpredictability of resources there is need for drafting a comprehensive financial-economic plan which can relatively safely project the 'size of the blanket' in view of the predictable changes in the broader context. This plan should also specify the size of the required external resources, as well as the municipal government's potential to draw on these resources in order to realize the goals that are justified by other – "content" – considerations. This is the only way for us to rank the projects, and it is only on this basis that we can schedule the realization of the major projects for the medium term, i.e., for a period longer than two years. [...] without such a comprehensive plan we cannot step forward and cannot decide on the nature (bond issuance, loan, concession, etc.) and size of the external resources we should rely on. Furthermore, in absence of a comprehensive consensus on the financing frameworks we must count on a series of potential conflicts caused by the time-consuming process of individual decision-making."[32]*

The other major innovation of the two-year capital investment plan was that it structured the decision-making process. This was the first time that the political and the professional decision-making processes were rationally and transparently distinguished. Based on "The Program of Joining Forces," professional work now had resort to an established set of values and priorities. It fell on the departments and experts to translate the established goals into professional proposals. Based on their professional convictions, the departments had the right to prioritize sectoral capital investment projects. Finally, the politicians could decide – within the bounds of financing possibilities – on the ultimate ranking of projects within each sector and also on the proportion of different resources that the sectors would receive. This

---

[31] We emphasize here the role of coordination. This was the first document that resulted from a long and detailed internal coordination process. In terms of content, the Priority Development Goals and the two-year Capital Investment Program may seem similar, yet their origins were quite different. The former document was drawn up by the deputy mayor in charge of urban development based on the wishes of the office departments, while the latter was drafted on the basis of prolonged professional and political negotiations conducted by the mayor's cabinet. The different character of the elaboration process strongly influenced the strength of the documents in influencing future decisions.

[32] The Office of the Mayor of Budapest, 1993: 2

way the process enabled the simultaneous presence of rational professional deliberation and freedom of political choice.[33]

The structure of the two-year capital investment program provided an accurate reflection of this financial, professional and political coordination process. It began with an assessment of the financial possibilities, continued with the definition of the values and priorities, and concluded with a list of the agreed sectoral capital investment projects. Capital investment projects were listed according to sectors and each sectoral list was prioritized. In each sectoral list there was a "line" to separate the projects into two groups. "Above the line" projects were considered to be achievable by politicians (based on the resource projections) and thus were to be elaborated in further detail. For all their significance, "below the line" projects had to be postponed. A political decision (based on changes in the resources or the points of view) was required to shift a project from one category to the other.

As we can see, the urban policy process that was applied in Budapest is not a textbook case of deductive strategic planning. Strategic goals were not broken down into programs, program-objectives, sub-programs, specific objectives, projects, and action plans. Instead, the process aimed to bring out concrete, realistic, and achievable agreements in the shortest possible time. These agreements promoted the previously agreed goals and established priorities, and guaranteed the continuity of the capital investment projects' implementation.[34] In order for this to succeed, both the priority medium-term investment goals and the two-year capital investment program had to be compiled in an iterative process. Their ultimate aim was to coordinate (to the best possible extent at the given moment) professional, political, and financing conceptions and possibilities.

ATTEMPTS AT INTEGRATION – 1994

The approval of the capital investment program did not result in the suspension of the comprehensive conceptual activities. In the period leading up to the municipal elections of 1994, conceptual work started along two lines, meaning that two groups independently started to develop two separate conceptions albeit with the same goal of integrating sectoral policies. The first line was governed by the city mayor's cabinet, and the second by the deputy mayor in charge of urban development.

The mayor's cabinet group continued with the approach detailed in the two-year capital investment program, trying to align the municipality's scope of activities with its objectives.

---

[33] The aim of the process was to respect professional work as well as to keep professional and political decisions apart. To a large extent these attempts proved successful. And yet, this statement entails a simplification. There is no denying that the departments' professional work is not independent of politics, as the committees and individual decision-makers exert their influence constantly through various formal and informal channels. Still, the key decisions (the approval of the development goals and plans) were made in a regulated process.

[34] Back in 1992, the planning process could not have got to a more sophisticated stage. But sophistication was not the aim, at the time it would not have made sense to postpone decisions. There was also political pressure for realistic and acceptable progress amidst the given conditions.

The group's goal was to draft a realistic urban policy strategy based on concrete achievables, weighing goals together with resources. The scope of the work was wider than the two-year capital investment plan in two respects. On the one hand, its resource assessment went beyond the plan's short-term approach by considering the municipality's financing and institutional possibilities over a longer period. On the other hand, instead of assessing only the investment goals, the approach was based on the operation and capital investment activity of the municipality as a whole. Strategic proposals and alternatives were formulated in this comprehensive urban policy context.

This broader approach was by nature less accurate than the two-year capital investment program. Its aim was not to lead to the drafting of a concrete list of capital investment projects. Instead, its sole aim was to go a step further, from the previously approved strategic goals towards professional programs. The sectoral chapters proposed minimal and expanded "program packages," which they deemed to be achievable. This way they "only" identified and programmed the sector and field specific priorities. And yet it was an extremely important development that – at least on the sectors' level – a consistent argument was drafted to connect goals and priorities with the program proposals. Furthermore, these arguments managed to keep the resource requirements of the sectors within realistic limits. The analysis of realities and the enforcement of priorities became organic elements of the document, and since then it has been impossible to avoid the inclusion of this type of argumentation in the strategic plans of Budapest.[35]

At the same time, the document failed to fully coordinate the sector strategies (notwithstanding that the conception approached the various sectors on the basis of the same basic strategy line). It was the other group – the one led by the deputy mayor – that undertook to synthesize strategies. The primary aim of this second group was to systematize the diverse requirements pertaining to urban development[36] along spatial and structural priority lines.

The urban development conception started out by defining the set of values to be observed during the capital investment projects, and also outlined the city's projected future state. The main aim of the conception was to create the supply of land uses determined in the vision – through infrastructure investments and appropriate regulations. To this end, the conception resorted to the previous infrastructure conceptions' supply-oriented approach and specified the required developments and regulations pertaining to the different areas and zones. However, as the planners' vision was not sufficiently grounded in reality, this conception turned out to be practically useless in promoting the continuation of strategic planning or substantiating the day-to-day political decisions. (At the same time this rather peculiar vision did exert a fairly strong influence on the capital city's new umbrella regulation[37] which was being drafted at the time.)

---

[35] Alliance of Free Democrats (SZDSZ), 1994

[36] The Office of the Mayor of Budapest, 1994b

[37] The umbrella regulation is the name of those elements of the city's zoning and master plan that can be defined by the municipal level of government.

Summing up, we can state that although in 1994 the municipality made some headway in making strategic planning more integrated, the two conception described above could only moderately contribute to the emerging synthesis of the city's urban policy.

The mayor of Budapest adopted the new urban policy program as his platform in the campaign leading up to the municipal elections in late 1994 and was reelected. After the elections, the mayor's liberal party concluded a coalitions deal with the socialist party. Since the local socialist fraction did not have a program for coalition cooperation, the liberal urban policy conception became the basis for the coalition's Work Plan.[38] The following four years however did not lead to the smooth implementation of the urban policy conception.

Although the coalition's work plan was accurate and to the point, it could not protect the city's leaders from the running debates. Although the mayor's program was adopted as the basis for the coalition's operation, it could not function as a mutually recognized agreement. On every single issue, the parties in the coalition had to fight again for an agreement. Nevertheless, this realistic work plan was still useful. It served as a starting point and point of reference for professional and the political debates.

THE MAIN THRUST: FINANCIAL STRATEGY – 1996

The next decisive step in the creation of new urban policies for Budapest was the reform of the municipality's financial management. As discussed in detail in the chapter on financial management reform, the liquidity crisis that coincided with the cancellation of the World Exposition preparations enabled the city's leaders to introduce a completely new financial strategy. The main aim of this strategy was to achieve and maintain a sustainable financial balance. To this end the city leaders introduced a seven-year financial modeling system and – based on that – the practice of rolling budgetary planning. Planning was based on long-term projections and it became a practice to prepare detailed medium-term forecasts. The introduction of financial modeling made the operation and investment financing deliberations inseparable, and the necessity of cardinal financial management measures could now be objectively proved (such as privatization, the rationalization of the institutions, the review of services provision etc.).

The chapter on financial management reform also reveals that after 1996 the municipality's operations became more transparent, easier to plan and efficient, and its financial system became more balanced and stable (despite the fact that the municipality's external financial prospects – i.e., independent of municipal financial management - did not improve at all). Simultaneously, the municipality's creditworthiness also improved, significantly broadening financing possibilities for investments. This way the municipality's financial system became a stable and predictable tool for the accomplishment of realistic urban policy goals.

---

[38] The SZDSZ and MSZP party factions of the Municipality, 1995

INTRODUCTION OF CAPITAL INVESTMENT PROGRAMMING – 1996

As part of the financial management reform process, the municipality introduced a new rolling system for programming its capital investments. This system initially covered four years, later seven years, and eventually became known as the seven-year development plan.[39] In terms of structure, the new system is similar to the previously discussed two-year capital investment plan. It features the investment goals in prioritized lists broken down into sectors, and it features above-and below-the-line projects.[40] This new system also adopted the rule that professional proposals had to be adjusted to the previously agreed conceptions and sectoral agreements. However, within these frameworks the city hall departments are free to make proposals following their professional convictions.

A new element is that the seven-year financial model contains longer-term and more accurate projections regarding potential resources. Another novelty is that the distribution of the resources among the sectors is based on the experiences of previous years.[41] The proportions of resources allocated to each sector can only be rearranged by the political decision-makers. Since the projections specify the amount of resources that are planned for, the only way to increase resources allocated to one sector is to reduce resources for another sector. This, clearly, results in tough political bargaining.

Although literature often requires that capital investment programming also function as an important means in the integration of development conceptions, the Budapest leadership did not find it necessary to apply this requirement in their investment programming process.[42] Their seven-year capital investment plan aims to adjust financing potential with demands, and is achieved by a strict view on financial constraints and a tough decision-making process.[43] The integration of investment goals can be performed by, on the one hand, keeping to the previously set agreements (on urban policy and sector conceptions) and, on the other hand, by the coordinating role of the political decision-making process to regulate allocations and policies from sector to sector.

---

[39] The municipality refers to its annually reviewed investment program as the seven-year capital development plan. The literature uses the term "capital investment program" to identify these types of documents, and refers to the related activities as "capital investment programming." This is why we use this term in the title of this section. Meanwhile, we had to stick with the term "development plan" in our references to the documents.

[40] The term of below and under the line projects are utilized only during the negotiations with city hall departments. The official plan and the capital budget of the municipality (that is accepted by the Assembly) contains only the above-the-line projects.

[41] The seven-year capital investment planning procedure is discussed in detail in the study entitled 'Elements of the Financial Reform.'

[42] Though individual political decisions are obviously motivated not exclusively by the desire to integrate policies, the Budapest system considers the "wisdom" of the political process prior to any other applicable algorithm. Due to the complex and sophisticated system of tasks to be performed by a metropolitan government, the Budapest leadership questions the relevance of the traditional project evaluating algorithms, even in the phase leading up to decision-making.

[43] See for details: subchapter 'Capital investment planning' in the study on the 'Elements of the Financial Reform.'

The seven-year planning process helped the strategic process enormously. Its importance is clearly shown by the fact that different actors' criticisms of it vary according to their role in the strategic process. Obviously, external planners and experts criticize political decisions that differ from their views, internal professional leaders occasionally object to the revisions of their professional proposals, and politicians are generally irritated by the inflexibility of the financial limits. Theoretically, all three types of criticism are justifiable, but critics often forget that the validity of these criticisms is only dependent on the extent of the political influence on the professional proposals, as a certain degree of political influence and a certain inflexibility due to financial constraints is a natural factor of investment planning.

From the point of view of the evolution of Budapest's urban policies, the capital investment program is important for two other reasons (besides its role in the planning of project financing). On the one hand, the seven-year capital investment program enables the municipality to prepare and implement its projects according to schedule, and on the other hand, it very clearly identifies the resources for the individual sectors, and thus defines cornerstones for sectoral planning.

CHANGES IN SECTORAL PLANNING

The financial management reform process, including the seven-year capital investment planning, has enabled the sectors to clearly identify the financial framework within which they can plan their strategies. It has become possible for them to draft realistic strategies based on their professional convictions and financial potentials. This method of planning, which is based on the contrasting of the professional plans with the available resources, was defined as strategic real planning in the introductory part of the present chapter. Strategic real planning requires – besides the quality input from the professionals – an appropriately advanced financial system. As we have seen, it took six years for these conditions to emerge in Budapest.

Since the mid-1990s, the sectors have been facing the challenge of having to draft task fulfillment and capital investment conceptions[44] that are adjusted to available resources and result in optimal institution, infrastructure and activity structures (within the given context).

In principle, these new conditions should have resulted in the unconditional adjustment of the professional plans to available resources. Of course, in practice the sectors continued to fight to increase their own importance.[45] Although the new system could not completely quell the sectors' struggle for better positions, the strict financial planning and financial discipline enforced by the city's leaders managed at least to keep these battles at bay.

---

[44] The task fulfillment conceptions are discussed in detail in the section on institutional reform, while the capital investment conceptions are tackled in the chapter on infrastructure.

[45] For details, please refer to the study on the 'Elements of the Financial Reform' and the chapter on utilities.

The chapter on financial reform will describe how difficult and time-consuming it was to create appropriate financial conditions for the municipality. Later on, we shall also see that the changes were even slower in the fields of urban development thinking and sectoral planning. Yet, some advances were obviously made in these spheres also. If we compare the development conceptions that were drafted in Budapest in the early 1990s with the ones dating from the end of the decade, we must conclude that the latter were more focused and showed less unrestrained ambition. "Professional planning" could indeed open up new solutions, although to varying extents in different fields of activity. By the end of the 1990s urban developers' dreams had become more or less aligned with reality. They planned to build only one new boulevard instead of two, two new bridges instead of five. For example, the forecasted consumption of drinking water has shrunk to less than 50 percent of that of earlier projections. In the field of transportation development, earlier plans that called for the creation of a "complete system" were replaced by a set of proposals that focused on a couple of prominent projects for demand management.[46] In health care, the focus of the plans calling for all-out institutional reconstruction was shifted to feasible elements within a regionally organized health care system. In education, for example, the conceptual renewal of secondary level vocational education is now clearly defined.

The clarification of the municipality's goals and possibilities exerted a strong influence on the evolution of the urban development strategy, which by definition synthesizes the results of different reforms, as well. The shape of the urban development conception in 1998 already bears the traces of the move towards strategic real planning.

THE URBAN DEVELOPMENT CONCEPTION – 1997–2002

It is intriguing to reflect on how relevant strategic real planning logic is to urban development, which by definition deals with long-term processes.

The logic of strategic real planning collides with the typical Eastern-European "urbanist" approach at several points. One reason for urban planners to object to strategic real planning has to do with their role in the planning process. Since, in principle, urban planners are the ones who integrate the diverse sectoral proposals, they are inclined to claim the conductor's stand and set urban policy themselves. Attributing such a "wisdom" to planners deeply contradicts with the logic of the strategic process that is built on the wisdom gradually developed during the iteration process.

Time is another problem. Urban planners inevitably think long term since the development of a city is a slow process. Yet at the same time, the longer the time span, the more obscure

---

[46] This statement simplifies reality. Though the planners' ideas continuously change, there are many stable elements in their conceptions and plans. The Transportation system plan accepted in 2001 is an excellent example of this. The plan contains nearly all projects that were developed by the earlier supply-oriented planning, yet is already based on a pronouncedly demand-oriented approach that guides its implementation schedule and provides clear priority ranking. The changes that occurred in the field of infrastructure are discussed in detail in the 'Infrastructure Development' study.

realistic forecasts are. Urban planners often feel entitled to freely think about the longer term projects and to forego reality in their visions, leading to unrealistic conceptions and goals. Actual capital investments built on such conceptions threaten to be inadequate and to launch development in the wrong direction.

Apparently consistent conceptions and strategies can be built on these mistaken starting points, but it would still be hazardous to make actual decisions based on these conclusions and proposals. As a consequence, urbanists are often at a loss to explain and understand the practical failure of their orderly ideas. They question why decision-making advances on the basis of seemingly individual deliberations and argumentation, instead of their "consistent scenario"?

Integrating urban planning into the strategic real planning process can be a way out of this conundrum. Only a realistic assessment of the scope of maneuvering and the context will enable us to define at least the scale of a realistic investment volume, to which the urban development strategy can be adjusted.

In Budapest, work on the urban development conception was started afresh in 1997. There were two markedly different approaches. The first aimed to pick up the thread of the "urbanist" 1994 development conception and to define all the items needed in the city on the basis of the conception vision and goals. The second approach relied on the logic of the 1994 urban policies. This approach emphasized the need to establish realistic goals and an inevitable selection between diverse proposals in the desire to advance towards the elaboration of an urban development strategy.

The first draft of the plan, which was subjected to a broad debate in 1998, adopted the "all-embracing" approach. It also included a financing projection[47] based on accessible municipal resources. It was obvious that the plan, which brought together all the dreams and visions one could think of, was anything but realizable. The plan was so rich that its presenters were "proud" to submit it to professional scrutiny. At the same time, the contrasting of the possible moves with the projected scope of action (based on the financial projections) elicited further thoughts on the characteristics and dimensions of a realistic strategy, i.e. it promoted a shift towards strategic real planning. This is reflected in the following quote from the conclusion of the chapter on financing:

---

[47] Of course, this resource projection was different from the seven-year financing model used in the municipality's budgetary planning, as the two estimations had different goals. The seven-year projection is used for planning budgetary obligations, and thus must be conservative in its approach. The projection of the financing possibilities of the urban development conception does not entail actual budgetary obligations. Instead, it provides the foundations for the drafting of optimal, long-term strategies. This offers more freedom. Two projections were made for the development conception: there was an "optimistic" and a "pessimistic" version based on the basis of the macroeconomic projections. The difference between the two versions was almost 100 per cent (measured against the total volume of resources projected until 2015). And yet, even this level of accuracy was helpful in choosing between alternative urban strategies. The need for more accurate projections arises when medium-term planning aims to approve a set of tools for the implementation of the given strategy, as well as to approve actual projects.

"The size of the estimated resources leads us to conclude that in the period at issue the municipality will be unable to complete the proposed infrastructure construction projects and the high quality rehabilitation of the districts. As an alternative, the municipality may choose to concentrate on a few appropriately selected major investment projects in order to compensate for the infrastructure gaps. It can also opt to improve the city's environment or employ any other future strategy to prevent the inhabitants from moving out of Budapest." [48]

It was definitely due to the sobering effects of these estimations that the 1999 version of the conception featured a markedly "prioritizing" strategic approach, really advancing towards a strategy. While the earlier urban development conceptions all started from the sectoral arrangements of the interventions proposed for the realization of the underlying visions, the 1999 strategic proposal evaluated the projects according to their urban development effects and ranked them according to these effects. Also the style was remarkably more concise. Here is a brief quote from the text:[49]

"To accomplish these goals, the Urban Development Conception focuses its strategy on the reorganization and differentiated development of the brown field zone. The key infrastructure element in the upgrading strategy of the brown field zone is the construction of the Körvasútsor boulevard [...]" [50]

From the point of view of strategic real planning, it is interesting to follow what happened later to this version of the urban development conception. As described before, the drafters of the 1998-1999 approach and strategy meant to align their work with the emerging trend and logic of strategic real planning. However, this is not what happened with the conception in the end. By 2002 (the completion of the conception in its final form), the formulation of the strategy became again less focused and concise than it had been in 1999. Rather than pursuing a definite line, the document had again evolved into an all-embracing and consensus-seeking mix.[51] As a result, the 2002 conception failed to outline a strategy. Yet, it appears that even this type of urban development conception can have its relevance. In this form, contrary to its drafters' intentions, it cannot exert marked influence on the decisions made on actual projects. Practically the only reason for its existence – in its present form – is political legitimization. It ranks among those "soft" elements that most likely exert some effect, but where it is difficult to state what that effect is.

In this respect it is welcome that it fails to fulfil the claim formulated in the introduction of the 2002 conception to "cover the way from long-term strategic thinking that produces strategic

---

[48] The Office of the Mayor of Budapest, 1998c: 136

[49] The quote is brief because our point is to highlight its style only. The analysis of the content of the strategy would go far beyond our goal, which is to review the evolution of the strategic process.

[50] The Office of the Mayor of Budapest, 1999b: 1-6

[51] To an extent, the 1999 strategy has survived in the sections on spatial structure, although without the original prioritization.

programs to the operative programs."[52] After all, there is no need for the programming part if the conception is to be used as a "soft" tool. As we have seen, the Budapest strategic process requires programming to come from the seven-year investment plan and not from conceptual planning. In this setup the urban development conception could gain a more important role if it moved towards strategy elaboration with definite priorities and realistic proposals.

THE STATUS OF STRATEGIC PLANNING – 2002

Having reviewed the evolution of the various tools and elements of strategic planning, let us now look at the forces and influences that shape the Municipality of Budapest's activities and urban policies today.

A key element in shaping a municipality's urban policies is the definition of long-term directions based on agreements on fundamental strategic goals. Since the creation of the 1991 urban policy document (never submitted to the Assembly) a consensus has evolved on two key urban policy goals: easing the transportation crisis and urban rehabilitation. The financial management reform that was officially approved as part of the budget conception for 1997 can already be considered a legitimate and long-term strategy in its own right. Since the reform strategy gives a concrete definition of its objectives as well, it can also provide directives for the municipality's short-term financial strategy.[53] The sectoral conceptions approved by the General Assembly during the past few years can likewise be considered legitimate attempts at defining the goals and further specifying directions. These conceptions always identified long-term sectoral goals and priorities, and occasionally also included scheduled medium-term objectives. The urban development conceptions and urban policy documents aimed at integrating these goals and objectives – and were more or less successful at that.

As a result of years of conceptual work, the agreements point to a more or less integrated – though far from being unified – system of medium- and long-term objectives. The comprehensive urban policy conceptions did not go beyond pointing out directions to be taken. Yet some of the sectoral conceptions went as far as identifying concrete programs and projects, and occasionally even included short or medium-term schedules for the planned activities. As a result, the Municipality of Budapest has accumulated a rather diverse set of objectives for its various activities.

For keeping to this set of objectives a plan coordination mechanism was set in the planning process in 1996. The aim of plan coordination is to guarantee that the proposals are drafted

---

[52] The Office of the Mayor of Budapest, 2002a: 3.

[53] The Office of the Mayor of Budapest, 1996c: 2-7. For details, please refer to the study on the 'Financial Management Reform.

in relation to[54] the already approved and relevant urban policy, sectoral, and financial decisions:

> *"[Plan coordination] has to make certain that the proposals submitted to the decision-makers are accurate and sufficiently detailed, that they comply with the previously approved conceptions and principles, or provide clear reasoning if they deviate from them."*[55]

Under ideal conditions, this filter serves a dual purpose. It can enforce the observance of the previously agreed strategic directions, and – if necessary – it can also signal the need to review the previously established directions and the earlier agreements.

Budgetary decisions are the necessary next step in the process of implementing the goals identified in the course of conceptual planning. Financial management reform created a system for planning the available resources for sectoral operation and investment over a seven-year period. Consequently, the implementation of the goals hinges on medium-term planning. The decisions that define the concrete steps implemented from the urban policy line are determined by the actual financing strategy, the seven-year capital investment program, and the annual budgets.

There is clearly no closed-end, direct relationship between conceptual planning and implementation. In other words, the conceptual-type comprehensive or sectoral plans do not as a rule directly lead to budgetary decisions (such a system would make no sense). The conceptual plans promote the definition of the strategic directions. As we have seen, it falls then on the sectors to adjust the proposals to the changing conditions, while the final decision belongs to the politicians. In principle, this system enforces the maintenance of the strategic course in a flexible manner and also integrates professional and political activities.

In the Budapest strategic process, decisions on implementation are influenced by the conceptual work that identifies strategic directions and by financial planning. Unless there is a reason for amending the strategic directions, the decisions must fall under these and within the forecasted scope of maneuvering. Activities are deemed in line with strategic directions based on an analysis of the decisions made. It is based on this analysis that decision-makers consider the system to be capable of adhering to the strategic directions and capable of accomplishing the required objectives on schedule and adjusted to potentials. At the same time, planners – who expect their plans to become realized in a consistent way – often criticize decision-making for inconsistencies. In response to this criticism, we can state that the strategic process and decision-making system elaborated in Budapest never aimed at "implementing the plans" according this strict interpretation of the planners' approach.[56]

---

[54] The term "in relation to" means that the conflicts between the old and the new goals had to be identified and clarified, while in the policy papers it was not compulsory to adjust the proposals to the earlier conceptions.

[55] The Office of the Mayor of Budapest, 1999b: 3.

[56] The demand for "realizing the plans" relies on the specific urban planner approach that strives to define an "ultimate state." As we have explained it before, this approach completely collides with the strategy-creating ideas of the municipal leadership. Further details on the different planner-approaches and on their possible integration into the decision-making process can be read in the subchapters on 'Integrated planning' and 'Urban development' in the paper on 'Infrastructure Development.'

Instead, it strives to reach (or implement) the identified goals, in each case taking into consideration the given and changing conditions, thus finding an optimal route to achieve the goals. Decision-making would deserve criticism within the frames of this system only if a significant part of the budgetary decision diverted from accepted strategic lines or went beyond the planned scope of maneuvering.

EVALUATION AND FURTHER COMMENTS

Why is the Budapest strategic process relevant and of interest? Perhaps because it is radically different from the idea of strategic planning that planners – educated in and influenced by the previous era – often instinctively propose. Twelve years after the change of the political system it is still a common occurrence that planners think of urban policy in terms of plans and documents rather than as a process. This mistake is often made not only by the local planners but by donor organizations as well. During the past twelve years, the international organizations have spent huge sums on drafting strategies for cities in the post-socialist region.

It is often easy to convince newly elected decision-makers that the involvement of noted institutions and famous experts in the drafting of their urban policy strategies will improve the credibility of their activities. After official approval the document then leads the process of decision-making to the beat, as a musical score would a piece of music.

This is a rather naïve expectation, if only because of the changing status of democracy at the local level. Amidst the nowadays intensively changing conditions it does not make much sense to produce documents that aim to guide decision-making in the long run, and political forces are generally not eager to subject their decisions to conceptions that are deemed optimal by experts and/or advisors. However attractive and well-presented the documents may be, only those parts tend to be implemented that both the professional and the political leaders understand and accept.

The Budapest strategic planning process provides a pattern that markedly differs from the "strategic plan-centered" model. Obviously, the example of Budapest (where there has been no officially approved strategic plan) does not aim to prove that advance is possible without any strategy and that a municipality could be managed by case-by-case political decisions. Instead, the city's example proves that a comprehensive strategy evolves through consecutive steps.

In the Budapest strategic process, the diverse conceptions and documents played a cardinal role. However, really worthwhile influence could be exerted only by solutions that answered the vital problems of the city and municipality, and not by accidental conceptions devised by urban planning experts.

The other studies in the present volume will testify to the fact that a document may play rather diverse roles in such fields as financial management reform, infrastructure development or various other fields. The positive elements in the final result originate from the intended and indirect consequences of the cumulated decisions made by the city's leaders – for twelve straight years in office – according to their own coherent strategy.

The continuity in the Budapest leadership is of crucial importance with regard to the adaptation process following the change of the political system, and is a salient feature of the Budapest model. The leadership was able to guarantee the consistency of the transformations. This was amplified by the cabinet system which supported the particular steps of the adaptation process.

The other salient – methodological – feature of the Budapest model is the logic of process regulation. The basic element of process regulation was the consistent, clearly defined thrust of the transition on the one hand, and a system that retained sufficient flexibility for adjusting the activities to ever-changing conditions on the other. From this point of view, it is also worth studying how the municipal leadership gradually created a process for articulating decisions and later for decision-making that fulfills both requirements of strategic direction and flexibility.

PROFESSIONAL WORK

No international institution or consulting firm has ever been involved in the drafting of Budapest's strategic documents.

The cabinets of the mayor and his deputies governed the elaboration of the cardinal elements of the Budapest strategic process. The counselors of the cabinets were expected to manage the new ideas and conceptions for adaptation from problem identification until the implementation of the solutions. The cabinets elaborated the great bulk of reform elements, while consultant firms working for the municipality often drafted the sectoral conceptions.

Essentially, the conceptions originated with the municipality's employees and decision-makers, or with their local experts. This internally developing process was a long and indirect way of getting to a strategy. At the same time, it enabled the municipality to firmly stay on its course as soon as it could overcome the difficulties of the first few years.

It goes without saying that even this internal process has never been free of tensions. In working together, the differences between the members of the administration, of the cabinets and the external experts can play quite an important role. External experts are inclined to introduce a series of new methods, thoughts, tools and objectives. However, while they have a comprehensive view of the "outside world," they often fail to accurately perceive the local government's internal conditions. The cabinet members stand in-between: their primary task is to seek new solutions, but at the same time they also seek to integrate these solutions into the operative work of the municipal administration.

The task of implementing and applying solutions always falls on the public employees. Quite often the success of a project depends on the involvement of internal expertise and on the internalization of the new ideas through informal approvals. For this reason, the learning process by which the office staff becomes acquainted with the new elements must be considered part and parcel of the conceptual work. This "professional participation" may ensure the acceptance of the new techniques not only on the formal level (by the decisions of the General Assembly) but also on the informal level (meaning that the individuals whose work schedule rests on those very decisions should also identify with them).

The present chapter could not go deep enough into the process to tackle the issues related to internal acceptance of new ideas. However, the following chapters will provide ample examples of how certain progressive proposals were blocked by the employees' "internal resistance."

POLITICAL PROCESS

In the post-socialist region, donor programs regularly raise the issue of public participation in the strategic process. For this reason, it seems appropriate to address the question of direct public participation and decision-making with regard to the strategic process in Budapest as well.

In general, theory identifies two distinct approaches to democracy: representative or direct. Each has its own particular mechanism for decision-making. In the former model, the election results legitimize the decisions of the elected majority. Here the politician's license is valid for an election cycle, and the voters pass judgment on his or her political decisions when they cast their votes. Meanwhile, the other – direct – model prefers consensus-based decision-making.

Both models have their advantages. Majority-based decisions encourage innovation and related processes tend to be faster and simpler. Consensus-based decision-making processes tend to be more time-consuming, but the acceptance of the decisions themselves is usually stronger and thus have a more lasting effect. On account of these differences, theory and practice alike prefer the consensus-based decision-making process in cases when the public is markedly divided or when conflicts abound.[57] In stable situations where there are no marked divisions, the benefits of the other – representative majority-based – decision-making process come out stronger.

If we accept the above statements, we cannot but argue that the conditions of Budapest's urban policy do not justify a broad use of community-based planning methods. Fundamental issues of development are hardly ever subject to debate in Budapest. To an extent this also applies to the election platforms. Differences tend to manifest themselves primarily on the level of detail, and also when there is a need to choose between alternatives. This way (although different political tendencies have their own particular priorities) the decisions on alternatives based on majority representation tend to reflect the electorate's will at least in principle.

Direct public participation may still prove to be useful for resolving certain issues that directly and perceivably affect citizens. However, the application of this method is hindered by the fact that for the time being, the change of the political system has not given rise to a broad, active and politically educated layer of citizens interested in public affairs and willing to take part in them.[58] Interest groups risk distorting decisions if this broad layer of politically active citizens is not present. By ending up being the only voice of the population their opinion may become over represented.[59] Such a minority opinion was counter-balanced by the so-called metro campaign organized in 1999,[60] where the local government itself organized a mass citizen campaign. However, there is as of yet no thoroughly considered and well organized participatory process in Budapest for solving local conflicts.

The majority of the population trusts the Budapest municipal leaders, although they did not apply forms of direct public participation within the strategic planning process. The popularity of the mayor, and also the fact that he was re-elected for the fourth consecutive term, prove that the public is content with the transparency of the strategic process.

THE ROLE OF THE POLITICAL LEADERS

The history of Budapest's urban policy process provides ample example for the importance of the elements of strategic planning and of politics in general in everyday practice. It is especially important to recount the story in view of the prevailing "political amnesia." Research proves that the average citizen's political memory span does not exceed one or two years, which means that people tend to quickly forget politicians' statements and deeds. It is thus natural that even the actively participating experts do not necessarily have such a structured picture of the value choices put forward in the first election platform or the arguments and stances of subsequent programs.

---

[57] There exists another justification for direct public participation in decision-making. As the example of many successful self-governments in Latin-America goes to show, public participation can also help to reestablish politicians' credibility in the eyes of voters, in cases where voters have lost trust in politicians, become disappointed with corrupted public life and with the deficient functioning of the representative forms of democracy. (An excellent example: Albers, 2001.)

[58] Direct public participation can also be useful when the institutions of representative democracy are properly functioning. However, this requires the involvement of precisely the layer of citizens who are aware of the basic principles and processes of the political system, of the connection between public services and taxation, fees, who are willing to cover the expenses of public services but expect services in return and who are willing to contribute to the solution of issues of distribution and supply.

[59] Popular protest against the building of the road-network connecting a new Budapest bridge to a national route offers a good lesson on this topic. In this case a small group of citizens halted the acceptance of a solution that would have directly benefited a much larger local community and indirectly the whole city. In such cases the involvement of the other, less vocal, citizens would be important and these should be given ample information and detail on the project (See for details: Pallai, 1998 b.)

[60] In 1998, the Government unilaterally cancelled the contract concluded with Budapest for building a new metro line. After the decision the government involved civil organizations in the argumentation against the metro. The Municipality of Budapest organized a mass citizen campaign against the Government decision and in support of the metro.

This detailed recounting of the events and trends can also provide examples for other local governments on how to shape a settlement's urban policy line step-by-step. In Budapest, this was a slow yet uninterrupted and consistent process, notwithstanding that an outside observer looking on at any given moment may view it as a mishmash of divergent elements. Which it was. This process occurred in a divided political field, amidst the constant clashes of divergent ideas and plans. The value choices and conceptions that we have identified in this chapter could never in themselves have kept the process under control. This control was the result of the staffers' unabated conceptual work, ensuing deals and agreements, the stability of the municipal leadership and their commitment to their goals. In this process the decisions were clearly not shaped by documents, and yet these documents played a key role as points of reference for the arguments and for progress in general.

Not long before the publication of the present volume, the mayor of Budapest was elected for his fourth consecutive term. This is an undeniable proof of the success of his record. The mayor now counts four successful campaigns to his credit. We have already referred to the first two campaigns. The mayor's 1998 campaign rested on a comprehensive and coordinated vision for the future, based on the urban development conception drafted in parallel to the campaign, which was conceptualized under the slogan "We are building a metropolis."[61] And yet, in his victorious campaign the mayor emphasized the realistic and concrete medium-term goals rather than the vision, which held so prominent a place in the conception. He also highlighted his approach to finance, thereby making the plans more credible. The 2002 campaign rested on the "Program for developing Budapest into a European capital."[62] This program spelt out his long-term goals, but also included concrete and detailed promises for the near future. The mayor's expertise – Gábor Demszky has been at the municipality's helm for twelve straight years – came through in his strongly buttressing the program.

Election campaigns play an unquestionable role in politicians' successes. Another lesson that can be drawn from the story of Budapest is that it is indeed possible to win an election with a program that identifies concrete goals and strives to remain (relatively) realistic.

And yet, it seems that the achievements of previous cycles played a more important role in the mayor's political success than his exceptionally concrete and realistic campaign. Similarly, the city's perceptible physical improvement, the definitive political statements, the credibility and the untouchable honesty of the city's leaders probably played a more important role in his re-election than the political documents and the campaigns, however professional they were.

To put it more bluntly: the mayor most likely was able to keep his position in the leading group of the political top lists because he remained credible in the eyes of the voters. He spoke the truth, did not promise the fulfillment of unrealizable dreams but fulfilled his

---

[61] Alliance of Free Democrats (SZDSZ), 1998

[62] Alliance of Free Democrats (SZDSZ), 2002

promises, and any suspicion of corruption concerning him or his direct political circle were out of the question.

SOURCES AND LITERATURE

Albers, Rebecca, 2001: *'Participatory budgeting in Porto Alegre'*, in Freire-Stern, eds.: *The Challenege of Urban Government, Policies and Practices.* WBI, Washington DC, pp. 129-145.

Alliance of Free Democrats (SZDSZ), 1990: *'A Szabad Demokraták Budapesti programja.'* *(The Free Democrats' Program for Budapest. Election program.) Budapest*

Alliance of Free Democrats (SZDSZ), 1994: *'Budapest Jövője: Várospolitika 2000-ig.'* *(The Future of Budapest: Urban Policy up to 2000. Eleciton program.) Budapest*

Foundation for a European Hungary, Local Government Experts' Office, 1991: *'Demszky Gábor programja a Főváros számára.'* *(Gábor Demszky's Program for the Capital City. Election program.) Budapest*

Inter-party document of municipal party factions, 1992: *'Az összefogás programja.'* *(A Program for Joining Forces.) Budapest*

Pallai, Katalin, 1998b: *'Dél-budapesti "közlekedési játék", avagy Dél-Budapest közlekedési problémájának stratégiai játék formájában való elemzése'*. *"Transportation Game" in South-Budapest, or the Analysis of the Trasportation Problems of South-Budapest in the Form of a Strategic Game. Tér és Társadalom, No 3-4, pp. 133-153.*

The Office of the Mayor of Budapest, 1992b: *'Budapest kiemelt középtávú fejlesztési céljai.'* *(Budapest's Priority Medium-term Development Goals.) Budapest*

The Office of the Mayor of Budapest, 1993: *'Fejlesztési program 1993-94.'* *(Budapest's Capital Investment Program, 1993-94.) Budapest*

The Office of the Mayor of Budapest, 1994b: *'Budapest Városfejlesztési Koncepciója, térszerkezet.'* *(Budapest's Urban Development Conception, Spatial Structure. Discussion document.) Budapest*

The Office of the Mayor of Budapest, 1996a: *'Tervkoordinációs csoport létrehozásáról.'* *(On the Creation of a Group for Plan Coordination. Presentation to the Cabinet of the Mayor.) Budapest*

The Office of the Mayor of Budapest, 1996c: *'Javaslat Budapest Főváros Önkormányzata 1997. évi költségvetési koncepciójára.'* *(Proposal for the 1997 Budget Conception of the Municipality of Budapest.) Budapest*

The Office of the Mayor of Budapest, 1998b: *'Javaslat Budapest Főváros Önkormányzata 1999. évi költségvetési koncepciójára.' (Proposal for the 1999 Budget Conception of the Municipality of Budapest.) Budapest*

The Office of the Mayor of Budapest, 1998c: *'Budapest Városfejlesztési Koncepciója.' (Budapest's Urban Development Conception. Coordination document.) Budapest*

The Office of the Mayor of Budapest, 1999b: *'Budapest Városfejlesztési Koncepciója.' (Budapest's Urban Development Conception. Draft submitted to professional and public discussion.) Budapest*

The Office of the Mayor of Budapest, 2002a: *'Budapest Városfejlesztési Koncepciója.' (Budapest's Urban Development Conception.) Budapest*

The SZDSZ and MSZP party factions of the Municipality, 1995: *'Budapest várospolitikai feladatterve, 1995-98.' (Urban Policy Work Plan for Budapest, 1995-98. Attachment to the coalition agreement.) Budapest.*

BUDGETARY POLICY

FINANCIAL MANAGEMENT REFORM
KATALIN PALLAI

Having discussed the inception, evolution and means of Budapest's comprehensive urban policies, we shall devote this chapter to summarizing the city's attempts to reform its financial management policies. This, clearly, is the most important element of the urban policy package. Below, we shall describe the way the municipal leaders have created a balanced and sustainable system for managing and financing the local services.

The main consideration governing our description of the strategic planning process was that the choice of the strategy to be pursued and the direction of the associated reform processes should be normally determined by the local politicians' value choices and the prevailing conditions. Although this appears to also apply to the field of local financial management, it is much easier to summarize the challenges and the local political responses in this particular sphere since the choices are more limited in identifying the strategic goals of financial management.

The importance of financial management reform, as an urban policy goal, hinges on the municipal government's independence: according to generally accepted professional principles, an independent financial management policy line is considered responsible if it rests on sustainable processes and secures the sustainable balance of the budget.

As we shall see, the local government conditions created by the Hungarian legal and public finance system in the 1990's were promising for the Budapest leaders and could enable them to take advantage of municipal independence, reshape urban policy corresponding to their own value choices and adjust it to the new context.

In the early 1990's, the Municipality of Budapest appeared to have a fair chance to launch comprehensive policy reforms and to utilize its resources in order to put its operations and financial management on a balanced and sustainable track.

Undoubtedly, the success of the 1990's reform process was that public tasks that had to be and could responsibly be performed by the municipal government were defined, the efficiency of the municipal government's operations was improved and a transparent, predictable, and plannable financial management system was introduced. This financial management system enabled the municipality to enter the international capital market and to build a strategic planning and management process for accomplishing the goals it set itself (as we saw in the previous study).

By the end of the 1990s the capital city's financial management system had become capable of managing practically any type of strategies aimed at long-term sustainability. However, in the early 2000's – during the period preceding the publication of the present volume – conditions prevailing in intergovernmental relations seemed to stop the municipal government from reducing the local structural deficit. The city leaders now expect the new state government (that entered in office in 2002) to carry out wide-ranging reforms such as reforming local government financing and restoring the conditions that had enabled local governments to pursue responsible local financial policies.

The present chapter aims to analyze the capital city's financial management reform process that is considered fundamentally successful but has lately been seriously challenged. Amongst other factors it has been challenged by, on the one hand, the hesitation of the central government in carrying out the necessary reform of the tasks and financing system of local governments, and on the other hand the absence of constitutional guarantees that could have prevented the state government from enforcing its politically biased measures towards local governments, especially in the capital city.

With regards to the lessons it may hold for other cities, the financial management reform process in Budapest may be split in two distinct stages. The first stage coincided with the first two election cycles. During this stage, the "old-style" financial management system, which served the purposes of the Soviet-type, deconcentrated "councils" of the day, was transformed into a system that could function rationally and responsibly amidst the new, decentralized set of conditions. The second stage occurred during the past two or three years, when the Municipality of Budapest had to devise a strategy to manage a short-term crisis. This stage provides important lessons for the analyst of the intergovernmental conditions necessary for the independent functioning of local governments. The analysis of the reform process in Budapest will likely also identify a series of constructive tools and solutions for reforms, and will certainly provide several interesting lessons.

The transformation of a municipal government's inherited financial management system and operations is necessarily a time-consuming process. In the case of Budapest, these reforms spanned several election cycles. During that period the general conditions were subject to continuous changes, and certain elements of the context were significantly altered. Consequently, although the strategy remained essentially unchanged during the period at issue, the steps to implement it had to be permanently adjusted to the prevailing conditions.[1] In this chapter we shall attempt to provide a brief but comprehensive summary of the Budapest municipal government's medium and short-term goals and the actual steps taken to implement them. We shall also attempt to order the elements of this rather complex process into a clear and logical picture.

UNDERLYING CONCEPTS

Prior to our analysis of the Municipality of Budapest's financial management policies and practices we should define a few underlying concepts. Besides facilitating understanding,

---

[1] As we shall see: the definition of goals, the adjusting of implementation to prevailing conditions and the management of the strategic process apply the same process regulation technique to the field of financial management reform that was described in the previous chapter (Strategic planning and management reform).

we also expect the interpretation of these definitions to shed light on the inherent logic of the financial management process.

The text below could have been taken from financial management reform textbooks. It may be seen as a simple, textbook-like introduction, but since the concepts and definitions at issue so very radically differ from the ones used during the previous post-socialist period (and, regrettably, also from the current financial management practices of several cities in Eastern Europe), we believe that it is justified to recapitulate these terms.

SUSTAINABLE FINANCIAL MANAGEMENT

Financial management reform aims to create the conditions necessary for sustainable service delivery. This requires setting up a financial management system that guarantees the long-term sustainability of the city's financial balance.

The financial balance may be construed as consisting of three different levels. These are: the operation's direct balance; the sustaining balance that sustains the organization's operation at a given level; and the adaptive balance that enables the city's operation to adapt to recurrently changing requirements.

Direct operational balance can be guaranteed by revenues covering every-day operating (current) expenditures. To keep up the sustaining balance, the revenues should cover not only the direct operating costs but also the costs of maintenance and refurbishment (to counter-balance depreciation in order to ensure operation at the given level). Finally, the adaptive balance requires not only revenues to cover direct operating costs plus the costs of maintenance and refurbishment, but also the costs of necessary service or infrastructure development or – if demand decreases – the costs of orderly cutbacks.

It goes without saying that adaptive balance alone can guarantee sustainability. A sustainable balance hinges on the municipality's ability to maintain the quality of its public services and continuously adjust them to the prevailing demands. This creates a favorable environment for the city's population and economic activities – thus ensuring that the city's revenue raising potentials will cover the costs of its future services.

If a municipality fails to maintain the quality of public services and to continuously adjust them to the prevailing demands, it becomes less competitive, its affluent residents and leading businesses move to other cities and eventually the city cannot stay afloat. There are several examples to prove this point, perhaps the best known being the decline of the downtown areas of large North American cities. Meanwhile, thriving major cities not only maintain their public services but also continuously renew and develop their servicing infrastructures and adjust them to the changing demand.

THE CONDITIONS OF SUSTAINABILITY IN PLANNING

The maintenance of a public service structure that is capable of continuously adapting to the changing demand requires the existence of a strategic planning mechanism. Sustainable financial management hinges on the presence of:

- relatively stable and predictable external conditions;
- a professional planning mechanism that takes account of the projected revenue sources and defines the desirable – adjusted, optimized – servicing conditions for the future;
- a financial planning mechanism[2] that considers the prevailing level of financing and the projected tendencies by transforming the findings of professional planning into revenue and expenditure projections;
- a financial management system that is capable of coordinating the professional and financial aspects of planning and the various associated decisions;
- strategic management that guides a goal-oriented process and can guarantee prudent decision-making.

The ultimate goal – the conditions for sustainable balance – can only be gradually reached through a process of strategic planning that entails both professional and financial elements as well as through a decision-making and operation process appropriate to the consequent implementation of the strategy.

CORNERSTONES FOR SUSTAINABLE FINANCIAL MANAGEMENT

Local governments all over the world have a factor in common: their resources are limited. (This statement is true even if we add that their actual tasks differ according to country, and that each settlement has its own particular resource base.) Due to scarce resources, local governments must carefully consider the way they utilize their resources in order to satisfy the triple requirement of direct operation, maintenance, and adaptation. To guarantee the sustainability of their financial management, local governments must create a system that is transparent, plannable, and can adapt to and reflect changes. The first cornerstone for sustainable financial management is therefore the existence of a transparent financial management system.

According to commonly accepted professional opinion, a budget should be (technically) divided into operating and capital expenditures, and revenues, in order to guarantee the most transparent accounting system possible. This type of system provides the clearest reflection

---

[2] The terms financial planning, budgeting and budgetary planning that appear later on in this chapter should not be construed as accounting terms. Instead, they are used in a broader sense and refer to a more comprehensive policy activity.

of the state of the balance. On the revenues side, the current (operating) revenues, which continuously (or periodically) flow into the local government's budget, are clearly separated from the accumulation or capital revenues. The latter are typically one-off revenues, i.e., they can be accessed only once from any given source. Similarly, on the expenditures side, the permanently binding recurrent or operating expenditures are separated from capital expenditures, which are typically larger, investment-type expenditures based on individual decisions. This budgeting system, divided into four main parts, is simple and transparent. It not only reflects the state of the balance at any given moment, but also signals possible future trends.[3]

The balance of the (current) operating expenditures and revenues (later to be called operating budget) plays a key role in promoting sustainability.

The importance of a balanced operating budget may seem obvious, since only revenues that flow incessantly into local government budgets can be expected to cover recurrent operating costs. When the recurrent revenues are not sufficient to cover the operating costs, and thus the difference must be covered from the capital revenues, we cannot talk about sustainability even on the direct operating level. In these cases, the one-off revenues originating from the sale of assets are available only temporarily, since the marketable portfolios are bound to be gradually exhausted.[4] Consequently, attempts to cover the operating costs from capital revenues are doomed to fail, since using these marketable assets eliminates the resources, while the operating costs of the operation are bound to remain.

However, if the direct operating costs consume all the recurrent revenues, it is likewise untenable in the long term to try to cover operating costs from the recurrent revenues. In such a situation the direct operating budget might remain balanced for a short while, but (since maintenance and adaptation are financed exclusively from the capital revenues) the revenues from the sale of assets will quickly dry up and the sources of maintenance and adaptation will become exhausted.[5] The results are predictable: deteriorating infrastructure, increasing operating costs and ultimately the inevitable choice between the need to cut back the quantity or the quality of the services.

These two examples should sufficiently prove that the second cornerstone for sustainable financial management is that recurrent revenues must exceed operating costs, i.e., there must be an operating surplus that is produced.

---

[3] In Hungary, the appendix to the local government budget specifies the operating and capital balances. However, in most of the other transition economies it is not a legal requirement to specify these balances either in the appendix or elsewhere.

[4] Capital grants generally can not be utilized for operating purposes. Local governments that have no asset reserves and produce a negative operating balance have no chance to raise loans either.

[5] Here we refer only to the drying up of the local governments' own capital revenues. However, we must also realize that in such a situation – when the recurrent revenues are fully eaten up by the operating expenditures – there is practically no other source of revenue for capital expenditure either. The local government that finds itself in this situation is not creditworthy, and cannot add its required contribution to the investment grants.

Previously, we defined sustainable financial management as one under which the revenues continuously cover direct operating costs, necessary maintenance and adaptation to the changing external conditions. The local government's own capital revenue sources are limited, as they can be drawn only from the local government's own assets. They are bound to eventually disappear if they are used to cover the operating costs. For this reason, only capital revenues can be used to cover capital expenditures. This is the third cornerstone of sustainable financial management. However, we must also see that even capital revenues cannot continuously cover the costs of refurbishment and adaptation. Consequently, the local governments must create the conditions for using the operating surplus (which draws on the recurrent revenues) as the source for their capital expenditures. This is the next reason for monitoring the balance of the operating budget.

Although the operating budget is the key to sustainability, capital revenues may also play a cardinal role in the grand transformation projects that characterize the post-socialist transition period. Local governments might be able to complete previously postponed refurbishing and investment projects and set their services on a sustainable course, if they spend the revenues originating from the sale of their assets and from the privatization of part of their services on transforming and upgrading infrastructure. This step (which qualifies as a peculiar "transitional scheme") may also provide remarkable leverage to shape the necessary conditions for balanced financing management.

We have yet to identify one more principle crucial to the financial management of Budapest's municipal government: a local government is not a business venture. The paragraphs above did not imply in any form that a local government could or should invest its own capital in lucrative businesses in order to generate extra revenues for operating or for other purposes. The leaders of the Municipality of Budapest believe that this is out of the question for the following reasons.

The prime reason is that only high-risk transactions can be expected to generate significant capital gains. A local government is in no position to run risks as a company might in the private sphere. Business risk implies the risk of failure, and a local government can under no circumstances risk the quality fulfillment of its public service obligations. Local government funding comes from public sources, which raises strong political and moral prohibitions to risking public money in business ventures.

Other rather significant practical considerations, that were regrettably not observed by the few local governments that had ventured to run business risks, may be enlisted besides this main reason: a local government is not a business organization, it does not have the kind of special expertise at its disposal that would enable it to successfully operate in a free market environment. In fact it is not advisable to develop such (rather expensive) capacities, as local governments were not designed to this end. Besides, the local government decision-making system is less dynamic and flexible than that of a business venture, and lacks the necessary consistency that a private owner has.

It is only natural that local governments (and thus also the Municipality of Budapest) from time to time posses liquid financial resources. Heeding the principles of financial prudence, the Municipality of Budapest invests these funds into securities guaranteed by the state. The gains from these securities are relatively modest (though definitely positive in real terms), and are too small to enable the municipality to expect them to continuously contribute to the city's operating costs. At the same time, they are not risky and are available at any time for investment expenditures.

THE OPERATING SURPLUS

As we have seen, the operating surplus (i.e., the recurrent revenues not committed to operation) can serve as the resource for the city's longer-term non-operating expenditures. The operating surplus may also serve as coverage for debt amortization, i.e., it may be considered a key factor in determining the city's creditworthiness.[6] The operating surplus constitutes an important element of the analysis of a local government's financial activity, and it is widely agreed that the local financial management strategy must specify its targeted level.[7] At the same time, there is no universally accepted and applicable benchmark[8] that can be used as reference, primarily because its expected level is always determined by the context (the structure of assets, tasks, funding; strategies etc.).

The operating balance of the budget and its projected fluctuations represent one of the main elements in the planning of local government financial management.[9] At the same time, we must recognize the fact that the attempts to increase the operating surplus always entail sacrifices. In a given intergovernmental framework, there are two ways to increase the operating surplus: the local government can either increase its own revenues and/or it can reduce its operating expenditures. Every step aimed at increasing revenues (tax or fee increases), and practically every method used for reducing operating costs is bound to lead to discontent from affected constituencies.

From a political point of view, the least disadvantageous option for a local government is to launch investments that promise to reduce operating expenditures. However, these investment projects might distract funds from other spectacular development projects that promise direct political gains. Therefore they often get pushed into the background. It is thus no surprise that, due to the high political "price" entailed, politicians who tend to think in terms of election cycles and usually do not look far ahead, dislike taking such steps that only pay off in the longer run. This is especially true for the new, evolving democracies.

---

[6] According to the logic of financial management this statement may be considered accurate. However, a more precise definition would be to say that the adjusted operating surplus can serve as the debt service of any newly raised loan. This is the part of the recurrent revenues which is not committed to financing the operation or repaying the earlier debts. Under Hungarian regulations this is identified as corrected own revenue which equals that part of the previously mentioned sum which comes from own resources.

[7] The capital city's financial management strategy, which was approved in 1996, prescribed the accomplishment and maintenance of a 20 percent operating surplus.

[8] A benchmark is an index that is generated from a series of values experienced in similar situations, and is used as a point of reference.

[9] It is important to note here that, to our knowledge, this basic consideration has never been raised during the setting up and the evolution of the post-socialist local government systems. The legislators did not reckon with it, and most local governments likewise have not included it in their financial strategies and planning.

Symbolically speaking, we might say that the operating surplus marks the crossroads between long-term and short-term political thinking. Maintaining or improving a positive operating result is a long-term "investment," while its reduction is often the product of the prevalence of short-term objectives. To improve the chances of realizing their longer-term goals, local governments should specify the need for a positive operating result as an objective in their financial management strategy.[10] This is the only way that they will be able to avoid "conflict-avoiding" short-term approaches taking over during the annual budgetary debates and decisions.

THE STRUCTURAL DEFICIT

Bearing a structural deficit means that – with constant external conditions – there is a negative discrepancy between the dynamics of the expenditures needed to fulfill the required tasks and available revenues. From the point of view of planning, with reference to any tasks structural deficit occurs when the fluctuations of the projected resources available for a given activity fail to guarantee coverage for the projected expenditures.

The concept of structural deficit can apply both to individual activities and to the whole operation of a local government. To quantify it, we have to determine the expenditures needed to fulfill a given task or group of tasks, and contrast them with the available resources. Similarly to the analysis of financial balance, the assessments of costs can be limited to the direct operating costs, or can also include depreciation or the costs of adaptation. Accordingly, structural deficit can occur in direct operation, in operation at a given level, or in qualitative adaptation.

With reference to the arguments concerning sustainability, we can also state that, from the point of view of sustainable financial management, a structural deficit is bound to remain as long as available resources fail to cover the costs of continuous adaptation. (Later in this study we will identify structural deficit as being one of the main problems of both Hungary's state budget, and the capital city's financial management.)

PROCESS REGULATION

The conditions that influence a local government's financial management are subject to continuous changes. Consequently, the financial model applied must be dynamic rather than static and must always enable the local government to adapt to an ever-changing environment.

Process regulation is the technique of adaptation to the dynamically changing external conditions – similarily to the strategic process reviewed in the previous chapter. This technique does not start with individual decisions or a long-term action plan but with the clear-cut, principled definition of the goals and necessary conditions conducive to their

---

[10] In strategic planning, objective means that the targeted performance is spelled out precisely, specifying what, when and how should be reached. In this specific case, the city must specify the targeted level of its operating surplus, as well as the accomplishment deadline and schedule.

realization. The clarification and approval of the principles and goals constitute the basis to rely on during the subsequent processes and the necessary adjustments. In this way, a single act of agreement can most effectively guarantee the evolution and implementation of a clear-cut strategy.

This interpretation of process regulation is in full harmony with the method of strategic planning presented in the chapter on urban policy. Strategic planning there also started with the drafting and approval of longer-term goals. The aim of this approval is also to create an underlying agreement that will help guide decision-makers in taking later decisions in volatile conditions.

NORMATIVITY IN FINANCING

A properly established normative financing system for performing public tasks is capable of simultaneously guaranteeing both predictability and equity according to a predetermined set of values. Furthermore, it can include incentives for applying efficient financial policies.

Normativity can best be construed in contrast to the discretionary method of management based on case-by-case decisions. It means that a minimum set of uniform rules is applied to a given group of activities. Ideally, this set of rules applies not only to the resource allocation model for the given year, but also offers guidance for the adjustment of this model when, subsequently, conditions will change. This longer-term regulation is the guarantee for predictability. Of course, genuine predictability requires that the rules be associated with relatively predictable variables (for example, in the case of an intergovernmental financing system, with the GDP or with the total of public expenditures).

A properly functioning, fully normative financing system rests on three fundamental principles: (1) its elements should be proportionate to the required tasks,[11] (2) it should provide guarantees for resource localization,[12] and (3) it should pay heed to resource capacity.[13] Although these principles may occasionally restrict each other, they must be observed and enforced simultaneously.

In current Hungarian terminology, the term "normative" is often also applied to "quasi-normative" systems where the budget assigns "norms"[14] (i.e., specific resources) to the individual local tasks. These systems rest exclusively on principle (1).

---

[11] A financing system is proportionate to the tasks, if it allocates resources according to a key parameter (or parameters) of the given tasks (i.e. on the basis of an algorithm, such as the number of those provided for, the number of students, or the quantity of the service at issue).

[12] Under the principle of resource localization, generated resources are left in the place of origin, thereby stimulating the creation of further revenues.

[13] The principle of resource capacity means that in the process of the distribution of central resources the given unit's own income producing potentials (resource capacity) are also considered. The related calculations are performed with an algorithm based on the unit's characteristics.

[14] Norms: annually specified sums tied to units associated with a given task (e.g., the amount with which the education of a primary school student is subsidized in a given year).

These quasi-normative systems in practice never provide coverage for the full cost of the given service. In consequence, they need local resources. This, in turn, requires the balancing of the individual economic entities' resource capacities (income generating potentials) in order to allocate evenly minimum level resources for the same type of tasks.

Based on principles (1) and (3), it is possible to establish and operate an equitable system. However, even such a system is likely to fail in providing incentives for independent financial management. These simple, quasi-normative systems can encourage savings and financial rationalization only by enabling local governments to allocate the residual resources from their annual savings to areas where resources are scarce within the same year. This is not a real incentive for creating resources (i.e. increasing own revenues), as these own resources are eventually withheld[15] by the equalization, and cannot be used for strategic purposes beyond the fiscal year.

Consequently, a fully normative system must also entail incentives for utilizing own resource capacities through resource localization. In addition, resource localization is also important from the point of view of the units affected for enhancing transparency and accountability.

We must not forget that in a system that simultaneously draws on these three principles, the principles of resource capacity and resource localization tend to restrict each other. For this reason, their simultaneous application requires a careful consideration of the possibilities that are available. Withholding (although it runs counter to the principle of resource localization) may be seen as an acceptable way of compensating the differences between individual resource capacities, but only to the extent that the motivation for own revenue creation is also retained. The real challenge in planning fully normative systems lies in finding this delicate balance.

Of course, normativity can occur in any relationship where a central budgetary organ finances a subordinate unit (and thus in intergovernmental financing or between a local government and its institutions). In consequence, it is possible to analyze and evaluate all these financing systems on the basis of these three principles, i.e., on the way they are observed and enforced.

THE CONTEXT – INTERGOVERNMENTAL RELATIONS

LOCAL GOVERNMENTS' TASKS

Act No. LXV of 1990 (Act on Local Governments – ALG) spells out local governments' obligations. The specifics of these tasks, associated requirements, and the division of related responsibilities and scopes of authority are normally defined in functional and sectoral laws. Consequently, Parliament's decisions on these laws may lead to changes in the conditions that regulate the fulfillment of local governments' tasks. In turn, these may affect the latter's expenditure assignments.

---

[15] Usually this means "indirect withholding," i.e., the proportionate reduction of subsidies.

The local governmental tasks relating to infrastructure services were regulated rather early, in the first half of the 1990s. In 1990, the ALG defined the infrastructure services that had to be provided by the local governments. The so-called Asset Act of 1991 contained stipulations pertaining to the transfer of assets associated with the decentralized services and in 1993 and 1994 the price setting authority for certain services was transferred.

Local governments set the rates for water, sewage, waste disposal, district heating and chimney-sweeping services. They also set local public transportation rates, although this requires the Finance Ministry's consent. The rates for gas services are still set by the state. In the field of infrastructure services, the rational decentralization of tasks, transfer of assets and the relegation of rights to decide on revenues have created a system that makes planning and envisioning strategies possible on the local government level.

In the field of human sector services, certain educational, welfare, health care and cultural tasks have been decentralized, and the assets needed for their provision have been transferred to local governments. These human services are partly financed by "normative grants,"[16] and partly by local resources. State investment grants as well as local sources finance investment into these services. Sectoral laws approved between 1993 and 1997 established the related quality requirements in the fields of education, welfare and childcare.

Logically, the aim of these national regulations is to ensure that all citizens can access public services independently of their domicile, at a level of quality that is prescribed by law. It is up to local governments to create the conditions thanks to which citizens will access these services. This often burdens them beyond their financial means. Although this system is also rational from the point of view of functional decentralization, some of the new sectoral laws have still created serious tensions, as the state has failed to offset the obligatorily increased expenditures.

Healthcare is the only system that defies rational policy logic. Here the local governments function as owners of the assets tied to the services. Consequently, they are responsible for maintenance and investments (hospital buildings, instruments and equipment). The operating costs are covered by the National Health Insurance Fund (NHIF). Although these sums are transferred to institutions through the local governments' budget, the municipality has no say in the way the money is spent (the sums appear in a separate column).

Omitting the small private healthcare providers, Hungarian healthcare institutions are owned either by the state or by the local governments. The owners decide on their respective institutions' spheres of activity, and they are in charge of assets and investments. However, the state alone determines the system of norms that covers operating costs. This system is often changed haphazardly, without the involvement of, or consultation with, the other owners (e.g., the local governments). The NHIF is also entitled to decide whether it will finance operating costs deriving form local government investments (e.g., new diagnostics equipment). This division of assets and operation financing is unfavorable for local governments (and for the healthcare system as a whole). It does not sufficiently allow for planning and for the chance to improve efficiency. This framework does not encourage a search for optimal solutions. Progress is not incited, but depends only on both sides' commitment to serve the public interest.

---

[16] A normative grant is a resource allocation through annually specified sums tied to units associated with a given task.

Under the ALG, local governments are free to undertake tasks beyond their mandatory responsibilities. However, these tasks must not in any form threaten the fulfillment of their legally prescribed responsibilities.

Besides mandatory and voluntarily assumed tasks, local governments also have delegated powers. The exercising of these powers may have serious financial implications. E.g., the regulations pertaining to land use and zoning may lead to expropriations, and the value of certain properties may appreciate or depreciate in the process. While it falls on local governments to cover the costs of expropriations and compensate those who are negatively affected by the regulatory changes, they partake in the profits (coming from appreciation) only indirectly – if at all.

In the case of large cities, local government tasks are influenced by two more factors.

First, the financing system does not recognize the tasks and services particular to large cities. The existing system does not compensate for the extra costs of these services (e.g., local public transportation), and does not recognize the fact that large numbers of non-local residents also use some of the subsidized services.

Second, it is important to note that, at its inception, the middle tier of the Hungarian system of local governments was based on the traditional intermediate units of public administration – counties. However, counties do not square with society's and the economy's organic, regional units. The creators of the new system divided the tasks of this "missing level" (i.e., the legally non-existent organic region) between the large cities and the "non-organic" counties. Yet they failed to properly regulate the provision and financing of these services and did not include appropriate resources in the cities' subsidies to ensure that they could fulfill these tasks beyond their borders. This situation has generated a spider web of conflicts (riddled with clashing interests, requirements, and conflicting tasks). Attempts to resolve these conflicts through fair and positive-sum solutions are only slowly evolving in the Hungarian public administration system.

THE LOCAL GOVERNMENT FINANCING SYSTEM

Alongside the tasks outlined above, the ALG also specifies local government resources. These are composed of state transfers and own source revenues. The main source for the former is the personal income tax (PIT). In 1990, PIT revenues were fully channeled to local governments but these soon became shared revenues between local governments and the state. Since 1997, PIT revenues have also become a source for the local governments' "normative grants" (i.e., a part of the PIT covers intergovernmental transfers for the local governments' operation). In 1990, 100 percent of the PIT revenues were allocated to local governments on a derivation basis. By 2002, this figure had gradually decreased to 5 percent.[17] Meanwhile,

---

[17] In principle, the percentage of PIT revenues directly re-channeled to local governments who collected them rose to 10 percent in 2003. However, the rise remained fictitious for those settlements where the change would result in substantial extra revenues. On the one hand, withholdings grew due to the change in the method for calculating tax potentials, and on the other hand a new regulation reduced (in proportion to the local tax potentials) the very state subsidies that ought to have been guaranteed in accordance with the change of mandatory tasks. Thus the growth in PIT revenues is practically withheld by the reduction of central revenues resulting from these two measures.

35 percent of the PIT revenues are used as coverage for "normative grants" and equalization transfers. As a result, the local governments' share of the PIT revenues collected from their respective jurisdictions is now a very small entry in their budget.

Chart 1
THE RE-CHANNELLING OF PIT REVENUES TO LOCAL GOVERNMENTS (%)

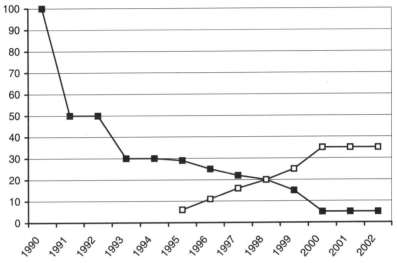

-■- On a derivation basis   -□- On a task basis
Source: Finance Ministry

Chart 2
SHARE OF PIT REVENUES IN LOCAL GOVERNMENT BUDGETS (%)

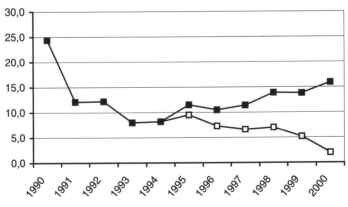

-■- On a task basis   -□- On a derivation basis
Source: Finance Ministry

Chart 3
STATE SUBSIDIES AND OWN SOURCE REVENUES IN LOCAL GOVERNMENT BUDGETS (%)

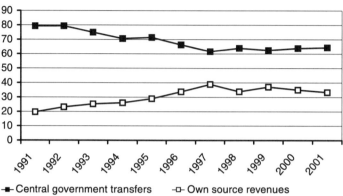

—■— Central government transfers   —□— Own source revenues

Source: Interior Ministry web site, August 22, 2002

The aggregate share of state subsidies in local government budgets has also been steadily decreasing. In 2001, state subsidies accounted for 64 percent (on average) of local governments' total revenues. In Budapest, the respective figure was 30.5 percent. The charts clearly illustrate the decrease in state subsidies, which is especially drastic in the case of Budapest.

Chart 4
SHARE OF STATE SUBSIDIES IN LOCAL GOVERNMENT BUDGETS (%)

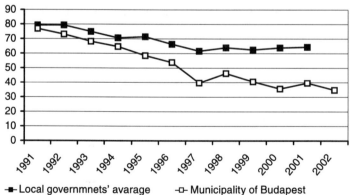

—■— Local governmnets' avarage   —□— Municipality of Budapest

Source: Interior Ministry web site, August 22, 2002;
The Office of the Mayor of Budapest, 2002b

The new system also has a rational side: the earlier practice of cost financing[18] has been replaced with a basically normative system of resource regulation.[19] In this new system the operating state subsidies are awarded in a normative manner, and only the investment subsidies remain to be decided on individually. This discretionary part of investment subsidies, however, accounts only for a mere 4 percent of the local government revenues.

Centrally regulated resources also include the sums transferred from the health insurance fund for the operation of the health care institutions. However, as we have seen, the local governments have no say in the use of these funds.

Alongside the normatively distributed operating funds, the central government also has the right to award investment subsidies to local governments based on discretionary decisions. These subsidies are identified as targeted and addressed investment grants,[20] and as contributions paid out from investment funds[21] outside the government budget. The investment subsidies are awarded through tenders. Certain aspects of this process are regulated,[22] but the discretionary character of the decision remains a key element. The discretionary element is needed, as not everything can be translated to normative rules. Though, unfortunately, from time to time it allows for the prevalence of certain parties or groups' interests.

Local governments collect their own source revenues from local taxes, as well as from fees, charges, stamp duties, fines and revenues from asset management. The local governments are free to decide the extent to which they draw on local taxes (within legally prescribed constraints). On average own source revenues account for 34 percent of the local governments' total revenues. In Budapest, the municipality's own source revenues in 2002 represented 65 percent of the total revenues (calculated without loans). Business taxes represent the most important form of local taxes: in 2000, these taxes accounted for an average 85 percent of the total local tax revenues. In Budapest, the respective figure was 98.6 percent. Revenues from stamp duties vary according to localities, the more active the real estate market is (typically in big towns) the greater importance they have. Revenues from fines and institutional fees are not significant. The user charge revenues from public utility services do not appear in the local governments' budgets.[23] The revenues from asset

---

[18] Under the cost financing mechanism, that had been in use until the late 1980s, the central budget covered the declared expenditure requirements of the councils. For any given year, the amount of subsidies was, as a rule, set on the basis of the previous year's figure. Any changes to this rule were based on individual decisions.

[19] The new name was meant to signify a conceptual change: the new system regulates the parameters according to which the operating subsidy part of the central budget is allocated to specific tasks. The new system was introduced before the change of the political system. 1989

[20] The sums earmarked in the central budget for targeted subsidies are allocated to the local governments on the basis of, and in proportion to, the latter's specific claims. The addressed investment grants are likewise tied to specific goals. These grants are allocated by Parliament through tenders and based on case-by-case decisions. In general, these grants cover 70-90 percent of the actual investment costs.

[21] The bulk of these funds were eliminated in 1995, while some of them were referred to the competence of the ministries.

[22] These regulations affect the procedures and the general aspects of judgment. In general, the peculiar aspects of judgment are spelled out in the individual tender documents.

[23] The 'Infrastructure policies' paper gives a detailed account of these revenues in the case of Budapest. This account reveals that the aggregate size of the budgets of the public utility service providers in Budapest is larger than that of the municipality.

utilization vary rather widely according to local government and period. After all, these revenues are determined by fundamentally diverse asset structures, the financial transactions applied and the pace of the privatization process. In Budapest's budget, the revenues from asset utilization were highest between 1995 and 1997, at the time of the privatization of the large public utility companies.

Chart 5
COMPOISITION OF OWN SOURCE REVENUES IN THE LOCAL BUDGETS (%)

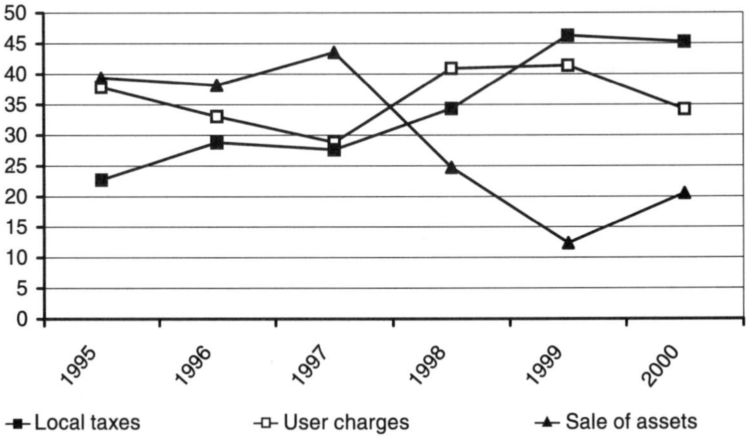

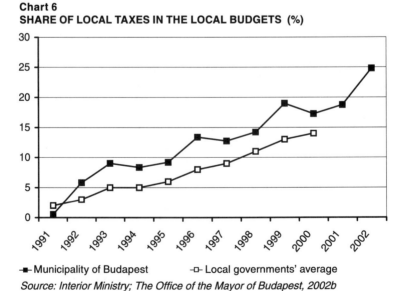

- ■ Local taxes   -□- User charges   -▲ Sale of assets

Source: Consulting, 2002

Chart 6
SHARE OF LOCAL TAXES IN THE LOCAL BUDGETS (%)

-■- Municipality of Budapest   -□- Local governments' average

Source: Interior Ministry; The Office of the Mayor of Budapest, 2002b

FINANCIAL REGULATIONS FOR LOCAL GOVERNMENTS

Under the ALG, the local governments are independent financial entities, i.e. their decision making bodies independently decide on their annual budget drawn up according to the relevant laws. This budget is an annual financing plan for fulfilling the local governments' mandatory and voluntary tasks. For this reason it must specify the revenues and expenditures of the local government and its budgetary institutions, as well as the subsidies granted to its independent economic units. This ledgered, line item budget is cash based, and must be balanced at the end of each fiscal year. On the revenues side resources are listed according to types of own and transferred revenues, while the expenditures are broken down by groups of operation, refurbishment and capital expenditures. The appendix to the budget includes a balanced summary of projected revenues and expenditures on operation and accumulation.

The local governments are entitled to borrow (draw loans and issue bonds) as prescribed by the Act on Public Finance. In a given year, the amount of credit that can be drawn by a local government must not exceed 70 percent of its own current revenues minus the short-term obligations. Furthermore, the local governments are entitled to deposit their temporarily liquid funds (excluding state subsidies) in banks or invest them in securities.

The Act on Debt Settlement (Act No. XXV. of 1996) was a pioneering attempt in regulating the local governments' financial activities. It regulates the process aimed at restoring the liquidity of insolvent local governments. The law aims to guarantee the provision of local governments' basic services, and to satisfy the debtors' interests within realistic and feasible boundaries.[24]

WEAKNESSES OF THE LOCAL GOVERNMENT FINANCING SYSTEM

It is most likely impossible to create a perfect system for local government financing. The weaknesses of the emerging systems occasionally present serious problems to the municipalities.

The system employed in Hungary for local government financing has three fundamental weaknesses that are worth highlighting and discussing in detail in the context of our analysis of the municipality's financial management reforms. The first is the constitutional and legal interpretation of local government independence. The prevailing interpretation fails to provide sufficient legal ground for the local governments to resist the central government's attempts to siphon off their resources. The second one may be identified as the unpredictability of the financing system, and the third as the financing system's limited normativity.

INTERPRETATIONS OF INDEPENDENCE AND THEIR CONSEQUENCES

The local governments' independence derives from the decentralization of public tasks, their resources and decision-making rights. In this respect Hungarian local governments are in an advantageous position since they are entitled (within the bounds of relevant laws) to freely decide on the allocation of their own resources, on their budgets and on drawing loans or issuing bonds in accordance with their capabilities and strategies. One logical but unfavorable consequence of this independence is that the central budget does not provide guarantees for the repayment of local loans.[25] Since this normally increases the lender's risks, quite often local governments end up with more expensive credit costs.[26]

Another favorable consequence of the local governments' independence is that they enjoy almost complete freedom in determining the allocation of their resources to their various tasks. Although the past few years have witnessed an increase in the ratio of earmarked subsidies within the state's total subsidies, the municipalities' independence remains unquestionable.

On this topic, it is also important to note that the laws do not specify the depth of the local governments' obligation to fulfill their mandatory tasks. Consequently, in most instances local governments define the quantitative and partly also qualitative parameters of their tasks on the basis of their historic experiences, as a function of local requirements and their own financial potentials. The only exceptions to this are the areas (welfare, educational and juvenile protection institutions), where ministry decrees establish specific quantitative per unit minimum parameters in order to guarantee the quality of these services. For example, these decrees define the number of professional staff that must be employed per each citizen catered to by these institutions. However, in most cases, the decrees do not specify the number of citizens these institutions are supposed to supply with the given services.

In the fields of personal services, the local governments receive normative grants based on the number of the given service's recipients. In most sectors this subsidy does not cover the actual costs of the individual services. Under the constitution, the local governments must be provided with resources that, as an aggregate, are sufficient for the fulfillment of their tasks ("normative grants" are only an element of the resources). Hence, the state government is authorized to set the subsidies at such a level (far below the cost covering level).

At the same time, Hungarian local governments rightly take exception to the fact that they are supposed to provide new services without receiving additional resources. The volume of these new "burdens" is so high that they find it increasingly difficult to finance them from

---

[24] This means that the payments are made in proportion to the claims, up to the extent of available marketable assets.

[25] To be precise, the state guarantee is not automatic, but is based on individual considerations and agreements when raising individual loans.

[26] At the same time, this condition reduces the risk of economically unjustified loans, the so called "moral hazard" risks.

the "aggregate resources" available. Certain municipalities mistakenly simplify the problem by demanding that the state directly associate funds with the new tasks. They are obviously wrong: the application of this principle would lead to the restoration of the previous highly centralized system, which in turn would do away with the municipalities' relative freedom. The liberal leaders of Budapest want the state's normatively[27] (and not necessarily through normative grants) distributed resources to fully cover the total costs of local services.

Local government subsidies dropped substantially in the year 2000. At the time, several municipalities turned to the Constitutional Court, requesting adequate task-proportionate resource distribution. In its decision announced in November 2001, the Constitutional Court declared that it was not possible to bind individual tasks to individual resources in its interpretation of the municipalities' task-proportionate financing system. According to the court, task-proportionate financing was to be established based on the analysis of total tasks and total resources. This ruling codified the state's freedom to deliberate in allocating resources to the municipalities and took the teeth out of the municipalities' arguments against the state's reduction of resources. After all, a shortage in the sum total of resources would be demonstrable only through the insolvency of a given municipality, and even in many such cases the state could point out non-prudent local financial practices. This particular interpretation of intergovernmental fiscal relations (as it failed to provide grounds for defining the total resource needs of tasks) further decreased the predictability of local government resources (see further on), and made local governments yet more defenseless with regards to central government decisions.

THE STRUCTURAL DEFICIT OF THE STATE BUDGET[28]

As we have seen already, the socialist period left behind an oversized system of redistribution and an obscure and improperly regulated system of public finance. The obscurity of the public financing system was objectionable not only from a political point of view but also because it made it impossible to track the changes in the budgetary equilibrium (or the lack thereof) and in the state's debt.

It was already clear prior to the change of the political system that the comprehensive public finance reform could brook no delay either for professional or for political reasons. The main objectives of this reform were already outlined at the time. These included the reduction of the role of redistribution, the re-regulation of the state's tasks and its budgetary practices (in order to guarantee the sustainability of the state budget's equilibrium), and the modernization of the financing and planning processes and practices. However, it was practically impossible to realize these goals prior to the change of the political system. The introduction of the new system of taxation in 1988 only affected the revenues side of the state budget.

---

[27] Normativity here refers to a predictable financing system based on normative regulation.

After the change of the political system the new Act on Public Finance was approved in 1992. However, this Act introduced only a few of the previously planned reforms. It restructured the regulations pertaining to the central budget and introduced a more transparent system of detailed budgeting, affecting also the financial practices of the local governments and the institutions. The law also regulated the municipalities' operating and developmental subsidies, which entailed normative elements as well. At the same time, as far as the reduction of the role of state redistribution is concerned, only such measures were introduced (apart from the cuts in investment and the reduction of the producer and price subsidies) that enabled the state to reduce the real value of its subsidies without a perceptible drop in its nominal value by capitalizing on the high inflation rate.

As a result of the deferral of the central budget's reform, by 1995 the deficit of the state budget had reached a level that raised the specter of a "debt trap." The deficit of the central budget reached 8.5 percent of the annual GDP, and the state's debts amounted to 85 per cent of the GDP. It thus became inevitable for the state to launch a strict stabilization program. Unfortunately, even the so-called "Bokros package" – named after the then Hungarian finance minister– refrained from embarking upon a comprehensive public finance reform, though it undertook measures that took a heavy toll on the population.

The stabilization program launched the process of privatizing state companies. The revenues from the privatization process were used to repay a part of the state's debts. The package introduced cuts in the budget's operating expenditures, thus reducing the municipalities' subsidies at the same time. It further improved the central budget's transparency and procedural discipline by consolidating the state budget. The package brought all but one of the off-budget state funds under the central budget's umbrella. However, the Bokros package did not undertake the restructuring of the largest redistributive systems (such as health care, social security, or education). Consequently – although by 1997 the central budget deficit had been slashed to 3.2 per cent of annual GDP, the state's debt stock to 65 per cent of the GDP, the ratio of redistribution had been reduced to 50 per cent, and the system of state financing had generally improved – the relatively high structural deficit of the state budget survived due to the failure to restructure the above-mentioned welfare systems.

The next government, which was in office between 1998 and 2002, completely abandoned state budget reform. In fact, that government introduced a number of restorative measures. The statist policies of the government were coupled with anti-decentralization policies. Since the government did not want to increase the role of redistribution but strove to boost the role of the central government, it eventually shifted the increasing structural deficit of

---

[28] As earlier defined, structural deficit means that – with constant external conditions – there is a negative discrepancy between the dynamics of the expenditures needed to fulfill the required tasks and the available revenues. From the point of view of planning, with reference to any task, structural deficit occurs when the fluctuations of the projected resources available for a given activity fail to guarantee coverage for the projected expenditures. In financial management, structural deficit is bound to remain until the available resources can provide coverage for the direct costs of operation, maintenance, and adaptation to changing demands and conditions.

the state budget on to the local governments. By the end of the third government cycle the entire Hungarian municipalities sector had had to face a general shortage of resources.

In 2002 it had already become clear that structural deficit in the public sphere could not be eliminated without successfully reforming public finance. It also became clear that, in the absence of such reform, successive governments would always try to shift their structural deficit on to local governments. In other words, governments will continue to try to balance their share of the central budget's deficit by limiting the local governments' access to resources. Consequently, in the absence of public finance reform there seems to be no limit to the reduction of local government resources, which in turn must result in an inevitable decline in the quality of local services.

LACK OF PREDICTABILITY IN THE SYSTEM OF FINANCING

The legal stability of the Hungarian system of local governments is guaranteed by the Constitution and the Act on Local Governments (which can only be amended by a two-thirds majority[29]). At the same time, the key financing parameters are stipulated by simple-majority acts.[30] The most important of the latter is the act on the state budget. Each year this act specifies the sums allocated to local governments in the various resource categories. Accordingly, the governing majority can alter (sometimes significantly) local operating conditions at will.

The established system of financing does not in any form tie the regulation or central subsidization of the local governments' resources to any macroeconomic or public finance indices. This makes it rather difficult to prepare projections for the availability of local resources, and it enables the political circles to influence the local government sector, occasionally through voluntary party policy decisions. The paragraphs in Parliament's annual budgetary decisions pertinent to local governments easily fall victim to short-term political maneuvering. In the absence of "financial constitutionalism" the system is simply unable to guarantee predictability, which is key to efficient local planning.

In connection to the predictability of the financing system, it is also important to note that investment subsidies are also allocated on the basis of discretionary decisions.[31] Although some elements of these decisions are regulated (procedure and certain decision criteria), the whole process is still dependent on the politicians' discretion, which does not help to make the system more predictable. The regulation of the decision-making process has remained unchanged over the past decade, and the extent to which politicians abuse of their discretionary power varied according to political elites' adherence to the unwritten laws of democracy. For example, discretionary elements were more marked during the previous government cycle due to the increased influence of political forces that favored them simply as ingrained practices or more distressingly as tools to enforce their political goals. This trend also clearly did not help to make the system more predictable.

---

[29] The approval or amendment of this type of acts requires the support of at least two-thirds of the MPs present at the vote.

We must draw a clear difference here between the reduction of resources and the concept of predictability. From the point of view of predictability, the 1995 stabilization program's effects were less serious, although it introduced strict restrictions with regard to both the allocation of resources and the relevant regulations. Strictly on grounds of whether it helped increase predictability in the system, the "Bokros package" can be considered acceptable. The package did not heed short-term, particular interests when it reorganized local resources. Instead, it implemented a series of inevitable measures to manage the fiscal crisis that had been awaited for a long time. The introduction of the restrictions and also of the system of net financing[32] clearly reduced local governments' revenues. And yet, since its consequences were predictable, it was still acceptable. The package gave local governments a chance (and also a boost) to introduce rational cuts in their expenditures. The other elements of the package that affected local governments (such as the regulation of borrowing and debts settlement) were not only inevitable in the interest of protecting the macroeconomic equilibrium, but were also welcomed by the municipalities as they created acceptable guidelines and clear and fair conditions.

WEAKNESSES IN THE NORMATIVITY OF THE LOCAL GOVERNMENT FINANCING SYSTEM

The normativity of the intergovernmental system of financing is closely related to the previously discussed expectations of predictability. We cannot emphasize enough the importance of a normative and predictable system of conditions, as this is a precondition for local planning, for rationalizing reforms and for a stable and balanced local financial management.

Since the literature offers different interpretations of the normative financing system concept, we would like to make it clear that we adopt the definition spelled out in the 'Underlying Concepts' section above. According to this definition, a systemic and universally enforced (i.e., normative) set of regulations must rest on the following principles that occasionally limit the applicability of each other: (1) the principle of task proportionate financing, (2) the principle of resource localization and (3) the principle of resource capacity. A fully normative financing system is a system that meets all these three requirements.

The 1990 AALG created a system that was operable. However, it was obviously not possible to create a satisfactory normative system for local government financing in just one try. There was clearly a need for adjustments on the road to full normativity. However, these adjustments were never implemented. As a result, the system developed following a series of uncoordinated (and quite often counter-productive) measures, rather than developing

---

[30] This type of law requires the support of at least half of the MPs present at the vote.

[31] Targeted subsidies are exceptions. Under certain conditions, municipalities can directly access these funds.

[32] This means the simultaneous management of the payments and the subsidies, under which the treasury transfers only the net sum (i.e., the difference between the payments and the subsidies) to the local governments.

systematically. Over the past decade, the share of discretionary elements has increased, which has reduced the system's normativeness as well as its predictability.

According to our definition, a system would be normative if it treated the centrally regulated normative grants, the personal income tax (PIT) sharing and local governments' own revenues with a systemic approach and if it enforced principles (1), (2) and (3) outlined above. However, in several respects the current system fails to meet these requirements. Thus its normativity is limited.

A basic inadequacy of the financing system is that it is deficiently adjusted to the tasks of the local governments. While most of the tasks that affect the metropolitan region (i.e., beyond the local jurisdiction) are to be performed by the central cities, the financing system does not encompass these tasks, and the accidental discretionary subsidies granted to urban public transport are not of systemic nature either. (This task is completely disregarded by the prevailing norms set for the local government financing system.) The introduction of a type of metropolitan normative grant would most likely be a step towards finding a systemic solution to the problem.

Although the normative grants pertaining to the municipalities' human sector services are distributed proportionately to their tasks, the prevailing system violates another area that in principle should also be normative: the re-channelling of a set part of PIT revenues into the local governmental sphere. As it is now, every year the state budget ties a part of the local governments' share of PIT revenues as a resource base to a certain part of the normative grants subsidizing local services – without defining any principles or regulations for this process. That is, by "renaming" a part of the originally local revenues, these become resources for state transfers without there being any actual state expenditure. This technique, while easing the burdens of the state budget, obviously withholds revenues from the local government sector.

In principle, PIT revenues that constitute a part of the shared tax system might also be taken into account in revenue localization, but due to recent changes in the system PIT revenues have practically lost this function. The shared part of the PIT revenues has become all too small, and the part distributed on a derivative basis has become so minimal (5 per cent[33]), that they have practically no resource localization effect.

Another weakness of the system as regards the local governments' own source revenues is that business tax, that accounts for the bulk of these revenues, is not an ideal type of local revenue. It would be more favorable to base local taxation on real estate taxes, project taxes, and perhaps also on sharing VAT.

The system does not entail regulations concerning adaptation to the potentially divergent dynamics of the various resource types either (e.g., the calculation of the revenue increases resulting from the inflation of the PIT brackets).

Summing up, we can state that the prevailing system of resource allocation and equalization is improperly engineered as it fails to accurately consider the differences in the tasks of the settlements of various sizes. Moreover, the cost of services provided by larger cities for the metropolitan region (i.e., beyond the local jurisdiction) is not covered. Due to these weaknesses, the local government financing system cannot be simultaneously proportionate to local government tasks and able to manage the divergent tasks and potentials. At the same time, the resource localization component of the system is also decreasing.

It was obviously not possible to create a "proper" system of normative financing "overnight" in 1990. The absence of subsequent corrections, and also the fact that changes in the regulations were not aimed at improving the system's performance, provide us with important lessons for situations when democratic local government systems must be created following sudden historical changes. One key lesson is that the system must admit the necessity of later adjustments, must define the objectives of the adjustments in advance and must determine the procedures necessary for realizing those adjustments.

INITIAL CONDITIONS OF LOCAL FINANCIAL MANAGEMENT

Alongside the external conditions, another important consideration pertinent to the evaluation of Budapest's financial management reform strategy is the set of internal conditions and financial management techniques which the city's new leaders inherited from their predecessors following the change of the political system. The following review does not touch upon the topic of supply-oriented, uncoordinated planning that was reviewed in the previous study, but focuses only on financial management.

THE INHERITED SYSTEM

Prior to the change of the political system, the local councils (in their role as "deconcentrated" state organs) operated amidst conditions radically different from the present-day ones.

In the earlier hierarchical state apparatus, key strategic decisions belonged to the ministries. The local councils were expected to execute these decisions. Implementation was financed primarily through discretionary, state-level decisions, and there were only "soft" constraints on financing. Accordingly, the local strategies' primary goal was to access investment subsidies. A settlement could expect to show results through investments, which in turn enabled it to further increase its future operating base budget. Of course, the techniques of financing and the practices of budgetary planning were adjusted to the highly dependent system of financing and also to the subsidy-maximizing local strategies. In practice,

---

[33] This holds true for the period of time discussed in this volume. However, in 2003 the PIT share directly left with local governments grew to 10 percent. The significance of this change is annulled by centrally defined, mandatory extra wage hikes on the one hand, and on the other hand this revenue is withheld from the more affluent cities through the calculation of tax potentials.

local financial management was restricted to keeping the books of the individual local organizations and institutions, and allocating the small savings within a fiscal year to various purposes.

The previous financial system proved unable to create the conditions for prudent financial management within the framework of local government independence – when local authorities have the right to decide on most of the future projects, but they also have to shoulder the financial responsibilities their decisions might entail. The partly normative state financing, the increased level of own source revenues, the introduction of hard financing constraints, and the financial responsibilities resulting from independence have made it possible (and imperative) to introduce a genuine system of financial management.

In this new system financial management entails tough deliberations and determined choices, and requires the optimization of the available resources. The aim is to achieve a sustainable balance, which requires multi-year financial planning.

THE STRUCTURAL DEFICIT OF LOCAL BUDGETS

As it has already been repeatedly stated, structural deficit refers to a situation where there is a negative deviation in the dynamic of the required expenditures and the available resources. Structural deficit can occur in direct operation, in maintaining a given level of operation, or in operation with qualitative and quantitative adaptation included.

According to this definition, Budapest's financial management has been constantly struggling with the two latter types of structural deficit since the change of the political system.

Before the launch of the financial management reform in 1996, structural deficit even occurred in direct operation. This structural deficit could not be estimated in figures due to deficient accounting practices and to poor asset inventories. Moreover, professional sectoral concepts did not identify adaptation requirements. Anyhow, reasonable guesses as to the existence of such a deficit could be made by analyzing the inner structural relations of the budget and the revenues–expenditure expectations. (In those years there was practically no operating result, and capital revenues, amounting to 5-10 percent of the budget, came from subsidies and sales of assets.)

From the beginnings of the 1990's there was obviously a trend whereby local governments' state subsidies were decreasing. The increase in own source revenues would not be sufficient to keep up total revenues at real value. Meanwhile, due to changes in the structure of public service delivery, the volume of the decentralized expenditure assignment was expected to grow.

With regard to these conditions, the leaders of the city – intent on creating the conditions for a sustainable financial equilibrium – had no choice but to seek to radically reshape the financing management system, and to eliminate structural deficit at all the three levels indicate above.

OBJECTIVES AND STRATEGY

As we have seen, by definition a sustainable equilibrium can be reached only when resources are also available for adaptation to changing demands. As a targeted condition, a sustainable equilibrium also presupposes the creation of a municipal task structure that is operable from the available revenues, the emergence of a transparent system of financing, and strategic management that constantly adjusts the financial decisions to the changing conditions.

As we have seen, an appropriate operating surplus plays a key role in financial management. The conclusions follow logically. Amidst changing external conditions, relatively predictable conditions and (at least) medium-term planning are necessary to safely maintain the operating surplus. The appropriate operating surplus and the transparent and reliable planning process lay the foundations for the municipalities' creditworthiness, and the drawing of loans increases the predictability, efficiency and equitability[34] of municipal financing. If local governments are independent, the above expectations (each based on rational professional considerations) are difficult to challenge. Still, unfortunately, for the time being, they are rarely taken into account in the municipalities of the post-socialist region.

In the field of financial management, political values are only supposed to play a cardinal role beyond this point. Values and political attitudes tend to mostly determine the transition strategy and the emerging policies of service provision (i.e., the specification of the desired circle of public services and the techniques of service provision). The definition for what we identify as the Budapest model is precisely this: an urban policy strategy rooted in political values and applying a given set of methods such as those employed in Budapest during the period of post-socialist transition.

With regard to financial management, the Budapest model's primary goal was to create the conditions for sustainable equilibrium. This could only occur gradually, over several years, as it also took a few years to create transparent conditions and understand the situation.

The comprehensive strategy aimed at creating a sustainable financial equilibrium was drafted and approved in 1996 within the frame of the budget conception.[35] This document entailed a full-blown strategy for the transition period, and thus we draw on it in our description of the strategic goals, tasks and the strategy itself. We deduce the strategy – in other words, the ways the municipal leadership devised for accomplishing their objectives and how they systemized the set of tasks ahead – from the strategic objectives as defined in 1996. Still, in our further analyses, we shall also revert back to the reform attempts of the pre-1996 period, and we shall also discuss the modifications of the original strategy during the third government cycle.

Besides trying to give a full description of the Budapest municipality's thinking on sustainable equilibrium, we have another reason for focusing our discussion on the 1996

---

[34] For details, see the subchapter on "Borrowing Policy" in the study on the 'Elements of the Financial Reform'.

draft. This was the first document based on a multi-year financial planning model. As we know, such a model must also remain a cardinal tool for the balanced financial strategy in the post-reform period as well. In other words, through this document we can introduce both the reform strategy and the strategy to be employed for maintaining the equilibrium.

VALUES

According to the liberal leaders of the Municipality, the public sector must play a limited role in society. It should function responsibly, in a transparent and predictable manner, and according to clearly established rules. With regard to the financial management reform process, the liberals emphasize three values: public authority entails responsibilities, requires regulated process management, and should prefer competition and market-conform methods in order to ensure the most efficient utilization of public funds.

A responsible public player strives for transparent, prudent financial management and for the utilization of the available resources in an optimal manner to promote the welfare of the community. This in turn requires the careful selection and identification of public roles (but this must not result in lower-quality performance) on the one hand, and the creation of the conditions for independent and responsible financial management and the introduction of transparent methods, on the other hand.

The value-based definition of the goals and the system of regulations pertaining to process management ensure predictability and create the conditions for rational operation. These also create the conditions for the drafting and implementation of longer-term strategies. The accurate codification of goals and their approval may provide guarantees against their eventual cancellation by short-term political or lobbying interests (the political leaders are certainly familiar with these types of – often strong, occasionally also "internal" – pressures). Especially in the case of a sensitive financial equilibrium, these interests and pressures may easily destroy the whole strategy. However, once the goals and the (review) processes are codified, it is easier to guarantee stability, i.e., to make certain that the strategy really functions as a strategy.

Accordingly, the primary aim of the system of regulations is to ensure the coordination of individual decisions. According to the liberal logic, the regulations and reforms cannot and should not aim to create the "final result" in one single step. Instead, they should produce a system of regulations and conditions – and also a set of structural changes – that alter the operation of the institutions and the behavior of the players, and elicit a positive-sum[36] type of cooperation.

---

[35] The Office of the Mayor of Budapest, 1996c

[36] This term has been adopted from game theory. It is used to describe situations in which there exists a strategy that has the potential to create a better outcome for all affected parties. In our case, this better outcome also means social benefits.

According to the liberal thinkers, the market is important because of its role in promoting welfare and increasing efficiency, and also because it provides an organizational pattern that sets an example. The liberals would let the market play a direct role in (financial and service) management. They are inclined to employ market-based techniques, and tend to prefer a "privatization" of public roles, i.e., an increased involvement of the private sector in public services delivery. The market's role as example can best be construed in the effort by decision-makers to adopt the market's efficiency-boosting elements to the public sphere. On the supply side, the liberals encourage competition between suppliers, while on the demand side they call for more information and advocate greater freedom of choice.

THE CHALLENGE

In the early nineties, coordination between the activities of the local governments and their financial planning mechanisms was fairly rudimentary. In practice, the local governments' budgets were based on plans valid for the given year only, and the financial system did not make the structural deficit perceptible.

The previous chapter described the strategy that successfully resulted in improving coordination between planning and financing. In that chapter we also discussed strategic real planning and outlined the municipality's experiences. Since the previous paper on "Strategic Planning and Management Reform' provided a detailed description of how comprehensive urban policy planning and planning in the various sectoral branches have enabled coordination between professional planning and project financing, here we shall focus our attention on the specific issues of the budgetary system. We shall touch upon professional planning only to reveal the ways the financial planning process is able to translate and calculate the specific goals and plans into revenue and expenditure projections.

The inherited state of the budget presented the Municipality of Budapest with a triple challenge:

– the budgetary system had to be made transparent and plannable in order for the actual balance to become perceptible and the future trends projectable;

– the resource structure and the task fulfillment processes had to be reformed to ensure sustainable balance;

– planning and decision-making had to be made fit for realizing the goals laid down in the strategy.

THE STRATEGIC GOAL

The leaders of Budapest specified most of their goals relating to the city's financial policies and practices back in the early 1990s. Under the two-year development plan, which was approved early in 1993, the municipal government's strategic goal was to keep the city operable. Toward this end, the city's leaders considered it imperative to "draft a comprehensive financial-economic plan" for the years ahead, and on that basis to create a coherent system for decision-making.[37]

Since due consideration of the projected financial processes is inevitable for the correct analysis of the situation, for planning and for establishing strategies, this multi year and comprehensive financial plan was indeed the key for launching the financial management reforms. The two-year development plan, which concentrated on investments, identified the projects that seemed realistic at the time, and thus laid the foundations for the creation of a more rational decision-making mechanism.

The still valid formulation of the strategic goals and the strategy itself were approved by the General Assembly of the Municipality of Budapest in 1996, as part of the budget conception for the year 1997. The approval came on the heels of the institutionalization of the seven-year financing projections.[38] According to the 1996 text, "it is a strategic goal for the local government to accomplish a balanced budget" (i.e., besides ensuring direct operability, the city also aimed to preserve its assets and to guarantee continuous adaptation).[39]

The financing strategy specifies two conditions for the accomplishment of the strategic goals. These are:

- the scheduled accomplishment and permanent maintenance of an operating surplus amounting to 20 percent of the current revenues; and
- *"the preservation of the real value of the capital expenditures, and especially the ones that improve the conditions for financing operations."*

The assumptions behind these two conditions rest on the cardinal numbers of the budget. The targeted operating surplus indirectly implies that 20 percent of the current revenues provides sufficient coverage for the costs of refurbishment and adaptation. Nevertheless, this figure was specified on the basis of prior experiences and not as a function of projected expenditures.

This rate was specified on the basis of proportions drawn from the preceding years' budgets. Experience showed that this level of development could guarantee sustainable operability, and also allowed for adaptation-related investments. The trends in asset depreciation were assumed to be unchanged. Experience also showed that the municipal government could realistically expect to undertake a manageable amount of projects from a capital budget amounting to 20 percent of the total budgetary expenditures. This was also seen as a burden that the city could bear.

---

[37] The Office of the Mayor of Budapest, 1993: 2

[38] The seven-year financial simulation model will be discussed in detail in the following study, within the context of financial planning.

[39] The Office of the Mayor of Budapest, 1996c: 3

Of course, this experience-based method was not able to prove that a 20 percent operating surplus is sufficient for eliminating the structural deficit in the long run and for keeping the budget balanced. At the same time, it was assumed that through the continuous improvement of strategic planning on this volume of investment it would be possible to better utilize resources and to adjust the task and asset structures to available resources. This process is promoted by the other condition specified above: priority must be given to capital expenditures that are expected to improve the conditions for financing operations.

Undeniably, this experience-based method did not start out with the assessment of the operating surplus needed for the elimination of structural deficit, calculated based on the costs of refurbishment and adaptation. This was only understandable, since back in 1995 several key conditions were still missing for the long-term projection of the municipality's structural deficit. On the one hand, the municipality would have needed an accurate assessment of the status and depreciation of the city's assets, and on that basis a quantifiable strategy for development and adaptation. On the other hand, the projected task structure would have had to be stable (predictable) in order for the municipality to be able to calculate a fair estimate of the costs of eliminating the structural deficit.

But irrespective of the way the 20 percent value was actually determined, the fact remains that the establishment of a targeted level was crucial to the implementation of the strategy. In this respect, the only important development was that the strategic goals and the related conditions were set in a way that also determined the course for managing the ensuing processes.

The two conditions for the accomplishment of the strategic goals (the 20 percent operating surplus and the preservation of the real value of the capital expenditures that improve the financing conditions of operation) accurately identify the cornerstones for the strategic process and the targeted strategic objectives. They also specify cornerstones for the planning of the annual budget, which enables the municipal leaders to accurately determine certain other key indices in this budget. In the course of annual budget planning, on the basis of resource projections – calculated with the aim of achieving the targeted operating surplus – planning limitations and obligations can be clarified, and revenue and expenditure projections become adjustable. Furthermore, the second condition ("the preservation of the real value of the accumulation expenditures, and especially the ones that improve the conditions for financing the operations") provides certain guidance for establishing priorities among the capital expenditures. All these lay the foundations for a coherent, short-, medium- and long-term strategic management, and can also direct the planning of medium- and long-term tasks.

THE STRATEGY

The assumption that the specified proportions of the cardinal numbers of the budget can provide coverage for the costs of operation, maintenance, and adaptation in accordance with permanently changing requirements, and that these proportions are conducive to the accomplishment of the strategic goal, i.e., the balanced financial management of the municipal government, lies at the core of the strategy.

Before drawing up the strategy, the municipality did not pay attention to the calculation of the operating result. Moreover, its budget – in conformity with the accounting regulation in force then – did not lend itself to direct conclusions concerning the operating surplus. Nevertheless, we may well assume that before the strategy and at the time of drawing it up, the cardinal element of the strategy, the operating surplus, was practically null. Thus, the municipality decided to focus its strategy on increasing the operating surplus. In principle, this can be achieved by increasing current revenues and/or simultaneously reducing current expenditures.

At the time of the strategy's approval it was already clear that the revenue increase was strongly limited and that the gap between expenditures and resources was increasing, although with fluctuations in this increase. The municipality did not have tools at its disposal to arrest the decline of the real value of the operating resources originating from the central budget. (It was assumed that the devaluation of current state revenues would continue in the short run, but this trend was expected to stop in the long run.) By that time the capital city had practically exhausted the potentials inherent in its own source current revenues, so chances for increasing their real value were modest at best.

In such a situation, reducing current expenditures is the only way to increase the operating surplus. Accordingly, the municipal strategy had to concentrate on this task.

There are two ways for a city to reduce its expenditures: it can either curtail per unit costs, or filter its services. The strategy of Budapest aimed to adopt both methods, but without jeopardizing the quality of the remaining services.

A strict review and reconsideration of the scope, content and the quality of the services considered is indispensable in order to filter public services. This in turn requires that each sector establishes the principles for fulfilling its own tasks, and works out a concept resting on financial realities, defining the associated requirements for human resources and physical infrastructure, and containing proposals for the restructuring process.[40] (In the Budapest municipality the so-called "task fulfillment concepts"[41] served this purpose.)

Per unit costs may be reduced through increasing efficiency. The municipal government hardly had any chance to increase the efficiency of its units' resource management through direct "manual" control. It lacked information, and did not have adequate management capacities either. The other method, namely to enforce rationalization exclusively through

---

[40] The following chapter will discuss in detail the process for evaluating tasks, obstacles in the way of the process, and partial successes in the Budapest municipality.

[41] Their analysis will be offered in the next chapter.

[42] The inevitable cuts in per unit resources can be considered "safe" only if we know the real resource requirements of the services and keep the cuts proportionate. This requires information on the individual economic units and careful consideration on the basis of the sectoral strategies.

111

cutting resources, is politically burdensome, and also dangerous, since it is very difficult to set the limits within which the quality and stability of the services remain intact.[42] The third option is to create a normative system that strongly promotes efficient financial management. Once such a system is operational and is adapted to the available resources, its framework makes it possible to force rationalization through cutting off resources.[43]

In order to reduce per unit costs and to promote a more efficient use of resources by the institutions, the municipality made an attempt to introduce a system of normative task financing. A zero-base task financing system was devised to be the starting point to guarantee task-proportionate financing, while the institutions' own source revenues were to be taken into account for calculating resource capacity, and resource localization was to be realized by leaving the bulk of the revenues produced "on location"[44] or within the given sector.

A properly established task financing system promotes an efficient utilization of resources by economic units within the given structure. However, cutting per unit costs is not only possible through enforcing a correct task financing system within the individual economic units. Huge savings can be achieved through the modernization of the services' infrastructures. In most instances, this method of reducing operating costs requires serious one-time investments, the return of which may take years. Since the economic units do not always have access to the resources needed for these investments, the reform process necessarily entailed the creation of a financial scheme that provided the required coverage. The municipality has thus established the so-called Institution Rationalization Fund[45] which advances resources towards these investments.

Transformations of the institutional and service infrastructure were also made imperative by changes in the tasks identified in the task fulfillment concepts. The financial strategy had to provide coverage for these investments partly from resources allocated for new investments – besides the rationalizing funds.

The second condition associated with the strategic goals of 1996 followed from this need to modernize the infrastructure and to meet the revised professional requirements. Accordingly, the city has had to preserve the real level of its capital expenditures with special regard to the investment costs related to the rationalization of the operating conditions.

It was obvious to the drafters of the strategy that the boom in the privatization of public utility companies and the consequent increase in capital revenues between 1995 and 1998 were to be followed by declining capital revenues, and that the coverage for the subsequent investments was to be expected from the operating surpluses. At the same time, the operating costs could be reduced only gradually, over a period of several years (in order for the quality of the services to remain constant). As a result it was feared that a "financing gap"

---

[43] The Office of the Mayor of Budapest, 1995b

[44] "On location" means the institution in the case of current revenues, and the sector in the case of accumulation revenues.

[45] Detailed analysis of the Fund will follow in the next study.

(or "investment gap") had been created in the years when the capital revenues were already down but the operating surpluses were yet to reach the required level.[46]

For this reason the spending rate of the capital revenues had to be adjusted to the rate of increase in the operating surpluses, and reserves had to be created to fill the "financing gap." Besides, loans for capital investments played an important part in the policy of transition, as they helped to fill the "financing gap" and enabled flexibility and timing in financing investment projects.[47]

The appropriate deliberation and timing of the investment projects requires systemic thinking covering several years and considering all the investment plans for each sector. For this reason, the strategy prescribed a four-, later a seven-year investment program based on the seven-year financing projections.

Summing up:

The municipal strategy identified the accomplishment of a 20 percent operating surplus as the key element conducive to the realization of its main goal: a sustainable financing equilibrium. Since the previous practice of annual planning could not be expected to produce such a result, the strategy foresaw a planning process spanning several years and the introduction of a comprehensive financial management reform.

The reduction of the operating expenditures was identified as a key element in the process. According to the strategy, this was to be achieved through revising the tasks to be fulfilled. Furthermore, the strategy prescribed special support for a new normative financing system that pressed for cost savings and priority to be given to a series of investments aimed at rationalizing operations.

The responsibilities associated with the transformations in the structures of task and assets (which was made imperative by the newly defined public service role after the change of the political system), along with the efforts to make up for the outstanding rehabilitation projects have placed a heavy cost burden on the municipal government. At the same time, the asset sales and the privatization deals made possible by political transition generated considerable accumulation revenues. It was a key element of the strategy that these (accumulation) revenues – the "products of the transition" – were to be used to cover the capital expenditures associated with transition. In addition, the strategy attached tight deadlines to the investment projects, prescribed the scheduled appropriation of capital revenues, and introduced an active borrowing policy. (The tools associated with the implementation of the strategy will be discussed in detail in the following study.)

---

[46] The Office of the Mayor of Budapest, 1995c

[47] The Office of the Mayor of Budapest, 1998a

THE ARCHITECTURE OF THE REFORM PROCESS

THE INITIAL STAGE – 1990-1992

As we have discussed above in connection with the prevailing external conditions, the late 1980s and the early 1990s witnessed significant changes in the revenues side of the state budget. Fundamental reforms were carried out in the tax system: personal income tax and value added tax were introduced. In the first few years of the new period even the finance ministry found it difficult to estimate the projected tax revenues.

The local governments were established in 1990. At the time the personal income tax revenues were transferred in full to the budgets of the local governments where the taxes were collected. Later on – as a result of the increased revenues and the central government's centralizing efforts – this ratio was drastically reduced. By 1991 it had dropped to 50 percent, and by 1993 to 30 percent. Consequently, the real value of the local governments' share in the PIT revenues also declined. Besides the personal income tax revenues, the local governments' other revenues were also difficult to calculate, and thus it was hard for them to predict their future revenue stream.

The new elements in the state's financing system created a rather precarious situation, since at the time of their introduction it was difficult to predict their effects. In addition, neither the central government nor the local governments had experience regarding the new system's operation and its potential effects.

One new element was the partial state coverage for the costs related to the fulfillment of the local tasks through the normative grant system discussed above. Another important element was the local tax revenue. In 1990, Parliament passed the Act on Local Taxation that authorized local governments to levy business tax – later a key element in the local governments' own revenue structure. In a transition economy, without proper databases it was impossible to predict this tax revenue potential. Furthermore, the space of financial maneuvering, due to the uncertainty in the amount of revenues collected from fees and duties, lacked clarity. The effects of the new system of state subsidies for local investments were also unclear. In short, with the economy and public financing in transition it was very difficult for the newly established local governments to come up with correct estimates of their projected resources.

However, the lack of local planning could not be blamed solely on external conditions. The survival into the early 1990's of the practice of local budgetary planning limited to "resource distribution" within the fiscal year could be explained by the survival of the "good old" accounting practices rather than by largely unpredictable external circumstances.

These "good old" practices became ingrained because the various sectors adjusted their adaptive mechanisms to them. Eventually, the sectors became interested in maintaining them. It was part of their tactics to squeeze even the smallest sum earmarked for kicking off their investment projects (which were expected to span several years) into the annual (state and local) budget. These sectors were aware of the fact that the projects could not be concluded within a year. However, since the initial sums were too small to make a difference, they could expect easy approval for their budget. Within the framework of annual financial planning they did not have to seriously consider longer-term financial implications, and there was no need either to weigh these entries against the others in the budget. And once these sums got into the budget, they had every reason to expect that the projects would sooner or later be completed. Earlier we called this method "hanging on the plan," which coupled a most likely truly felt feeling of responsibility for the development of the individual sectors, with irresponsibility towards the budget as a whole.

Initially (between 1990 and 1992) there was no financial planning at the municipality of Budapest either, at least not in the sense that was later identified as medium- and long-term planning. In those years the municipal drafters were concerned only with balancing the budget for every fiscal year. The columns in the municipal government's budget were filled with the cardinal numbers submitted by the various departments. Planning was based on the previous year's values, i.e., the annual subsidies were determined and distributed in proportion to the previous year's figures. The municipal government did not split its subsidies into operating and accumulation brackets. In practice, the subsidies covered the difference between each budgetary unit's revenues and expenditures. The budget specified the institutional ratios for distributing the resources, but did not identify the projects and activities which were financed from these resources.

At the municipality "professional" planning also reflected the earlier described, then general pattern: its outcome had no relation whatsoever with financial possibilities. The drafters of the developmental plans were building castles in the air. They drafted oversized and "supply-oriented" projects that (randomly or under the pressure of necessity) eventually received the required financial allocations.

In an environment where local governments were independent – where investment decisions had to be made locally, independently and taking into account resource limitation –, a simple confronting of sectoral and accountant approaches could not lead to solutions since longer term sectoral plans and demands could not be met without rational, multi-year financial planning. Due to the extraordinary differences between sectoral plans and financial possibilities, in the first years after the change of the system, sectoral and financial leaders turned a deaf ear towards each other.[48] The system of financing, planning and decision-making obviously needed re-shaping, but this required changes in views and paradigms far beyond the affinity of the main actors who were socialized to the old system. It was a task typically tailored for the cabinet of the mayor[49] to work out a system for the coordination of the elements of planning and for guaranteeing responsible decision-making.

---

[48] The sectoral leaders – disregarding financial limits – were unwilling to adjust their investment plans to financing limitations, while the financial leaders were not authorized to influence sectoral planning. Their accountant approach could not produce perspectives and persuasive arguments for the decisions of the politicians either. Thus, resource allocation was determined more or less merely by interest enforcement capacities instead of being driven by urban policy conceptions.

[49] For the role of the cabinet system see subchapter 'The cabinet system' in the previous study on 'Strategic Planning and Management Reform.'

The city leadership got a short postponement for fulfilling this task, as sectoral lobbying for investment resources became somewhat ambivalent in the first years of the new local government system: during the period when the financing system was in transition it seemed worth hanging on both state and local plans. However, a general lack of resources hindered the launching of big investment projects.

It is a matter of curiosity, that an external event enhanced both the revival of "hanging on the plan" and the change of the "good old practices." In 1991, the country's Parliament decided to host the World Exhibition in Budapest in 1994 (later postponed to 1996). Although the leaders of the municipality of Budapest (citing the city's lack of capacities) rejected idea of the monumental national project, the municipal leaders could not stop the preparations. From another point of view, they did not really want to stop them, since the preparations held out the promise of state subsidies for a series of important infrastructure investments. The World Exhibition revitalized both sectoral planning and the "hanging on the plan" practice that now primarily took place, and had to be handled, on the local government level.

The city leaders aimed to utilize the resources connected to the World Exhibition in a responsible manner. This implied a thorough consideration of the projects, and financing in line with the city's long term interests. The municipality had no previous experience in harmonizing plans with financing possibilities, thus the Cabinet of the Mayor had to undertake a coordinating role.[50]

A significant condition was that the Municipality of Budapest was expected by the central government to finance part of the preparatory investments from its own resources.

The city had to estimate its potential resources before launching the large multi-year investment projects. Although the central government did not yet use a strict financial evaluation and control system for allocating its investment subsidies, such as those employed in the banking sector, it did require the municipal government to assume responsibility for its own share of the funding.[51] At the same time it was also clear that the investments would require longer-term loans, which in turn would necessitate the introduction of a medium-term planning mechanism. Based on these considerations, the leaders of the Municipality of

---

[50] The mayor could break the earlier practice of a "dialogue of the deaf" and implemented new, constructive solutions relying on his Cabinet that worked out the steps for the reform of planning and those of the internal coordination process, thereby enhancing previously poor internal coordination. Similarly, the experts working for the cabinet directed the external coordination connected to the World Exhibition as well.

[51] Although it is not directly relevant to developments in 1992 and 1993, we believe we should add that both sides made several "peculiar" attempts at financing the World Exhibition project. The municipality submitted a formal application for support from the World Exhibition Fund (WEF). The WEF – although it had some resources for real estate development preparation – was to provide pre-financing aid to the preparations through temporary government support, which would then be debited from the projected revenues. The WEF based itself on highly questionable feasibility calculations and included a bulk of uncoordinated elements, which features anticipated the exposition's subsequent cancellation. The capital city did not have access to resources to cover its own share of the project, and thus tried to secure coverage from the state's targeted subsidies and addressed grants.

Budapest convinced the General Assembly of the need to introduce medium-term financial planning.[52]

THE TWO-YEAR DEVELOPMENT PROGRAM – 1993

The two-year development program,[53] approved in early 1993, aimed to systematize the investment-related tasks on the basis of the city's projected resources and by defining values and priorities for the urban development process. The plan spanned only two years, which was not a significant period from a planning point of view. The real significance of the program was to be sought in its fundamental conceptual and methodical innovations.

During the drafting of the two-year development program each sectoral department of the municipality had a chance to compile a full project list based on targeted interventions (in accordance with the earlier practice). It was a new element that these lists had to be prioritized by the municipality's sectoral leadership, as it was clear from the outset that the costs associated with the projects that were claimed to be professionally justified far exceeded the municipality's limited resources. Another new element was that the program listed the investment plans of the various sectors side by side, and thus the city's leaders could comparatively evaluate the projects and the priorities behind them and on this basis could decide on the distribution of the resources among the sectors. Entries in the investment program got broken down into two categories according to resource allocation: (1) "Above the line" projects were considered realistic with regard to resource projections, and so the leaders gave the go-ahead to their detailed elaboration and execution, and (2) "below the line" projects were deemed realistic only upon access to supplementary resources.

Compared to the earlier practice, these steps toward independent and responsible planning have:

- introduced the practice of estimating both the municipality's resources and commitments in investment planning beyond the fiscal year;

- established urban policy priorities for laying the foundations of financial planning;

- encouraged the change to clear and established priorities in professional sectoral planning;

- encouraged the optimal utilization of local resources through collecting all the investment projects of the municipality and making the decision on distributing resources among the sectors on the basis of the comparison of the sectoral proposals,

- separated – to an extent – professional planning from political decision-making, thereby enabling the professionals to formulate proposals on the basis of professional considerations, and referring the ultimate decision, based on weighing sectoral priorities against each other now that this was possible, to the political decision-makers.

---

[52] The meaning and significance of this process in urban policy, as well as the process of inevitable coalition-building are discussed in details in the previous study on 'Strategic Planning and Management Reform'.

[53] The Office of the Mayor of Budapest, 1998a

Consequently, the two-year development plan was significant not only from the point of view of planning but also with regard to the rationalization of the decision-making process.

Since the approval of the program implied that the projected investment resources would be tied up, in principle the municipality ran out of liquid investment resources. For this reason it became inevitable to approve a rule under which the proposal (or approval) of a new project to be implemented during the duration of the program had to be preceded by its drafters (or ultimately by the General Assembly) having to identify an already approved entry in the program which would then itself provide the project's financing. The original project attached to the budget would then be deleted and the resources reallocated to the new project. From this moment on any proposal drafter has been bound to carefully consider the necessity of a new project and to professionally prepare it for decision by others and not only his or her general responsibilities as an official and a decision-maker. It became clear that the approval of a project proposal hinged on its comparison with the utility of a number of other proposals, and thus the approval process entailed a more or less open clash of interests. Accordingly, the new system required better arguments and more solid professional grounding, notwithstanding that the decision was ultimately also based on political considerations.

As a result of this new approach and methodology, the earlier lobbying strategy that aimed to maximize support based on vertical subordination was replaced by a more responsible culture of decision making that aimed to optimize the use of available resources.

The next step to further improve resource utilization was targeted by the new urban policy concept which was drafted in the years following the approval of the two-year development program. Eventually, this policy concept provided the foundations for the mayor of Budapest's election platform in 1994.[54] The concept contrasted the municipality's projected potentials with the various sectoral strategies, and attempted to identify the main priorities. This approach evaluated operation and development simultaneously, and took into account the associated structural changes. It represented a major step toward identifying the realistic dimensions of the sectoral plans. The document was eventually used by the drafters of the succeeding coalition's work plan, and could serve as a point of reference during the ensuing debates. It also played a key role in shaping the decision-makers' approach and way of thinking.[55]

THE LIQUIDITY CRISIS – 1994–1995

The municipality's resource projections clearly improve the security of financial planning, but they are not free of error. The projections entail decisions on which of the trends and

---

[54] Alliance of Free Democrats (SZDSZ), 1994

[55] The SZDSZ and MSZP party factions of the Municipality, 1995

changes identified at a given point of time should be considered relevant, and establishes a framework for planning on their basis.

While preparing the blueprints for its investment projects - within the frames of the two-year program - and assessing its obligations related to the World Exhibition in 1993, the municipality worked based on a series of assumptions for that period. These assumptions could have been considered conservative at the time but eventually turned out to be fairly optimistic. Though the drafters made allowances for the expected increase in municipal expenditures associated with the changes in the resource and task-sharing schedules with the districts, and also for losses in the centrally regulated resources, they did not expect the central government to introduce disproportionate reductions to the local governments' year-on-year resource-base as compared to the average changes in public expenditure.

The leaders of the municipality opposed the idea of organizing the World Exhibition in Budapest from its very beginning and later at the 1991 approval of the project. They opposed it partly on grounds of principles, but also for practical reasons. The municipal leaders saw that the capital was not well enough prepared for the event. Later on, they did not believe that the organization and financing models that were being elaborated were realistic. Therefore, when the government started its preparations for the World Exhibition, the municipality focused it efforts on investments (as preparations for the event) that, whatever future developments, would be important for the operation of the city in the long run. However, by 1994 – owing to the reduction of resources in the local government sector – Budapest had not been able to finance these investments either.

There was reason to believe that a change of government in the spring of 1994 would mean the cancellation of Hungary's plans to host the World Exhibition. By this time it had become obvious that the event placed "disproportionate burdens on the public expenditure of the Hungarian Republic" and that it could not be undertaken.[56] In parallel with the cancellation of the World Exhibition, the World Exhibition Fund (WEF) that had been created for financing the investments necessary for holding the exposition was dissolved without a legal successor.

The leaders of the capital initiated negotiations with the government to force it to recognize its earlier commitments to the WEF. They also wanted the government to acknowledge that the erosion of the city's own share in the jointly planned projects was the result of the previous years' withdrawal of resources by the state. The city wanted the government to compensate for these losses. The municipality's aim was to get the investments that were important for Budapest with or without an Exhibition held in Hungary, and to get more government subsidies than was initially projected for the completion of the projects already launched. (The government was supposed to acknowledge not only the earlier withdrawal of resources, but also the outstanding national importance of developing and financing the capital city.)

---

[56] Acts and Decrees, 8

Negotiations took place in difficult financial conditions for the local government, as by 1994 it had become clear that the municipality of Budapest was threatened by a liquidity crisis in the short run. The leaders of the city made a twofold effort to avoid a crisis: on the one hand they urged quick agreement with the government on the projects that may get supplementary central support, and on the other hand the mayor – going so far as to freeze or amend contracts – immediately halted a great part of the investment projects started by the municipality,[57] thus gaining time for solving financial problems.

The municipality and the Minister of Finance negotiated an agreement in principle on the supportive government subsidies as early as August 1994.[58] It took four months to work out the details. In this process the actual municipal resources had to be presented, the claims for subsidies had to be clarified and justified, and deliberations had to be made on the importance of the projects retained and on the cancellation costs of the ones to be given up. This process resulted in a final list of projects. The HUF 8.5 billion total amount of government subsidies had been fixed by December 1994. This served as the basis for the agreement of February the following year on the technique of financing.[59] Thus, theoretically, the municipality was relieved of paying its own share, and financial strains could have been eased, yet the actual transaction[60] was delayed by almost a year.

Due to the delay in making the government guaranteed loan payable, the capital city found itself in a direct liquidity crisis in 1995. This financial crisis meant that the city did not have enough resources to pay off its debts according to the agreed schedule and to cover its own share of the investment projects that were jointly planned with the state.

In the fall of 1994, the mayor of Budapest was re-elected, and the mayor's liberal party concluded a coalition deal with the Socialists in the General Assembly. The post of deputy mayor responsible for financial management remained with the liberals, but was filled in by a new person, the former head of the cabinet of the mayor. At that moment, the new leader did not submit his – already elaborated – ideas on financial management strategy to the Assembly. Passing them would demand more time than was left for drafting the next year's budget.

In absence of an authorization by the General Assembly, the comprehensive strategy could not be launched, and only an emergency budget reckoning with restrictions was drafted

---

[57] Under these difficult financial conditions, the mayor – supported by a minority party in the Assembly and with local government elections approaching – could never have got the approval of the Assembly, so he had to freeze projects under his own competence. His decision was legitimized later, in the fall of the same year, after the local government elections.

[58] Acts and Decrees, 15

[59] As the central government was also under pressing financial conditions and had neither resources to re-allocate nor the possibility to raise more loans, the only solution could be that the municipality raised the loans and the government undertook the amortization of the loan. Debt service increased the HUF 8.5 billion to an ultimate sum of HUF 13-14 billion. (Acts and Decrees, 16)

[60] Transaction here does not mean money transfer, but the signature of the document necessary for the municipal borrowing: the state guarantee for the municipal loan and its renunciation of the right to recourse.

for 1995. The Assembly had already approved the necessity of the emergency budget in its 1994 November session, when the budget conception was passed. That time, in a single session, the General Assembly "butchered" nearly 80 earlier investment projects,[61] and also approved the reduction of the city's operating expenditures to a minimum level, resorting – if necessary – to the "lawnmower principle."[62] Eventually, the budget for 1995 was drafted according to this emergency budget conception.

For all these developments, in 1995 the municipality had to draw liquidity loans on several occasions. Liquidity loans helped Budapest to survive. Long-term loans were not available for the municipality that time, because Hungarian commercial banks were not in a position to offer them in substantial volume and with proper conditions.[63] Taking up international investment bank loans would have claimed much time, and anyway, the reality of taking them up for suspense projects would have been questionable.

However, significant capital revenues received in the last days of the year eased the crisis. Later the government guaranteed loans could also be drawn to eliminate the liquidity crisis. The preparation of the 1996 year budget started among more favorable financial conditions.

Although the 1995 budget was produced under constraints, the year also witnessed important steps ahead. The city's near-bankrupt status improved the political and policy window of opportunity for financial leaders: it became possible to approve the financial management reform strategy which had long been in the making. The financial crisis made the first larger privatization deal and the main concepts and principles behind the emerging reform strategy acceptable to politicians. For this reason 1995 was a turning point. The financial crisis that lasted through the whole year brought about a "historical moment," in which it became possible for the decision-makers to build a coalition for supporting a fundamentally restrictive financial program that was markedly liberal in its long-term goals.

Besides the municipality's near-bankrupt status, which was arguably the most important spark behind these developments, we should mention the "Bokros package" of 1995 (named after the Minister of Finance), which we discussed in detail in connection with the broader financial context. We have reason to believe that the central government's restrictive measures (which created quite a stir throughout the country) also contributed to the decision-makers' realization that the cuts in expenditures and structural changes simply could not be postponed.

---

[61] This meant the subsequent approval of the mayor's spring decision freezing these investments.

[62] The "lawnmower principle" proclaims the even distribution of restrictions. It means a strictly financial consideration based withdrawal of resources. The withdrawals are proportionate to the base values. The method is dangerous in that it does not consider actual tasks or actual costs, and therefore in principle the withdrawals proportionate to resources may result in the crippling of some institutions.

[63] The reason for this lay in the difficult economic situation of the country and in the relatively underdeveloped Hungarian banking system: on the one hand there was no established practice for syndicated loans in the Hungarian market, on the other hand high inflation rates and the risks of the domestic money market were justifiably incorporated in the pricing of loans. These conditions together would have made the domestic borrowing conditions unacceptable to the municipality.

STRATEGIC BUDGETARY PLANNING – 1995

It became obvious that central budgetary restrictions were to continue in the wake of the "Bokros package." In this situation (due partly to the crisis and partly to other long-term considerations), ways had to be found for the local budget to manage the ever more pressing situation. Obviously, the restrictions, that were proportionate with the diminishing resources and were implemented according to the "lawnmower principle," could work for an extremely short term only. Meanwhile, resources were expected to continue shrinking. Under these conditions, the only way for the city to maintain the standard of its services was through rationalizing its task structure, task fulfillment and financing system. This rationalization would mean reconsidering the full scope of municipal activities and creating a financing system that would encourage restructuring.

The document entitled 'Draft Conception for the 1996 Budget' which was prepared for the mayor in 1995, made an attempt to lay the foundations of a reform strategy. (The official conception for the 1996 Budget, i.e., the document that had to be prepared each year, which was approved by the General Assembly in late 1995, was less detailed in its content. Under the relevant legal stipulations its only role was to lay the principles for the following year's budget.) The Draft Conception's main goal was to change the earlier practice, the "accountants' approach," that aimed to distribute the deficit or the surplus within a single year's budget as in the same way as a "bookkeeper." Instead, the Draft Conception suggested the introduction of "strategic budgetary planning," capable of envisioning and implementing a medium-term financing concept. According to the 1996 memorandum of the deputy mayor, strategic budgetary planning is defined in the long-term, whereby the long-term strategy guides short term decisions. The essence was formulated as follows:

> *"We attempt to position the given fiscal year in at least medium-term trends, to reckon with constraints and variable conditions, with the processes to be encouraged or restricted, with the space of maneuvering necessary for the rationalization of the municipality's operation structure for several years ahead, and to utilize the available scope of activity by clearly establishing priorities, and using financial constraints to enhance the desired changes in content."* [64]

It is clear from the goals that the ideas behind the draft concept were similar to the ones that defined the two-year development program: it is not enough to base budgetary planning on the assessment of the resources that are available within a fiscal year. Instead, the planning process must start out from the evaluation of the medium-term trends, and the decisions must be guided by establishing fixed priorities. The draft concept represented a major improvement over the two-year development program. While the latter focused on investment but ignored operation, the former looked at the budget as a whole and aimed to adjust the internal proportions of the budget to the prevailing goals and constraints. Furthermore, the Draft Conception identified budgetary planning and financing as the tools for implementing the planned reforms. The term "strategic budgetary planning" refers to this last goal (using budgeting as a strategic tool).

---

[64] The Office of the Mayor of Budapest, 1995c: 2

CREATING THE TOOLS – 1995

Besides proposing ways to change the method of financial planning, the Draft Conception also entailed strategic proposals for reforming the financing system. The 1996 budget conception foresaw further drops in the real value of central resources and proposed to compensate this by increasing the municipality's own source revenues and also by improving the operation's cost efficiency. By establishing these two goals while defining a new planning method, the Draft Conception created the foundations for the new financial strategy.

The Draft Conception also identified principles and methods for increasing municipal own revenues, introducing realistic planning, and implementing institutional reform. We shall now sum up the key elements of the strategy using the document's terminology.

RECKONING WITH THE PROBABLE TRENDS OF PUBLIC FINANCE REFORM

It seems natural that financial planning should be based on projections of expected revenues. And yet, the fact that the Draft Conception proposed to create resource projections for several years ahead counts as a major improvement over the previous practice. As far as centrally regulated resources are concerned, the only development that could be assumed was a decrease in the pace of the real value loss of central resources. At the same time, the good news was that the resources were expected to become more predictable. Decreasing central resources fundamentally defined the scope of possibilities for the municipal reform strategy.

BROADENING THE SCOPE OF POSSIBILITIES – OWN REVENUES

A city can offset the decreasing central revenues by increasing its own source revenues. According to the Draft Conception, this is important not only because it secures resources but also because it strengthens the municipality's financial autonomy. In the field of local taxation, the Draft Conception proposed to utilize the full legal scope for taxation to the extent of the inhabitants' tax-paying potentials. While there was practically no chance to boost revenues in the field of asset management, it still seemed important to restructure the marketable portfolio to reach positive yield instead of negative yield. (The explanation for the earlier negative yield portfolio is that stakes, securities were "inherited" in the process of asset transfers from the state.) Besides, creating the rules and conditions for avoiding the exhaustion of assets was an urgent task.[65] Although the municipality's 1994 privatization concept identified higher efficiency (and through this the cheapest possible provision of

---

[65] "The primary task on the one hand is to develop a proper system of asset management, including the conversion of assets into a portfolio that produces a positive yield in real terms. On the other hand, it is to promote financial balance with asset management means that minimize the loss in yield-producing assets and do not produce any loss for the total of municipal assets. This means that revenues from assets must not cover operation, or at the worst only a part of the increase in the assets that produce not direct yield can be covered from asset conversion, and even these only to enhance the 'shock absorption' that will be discussed later." (The Office of the Mayor of Budapest, 1995c: 6)

public utility services) as the primary goal of the privatization process, the city could also reckon with significant one-time revenues, that played a role in "shock absorption" that will be discussed later.

Alongside local taxes, public utility charges played a key role in increasing the city's own source revenues in an indirect way.[66] Although the municipality's prime concern in establishing public utility rates was to provide more efficient services, it heeded the consideration that it is more equitable to shift the costs of these services on to the customers in a proportionate manner than to redeem these costs through taxes spread over the city's entire population. The rates that are proportionate to consumption are more equitable and enable customers to save some of their money.[67]

In most instances, the introduction of cost-covering public utility charges resulted in rate hikes. By 1996, the municipality had introduced cost-covering rates for all those basic services (with the exception of public transportation) where it was possible to measure individual consumption. As a result, the city's budget was relieved from the need to finance the operation of these public services. The municipality could thus increase its redistributive activities within the frameworks of the systems that lent themselves to that (education, welfare policy etc.). In other words, the city covered certain (earlier rate subsidizing) expenditures from indirect revenues, and the resources freed this way were used to finance other activities.

"SHOCK ABSORPTION" IN INVESTMENT

According to the Draft Conception:

> "The 1980s created an 'investment vacuum' in the capital city, and this was one of the reasons behind the municipality's decision to subscribe to the development obligations presented by the World Exhibition and buttressed by surplus resources. However, these extra resources were accessible only through the mobilization of sizeable own resources. This required the city to draw large loans. An 'investment peak' of this kind tends to generate lasting burdens, and so for a year or two after, the city could only keep its budget balanced through a series of extremely tough cuts in investment and a practically complete freeze on further borrowing. 'Putting on the brake' will send wild and lasting shocks across the municipality's financial system. These shocks must therefore be absorbed as soon as possible, preferably during the first cycle."[68]

The tools for absorbing these shocks included the strict four-year work-plan, the coordination of the medium-term development concepts, and the shifting of the burdens of public utility development on to the corporate sphere simultaneously with an increase in the cost-coverage of utility charges.

---

[66] The term of indirect revenue refers to the fact that the user charges are collected by the service companies and not by the municipality.

[67] See the paper on 'Infrastructure Policies' for details on this issue.

[68] The Office of the Mayor of Budapest, 1995c: 5

REALISTIC WORK-PLANS AND MEDIUM-TERM INVESTMENT PLANNING

In its efforts to promote the emergence of an efficient financial system (in investment as well as in operation), the Draft Conception assigned a key role to strict and accurate planning. To this end, it proposed the introduction of three important tools: a model for analyzing the financial-economic processes, strategic and medium-term development concepts that heed the possibilities of financing, and the "rolling" method of financial planning that enables "fine-tuning" within the annual budgeting process.[69] These three tools were identified only as goals, and the Draft Conception did not yet elaborate on their content.

THE REFORM OF THE INSTITUTIONS

The Draft Conception asserted that leaving the financing system of the institutions unchanged, i.e., continuing base financing, would lead to complete disaster. The concept asserted that reforms were inevitable, and aimed to introduce them while maintaining the city's operability. Furthermore, the Draft Conception promised to introduce a series of methods that it said were capable of enforcing the reforms without trespassing on sectoral autonomies.

However, it was clear that this very sphere was the least receptive to the reform process. It was predictable that the actors would strive to protect their historically established positions by voicing professional considerations. To quote the Draft Conception, devising a way to "enforce the rationalization of operating costs without interfering in the content areas with our financial regulatory measures"[70] was a great challenge.

The Draft Conception defined only two new tools for the realization of these goals and expectations: the Institution Rationalization Fund, and the remittance of internal savings within the sectors. As regards the financing of the operating costs, the "lawnmower principle" was retained as a primary method, but the concept – improving the base financing approach – suggested including individual limits to institutions "at a technically safe level and in a way that does not violate content considerations" as a guarantee of safety for the operation.[71] In practice this meant that the fiscal leadership only determined the aggregate sum allocated to the individual sectors, and the sectors then had the right to decide on the spreading of the effects of the "lawnmower" (except wages) to various institutions. Thus, withholding resources could be effectuated unevenly, on the basis of a clear awareness of the conditions prevailing in the individual institutions.

It follows from the above that the Draft Conception managed to establish clearly defined goals for the various sectors of budgetary financing. These goals all had their roots in the original strategic goal (the maintenance of the city's operability), and also linked up perfectly with subsequent versions of the strategy.

---

[69] The "rolling" method of planning means that – alongside the plans for the given year's budget – a multi-year projection and plan is drafted each year, and in the following year this plan is adjusted to the changing conditions and another year's projections are added on. The result is an annually updated planning process.

[70] The Office of the Mayor of Budapest, 1995c: 7

[71] The Office of the Mayor of Budapest, 1995c: 7

Although the Draft Concept included several progressive principles and strategic elements, not all of thesione could make it into the 1996 budget conception. The basic change in approach – symbolized by the strategic budgetary planning method whereby the long term strategy guides short term decision making - could not be fully carried out because of the lack of proper financing projections and a model of planning.

The 1996 budget recognized the need to review the resource requirements of the city's operation and to renew its institutional structure. Still, up until the launch of these reforms, the drafters had resorted to the practice of the previous years in planning the budget's cardinal numbers. They defined the volume of the investments by assessing the city's potential revenues and the obligations associated with operation, refurbishment and debt servicing. At the same time, the budget adopted the measures coming from the Draft Conception that aimed to create a more rational institutional structure. These measures included the proposed launching of the Institution Rationalization Fund to support the restructuring process, or the decentralization of the right to dispose of the sectoral and institutional revenues based on the principle of resource localization. This last measure was meant to encourage the generation of own current revenues and the sale of unutilized institutional assets.

THE INTRODUCTION OF SEVEN-YEAR PLANNING – 1996

As we have seen, the underlying goal of the Draft Conception was to promote the introduction of strategic budgetary planning. However, the 1996 budget was not supported by proper financial projections and a planning model, and in the lack of a proper analysis of the trends, the structure of the budget could not be drawn up by applying the "counting backwards" method. From the point of view of the reform process, the next important step was the introduction of the seven-year financial analysis model.

In 1996, the city decided to adopt the financial analysis model developed by Credit Local International (hereinafter CLI Model), which was adapted to the Hungarian budgetary system later that year (and later fine-tuned several times). This computerized financial analysis model arranges the budget entries into a financially transparent and comprehensible structure, consistently separates the current and capital expenditures and revenues, and calculates the difference between current expenditures and current revenues, i.e., the operating surplus. The model relies on the trends of the preceding three years and on the projections for the following seven years. The model has to accommodate assumptions (such as the projected rate of inflation), which usually come from expert sources. Of course, the model treats all the projections and expectations as variables, and calculates the related functions. The computerized model is extremely fast and user-friendly and enables the simulation of a variety of assumptions and strategies. Regarding the hypothetical assumptions, the Municipality of Budapest has always based them on detailed professional consultations and thorough deliberations.

After 1996, the model became a tool for analyzing the situations underlying budgetary decisions and simulating the effects of these decisions. The model supported the systemization of the earlier reform concepts and also the identification of the areas that required further clarification. With regard to the creation of the reform strategy, the CLI Model's most important feature turned out to be the calculation of the operating surplus. The operating surplus[72] evolved into the central element or benchmark of the new financial strategy. As we have seen, the elements of the reform process were subsequently deduced from the targeted operating surpluses.

THE FINANCIAL MANAGEMENT REFORM STRATEGY – 1996–1997

The financial model is an excellent tool which allows to perceive trends, expresses expectations in terms of revenue and expenditure projections, and calculates the effects of the simulated steps seven years ahead.

The model has turned out to be a fundamental tool for evaluating projected situations and determining the steps to be taken. And yet, the most important effect of its introduction in 1996 was that it unquestionably proved that without significant restructuring the city's financial balance will disappear even in the medium term. Having entered the broadest possible range of hypotheses into the system, the conclusion was that the capital city's financial system could not be set on a sustainable course without significant cuts in the operating costs[73] (as suggested by the strategy). The city's leading political forces and bodies were all confronted with the need to introduce a comprehensive reform process. In addition, the concept that aimed to achieve a positive operating result was fit for laying the foundations of a comprehensive strategy, and the concept could also logically structure and unambiguously communicate it.

In 1996, when the first calculations were completed with the model, there was no ground to expect an increase in the real value of the municipality's revenues over the next few years. In the financing projections, the maintenance of the real value of the current revenues was treated as a realistic goal only for the period after 2000. Regarding the accumulation

---

[72] The literature and papers in this volume define operating surplus as the difference between current revenues and expenditure. Nevertheless, under the Act on Public Finance both current revenues and the Municipality's expenditure must include some "targeted" revenue items that are not directly connected to the municipality of Budapest (Items on which the municipality has no right of disposal, i.e., channeled through its budget only. These are sums connected to sharing of funds with the district governments and to company credits). As these sums are included into the budget figures, they must be included in the financing model, too. Therefore, to get to the value relevant for municipal financial management, the surplus of the balance of these "targeted" revenues and expenditures must be deduced from the operating surplus. The adjusted operating surplus is calculated this way in the model. As the adjusted operating surplus is relevant to the analysis of the financial positions of the municipality, its changes will be taken into account in the subsequent part of our review. Accordingly, as the adjusted operating surplus equals the concept of operating surplus used in literature, from now on we will consistently use this simpler expression for the concept.

[73] In order to give a clear picture, the model produces projections at real value. The reduction of operating costs is to be interpreted accordingly. This also meant that, due to the high rate of inflation, the increase in the nominal value of the operating costs was significantly curtailed, so its real value was reduced, and – temporarily – even its nominal value was diminished.

and capital revenues, these were expected to expire (privatization, sale of real estate and portfolios).

The municipality had to make a decision whether to strive to maintain the level of the operating or the accumulation expenditures during the period for which it could expect a decrease in the real value of its revenues. Another option was to reckon with a drop in the real value of both. To maintain the financing of its daily operation at real value, the city would have had to resort to accumulation-type revenues as well. This solution would have rapidly led to the exhaustion of capital revenues and consequently to an inoperable city. The simultaneous reduction of the operating and the accumulation expenditures would have led to the same result, albeit more smoothly and gradually. These two "cul-de-sac" strategies proved that the services were not sustainable with their given structure and status. In other words, the earlier "bookkeeper" approach (which strove to distribute the losses among the various budgetary entries) could not offer a solution.

The 1997 budget conception had the following to say about the reform strategy that promised to achieve a balanced budget:

> "The way out of the present situation leads through efforts aimed at maintaining, or even increasing, the real value of the capital expenditures (and also the equally important one-time cost-rationalizing operating expenditures) that improve the operating conditions in a cost-saving manner.

> "In general, and based on these criteria, [during the transition, i.e., the reform period the budget of the municipality can be considered balanced if it manages to keep the accumulation (and the one-time cost-rationalizing operating) expenditures – including the ones that improve the financing conditions of operation – at real value (and at an acceptable level).

> "Due to the 'expiry' of the accumulation and capital-type revenues, the operating surplus remains the only key 'resource' for achieving a balanced budget. From this it follows that our goals must be commensurate with the proportions of the operating surplus and the current revenues.

> "According to our projections, the municipality's budget will be balanced and the volume of the accumulation expenditures will be acceptable if the operating surplus reaches 20 percent of the current revenues, and stays at that level from then on.

> "However, we must understand that due to the operation's excessive vulnerability (high 'inertia') it is not possible to achieve this goal within one or two years (the 'deflection' of the real changes of the current revenues and the running expenditures cannot exceed a few percentage points each year).

> "We must use the projected temporary increase of the accumulation revenues in 1996-1998 to bridge the gap that will occur in the first years between the operating surplus and the required level of the accumulation revenues. The [accumulation resources]

should be technically spread over the years when the resources are expected to be rather scarce.

"At the same time, the level of this 'deflection' must be high enough to ensure – over a period of four or five years, and despite the changes in the trends – the accomplishment of the above goal, i.e., the balancing of the municipal budget."[74]

In order to guarantee an appropriate pace for the "deflection," the tasks undertaken by the municipality had to be filtered according to a previously agreed schedule (this had to occur simultaneously with the rationalizing measures). In addition, the Conception urged the optimal spending of the remaining investment resources:

"Following the scheduled filtering of the tasks, and in order to ensure that the operating surplus can be increased by means other than the intolerable reduction of the tasks or the likewise intolerable reduction of the real value of the expenditures... the resource capacities that will remain available after the cost-rationalizing developments will have to be earmarked for financing the strategically most important tasks. [...]

"Pending the completion of a balanced budget, the strategy to be applied in the field of budgetary financing should simultaneously apply an active borrowing policy and strive for the maintenance of the financial reserves. [...] The investments would require the creation of a credit portfolio that splits financing risks. In external financing it would be expedient to rely on the domestic as well as the foreign financial markets, and to involve resources from the banks' credit markets as well as the bond market."[75]

As the above quotes reveal, the reform strategy was practically ready in the fall of 1996 (at the time of the approval of the 1997 budget conception). In the next budget conception, for the fiscal year of 1998 (which was approved in 1997), the strategy aimed at reducing the operating costs added an important new element to the dual goal of task filtering and rationalization: it urged the municipality's preparation for the institutions' zero-based task financing system. With this, the tools aimed at encouraging the restructuring of the tasks and the institutional structure were supplemented by another one: to establish a more efficient financing system for the retained tasks. (The three tools aimed at reducing the operating costs will be discussed in detail in the following study.) Another new element, the aim of which was to promote the preparations for planning the capital budget, was the introduction of the four-year "rolling" investment planning (for details, please see the following paper, under the subhead 'Investment Planning'.)

---

[74] The Office of the Mayor of Budapest, 1996c

[75] Ibid.

RESULTS AND POSSIBILITIES – 1997-1998

The reform process should be discussed in the light of the comparison between the results and the goals laid down in the strategy. The accomplishments prior to 1998 should be contrasted with the goals specified in the first, 1995, draft of the strategy.

The strategy's main focus was to increase the operating surplus. The aim was to bring the operating surplus up to 20 percent of the current revenues by the year 2000. In 1995, the operating surplus was low – only 8 percent. In the period at issue the operating surplus increased (in 1998 it stood at 12 percent), and at that time the targeted 20 percent level appeared to be tenable, even if not by the desired deadline of 2000 but by 2003.[76]

The strategy aimed at increasing the operating surplus did not reckon on a real growth on the revenues side. The projections regarding the central revenues were partly proven right, as the resources had continuously lost their real value. However, the rate of this loss exceeded expectations: it reached 23 percent during the period at issue.[77]

Chart 7
**NOMINAL AND REAL VALUE OF THE CENTRALLY REGULATED REVENUES
(basis: 1991; billion HUF)**

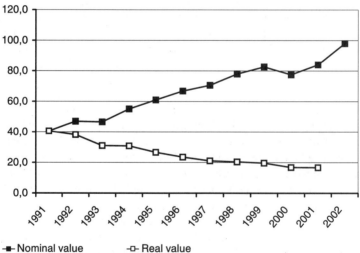

-■- Nominal value   -□- Real value

Source: The Office of the Mayor of Budapest, 2002b

From 1995 own revenues started to increase with a turning point in 1997, when they amounted to 288 percent of the 1991 own revenues. Then, they could counterbalance the decrease in the central revenues and exceeded the amount of the centrally regulated resources. (In 1997,

---

[76] Legal and financial information, 1998d: 81

[77] The Office of the Mayor of Budapest, 2002b: table pertinent to charts showing real values

the city's own revenues represented 55.3 percent of the budget, while the centrally regulated resources stood at 36.4 percent – or at 20.6 percent without the "transient" resources of the social security system). Regarding this indicator, the position was better than expected in the resource projection. Between 1995 and 1999 the city witnessed an increase (albeit modest) in the real value of its total revenues.[78]

Chart 8
REVENUES AT 1991 REAL VALUE (billion HUF)

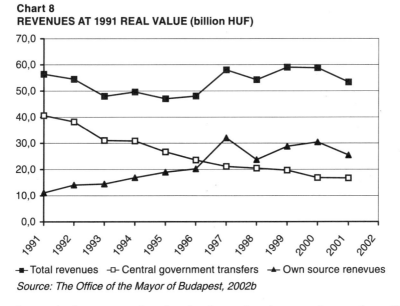

-■- Total revenues   -□- Central government transfers   -▲- Own source renevues
Source: The Office of the Mayor of Budapest, 2002b

The other element in the strategy that aimed at increasing the operating surplus called for the reduction of operating costs. This program proposed to apply two methods: filtering the tasks and boosting the efficiency of the tasks' fulfillment.

The process of task filtering and function reorganizing carried on, although not always with spectacular successes. Tasks were regrouped under three headings: "to be canceled," "contracted out," and "transferred between the city and districts."

Alongside the "lawnmower" method, which was considered a transitory constraint, two elements were expected to provide incentives for increasing efficiency: these were the Institution Rationalization Fund and the task financing concept. The Institution Rationalization Fund proved to be a major help in completing the changes aimed at increasing efficiency. (At the same time, as we will see later on, this tool, which was excellent at its inception, suffered some distortions over the years.[79]) The only real and complete fiasco of the program that was aimed at reducing the operating costs turned out to be the introduction of the zero-based budget (for reasons that will be discussed in detail in the next paper).

---

[78] The Office of the Mayor of Budapest, 2002b: table pertinent to the charts showing real values

[79] For details see the next study.

This was generally a successful process, even if all elements of the attempted reduction of the operating costs could not be implemented: while in 1995 the current expenditures amounted to 66 percent of the budget, in 1998 the respective figure was only 53 percent.[80] This was achieved without compromising the quality of the services, and by methods other than just by filtering the tasks.

The goals also included an active borrowing policy and a gradual entry to the capital market. The latter was to be done from an appropriately strong position, and with adequate timing. In the first cycle the only available solutions were to accept the loans offered by the international investment financing institutions, or the short-term loans of domestic banks in smaller amounts. However, the improvement of the capital city's financial position between 1995 and 1998 enabled the municipality to replace the previously drawn loans with cheaper ones and also to appear on the international bond market, where the interests are lower than for most other credits. The bond issue in 1998 showed the success of the city's borrowing policy (for details please see the following study under the subhead 'Borrowing Policy').

All in all, we can see that until 1998 the balance of results was definitely positive, and in the year of the elections the goals still appeared to be realizable in terms of both content and – the previously postponed – deadlines.

DRASTIC DROP IN RESOURCES – 1999–2002

The right wing party won the general elections held in spring 1998. However, in the municipal elections held in the fall, the liberal mayor was re-elected in Budapest and a Liberal-Socialist coalition could again be formed in the general assembly.

During the third election cycle, the right-wing government adopted statist practices and used every opportunity to interfere with the normative system by which public funds were distributed (and thereby to provide preferential treatment to its political allies). Furthermore, the gradual advance of the right in controlling the distribution of public funds by the government resulted in a gradual loss of resources for the local governments (the governing party's followers were again exceptions). After the elections it became clear rather fast that the right-wing central government aimed to undermine the Socialist-Liberal left-wing's credibility (which was stable in Budapest) by throwing obstacles in the way of the capital city's spectacular large investment projects and clearly trying to paralyze the city's financial management system.[81]

The 1999 central government budget was still based largely on the plans of the previous government, since the budgets are always drafted a year earlier. This meant that there was no time for the government to restructure its budget between the national elections and the approval of the new state budget. All it could do was to cancel a few major projects and reconsider the discretional resources. In its 1999 budget, the capital city managed to counter (to an extent) the drop in the real value of the central budgetary resources by increasing its

---

[80] The Office of the Mayor of Budapest, 2002b: table pertaining to charts 6-8

[81] Besides the efforts mentioned above, a crucial means of financially paralyzing the Municipality of Budapest was to ruin the public transport company BKV through withholding central subsidies and slowing down the pace of fee increase through the veto of the Minister of Finance. The issue of financing public transport played a cardinal role in the strategy of both sides, because it was obvious that the bankruptcy of BKV would have caused the insolvency of municipal finances in a short while.

own revenues. On the expenditures side it significantly restructured the obligatory public services and drafted measures for the various sectors with a view to reduce the costs and thus increase the operating surplus. Eventually the city managed to ensure the growth of the operating surplus, and it seemed that a date could be kept that would be even earlier than the postponed deadline for the accomplishment of the strategic goal (the 20 percent operating surplus in 2002).[82]

The 2000 central budget (and within that the regulations pertaining to the financing of the local governments) was already drafted completely in accordance with the new government's plans. The result was a sizeable withdrawal of resources from the whole local government sector, and within the financing of the sector significant restructuring was implemented at Budapest's expense. By this time the drop in resources in Budapest had meant not only the drastic loss of value of the centrally regulated resources (15 percent at real value) but also a decline of the city's own revenues.[83] Although the capital city's financial transactions significantly increased the figures in the budget's revenue side, in 2000 Budapest's total revenues shrank in real terms compared to the previous year. In response (and in order to maintain its operability) the city had to accept a slight – and, in intention, temporary – drop in the operating surplus (which had been steadily increasing until 1998).[84]

In 2000, the central government completed a two-year budget for 2001-2002. This budget changed the regulations pertaining to the local governments' revenues in several respects. First, a significant percentage of the duty revenues belonging to the municipality was channeled away from it. Second, to the detriment of Budapest, the new regulations modified the way of calculating the tax potentials.[85] Third – disregarding the established task proportionate distribution principle for revenue sharing –, benchmark figures[86] were

---

[82] The Office of the Mayor of Budapest, 2000c: 79

[83] The Office of the Mayor of Budapest, 2002b: table pertaining to the real value chart.

[84] The Office of the Mayor of Budapest, 2000c: 79

[85] The formula for calculating tax potential takes into account the volume of PIT share distributed on a derivative basis and the local business tax potential. These two calculated sums provide the basis for calculating the per capita tax potential. Each year a threshold value is established and the amount of tax above this value is withheld (also on the basis of annually established brackets and proportions) for financing resource equalization among local governments. The amount to be withheld and its distribution among the local governments can be modified by changing the following three indices: threshold value, brackets, and withdrawal percentages. As a result of the modification of these parameters, the sums withdrawn from Budapest (based on the tax potential) increased from HUF 876 million in 2000 to nearly HUF 5.5 billion in 2002.

[86] Due to Budapest's two-tier local government system, certain operating transfers must be shared between the districts and the municipality. The revenue sharing method was based on a task proportionate (which could be more accurately named as "deficit proportionate") distribution of funds in Budapest. In the new regulation, the central government introduced benchmark figures for revenue sharing. This means that the government legally regulated the minimum share that the districts would get from the various revenues under "revenue sharing." This was to be done irrespective of the tasks and despite the fact that the Act on Local Governments – which can be modified only by a qualified (i.e., two-thirds) majority – authorizes the municipality of Budapest to distribute central resources within the city. Eventually, acting on the capital city's petition, the constitutional court canceled this measure effective December 2002. However, these benchmark values were still enforced in 2001 and 2002, which caused serious resource losses for the capital city. By 2002, these values had canceled the practice of sharing funds between the municipality and the districts proportionally to the tasks. The municipal fund sharing system itself could remain task-proportionate in the distribution of funds only among districts.

prescribed for the districts' access to resources distributed through local "revenue sharing," which again had a negative effect on the Municipality of Budapest. In 2001, the real value of the city's revenues for the base year dropped by a further 10 percent over the previous year's figure. In 2002, the respective figure was minus 7 percent according to estimate figures.[87]

By 2001, the city's budget had reached the point where its resources could not cover the costs of retaining the level of its tasks. It became clear that the earlier strategy was no longer tenable. The operating costs could not be reduced along with the dropping resources any further, or else the standard of the services would have declined dramatically. On the other hand, continuing with the operations would have drained the resources for maintenance and adaptation. Thus, both obvious paths would have eventually led the city into deeper and deeper trouble. It was clear that without radical changes to the city's access to resources, the services were doomed to collapse.

The city's leaders found themselves at a crossroads. One option was to follow the strictly conservative route, according to which the consequences of the restrictive central measures would have to be spread linearly over the whole spectrum of the city's services without delay. This would have required reducing the operating surplus (which served as a resource for the indispensable refurbishment and adaptation projects) and channeling financing towards the (short-term) maintenance of daily operations. In essence, this would have meant the freezing of the investments that were financed (at least partly) from the city's own resources. Under this scenario, additional resources could have been involved only to the extent allowed by the city's creditworthiness calculated according to the new revenue trend. The latter option was strictly theoretical, since the city could not have secured coverage for the debt service of new loans. This route would have led the city to swift and total collapse.

The other option was identified as the dynamic crisis management strategy. Accordingly, the consequences of the restrictive government measures were included in the municipality's financial projection and plans only for the two-year state budget term, but were not extrapolated over the usual seven years. The explanation for this idea was that the drastic cuts in revenues were obviously manifestations of the government's intentions to paralyze the city. Facing this government strategy the municipality's only solution was to try to keep afloat. Keeping afloat in the long run was only possible if at least the earlier level of financing was restored. Therefore, the dynamic strategy rested on the assumption that the earlier financing conditions would be restored in 2002 – either due to the replacement of the government, or because no government could afford the complete destruction of the capital of the country. With regard to this assumption the municipal strategy was to endure its hardship until a change in the government strategy. The municipality did this through options that were still open to it such as reducing expenditures and seeking additional funds.[88]

---

[87] The Office of the Mayor of Budapest, 2002b: table pertaining to the chart showing real values.

[88] The Office of the Mayor of Budapest, 2000a

It was clear even at the inception of this strategy, that the failure of this assumption would also have spelled disaster. This strategy may seem irresponsible, but the road chosen by the municipality of Budapest may also be considered as rational and morally justifiable. This way they postponed the beginning of what would have been a sharp decline in the city's infrastructure and services, and hoped that future changes could then build on a city in a better condition.

The General Assembly of the municipality of Budapest decided to adopt this assumption regarding the restoration of the city's financing conditions and to build it into the municipal financial strategy. For the period following 2003 it presumed a restoration of the pre-decline level of financing, the elimination of negative preferences, and a compensation for the negative effects of the previous government's policies through a one-time correction measure. The dynamic strategy aimed to use the creditworthiness calculated on the basis of the above projections for countering the effects of the transitional decline of the operating surplus. Of course, this strategy was applicable only to the extent that the capital market would positively react. In other words, the strategy was applicable only if the market also rejected the government's strategy elaborated in 2000, and confirmed the city's assumptions about the necessity of its change.

Undertaking a transitory deflection from its earlier strategy, and with the aim of maintaining its operability, the city reduced its operating surplus[89] to 7.4 percent in 2001 and to an expected figure of about 7 percent[90] in 2002, and simultaneously launched a series of talks on its new loans. As a declining operating surplus shrunk the projectable coverage for debt service based on recurrent revenues, the municipality was forced to review its then considerable financial reserves and transferable (or potentially transferable) assets to prove its creditworthiness. The municipality undertook this review although it has not deviated from the principles of its earlier established borrowing policy, i.e., assets and reserves were not contracted as collateral, as the municipality continued borrowing under name financing, or negative pledge.[91] Besides the municipality also had to point out the possibility of canceling investment projects as an ultimate resort. This was justified partly by its continuously prudent financial management and by the precedent of the World Exhibition.

Based on its long-standing reputation and having considerable reserves, Budapest could initiate talks even in those conditions with respected international financial institutions. It was clear that the city's strategy was so very peculiar that its "authentication" required the

---

[89] Corresponding to the terms of the financial projection, here we speak about the adjusted operating surplus, because – as we have discussed earlier – this value is relevant from the point of view of the financial balance of the municipality.

[90] Though the financial projection posts 2.2 percent here, we use the expected 7 percent instead for the sake of comparison. The use of this figure is justified by the fact that every year the calculated figures of the financial projection differ remarkably from the actual figures due to the improper handling of residual funds. This is a technical deficiency of the model that financial leaders have already noticed, but have not managed to correct yet. Thus, owing to residual funds, the actual figure of operating surplus exceeds the planned figure at each annual closing.

[91] For details see the next study on the 'Elements of the Financial Reform.'

consent of a high-prestige international financial institution or a first-class international bank. It was likewise clear that Budapest's solicitation for credit would be duly considered only by such financial institutions that had prior knowledge of the city's financial record and respected its financial leaders.

The feedback from the capital market was positive. In 2001 (after the government refused to undertake a guarantee), Budapest used the guarantee of a commercial bank for signing a loan agreement with the European Investment Bank (EIB). In the fall of 2002, Budapest was assigned an issuer rating on a par with the country by two international credit rating agencies Standard & Poor's and Moody's.[92] A favorable rating could have contributed to the success of the negotiations with EIB on the next loan, if the new government also refused to be the guarantor of the credit. As for the syndicated loan from commercial banks also under negotiation at the time, issuer rating was unnecessary. Still, the ratings publicized between two turns of the negotiations improved the conditions that were offered to the municipality.

This dynamic strategy was justified by the success of both credit negotiations, and the municipality managed to keep afloat without great sacrifices until the change of government in 2002. Although – in spite of the pressure by the Budapest municipality – no structural reforms of the local governments' financing system were implemented in 2002,[93] the government stabilized the financial situation of the public transport company BKV by a one-off, considerable subsidy, undertaking its HUF 38 billion debt. This intervention provides the municipality – and eventually the government, too[94] – a further year for settling its financing problems. (It is most likely also clear for the government that one-off subsidies cannot resolve the operations problems of the capital city and those of the local governments in Hungary. The ability of the local governments to provide services in a decentralized system in a really self-governing way can only be exclusively sustained by a thorough revision of their financing system.)

Though the dynamic strategy proved to be successful, it is clear that a crisis management strategy is a temporary solution. Its implementation did not mean that the municipal government had altered its earlier goals. Under the given set of constraints, the municipality has simply postponed the deadline for achieving the 20 percent operating surplus by 2008.[95]

---

[92] For details of the rating see subchapter "Borrowing Policy" in the next study.

[93] In early 2003, when closing the manuscript, it was still possible to hope that the government had failed to start the reform of the local government financing system only due to lack of time.

[94] It is important to call attention to the government's responsibility. Justifiably, the municipality does not have the financial means to settle the problems of public transport. The State Audit Office – whose independence has never been questioned – came to the same conclusion after scrutinizing the problem. (State Audit Office, 2001)

[95] The financing projection attached to the 2002 budget conception put the deadline to 2006, in the next one, for the 2003 budget conception, the deadline was postponed to 2008.

THE STRATEGY FOR MAINTAINING THE EQUILIBRIUM

The strategy of "transition" outlined above was aimed at creating a method of task fulfillment and financing that enabled the municipality to guarantee a sustainable equilibrium for its budget thanks to the 20 percent operating surplus.

Should this goal be achieved, the city's budgetary planning process would in principle become simpler, since the municipality would "only" have to concentrate on maintaining its operating surplus. Accordingly, being aware of the resource projections, the first step in budgeting should be the definition of the cardinal numbers: the operating surplus and the sums earmarked for operation. Since the city is bound to continue its operations in the context of ever-changing conditions, the planned expenditures items within the limits of the cardinal numbers must be identified on the basis of the projected external conditions.

In this system of planning, where the long-term aim is to guarantee a sustainable equilibrium (which is not possible without allocating an adequate share for refurbishment and adaptation in the budget), the drop in resources results in a scheduled restriction of the operating costs. This method of planning is at complete variance with the previous practice, in which the planners of the budget heeded short-term interests when they strove to avoid having to pay the political price for the operating restrictions. It was for this reason that the investment expenditures were planned on a residual basis. (i.e., those resources were allocated to the capital budget that remained after all operating costs had been covered.)

EVALUATION AND LESSONS

EVALUATION CRITERIA

The financial management reform implemented within the framework of the "Budapest model," as well as the results of the process, can be evaluated on the basis of two different sets of criteria. On the one hand, we can compare the process and its results with the goals spelled out in the reform strategy. This way we evaluate only the internal consistency of the process. On the other hand, the process can be evaluated on the basis of general and external criteria. Here the process and its results are evaluated in relation to generally accepted professional expectations, and the results themselves are brought into comparison with the reference values of the internationally accepted and used indices.

The evaluation of the internal consistency of the process can entail four elements:

- the analysis of the goals, i.e., the evaluation of the initial objectives and whether the way these objectives were defined and formulated was conducive to the successful implementation of the strategic process;
- the analysis of whether the strategy was logically built on the initial goals, i.e., whether the strategy was conducive to the accomplishment of the original goals;
- the analysis of whether the implementation of the strategy was consistent and steadfast;
- the analysis of the relationship between the results and the targeted goals and objectives.

If the evaluation is based on external professional criteria, the results are normally analyzed on the basis of internationally accepted reference systems. In this case our evaluation can start from local governments' responsibility for managing public funds in a responsible, efficient and transparent way.

According to commonly accepted practice, the most detailed evaluation of the soundness of a financial management system comes from the issuer rating analysis, since this analysis is meant to determine the risks behind the investments of exterior partners. For this reason, the issuer rating analyses focus on the transparency of the financial management system, the methods of planning that are applied, the level of discipline in the system, and the projected operating surplus (which is the source of the debt service). For our purposes, the following elements of the issuer rating methodology can be considered relevant (as these evaluate the financial management system in a direct manner): the method of financial management, the financial performance, and the budgetary indices.

In the closing part of this study we shall evaluate the soundness and reliability of the city's financial management system on the basis of the above criteria. It is far more troublesome to evaluate the efficiency of this system. In this respect, improvement is defined as a per unit drop in the resources used for maintaining services at least at the same standard. However, it is difficult to accurately measure the standard of the services, and thus we would have to restrict ourselves to evaluating the changes in the costs associated with the fulfillment of the tasks. The findings will only be relevant for elements where the content of the task was unchanged.

IDENTIFYING THE STRATEGIC GOAL

Initially, in the first half of the 1990s, the maintenance of the city's operability was identified as the strategic goal. To this end, the municipality introduced comprehensive planning spanning a period beyond the fiscal year. When the introduction of seven-year planning made the budgetary processes and the city's financing status more transparent, it became possible to identify the goals with better accuracy. From then on, the goal has been to create the conditions for balanced financial management.

There were two conditions considered conducive to this goal: the 20 percent operating surplus and the maintenance of the real value of the capital expenditures, especially the ones that serve to improve the operation's financing conditions.

This "mature" version of the strategic goal successfully governed the municipal reform process and – as experience shows – guaranteed equilibrium. Thus, this phrasing is adequate from the point of view of professional practice, but it is far from being perfect theoretically.

The theoretical problem can be identified as follows: taken as a premise, the 20 percent operating surplus suggests that it is sufficient to continuously cover the costs of refurbishment and adaptation. However, the strategy fails to justify this inherent assumption on the strength of calculations. Instead, it builds on earlier expenditure-related experiences without providing further information on the structural deficit-reducing effects of this expenditure level. Consequently, the strategy avoids the quantification of the cost requirements of maintenance and adaptation (from the point of view of both the assets and the allocations).

Back in 1996, it was a logical decision to bypass quantification, as the drafters of the strategy did not have sufficient data and methods at their disposal to associate figures with the maintenance and adaptation-related cost requirements.[96] This would have required:

- an accurate registration of the state of the assets;
- an algorithm for the calculation of the continuous cost requirements needed for the maintenance of the assets (after the completion of the postponed rehabilitation projects);
- professional concepts to clarify the content of adaptation.

However, these theoretical deficiencies may be considered less important from a practical point of view. Detailed calculations may have smoothed the way for the political approval of the strategy (although this is far from certain), but after its approval this consideration would have had little or no effect on the capacity of the 20 percent operating surplus goal to guide the strategic reform process.

The 1996 definition of the goals of the municipal financial management strategy can be considered correct also from the technical point of view of professional planning. Indeed, it was accurate enough to lay the foundations of the strategic management concept for the municipal finances through an officially approved decision, and to guarantee the direction of the management until the decision was in force. At the same time – since the above two conditions specify "only" the ratio among the cardinal numbers of the budget – it was general enough to enable the municipality to adjust its short-term strategies and concrete measures to changing conditions. Thanks to these two features, the definition perfectly meets the requirements of process regulation spelt out in our introduction and in the paper on strategic management.[97] Besides, the targeted status specified in the strategic goals was a professionally correct approximation. The method relied on the so-called "second best" solution, as it specified the expected operating surplus not by quantifying the local requirements but instead by replacing them with approximations based on empirical values.

---

[96] These statements hold true even now, owing to the deficiencies of local government asset registration. Though from December 31, 2003 onwards, the Act on Public Finance requires local governments to set up a complete inventory of their assets registered at market value, this is probably bound to fail due to unsettled asset transfers (among other reasons).

[97] Although we have no room to discuss it here, we may say that the regulation of the financial decision-making process also corresponds to the logic of process regulation spelled out in the previous paper on 'Strategic Planning and Management Reform.' Decision-making approved the strategy for the long run. Every year, together with the approval of the budget conception and aware of the updated financing projection, the assembly adjusts the implementation process of the strategy to the given conditions. This means that it determines the following year's steps for the strategy's implementation, i.e., – the following year's tactics.

From a methodological point of view, the strategic goal was the achievement of a balanced budget. This does not include the identification of these two conditions, although their identification was exceptionally important in strengthening the process management role and capability of the strategic goal. The two conditions already belong to and are the key elements of the strategy. They could also only be defined once there was a realistic strategy for the accomplishment of the strategic goal. And yet, from the point of view of process management, it is justified to reintroduce these conditions here and to have them officially approved together with the strategic goal. After all, as we have seen, these two conditions play a crucial role in enabling and guaranteeing process management, i.e., that a one-time agreement can determine the content of the subsequent decisions.

CHOICE OF STRATEGY AND METHODS

It is a fact beyond dispute that – if local governments are independent – financial management aims to maintain a balanced budget. As we have seen in our discussion of the underlying principles, if the local leadership strives to create and pursue a responsible and sustainable political line, several key elements of the strategy can be unambiguously identified by relying on rational, professional considerations:

- The local leadership should inevitably introduce strategic planning based on the evaluation of multi-year trends and should inevitably bring the operating surplus to an appropriate level.

- If the goal is a balanced budget, central resources are declined and own resources are limited, it is a "professional commonplace" that the real value of the operating cost must be decreased and resource-optimizing strategic deliberations must precede investments decisions.

- Analysts often argue that the one-time revenues generated during the political transition may prove to be important resources for financing the costly elements of the inevitable reforms. Accordingly, there is no arguing with the strategy when it states that besides the (unpredictable) central resources for development it is important for a local government to utilize its own capital revenues for financing the reorganizations required by sustainable financial management.

All in all, we can state that the above elements are also included in the strategy of the municipality. These elements are of cardinal importance for the strategy as a whole, and are also inevitable because they logically follow from the decision that the local leaders want to pursue a responsible and sustainable political line.

In reforming financial management, strategy identification only amounts to a value choice beyond this stage. In Budapest, the choice of political values manifested itself in the decisions on the methods and priorities through which the municipality aimed to achieve the targeted status.

There are two elements in this value choice that are worth evaluating: the choice of tools for process management and the measures aimed at strengthening social equity.

In the field of process management, the liberal approach provides two distinct handholds: on the one hand it specifies the need for a process management system that is based on a set of predictable and transparent regulations, and on the other hand it prefers regulations that coordinate the decisions toward the public good while respecting the freedom to make case-by-case decisions. The liberal approach clearly rejects direct, "manual" control over the transformation process (the efficiency of which is questionable anyway). In Budapest, the financing management reform agenda aimed to respect the professional decisions of the individual sectors, and defined only the political principles, financial frameworks, and incentives behind the inevitable transformations. In this respect the reform of both the operations and the investment programming may be seen to follow a liberal course.[98]

Initially, in the absence of sufficient information and appropriate techniques, the city's leaders could enforce the improvement of the operation's efficiency only by withdrawing resources. They did this despite being aware of the risks and limited potentials of this method. At the same time, the municipality worked on the elaboration and the ensuing introduction of a normative system of financing to reduce operating costs. In addition to coercion, this system attempted to build on the dual method of motivation and assistance. The system attempted to guarantee the task-proportionate financing of the activities by introducing zero-based planning. The consideration of resource capacity manifested itself in the calculation of institutional and sectoral own revenues.[99] The Institution Rationalization Fund was identified as the prime tool for restructuring assistance, and the efforts for increasing income and savings were encouraged by the possibility of producing institution revenues and, respectively, by leaving part of the realized and saved resources with the given sector (based on the principle of resource localization). Thus, if the reform had been successful in every element, the result would have been a predictable system of regulations that complied with the liberal principles and respected professional independence. Although the system would have resorted to coercion by applying certain restrictions to the resources, still, it would have been by and large built on incentives and assistance. The extent to which the individual reform elements were realized and were able to meet the expectations will be discussed in the next paper in detail.

In the area of investment programming the separation of the professional and the political decision-making processes was meant to guarantee the rationality and transparency of the process and the prevalence of professional considerations. The value-choice based political element manifested itself in the identification of the developmental priorities (at the outset of the planning process). It thus played a crucial role in the management of the process. It was also responsible for the identification of the sectoral allocations of the development program and the final decisions on the projects themselves (at the conclusion of the planning process). In this system professional rationality can be "freely" enforced within the financial frameworks set by the municipal financial management and the political frameworks

---

[98] Of course, as the detailed analysis of the various tools and policies will show in the next two chapters, the transition from "manual control" to process management leads through bumpy roads, and our progress to date has been limited.

[99] The method will be discussed in detail in the following study.

defined by the priorities set by the decision-makers. This system allows for the drafting of rational professional proposals, and the coordination of the pertinent professional, financing, and political considerations. At the same time, the system does not violate the general assembly's decision-making rights, since the preparatory process only produces sound argumentation for certain decisions and still fails to put limits on the final decisions.

The prevalence of the principle of "the user pays" ensures the equitable allocation of the costs of services. The prevalence of this principle can be analyzed in two respects – concerning the allocations among various users at a given point of time, or across generations. Besides following the "user pays" principle, the principle of social equity should also be considered. Based on this second principle, social subsidies should be introduced for the needy social strata. Following these two equity principles, the municipal policy introduced a cost-based system of rates in the public services fields where the cost coverage from charging was not overridden by other considerations. At the same time, it also introduced targeted social subsidies to the needy. In accordance with liberal principles, the municipality grants all its social subsidies on the basis of needs, and not, say, on the basis of merits or spreading benefits for larger groups with the aim of maximizing votes.[100]

An equitable, inter-generational financing system generally manifests itself in the project development field. This means that the city finances its investment projects in a way that shifts the associated public burdens on to the potential or actual users of the given service. The active borrowing policy, which is defined in the strategy, is the tool for this. If the municipality manages to finance an investment project from a loan with expiration similar to the projected life span of the given project, the loan will then be repaid from the fees or taxes of those who actually enjoy the benefits of the given project.

During the change of the political system, there was one more issue where the notion of equity played a role in the local governments' financial management practices. This had to do with the previously postponed rehabilitation and development projects and also with the costs of transformations. It obviously cannot be considered fair and just to shift all the financial burdens of the previously postponed projects on to the generation of the political transition period. The municipality of Budapest acted equitably in the following ways: by spending the revenues that came from the assets transferred by the state and not tied to specific services on financing the improvement of its infrastructure, and by attempting to spread its one-time revenues over the whole period during which they strove to create sustainable conditions (using borrowing as a technical means). In practice, the city financed the previously postponed projects thanks to its revenues coming from previously accumulated assets.

---

[100] The equity considerations and the explanation and classification of subsidies will be spelled out in the 'Infrastructure Policies' paper of the chapter on 'Extra Budgetary Utilities'.

THE STRATEGIC PROCESS

As we have seen, the strategic goal and associated objectives were especially suitable for laying down the rules of the city's financial management (of course, as long as the goals and objectives are adhered to). At the same time, since the strategy specifies goals and principles and not a detailed plan for achievements, it grants ample scope of action to the decision-makers.

As the following study on the elements of the financing reform will reveal, the specific tools employed during the reform process were conceived and introduced according to a similar logic (that of process management). The strategy became operational thanks to the elaboration of those tools. The tools were built according to the goals spelt out in the reform strategy. This is how the individual tools became organic elements of the strategy's implementation. Whenever it was possible, the proposals for adapting the tools also aimed to identify the tools' relation with the financial goals in order to prove that the tools promoted the accomplishment of the goals.

Besides establishing the strategic goals and identifying the tools, the municipality also had to transform its decision-making mechanism in order to improve the consistency of the implementation of the strategy. This was an extremely tough challenge. Since the representatives had the right to freely make decisions within the bounds of legal regulations, it was necessary to approve a set of principles and regulations that could keep the decisions in conformity with the strategic goals.

The rationalization of the decision-making mechanism began in connection with the two-year development plan. Since the materials on which the decisions were based identified the trends beyond the fiscal year it was difficult for decision-makers to ignore these trends. Furthermore, the drafters of the new projects were obliged to specify resources for financing. The resources could come from sums earmarked for other projects, or new projects could completely replace older projects. All in all, this obligation greatly promoted better preparation and more efficient deliberation.

The above element of the regulation of the decision making process has never been codified in decrees, and yet it had been enforced by the system itself. Its importance points beyond the investment decisions. This regulation was the first manifestation of a culture that considers the previous decisions binding onto subsequent processes. This was also the basis for the 1995 introduction of plan coordination in Budapest. From then on, the proposals could only be deliberated in relation to the previously approved plans and regulations. Of course, this type of plan coordination does not trespass on the decision-makers' freedom. It only rationalizes the arguments and thus makes the decisions more coherent.[101]

---

[101] The function of plan coordination is discussed in detail in the previous study on 'Strategic Planning and Management Reform.'

Since 1996, the CLI model's seven-year financial projections and the strategy that was approved that year have been used as a basis for preparing, supporting and making the fundamental financing decisions needed for the maintenance of the municipality's financial balance. Since then the decision-making mechanism has been left practically unchanged. While the two-year development plan served to rationalize the investment-related decisions, the introduction of the model has elicited coherent preparations for decisions throughout the budgetary planning process.

Besides this fundamental method of strategic management we should mention another method that was applied. The comparison of the ways in which the central government and the municipality of Budapest took inflation into account for their cost-cutting policies throws a special light on the methods used for implementing the strategy.

In the years when the budget was subject to tough restrictions, the central government took advantage of the high inflation rate as it concealed the drop in the real value of the resources and allocations. This way inflation helped the government reduce the political price of its restrictive measures.

Exercising a very different approach, in 1996 the municipality shifted to the use of real terms in its planning processes. The real numbers accurately pointed out each withdrawal, but at the same time explained the need for these measures and provided a foundation for their explanation. Transparency and comprehensibility were exceptionally important since the municipal leaders wanted to implement a long-term strategy based on prior agreements. In exchange for transparency, however, they had to foot the political bill for the withdrawals.

SCHEDULING THE IMPLEMENTATION OF THE STRATEGY

From the point of view of the successful implementation of the strategy, the timing of the individual steps was a crucial factor. On the one hand, the drafters of the schedule had to consider the maturity of the organization at every step, and on the other they had to take stock of the external conditions. In the paragraphs below we shall first analyze the structure of the process and the progress of the changes. Then we shall evaluate the way in which potentialities and limitations arising from the surrounding context were taken into consideration. (We shall evaluate the strategy's implementation process from the point of view of its accomplishments in the following paper.)

THE INTRINSIC LOGIC OF THE IMPLEMENTATION PROCESS

The first officially approved strategy (the two-year development program of 1992) aimed to introduce a comprehensive multi-year financial-economic planning process and on that basis a consistent decision-making process in the field of investments.[102] The goal of the second strategy passed by the assembly – already encompassing the whole sphere of financial

---

[102] The Office of the Mayor of Budapest, 1993

management – was to achieve an operating surplus amounting to 20 percent of current revenues, and to protect the real value of the capital expenditures.[103] The second strategy already fully encompassed the field of financial management. The sequence was logical: back in 1992, it amounted to a challenge to simply take stock of the situation and assess the prospective trends. After decades of planning within fiscal years, it was a challenge in itself to have the concept of comprehensive multi-year planning accepted. The state of planning at the time did not allow for the introduction of methods significantly more refined than those employed by the two-year development program. One other reason behind these limitations was that the city's leaders did not have enough information at their disposal to conceive a more complex strategy.

The two-year development program could not go further than collecting and filtering the investment proposals, and also restructuring the subsequent decision-making process based on the approved program. Both steps required serious political determination, but they were fairly simple from a professional point of view. This is why the investment program could be successful at this early stage. At the same time, these steps had a determinative effect on the subsequent processes: after all, there can be no realistic strategy and consistent policy without comprehensive planning with a view to the future (at least several years).

The two-year development program was based on the assumption that the operating conditions would remain unchanged. On this premise it is fairly easy to project financial coverage for the investment projects. At this initial stage comprehensive development planning hardly meant much more than prioritizing and was only applied to new investment projects.

Running the actual operation of the services entails a significantly larger inertia factor, since it has to guarantee the continuity in service provision. Here the reforms must navigate in a sea of constraints and specifications. In the field of operation it takes more accurate and longer term planning to reduce the costs, and the scope for planning is tighter due to the various and highly specified content of the tasks. Logically, the restructuring of the financing of operations hinged on the introduction of more refined planning and the presence of a clear-cut political concept backing the plans. It was also logical that this process could only be implemented stage by stage.

In reviewing operation and investments as a whole, the next step was the 1994 comprehensive urban policy concept, which subsequently became the foundation of the city mayor's election platform and also of the coalition's work plan for the second cycle.[104] This program already evaluated the situation, potential goals and policies by analyzing both the operation and investment problems of the individual sectors. The aim of this program was to make medium-term sectoral strategies adjustable to the possibilities of political, legal and financial action. This program complemented the two-year development program's practices in resource estimation and investment programming by clarifying the principles and establishing the realistic goals that were deemed necessary for restructuring the

---

[103] The Office of the Mayor of Budapest, 1996c

[104] Alliance of Free Democrats (SZDSZ), 1994

operation amidst the projected conditions. The urban policy concept represented the next step in the iteration. Its function was to provide a basis for subsequent activities by roughly adjusting the goals to the scope of action.

The 1995 Draft Conception drew the inevitable financial management conclusions that arose from the increasingly clear and predictable possibilities and conditions governing local government operation.[105] The cardinal elements of the later comprehensive financing management reforms took their first exact shape in this document. Though the document was not submitted to the assembly, it served as the basis for reconciling views within the coalition governing the city, thus paving the way for the official approval of the financial management reform strategy.

The seven-year financing model was the other element in the set of tools behind the reform strategy. This model already accurately reflected the feasible and necessary changes in the budget's cardinal numbers. The model, together with the preceding clarification of the concepts behind the potential strategic elements, was able to identify the constraints, and lay the foundations of the 1996 strategy, which could find a way out of the structural deficit by evaluating the information gathered during the preceding steps.[106] In the given situation, the strategy was logical, apparently obvious, yet its creation required all the elements of the preceding process.

The financing management strategy that was formulated in 1995 and 1996 justified the need to concentrate on institutional reform and to create and introduce the tools necessary to implement it. In the absence of the unquestionable justification of the need for a financing management reform and without the preliminary approval of its strategy it would have been impossible to push through a set of tools that went against specific sectoral and institutional interests.

With regard to the tools, the task fulfillment concepts could logically be expected to be adjusted to financing possibilities only upon the identification of the scope of financing action, and it was also after this that the Institution Rationalization Fund (which aim was to promote restructuring) could be fully exploited. Of all the elements of the institutional reform, the only one that could have been created prior to this point was zero-based financing. However, this method was too refined and complex to be introduced at an earlier stage of the transition process. We must add that zero-based task financing went against so many interests and ingrained practices that it could not either have been defended politically without the whole strategy to back it. Logically, the municipal leaders tried to introduce this only as a "last resort" in their reform drive, which by then had already produced some successes as well.

As we have seen above, an effective borrowing policy is also an important tool in promoting equity in financing. This tool could be applied throughout the transition process. The conditions of borrowing improve simultaneously with the strengthening of creditworthiness,

---

[105] The Office of the Mayor of Budapest, 1995c

[106] The Office of the Mayor of Budapest, 1996c

and thus it was crucial from the point of view of timing that the city's gradual appearance in the credit markets – raising loans of remarkable size – coincided with the results provided by the ongoing financial management reform.

THE EFFECT OF THE EXTERNAL CONDITIONS

The relationship between the strategic process and the changes in the external conditions is also worth analyzing. Of the external conditions, we highlight only two types here: the ones that convey general messages, and the ones that have elicited such positive responses from the city's leaders that may be applied by other local governments as well.

During the whole period at issue, the unpredictability of intergovernmental financial relations[107] presented a serious obstacle to the reform process. The financing system hardly leant itself to planning in the first few years, and thus it was not possible to draft longer-term strategies. Later on changes in the tasks and also in the financing conditions established by the state budget decisions made it impossible to keep some of the ongoing positive processes alive or to launch new reforms. Finally, after 2000, the central government's markedly centralizing and dynamically anti-Budapest policies made it impossible to pursue a sustainable financial policy line.

Consequently, the "Budapest model" in all its stages of realization reveals the determining effects of the intergovernmental framework on local strategy. If it is not properly regulated (and therefore unpredictable), the system of intergovernmental relations can become a major obstacle to local efforts, strategies and accomplishments. This is why the basic framework of operating conditions for the local governments must be regulated through laws of constitutional force rather than by laws adopted with simple (i.e., 50 percent plus one vote) majority.

Although the drop in the Hungarian local governments' resources exceeded the tolerable level during the three cycles at issue, initially this drop undeniably served also to elicit a series of rationalizing measures. It is clear that the "good old" conservative strategy – according to which diminishing resources tend to compel actors to introduce rationalizing measures – generated positive results in the early stages. The drop in the local governments' resources was a major driving force behind the revision of the task fulfillment processes, and the institutions were also compelled to rationalize their activities as they too had to shoulder their share of this negative trend. There is no denying that the "lawnmower method" proved its worth in Budapest as well, as the rather serious drop in the real value of the per unit resources did not bring about a perceptible decline of the servicing standards.

At the same time, the Budapest scenario also shows that there is a limit to the centrally sanctioned withdrawal of resources, provided that we aim to respect the goal of guaranteeing conditions for the local governments' prudent and sustainable financial management. As we have seen, in order for the local governments' financial management to remain sustainable

---

[107] The intergovernmental framework is used here as an aggregate for the local governments' expenditure assignments, revenue assignments and local discretion.

a certain percentage of the resources must be spent on capital expenditures. Therefore a drop in the total revenues of a local government necessarily reduces the amount of revenues allocable to operation. However, the prudent financial management strategy comes to a deadlock when operating expenditures cannot be reduced in proportion to the drop in total revenues without risking a significant deterioration of the standard of services.

As we have seen, this is what happened in Budapest in 2001. At that point the city's leaders had to realize that shifting the effects of the drop in their resources on to the institutions would jeopardize the city's operability. The dynamic strategy that was worked out in Budapest in 2001 can under no circumstances be considered a panacea. Obviously this method is applicable only if adverse external conditions can reasonably be described as transitory, and also if the municipality still has reserves, and its leaders have already earned an appropriate level of reputation in the international financial markets. Under such conditions it is possible for a city to survive the effects of even a drastic government strategy for a year or two. However, only a handful of the post-socialist local governments have established a strong enough position for themselves to be able to counter – if only for a short while – the effects of the central government's anti-decentralization measures.

Alongside the drop in resources, the externally imposed changes in tasks and the reregulation of the content of the tasks were the greatest burdens on the local governments' budget. Throughout the three cycles, the local governments' tasks were subjected to continuous changes, and these changes practically always resulted in greater expenditure assignments while resources remained unchanged.

The content of the tasks also changed as a result of the new sectoral laws that were approved between 1993 and 1997. The timing of these changes differed according to sector. The new central re-regulation prescribing mandatory minimum levels for the services in the human sector represented a positive development from the point of view of functional decentralization. The only problem was that the extra costs of guaranteeing these minimum conditions had to be covered by the local governments alone. Consequently, the central budget imposed unfunded mandates on the local governments through changing their tasks by amending the sectoral laws. The effects of this change were similar to those of the resource reduction. Here was budgetary pressure at work. Coupled with the changing tasks, this pressure clearly showed the weakness characteristic of intergovernmental relations, i.e., the lack of a predictable and stable framework.

In some instances external constraints exerted a positive influence on local governments' reforms. In principle, the World Exhibition preparations compelled (in practice helped) the municipality of Budapest to introduce comprehensive multi-year planning. The essence of this constraint was that the municipality had to assume an obligation to cover a specific part of the investment costs from its own resources. Although under the relevant laws the municipality was obliged to plan only within a fiscal year, the city could not have determined its own resource requirements for the multi-year projects without planning ahead for several years. This is why we said that in principle the World Exhibition was the spark that lit the multi-year planning fuse. At the same time, owing to the central government's weak monitoring activities, the city could have also concluded the contracts without planning ahead. And yet, we believe that the obligations related to the exhibition were in practice a help to the city. After all, these obligations were crucial arguments behind the municipality's efforts to push through its two-year development plan (which was logically inevitable anyway). In retrospect it seems that – at such an early stage – without these arguments it would have been quasi-impossible to break with the ingrained practice of planning within a fiscal year.

The city's borrowings presented another set of more serious constraints for introducing more accurate planning. Since access to loans was conditional on multi-year planning, it became inevitable to introduce this practice during the preparations for Budapest's first loan agreement with the World Bank. In addition, the loan agreements often include financial stipulations that aim to keep the debtor's financial management status at a level to be able to repay its debts. Consequently, raising loans can support the reform process, as a great part of the contractual terms are also important from the point of view of the reform process, and are rather difficult to be subsequently challenged by politics.

Among the effects of the changing elements of external conditions the 1994-95 financial crisis was probably the most relevant in the general message that it conveyed. As has already been discussed, the threat of insolvency strongly contributed to making the assembly approve the fundamentally liberal and restrictive reform strategy.

RESULTS

Perhaps the most important result of the Budapest financing management reform was the emergence of a financial planning method that could support strategic management. As part of the planning process, a seven-year financial model was introduced that arranged the various elements of the budget into a transparent system. The budget decisions can now be based on the refined analysis of the fiscal year's balance and also on the evaluation of past and future trends. The financial model is a tool for planning: it enables the city to simulate the effects of any policies. This way, in principle, the debates on the financial strategy and the budget conception can be kept within the limits of rationality. (Transparency, of course, is a key element of municipal creditworthiness as well.)

It is an important result, too, that the city has created and officially approved a financial strategy that specifies the long-term goals, defines the objectives for the medium- and short-term strategies, and establishes the principles to be adhered to during their drafting. Thanks to this, it adequately aligns the medium- and short-term decisions with the long-term goals.

During the past twelve years at issue, and especially since the introduction of the strategy and the new planning method, the key indicators of the budget have improved significantly (not taking into consideration the period of drastic interference by the government).

As is shown earlier in Chart 8, the real value of the transfers from the central budget has markedly decreased. The marked increase in the city's own revenues – especially after the approval of the 1995 reform strategy – not only compensated for the diminishing resources but also prompted an increase in the real value of the municipality's total revenues. In this respect the strategy was successful. However, the third cycle brought this positive trend to a halt, as the prevailing set of intergovernmental financial relations made it impossible to continue with the strategy. In that period – and especially between 2000 and 2002 – the drastic drop in the real value of the central transfers was accompanied by measures by the central government that significantly stymied the municipality's chances to generate its own resources. These two developments together resulted in a significant drop in the real value of the total revenues: in the draft budget for 2002, the projected total revenues amounted to only 75 percent of the actual revenues in 2000.[108] Corrections during the year are expected to reduce this figure to below 70 percent.

Chart 9 shows that the drop in the central transfers and the increase of the municipality's own revenues were so marked that their ratio became reversed in the budget. The share of central subsidies in the base year's revenues dropped from 76 percent to 35 percent, while that of the municipality's own revenues increased from 23 percent to 65 percent.

Chart 9
CENTRAL AND OWN REVENUES IN THE BUDGET (%)

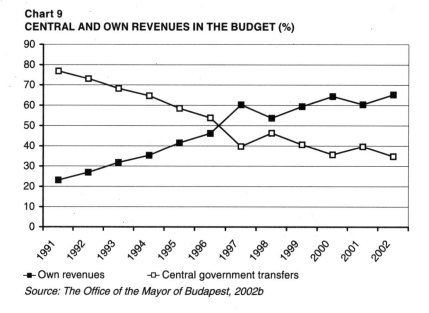

-■- Own revenues   -□- Central government transfers
Source: The Office of the Mayor of Budapest, 2002b

---

[108] The Office of the Mayor of Budapest, 2002b: tables for the chart showing real values

The expenditures chart shows that the gradual reduction of the real value of the operating costs enabled the city to maintain its level of investments *(Chart 10)*.

Chart 10
EXPENDITURES AT 1991 REAL VALUE (billion HUF)

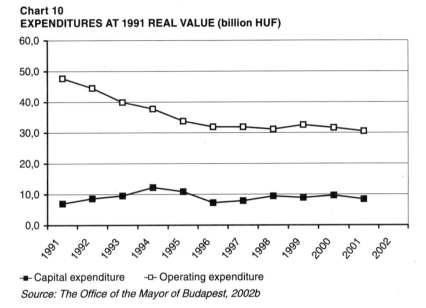

—■— Capital expenditure   —□— Operating expenditure
Source: The Office of the Mayor of Budapest, 2002b

Chart 11 shows the changes in the operating surplus, which is the focus of the financial management strategy. The chart reveals that as a result of the gradual implementation of the financial management strategy that was approved in 1996 together with the annual budget conception for that year, the operating surplus increased between 1997 and 1999. However, the cuts in resources that occurred during the third election cycle reversed this trend. The chart also shows the effects of the so-called dynamic strategy that was approved in 2001. While in 2002 the operating surplus is expected to drop to 2.2 percent,[109] the projections suggest that (due to the expected restoration of the level of financing) it will increase to the targeted level of 20 percent by the year 2008.

---

[109] As we mentioned earlier, the actual operating result is expected to be 7 percent instead of the projected 2.2, so we felt justified to include this figure in the chart.

Chart 11
THE OPERATING SURPLUS AS A PERCENTAGE OF THE CURRENT REVENUES (billion HUF)

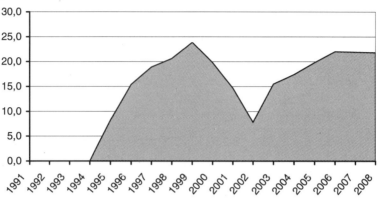

☐ Operating surplus

Source: Legal and financial information, 1998 and 2002

The city's borrowing policy was another key element of the reform strategy. Budapest has managed to gradually appear in the credit markets, and by justifying its prudent financial policies it improved and then retained its creditworthiness even at times when external conditions gravely damaged the revenue buttress of its financial management system.[110]

In general, one can say that the municipal management has adopted a set of transparent rules complying with liberal principles that secure a predictable process management. Furthermore, the Budapest leadership has taken a few key steps towards replacing the direct intervention approach in specific decisions (i.e., the earlier practice of "manual control." whose efficiency is rather questionable) with reform strategies that honor the professional views of the sectors.

While discussing the accomplishments of the reform process, regrettably, it is rather difficult to quantify the efficiency increase, as the city has not developed a method for measuring performance. Furthermore, the financing system cannot yet automatically generate values and indices for a monitoring system. Accordingly, the only way for us to gauge the increase in efficiency is to recognize the fact that the institutions are still operational despite the significant drop in resources, and that no perceptible changes have occurred in their operating standards.

The evaluation of the increase in efficiency will be easier in the case of public utility services. Later we shall see that in the case of the "off-budget" public utility companies, when working out the fee formulae, the municipality introduced a certain kind of quantified efficiency calculation in each case – either incorporated in the calculation method of the fee or connected to it. This method of calculation – if we find it acceptable – enables us to satisfactorily assess and demonstrate that there was an increase in the efficiency of public utility companies in Budapest.

---

[110] See the next study for details.

SOURCES AND LITERATURE

Alliance of Free Democrats (SZDSZ), 1994: 'Budapest Jövője: *Várospolitika 2000-ig.' (The Future of Budapest: Urban Policy up to 2000. Election program.) Budapest*

The Office of the Mayor of Budapest, 1993: *'Fejlesztési program 1993-94.' (Budapest's Capital Investment Program, 1993-94.) Budapest*

The Office of the Mayor of Budapest, 1995a: *'A Főváros hitelpolitikája.' The Borrowing Policy of the Municipality. Memorandum of the deputy mayor.) Budapest*

The Office of the Mayor of Budapest, 1995b: *'Fővárosi fenntartású intézmények gazdálkodási reformja.' (The Financial Management Reform of the Municipal Institutions. Presentation to the Cabinet of the Mayor.) Budapest*

The Office of the Mayor of Budapest, 1995c: *'Koncepcióvázlat az 1996. évi költségvetéshez.' (Draft Conception for the 1996 Budget. Memorandum of the deputy mayor.) Budapest*

The Office of the Mayor of Budapest, 1996c: *'Javaslat Budapest Főváros Önkormányzata 1997. évi költségvetési koncepciójára.' (Proposal for the 1997 Budget Conception of the Municipality of Budapest.) Budapest*

The Office of the Mayor of Budapest, 1998a: *'Hitel- és beruházáspolitika.' (Investment and Borrowing Policy. Memorandum of the deputy mayor.) Budapest*

The Office of the Mayor of Budapest, 1998b: *'Javaslat Budapest Főváros Önkormányzata 1999. évi költségvetési koncepciójára.' (Proposal for the 1999 Budget Conception of the Municipality of Budapest.) Budapest*

The Office of the Mayor of Budapest, 1998d: *'Legal and Financial Information.' Yearbook. Budapest*

The Office of the Mayor of Budapest, 2000a: *'Alternatívák' (Alternatives. Presentation to the Cabinet of the Mayor) Budapest*

The Office of the Mayor of Budapest, 2000c: *'Legal and Financial Information.' Yearbook. Budapest*

The Office of the Mayor of Budapest, 2002b: *'A Fővárosi Önkormányzat gazdálkodása az 1991-2001. évi tényleges teljesítések és a 2002. évi tervadatok tükrében.' (The Economic Management of the Municipality of Budapest on the basis of the 1991-2001 records and the planned figures for 2002.) City-hall Papers, Budapest*

The SZDSZ and MSZP party factions of the Municipality, 1995: *'Budapest várospolitikai feladatterve, 1995-98.' (Urban Policy Work Plan for Budapest, 1995-98. Attachment to the coalition agreement.) Budapest*

ACTS AND DECREES

Act LXX., 1994 on the Cancellation of the "EXPO '96 Budapest" International Exhibition

1071/1994. (3 Aug.) Government Decree on the realization of certain outstanding investments of the municipality of the capital city through state financial means

2067/1995 (6 March.) Government Decree on the effectuation of the Governmnet decree on concluding agreement to realize certain outstanding investments of the municipality of the captal city through state financial means

ELEMENTS OF THE FINANCIAL REFORM

KATALIN PALLAI

The previous two chapters discussed the evolution of Budapest's urban policies and the reform of the municipality's financial management system. Since both studies focused on the historic aspects and the interplay of the various measures, they could not present the key elements of the process in sufficient detail. The present chapter aims to introduce the tools and instruments that have played a cardinal role in the process of financial management reform and are pertinent to financial planning, institution financing, investment planning and borrowing policy.

Although the reforms of these four areas are undeniably interwoven, we shall refrain from repeating these interactions. Instead, we sum up the goals, strategies, and accomplishments in each area separately.

FINANCIAL PLANNING

At the time of the change of the political system the Municipality of Budapest engaged in financial planning only to a very limited extent. In those years, financial planning equaled the drafting of the annual budget. The aim of that process – similarly to the previously mentioned intergovernmental "expenditure financing" practices – was to finance the expenditures of the institutions and the departments,[1] and thus the main purpose of the budget was to indicate the amounts allocated by the municipality to each budgetary unit.

The local budget did not break up the revenue and expenditure totals into operating and capital columns. The detailed budget consisted of entries for the various institutions and departments. For each institution, the budget totaled the expenditures and the own revenues. The latter figure was usually minimal. The difference between the two totals was featured as subsidy. The budget did not even reveal whether this subsidy was supposed to cover the operating or the capital expenditures, and the expenditure goals were not specified at all. This period generated un-transparent line item budgets, which were closer to accounting reports than to financial plans.

The local government financial management reform inevitably had to address the issue of transforming this practice, whose only purpose was to "distribute funds within a fiscal year."

---

[1] The chief departments of the earlier council apparatus· had their separate, "independent" annual budget. The financial department of the council served essentially as the accounting department of these chief departments. With regard to the needs of the independent local government system, the whole of the local financing management had to be made transparent, and breaking down the chief department structure as well as embedding it in the local budgetary planning process was an important step forward. However, transformation was gradual, and department financing followed the earlier line for a while.

A responsible financial management cannot operate without transparent financial planning which thinks beyond the confines of a year. As we have seen in the chapter on the financial management reform, after the change of the political system the leaders of Budapest managed to transform financial planning into a system capable of supporting the planning and execution of the municipality's financial management strategy. Since we have already discussed the process itself, we will now concentrate on the financial planning model which the municipality introduced as the backbone of its financial management reform. This model is still in use in Budapest.

The model was originally devised by the French Crédit Local International Conseil (herewith called CLI). It was used for analyzing the local governments' financial status, long-term viability of financing strategies, and creditworthiness. In 1995, the municipality signed a contract for the adaptation of CLI's computerized model to its own financial projections (herewith called CLI model).

THE CLI MODEL

The CLI model rests on a methodology for financial analysis that goes beyond the comparison of total revenues and expenditures within a fiscal year. By systemizing the various resources and expenditures, this method arranges the entries in the budget following a transparent structure. It analyzes the budget's long-term viability through a series of time sequences based on past budgets and future budget projections, and it also evaluates the internal proportions of the budget through indices calculated based on the cardinal figures.

The model divides the budget into three parts:

- Operating revenues and expenditures (hereby called operating budget). The operating budget includes all recurrent revenues and expenditures.[2] The aim of the analysis of these entries is to calculate the operating result (the difference between the operating revenues and expenditures that is normally called operating surplus), that shows the amount of current resources available for debt servicing and capital expenditure.

- Loans and debt service (hereby called borrowing). The analysis of borrowings concentrates on debt servicing (on principal and interest). Although these are recurrent expenditures during the terms of the individual loans, registering them separately from the operating expenditures is justified by the system's aim to also reveal the municipality's level of indebtedness. Loan and debt service items are classified as existing and new loans, because this way the model can separate the burdens presented by the existing loans from the ones that can be drawn in the period at issue.

- Accumulated and capital-type revenues and expenditures (hereby called capital budget) The capital budget includes all one-time (i.e., not annually recurrent) revenues and

---

[2] The municipality's budget includes the following current revenues: normative state grants, health care transfers from the Social Security Fund, shared personal income tax and vehicle tax, local taxes, stamp duties, operating revenues of institutions. The operating expenditures include the operating costs (like wages, bills, etc), the health care payments and other miscellaneous expenditures and transfers.

expenditures.[3] The balance of the capital revenues and expenditures indicate the fluctuation of the municipal assets.

Based on this tripartite budget one can define a number of fundamental budgetary indices. These include the operating surplus, the net operating surplus, the investment deficit and surplus, and the annual result.

- *The operating surplus* reveals whether the municipality has sufficient current revenues to cover its operating expenditures. The net operating surplus equals the operating surplus minus debt servicing. If the operating result is negative, the municipality has to cover its operating expenditures from its capital revenues, which results in the exhaustion of the assets and leads to the municipality's impoverishment in a short time. If it is only the net operating result that is negative, only the according part of the debt service of the earlier loans must be repaid from the assets.

- *The investment deficit* shows whether the municipality's capital expenditures exceed its capital revenues. If they do, the municipality's assets are increasing. If the capital expenditures lag behind the capital revenues (i.e., in the case of an investment surplus), the municipality's assets are decreasing.

- *The total annual resource deficit or resource surplus* shows the difference between the investment deficit and the operating surplus. Resource deficit occurs if the investment deficit exceeds the net operating surplus. In this case the municipality can decide whether to draw loans for its investments on a case-by-case basis. If in a given year the resource deficit occurs against a positive net operating surplus, as a result of the higher than expected investment deficit, it is financially justifiable for the municipality to draw loans, which in this case serve to increase the municipality's assets. If the term of the long-term loan is identical with the life-span of the investment, the municipality can enjoy the financial and political benefits of a situation in which the costs are covered by the actual users.[4]

- *Savings* exist when total revenues exceed expenses. This sum shows the temporal difference between revenues and expenditures, and therefore is featured in the following year's budget as a separate entry from the other annual revenues. This sum can be used for financing the deficit or for moderating debt servicing.[5]

---

[3] Accumulation and capital-type revenues come from the sale of the municipality's assets and from investment grants. The capital expenditures include the renewal and accumulation of material assets, as well as the accumulation of land property, financial investments, company shares and immaterial assets. (The Office of the Mayor of Budapest, 2002e. 28)

[4] For a detailed discussion of this point cf. the chapter on "Borrowing Policy".

[5] In the municipality's budget, up to 2002, this line featured an extremely large figure (amounting to almost half of the annual revenues). The bulk of this sum was "reserved" from earlier capital revenues for financing certain fundamental investment projects. Part of this reserve was used as coverage for ongoing (occasionally multi-year) projects, while another part served as coverage for planned but as yet not launched investment projects. The reserve with the latter function is justified by the fact that most of these revenues came from one-time privatization deals, and thus in principle cannot be used for financing operation. Moreover, the operating surplus that can be attained under the established financing system for local governments falls short of the capacity needed to cover these urgent investments, not even as debt servicing capacity. Consequently, while the financial leaders of Budapest were often criticized by professionally unprepared but politically motivated voices for insisting on this reserve, this practice – as long as it was applied – clearly followed a rational strategy.

As we can see, the CLI model's structure "separates" the operating surplus from the operating budget, and generates projections for its future fluctuations. The model attaches the operating surplus to the capital budget, because the net operating surplus and the capital revenues together may serve as coverage for the new investments and loans. This "restructuring" introduces a new paradigm in financial planning. The operating surplus becomes a key element of budgetary planning. First, it immediately reveals the loss or depletion of assets,[6] second, its separation enables the municipality to allocate the planned capital expenditures in proportion to the sustainable operation rather than on a residue basis; third, through this it imposes strict financial discipline upon the planning of the operating expenditures. As we have seen in the chapter on financial management reform, codifying the targeted size of the operating surplus in a strategic decision facilitates the maintaining of the direction of the sustainable financial management strategy.

Since the computerized model automatically rearranges and calculates the indices, it continuously enables analysts to shed light on the financial positions of the local government, and it also provides transparent information to both decision-makers and external partners on the projected amounts of loans that can be drawn to replenish the limited resources (of course, all this in light of the municipality's debt servicing capacities).

THE OPERATION OF THE CLI MODEL

The CLI model presents the factual data of the preceding three years and the projections for the following seven years. The user must first feed the budgetary data of the preceding years and the planned figures for the actual year into the application. Using these figures, the model calculates the indices mentioned previously. Then the user has to define hypotheses for the future. The model grants total freedom to the user, who can come up with any kind of hypothesis based on factual or calculated figures in order to get the other relevant values calculated. For the accomplishment of an objective specified in the hypothesis by figures the model shows the required changes in all the other related values.

If our hypothesis concerns the changes in revenues and we feed our expectations towards the operating surplus into the model, we can then study the resultant and necessary changes in the operating expenditure. If we start out from the projected capital expenditure along with the revenue hypotheses, we can make the model calculate the resultant changes in the operating surplus and the operating expenditure. Besides these two functions, the model is capable of calculating a wide variety of scenarios. If the user wants a sobering experience, he can even make the model calculate the seven-year financial effects of any proposal raised during the preparation of the budget.

The CLI model is an excellent tool for testing strategies and scenarios. But it is not more than a tool, which sheds light on certain trends, and translates the expected conditions

---

[6] Naturally, the model itself only shows whether the local government finances its operations to the detriment of its assets. Keeping precise track of the loss or growth of assets also requires defining and calculating asset amortization.

and planned measures into revenue and expenditure projections. The real importance of this tool lies in the fact that it leads to conclusions, and the analysis of these conclusions enables to choose among various policy alternatives. In Budapest, the decisions behind the 1996 reform strategy were based on the model's simulations, and the simulations were also crucial in promoting the strategy's approval. The municipality plans to use the model even following the creation of the conditions for a balanced financial management system. It will continue to be a cardinal tool for adjusting the process of annual planning to changing circumstances.

UPGRADING THE CLI MODEL

The CLI model was originally developed by the French for analyzing the financial status of local governments in Western Europe whose main effort was merely to maintain their proper operating surplus and equilibrium. Two important consequences stemmed from this for the application of the model for the Municipality of Budapest. On the one hand, the assessment of the external conditions had to be refined for making the model applicable to Hungarian conditions that changed more dynamically than in Western Europe. Originally, the model used simplifications that had an effect on the accuracy of the calculations.[7] (This conclusion obviously does not mean that, amidst stable conditions, the original model could not provide a satisfactory basis for strategy formulation and planning.) On the other hand, the model was created for local governments with balanced finances, so a sole focus on operation surplus was justified. In Budapest, the aim was to attain a balanced state of finance, thus the model had to focus on the conditions necessary for it. During the transition period, the decision on the level of the operating surplus is strictly limited by the extent to which it is practically possible to reduce operating expenditure. Consequently, decisions will be made by scrutinizing the operation result in relation with the cuts in operating expenditure. The adaptation of the CLI model to the conditions in Budapest concerned these two points.

On the one hand the upgrading included the distinction and more exact definition of the exogenous indices that are used for simulating the effects that projected changes in external conditions will have on the budget. This meant the elaboration of fluctuation indices for each of the revenue and expenditure entries. In the original version the indices were calculated by a method that drew on the GDP and the consumer price index. The streamlined version replaced this with more sophisticated economic analyses. The upgraded model calculates the projected changes of each item individually. (For example, if the task is to calculate projections for the local tax revenues in Budapest, the model does not simply use the GDP, but calculates based on the "local GDP" – i.e., a calculated figure on the city's gross product – and takes the projected local structure of this figure into account as well. It calculates the personal expenditures on the basis of the wage index particular to the given sector, and the material expenditures on the basis of a "consumer basket" adjusted to the specifics of the public service at issue.) Thus, the model can calculate more exactly the effects that changes in external conditions will have on the budget.

---

[7] E.g., for the calculation of inflation rate it used only the consumer price index, and the only factor taken into account for projecting growth was the GDP.

On the other hand, upgrading meant scrutinizing ways in which the content of the basic financing decision could be made more explicit. This was urged by the deteriorating financial conditions that jeopardized the attainment of the 20 percent operating surplus. At the start of the financial reform this rate seemed to be attainable by 2002. That time the model – as it was originally designed to do – had to present the value of the operating expenditure that would enable the attainment of this aim. After 1998, the 2002 deadline was supposed to be postponed, which altered the basic policy issue. The main question was: by what point of time can the municipality undertake to reach the 20 percent operating surplus without reducing municipal expenditure to a dangerous extent.[8] For preparing such a decision the model has to be able to show the extent to which the dynamic of current expenditures should be diverted from that which is projected at stable conditions in order for the given operation surplus to be attained. In order to present the proper set of conditions for decision-making a so-called correction factor has been added to the model expressing the relation between the deadline of the 20 percent operating result and the necessary diversion of the original current expenditure entries. By applying this factor the model is able to simulate the (expenditure reduction) assessment necessary for the desired increase in the operating result, and presents the contents and weight of the expected political decision to the decision-maker in a direct form.

APPLYING THE CLI MODEL IN A CRISIS SITUATION

In the fall of 2000, the choice between conservative and dynamic crisis management strategies (discussed earlier, in the chapter on "Financial Management Reform")[9] was prepared by using the upgraded CLI model.[10] The data pertinent to each of the alternatives were fed into and ran by the system.

The simulation of the conservative strategy, having spread the parameters of the discriminative resource regulations over the full seven-year term, showed that the inevitable cuts in operating expenditures were bound to jeopardize not only the projected investments but also the quality and safety of basic urban services. According to the results, the municipality could expect total financial collapse within a year or two.

Simulating the dynamic crisis management strategy, the model spread the parameters of the discriminative regulations over only two years (i.e., until the end of the government's term). For the remaining five years, the model used parameters that had been applied under

---

[8] Earlier, the model scrutinized the extent to which current expenditure should be cut in order to keep to the original 2002 deadline. This could be justified as long as the municipal institutions had enough reserves to accomplish this goal. When it became clear that this goal could not be accomplished by the given deadline without threatening operations themselves, the issue to be scrutinized had to be altered: a realistic deadline had to be found for attaining the 20 percent operating surplus without endangering the institutions' operation by the cuts in revenues.

[9] The conservative and dynamic strategies for the municipalities' finances are discussed in detail in the chapter on financial reform, under the subhead "Drastic drop in resources" – 2000–2002.

[10] The Office of the Mayor of Budapest, 2000a

the preceding government. Of course, this scenario was based on the assumption that the government would change and as a result the municipality's financial conditions would be "restored."

This simulation projected an operating surplus that would have made it possible for Budapest to stay afloat. Furthermore, the use of the correction factor showed the (still acceptable) extent to which the operating expenditures would have to be reduced (or which would have to be covered from loans) in order to compensate for the negative effects of the central government's policies. Accordingly, the model greatly facilitated the decision-making process, and also provided important information on the further borrowings that were inevitable under the dynamic strategy by clearly showing their consequences on the budget.

Simulations produced by the model enabled politicians to see not only that the conservative strategy was bound to lead the municipality to financial disaster, whereas the dynamic strategy held out the promise of survival. The upgraded CLI model could also show the "price" of staying afloat that would have to be paid in the field of operation and borrowing.

THE STATE OF FINANCIAL PLANNING

The municipality's financial and budgetary planning is cash-based.[11] The annual budget enlists the following year's expected revenues and expenditures and balances the two, by force of law. In this respect it presents the accrued revenues and expenditures. Alongside the mandatory equilibrium of the total budget, the current and capital balances (i.e., the balances of the current expenditures and revenues and of the capital expenditures and revenues) attached as appendix to the official budget shed light on the municipality's financial position. The municipality uses the CLI model to analyze its financial status, but has no similar model to analyze the state of assets. The asset registration system[12] of the municipality is not informative enough on the value of the assets as to be suitable for feeding in a similarly sophisticated model,[13] and the calculation of asset depreciation is still a standing problem. Besides, Hungarian regulations do not prescribe a more sophisticated system of asset registration. Thus, introducing a system of double-entry book-keeping based on accrual basis accounting is out of question for the time being.

After 1996, the use of the CLI model as a tool for financial planning within the framework of the drafting of the budgetary conception fundamentally changed the nature of financial

---

[11] Note that several donor programs suggest the implementation of accrual basis budgeting, which can provide a simultaneous description of the state of assets and that of financing management better than cash-based budgeting can.

[12] Assets are mostly registered on book value.

[13] In principle, the Act on Public Finance obliges local governments to set up their inventory of assets at market value by December 31, 2003. However, they most probably will not be able to meet this requirement due to the immense expenses of asset valuation and to the still unsettled cases of asset transfers.

planning at the municipality. By assembling the past trends and translating the projected conditions and planned steps into expenditure and revenue projections, the model enables the municipality to evaluate long-term financial strategy options and promotes prudent and responsible decision-making.

The introduction of the CLI model fit perfectly well into the city leaders' strategy, which aimed to improve the political culture and associated processes. The model has become an integral part of the attempts to create a transparent system of decision-making that draws on substantiated information. The transformation of the CLI model proves that – in this respect – the practice of modeling is more important than the model itself, as modeling is an excellent tool for simulating the results of any strategy or scenario, and also for preparing materials for the decision-makers and thus for influencing political decisions.

Accordingly, we can consider the CLI model as a technical as well as a political tool. The fact that the model is capable of simulating the longer-term consequences of any kind of proposal proved crucial not only in the approval of the municipality's financial reform strategy in 1996 but also in rationalizing the subsequent political debates.

Of course, this does not mean that the conclusions drawn from the model can be directly translated into political decisions. Political forces still campaign for proposals that run counter to the prior agreements on the operating surplus during the ensuing drafting of the actual annual budget and related budgetary debates. They do this notwithstanding that since 1996 the Assembly each November approves the following year's targeted operating surplus as part of the annual budgetary conception. Up to 2003, these intra-coalition disputes could in most cases be kept within the frames of the previously approved cardinal figures. Occasionally, certain proposals were pushed through by way of the more or less substantiated increase in targeted revenues, or by slowing down the targeted pace of the accomplishment of the operating surplus. The second "assault" on the limits of the budget usually begins right after the approval of the budget. This is the time when proposals that have been discarded (as unrealizable) during the original budgetary debate suddenly "resurrect." The proponents of these proposals usually attempt to enforce their goals by finding the resources to finance them within the tightly allocated general reserves. The bulk of these proposals are eventually rejected as financially irrational, but some of them are approved as a result of political compromises. All in all, to date, this phenomenon has been successfully kept under control and has not endangered the equilibrium of the budget.

REFORMING THE OPERATING BUDGET

The municipality's financial management strategy is focused on the operating surplus (which shows the difference between the revenues and expenditures sides of the operating budget). During the period at issue, the municipality's aim was to increase the operating surplus. This can be achieved by increasing the operating revenues and/or by reducing operating expenditures.

We have already discussed the strategies related to the revenues and expenditures sides. We have also described the way the central government attempted to prevent the Municipality of Budapest from increasing its revenues, and therefore will now focus only briefly on the municipality's strategy for increasing its current revenues.

Our discussion of the municipality's financial strategy has yet presented only the general aspects of the operation and the interdependence of policies. We have not yet talked about the three fundamental elements of the reform of institutional financing (the task fulfillment conceptions, the Institution Rationalization Fund, and the zero based task financing method), and must therefore discuss in detail these policies aimed at decreasing the municipality's operating expenditures.

INCREASING THE OPERATING REVENUES

The municipality's hands are tied when it comes to increasing its current revenues, as the central government's policies put a limit on both the resources accessible through transfers and the municipality's chances to create resources for its own purposes. The municipality has no direct influence on the allocation of central subsidies. Over the past decade, the municipality's role in this respect has been limited to lobbying – alone or together with local government associations or political allies – for the maintenance of the stability of the local governments' financing. In the field of resource generation, the Municipality of Budapest has had to pursue different strategic lines depending on the different revenue types in its quest for exploiting them to its maximum advantage.

LOCAL TAXES

In all but the first few years, the municipality imposed local taxes (at its own discretion)[14] which were set at the legal maximum. Tax allowances for municipal taxes were few and the municipality used every legal means at its disposal to improve the efficiency of tax collection (subsequent tax control, collection of declared but unpaid taxes via incasso). Through this strategy, the municipality reached a 97.5 percent collection rate with regard to declared taxes. The local tax revenues (mostly from local business taxes) account for one quarter of the municipality's total annual revenues.

PUBLIC UTILITY FEES

Since the public utility fees are extra-budgetary revenues collected by the utility companies, they do not have a direct effect on the operating surplus. However, their indirect effects are so very marked that we must include the city's public utility policies into our discussion of

---

[14] The municipality only imposes a certain part of the local taxes. The key resource at its discretion is local business tax. It can also decide of the rate of the tourist tax, but the real estate and communal taxes are at the discretion and collection of the districts.

the operating budget. In the 1990s, local taxes and the public utility fees formed part of the municipality's most dynamically increasing revenue sources.[15] Since the mid-nineties, the public utility companies' annual fee revenues have generated resources in the order larger of the municipality's total budgetary revenues, practically covering the costs of the public utility services.[16] As a result, since 1996 the municipality's budget is exempted from the need to finance most of these utility services (except some large investment projects), and can allocate more of its resources to finance services included in its budget.

INSTITUTIONAL REVENUES

Over the past few years, institutional revenues[17] have amounted to an average 15 percent of the municipality's total annual revenues. The reform of the 1996 budget introduced a number of important tools. On the one hand, it introduced tools for preventing the institutions to plan their revenues below the level that was deemed realistic. On the other hand, it introduced tools for instigating or coercing the increase in these revenues. Under the Hungarian laws, the founder of the institution is not entitled to draw funds away from it. However, an increase in institutional revenues can logically reduce their need for direct subsidies from the municipality. In order to reduced the municipality's direct financing burdens (i.e. for increasing the operating surplus), the municipality had to find a technique that would both influence the increase in institutional revenues in order to reduce the need for subsidies, while at the same time preserve the institutions' interest in increasing their own revenues. To this end, the municipality introduced the following measures:

- Institutions were obliged to plan revenues for the following year by at least 10 percent over the previous year's expected actual revenue.
- The municipality decided to reduce subsidies in a regressive manner rather than in direct ratio to the increase of the institutions' revenues.
- If the institutions' actual surplus revenues exceed their planned revenues by at least 10 percent, the institutions can dispose of only 50 percent of the surplus in their own right.

These measures meant the introduction of a degressive system for taking the own revenues of the institutions into account. Thanks to this, the municipality aimed to keep the institutions interested in generating surplus revenues.

---

[15] The municipality's strategy with regards to public utility charges is discussed in detail in the following chapter.

[16] However we must also see that cost coverage was not a goal for all services. Reasons for and against charging cost covering rates some services are discussed in the "Infrastructure Policy" paper.

[17] Such as the fees paid by the users for the services, the revenues from the utilization of institutional assets, interest revenues, etc.

REDUCING CURRENT EXPENDITURES

During the 12 years at issue, the municipality has made relentless efforts to reduce the operating costs of the public utility services. (In the municipality's budgetary policy the emphasis has been shifted to the human services, since – as we have seen already – the bulk of physical infrastructure services were taken out from the budget and had become practically cost-covering by the mid-nineties.[18]) In order for Budapest to reduce the budget's operating expenditures, the city had to implement a series of operational changes aimed at adjusting the system of institutions and their services to the liberal interpretation of public roles as well as to actual demands. It also had to improve the efficiency of the institutions' financial performance.

Obviously, the sectors were reluctant to voluntarily give up their "hard-won" resources. It is a universal experience that the human sector institutions produce the most hostile resistance to changes inducing rationalization. The representatives of the human services tend to be the "smartest" in utilizing the "professional considerations", and are also the most adamant in rejecting changes aimed at reducing costs.

And yet, the institutional reform was bound to align professional goals with financial goals. In view of the predictable resistance from professional circles, the financial side was to launch this process alone. The aim was to spark off a transformation process that would elicit the rationalization of operating costs without trespassing on the sectors' professional autonomy or damaging the quality of the services. The challenge was to create a financial system that would remain neutral in the professional and content-related field, but would be able at the same time to enforce cost efficiency, thus inducing the sectors to draft and implement conceptions aimed at rationalizing task fulfillment and operation.

The institutional reform had three fundamental goals. It aimed to:

- define a new structure of activity and services in accordance with the new interpretation of the role of the public sector;
- create an institutional structure and infrastructure capable of fulfilling these tasks in an efficient manner;
- introduce a system of financing that would promote the institutions' efficient operation.

To accomplish these goals, the institutional reform has introduced three fundamental tools. The 1996 conception aimed to adjust the activity and servicing structure corresponding to the new public sector approach by drafting a series of sectoral conceptions for task fulfillment. It planned to promote the creation of an institutional structure and a matching infrastructure for the efficient fulfillment of the tasks via the Institution Rationalization Fund. It further proposed to introduce a zero-based, normative system for task financing to promote the efficient financial operation of the institutions.

---

[18] Cf. the following chapter.

As we shall see, none of the three tools have brought about changes of decisive importance. The introduction of task financing turned out to be a complete fiasco. The task fulfillment conceptions have produced partial results, but have failed to accomplish their original goals. The Institution Rationalization Fund may be considered a success, as it has elicited the incremental, progressive changes it was supposed to elicit. Still, independently from the limited nature of accomplishments, there are many lessons to be drawn from the original ideas and their successes or failures.

TASK FULFILLMENT CONCEPTIONS

Defining the structure of activity and servicing corresponding to the new public sector approach is a fundamentally professional task. Politics can point out directions and financial planning can define the limits, but it clearly requires sector-specific professional knowledge to draft the conceptions and propose the necessary steps. According to the methodology of strategic real planning discussed in detail in the chapter on strategic planning, the activity structure can be defined through a process that iterates between the professional and the financial planning processes.

Pre-conditioned sectoral professionals who play a cardinal role here hinder this seemingly simple process. These professionals oppose rationalization in almost all cases when the filtering of activities is the obvious option. This way the clarification of the goals and the financial frameworks does not in itself provide sufficient incentives for the sectors' adjustment.

Under the institutional reform process launched in Budapest in 1996, it fell on the sectors to filter the services, i.e. to adjust them to the new public requirements and to define their scope, contents and qualities. To this end, each sector had to devise principles and conceptions for the definition and fulfillment of its respective servicing tasks. In these conceptions, they were supposed to side with professional proposals that were adjusted to the financial realities. The sectors also had to define the associated human and physical infrastructure requirements, and were expected to draft proposals for the implementation of the transition process.

The task fulfillment conceptions that were completed in 1997 and 1998 could only partly meet these requirements. The definition of the principles of task fulfillment turned out to be a less problematic area. Based on these principles, a number of professionally sound conceptions were drawn up, and program proposals were also presented for the transformation of the human and physical infrastructures. However, practically none of these managed to observe the prevailing financial realities. Especially in the human fields, the sectors attempted to prevent the reduction in their resources by emphasizing their professional considerations. The conceptions generally did not concentrate on this need, although a few steps were made towards rationalization. Instead, they served as vehicles for announcing new claims. Genuine rationalization occurred mostly in those areas where long-standing professional needs also pointed in this direction (e.g., the transformation of the education system according to vocational categories, school mergers in response to the shrinking number of students, creation of home-housing for the juvenile care system, etc.).

166

In retrospect it appears that despite the clarification of the financing potentials, sectoral planning continued to fight mostly for boosting the given sector's recognition and weight rather than attempting to optimize its strategy within the given financing possibilities. The ongoing fight among the sectors for access to the largest possible slice from the budgetary cake may be considered natural. It is most likely not simply a question of increasing their bureaucratic powers.[19] Instead, it is rooted in benevolent, and to an extent ingrained, professional convictions. At the same time, we must admit that these "inter-sectoral clashes" may undermine the finding of "solutions." On the one hand, the sector forgoes its chance to plan for professionally optimal solutions within the bounds of the available resources. On the other hand, the "belligerent" sector puts itself into an insecure situation: if sectoral planning serves as a tool in the competition and lobbying for municipal resources, it will not provide proper information for the deliberation of priorities among projects and for helping define how much resources should really be devoted to each sector. The municipal leaders have no choice but to apply the potentially insensitive "lawnmower method" again, and to allocate resources on a practically ad hoc basis. This way the distribution of resources becomes more power-based, and quite often fails to meet the professionally rational optimum level. Finally, in the longer run, ignoring the financing potentials of the sectors jeopardizes the financial system as a whole, and thus the sector itself.

The question of how rationalization may be promoted through the planning of task fulfillment has not been answered yet in the course of Budapest's experience in the matter. Although the task fulfillment conceptions have certainly made some professional headway towards rationalization, they obviously did not generate strategies that are simultaneously comprehensive and realistic. A longer period with both financial and professional yields may contribute to a common understanding of the new financial approach. However, realistically we cannot expect the sectors ever to behave in a fully and rationally self-restraining manner. The outcome will always be the result of general value choices and professional-political power relations. However, it can be strongly influenced by persuasively presenting the perspectives of rational financial limits and practices.

THE INSTITUTION RATIONALIZATION FUND

To promote the reduction of the operating costs, the financial reform ventured to introduce a ..1ore efficient institutional structure and operation.

In general, this type of rationalization drive is bound to hit two kinds of obstacles. First is the lack of resources. Rationalization may require significant one-time investments, since the transformation of the institutional structure often involves reorganizations or extra investments. The improvement of the operation's efficiency also often requires modernization investments. In addition, the affected institutions often cannot afford to foot the bill for required one-time major investments or the reorganization process. Thus, they

---

[19] Public administration theories often attempt to explain this behavior by looking at competition for ever greater power that manifests itself in the discussions over the sectoral budget.

are unable to lay the foundations for their subsequent cheaper operation. The asymmetric possession of information is the other obstacle. Through rationalization, the municipal leaders attempt to save operating costs, but have no accurate information on the savings potentials of the various interventions. This – more or less accurate – information normally rests with the leaders of the institutions. However, they are not interested in assisting in the reduction of operating subsidies. Instead, they are inclined to use their professional expertise for securing yet more funds for the development of their institutions' range of activities.

Clearly, there is a need for cooperation between the municipal and the institution's leaders. The municipal leaders should allocate resources for the rationalization process, and the institution leaders should explore the possibilities of cutting costs. The one-time resource injections can be justified by the permanent drops in operating costs, and can induce the institutions to "publicly identify" the areas where costs could be cut. The aim of the Institution Rationalization Fund, launched in 1996, was to elicit this type of cooperation in order to promote rationalization. The fund's longer-term objective was to make the reduced costs manifest themselves in the municipality's budget as well.

The aim of the Institution Rationalization Fund was to:

> "... provide incentives for reducing the per unit operating costs through subsidizing one-time investments. In the longer run this makes it possible to maintain the quality of the services while continuously reducing the real value of the associated expenditures."[20]

The Operation of the Institution Rationalization Fund

The Institution Rationalization Fund constitutes a separate entry in the municipality's budget. The Fund accepts applications from municipality-owned institutions. According to the standing regulations, the institutions can apply with projects that can obtain return on investment (ROI) in less than ten years. In addition, the institutions must undertake to reduce their operating costs upon the realization of their projects. The Fund covers the costs of the transformations specified in the winning projects. At the same time, the municipal budget automatically deducts (at least part of) the committed cuts in operating costs from the applicant's subsequent operating subsidies. As a matter of fact, this way the Fund grants interest-free investment loans. The Municipality of Budapest does not check if the projects are realistic (doing so would lead to endless and boundless debates). Instead, after the realization of the project, the city begins to deduct – in installments – the previously committed cost reductions from the institution's subsidies.

The Institution Rationalization Fund works according to a simple pattern. The basic principles behind the Fund were laid down upon its inception. Following consultations with the professional staff, the municipal leaders each year make a decision – included in the budgetary conception – on the areas of which the Fund should subsidize the projects.

---

[20] The Office of the Mayor of Budapest, 1998b:4

Simultaneously, a decision is made – based again on financial and professional consultations – on the detailed conditions of the tenders. The financial criterion for the subsidy is the per unit return, i.e., the rate between the one-time investment and the yearly reduction in the operating costs. The other conditions serve to enable the municipal leaders to enforce their professional priorities. The total resources allocated to the Fund are decided upon during the annual budgetary debate. Based on a set of previously established criteria, the professional committees of the General Assembly make proposals for the distribution of the available resources among the applicants. Those committees have the competence to compare the professional qualities of the applications that meet the general requirements.

The system leaves the decisions to those who have the necessary information. The structure was devised by the financial leaders: they are the ones who submit proposals for the resources required and for the returns criteria, in light of the municipality's financing potentials. The professional leaders decide on the content criteria of the selection, and are also in charge of identifying the projects to be supported in view of the sectoral objectives and strategies. Finally, it falls on the head of the institution to work out the project details and to analyze the projected returns, since he or she is best informed of the situation within the institution.

For the institution it is worth losing part of the subsidies in exchange for access to investment resources. The incentives for the sectoral leaders to explore the possibilities of rationalization include the latter consideration, as well as the fact that 60 percent of the savings can be used by the sector to finance its future quality investments. Consequently, the system provides ample incentives for cooperation with the financial leadership and – unlike the earlier "irresponsible" practice of professional lobbying – it endows the institution and the sector leaders with genuine decision-making responsibilities.

As a tool, the Institution Rationalization Fund is simple, and its structure enables the participants to make decisions on issues in which they are best informed. Furthermore, the participants are motivated to work towards rationalization (i.e., towards the public good). The Fund has made it possible to replace the earlier practice of "irresponsible lobbying" (which we have discussed in detail in connection with the task fulfillment conceptions) with informed and responsible institutional and sectoral decisions. At the same time, the right of the competent and professionally recognized committees of the General Assembly to come up with proposals unburdens the budgetary debates from the need to discuss each smaller rationalization project separately.

The Demise of an Attractive Idea

In its original form, the Institution Rationalization Fund extended one-time support to two types of processes: it subsidized sectoral restructuring, institutional mergers, and institution closures on the one hand, and infrastructure developments on the other. Of course, the Fund's primary aim was to extend support to larger restructuring projects. However, it also catered to "smaller" projects like the cost-saving modernization of heating or lighting systems. After all, the latter also pointed towards improving financial efficiency.

After the mid-1990s, Parliament redefined the mandatory conditions of the local governments' activities within the framework of its debates on human sector public services laws.[21] From the point of view of the sectoral policies this was a completely correct and necessary move, since citizens – irrespective of their domicile – had to be guaranteed access to quality public services. The only problem with the new sectoral laws was that the government failed to provide resources for meeting the so-called minimum conditions. The local governments had two choices: they could either restructure the affected institutions by reducing their capacities,[22] or could develop the institutions so that they perform better at the same capacity level. In the municipality, the sectors almost always chose the latter option. However, this also entailed rather significant costs. From then on, the sectors – citing their obligation to meet the minimum conditions – began to exert enormous pressure on the budget.

Following its apparently successful launch in 1996, the General Assembly increased the Institution Rationalization Fund's budget for 1997 eightfold.[23] However, the projects that were eventually realized took up only half of this increased purse. In the following years the sectors could submit less and less projects that were clearly designed for rationalization.[24] At the same time the municipal budget had no available resources to be allocated to enable local governments to meet the minimum conditions. It seemed politically impossible to eliminate the successful Institution Rationalization Fund and to create – within the limits of free resources – a new fund or other allocation tool for the investments necessary to meet the minimum conditions. The fact that available resources would only have been enough for meeting a fragment of the minimum conditions by the prescribed deadline was also an obstacle to this clear-cut solution. In this situation, giving in under sectoral pressures and facing a lack of other resources, the city's leaders "adopted" the realization of minimum conditions as part of the Fund's support objectives.

This turned out to be a wrong decision in more than one respect. On the one hand, in most instances the creation of minimum conditions has nothing to do with specific cost reduction, and therefore the projects of this type do not fit into the Fund's objectives. On the other hand, since it is not possible to tie the creation of minimum conditions to any kind of return criteria, the drafter of the proposal ceases to be responsible. Finally, it is rather difficult to define minimum conditions. The law does not define in adequate detail all relevant aspects of the mandatory conditions, hence these inaccuracies tend to elicit fierce sectoral lobbying.

---

[21] Acts and Decrees, 12, 13, 14

[22] In the field of welfare policy this would have been possible since the law (while prescribing certain mandatory specific parameters) did not specify the number of people the network of institutions were obliged to cater to. In education and juvenile care, the situation was different because of compulsory enrolment and care; notwithstanding that certain services are similarly not defined in this field either.

[23] The Institution Rationalization Fund was replenished by 445 million forints in 1996, and by 4 billion forints in 1997. Of this sum, only 1.857 billion forints were spent.

[24] We must emphasize that here we record only the fact of the decrease in the number of the clearly rationalizing projects submitted by the sector leaders or by the heads of the institutions. We by no means state that the goals of institution rationalization have been realized (e.g., some causes of the financial crisis affecting certain hospitals surely could have been eliminated by the support of the Fund, if the institution leaders had been able to devise rationalizing interventions and enforce them in spite of the counter-interests of the inner opposition).

Under these circumstances it comes as no surprise that in their proposals the sectors tend to describe practically every claim as justifiable on the grounds that they "meet the legal requirements."

The fact that lobbying reappeared as a method of access to the Institution Rationalization Fund's resources has eliminated one of the Fund's most important characteristics. Under these new conditions it is no longer possible to expect goal-oriented cooperation between the financial and the sector leaders based on responsible proposals.

The "adoption" of minimum conditions as one of the Fund's support objectives was an inconsequent decision on the part of the leaders, despite it being dictated by actual constraints and aimed at preserving the balance of the budget as a whole. It comes as no surprise that the sectors do not miss a chance to capitalize on it. Each sector demands access to a multiple of the available resources, and in most cases they cite their respective legal obligations. This "adoption" has practically eliminated the Institution Rationalization Fund: it has also been eliminated from the municipality's 2003 budget. As a result, the system based on rational deliberation and decisions had to be again replaced by the "blind" lawnmower method.

NORMATIVE TASK FINANCING AND ZERO-BASED BUDGETARY PLANNING

By the mid 1990s it had become clear that the subsidies and growth in expenditures expected by the institutions maintained by the municipality – given their number, structure and financing management system – could not be covered by the municipality budget. At the same time, the creation of a municipal task system financed in a sustainable manner was the goal of the financial reform process.

The gist of the problem is explained by the conflict between the two sentences above. While the municipality was unable to finance the increase in the institutions' projected expenditures, it had to find a solution for financing the mandatory tasks fulfilled by the institutions.

The previously established base financing system[25] regarded the institution as the basic unit, and thus – without analyzing the fulfilled tasks – financed the costs of the institution. In terms of its logic, this method resembles the intergovernmental "expenditure financing system" of the socialist era, which we have discussed in connection with the context of local government financing. As we shall see, the essence of the municipality's task financing experiment was to change the paradigm: rather than focusing on the institutions, it aimed to introduce a system that concentrated on (and financed) tasks. The goal of revising the system of financing was to maintain a network of institutions that use municipal resources (i.e., public funds) in an economical and controllable manner. The other aim was to:

> *"Eliminate the misinterpreted equalities which, through automatism, cause distortion in the per unit indices."*[26]

---

[25] Base financing means that the institutions are allocated subsidies in the municipal budget on the basis of the previous year's figures (i.e., according to the previous year's proportions).

[26] The Office of the Mayor of Budapest, 1999a:2

The municipality aimed to accomplish these goals through the introduction of normative task financing and zero-based budgetary planning.

> *"Normative financing means that the end results are defined by normative values based on sets of primary data and calculated through normative processes. The essence of task financing is that we do not finance a given institution as if it were a closed system, but instead we look at the tasks that the given institution was meant to fulfill according to the founder (owner). Taking into consideration the central and local norm regulations underlying the normative calculation processes, we calculate for each task the required staff size (human resources and number of positions) and the quantity of services and products (the so-called naturalia), and then we translate the results into budgetary allocations (wages, material expenditure, etc.). Based on this calculation the full budgetary allocation for each institution becomes the sum total of its task-specific allocation figures. The distribution of this sum among the various budgetary entries within the same task category depends on the way the given institution fulfills its specific task.*
>
> *Zero-based means that we perform the calculations after each major change in the task structure. In other words, we 'zero' the lines, since the new results will be produced by the new calculations, and not by the indexing of the previous results."* [27]

An Attempt at Drafting a System for Task Financing

In essence it was a logical step to push the municipality towards task financing, as the state also supports the local governments' activities in a normative, task-proportionate way. There was another (yet more serious) argument for eliminating the previous system of base financing. The long-established practice of base indexing had already separated the resources (which, let us suppose, were originally proportionate to the tasks) from the changing tasks, and the result was an often unjust distribution of resources among institutions [28] and also a non-transparent financing management system within the institutions. At the same time, the non-transparent nature of base financing makes it impossible for the maintainer (founder) to safely identify the reserves hidden in the system, and thus it cannot safely force the institutions to increase their efficiency through limiting their access to certain resources. [29]

---

[27] The Office of the Mayor of Budapest, 1999a:2

[28] If an institution manages to secure higher subsidies for itself by registering higher expenditure figures, base financing automatically "rolls on" this extra expenditure to the following years, irrespective of the actual tasks fulfilled. The result is a marked diversity among the financing levels of the various institutions.

[29] Based on the information used for planning a base financing system it is not possible to specify the individual resource requirements of the tasks to be fulfilled by the individual institutions. Accordingly, the maintainer has no choice but to mechanically reduce subsidies "across the board." This is identified as the "lawnmower principle." The lawnmower may represent coercion for rationalization, but it is clearly insensitive to the differences. As a result, its application may lead to unacceptable drops in the volume or quality of certain services rendered.

In Budapest, the spark behind the transition to the new system came from the fact that even the old system could generate data the analysis of which could prove that the municipality was financing the basic tasks differently at each institution. By splitting up the institutional expenditures the municipality could distinguish the causes behind the differences. These difference could be infrastructure-related (building, equipment, etc.) or directly task-related, such as personnel-related and material expenditures.[30] By contrasting the directly task-related expenditures (that are not infrastructure dependent) and the number of people employed with the number of people cared for at each institution the municipality could generate important and comparable per unit financing indices. The ratio of the funds spent on running costs and maintenance of the buildings and task fulfillment allowed for important conclusions on the efficiency of asset management.

The significant differences between the indices of institutions with identical tasks proved that the positions that were established on the basis of the base financing system were unjust, especially in those cases when an institution that provided lower quality services received higher support. (Had the system been eventually introduced, the indices could have been used in effect analyses as well.)

Based on the findings of the preliminary analyses, the General Assembly decided in 1997 to launch preparations for the transition from base financing to task financing. For this end it initiated the screening of the complete institutional network, which entailed detailed analyses of the fulfilled tasks as well as the resources spent on these activities. The results of this screening made it possible for the municipality to create a detailed map of the municipality's task structure, and to evaluate each institution's financial coverage. The accurate and detailed analysis of the tasks enabled the municipality to model the structure of the expenditures directly tied to specific tasks, and on this basis it could establish norms for subsidies associated with specific tasks. The analysis of the level of actual financial coverage made it possible for the municipality to schedule the gradual elimination of the long-standing inequalities (i.e., to gradually bring the individual institutions' level of financing closer to the calculated values).

Based on these data and the relevant regulations, the municipality could calculate norms for at least a part of the components of the institutional expenditures. Regarding the other part of these components (e.g., certain material expenditures) it was practically impossible to establish norms "based on calculations." In the latter type of cases the decision on the norm to be applied could be based only on the analysis of the preceding year's expenditures. The normative regulations of the zero-based budgetary planning system were defined on the basis of norms and deviation rules, which in turn enabled the municipality to calculate specific subsidy figures for the individual institutions. In this system task financing means that the norms are associated with specific tasks and normativity is guaranteed by the firm association of the norms with the parameters that describe a specific task.

---

[30] The institutions are bound by the laws to include these data in their budget reports.

In 1998, the municipality completed a "shadow budget"[31] alongside the official budget. The aim of the shadow budget was twofold: on the one hand it allowed control and necessary refinements of the new system; on the other hand it enabled the municipality to compare and contrast the subsidies resulting from the old system with ones resulting from the new system, and plan the possible deflection of subsidies towards the calculated figures. The plan was for the municipality to verify and refine the new system for 3-4 more years, and to gradually adjust the exorbitant values to the calculated values during this transition phase.

Following the evaluation of the system in 1998 and 1999, it was possible by 2000 to define the required material and personnel expenditures through calculations. The package still lacked modeling for the expenditures associated with buildings and equipment and the revenues of the institutions since there was no accepted method for calculating them. At the same time, it was already clear that the full analysis of the whole institutional sphere would present an enormous challenge to the professional staff working on the issue. In addition, there was a perceptible resistance from professional and political circles. This resistance was fueled partly by a lack of comprehension and partly by the affected circles' fear of losing their previously secured resources. The 2000 budgetary conception came up with the following – compromising – proposal:

- *"There is need to reduce the number of institutions involved."*
- *"There is need to define the circle of sectors where zero-based budgeting can be introduced, and dates should also be specified for the transition."*[32]

Though the General Assembly had approved the proposal, the consultant firm in charge of elaborating the system could still not meet the requirements concerning the content elements in 2000, even by postponed deadlines. Gradually it became clear that the firm's professional resources were insufficient to solve the problem. Since the municipality could not find another consultant firm fit for accomplishing the task, the implementation of zero-based task financing ended in failure at the municipality.

The Causes of the Fiasco

The causes of the fiasco were manifold. By introducing zero-based budgetary planning, the municipality attempted to employ a method that had never been introduced before in its full form. Accordingly, it fell on the municipality to devise each element of the system on its own, and to push the new system through without ever being able to refer to previous experiences or successful implementations.

---

[31] "Shadow budget" means that the city drafts another budget along with the official budget. The aim of the shadow budget is exclusively to test and analyze certain hypotheses. The figures in the shadow budget do not in any form affect the allocation of budgetary resources.

[32] The Office of the Mayor of Budapest, 1999a:4

The fully calculation-based system of normative task financing presupposes the existence of an extremely complex data management and calculation system. This complexity required the users to employ an intricate system of data processing that was extremely difficult to use for the staff of both the municipality and the institutions who had been accustomed to old-established algorithms. Further resistance was generated by the recognition that the new system would prevent the institution and sector leaders from using their usual techniques for enforcing their interests.

Besides requiring a radical departure from usual practices and canceling the long-established strategies for accessing resources, the new system also ran counter to the interests of sectors and institutions that enjoyed relatively good positions in the past. We have every reason to suppose that even in the past the access to higher resources (even if it was not justified by greater tasks) was not merely the product of blind fortune. Most likely, groups that had better capacities for interest-enforcement or that led activities that lent themselves more easily to acceptable argumentation could reach better financial positions. Normative task financing would have affected these "stronger" fields and institutions negatively, albeit justly. At the same time it would have been practically impossible to equip the new system with incentives that would have elicited their cooperation, as the beneficiaries of the old inequalities would remain counter-interested anyway, as these incentives could never equal their comparative advantage under the old system.

In fact, the zero-based method was not even attractive for the earlier "losers," as it did not promise more resources for them, "only" a more just distribution of the shrinking total resources.

The sectoral actors did not realize the most important contextual element: the urgent need for the reduction of operating expenditures within the municipal budget. Consequently they did not feel threatened by the consequences of postponing reforms. Thus, the more secure and fair distribution of resources offered by the new method instead of insensitive cuts did not appeal to the sectors: the institutions had more to gain in the short run from the "lawnmower" method that had to be applied much too cautiously, as well as from the option to retain their own non-transparent, protective financial management system.

Besides the counter-interests of the affected professional parties, political interests also worked against the introduction of the new method. As was the case with the sectoral leadership, most politicians did not want to leave the good old methods of budgetary bargaining behind. The introduction of the zero-based method required a stable political agreement as well as consistency in enforcing the agreement on the individual fields.[33] Political approval was facilitated by the fact that the objective of task financing could be easily drawn from the long-term financing reform strategy already approved. It was incorporated into the strategy in 1997 by the approval of the 1998 budget conception.[34] From this point on, the stability of the long term financing management reform strategy could provide a steady backing for accomplishment. Thus, the municipal leaders, consistent in their effort to accomplish this task, could continuously keep up the necessary pressure as long as the gradually developing system was able to justify it.

The pioneering work was promising in elaborating the set of norms for the relatively easily calculable personal expenditure, and in formulating proposals for the calculation of material expenses in the sectors which activities could be classified into bigger, homogeneous groups and where the size of these homogeneous groups was large enough to safely filter the unjustified extra payments and to establish per unit costs. However, the activities of many Budapest institutions are of individual character (Budapest Archives, Budapest Zoo, etc.). Due to their non-typical activities, it was impossible to classify these institutions into homogeneous groups, consequently it was hopeless to deduce algorithms on the basis of available data for the financing of these specific activities. For similar reasons, it was impossible to translate the expenses associated with institution assets into norms. Except for individual cases, the calculation of the resource needs of asset maintenance based on algorithms also proved to be too difficult, and the calculation of the resource needs for adaptation in the form of norms was an utter failure.[35]

Since the contract that demanded the setting up of a full system was not performed, and parallel and partly in connection with this the company (which at that time was seen as the only one qualified for the task) was dissolved, the introduction of zero-based task financing at the municipality ended in failure. Finally, it was not professional or political resistance that blocked the way for realizing this basically good idea. The question remains open whether it is possible to finance a divaricate set of tasks purely on the basis of calculated values.

CAPITAL INVESTMENT PLANNING

In the preceding chapters we have made several references to the reform of the capital budget.[36] The first chapter, which introduced the transformation of the municipal govern-

---

[33] The success of the earlier introduced elements of the financing management reform was reached not on the basis of unanimous concord by the affected parties, but often – as we have seen – due to external pressures (World Exhibition, the danger of insolvency, etc.). We have to note that at the time of the elaboration of the task financing system, the realization process of this important goal could already be kept going without external compulsions, on the basis of the proper financing strategy and thanks to the consistency of the municipal leadership.

[34] The Office of the Mayor of Budapest, 1998b: 3

[35] While it is easy to calculate the amortization of new, classifiable equipment, it is significantly more difficult to classify and to express in norms, for example, the labor and costs required for the maintenance, reconstruction and adaptation of several buildings of different ages and in different conditions. We are not aware of any operable system that would encompass all the necessary components in proper detail – which was the need of the Municipality of Budapest.

[36] Capital budget means the part of the budget that includes the capital and accumulative type revenues and expenditure.

ments' policies as a whole, highlighted the relationship between urban policy planning and the programming of investment projects.

At the outset of our discussion of the capital budget, let us define three underlying concepts:

–   The contents of the term development, or investment program[37] are significantly more concrete in meaning than the urban development concept or strategy is. This program entails all those concrete development - and investment projects that are foreseeable at a given point of time. In general, the municipal governments prepare medium-term (3 to 7-year) development programs,[38] as this time-span enables them to associate relatively realistic budgeting schedules with individual projects. (In Budapest, the seven-year development plan serves as the city's investment program. For practical purposes, instead of the development plan we would remain with the term "investment program" as suggested by the literature.)

–   The term "investment programming" identifies the process of the drafting of the investment programs. During this programming process, concrete development and investment projects are created out of comprehensive conceptual plans. The final "investment program" consists of a number of such projects.

–   The terms "capital budget" or "investment budget" identify that part of the invest-ment program which the municipal governments decide to undertake during the forthcoming fiscal year and thus include into their budget. Obviously, only the budget entries entail commitments in the legal sense. These provide the coverage for the costs of the given project in the given year. All the other "preliminary" steps serve only as preparation.

In the second chapter describing the municipality's financial management reforms, we made several references to the role and significance of the development program and the capital budget in the municipality's financial strategy, as well as those of the seven-year financial analysis. We also summed up the history of the municipality's investment programming process. Perhaps the only important aspect that we have not introduced and evaluated yet is the relationship between the seven-year budgetary analysis model and investment program-ming, and through this the method employed in the municipality for capital budgeting.

In Budapest, capital budgeting is prepared by a seven-year investment programming process that rests on the seven-year financing projection. From a financial point of view, programming is performed in two distinct steps. First, the municipality prepares its resource projection. The resource projection also identifies the sums assignable to capital expenditure over the next seven years. With reference to the total amount of available resources, and considering the earlier trends in expenditure, the city's financial leaders determine starting

---

[37] The English literature uses 'capital investment program' and 'programming', and this corresponds to the meaning of the looser Hungarian term of development plan or program, but both usages intend the 'program' to cover the investments of adaptive and maintenance character alike.

[38] Note that only a part of the investment programs are of really adaptive character. The other part consists of reconstruction as well as investments for maintaining the level of the given service.

values for the allocation of investment resources to the individual sectors. During this step the city's financial leaders do not consider the contents of the potential projects and they do not deal with other sectoral or professional issues either. This is because the distribution is based on a prior agreement according to which the expenditures must be aligned with the earlier sectoral quotas (with the exception of the cases when new legal or General Assembly commitments overwrite this rule). The seven-year projection and the associated allocation framework are revealed to the individual sectors at an early stage of the budgetary planning process.

The second step includes the drafting of sectoral proposals for resource utilization on the basis of the allocation frameworks. These proposals reflect concrete projects with definitions regarding their technical contents, costs and timeframe. Each sector creates a prioritized list of its proposals. The financial leaders do not consider the contents of these proposals, as that belongs to the competence of the individual sectors. The sectoral project lists can be easily adjusted to the allocation framework as the lists are organized in order of priority. Projects from the list can enter into the program up until the limit of the given allocation frame. The projects that do not fit into the allocation frames appear as "below the line" items during the internal negotiations. (The importance of the below the line projects is not called into doubt, only they cannot be launched under the prevailing budgetary conditions.). The sectors usually do not challenge the positioning of the "line," i.e., they adjust to the established financial frameworks. They know that any additional projects of their own could be accommodated by the budget plan only to the detriment of the projects of other sectors.

Any modification to priorities or to the proportions of sectoral allocations can be decided only by political agreement. Proposing such modifications falls in the competence of the deputy mayors in the first round of budgeting preparations. Then the draft budget is submitted for debate to the committees of the General Assembly. Although the committees may keep track of the apparatus' project proposals from their inception, they have the right to propose amendments during the Assembly debates as well. Finally, the General Assembly decides on the proposals set forth in the budgetary conception and approves the city's investment program.

Apart from the basic steps of planning, our analysis of the process of investment programming and capital budget planning should focus on three key aspects: the planning of financing, the preparation and scheduling of the projects, and the selection of the projects according to their content and utility.

PREPARATION AND SCHEDULING OF PROJECTS[39]

The process of project preparation is regulated by a decree of the General Assembly.[40] The sectors have the right to make proposals for·the drafting of projects on the basis of conceptual plans, strategies or other considerations. If the General Assembly accepts a project proposal, the expenses of more extensive drafting can be covered from a specific reserve budget entry for target documents.[41] The target document is re-submitted to the General Assembly and if approved, it is incorporated in the seven-year development program as an entry in the specified reserves category. This gives way to minute preparations for the implementation of the project (getting licenses from the respective authorities, execution planning, detailed pricing) – following the schedule set out by the seven-year development program. The costs of preparations of this detailed document, called the "license document," are covered from the specific reserves entries that sectors have in the budget. The so-called "license document"[42] elaborated in this process presents the details of the implementation and includes the necessary licenses from the authorities. This document is submitted to the General Assembly. After its approval, the project is moved from the specific reserves of the seven years development program to the status of approved investments.

The seven-year development program essentially includes projects with target documents or license documents.[43] The revision of the development program may cancel or postpone certain projects the target documents of which have already been approved. In a period of financial crisis even projects with license documents may be cancelled in if no contractual or other legal commitments have been made for the project.[44]

In principle, resources for the projects with license document are allocated by the annual budget.[45] Concerning investments, the annual budget imports the entries of the seven-year development program for the given year. Naturally, the budget can allocate resources only

---

[39] The Assembly decree regulation for the big projects with more than HUF 500 million total expenditure is presented here. This general regulation is also applied to the investments between HUF 500 and 15 million with the modification that the decision on the relevant so-called target documents fall in the competence of the committees of the General Assembly. Minor investments below HUF 15 million do not necessitate the submission of target documents.

[40] Acts and Decrees, 18

[41] Target documents are detailed documents on specific investment projects. Their drafting means the elaboration of details to the extent that – on the basis of the essential features, the assessed costs and expected effects of the project – decision-makers are able to thoroughly deliberate and, if it is proper, to proceed with the project as an "investment target."

[42] This document contains detailed information on the planned project, including a comprehensive budget that serves as the basis for the execution tender as well. The approval of this document by the General Assembly may signal the start of the project's implementation.

[43] Later we shall see that projects that have no target document but rendered to be prepared by the municipal leaders and the General Assembly can be also included as an exception in the seven-year development program.

[44] In 1994, as the financial crisis was imminent, even projects already launched had to be postponed or their contractual conditions had to be changed. This exceptional situation was reviewed in the previous chapter.

[45] As an exception, the General Assembly may associate resources to the project when it approves its license document (in the case of meeting legal obligations, or of unexpected, inevitable conditions, or if the direct preparations would take an excessively long time). In practice, this is an advanced commitment of budgetary force, the role of which will be spelled out later.

to projects that have a license document. The projects that have only a target document are treated as specific reserve entries – similar to the seven-year development program. Thus, the annual budget covers the ongoing investment projects, the projects endowed with license documents for the given year, and also programs that have been elaborated up to the level of target document or have become urgent and may be launched depending on financial resources.

Following resource allocation the apparatus may set out to accomplish the project (tendering, contracting etc). From this turn on the departments have no obligation to apply to the General Assembly for further authorization; in practice, resource allocation means a final commitment on the part of the Assembly.

The sectors' gradual authorization for the elaboration of the projects, as well as the preparation of decisions with regard to the full life span of the projects serve to prevent the sectors from applying the old strategy of "hanging on the plan." In this respect, the fact that the two-year development program in 1993 removed all those projects from the agenda that were deemed unrealistic was of strategic significance. The license to gradually elaborate the projects prevents the sectors from compiling overly ambitious investment project lists. In this respect strict regulation is welcome.

At the same time, certain investment projects can suffer significant delays due to the condition that the often time-consuming process of tendering and contracting may start only after having the respective budget commitments. In an attempt to solve this problem and launch the process in time, during the last few years the General Assembly has been allocating resources before the following year budget debate – and parallel with the approval of the license document – to certain investments the importance of which are unchallenged and for which budgetary allocations are assured.[46] The major investment projects that require longer planning and preparation are incorporated in the seven-year program together with the associated planning schedules and costs. In these cases the annual budget entries for the given investment projects (before the final approval of the projects license document) include only the planning-related expenditures that may amount to hundreds of millions of forints.

PLANNING INVESTMENT FINANCING

In Budapest, the seven-year financing projection has introduced a "rolling" method of planning; meaning that planning looks ahead for a seven-year period and is upgraded every year. The seven-year period is the upper limit in municipal planning methodology. It is the longest period that economics can accept for financing projections.[47] The projection method

---

[46] In principle, only the annual budget includes legally binding resource allocations. Such an earlier commitment to the project entails high risks, since at the time of drafting the next year's budget – e.g., facing a financial crisis situation – it may cause difficulties and perhaps lead to the cancellation of the project.

employed in Budapest considers the budget as a whole, and so it "keeps the individual sectors' investments within plannable frameworks and provides appropriate room for the investments aimed at rationalizing operations while respecting the city's most important strategic urban development projects."[48]

The drafting of the investments program (i.e., the drafting and assembling of sectoral project lists) also employ the "rolling" method of planning and annual upgrading. Financing possibilities for new projects are defined by deducting earlier obligations from the forecasted resources. In principle, the projected resources of the seven-year investment program are filled in with projects with target or license document only for the next year. However, it is important to note that inclusion in the investment program alone does not mean that the project will be implemented.[49] Legally binding obligations can only be made after the Assembly has also made a financing decision on the project.[50]

The financial positions that are projected to be free can be tied to projects by mid-year commitments of legal force – according to the 1997 budgetary conception – up to 80 percent for the following year and up to 60 percent for the years after. Filling in the financial frames up to 100 percent can only happen if and when the following year's budget is approved. This method by which projects are gradually filled in the program aims to provide ample time for preparation and also gives the decision-makers room to maneuver up until the final approval of the budget. A third aim of the method is to allow making legal commitments to all the future resources only when their existence is assured.[51] The development program breaks down the costs of individual projects according to years and resource types (own resources, loans, government subsidies, transferred funds). This follows the pattern used by the financing model, which includes projections for the municipality's own resources and models its borrowing potentials.

---

[47] Municipal governments generally draft 3- or 4-year plans. Budapest uses the seven year financing projection and planning due to its specific metropolitan task structure that necessarily entails long-term investments.

[48] The Office of the Mayor of Budapest, 1996c: 35

[49] The investment program is a tool for planning. Consequently, inclusion in it is not yet a legal commitment to implement the program. In order for the project to be implemented, resources must first also be allocated to a given project. Routinely resource allocations are made in the yearly budgets when the investments programmed to the given year are accepted within the frame of the capital budget. In principle, legally binding obligations can only be made for these projects. Though, as we will see, there are exceptions.

[50] Here we refer to either the yearly budget decisions, or to mid-year Assembly decisions allocating resources to a project (or undertaking financial commitments) that give way to tender and contract for the project. From the point of view of financial planning this event may be considered as the point at which a legal commitment is made. This is because – though still with contracting ahead – the documents approved do not necessitate any further decision by the Assembly on payments included in them.

[51] Practically, this means the date of the annual budget's approval.

SELECTION AND COORDINATION OF PROJECTS

The literature considers capital investment programming to be an instrument for realizing the urban policy goals. For this reason, the primary tasks attached to investment programming are often: first, the selection of investment projects that best correspond to the approved urban policy goals, and subsequently, the coordination of the implementation of the selected projects.

In the municipality of Budapest, the departments have the right to launch proposals for the drafting of investment projects. Here the departments work under the guidance of the political leaders who exercise professional control over the given sectors. In principle, the proposals must be based on already approved conceptual documents and on the relevant sectoral programs. Plan coordination (already described in the paper on 'Strategic Planning and Management') should ensure this conceptual harmony, i.e., the coordination of strategic planning (taken in a broad sense) and capital investment programming. Of course, it falls beyond the competence of plan co-ordination to check whether the proposals offer an optimal route towards the approved goals, corresponding to the accepted view in literature. The role assigned to plan coordination in Budapest is restricted to contrasting the proposals with previous decisions in order to filter out any potential conflicts. If there is a conflict, before the proposal is presented to decision makers, plan coordination is meant to verify the existence of appropriate arguments and justifications.

Once the project's target document is approved, the investment objectives are incorporated by the General Assembly in the seven-year development program. As was discussed in the first chapter, the recommendation, even in its initial form, is the result of professional and political considerations. Both forces also supervise its detailed elaboration. The content of the proposals is not reviewed (officially) by the financial leaders in charge of compiling the development program. Neither does the municipality employ other methods of project selection and integration (decision matrix, project evaluation sheet, participative methods, or specific programming committee, etc.).

The subsequent steps in drafting the seven-year program are based on political decisions, and thus the final project list is bound to be the product of a series of political "adjustments" and bargains. Thus, two interesting and often debated questions are raised concerning this process: (1) to what extent can the final capital budget implement the strategic and sectoral plans, and (2) to what extent can the final capital budget be seen as implementing the strategic goals.

In order to answer the first question, we return to the underlying issue behind the chapter on strategic planning, i.e., to the difference between plans and the strategic processes. In that chapter we defined strategy as an agreement that guides the subsequent decision-making processes by defining values and goals, and if possible also through passing a series of concrete decisions. We also established that the aim of the strategic process is to implement the goals laid down in the strategy. To this end (i.e., to keep the process on to its established course), the strategic process continuously adjusts medium and short-term decisions to the changing conditions. Accordingly, the aim of the strategic process is not to create and implement a plan with fixed end state and ultimate actions but instead to bring about the goal-oriented coordination of the municipality's activities. The relevant question concerning the process of capital budgeting can only be whether it corresponds to the municipality's idea on the strategic process and whether its specific system is harmoniously adjusted to it.

Nevertheless, the experts working on the sectoral plans and conceptual works often feel that the municipality is not moving towards the realization of its plans. In their opinion a straight path should lead from professional plans to budgetary decisions. This view is rooted in a planning approach that defines an ultimate state and considers sectoral and urban development plans as if they were quasi long-term working plans. Consequently, this criticism is based on a planners' attitude alien and essentially contradictory to the planning approach of the municipality's leadership. This criticism is all the less relevant here since – as we have already seen – the sectoral plans still reach far beyond actual financial possibilities, and thus asking whether investments implement the sectoral plans is an irrational question and cannot be properly answered. Anyway, the decision-making process could not function directly on the basis of the plans. The aim of investment programming within the planning process system developed at the municipality is clearly not the implementation of "the plans", but to implement the previously approved goals by adjusting sectoral conceptions to prevailing conditions. Keeping implementation in the direction of the goals is cared for through the regulation of the decision process.

If we evaluate the outcome of capital investment programming from this point of view, we can see that investments do indeed fall in line with the sectoral plans, and that they do not run counter to the goals laid down in the urban policy and urban development conceptions.

Another reasonable criticism may come from the academic analyst who may find that the role of political considerations is excessive in the selection of projects, and consequently argue that the process of development programming does not help developments become integrated. It is nearly impossible to react to this summary criticism by considering it by itself. True enough, individual political decisions do not necessarily promote coordination. Quite often they do not even correspond to agreements on the plans. Still, as investment programming is part of the strategic and decision making process, the political factor is inherent. The process of investment programming is part of the strategic process outlined earlier. Consequently rejection or acceptance should start out from the evaluation of the strategic process.

BORROWING POLICY

On the current financial scene, investments (and investors) are usually backed up by external financial resources. These resources come from financial institutions, funds, or consortia, which draw on their experience and sophisticated risk assessment methods in determining the creditworthiness of an investor or an investment project.

Since the local governments cannot finance their major investment projects from their own capital or operating cash revenues, they often borrow funds on the market. Usually, due to the short and cost intensive executing period it is difficult to finance major investment projects from budgetary resources or from extra budgetary revenues both generated during the executing period. Besides, it would indeed be a mistake to attempt to finance the costs of a major utility investment directly from increased user charges, as they ought to be adjusted to the peak demands of the investment process. Financing from loans opens the way for a plannable, even spreading of the burdens of investment over a longer period. Under ideal circumstances, borrowing also gives a chance to harmonize debt servicing with the given investment project's direct or indirect return period or "whole life."[52] This financing method that spreads the burdens over a longer period is also fairer, since the beneficiaries of the investments cover the costs.

For these reasons the planning of long-term investment projects is inseparable from associated financial planning and the financial policy processes. Long-term investment projects require firmly plannable resources and also the creation of a credit portfolio in which financing risks are spread.

Modern financial interpretations consider borrowing not only a necessity but also an opportunity. Borrowing is a natural practice of players in economic life. The question is not whether to borrow, but when, for what, and under what conditions to borrow. Of course, the borrower's financial positions and prospects determine the conditions for the loan, and therefore it is in the borrower's best interest to enter the market in a financially balanced, stable position relying on a well-considered, long-term strategy. In the evaluation of the stability of the borrower's financing management the purpose of the loan and the adequate regulation of spending are also of basic importance. While it is economically justifiable to finance investments with positive operating returns from loans, the drawing of sizeable loans for operating purposes[53] is considered a signal of financial difficulties.

In free market economies, borrowing (and bond issue) is also considered a basic financing facility of the municipalities. It is absolutely normal for a city to issue bonds. In fact, it would be rather unusual for a settlement to refrain from raising funds from the capital market for financing its investments. Should a city of the stature of Budapest fail to borrow money from the capital market, it would certainly raise a few eyebrows. Since borrowing is considered a rational move, the international financial circles would look askance at the city and would wonder if it simply lacked the expertise or if it faced other financial problems or anomalies behind the scenes.

---

[52] "Whole life" here is used to mean the scheduled duration of the total depreciation of the object in the financial calculations.

[53] Of course, these comments only apply to medium - and long-term loans. They are not relevant for short-term liquidity credits.

THE PRINCIPLES OF BUDAPEST'S BORROWING POLICY

Borrowing has always played a key role in the Municipality of Budapest's financial credo. The municipality's financial leaders defined the principles, goals, and strategies associated with their borrowing policy in the early 1990s, notwithstanding that at the time the municipality's financial status was still not ripe enough to enable it to utilize the instruments that serve to raise loans. And yet it was important for the municipality to define these objectives and establish its long-term strategies at such an early stage. This could provide a guideline for future borrowings and contributed to the consistent effort to gain respect in the international capital markets.[54]

Budapest's financial leaders view loans as an active facility. This means that – as far as its purpose is concerned – borrowing is not an inevitable act of debt assumption, but instead a positive facility for pre-financing or for spreading the burdens of payment. According to this philosophy investment financing is the only purpose of borrowing.[55]

An active borrowing policy is justified by theoretical considerations as well as by financial rationality. Of the former, equity is the most often cited reason. With regard to borrowing, equity means that the costs of the investments should be charged on those who will eventually profit from them, and that the burden of investment should be proportionate to individual benefits from the services they provide. Accordingly, a development is equitable if it is financed from a loan which expiration equals the given project's amortization, with the debt serviced from charges proportionate to usage. This type of loan helps avoid cross financing among generations (when currently active taxpayers finance an investment project to provide services in the future). Furthermore, this loan type clearly associates burdens with the utilization of the loan. This also makes the decision on the competing utilization objectives more transparent and democratic. Loans – when they are associated with projects –, through transparency, facilitate the predominance of such democratic values as accountability and the responsibility of decision-makers.

Finding the appropriate borrowing policy is also beneficial for financial management. So-called project loans[56] necessitate the improvement of project preparation and investment management processes, which in turn has a beneficial effect on the municipality's investment process as a whole. General purpose loans can also be "addressed" to specific projects, and thus may exert a similarly positive influence.

---

[54] The Office of the Mayor of Budapest, 1995a

[55] This statement naturally does not refer to short-term liquidity credits that play an absolutely different role in local government financing.

[56] With regard to their objective, the loans fall into one of two basic types: so-called "project loans" are used for financing certain projects (the analysis of the project forms part of the evaluation of the application), while general loans are freely dispensable by the borrower. The conditions for the latter type of loan are dependent on the general creditworthiness of the borrower.

In general, borrowing requires the existence of a financing management system built on projections for several years ahead and on the transparent planning of resource utilization. The urge for applying projections and for disciplined decision-making that rests on priorities demanded by the creditor has its internal effect as well. It makes decisions more substantiated, better prepared, more cost effective and planning more disciplined. At the same time, the local government's arguments against any central government policy decreasing local resources are also buttressed by the existence of loan agreements that technically fill the projected borrowing capacity (e.g., in the case of the conclusion of the World Exhibition project). In this is the case, the central government must share responsibility if decreasing resources create insolvency or financial crisis at the local level.

THE MUNICIPALITY'S BORROWING STRATEGY

Besides defining the principles and goals of its borrowing policy, the early shaping of a strategy was of cardinal importance. Budapest incorporated its borrowing policy in its financial reform strategy. It was already clear at the launch of the financial reforms that the municipality's creditworthiness would improve in parallel to the results of the reform process, and that expected changes would enable the municipality to gradually appear on the credit markets and would gradually increase the range of its credit facilities.[57] The underlying goal of Budapest's borrowing strategy was to consistently build up its reputation on the money market utilizing credit facilities corresponding to the current state of its financing management, to constantly improve the perspectives of its credit portfolio, and to keep this portfolio in the best possible shape.

The strategy also attempted to identify the factors that could be expected to enable the municipality to utilize the potentials inherent in its prestige and financial strength in the long run.

A decision was made that Budapest would exclusively raise funds according to the negative pledge clause[58] and only from partners of comparable prestige. The municipality would always enter the credit markets in an active position (i.e., having an ample scope of maneuvering both in resource capacity and effective financial means), and would also avoid being "cornered" by time pressures[59] in order not to be at the mercy of market fluctuations. To this end, the municipality would employ conservative methods for calculating debt-

---

[57] Gradualness manifested itself in two elements: on the one hand the municipality's loans were more and more adjusted to the life span of the projects, and on the other hand it involved the different segments of the credit market step-by-step (a general purpose loan from domestic commercial bank, a general purpose loan from a foreign commercial bank, a closed-end bond, a project loan from an international development bank, a retail bond, an open credit line from an international development bank, a global credit line).

[58] The negative pledge clause – a negative covenant – is an indenture. It states that the borrower will not pledge any of its assets if doing so would give the lenders less security. The covenant is the reputation of the borrower originating from its prudent financing management and contractual discipline.

[59] This means borrowing planned in advance, never initiating it at the last moment.

servicing benchmarks; it would create diversified portfolios with regard to its partners and its instruments; and it would continuously optimize and adjust these portfolios to changing circumstances.

During the transitory phase towards strengthening creditworthiness, Budapest had a dual task: it had to make the credit transactions financially secure, and it also had to improve the city's reputation. The coverage for debt servicing was expected to come from the gradually increasing operating result. Meanwhile, the municipality also built up financial reserves (or a kind of "secondary shield") through the conversion of the municipality's liquid resources into state securities.

The active position was demonstrated for the first time in 1997-1998, when – due to the municipality's improved financial positions – Budapest could raise funds at more favorable conditions than it could earlier. In its new position the municipality called on its creditors to adjust their conditions to the prevailing conditions on the money market, as well as to the growing reputation of Budapest or, in other words, to the reduced risks associated with this growing reputation. In cases where this was not possible, Budapest used its one-time privatization revenues as anticipated payment, and replaced its loans with ones that offered better conditions.

As the credit record will show, the issuing of Euro-bonds and the creation of a diversified loan portfolio with high-prestige partners was the next step in the Budapest strategy. At the time when this book was about to be published, Budapest signed a major general loan agreement with the European Investment Bank (EIB) for infrastructure development and a syndicated loan agreement with commercial banks.

BUDAPEST'S CREDIT RECORD

In the first half of the 1990s, the Municipality of Budapest (similarly to other local governments in the region) was obliged to draw loans clearly because it lacked funds.

As we have seen, the municipality was compelled to realize a series of major investment projects in connection with preparations for the planned World Exhibition. Although initially, part of the coverage for the planned investment projects came from the World Exhibition Fund, the city could not expect to cover the rest of the costs from its own scheduled revenues, and thus had to replenish its own resources with loans. We have already mentioned that by 1994 the changes initiated by the central government in the local governments' financing system led to the withdrawal of resources from the sector to such an extent that the revenues generated at the municipality of Budapest drastically fell behind expectations. This made further borrowing necessary.

In this period Budapest drew primarily forint-based bank loans and hard currency credits from international financial institutions. The international financial institutions[60] required sovereign guarantee, thus, raising loans was not the municipality's sole decision.[61] There were two further limitations to raising loans from international financial institutions (beside the government guarantee): on the one hand these credits could only be extended to certain projects,[62] and on the other hand the preparation of these credits was relatively time-consuming, while needs were urgent.

Therefore, early on, the domestic money market also played an important role in municipal borrowing. The domestic market did not apply limitations to Budapest's borrowing. Nevertheless, the municipality experienced an overall shortage of medium- and long-term credits. Consequently, for credits of remarkable volume resources were available at increasing interest surcharge, i.e., with seriously worsening conditions.

Furthermore, the domestic financial market did not yet have a generally accepted reference interest rate. Thus the changes elicited by the financing demand of the central government budget quite often sent the yield interest of government bonds and treasury bills above the interests on the credit market, also constraining the latter ones to follow the trend. Consequently, diversifying the portfolio to foreign money and bond markets was seen as a rational step even at that early phase. However, this required a prior strengthening of the creditworthiness of the municipality.

The municipality drew its last forced loans in the mid-1990s. As we have seen, the primary goals of the financial reform were to create a sustainable financial equilibrium, to shift to active borrowing policy and to pay special attention to the coordination of investments and related financial processes. The gateway to this transition (and to the demonstration of the active position) was opened up by the 1994 launch of the privatization process of the public utility services as well as the transformation and privatization of the state owned companies. The local government privatization process (especially between 1995 and 1997) and the transformation of the state owned companies[63] generated sizeable revenues for Budapest. This improved the municipality's financial status significantly. On the one hand, these sizeable one-time revenues could be used for anticipated payments of loans in cases when such a move entailed calculable financial gains. On the other hand, the municipality could use them to build up sizeable financial reserves in the form of government bonds and treasury bills.

---

[60] In the first half of the 1990's the municipality opened a credit line with the European Bank for Reconstruction and Development (EBRD) and began the preparation of a World Bank loan for the purposes of public transport investments.

[61] The sovereign guarantee was denied only once, in the preceding government cycle. That time the municipality had to obtain a more expensive commercial bank guarantee. The new government, assuming duties in 2002, has several times declared its will to refrain from such senseless and harmful discrimination

[62] The scope of the negotiable projects was relatively narrow.

[63] By force of law, the municipality had to receive compensation associated with the transformation of the state owned firms into limited companies, since part of their assets (previously non-private real property within the boundaries of the city) were transferred to the local governments after the change of the political system.

In 1996, during the credit swap process, successful negotiations with commercial banks affected several billion HUF of municipal loan stock. An average 0.3-0.5 percent annual savings could be attained on interest surcharges. Anticipated payments were carried out for loans that could not be renegotiated.[64]

Since the municipality could not renegotiate the interest surcharge of the loan drawn from EBRD in 1993, in 1998 it carried out anticipated payment for the whole loan. The ensuing shortage of available resources could be balanced by an EIB credit line at much more favorable conditions (the interest surcharge equaled the LIBOR-level of the Hungarian National Bank). This loan swap resulted in an approximately 1 percent saving on the interest surcharge.

As a result of anticipated payments at the end of June 1998, the Municipality of Budapest, as a true addressee of debt obligations, had no debts at all.[65] Moreover, due to its firm financial positions and reserves, the municipality's creditworthiness had improved to the extent that it was in a position to consider all possible forms of loans from an active position – adjusting to the practices of modern market economy. The gist of this policy was that the municipality drew loans to finance its investments from a favorable financial position, at the most advantageous conditions, relying on its reserves, and planning ahead – not as coverage for investment deficit.

The logical next step of the municipality was to appear on the international bond markets. The timing of this decision was based primarily on strategic considerations. Owing to its strict and transparent financial practices, Budapest had gained a rather good reputation on the international markets by 1998. Thus the conditions of its loans were similar to those of the National Bank of Hungary. Based on this position, the municipality could include the international bond market in its resource base. The issue of the municipality's 150 million DM Euro bond package in 1998 marked the introduction of an important new financing facility in Budapest. To a large extent, the success of the issuance[66] was due to the municipality's ability to schedule it for a favorable market period. This open-ended Euro bond with a five-year expiration and fixed interest rate represented a landmark in the evolution of the municipality's borrowing policy.

The last major development in the period at issue was the municipality's decision to draw a second loan from the EIB as well as a syndicated loan. These moves were initiated under the "dynamic strategy" discussed in detail in the chapter on the municipality's financial management reform. It is also worth mentioning these transactions since they have features that differ from earlier borrowings.

---

[64] Anticipated payments amounted to HUF 6.2 billion in 1996 and to HUF 2.8 billion in 1997.

[65] For legal-technical reasons, the public transport World Bank loan was registered in the capital's books, but debt service was covered by money transfers from the public transport company BKV Co.

[66] See below for details.

This dynamic strategy entailed a shift in borrowing as the municipality intended to raise loans at a time when local government revenues decreased in a drastic – though supposedly transitory – fashion. Loans were supposed to partly balance this shortage. By 2001, when the municipality approved the dynamic strategy, its operating surplus projected for the following two years (until the expected change of restrictive government policy) was not foreseen to cover the debt service of a large loan. However, the municipality expected its operating surplus to be restored following the next parliamentary elections. As a "security back up" the two-year gap could be covered by the municipality's reserves. At the time the municipality had considerable financial reserves (although a great part of those reserves was tied to investments by resolutions but not by legally binding contracts). The municipality's transferable and potentially transferable real property, as well as the incomplete privatization process could also be taken into account as potential reserves for revenue generation. Moreover, by that time the municipality had gained an excellent reputation on the money markets as a consequence of both its consistent financial management record and its performance in connection with earlier borrowings.

It is the success of the dynamic strategy that the municipality managed to raise loans at favorable conditions even at a time when transitory revenues were decreasing. It was naturally only able to raise loans to the extent of its debt servicing capacity, the elements of which had been pointed out for the lender.

Even with these conditions, applying the dynamic strategy and borrowing was possible only based on the grounds that the municipality presumed that revenue reduction was transitory and that earlier financing conditions would eventually be restored.[67] Thus, borrowing on a drastically tighter resource base implied driving the municipality's financing system back to the earlier devised trend, minimizing the long-term effects of the short-term drop in resources.

During the course of the credit negotiations, the municipality gave its partners a fair picture of its situation and of the dynamic strategy and its presumptions. It also declared its determination to stick with the practice of the negative pledge clause and to refrain from furnishing its credit deals with any collateral.[68] The municipality's international reputation and its prudent, conservative financial management practices qualified the presented municipal guarantees as satisfactory without mortgaging assets.

There were two other factors behind the success of the municipality. First, there was the replacement of the government during the 2002 parliamentary elections. Although the new government did not introduce the expected changes during the year at issue, some key corrections were made (partly in response to the municipality's efforts), and the general

---

[67] I.e., the government would be replaced in 2002, and the new government would restore the earlier level of the local governments' revenue potentials, as well as compensate Budapest for its losses.

[68] The financial institutions could take into account the transferable assets of the municipality and the potential revenue from the incomplete privatization process as indirect collateral, but Budapest did not offer mortgaging its assets.

political climate also changed perceptibly. Proof of this change of circumstances was that Budapest could again start lobbying. Unlike during the previous government cycle, Budapest could present its stance several times as a negotiating partner at appropriate forums. Of course, the elaboration of systemic solutions to most of its problems is still ahead, but the new government appears ready to be a working partner for the municipality.

Second, there was the fact that Budapest received a favorable issuer rating[69] in the summer of 2002 from the internationally recognized credit rating agencies Moody's and Standard and Poor's.[70] Budapest's hard currency issuer ratings equaled that of the Hungarian state, while its domestic rating was one grade lower due to the municipality's strong dependence on the central government's movements.

Moody's assigned A3 issuer ratings to both the international and domestic markets. In the attached report it appreciated the municipality's good financial performance over the preceding five years. The report underlined its large operating balances, high level of self-funding capacity and emphasized the importance of its prudent budgetary policy that strengthened its creditworthiness (i.e., remarkable liquid reserves that in emergency can be used for repayments).[71]

Standard & Poor's forint-based rating was A+/Stable/A-1, and the international was A-/Stable/A-1 with arguments very much similar to those of Moody's. It qualified the budgetary performance of the municipality as basically firm with low levels of direct debt. It also found the financing perspectives of the municipality favorable. Quotation from its Outlook: "Standard & Poor's expects the city to continue to benefit from dynamic economic growth, from increasing wealth, and from prudent financial management with only slight deficits after capital expenditures. Increasing projected debt levels should remain manageable at this rating level."[72]

Issuer ratings would have gained strong significance if the government had refused to extend a guarantee on the EIB loan. The guarantee was given by the new government. The signature

---

[69] It is important to differentiate issuer rating from credit rating, though they are often mixed up in everyday usage. The issuer rating process scrutinized the creditworthiness of the municipality and had nothing to do with any actual financial transaction. In the case of evaluating an actual financial transaction, credit rating, i.e., the scrutiny from the position of the creditor, would have played an important role.

[70] On August 29, 2002, Moody's assigned A3 issuer ratings to both the international and the domestic markets. Standard & Poor's forint-based rating was A/Stable/A-1, and the international was A-/Stable/A-1.

[71] Moody's Investor's Service, 2002: 1. Quotation from Moody's: "City's finances have recorded good performances over the past five years, including large operating balances and high levels of self-funding capacity. Due to unfavourable changes in the intergovernmental relationships however, these performances dropped slightly in 2001, a trend expected to worsen this year. Stock of debt and debt service burden have remained moderate and well within the city's repayment capacity, despite substantial annual borrowing increases over the past five years. In Moody's view, Budapest's credit quality is also strengthened by cautious budgetary management, notably in the form of substantial liquid reserves that the city would be able to use for debt repayment."

[72] The Office of the Mayor of Budapest, 2002c

of the new EIB loan agreement (signed in 2002) leads us to conclusions similar to the ones drawn from issuer ratings.[73]

Alongside its preparations for the EIB contract, the municipality also arranged for a syndicated international loan agreement to the tune of €130 million. The contract to that effect with conditions very much similar to those of the EIB was signed in December 2002. Although the issuer rating was not a condition for the syndicated loan, it had its advantageous effects. The ratings – made public before the second turn of the negotiations that finalized the offers – could improve the conditions offered to the municipality. The parties contracted the agreement on a general purpose loan but its primary function is to finance infrastructure investments.

In the Appendix to this volume, a table summarizes the nature, amount and maturity of the major loans taken up by the Municipality of Budapest in the period at issue in order to demonstrate the changes in conditions (Appendix, Table 3). Of course, it would be worth to compare the financial conditions of the individual credits in order to scrutinize the success of the municipality's borrowing policy, but these figures are not public. The leaders of Budapest may assert that in each case the municipality has managed to take up loans in the past years with the same conditions as the Hungarian State.

During the negotiations the municipality strove for conditions approximating the conditions of the EIB loans. According to the leaders of the municipality, by now the conditions of the commercial bank and syndicated loans have met this aim, Budapest can practically take up loans at cost-level.

Finally, it is to be noted that despite the fact that expenses on the EIB loan are the lowest, the municipality – in its effort to retain its diversified portfolio and borrower positions – intends to continue raising funds from other sources. The idea is also backed by the fact that EIB extends financing to a definite class of investment projects. Other projects thus require other institutions to finance them.

CONSIDERATIONS BEHIND BUDAPEST'S BOND ISSUANCE

Since only a few of the post-socialist local governments have ventured into the field of bond issuance to date, and the lessons of these deals are yet to be summarized, it appears justified to sum up and evaluate Budapest's experiences with its Euro bond issuance.

We must first reiterate that the idea for Budapest to enter the international bond market postdated the establishment of its solid financing management system, and that its financial record was on the upswing at the time. Issuing bonds had a double strategic drive: the municipality wanted to supplement its credit-related facilities and intended to achieve better conditions for its loans.

---

[73] It is not the conditions of the EIB loan but the fact of the agreement that matters. Namely, the EIB provides funds only for borrowers with proper creditworthiness but then according to principle of costs, charging no profits or risks because an essential condition of extending loans is government or bank guarantee.

Budapest's appearance on the bond market was facilitated by the following factors:
- the municipality was considered to be a good debtor;
- it had a relatively small credit portfolio and a large investment portfolio;
- Budapest had a positive record in privatization and urban development;
- on the eve of Hungary's accession to the European Union, the country was considered a trustworthy partner;
- owing to the hard currency reserves of the National Bank of Hungary there was no need to fear a crowding out effect.

The choice of the Euro bond market was supported by the following considerations:
- rating was not mandatory, and thus the municipality could avoid the costs and risks associated with the credit rating process,[74]
- the broad choice of currencies enabled the municipality to issue its bonds in German mark, the currency to which the rate of HUF was pegged. This reduced the associated financial risks;[75]
- Budapest was well known to the German population, and thus the municipality could target those investors who (unlike the institutional investors) tend to rely primarily on their own experiences. These investors are less sensitive to the volatility of the country risks, and tend to maintain their investments until their expiry.

Budapest issued its Euro bonds in Frankfurt in July 1998. The issuance was worth 150 million German marks. The open bonds had a five-year maturity date and a fixed rate of interest. The trading price of the bonds was 99.35 percent, and the offer price was 101.55 percent. The bonds drew an interest of 4.75 percent. Compared with the yield of the German government bonds, which had the same maturity date, the municipality's Euro bonds had a 57 basis point surcharge and its yield had a 35-point premium over the LIBOR rate. The yield of the National Bank of Hungary's five-year floating rate bond, which was issued in February 1998, exceeded the LIBOR rate by 31-33 basis points. All these go to show that the market considered the risks associated with the Municipality of Budapest's bonds comparable to those of the bonds issued by Hungary.

---

[74] Budapest could not have received a better rating than Hungary. Prior to the bond issuance, Moody's assigned Baa2 issuer rating to the country, and shifted Hungary from the speculative to the investment category. At the same time, since the targeted private investors predictably prefer to rely on their personal experiences, the rating was not expected to improve the conditions. The rating informs the investors in a comprehensible and standardized form. In absence of a rating, the municipality compiled a comprehensive information kit which outlined Budapest's legal and financial risk factors. This publication has been issued annually since 1998 (Municipality of Budapest, Financial and legal information).

[75] The currency basket that determined the rate of HUF consisted of 30 percent USD and 70 percent DEM after 1997. Since 2000, the Hungarian currency's rate is pegged 100 percent to the Euro.

EXTRA-BUDGETARY UTILITIES

INFRASTRUCTURE POLICIES
KATALIN PALLAI

In this chapter we shall focus on the infrastructure services that are assigned to the local governments by the Act on Local Governments (ALG). Budapest provides these services as part of its extra-budgetary activities, through independent companies. These public utilities (gas and water supply, waste water management, district heating, solid and liquid waste management, public transport, etc.) are key determinants of the capital city's urban policies since the quality of these services determines the quality of life in Budapest and affects the city's competitiveness. Furthermore, the total annual cost of these services is considerably more than the cost of all other activities directly delivered by the Municipality of Budapest *(see Appendix, Table 2)*.

Besides the importance of the physical infrastructure services, their difference from other local public services also justifies their discussion in a separate chapter.

The present chapter will analyze and evaluate the most important challenges and policies associated with infrastructure services (such as user charges or privatization), and will also discuss the transformation process both of the individual companies and of the services. Since the studies in this chapter focus on particular issues, it appears appropriate to introduce the general goals and inherence of Budapest's infrastructure policies at the start of the chapter.

THE LEGACY

In the highly centralized state socialist systems of Eastern Europe (where the councils only played an executive role), the state was the ultimate landlord providing everything and setting all standards. In the "classical" state communism of the 1950s, the rational rules of market economy were ruthlessly overruled. They were also distorted later on, albeit to a gradually decreasing extent.

Prior to the change of the political system, the central power, i.e., the state and local councils, operated local public services through public utility companies, which they founded and ran. These public utility companies had independent budgets. The councils' budgets only recorded the subsidies granted to them. And yet, the central government's will was easily enforced on these companies through centrally established operating and developmental subsidies, and also through the right to appoint their top leaders (and through influence on the appointment of the other key managers).

As the central power (the state) had a genuine interest in developing the capital city's public services, public utility companies enjoyed special treatment and held strong bargaining positions due to their importance, monopolistic positions and asymmetry in information distribution. The confidential relationship generated by this mutual dependence made for a fraternal bargaining atmosphere – in the pattern of the large-scale works typical of the socialist period.

At the end of the 1980s, the public administration could only have rather distorted and semi-market signals on supply-demand relations and on the real costs of public services. The lack of information on real costs of individual services and activities prevented the emergence of a system resolutely enforcing the efficient use of public funds.

In the absence of genuine market pricing and conditions, public authorities and company leaders could not obtain realistic information on the real costs of activities and could not determine the efficiency of service provision even if they had wanted to (in spite of a few, indeterminate attempts that collided with opposing interests). Furthermore, since the authorities set all the conditions, they did not feel compelled to obtain proper information either. On the other hand, there were ample possibilities for concealing the deficiencies of economic management and postponing solutions:

– The economic "lifeboat", that is the individual, discretional decisions on additional resources, i.e., the soft budget constraints inherent to non-transparent centralized systems that are vague on the issue of costs, encourage voluntarism, and at the same time see the tolerable level of public services as a prime interest.

– Another way out of situations with scarce resources is to defer the replenishment of amortized equipment. Quite often this is motivated by political considerations to save resources for more spectacular investment projects. This approach can generate vast "virtual" resources (for example, neglecting the maintenance of Budapest's apartment stock enabled the state to spend hundreds of billions of Forints on other projects).

– The non-democratic system itself was the ultimate resource that enabled state leaders to retain power in spite of great failures in managing the public sphere.

The change of the political and ownership system, i.e., the prevalence of free market conditions, radically altered the situation.

Under the new system, local governments were bound to realize that:

– they had become fully responsible for their financial management as they had lost the umbrella of the "paternalistic state," i.e., they had to do without a "lifeboat";

– their resources were restricted, and they had to face hard budget constraints (in practice the real value of their resources was decreasing);

– they could not continue with their non-transparent – and thereby unmanageable – practices. The only way for them to prevent the decline of public services was to increase efficiency;

– the acts of the local political leaders entailed direct political risks (and potential benefits to their opponents).

The essentially liberal program underlying the change of the political system included the goals and strategies that could also offer guidelines for local politics to manage this situation. Nevertheless, most of the local political forces tried to bypass conflicts and postpone changes. But since the state continued tightening the financial screws on the local governments, by the mid-1990s it became imperative to address the problems and reform the system.

There was no avoiding the fact that monopolistic positions had rendered the service providers inert and had led to inefficient operation; that supply-oriented investments quite often had produced prodigal systems; that network losses due to deferred maintenance had increased operating costs; and that the symbolic charges encouraged wasteful consumption. As a result of all these factors, per unit public services had become expensive, placing enormous burdens on public resources.

THE CHALLENGE

In Hungary, local governments became responsible for public services following the change of the political system (Act on Local Governments – Act No. LXV of 1990). Local governments were also transferred the (company) assets needed for the provision of these services (in 1991-1993) and from 1994, have been authorized to regulate the rates of certain public services. In principle, these changes created ample possibilities for the local governments, since they assumed control of all the key aspects of public service provision. However, they also had to assume all the burdens associated with this task.

SUSTAINABLE, MARKET-ORIENTED AND EQUITABLE SERVICE PROVISION

The challenges that local governments had to face under these circumstances may be told and seen from two different angles: from a functional or a political approach. From a functional approach (i.e., strictly on a utilitarian basis), the main challenge of the 1990's for the Municipality of Budapest in the field of public service provision was the maintenance of universal service while reducing the burdens on the municipal budget and improving the quality and efficiency of the services as much as possible.

Universal access to service is justified by the fact that public services are a public good. In the field of infrastructure services, the obligation to provide universal service applies primarily to access, i.e., these services must be provided at a high quality level and the rates must be affordable for all. In other words, access must be secured for the socially, economically or physically handicapped as well.

Reducing the burdens on the budgets of the local governments requires cost covering pricing of the services. If pricing can take up market functions, it can produce several other benefits as well: it boosts corporate efficiency and elicits rational consumer behavior. As we shall see later, this facilitates privatization either through competition on the market or through competition for the market (i.e., a privatization race).

At the same time, it must be acknowledged that cost-covering prices are clearly unaffordable for certain social groups, and this violates the principle of universal access. For this reason, market-based pricing must be accompanied by a system of targeted subsidies, which guarantees access to public services for the socially and economically handicapped strata as well.

In principle, the goal of imposing cost-covering prices may not only run counter to the principle of universal access, but may also clash with the preferences assigned to certain services on the basis of their social costs and benefits: it may be justified to subsidize certain public services for the sake of their positive overall social effects. E.g., subsidizing public transport may be justified even from a strictly utilitarian viewpoint, as its per unit social costs are lower than those of its only alternative – individual transport. At the same time, the costs of using private cars remain latent since the bulk of the social costs associated with individual transport can hardly be burdened on to the individual users.[1] In this situation, the cost-covering pricing of public transport would render this service non-competitive. Had there been no general subsidies granted to public transport, the citizens would most likely prefer individual transport to public transport. This, in turn, would place much heavier burdens on the environment and on the public budgets.[2]

Captured from a political point of view, the main challenge of the 1990's in the field of Budapest's public utility services was to provide sustainable, market-oriented and equitable services. This analysis should also take cost-covering pricing as a basis, since this is a common denominator for the above three requirements. If the rates charged for a service (i.e., the service's revenues) are sufficient to cover the operating, maintenance, and adaptation costs, the service can be described as self-financing and sustainable. Cost-covering user charges – as they are higher than subsidized charges – make the user sensitive to costs and influence the volume of consumption. Market prices also inform the service provider of the actual status of demand and make the provider sensitive to the consumers' requirements. At the same time, they enforce accountability, which in turn boosts the efficiency of the provider. As a result, adequate pricing mechanisms can urge market-oriented service provision that is more responsive to demand and more efficient in its delivery. In other words, it urges simultaneously the improvement of allocative efficiency and operational efficiency.

The cost-covering rates also render the system more equitable, since they enable consumers to pay in proportion to actual usage (whereas the publicly funded services may be seen as

---

[1] Due to the difficulties in collecting the costs of pollution, of the time lost in traffic jams or of the use related amortization of the city roads, etc.

[2] The larger costs of road building and maintenance represent only one (obvious) element of these public burdens. At least as important as these are indirect effects, such as the loss of efficiency of urban structures caused by the sprawl of the settlements due to the increasing use of privately owned cars, and also the markedly higher associated costs of geographically dispersed patterns (see the last study in this chapter for details).

regressive taxation[3]). From a political point of view, the principle of cost-covering pricing is justified and dictated by social equity.

There are two arguments in the liberal approach that rest on the principle of equity and that explain the deviation from strictly cost-covering rates. The first is the principle of indigence. According to this argument, consumers with no chance to access basic public services on their own may be subsidized.[4] In order to avoid violating the principle of equity based on the consumption-proportionate payment rule, the needy must be supported through targeted subsidies[5] and not through reduced service rates.

The second argument is the positive social effect, or the optimization, of social costs.[6] Here subsidies aim to drive consumption towards services that have lower social costs or favorable social effects. Either way, the subsidies should go to the affected services as a whole in order to ensure that the consumers have equal access to the subsidies.

Whether we pursue the utilitarian or the political line, it is very important to separate the logic behind the two types of subsidies. While the subsidization of the needy reduces social inequalities, general subsidies usually increase them, so they can be applied only in cases where social benefits are clearly justified. This difference (along with the consequences of the subsidies) must be emphasized and accurately considered since the ingrained practices of the past along with short-term political interests (vote maximization) tend to push decision-makers, often unconsciously, towards general subsidization.

Of course, we have only outlined the explanation of the principles and logic behind the choice of tools. In concrete decision-making situations it is up to the decision-makers and the value choices that they make to decide on how the principles will be applied and the proportions according to which they will be applied. However, in most cases the enforcement of the set of values entails compromises. The rest of this chapter will describe these particular decisions. As we shall see, the decisions that could have been made purely according to the liberal philosophy of the Budapest leaders have often been led astray by prevailing political realities.

---

[3] In essence, public funds come from tax-type revenues paid by the public definitely not in proportion with their use of the public services. In the case of most of the public utility services discussed in this study the rich tend to consume more than the poor do (i.e., they consume more electricity for larger houses, or more water for gardens, etc.). If – at least partly – these public services are covered from public funds, the rich get the bulk of the subsidies. Accordingly, the progressivity of public burden sharing through taxation is certainly reduced by public funding of public utility services. In a slightly populist manner, we might sum up the gist of the problem as follows: the rich citizen who heats the water for his private swimming pool gets more out of the "common purse" than the poor citizen who has trouble keeping his apartment warm in winter.

[4] Of course, it is always a political challenge to define the contents of basic services or indigence. This issue always elicits tension among those who are left out of the benefits of the services.

[5] Besides the difficulties in defining indigence, it is likewise very difficult to create a system of targeted subsidies that successfully focuses on the politically defined group and gives the required level of support.

[6] Education is a good example of subsidies for aiming at positive social effects, while the earlier mentioned public transport subsidy may be seen as an example for the optimization of social expenditures.

STRATEGY

The challenge for sustainable, market-oriented, and equitable public services could be met through combining three basic measures: on the supply side, the efficiency of the service could be improved (meaning both the improvement of the service structures and the reduction of the unit costs); on the demand side the volume of the necessary services could be reduced through the rationalization of consumption;[7] and the reform of the financing system could produce more equitable, usage proportionate coverage for the service. The municipal strategy aimed at accomplishing these goals through the rationalization of the servicing companies' operation and through the restructuring of the pricing of the services.

The international experiences of the 1980s furnished two important lessons to the drafters of Budapest's public utility service policies. First, experience showed that it was indeed possible to create competition in the field of public services as well; and second, it became clear that appropriate regulation was much more efficient than manual control in compelling the public service companies to improve their efficiency.

Ideally, the market generates competition. However, in those cases when it is technically difficult (or impossible) to split up the services between two or more service providers, competition cannot arise from the market itself. In such circumstances, it is still possible to make the providers compete for access to the market. In practice, this means that there are two ways to create competition: either through splitting up the service itself, or through competitive privatization, which is a limited substitute to later market competition. In these scenarios, price (both service price and privatization price) represents the key tool for enforcing efficiency.[8]

As we shall see, the Budapest reform of public utility services drew on practically all the above lessons. In the early 1990s, Budapest began to split up (in some cases contract out or privatize) certain activities from the large servicing companies' portfolios. Between 1993 and 1995 the companies were transformed into independent economic entities (share companies or limited liability companies). The privatization of these companies began in 1996. Simultaneously, the role of "price" in local politics has altered and assumed a new meaning: from a purely "political" tool it has gradually become an "economic" and policy tool.

---

[7] This rather simplified statement is only meant to explain the logic behind the changes. Of course, the situation is far more complex. For example, the drop in water consumption – due to the fixed part of the costs - immediately increase the per unit costs of the service, while savings on the fixed elements of the costs accrue on the longer run due to the decreasing investment needs.

[8] See the other studies in the present volume.

In the field of public utility services (with the justified exception of public transport[9]), prices gradually reached the cost-covering level. In other words, actual users increasingly shouldered the costs of these services. Meanwhile, a system of targeted social subsidies was also introduced separately from the pricing system. This new, double system was suitable to address economic problems as economic ones and social problems as social ones, and to reckon with their costs accordingly. Costs and subsidies that played an important role in the adaptation to market conditions have become transparent.

Thus, the price of public services ceased to be politically defined and deliberated as "allowances" and was defined economically. Under this new economic logic, pricing became an important infrastructure policy tool. This new role of prices differed from the earlier one: it was no more an across-the-board, non-transparent subsidy based on ideological considerations instead, it has become a basic tool for creating a more efficient and equitable system. In a system of cost-covering rates, the price of the service is shouldered by the consumer, and all the other economic and political objectives are addressed through goal-oriented incentives calculated on the basis of transparent cost analyses. As we shall see, the rates and the pricing schemes played a key role in the accomplishment of practically all of the municipality's infrastructure policy goals.

UTILITY RATE REFORM

Since the change of the political system, the liberal municipality leaders have considered the establishing of cost-covering prices wherever possible as a fundamental priority. Simultaneously, they created a system of targeted subsidies for the needy.[10] The only exception was public transport – as we have seen above. There were also certain investment projects that the municipality could not realistically expect to be financed by the citizens themselves (for a while, the completion of the wastewater management system seemed to be such an investment).

The rise in public service prices started in the early 1990s. Their revenues could gradually cover the operating costs of the services – and later even the maintenance costs and, at least partly, adaptation costs (with the only exception of public transport). This put an end to the system of open subsidies of the socialist era. At the same time, rate hikes meant that housing maintenance and public service expenses increased faster than the citizens' income (see

---

[9] The subsidization of public transport from public funds may be primarily justified since, compared with individual transport, it is less damaging to the environment and its per unit traffic burdens are smaller (road use, traffic jams, etc.). Another argument in favor of subsidizing public transport is that the bulk of the costs of individual urban transport are also financed from public funds (road building and maintenance, traffic management, etc.). However, these costs do not appear as user charges, and thus an unfair price competition would occur between individual and public transport if the total costs of public transport were shifted on to the users. The subsidization of public transport, which is politically favored, aims to increase the use of this public service.

[10] Alliance of Free Democrats (SZDSZ), 1990: 16, 22

Table 1 below). Part of the consumers were then unable to pay the increased housing-related expenses. These handicapped strata receive support from the districts' welfare budgets, and also through the municipality initiated system of utility cost allowances that provides targeted allowances in order to buttress the citizens' capacity and willingness to pay their utility bills.[11]

Table 1
HOUSING MAINTENANCE AND TRANSPORT EXPENDITURES IN BUDAPEST HOUSEHOLDS
(per capita/per annum, HUF)

ITEM	1993	1994	1995	1996	1997	1998	1999	2000	2001
Total expenditure	152904	158310	187431	273473	315703	369243	412428	467490	564960
Housing maintenance	19128	21329	27449	53434	64523	72442	85601	101002	108094
Housing maintenance in total expenditure (%)	12,5	13,5	14,6	19,5	20,4	19,6	20,8	21,6	19,1
Transport and telecommunication	20760	22323	27819	38155	48519	51741	65526	76538	95589
Transport and telecommunication in total expenditure (%)	13,6	14,1	14,8	14,0	15,4	14,0	15,9	16,4	16,9

Source: Budapest Statistical Yearbooks, KSH, 1994-2002

The reform of the pricing system was not only restricted to rate hikes. In its relation with the companies the municipality made efforts to replace the system of annual political bargaining for subsidies and micro-management, with a system resting on long-term price schemes (price formulae) and detailed servicing contracts. The servicing contracts regulate the operation of the companies and create transparent and predictable conditions for the management of the servicing companies. According to the literature, it is rather difficult to create pricing formulae and establish the initial price level for the non-privatized public utility companies as it is practically impossible to safely determine an acceptable level for costs. Since these companies enjoy a monopolistic position, there are no comparative prices to rely on. Furthermore, asymmetric information prevents the identification of the efficiency reserves, and makes the determination of the price level through calculations uncertain.

However, experiences in Budapest are different. With the exception of public transport, the municipality succeeded in drafting and implementing formulae for the pricing of public utility services. As the paragraphs on the individual companies will reveal, these formulae have generated sufficient revenues for the operation of the companies and have led to improved efficiency. The application of such a formula for public transport was not prevented by technical difficulties either, but rather by the lack of the availability of funds that are inevitably needed for subsidies in this special field.[12]

---

[11] The goal and operation of the housing-related allowance system will be discussed in detail by another study in the present volume.

[12] This statement will be explained under the heading 'Non-Privatized Companies'.

Today, the rates of all but two of Budapest's public utility services are based on a "rate of return" type calculation relying on costs (the exceptions are the price of natural gas that is set by the state, and the rates of public transport). The price formulae normatively regulate the calculation of the associated operating, depreciation, and overhead costs of the servicing companies. The formulae also include incentives for improving efficiency. For privatized companies, this incentive is incorporated in the calculation of the dividends or in the so-called management fee.[13] Both are tied to the calculation of the improvement in the company's efficiency, and serve the return of investment. For non-privatized companies, the incentive is represented by the companies' right to retain part of the savings that result from their improved efficiency.[14]

Beyond these normatively regulated elements, the rates also include a so-called investment quota to cover the costs of certain major reconstruction and development projects. The setting of these quotas is at the discretion of the municipality that decides it annually.

The introduction of these formulae significantly altered the pricing process that was earlier based on political bargaining. The price setting negotiations between the pricing authority (the Municipality of Budapest) and the servicing companies have been altered to factual, professional debates on the values applied for the parameters of the formulae. The components of the formulae are fixed, thus the dialogues primarily focus on the extent to which the fluctuations of the parameters can be recognized by the formulae. The servicing company tries to justify its proposal for the value of the relevant parameters with detailed calculations. The pricing authority likewise buttresses its observations on the individual parameters with (generally) two sets of calculations made by independent experts. In this process, argumentation refers to the processes behind the parameters and not to the values of the parameters or the actual rates themselves. Limiting debates to real processes affecting the parameters guarantees the consistent application of the formulae.[15] Of course, in this system the computed result of the formula is not questioned, i.e., the normative cost element of the rate is strictly generated by calculations. In this process, the local government's scope of political activity is restricted to deciding the development quota.

---

[13] The management fee is discussed in detail in the study on privatization.

[14] The other part of the savings from increased efficiency is used by the owner (the local government) to moderate the increase in consumer prices.

[15] Of course, this type of calculation requires a lot of expertise and work each year. However, the formulae can not work without this effort. Even the most brilliant formula produces faulty results if the data entered are incorrect or distorted to satisfy the particular interests of any of the parties. The Municipality of Budapest – in its capacity as an elected body charged with representing the interests of the public – strives during the negotiations to reduce the fees to a realistic minimum level. According to the leaders of the municipality it would be even more preferable to leave negotiation to an independent body instead of the municipality that is owner or part-owner of the provider company. In this body the representatives of the service providers, of civilian and interest groups as well as independent experts could negotiate upgrading. As the members of the body have utterly colliding interests, each member would mobilize all the professional expertise at hand to defend the differing standpoints, thus providing the potential maximum of professionalism. Under such circumstances, the participants in this body would be compelled to come up with well-founded professional arguments. Eventually, this body could make a professionally sound proposal for the justified cost levels.

Of course, the maintenance of this system of price regulation (due to the need for detailed price and cost analysis) entails transaction costs. However, these transaction costs are always considerably smaller than the savings achieved via the annual debates. Consequently, this practice would generate net profit for the consumers even if the municipality decided to include the expert fees in the final rates.

The experiences of the past few years have shown that the charges calculated with the formulae were adequate to maintain the stability of the services and also the consumers' willingness to pay their utility bills. Most companies have accomplished around and above 95% collection rates even from inhabitants and "small consumers." Larger and increasing loss in collection (and on factoring) has only occurred in the case of district heating (see Appendix, Table 6). This fact supports the description of the problems related to this specific service that are discussed later.

Beyond the stability of the price formulae, we must also recognize that the initial agreements on the computation methods of formulae had to be repeatedly corrected since their introduction. Proposals for correcting the formulae (i.e., for refining the system of related rules) have been drafted by both sides. This was a natural and beneficial development, since its aim was to include the latest experiences, facts, and knowledge into the formulae. In this respect not only the initial adjustments were natural and welcome (which helped the system to overcome its "teething pains"), but we should also recognize the beneficial effects of subsequent and fairly regular corrections. Therefore the municipality incorporated the option of corrections in contracts with the service providers along with the rules and procedures applying to the corrections. However, in order for the system to properly function, the proposals and debate on the possible corrections of the regulatory framework and the argumentation on the calculation of the individual values during the price setting negotiations must be separate to the greatest possible extent.

The ensuing analyses in this chapter will reveal that the change of the pricing policy was beneficial to the operation of the sectors in more than one respect. The improvement of cost coverage ratio realized through the rate increases has today rendered prices fully cost covering (with the exception of public transport).[16] Cost-covering prices have rationalized consumption and strengthened the servicing companies' accountability. In certain areas the restructuring of the pricing system has enabled privatization, which in turn boosted the efficiency of the services. Consequently, pricing policy and pricing reform have become key elements in the implementation of all the strategic goals of the municipality in the field of its public utility services.

---

[16] Notwithstanding significant price increases, the real value of the total revenues of companies has not increased due to the effect of the consumption decrease and the redressing of the companies activity profiles. (see Appendix, Table 4)

RESTRUCTURING THE COMPANIES' OPERATION

The restructuring of the servicing companies' operation is another key element in Budapest's public utility policies. The reforms started out from the understanding that the municipal regulations should guarantee the optimal utilization of available resources, i.e., the costs of stable and quality service should be kept at the lowest possible level.[17] The only way to accomplish this goal was to improve the servicing companies' efficiency. Acknowledging these facts still leaves the question open of how company efficiency may best be improved.

In principle, the servicing company itself is interested in improving the quality and stability of its services. However, if the company has access to appropriate resources and is not operating under financial constraints, it is not necessarily interested in generating coverage for its operation and investments through increasing efficiency, as this is clearly the most painful alternative. The optimization of service provision becomes a key consideration only if the company is forced to operate amidst clear and hard financial constraints. Accordingly, the aim of municipal regulation must be to create these hard constraints. In other words, we could rephrase the previous question by asking how best to create the conditions required for boosting efficiency. Which path is more promising to reach this end: the reorganization of the companies and the gradual reform of the regulations pertinent to their operating conditions, or privatization?

The liberal leaders of the municipality clearly opted for the latter method as they were aware of the conflicts inherent between the roles the municipality plays vis-à-vis a non-privatized company.[18] They recognized that a local government – paradoxically – may not fulfill its most important public role, the protection of the interests of the consumers, i.e., public interest, due to various reasons: first, simply because of the inherent limitations that pertain to the acts of public bodies; second, as the local government may not function as a good, genuine owner of the servicing companies, and thus could not force the companies to function efficiently. By opting for privatization, the municipal leaders aimed at creating a clear situation: they tried to select the private investor who could function as an efficient owner of the servicing company. They tried to make this investor interested in improving the company's efficiency through appropriate regulations. And they tried – at least partly getting rid of the role of the owner – to concentrate municipal activities purely on the political role of representing public interests.

In principle, the surest way for privatization to lead to improved efficiency is if the monopolistic nature of the given service can be eliminated or at least loosened prior to the actual privatization. The fact that (as we shall see later) on certain occasions the leaders of the municipality have opted for privatization even in cases where the prevailing political conditions prevented the emergence of a privatization scheme required for weakening monopoly is indicative of the liberals' strong commitment to privatization.

---

[17] In this respect, expenditure means both the financial burdens of the users and of the municipality.

[18] See below under the sub-title 'Privatization'

During the past three cycles, the privatization of most of the local public utility companies has been launched or completed in Budapest. In certain cases, prevailing conditions (the servicing context or local political circumstances) prevented privatization. Therefore, following the review of the logic behind the privatization process, we shall discuss some of the obstacles encountered during attempted privatization transactions, and we shall also summarize achievements in the field of non-privatized services.

PRIVATIZATION

The attempt to incite efficiency via privatization starts out from the conflicting local government roles of being a public authority and the owner of the servicing company at the same time. The local government is primarily a political body, whose task in this capacity is to protect the interests of the public. That is on the one hand to guarantee and control the stability and quality of the public services, while on the other hand to keep service prices low. At the same time, in the case of the non-privatized companies, the local government is a company owner and service provider. In this capacity, its goal must be (though excluding extra profit) to keep company revenues high enough to cover the operating and investment expenditures. After all, in this scenario the local government is simultaneously the operator and the regulator of the very service that it provides. This conflict makes it inevitable for the local government to simultaneously consider a number of clashing goals during decision-making. This in turn may result in inconsistent decisions and a loss of efficiency. A logical way out of this conflict is to (at least partly) relinquish ownership.

International experience has furnished three relevant reasons for considering the privatization option. First, it has been proved that private capital is more efficient in utilizing resources than the public sector (provided that it finds appropriate operating conditions). Second, experience has shown that services can be provided through private companies also in fields that fall under the responsibility of the local governments. And third, it has been pointed out that the one-off price competition sparked by the privatization tender (through long-term pricing formulae built into the contract terms) may exert continuous efficiency pressure even in the case of monopoly services.

During the privatization process, the Municipality of Budapest was looking for partners who could be expected to introduce the efficiency and expertise of the private sector into the company's management. Another aim was to clarify conflicting interests and create positions that would enable the municipality to clearly represent the interests of consumers on the one hand, and the company to strive to reach its own best business and development pattern on the other hand. Once these roles are separated, it becomes much easier to identify – and ultimately to solve – a number of anomalies and problems. In this bipolar scenario, a dynamic tension occurs between the two markedly different sets of interests, and this in turn may boost efficiency. Under the new circumstances it already falls onto the investor (who seeks a return on his investment) to ensure cost efficiency by prescribing it as a key consideration for the new management. If the local government is able to draft and approve regulations to protect its own interests, the company has no choice but to increase its efficiency in order to reduce its expenditures and optimize its services by adjusting them to demand.

On top of all these issues, privatization may generate sizeable one-time revenues for the local government. However, we must add that the goal of increasing one-time revenues and urging efficiency constraints can only be achieved to the detriment of one another.

Privatization in Budapest intended to free the municipality from earlier local council activities that did not necessarily fit its public role, as well as to improve the efficiency of the remaining activities. The prime goal was clearly to boost the efficiency of public services. The other privatization-related goals included the reduction of the budgetary burdens of local public services and the involvement of new expertise. At the same time, the 1994 Conception on Privatization emphasized that the "economic benefits from privatization cannot be prior to the operation safety of the given service."[19]

Deliberation on the various objectives (which in some instances would have justified conflicting decisions) and their prioritization took place simultaneously with the approval of the given company's privatization conception. Usually goals considered of prime importance in the given case determined the choice of the constructions applied. The chapter on the "Privatization of Certain Public Utility Companies" discusses various privatization models applied to diverse service companies in Budapest that were in different condition, operated in different contexts, and therefore had to have a different privatization model. At the same time, the ensuing studies also reveal that, regrettably, in some cases purely political considerations and interests, resulting in compromise solutions, overrode principles and potentials.

The Pharmafontana Pharmaceutical Co. was the owner of the retail pharmacy network in Budapest, and was also a wholesaler and producer of pharmaceuticals. The company's activities were not in any form associated with legally prescribed municipal obligations, and the municipal leaders did not consider the above activities part of the local public services. In the opinion of the liberal leaders, this company was to be privatized purely through market-based solutions. Prior to launching the privatization process, the pharmacies were separated from the company.

Concerning the pharmacy privatization process, it was clear that the end result of the transaction was to be determined by the market and not by a local government decision. And yet, political logic forced for a compromise solution. The tender did not call for the best offers (i.e., the foreign companies already present in Hungary who were interested in taking over a large retail network), but targeted the employees (the pharmacists), who quite often resold their newly acquired property. This solution could not "protect" the pharmacists, but only lead to what was the logical outcome in several stages and in 3-4 years. On top of this, the municipal revenues from privatization were lower than they could have been.[20] At the same time, through this compromise the local government managed to avoid the fierce attacks that could have turned public opinion against the ensuing privatization transactions in general.

---

[19] The Office of the Mayor of Budapest, 1994a: 5

[20] Through this compromise, the municipality indirectly transferred profits to the pharmacists (the difference between its revenues and the market value of the retail units), who could realize this upon the resale of the pharmacies.

The privatization of the pharmaceutical wholesaler and producer Pharmafontana Co. was a similar, albeit smaller volume transaction. The first attempt failed, because the offer of the tenderer who seemed to be the best was inaccurate, and would have ultimately resulted in lower-than-promised revenues. There were doubts raised against the best bidder during the second round too, but a privatization decision was made all the same, enforcing tough contractual conditions to minimize risks. This, again, was a compromise solution: though the sales price was lower than the company's liquidation value, the transaction freed the municipality from the political burden of liquidating the company on its own and from firing the employees. Thus the transaction did not worsen the public's attitude towards privatization. This, clearly, paved the way for the ensuing important privatization projects.

Prior to its privatization, the Budapest Gas Works had sufficient infrastructure and offered quality services to the public. Although the company fulfilled a municipal task, its performance was practically under state control through its centrally regulated prices. In this case a profitable monopoly was to be privatized. Accordingly, privatization revenue was a top consideration besides maintaining the stability of the service and boosting its efficiency in the contractual framework.

In the cases of the privatization of the water related utility companies[21] – that are discussed in detail in the chapter on public utility privatization – the Municipality of Budapest was allocated both the responsibility for the services provision and the price setting authority. Here the municipality had every chance to come up with schemes that focused on improving efficiency. Though Budapest has retained its majority share in both the Waterworks and Wastewater Management companies, both privatization models assigned the right of operation – in essence the management of the companies – to the investors, opening up the way to the rationalizing of interventions. The pressure for efficiency was left to the pricing formula, which had already been laid down in the tender documents. The formula specified the company's potential revenues and regulated the profit making capacity in relation to, and dependent on increased efficiency. The tenderers were aware of the formula when making their bids. In the given conditions the bidding process on the privatization price was a competition between offers to assume financial responsibility, where the intensity of the competition urged investors to bid up to the limits of their calculated return.

The privatization models applied were also expected to ensure the return of the invested capital that could be guaranteed in different ways depending on the general state of the two companies. There was a fundamental difference between the two companies: while in the field of water supply there was no need for large investments, the sewage and wastewater management systems had to make up for major missing investments. The municipal leaders wanted to minimize the subsidies necessary for these investments. For this, profits had to be generated in the balance sheet of the Sewage and Waste Water Co. that could be invested in the service development projects. As profits were produced on the balance sheet, the applied price formula allowed the return of investment on the privatization price in the form of a dividend and had to be able to normatively regulate the development and dividend brackets within the company's revenues.

---

[21] Water supply and waste water management.

The Water Works had been in the red for a few years prior to their privatization, and the same was expected for some years after their privatization. Since this company required no significant investments, the Municipality of Budapest had no intention to immediately eliminate the losses with a shocking rate hike. Accordingly, the investor could not expect returns from dividends.[22] The possibility of return was established by the so-called management fee[23] determined in proportion to the verified savings in expenditure[24] that could not be attained to the detriment of the service itself.

As we can see, Budapest has had to manage simple as well as complex privatization transactions. The above examples sufficiently prove that privatization may pursue different goals and take different forms depending on the actual case.

THE NON-PRIVATIZED COMPANIES

In view of the liberal municipal leaders' commitment to privatization, it might be of interest to briefly sum up the reasons behind the fact that three very important public services (public transport, district heating, and waste management) were not privatized and have remained in the hands of the municipality.[25]

A key condition for the privatization of public services is the availability of the resources required for the service provision. In this respect it is generally best if the fees paid by consumers cover costs, but in principle it is also possible to cover a certain part of the costs through public subsidies. In both cases, the most important consideration is that the resources should be reliably available under long-term normative regulations, since only in this case can the investor calculate the returns and risks of his investment with relative certainty.

Of course, from the point of view of privatization, the situation is considerably simpler if the costs are covered by the utility rates. Under this scenario, the rates must be commensurate with the consumers' willingness to pay. Here – under a proper price formula – the investor has only to face the operating risks, which he is ready to undertake. In general, the investors tend to be rather cautious when it comes to assuming risks that are extraneous to their activities.

---

[22] In retrospect we can conclude that even in this situation it would have been possible to come up with a privatization model that could have guaranteed a dividend proportionate with the efficiency increase without an unjustified rate hike. However, at that time the municipality still lacked the required expertise.

[23] The management fee is discussed in detail in the study on privatization.

[24] Similarly to the price formula, expenditure savings are calculated on the basis of the pre-privatization figures, applying the formula laid down in the contract.

[25] In this chapter, we discuss only these cases because they are closely related to the logic of our argument. The selection is also justified by the importance of these local services. The other unsuccessful attempts at privatization are discussed in detail in the study on privatization.

The municipality's failure to privatize the district heating service was most likely due to the external risks.[26] The state regulation of gas prices constitutes one element of the risks[27]. The district heating system caters primarily to "constrained consumers" who practically cannot shift to alternative heating methods. Consequently, the main threat to the service is not so much the relative competitiveness of the alternative methods of heating – a frequent argument made by analysts – but the threat of an unpredictable and significant energy price hike, the consequences of which the consumers would be unable to shoulder.[28] Other major risks stem from the potential changes in the relevant legal regulations, and from the service's dependence on the heat energy suppliers.[29] In principle, the legal regulations may prescribe the installation of individual meters at each consumer, which – as the chapter on infrastructure development spells out – may mean that large groups of consumers become unable to pay their bills.[30] The dependence of the district heating service on the heat energy suppliers may cause a radical increase of district heating rates – due to the hikes in heat energy prices purchased for the service – that would jeopardize the service itself.

A few years prior to the announcement of the privatization tender, cost-covering district heating rates were introduced in Budapest. In principle, this paved the way for the service's privatization. Similarly to the other earlier major privatization tenders, this tender also invited investors to bid both for the assets and the operation. For all the preliminary interest, the privatization attempt failed – most likely because the investors were not satisfied with the conditions laid down in the tender. It does not seem far off the mark to say that this privatization model is not fit for addressing the risks inherent in this specific service.

After the failure of the first privatization round, the municipality leaders attempted to have an alternative privatization model drafted by the Finance Research Company.[31] The new model focuses on improving the service's competitiveness and proposes a gradual, multi-player privatization process, carefully deliberating the risk-management capabilities of both the investors and the municipality. By separating assets from operations, the new model minimizes the need for the investor to tie up cash for a longer period, and it also reduces

---

[26] The ensuing arguments may be difficult to follow for those who are not familiar with the situation of Budapest's district heating service. To facilitate understanding, it is worth reading the paragraphs on the district heating service in the studies entitled 'District Heating – a Non-Privatized Utility', and 'Infrastructure Development', and then return to our arguments.

[27] The state regulation of energy prices still fails to follow a predictable method and practice and to set cost covering prices as is discussed in the paper on utility pricing.

[28] The concluding study of this chapter on 'Infrastructure Development' describes in detail that the majority of the district heating service's customers are low-income citizens living in housing estates. Accordingly, the introduction of market-based gas prices is an imminent risk and would render these people insolvent.

[29] For details, see the study on "Infrastructure Development."

[30] The current system is based on cross-financing both between individual heating districts and between individual consumers. The elimination of this system may easily render larger groups of consumers insolvent. The liberal principles of the municipal leaders run counter to this cross-financing system, however, as we shall see, the elimination of this system is conditional on solving a series of problems and dilemmas.

[31] Finance Research Co., 1991

the municipality's risks arising from its potential dependence on an exclusive partner. Furthermore, the model also separates the process of heat production from the transmission of heat to the consumers, and in both areas it enforces the principle of free access (as much as possible). In the field of heat production, the model creates the conditions for a competition among suppliers[32] – thereby minimizing the chances for a monopolistic supplier pricing mechanism. In the field of heat transmission and distribution, the creation and individual privatization of "heating districts" would facilitate the access to the market, thus creating competition among service providers.

According to this model the municipality would retain ownership of the heat distribution network, and would invite open bids for the operation of the "heating districts" established under uniform conditions. In this system the company would supply heat energy to the entrepreneurs on a contractual basis, and would rent out the required distribution infrastructure. The entrepreneur would pay a fee to the company, that would cover energy costs, the costs of the depreciation and development of the assets, as well as cover the overhead.

After the privatization transaction, the new operator would be in direct contact with the consumers. The operator would be responsible for the quality and quantity of the service, and would also collect the service fees. The gist of the alternative model is to use the price competition that emerges during the tender process as a booster for cost efficiency. The bidders would quote prices calculated from a fixed price formula – these prices should be lower than the actual price. Consequently, the system guarantees price reduction (provided that the tender is successful).[33] Since the model does not require significant investments from the entrepreneur[34], his risks are reduced and thus a smaller increase in the efficiency of the service can guarantee lower consumer prices. At the same time, the municipality's risks are also manageable since it rents out each heating district separately and retains its ownership rights and associated decision-making rights. Another favorable aspect of the model is that the municipality would most likely contract with different entrepreneurs in the individual heat districts. This would facilitate the replacement of laggard partners.

---

[32] It is important to note that this model is not exactly the same as the heating ring model developed by the District Heating Company and described in detail in the study on 'Infrastructure Development.' The ultimate aim of the model devised by the Finance Research Company is to replace monopoly conditions with competitive ones. For this reason, the model focuses not on the heating ring itself (i.e., the creation of the largest possible (macro) network), but instead on the facilitation of the suppliers' economical and unrestricted access to any heating district (i.e. local part of the heating network).

[33] For political gains, the District Heating Company may apply an appropriate price balancing mechanism to establish uniform user rates in the capital, despite the different heating district prices charged by the entrepreneurs. At the same time, we must add that the liberal approach of the municipality would suggest the gradual elimination of price balancing (and thereby of cross-financing).

[34] The one-time privatization fee may as well be left out of the model, and thus its capital costs do not have to be shifted on to the business. (Of course, in exchange for the lower costs, this would also eliminate the motivating force of the responsibility assumed with the one-time investment.)

Thanks to the gradual hand-over of operations, the Municipal District Heating Company and the Municipality of Budapest can increasingly concentrate on their strategic and managing roles, thereby easing the identity crisis that characterizes non-privatized municipality-owned companies. However, since the General Assembly has not yet approved this model, the above thoughts are of theoretical significance only. This train of thought attempted only to offer an alternative solution to the previous privatization model of the District Heating Company that failed due to the excessive risks that investors faced.

As for the privatization of the Budapest public transport service, it fell through because the other key player, the municipality, could not assume it's related risks and due responsibilities. The study on the Budapest Public Transport Company (from now on: BKV Rt.) discusses the company's privatization attempts in appropriate detail. Here, we will concentrate only on the major obstacle to privatization relevant to our discussion on general principles of infrastructure policy.

Perhaps the most important of the privatization attempts was the one which aimed to privatize specific lines in the city, in the frame of a gross-cost franchise widely used in other cities throughout the world. In Budapest, BKV Rt. managed to contract operators for some of the city's public transport lines. In the first round, the price limit was determined at the level of the company's own direct costs determined individually for each line and did not include the proportionate share of the company's losses. The bidders were expected to quote a price below the price limit. As a result, contracted lines reduced the company's operating expenditures.

As a next step – acting on the municipality's request – the company made an attempt to privatize certain lines at a price limit which already included the proportionate share of the company's losses. This attempt failed.[35] In response – as an apparent paradox – the whole process was halted by the municipal leaders, who otherwise were committed to privatization.

It is fairly easy to understand the motives behind this decision. Due to the regulations in force, public transport is suffering from a lack of resources in every large city in Hungary. In spite of their legal obligations, local governments are unable to finance the losses generated by the public transport companies under the prevailing conditions of financing[36] (which fall beyond their competence). Consequently, they "have no choice but to supplement their resources with revenues from the sale of the company assets or to postpone necessary refurbishment and investments."[37]

---

[35] The inclusion of the losses would most likely prevent the privatization of even the most profitable lines.

[36] "The stipulations of the law on pricing are not enforced, since the Finance Minister approves the maximized official prices taking into account welfare and anti-inflationary goals, as well as the burden-bearing potentials of the state budget that is affected through the system of price subsidies. If the price increase is lower than required, the difference increases the local governments' obligation to compensate the losses." (State Audit Office, 2001: 4)

[37] State Audit Office, 2001: 6.

In this situation, a line privatization transaction that does not calculate with company losses is dangerous, even if it reduces the direct costs of public transport services. Should the company continue with the practice of excluding losses in the price limit, this "uncovered" loss is retained even after the privatization transactions. At the same time, in parallel with the progress in the privatization process, the assets of the company are gradually running low, narrowing down the possibility to take the "emergency exit" of selling off assets. The local government, bearing the final responsibility for the service, cannot afford to go down this path until it finds an alternative source for financing the losses. In other words, this type of line privatization is not the right way, until a long-term, normative solution is established for subsidizing public transport to the extent that eliminates losses produced under the prevailing subsidy system.[38]

To understand the implications of this problem, it is worth referring to the chapter on financial management. Public transport financing is a problem of such magnitude that it directly affects the sustainability of the Municipality of Budapest's finances.[39] And yet, despite their decade-long efforts, the municipal leaders could not get the government involved in hammering out a satisfactory, normative solution to this problem.[40] In this situation – for all the municipal leaders' principled refusal of the idea of asset consumption for operating purposes – the public transport company could be saved from bankruptcy during the "hardship years" only by selling assets and deferring the amortization of expenditures.[41] In Budapest, the city leaders blocked further transport line privatization because they saw clearly that the

---

[38] "The strategy of the companies is aimed at maintaining their operability and expected standards of services, since their general financial state and conditions do not allow them to carry out the necessary and technically justified upgrading of material assets and investments. [...] Without the transformation of the current system of financing and subsidization the companies cannot overcome their financial problems through the mere reorganization of their own resources. It is futile for them to seek further alternatives." (State Audit Office, 2001: 6)

[39] Tables 4 and 5 of the Appendix show clearly that the provision of public transportation is not only the most expensive among municipal infrastructure services, but it also receives by far the highest amount of subsidies each year. The provision of public transportation covers more than 30% of the costs of all municipal infrastructure services.

[40] The creation of a system of normative financing would require, on the one hand, the identification of which entries in the expenditures column are rational to be subsidized (and to define their proportions), and defining whether the subsidies are aimed at supporting operation only, or operation and development under a normatively regulated scheme. On the other hand, the resource elements to each subsidy component are to be decided as well. One possibility is to grant state subsidies for operation under a normative system; another is to introduce local taxes to finance public transport (in principle, the latter should apply to the urban region, and should be excluded from the taxpaying capacity calculation). It would also be logical to retain the financing of development in the municipal budget, because this way investments could be harmonized with other urban policy goals and a wider scope of financing techniques could be provided.

[41] The undoubtedly independent State Audit Office has reviewed the financing of public transport in the cities of Hungary that operate independent companies to this purpose. According to the Office, these activities are underfinanced, and thus their volume is declining. One major recommendation of the Audit Office chimes with the opinion of the Municipality of Budapest: the government should "consider the introduction of a system of normative subsidies in order to promote the development of public transport services." (State Audit Office, 2001: 9)

"emergency exit" of – inevitable – asset consumption would have been closed off in the absence of a solution to its financing problems.

The third case where privatization was likewise unsuccessful is solid and liquid waste management. Here we discuss only the problems related to waste transportation (the issue of waste disposal is tackled in the study entitled "Infrastructure Development" at the end of this chapter).

The area of solid and liquid waste management is peculiar among public utility services since its elements – collection, transportation, and disposal – do not constitute natural monopolies and are thus easy to privatize. In Budapest, private ventures had been responsible for a large part of these services already prior to the change of the political system. At the same time, in a rather peculiar way, the events of the 1990's pushed the provision of these services deeper into the public sector rather than leading to further privatization. Therefore it appears worthwhile to briefly summarize the reasons behind this atypical trend and to recall a few interesting episodes.

In the capital city, solid waste management is the responsibility of the 100 percent muni-cipality-owned Public Space Maintenance Company (from now on: FKF Rt.). (Liquid waste management belongs to the competence of FTSZV Kft., another municipality-owned company.) Besides waste management, FKF Rt. is also responsible for providing road maintenance and public area cleaning services. During the socialist era, FKF Rt. was developed into a huge company responsible for a diverse set of tasks, and the company has retained its dimensions to the present day. The company's scope of activity includes fundamentally "public good"-type of services that are rather difficult to measure and are publicly financed, as well as services that are easily measurable and can be supplied by market-based, fee-based methods. Since the change of the political system several attempts have been made within the company to improve efficiency. However, it remains extremely difficult to measure the results of these efforts in view of FKF Rt.'s complex portfolio and intricate financing system.

It would have been logical to separate certain activities from the company and to draft individual strategies for each. However, ingrained practices, established interest structures and often also relevant regulations themselves prevented these attempts. The liberal and pro-privatization leaders of the municipality were unable to build up a coalition to elicit a drastic change towards competition or towards separation of certain activities for privatization. Moreover, not only privatization was taken off the agenda, but changes have also taken place – oddly enough – in a direction contrary to market-based operation.

Act No. XLII of 1995 (on the mandatory acquisition of certain local public services) regulated the "collection, transportation, and safe disposal of solid and liquid community waste" as well as chimney sweeping, all under the responsibility of the local governments. Under the Act, the local government can sign a public service contract with only one service provider, who then is "obliged to provide regular and full public service for all the owners." (Paragraph 2. b)

Prior to passing the Act, market conditions were already established in Budapest to a certain extent for the transportation of solid and liquid waste, as FKF RT. and FTSZV Kft. provided these services in parallel with private ventures in a partly competitive way. (While the municipality-owned company had exclusive rights in the field of communal solid waste transportation, a number of private and municipality-owned businesses were active in corporate solid waste market and communal liquid waste transportation.)

Thus, the Act has created monopolies replacing the competitive market for these services, and compelled some of the earlier players to dissolve. This generates problems not only because the Act has granted monopoly rights for a set period, but also because the 10-year term specified in the contracts will certainly be long enough to squeeze earlier players out of the field.

Obviously, under the legal stipulations only the municipality-owned companies had a realistic chance to win the tenders, since only these companies could demonstrate references for having operated the full spectrum of the service at issue. They could tackle the problem of no longer being able to provide services for the full volume on their own by subcontracting – after winning the tender – all the ventures that had been squeezed out from direct service contracts. The case provides an excellent example for the restoration of a monopoly position exclusively by legal means.

After the Act came into force, in 1997-1998 the Municipality of Budapest invited tenders for the provision of the respective public utility services. The tenders were won by FKF Rt. and by FTSZV Kft. (previously council- and then municipality-owned companies) who led consortiums of a few private businesses. The term of the tenders was ten years. The signing of the contracts elicited fierce opposition from other players in (what used to be) the market.

The roots of the problem are identical in both areas: the protesters believe that the contracts amounted to a forceful transformation of a competitive service market into a monopoly one. In their arguments they emphasize the negative effects of a monopoly, the limitation of free-market competition and the adverse effect of monopoly prices on consumers.

The drafters and advocates of the Act neglect the problem of creating monopolies and assert that relevant public health regulations can only be enforced this way. They argue that the consortium, which is dominated by a fully council- and then municipality-owned company, is the best way to minimize the risk associated with illegal solid and liquid waste disposal.

In their opinion, in absence of efficient control there is nothing to prevent the service providers, in order to cut the costs of transportation or disposal, from, for example, dumping the liquid waste into the city's sewage system or straight into the Danube river rather than transporting it to the designated disposal areas. They argue that a fully municipality-owned company with exclusive rights would never do this, and that it is anyway always easier to keep an eye on this type of a company.

Opponents, however, remain convinced that it is equally difficult to control any company, and argue that soft sanctions are not an efficient weapon against a monopoly. If there are several players, it is possible to apply tough sanctions, one being the exclusion of the repeat offenders from the service. The service providers who have invested in their business by purchasing waste disposal vehicles and other equipment will likely think twice before violating the relevant regulations. Meanwhile, the large and monopolistic company will enjoy its position and will be impossible to exclude from the service.

The advocates of the Act also cited the higher comfort level of the consumers: the citizens are not "constrained" to choose – they just call the service, and the familiar truck arrives. There is something to this argument, since predictably the same companies will continue to provide the service as subcontractors. The consumers will not "choose," but irrespective of that, they will have no choice but to use the same provider's services. Meanwhile, the service rates will also include the margin between the rates of the main contractor and the subcontractor, and the price hike resulting from the "comfort" of a monopolistic service.

The Act almost completely counters the logic behind the privatization processes in Budapest. The lawmakers did not want to separate the regulating and controlling role associated with the municipality as a public authority from the role of providing the service.

The critics of the Act would apply the logic of economic policy: they would keep the role of regulator and controller with the public authority, and would leave it up to the competing (municipality-owned and privately-owned) businesses to organize an efficient public service provision. Under this scenario, the services and rates of the participating business would most likely be regulated by the market itself. According to this logic, the problem of illegal disposal and dumping should be addressed through appropriate regulations and sanctions.

The businesses previously engaged in liquid waste disposal made repeated attempts through the media and by organizing demonstrations to force the amendment of decisions that they considered not only as being against their interests but against their rights as well. Still, the public service contracts have entered into force. In the field of solid waste disposal, experience seems to justify the arguments that cite the benefits of market competition. Right after signing the contract, the FKF Rt. increased the waste transportation fees for its corporate clients by nearly 50 per cent to bring these prices on par with communal rates.[42] Since the signing of the contract left only one legal waste transporter in Budapest, the company's clients had no choice but to accept the higher fees.

In principle, there could have been an in-between solution as well – one that, while keeping to the law, would have satisfied both "market-based" and "single-provider" camps. Under

---

[42] Although this cost increase could in principle be described as taking advantage of the monopoly position, we must add that the acquisition of a market of this size may have entailed price hikes resulting from the real cost increase of the service. One factor to be considered here is the higher cost of the deposit areas used by the new service provider. This note is meant only to satisfy the requirement of professional correctness, since from the consumers' point of view the actual reasons behind the rate hike are hardly relevant.

this scenario, the city would have had to be divided into service districts, with separate tenders invited for each district from individual businesses or their consortia. This solution would have satisfied the proponents' desire for a system in which there is just one business responsible for a given district. At the same time, it would have kept a number of businesses on the market, which would certainly have been a more market-conform solution. Furthermore, this system would also have improved the chances of sanctioning, and would have enabled the city to exclude grave offenders of relevant environmental, safety, or business regulations from the service as there would have been other businesses to take over the tasks.

This compromise solution would have been conceivable under the relevant laws, but it died as a result of political infighting in the municipality. The idea of creating service districts and inviting separate tenders ran counter to the previously established interest structures, as all this would have pushed the city towards the splitting up of the largest servicing company and eventually towards the privatization of its activities. The compromise solution would have violated the interests of those who were keen on preserving their jobs and maintaining the status of a closed large company. In this conflict, the liberal forces proved to be too weak to get this job done.

RESULTS OF RESTRUCTURING OF NON-PRIVATIZED PUBLIC UTILITY COMPANIES

For cases when it was not possible to privatize the service providers, the municipality's strategy was based on the condition that the municipality should hold practically all the rights relevant to the company's management. After all, the municipality was not only a political player and a regulator, but also the owner of the companies at issue. In principle, this status enables the municipality to make any rational intervention. It can restructure the business in order to improve its efficiency and to optimize its resource utilization practices. Being the owner, the municipality – in principle – has sufficient information at its disposal to determine the size of the resources that are appropriate to provide the service. At the same time, the municipality as public authority is able to guarantee the required resources, as in principle it has the possibility to create an optimal pricing and subsidy policy. The description of the case of the two non-privatized companies (BKV Rt. and Főtáv) in the present chapter sheds light on the municipality's attempts at rationalization and analyzes the successes and limitations of these efforts.

An analysis of the operation of the non-privatized public utility service companies in Budapest shows that while the municipality's license as owner entitles it to implement certain measures aimed at increasing efficiency (e.g., to transform the capital and activity structure or the organizational structure), this cannot solve the problems that result from the asymmetry in information. These problems remain a major obstacle to the introduction and codification of tougher regulations, and thereby to the further improvement of operational efficiency. Meanwhile, the power splits within the municipality, as well as its multiple roles, tend to point to conflicting goals, which makes it rather difficult to approve and pursue a coherent strategy. In such a situation the company's efforts to retain earlier positions and to postpone changes can easily prevail.

THE CONTENT OF THE STUDIES IN THE PRESENT CHAPTER

The studies below evaluate the policies related to public utility services from the point of view of the individual policies and also at the level of the different companies. As we have said, the strategy of the Municipality of Budapest rested on three closely related conceptions and goals: pricing policy; the restructuring of company management; and development management. The first two studies in this chapter look into the room for maneuvering in pricing and subsidy policy and analyze Budapest's choices among the available alternatives. The next three studies focus on the questions and possibilities of company management (they look at both the non-privatized companies and the privatized ones, with comments and evaluations). The last study reviews the lessons of infrastructure development.

The paper on price regulation offers a detailed description of the pricing of public services through analyzing the problems of the monopolies, universal servicing, and pricing. It presents the internationally approved criteria for the regulation of public utility service rates, then discusses the evolution and the current state of Budapest's pricing policies. Besides highlighting Budapest's experiences in the changes of cost coverage and in the application of various price-calculation schemes, the study also looks at the problems associated with investment financing and efficiency-boosting measures. The paper on price regulation is followed by a study that presents the utility charge allowance system that has been developed by the Municipality of Budapest in parallel to the process of increasing prices.

The next study deals with the transformation of the operations of the Budapest District Heating Works, which is a model example for getting to understand the district heating problems typical of cities in the post-socialist region. After the change of the political system, most off the municipalities in the region had to live with district heating systems inherited from the previous era. Most of these systems are uneconomical, out-of-date and worn out. This makes district heating markedly expensive, while the absence of metering induces wasteful usage.

In Budapest, over half a million people depend on the district heating system. For many citizens, this service presents insurmountable financial problems, which neither the districts' housing related cost allowances, nor the municipal fund for utility charge allowance can efficiently handle. Though district heating burdens the households with disproportionately larger costs than individual heating systems, the users of the former cannot exit from district heating due to technical and financial problems. Thus, they are "constrained users" of the district heating service. Under these circumstances, the maintenance and gradual development of the huge district heating system (one quarter of Budapest's households are hooked up to the pipe network) presents enormous challenges to both the company and the municipality (in its capacity as owner). In the 1990s, a program was started to improve the system's technical infrastructure, rationalize its operations (heat production, transfer, and metering), and boost the company's overall efficiency.

The study of the Budapest District Heating Company focuses on the latter goal. It describes the transformation of the relationship between the municipality (the owner) and the company, and also of the company's operating conditions and practices. The chapter focuses on the relevant contracts regulating the company's operations, and also on the methods employed for rationalization and for pricing. It also describes the system of factoring the company's outstanding debts, and acquaints the readers with the annual rate bargaining process. The other questions pertinent to district heating are tackled elsewhere in this volume. The obstacles to privatization are discussed here in the first introductory paper to the chapter and also in the study on privatization. The relevant technical issues (such as individual metering, or the "heating district" and "heating ring" conceptions) are covered in the closing study of the paper entitled "Infrastructure Development."

The Budapest Public Transport Company (BKV Rt.) is responsible for operating the capital city's public transport services. Public transport is a crucial service in a city of two million inhabitants, and its quality greatly determines the city's competitiveness as well as the sub- and re-urbanization processes. The 1990s witnessed a drastic increase in the number of privately owned vehicles (an alternative to public transport), and this has logically resulted in a decline in the use of public transport services. At the same time, the city's road network development efforts could not keep abreast of the ever increasing traffic of vehicles,[43] and the emerging environmentalist forces also became louder, increasingly criticizing the resulting environmental burden. The only way to keep the city livable amidst dramatically increasing motorization is to improve the standards of public transport. However, the available resources are extremely limited, thus the major instruments left for the above-mentioned goal were to improve the efficiency of the service and to rationalize the network. Of course, it fell on BKV to realize these objectives, and thus the reorganization of the company became a key issue for the transport policy of the 1990s.

The study analyzes the transformation of BKV. The case furnishes an excellent example of the difficulties associated with the management of a non-privatized company: the results of the information asymmetry between the owner and the company; the difficulties encountered during the drafting of a coherent strategy and its communication to the company; the power and interest relations which have the potential to block changes. The study offers a detailed introduction to the partially successful reorganization process in Budapest, in the course of which a series of important steps were taken towards the rationalization of the company's capital and activity structure and its internal organization and management.

The study lays special emphasis on the issues of service provision and company financing. It presents the way the company could finance the measures aimed at rationalizing its operations and reducing its operating losses by clearing its own portfolio and reorganizing

---

[43] This simplified statement refers to the increase in the volume of traffic and to the need for movement. As this is discussed in detail in the study on "Infrastructure Development", the development of the city's road network to a level that could satisfy the increased total demand in every part of the city is not an objective. However, in those areas where the city has no plans to develop the road network, it should certainly make sure that public transport can offer a practical alternative.

its capital structure. The study also highlights the possibilities and drawbacks of tightening budgetary constraints. Finally, the study discusses the associated responsibilities and the division of financing burdens between the municipality and the state.

The study entitled "Public Utility Privatization" offers an insight into the full process of the privatization of Budapest's public utility services, from the initial company screenings to the latest lessons coming out of the process. The author of this study sums up the techniques applied, discusses successful transactions and also outlines cases when privatization could not occur. The analysis touches upon the disputes that surround the privatization process and lines up arguments in favor of Budapest's stance on such key issues as the selection of a privatization method, the choice between professional and financial investors, or the main issues of pricing and contracting.

The closing study of this chapter (on infrastructure development) discusses the effects of the reforms on the state and development of the existing infrastructures. The study refers back to the paper on strategic planning and management in the first chapter of the volume, which deals with the municipality's general urban policies and the particular method known as strategic real planning. This study evaluates the changes in the approaches to physical planning and the way planners have gradually drawn closer to the method of real planning. The author looks at the emergence of the urban policy context that enabled individual service areas and various "professions" to abandon the earlier, markedly supply-oriented methods of planning and to eventually "find their place" in the process that shapes Budapest's new urban policies. The study summarizes the evolution of network development and service content as a result of the financing and organizational reforms of service provision, i.e., it reviews the changes that have occurred in the field of infrastructure development (including engineering solutions) and the effects of these on the services themselves.

EVALUATION AND LESSONS

Budapest's public utility policies and their results should be evaluated in the light of the objectives outlined above. There have been a few undeniable accomplishments: during the past decade, through universal provision public utility services have remained available to all by Budapest, and in certain areas the quality of these services has also improved. Meanwhile, the service-related burdens of the public sector have decreased. Public funding of these services is increasingly replaced by user charges. Consequently, the financial burdens of service maintenance and development (with a few exceptions) are shifting from the "public in general" to the actual users, which is undeniably a fairer solution. In general, utility rate revenues are increasingly sufficient to cover the costs of these services,[44] and the reorganization and privatization of the servicing companies has clearly improved the services' efficiency.

---

[44] Since 1995, the Municipality of Budapest has been granting operating as well as developmental subsidies only to two services: public transport and public baths (in the latter area, operating subsidies are granted only to certain special medicinal services). In certain fields, developments of an exceptionally large size are also financed in part from municipal funds (wastewater treatment facility building and reconstruction, certain waste management-related investments, etc.).

UTILITY RATE POLICY

In Budapest, the public utility charges (as much as possible) are tied to consumption. In the case of gas, water, sewage, and waste disposal services, the municipality applies a volumetric method for measuring consumption. In public transport, Budapest has a multi-level ticket system. The district heating service gradually introduced metering by block, and the service company is about to make steps towards metering by apartment. In the case of the services where the adoption of a new consumer requires fresh investment, the system treats the connection fee separately from usage fees.

Consequent to the increase in the real value of the prices, utility charges have practically reached cost coverage in all utility services except for public transportation. The share of user charge revenue has increased on average from 70 to 75% among the revenues of the utility companies. Calculating the share of user charge revenues only related to the price and subsidy part of company revenues, the increase already figures between 76 and 85%.

At the beginning of the 1990's, user charge revenues only tripled the amount that the municipality spent on subsidizing the services. Until the end of the period at issue users already paid eight times the amount the municipality contributed to the whole of infrastructure services. The fact that the aggregated user charge revenues of the companies have increased from 80% of the other direct revenues of the municipality, to more than 100% demonstrates the considerable increase of charges and the crucial importance of user charges in municipal finance *(see Appendix, Table 4)*.

Via the introduction of cost covering and two-part tariffs, a transparent financing system has been created for the utility companies. As a result of these changes, the previously supply-driven policies are increasingly becoming market- or demand-driven, where fees can adjust supply and demand. In several areas, the increasing fees have perceptibly rationalized consumption,[45] and have enabled the planners to cut back on the (often exaggerated) investment projections of the earlier development plans. For example, in the field of wastewater management, the development plan for 1993 calculated with a daily demand of 1.5 million cubic meters. By 1999, this figure had decreased to 600,000 cubic meters. More realistic plans and their implementations have resulted in serious savings.

In the field of utility rates, the other key objective besides making them cost-covering has been to replace the practices of discretionary price regulation and annual price bargaining with a system based on regulated and regularly reviewed price calculation formulae. This system creates a predictable environment, facilitates planning and promotes privatization. Of course, the determination of a pricing formula that is capable of reflecting the actual costs or expenditures, of boosting efficiency and at the same time resulting in a "justifiable" price level is a key element in this process. Attempts aimed at fixing these formulae tend to meet resistance from the company and also from those political forces who prefer "direct

---

[45] This decrease of consumption was one of the main factors that explain why the real value of company revenues has not increased during the price increasing period (see Appendix Table 4).

control." The absence of comparative prices and the prevalence of information asymmetry present another obstacle. Via the tenders, privatization eases the tension, and also enforces the codification of the formula. In Budapest, the formulae have been codified in the majority of the non-privatized areas as well. The only major exception is public transport, where the codification of the formula was prevented by the lack of financial coverage.

In Budapest, the public utility companies' rate calculation formulae always include efficiency boosting elements. For the privatized companies, the dividend revenue (or its replacement, the so-called management fee) represents this element. Since these resources are calculable on the basis of the increase in efficiency, the formulae present real incentives for the investor to increase efficiency. For the non-privatized companies, the savings resulting from increased efficiency are split up between the company and the local government. The latter uses the savings to reduce utility fees, and the other part it leaves with the company in order to boost its interest in increasing its own efficiency. Though real value of utility charges has increased in all services during the whole period at issue, during the last years their real value has decreased in some fields due to increase in efficiency of service provision.[46]

The pricing system of Budapest's public utility services always treats developments in a separate bracket. The developments are financed either from municipal subsidies or from the part of the rate revenues flagged for development. In either case, it falls on the local government to consider and decide on major investment projects. Under this system, each investment requires an individual decision, which can thus be adjusted to the prevailing financial situation and also to the city's urban development strategy. Another advantage of this system is that it clearly separates investment resources from operating resources. There is no way for the former to be used for operating purposes.

UTILITY CHARGE ALLOWANCE

Another advantage of the new rate policy is that the increase in the rate (and also in its cost-covering ratio) has clearly eliminated the previous system of general and hidden subsidies.

Simultaneously with the rate hikes, the public utility companies and the capital city have set up a foundation for establishing a targeted utility charge allowance system (the colloquial term is Rate Compensation Fund), whose aim is to compensate the needy. Allowances are based on their family revenues, social needs, and on their willingness to pay the bills. This rate compensation is offset in the given service's utility bills. This practice guarantees that the compensation cannot be used for any other purpose.

In Budapest, companies' contributions mostly fill up the Compensation Fund. Since they want to maintain their consumers' paying discipline and also to retain their customers,

---

[46] The decrease of real value during the last years will be discussed in the papers on 'District Heating' and 'Utility Privatization.'

the companies are interested in contributing to the Fund.[47] The targeted subsidies utilizing approximately 1.5 per cent of the companies' price revenues through the Fund have proven sufficient to maintain the consumers' willingness to pay. Despite the rate hike the efficiency of collection has remained practically unchanged and in certain cases has improved (except for the district heating). For this reason, the local government has every reason to consider it a success.

Table 3
EXPENDITURES ON LOCAL SERVICES AS A PERCENTAGE OF THE HOUSEHOLDS'
OVERALL EXPENDITURES

SERVICES	COUNTRIES		
	OECD	POST-SOCIALIST, PRIOR TO REFORMS	POST-SOCIALIST, AFTER REFORMS
Housing	20-25	3	3-9
Public utilities	3-6	3	5-9
Transportation	10-12	2	7
Local public utility taxes	15-20	3	8
TOTAL	48-63	11	23-30

Source: World Bank, 2001

Notwithstanding the results of the compensation system, public utility fees clearly present an ever increasing burden on households. During the past few years, 20-21 per cent of the total household expenditure of an average Hungarian household went to housing related costs. As the comparison in Table 3 shows, in the post-socialist region the average utility charges, and the expenditures on housing and local public services are still way below those in OECD countries. According to Table 2 above, these expenditures are also below the OECD average in Budapest, although the difference is minimal. And yet these fees are very high if we compare them to the income of those social layers that were detrimentally affected by the political transformation. In several instances, housing-related expenditures exceed 27 per cent of the household's total expenditure.[48]

COMPANY MANAGEMENT

The past decade also witnessed positive changes in the management of public utility service companies. By 1995 all the companies had been corporatized (transformed into

---

[47] The deterioration of the consumers' willingness to pay or the loss of the customer-base would result in increasing per unit costs, which would speed this process up.

[48] Central Office of Statistics, 2002: 18

limited liability companies or share companies). This reorganization also affected the local government's behavior. The previous practice of direct control was replaced by a legally regulated relationship between the company and the owner (deed of foundation and servicing contract). The Ownership Committee of the Municipality of Budapest's General Assembly represents the owner, and the delegates to the company's control board directly represent the interests of the capital city.

Despite the formalized relationship system, the local government could not significantly improve its record as an owner. Ingrained company practices and ossified power structures are extremely difficult to overcome, and the (previously mentioned) conflicting municipal goals and responsibilities hinder the representation of a clear strategic line. The local government's organizational and decision-making structure means that it is practically impossible to make fast and consistent decisions. The decisions in the assembly bodies are usually reached via compromises between lobby groups with fluctuating power positions. This way the enforcement of certain political interests often comes prior to rational company management, while the companies' best interest would be to function amidst politically balanced and predictable conditions.

PRIVATIZATION

Although the study entitled 'Utility Privatization' concentrates on the privatization of large public utility providers, privatization has a wider meaning. Privatization is a process whereby the local government moves from keeping public services within the public sector towards involving the private sector, with the aim to ultimately provide these services via private businesses. In this sense, privatization also includes portfolio cleaning measures and company restructuring, as well as the transfer of part of the service to private hands.

The aim of the public utility service privatization in Budapest was clearly to improve efficiency. But in the case of the activities and companies where the municipality had no service obligation or service responsibilities were not supposed to provide a full coverage of demand, privatization could have other goals (e.g., revenue).

The results of privatization can only be evaluated in light of the goals set out at the start of the process. In Budapest, portfolio cleaning measures and the unbundling of the services were successful because they succeeded in splitting up the functions that could also be contracted on the market. Thus the service retained has become simpler and more transparent. The primary aim of this process was to clear up the structure of the companies, but in addition, the process also reduced the acquisition price of certain auxiliary products and services. In some cases, portfolio cleaning generated sizeable revenues, which could be used to finance further reorganizations. The study on privatization also cites examples of special cases: the key consideration behind the privatization of Budapest Film was a cultural mission, while at Pharmafontana purely financial considerations were overridden by a quest for "political peace."

In Budapest, the largest privatization transactions affected gas, water, and sewage service providers. The ultimate declared goal of the Waterworks' privatization was to improve the service's efficiency. The financial rationality of the private partner, the clear interest profiles resulting from the diminishing ownership role of the municipality and a series of tough regulations based on the clearly separated interests of the parties were all conducive to the realization of this goal.

It is extremely difficult to quantify the results of these efficiency-boosting measures. In the case of the privatization of the Budapest Water Works, the formula for the management fee attempted to calculate the savings as a function of the pre-privatization base figures. As the study on privatization reveals, in its original form (as featured in the privatization contract) this extremely complex formula was riddled with inaccuracies. The formula has likely been more accurate since 2001, when the investors and the local government reached an agreement on corrections. The fact that the currently used formula is acceptable to both sides (even they have conflicting interests), leads us to conclude that it can accurately measure the savings associated with efficiency increase. The other fact – namely that the calculated annual figure of savings has been positive since the completion of the transactions – goes to prove that privatization was successful from the point of view of efficiency increase. There are similar efficiency elements in the formulae applied at the Sewage Works and the District Heating Company, both falling under the pricing authority of the municipality. At the Sewage Works, the calculation of the dividend is tied to the calculated efficiency increase. The mere fact that there is a dividend (especially after the rate correction) allows us to believe that efficiency has indeed increased.

The price formula applied at the District Heating Company also includes an efficiency-boosting element. As long as the company can successfully operate based on user charge revenues calculated by such a formula, we have reason to suppose an increase in its efficiency. Following the introduction of this element, the owner (i.e. the municipality) conducted an analysis of the company's financial experiences. The results showed that the efficiency increase was faster than was originally expected. Accordingly, the municipality has reviewed and increased the efficiency element in the price formula.

In the case of the Gas Works, we cannot conduct a similar evaluation since state gas prices have been kept at an artificial level.

Beyond the conclusions that can be drawn from the user charge formulae there is another consideration worth noting here. The revenues of the companies at issue since privatization have been sufficient to allow major investments and occasionally even dividend payments and this without a drastic rate increase. By 2002, the increase in the sewage and drinking water rates had dropped below the general rate of inflation (as calculated by independent experts). In 2002, the final result calculated based on the price formula for both companies[49] was lower in real value than previously, while growth continued to stay below the inflation rate for 2003. Meanwhile, the Water Works company also managed to eliminate its accounting losses.

Besides the savings resulting from increased efficiency, the transactions have also produced sizeable one-time revenues for the municipality. The chances for this revenue to be very

---

[49] Only that part of the official consumer price is relevant which results from the scheme with regard to the question of whether the privatization of the company has resulted in an increase in efficiency,. The local government, on a case-by-case basis, irrespective of efficiency indices, determines the other part that is earmarked for development.

high were boosted not only by the companies' monopoly position but also by the fact that the transactions occurred at the right moment, i.e., when investors were seriously interested. Furthermore, Budapest had a good reputation on the international capital market, and investors regarded the municipality as a good and rational potential partner in the light of its earlier steps towards operating and financial stability.

In the years of the grand transactions, privatization-related revenues accounted for 15-20 percent of the Municipality of Budapest's total revenues (see Table 4). These revenues represented a significant one-time resource for the municipality to finance its capital expenditures.

Table 4
PRIVATIZATION-RELATED REVENUES
UNDER THE COMPETENCE OF THE MUNICIPALITY OF BUDAPEST (HUF billion)

	1995	1996	1997
Revenues of the Municipality of Budapest's budget	107,50	136,00	194,00
User charge revenues			
Gas	29,82	41,94	54,19
Water	8,87	10,19	12,07
Sewage	7,32	9,19	12,88
Privatization revenues			
Gas Works	13,12	4,58	0,17
Water Works			16,47
Sewage Works			16,91
Gas, water, and sewage-related privatization revenues, total	13,12	4,58	33,55

Source: Annual budgets of the Municipality of Budapest and data supplied by the Municipality of Budapest's departments

And yet, the real success of the privatization process in Budapest is not the revenue it has generated. The one-time revenues were but a secondary consideration in most transactions. The creation of conditions aimed at boosting efficiency enjoyed priority over the drive to maximize one-time revenues. Consequently, in the case of the Water Works and the Sewage Works (where the Municipality of Budapest acted as the pricing authority) the price formulae played a cardinal role. The privatization of the Gas Works was slightly different as there the one-time privatization revenue carried more weight, for two reasons. On the one hand, the municipality's financial problems (liquidity crisis) at the time of this transaction strengthened the need for maximizing revenues, and on the other hand, since pricing in this case fell beyond the competence of the municipality, it was not possible to apply permanent efficiency incentives through the price formula.

Following a strict, self-imposed rule, the municipality only allocates privatization revenues to investment projects. These resources greatly contributed to infrastructure investments and also to the transformations needed towards sustainable financial management. Consequently, these privatization revenues were pre-calculated and cardinal elements of the reforms were carried out in the municipality's financial management and operations.

The privatization process also resulted in the partial separation of the municipality's conflicting roles. Today, the companies have their own directorates and control committees. Although the municipality has retained a say (commensurate with the size of its ownership stake unless specified otherwise in the transaction contracts) in the management of these bodies, the companies' management has become markedly more independent. The municipality, hardly fit for wielding any monitoring and incentive powers, has found determined and efficient partners in the private investors. And yet, the separation of the roles is still far from complete. The Municipality of Budapest continues to be a majority owner, and thus in principle the conflicts (gentler as they are) remain. In practice however, they are considerably lessened.

The resources for the system of utility charge allowance essentially come from the public utility companies (beyond the contribution of the municipality itself). There are two reasons behind this unusual set up, i.e., behind the fact that allowances are not covered from the general funds of the municipality, but from company contributions. The first reason is that the basic social allowance is not the purpose of the fund. Under the relevant laws, it is the individual districts' obligation and not the Municipality of Budapest's obligation to provide welfare allowances to households. The districts meet this requirement to varying extent and the Municipality of Budapest has no obligation in this field, neither does it have the opportunity to play a coordinating role here. The second reason is that it is in the companies' business interest to contribute to this system. Only those consumers who pay their bills (or amortize their debts) receive subsidies, and the subsidies improve (or at least maintain) the willingness to pay and paying discipline. Accordingly, the companies' contribution to the system is based not on welfare considerations but instead on their desire to maintain their markets through liquid demand.

Following the evaluation of the results of the privatization process it is also worth looking at a few details which constituted key dilemmas and issues during the planning and execution of the process, as these may also provide us with important lessons.

One objective of the municipality's 1994 privatization conception was to increase expertise capacity and to import know-how. However, the experiences in Budapest do not seem to justify this goal in two respects. First, we have found that in the field of engineering Hungarian experts are at least at level with their foreign counterparts. There is one major difference though: foreign professionals follow different practices,[50] and are more aware and acceptive of the particular constraints governing their work. For them, cost efficiency is a key consideration underlying all decisions. Second, in general the investors have only dispatched special experts to Budapest on a few occasions, and then mostly to resolve conflicts or handle crises.

---

[50] They have been socialized to accept a different logic.

The dilemma of whether to choose a financial or a professional investor is a related issue. The choice apparently depends on identifying the weaknesses of the municipality. If "only" expertise is missing, then the municipality needs a professional investor. A financial investor would also be sufficient if the enforcement of the owner's interests is considered to be weak, since this investor normally has appropriate professional backing. The only difference between the two is that the financial investor subcontracts professional experts – and his choice in this matter can be mistaken (the same also applies to the municipality). If the subcontracted professional turns out to be unfit for the job, the resulting crisis is bound to be only temporary, since the investor has the right to find new subcontractors. If we identify with the opinion that the municipality is a "weak" owner, we cannot but conclude that it does not make much sense to insist on professional investors. Contrary to all these logical considerations, it is a common practice that, for political reasons, local governments (similarly to the Municipality of Budapest) are not willing to admit their weakness as an owner and are inclined to seek out professional investors in the tender documents. In Budapest it was clear to the financial leaders of the municipality that this requirement did not make any sense. Nevertheless, in an attempt to avoid blocking the privatization process, they settled for a compromise.

The other fundamental question behind the public utility privatization processes is known as the "construction dilemma."[51] The key question in the architecture of the privatization scheme is whether the municipality should sell the companies with or without the associated utility assets. The disadvantage of selling the companies with the assets is that, in this case, monopolies are sold as companies that surely retain their monopoly positions. Later corrections seem almost impossible due to the long-term contracts. It is more flexible to retain the assets and privatize operation. In certain services this opens possibilities to remove the monopoly, and it also becomes easier to cancel the privatization contract. In Budapest, the advisors and the politicians in charge of the privatization process have agreed that it is more advantageous to separate assets from operation. And yet, only the other scheme could generate political consensus, and thus the major transactions all treated the companies as a package together with their assets. The broad opposition of strong political forces to the idea of separating assets from operation later became a major obstacle to the continuation of the privatization process.

As we have seen, the one-time privatization-related revenues constituted a very important resource for the municipality. Nevertheless, critics of the privatization process in Budapest quite often argued against "privatization for money." In their opinion, consumers must eventually shoulder the privatization price. They argue that the cost of privatization revenue is higher than that of an average bank loan, since the investor also covers his expenditures from bank loans but adds his own margin to the related costs.

However, this logic fails in cases where the major goal of the privatization transaction – i.e., increased efficiency – is buttressed by appropriately worded contracts. In these cases the

---

[51] I.e., the dilemma related to the architecture of the privatization model to be applied.

consumer is not obliged to "finance" the difference between the bank loan and the investor's financial calculations. Instead, the consumer is a beneficiary of the company's increased efficiency (in reality, the result should be calculated as the difference between the efficiency increase and the investor's profits). The compulsion to increase efficiency depends not only on the privatization price but also on the other conditions of the tender and the contract (including the price formula).

Another argument in favor of the privatization price is that the sum paid out upon the signing of the contract constitutes a financial risk for the investor, and this clearly increases his incentives for efficient and successful operation.

It is especially difficult to justify the rejection of "privatization for money" in cases where the municipality sells out a profitable monopoly whose pricing policy does not belong to its competence (e.g. Budapest Gas Works).

Another very important lesson to be drawn from the privatization process in Budapest is that during the initial transactions, a local government is bound to be weaker than the other contracting party or parties are (and this will not change unless the municipality learns from its experiences). Necessarily, the municipality has less knowledge regarding privatization than the investor, who most likely has already concluded other such transactions. During the initial phase, the municipality does not have reliable and time-tested models and solutions at its disposal that could serve to quickly and accurately evaluate the effects of its decisions on particular elements of the transaction (e.g., financial analysis model for investments). On the other hand, it does make a difference whether the municipality is large or small, or whether it is able to draw on appropriate intellectual capacities. It is imperative to employ well-prepared and experienced advisors who properly represent the municipality's interests. This expertise cannot be accumulated in the municipal bureaucracy. This is the case not only due to the high market price of this expertise, but because this particular type of expertise requires continuous upgrading, which is achieved through taking part in a number of transactions that simply cannot be attained when working for one single municipality.

The transactions also teach the municipality lessons, making it more and more capable to meet the requirements of subsequent transactions. However, the expertise that the municipality gains in this way requires permanence in management in order to be effectively maintained. Once there is a new set of leaders in charge of the privatization process, as the new leaders tend to employ new advisors, the learning process must start afresh.

The last experience we wish to highlight here deals with contracts. In this field it is very important to make certain that the contract allows for subsequent reviews and corrections. We recall here the logic of process regulation that has been discussed several times before. There is a need to lay down in the initial contract the fundamental goals and principles under which later corrections can be carried out in a regulated manner. In other words, if the initial contract turns out to be imperfect, there should be a possibility to correct it. This system can guarantee that solving problems – on appropriately established goals and principles – may be left to experts.

QUESTIONS OF INFRASTRUCTURE DEVELOPMENT

The last paper of the chapter titled "Infrastructure Development" seeks answers two funda-mental questions. First, it strives to evaluate Budapest's successes in using the financial reform process for creating clear conditions for infrastructure planning and for integrating the financial, political, and professional aspects of the planning process in the infrastructure field. Second, it assesses the diverse types of influences that have affected the infrastructure services. The highlighted areas and cases sufficiently prove that urban policies evolve under diverse influences. Furthermore, it is also clear that while the two key elements of the municipality's urban policy methodology (strategic real planning and process regulation) are present in all areas of the infrastructure services (to varying extents), their meaning and significance differ according to sector. It takes diverse influences to elicit and to enforce them.

In our discussion of the methods of strategic real planning, we emphasized the need for iteration between professional and financial approaches. In the field of infrastructure development, it is likewise very important to iterate between the diverse sectoral and the general urban development conceptions. Ideally, the financial reform process is buttressed by the modern sectoral approaches, and these in turn elicit realistic strategies. From the point of view of development, the clarification of the municipality's resource-base, the introduction of cost-based pricing, and the privatization process itself have together pushed in the same direction and have transformed the content of planning. At the same time, we may also assert that the municipality has also had successes in the areas where it could not elicit competition either on or for the market (e.g., district heating or waste management). We have reason to believe that privatization could also result in further improvements in these specific areas.

* * *

The present paper, as an introduction to all other papers in the chapter, has summed up objectives, strategy, and accomplishments. It has discussed these issues in the general context of urban policy-making, and has evaluated the results to date. The ensuing studies will consider individual processes – i.e., they analyze the complexities of the practice of public policy making among different physical planning sectors in Budapest.

SOURCES AND LITERATURE

Alliance of Free Democrats (SZDSZ), 1990: *'A Szabad Demokraták Budapesti programja.'* *(The Free Democrats' Program for Budapest. Election program.) Budapest*

The Office of the Mayor of Budapest, 1994a: *'Privatizációs koncepció.'* *(Conception on Privatization. Presentation to the General Assembly, July 14, 1994.) Budapest*

Central Office of Statistics, 2002: *'Háztartás-statisztikai közlemények, 2001.'* *(Statistical Findings on Households, 20. 2001. Q1–Q4) Budapest*

Finance Research Co., 1991: *'Összefoglaló a tíz önkormányzati tulajdonban lévő közüzemi vállalat szervezeti és pénzügyi átvilágításáról.'* *(Summary of the Organizational and Financial Due Diligence of Ten Public Utility Companies Owned by the Municipality.) Budapest*

USER CHARGE POLICY FOR PUBLIC UTILITIES[1]

PÁL VALENTINY

An increasing number of people believe that access to high-quality public utilities at reasonable prices is a basic right. This applies equally to market-based public utilities (such as telecommunications, energy and water supply, transport, etc.) and to non-market based services (e.g., compulsory education, social security and other public services of national interest such as jurisdiction, public security or registration).

The past few decades have seen significant changes both in the way public services are delivered and in citizens' expectations. Consumers have become more steadfast in practicing their rights, and are particular about their choices, and the quality and price of the services. Competition has become common among public utilities that are now interested in charging rates that are attractive to consumers. Previously, the private sector was reluctant to participate in the financing of these services. Service providers had therefore to draw primarily on public funds. Today, the private sector is considerably more inclined to consider the financing of public utilities as a lucrative undertaking, while in several countries public funds have more or less dried up. Simultaneously, we have witnessed spectacular technological developments, which even lead to the challenge of earlier monopolistic situations in certain sectors.

Monopolistic service providers evolve under specific legal or economic conditions that make it possible for them to become the exclusive supplier in their specific fields of activity. Out of sheer economic considerations, monopolies are not interested in extending their goods or services to all consumers. Quite often they do so if they are subjected to universal service obligations. However, there is a limit to these obligations, i.e., they cannot disregard related costs. In other words, these obligations are applicable only within "reasonable" limits.

Regulatory reforms that have been launched in more developed countries were rooted in the realization that earlier regulations violated certain fundamental interests. In most cases, these earlier regulations were aimed at maintaining or limiting the cross-financing potentials of the monopolistic state or local government-owned service providers that were obliged to provide universal services. Those regulations failed to force providers to cut their costs and improve the quality of their services. They also proved unfit for ensuring diversity and a quick reaction time to changes in demand or technology.

In most cases the regulatory reforms strove to separate the individual servicing activities organizationally or at least from an accounting point of view. They also aspired to disaggre-

---

[1] The author finalized the manuscript in April 2002. (*The editor*)

gate and balance the rates (i.e., to eliminate cross financing), and to unbundle the services and introduce a pricing system based on marginal costs.

Accordingly, several requirements must be met simultaneously in regulating the prices applied by monopolistic service providers. First of all, prices must be cost oriented, and must spur efficiency both in productivity and in quality improvement. This coincides with consumer interest. Prices must be transparent, i.e., pricing principles must be clear and consistent, and the rates charged to consumers must be easy to comprehend. The regulation of prices must strive to be just in that it must guarantee that services are universal and free from discrimination. Furthermore, price regulation must establish reasonable constraints for service providers, as an adaptive and innovative price regulation is conducive to the approximation of supply and demand.

The above principles should apply whether a state authority or a local government sets the prices. No doubt that the local government acts differently if it has to accept exogenous price regulation instead of being free to set the prices itself. The present paper analyzes the differences between these two approaches. We shall discuss the professional tasks behind price regulation and evaluate correspondence between theoretical requirements and practical achievements. The paper outlines the theoretical and practical consequences of the choice between the various methods of price regulation, and it discusses in detail the problems and theoretical and practical financing solutions associated with the (universal) service obligation. We shall highlight the need to separate the financing requirements associated with universal service obligation from the actual price setting process.

CHARACTERISTICS OF MARKET-BASED PUBLIC UTILITIES

In most cases these services are organized vertically, i.e., they consist of separated but hierarchically and functionally related activities. A service provider qualifies as fully vertical if it entails either the phases of production, delivery, and distribution (such as with gas, electric energy, or water supply), or the phases of collection, transport, and storage/elimination/procession (e.g., waste or sewage disposal). Certain services entail only delivery and distribution activities (e.g., telecommunication or public transport). These systems require large and in most cases exclusive physical infrastructure networks and/or sizeable logistical backing.

Public utilities mostly evolved from local needs. These services were usually provided by the local governments themselves, or by certain private ventures that received concessions from the local authorities. The ownership and organizational structures of these services (i.e., the national or local forms of communal management and operation) differed according to the peculiar administrative setting of the individual countries. Much depended on whether the central authorities were willing to grant independence to the local governments, or considered them executives instead. The latter question had a bearing on the financing system as a whole, i.e., on the division between revenues and expenditures.

In most countries, certain types of services (such as public transport, or more specifically urban transport) require permanent subsidies from the state, as the burden of cost increases can only partially be shifted on to the public.

A series of political, legal, and economic factors determine whether a given public utility is organized centrally or locally. The local governments have significantly more information about the affected communities' expectations and requirements, and can thus react faster and more efficiently to the demands. Due to their identical organizational frameworks and operational environments, the locally organized services tend to cooperate much more closely than the regional units of the national services. Achieving synergy, this is why the various services are often concentrated into a single organizational entity (local government department, independent holding, etc.). Meanwhile, the national networks can exploit their advantage in economies of scale, and market failures remain correctable mostly at the central authorities level only.

The organizations that provide public services usually operate as local, regional, or national monopolies. Initially, their monopoly position was ensured by their exclusive rights to service a given area (which, occasionally, were coupled with certain obligations to serve). The extension of the served area has transformed some activities (transmission, distribution) into natural monopolies.

It follows from their monopoly position that in principle they can detach their charges from their costs, determine the quality of their services independently of the consumers' demands, prevent competitors from entering their markets, and prefer or exclude certain consumer groups. To counterbalance these powers, the central or local authorities make every effort to regulate the activity of these service providers.

In response to the changes in the market and the technologies employed, the principles and practices of regulation have been significantly transformed during the past decade. It has been proven that public services can also be provided reliably and more cheaply in competitive environments. Alongside the traditional methods of cost cutting, a series of new approaches (joint billing, joint procurement, etc.) has been devised to boost the public utilities' efficiency. Coupled with the beneficial effects of the incursion of information technology into the sphere of public utilities, these new methods have resulted in the appearance of multi-utilities.

The regulatory reforms that follow (or elicit) these processes codify a series of new rules for the separation of the network infrastructures from services, the unbundling of services, the interconnection of service providers and access to essential facilities.

TYPES OF PRICE REGULATION

Monopolies may abuse their powers. They do not as a rule do so, but their inclination is rather strong. If the owner is the state or the local government, the motives are mostly political, while other owners might expect that the public utility will satisfy certain particular business interests.

The monopoly public utility has a chance to realize "abnormal" profits, i.e., to take advantage of consumers. The most common way to do this is not through generally increasing prices well above costs but through unjustified (i.e., not cost-based) discrimination between the various consumer groups. Accordingly, one of the goals of price regulation is to protect the consumers.

However, regulation would fail to meet its fundamental purpose (the maximization of social welfare) if it neglected the interests of the investors, because – as we have said above – these investments are embodied in assets that are difficult to convert. In this respect price regulation must guarantee a reasonable return on the capital invested.

As a result of these two approaches, price regulation is expected to seek a price that, by enforcing efficiency, protects the interests both of consumers and investors. In a sense, regulation can be considered as a bargaining process whose end result is a set of conditions which mostly appear in the form of concessions or other types of contracts. Price regulation is perhaps the most important, although not the only, element in a contractual system: the definition of the quality of the service and the prescription of a phase-by-phase control mechanism are at least as important.

Over the years, two distinct approaches have emerged for managing price regulation. Initially, the rate-of-return regulation, which defined the rate of return as a function of the approved costs, was used almost exclusively. The identification of the costs that were allowed was an extremely time-consuming and labor-intensive procedure. Even in its most elaborate form, this process was not able to completely eliminate the intentional exceeding of costs that is called gold plating.

The price-cap method is the alternative to the rate-of-return regulation. In this method, price increases are tied to the rate of inflation, and are modified by the given service's productivity factor. The price-cap regulation usually defines pricing mechanisms for a long-term (4 or 5-year) period and thereby enables the automatic approval of the inflation-based cost increases. At the same time (also automatically) it allows for the sharing of profits resulting from increased productivity between the service provider and the consumers.

The price-cap regulation is remarkably simple and thus labor-saving. Nevertheless, the changes in the market or the technology employed (or, for that matter, the poorly defined price formulae) may produce unexpected and unwelcome situations. To prevent these, the authorities must regularly review the regulatory process (i.e., the price formulae). These reviews might necessitate the completion of detailed cost analyses that are normally associated with the rate-of-return regulation. Here the two methods overlap.

In both price regulatory systems, access prices and usage prices are calculated separately when and if it is economically justified.

Professionalism and an expert staff are required to observe and especially to enforce the principles behind the price regulation of market-based public utilities. In the economies of transition, and also with certain national authorities, these factors are often missing. The situation tends to be even worse with local governments.

There are alternative procedures that may prove especially useful in such situations. The characteristic of these procedures is that they define prices on the basis of information that is mainly collected not from the regulated firms. One common method is to regulate prices on the basis of international comparisons. This may be complemented or, in the case of several domestic service providers, it may even be replaced by conclusions drawn from domestic comparisons (yardstick competition). Based on the information collected, the method for price regulation, or the prices themselves, are often identified on a basis considered as best practice.

SERVICE OBLIGATION, FAIRNESS

We believe that the concept of public utility service entails the right to access these services through reasonable conditions. However, in several countries, among them in the Eastern European transition economies, this requirement was often not applied (to a varying degree for different services). The inhabitants of large cities – among them the population of Budapest – were in a more advantageous position. This phenomenon can in certain respects be connected to the fact that local or national monopolies traditionally resorted to cross-financing between the services that operated in favorable business environments and those that were constrained by more backward conditions in order to sweeten the pill of their service obligation.

CROSS-FINANCING

Besides cross-financing between services with diverse financing needs, the most common form of cross-subsidization has been the unjustified (i.e., not cost-based) discrimination among the various consumer groups. A well-known example of the latter is cross-financing between residential and business consumers. In the Eastern European transition economies, the welfare effects of the suppressed residential user rates have long been questioned. However, partly out of political considerations, the rebalancing between residential and business user charges was a prolonged process that proceeded by fits and starts. Prices are still unrelated to costs, albeit the known models of price regulation for monopolies consider it as a basic requirement to balanced, well-functioning price regulation.

Cross-financing within a monopoly is known to entail several negative effects. It distorts the real cost coverage proportions of individual activities, and thus sends wrong signals to guide service providers' business decisions, risking the efficient operation of the services. In less attractive markets, unbalanced rates fail to prompt service providers to invest and develop. Cross-financing renders the system of internal subsidies obscure and voluntary, replete with hidden subsidies that lack specific targets. The effects of these subsidies are unpredictable. They often get extended to people with high income, which is an unwelcome development from a welfare policy point of view.

Price regulation has never meant the elimination of cross-subsidization. The methods of price regulation employed and the types of regulated services have determined the extent to which cross-financing has survived in any one system.

At the same time, there have always been and always will be loss-making services, that are important to maintain from a social-welfare point of view. These loss-making (i.e., unprofitable) services must be properly identified, and the amount of subsidies needed must be preliminarily assessed.

Once we know the latter figure, it is possible to seek alternative financing sources. It is rather common today (especially in public transport) to invite tenders for subsidies. Here the company that claims the smallest amount has a chance to be granted the servicing license. Another common method is the creation of central funds to subsidize those public utility services that must be maintained out of social-welfare considerations. The organizations that manage these funds may decide to subsidize the service provider or the customer. In the latter case, the subsidies may be given out directly, in the form of vouchers. Depending on the goals (e.g., the spreading of the service), the provider may come up with easy-access rate packages, that may be introduced with the help of subsidies coming from independent financing systems.

UNIVERSAL SERVICES

The types of subsidies outlined above are now identified with the concept of universal services. The documents of the European Union on public utilities emphasize that the requirements of public utilities must be neutral to ownership, and that each EU member state has the right to define the range of public services and to determine if a given service provider is eligible to certain special rights or competitive financing. However, the declaration of obligation must not prescribe how the obligation should be performed. At the same time, the principle still applies that the methods chosen must be commensurate with the goals.

The concept of universal service is normally applied to market-based public services. In short, the universal service obligation means that the services provided by public utilities must be of high quality and easily accessible to all at a reasonable price. For a more detailed definition we should resort to certain well-known principles such as equality (the users of the service must be treated as equals), universality (the service must be accessible to all), continuity (the service must always be accessible), and adaptability (the service must be adaptable to any given environment, under realistic conditions). The enforcement of these principles may be promoted by the transparency of the managing and pricing of the universal services, and also by the presence of an independent organization that oversees their financing and provision.

The concept of universal service is evolutionary and is considered to change over time. It is dependent on changes in the technical and structural characteristics of the given sector, and also on the prevailing social definition of what the concept of universal service should entail. Finally, it is also dependent on changes in consumer demand. The regulations of the European Union enable member states to specify additional obligations above and beyond those laid down in the sectoral directives. Member states are free to define a public service as obligatory, and also have the right to set up a specific financing system to this purpose.

The concept of universal service therefore may be interpreted and implemented differently, as reflected by the relevant directives of the European Union. For example, in telecommunications it was explicitly declared that in EU member states, socially, economically, and/or physically handicapped people must also have access to these services at a reasonable price. EU directives also aim to keep postal services accessible to all. For this reason, and to maintain a uniform pricing policy, the EU is in favor of applying a limited cross-financing approach, adding that the postal services may retain their oft-challenged monopolies in certain weight and price categories. Just as in telecommunications, the new entrants to the postal market (may) take a share in financing the universal service. In the fields of transport (public transport) and electricity supply, EU regulations likewise enable member states to impose public utility service obligations.

With regard to most public utilities (at least where the services are not particularly diversified, such as in water or electricity supply) the concept of universal service applies primarily to the right of access. In most areas, water, gas, and electricity suppliers are obliged to provide services, which means that they do not have the right to deny access to interested consumers. Of course, the principle of "reasonability" may still hold, i.e., the obligation may require the presence of certain conditions. In general, only those consumers can have access to these services who live within a certain distance from the distribution pipes or cables. Others have to pay for the access pipes or cables themselves.

Besides issues of access, the principle of universal service also entails regulations pertaining to exclusion from the service. Although the conditions under which consumers can be disconnected from the service were specified previously, those regulations were rather strict, and reflected primarily the interests of the monopoly service providers. However, due to the reduction or even the disappearance of the monopolies and the simultaneous spread of the concept of universal service, the situation had changed considerably by the early 1990s. Out of business considerations, and also pressured by the regulatory agencies, the service providers were obliged to devise more refined methods that could address the relevant social and other issues in a gradual manner.

The universal service obligation (whether legally prescribed or contractual) places extra burdens on the service provider. However, the provider can also benefit from this obligation. Most of these benefits are not financial: the company can promote its brand and gain recognition and respect among consumers, employees, shareholders, or regulators. From a marketing point of view, it is another advantage that potential consumers are aware of the fact that they can access the given service anywhere within the company's geographical area of activity. Another advantage is that the company can enjoy exposure in public places. The service provider may also undertake this activity in the hope that the initially unprofitable venture will later turn profitable. These advantages can be quantified, albeit not easily.

It is likewise difficult to express the extra burdens in figures. According to a simplified calculation method, the costs of the service without the obligation are deducted from the net costs (i.e., minus the benefits) of the service with obligation. Once the costs are known, it is worth considering the available methods of financing. The economically most favorable method would be to finance the extra burdens of the universal service through taxes. After all, in this case the social costs accrued are independent of the servicing company. However, this method is only rarely used. Setting up support funds, issuing vouchers, or inviting tenders for subsidies are more frequently used methods.

BASIC PRINCIPLES OF PRICE REGULATION IN PUBLIC UTILITIES

- There is a need to specify who the stakeholders are in the price regulation process, as well as whose authority is affected by the process.
- The regulations must prescribe schemes for calculating, rather than identifying prices.
- To improve the efficiency of the regulations, the consumers must be made familiar with the reasons behind, and the essence of, the changes. Irrespective of the range of justified costs approved by the regulator, it is crucial to make public the full cost structure of any given service, in order to determine the subsidies needed.
- The characteristics and efficiency of the rate collection systems (simplicity, deadlines, minimal collection fees, non-payment procedures, etc.) are also crucial for the credibility of the price regulations.
- To evaluate the price regulation of public utilities, one must take into consideration the quality parameters of the given services. For this reason, the regulation process must entail the regular evaluation of these parameters.
- In all those areas (their number is increasing) where it is already possible to create competition, the authorities must make sure that service providers with monopoly power in certain areas cannot cross-finance their activities in a competitive environment.
- If rates are based on full costs, large numbers of consumers might find it disproportionately difficult to use the services. Subsidies are offered in such cases. However, the authorities must check and verify the customers' eligibility to benefit of these subsidies in a transparent and controllable way. The amount from subsidies must be clearly specified if rates are not equivalent to full costs.

PRICE REGULATION AT THE MUNICIPALITY OF BUDAPEST

Prior to the 1990s, regulations in the transition economies of Eastern Europe were implemented through property rights, which in practice meant direct command. This process entailed imposing public service obligations, financing the investments needed for performing the service, and defining the service's quality parameters and rates. These were rather conflicting goals, and the priorities among them were usually set according to the prevailing government's preferences. The results are known: monopolies were fairly inefficient and insensitive of costs; the development and reconstruction projects were often scrapped; shortage was a fact of everyday life; and consumers were at the mercy of the service providers.

The changes of the early 1990s in Hungary proved that, in most areas, public utilities continued to increase their independence – a process that began in the 1980s - and tended to strengthen their monopoly position. During the early 1990s, huge organizations and trusts were dismantled, enterprises were transformed into joint stock or limited companies, property rights were clearly defined, the privatization process was launched, and the authorities of the regulatory agencies were further defined (on state and local level as well). However, these developments were not enough to weaken the position of the monopolies. The absence of politically independent regulatory structures meant that the service providers themselves were to assume very influential roles in creating the regulatory environment. The governments' behavior can be explained by certain – primarily privatization-related – considerations. However, as a result we now have to face drawbacks resulting from the monopolies' market power advantage.

The past few decades have witnessed the emergence of non-cost-based rate systems practiced by virtually all public service providers. These rates disorient consumers and decision-makers alike. As a first step towards re-regulating these rates, most providers introduce rate increases and restructure their user charges. The thrust of this process differs according to specific services.

The emergence of cost-based prices does not as a rule have to entail astronomical rate increases. With several public utilities the conditions are ripe for competition (or there is competition already). The vertical disintegration of the large monopolies in these areas, and also the concession-based operation of certain activities, will create the conditions for competition, which in turn will lead to lower prices and better service quality. Meanwhile, in those areas where market competition is less prevalent, the public utility must be controlled by efficient price regulations based on a thorough examination of the actual costs.

In the early 1990s, the situation outlined above applied to the public utilities owned by the Municipality of Budapest. The charges did not cover the costs, and thus revenues were not enough to finance required developments. Meanwhile, consumers were not encouraged to use resources economically. In effect the ministries exercised the rights of a pricing authority. In most cases they subsidized the service providers' prices in order to cover their (operational) costs. Quite often the service providers' economic performance was further burdened by a series of other unrelated activities that they pursued alongside their core activity (production, shipping, assembly, construction, repair, design, loaning, retail, sports financing etc.).

The first three years of the 1990s witnessed radical changes in the service providers' activity, and also in the broader economic environment. The service providers that had earlier functioned as enterprises owned by the local government were transformed into joint stock or limited companies. This transformation enabled the local governments to clean the service providers' business portfolio and remove most of the activities that were not part of their core function. The elimination of open price subsidies (primarily concerning water, sewage and district heating services) changed the conditions of pricing as well. The bulk of the price regulation was transferred to local governments. During the partial privatization of public utilities a series of investors became shareowners (alongside local governments) who were (or were forced to become) interested in cutting costs.

With the exception of electricity and gas prices, the Municipality of Budapest sets the rates of public utilities for the capital. Public transport rates require the consent of the government.

Fully aware of the conflicts of interest resulting from its dual role as owner and regulator, the Municipality of Budapest holds a majority stake in these public utility service companies (the only exception is the electricity supply, which was transformed from a majority state-owned venture into a majority foreign-owned company, with the Municipality of Budapest holding a minority – 10 percent – stake). Today, rates are generally high enough to cover not only operational costs but also those of certain minor developments and investments. Public transport remains the only subsidy-intensive field. The current system of price regulation may be associated with the privatization process and the entry of foreign investors onto the scene. This necessitated the transformation of the earlier, rather voluntary system into today's more predictable and strategically applicable price regulation.

To see the motives behind these changes, it is instructive to go through the moves that characterized and shaped the price regulation system within the energy sector both on the central and on the local government level.

GOVERNMENT LEVEL

In 1989, the district heating and electric energy rates charged to households amounted to a mere one third of the justifiable costs. Following a series of electricity price increases this proportion still stood at two thirds in 1992. To finance its huge international debts, the government concluded agreements with the World Bank and the International Monetary Fund in the early 1990s. In these agreements the government obliged itself to eliminate direct subsidies for energy prices, and undertook to raise prices to economically justified levels of costs. The government also pledged to modify the rate structure in order to eliminate cross-financing between business consumers and households. The deadline for accomplishing all this was the summer of 1995.

In the energy sector, the aborted privatization attempts of the early 1990s as well as potential foreign investors convinced the government that nobody would invest in Hungary's energy industry in the absence of a reliable system of institutions and regulations. The Act on Gas and Electric Energy and the establishment of the Hungarian Energy Office (1994) were important stages in this process. The relevant laws prescribed the principles of pricing as well. Most of these were on par with the previously mentioned international standards: the regulated prices had to cover the costs of efficient operation, of justified investments (which included investments into environmental protection and supply security), and also lead to reasonable profits, based on the least-cost principle. While it is against the law to discriminate between consumers, the laws do not explicitly prohibit cross-financing between business branches. However, the activities must be accounted for separately. The principles of price enforcement originate with the Office, but the minister is the ultimate decision-maker.

It was rather difficult to translate these principles into practice. The privatization process greatly facilitated work on creating the regulatory frameworks. Work began in 1995 in the energy industry when large stakes of the industry were sold.

The process of price regulation entailed two consecutive phases. First, the so-called starting price was determined. To this end, costs were reviewed. The deadline was January 1, 1997. In the second phase, price formulae were determined for the next four years. The new system can best be described as a mixture of the rate-of-return and price-cap regulations. It was rational to consider the starting price as a peg on which all subsequent price changes were to be hung. In accordance with international practice, the principle of cost-pass-through was incorporated into the price formulae. However, correctional factors due to changes in productivity played a smaller part. The four-year price structure was anything but a simple and predictable method of price regulation. In fact, it was rather complicated and gave rise to a series of interpretive arguments.

The prolonged debates over price increases, and the successive governments' reluctance (often unfounded and politically untested) to introduce radical price increases, resulted in the degradation of what was meant to be a long-term, transparent, and non-discriminative price regulation system to the level of the previously applied annual price bargains. The planned level of the starting prices was expected to be reached sometime between September 1995 and October 1996. However, the government decided against implementing the last phase of the price increases, and appointed instead a government commissioner and thus laid the table for a series of quarterly bargaining sessions with investors. The starting prices that went into effect on January 1, 1997, turned out to be unacceptable for most of the service providers. In fact, they prompted a series of legal disputes, many of which lasted for years and ended up in court. It was only in early 1999 that all the energy industry companies gave their consent to the starting prices, acknowledging them as covering justified costs and being sufficient to lead to appropriate profit margins. Meanwhile, the price regulator reverted to the practice of defining prices on an annual basis.

Alongside the general price increases, most of the 1990s were characterized by efforts to balance the price-cost ratio with the interests of various consumer groups. As a result, the energy rates charged to households increased faster than those charged to businesses, notwithstanding that in 2000 rates were still lagging behind required levels. At that point, the trend changed and the government began to increase business rates faster. After 1999, the regulation of the energy prices took another turn. From then on, rates were adjusted to the ex ante inflationary expectations. The history of energy price regulation – at least in Hungary – proves that even a theoretically flawless regulatory system is unable to filter out political influences, and that the relative complexity of the price formulae applied serves only as a playground to the bargaining processes.

MUNICIPAL LEVEL

The developments on the national level in the field of price regulation of public utilities have affected the Municipality of Budapest in several respects. One of them is that a number of companies (e.g., the majority local government-owned gas provider, or the majority private-owned electricity supplier) operate under direct government regulation, or are affected by the prices of these companies (e.g., district heating). Another important factor is that the possible scenarios for price regulation in the domestic market have evolved from national debates. An example of this was the way district heating rates were established. In its present form, this system rests on a rate-of-return price regulation, and is reviewed annually by the local government, which is a political body, but which here acts as the price authority.

The Municipality of Budapest has made a series of often pioneering attempts to introduce automatic procedures in price regulation. One motive behind this was to reduce the role of non-professional considerations and debates. Another was the privatization process and the pressure and expectations of potential investors in public utilities. These companies wanted to operate under predictable regulations. Since the mid-1990s, the price regulation has been determined by the price formulae that were established according to agreements with the public utilities. The formulae that were devised partly with the involvement of outside experts were already employed in 1996-1997 at the majority of the public utilities that operated under the Municipality of Budapest. These formulae have been in use at the Municipal Sewerage Works Co. (FCSM), the Waterworks of Budapest Co. (Vízművek), and the Budapest District Heating Co. (Főtáv) since 1997, and at the City Public Space Maintenance Co. (FKF) since 1996.

The structure of the price formulae differ from company to company, but all are characterized by the rate-of-return approach, under which the rates charged to consumers are determined on the basis of the changes of categorized costs. This method is different from the price-cap calculations where the consumer rates are tied to inflation and to the improvement in efficiency. They are, however, maximized.

Expert analyses show that the price formulae and the whole mechanism of price determination guarantee local government control on prices as well as the viability of the service companies. The local government is also able to enforce welfare considerations, and the process of price regulation has become more transparent and predictable. Adopting the instrument of price formulae has contributed to the establishment of a more precise framework for the annual process of price determination. The system of price regulation made the conditions for employing the price formulae disputable in details and regulated the process of systematic revisions. Naturally, the maintenance of the price regulation system and the regular reviewing of the costs required the contribution of independent experts, and created extra burdens too.

The initial agreements between the Municipality of Budapest and the service companies have practically had to be modified gradually since their signing. These modifications were initiated either by the local government or by the companies themselves. The 1997 agreement with FCSM was modified in 2001, and the syndicate and management contract that was concluded with the investors at the Vízművek in 1997 was amended by an agreement in 2000. Since 1997, Főtáv has made repeated attempts each year to modify its cooperation agreement, which finally it managed to do in 2000. Later, in 2001, a new cooperation agreement was signed. At FKF, a few principles of price calculation were modified in 1999.

The introduction of the price formulae – which was considered an innovation at the time – was preceded by long coordination sessions and debates. It goes without saying that the formulae were far from perfect, and their application highlighted a series of problems and shortcomings. The formulae were then fine-tuned through a series of corrections. At Főtáv, for example, five different types of price indices were already used in 2001 instead of one general index as in 1997. However, there were a number of other problems as well. The companies were very good at identifying new interests and considerations, and the corrections also had to keep track of the changes in the economic environment. In general, we can state that the new formulae and elements that were reconsidered in the process have enabled service providers to practically cover their operational costs from the rate revenues.

At the same time, practically all these public utilities are struggling to address the issues of development and expansion, and some even to maintain the recent level of services. These are the most difficult considerations drafters have to face when compiling and evaluating the price formulae. After all, it is extremely difficult to give estimates for the required reconstruction, intra-company efficiency reserves, and strategically important developments.

In this respect, the results concluded in the agreements between investors and the Municipality with the two partially privatized companies (FCSM and Vízművek) are more reassuring than in the case of the other two companies (Főtáv, FKF) that are fully owned by the local government. In the latter case we are witnessing a clear conflict between the Municipality of Budapest's short-and long-term interests. The problem of this dual commitment can be summarized as follows: the local government aims to become the owner of companies with good business prospects, while at the same time it wants to raise the public utilities' rates by the minimum required amount. The latter goal is rooted in political as well as welfare considerations. This approach often overrode the other approach that aims to heed the strategic development goals of the public utilities. In the case of FKF, the local government regularly approved the smallest of the submitted price increase proposals, while with Főtáv the charges that got approved were lower than those set on the basis of the price formulae.

Another recurrent problem was how to improve the efficiency of the companies. Some of the price formulae include elements that account for efficiency. At those companies that were not fully owned by the local government the dividend structure (e.g., FCSM) or the so-called management contract (e.g., the Vízművek) guaranteed the investors' interest in permanent cost cuts. These clearly promoted efficiency. However, at companies where the financial benefit of the improved efficiency has to be used for minimizing rate increases (e.g., at Főtáv), the incentive to improve efficiency remains negligibly small. Improving efficiency can be slowed down also in the case where companies feel there is a chance to solve their economic problems through annual price bargaining and price formula modifications.

The Municipality of Budapest's efforts toward modernizing price regulations for public utilities and introducing automatism in this field can be described as following domestic trends and often even pioneering. Due in part to changes in the relevant legal regulations (such as the Act on the Obligatory Use of Certain Public Utilities – 1995, the Act on District Heating – 1998, or the Act on Waste Management – 2000), the number of those factors that had to be decided on during the annual pricing procedure has increased significantly. This in turn has increased the chances for differing interpretations, as the service provider and the local government often held different views on the effects of the changes that occurred during a given period.

As we have already seen, the steadfast observation and enforcement of the principles of price regulation requires the presence of well-trained and experienced professionals. Due to the complexity of the pricing formulae, the local government quite often has to involve external experts in its decision-making processes. Contrary to the situation that had previously prevailed, the laws that were passed in recent years specified (though to varying extent) the principles that the local governments were supposed to heed while shaping their price regulations. This has not yet happened in the areas of water and sewage services. However, irrespective of the presence or absence of regulations in the different branches, it would definitely be expedient to evaluate and collect the gauges and standards that reflect the relevant practices of the local governments in a comparative manner, as these could offer valuable guidance on the best practices available.

PRICE REGULATION AND SUBSIDY SYSTEMS

The partial adoption of prices that cover the full costs of a given service coincided with the elimination of the previous system of open price subsidies. By 1999 the energy providers (gas, electricity) had reached a stage where their costs were fully covered by the prices. Meanwhile, the balancing of the rates had gradually reduced cross-subsidies between various consumer groups.

In 1997 and 1998 the state government made successful attempts to collect subsidies from the privatized companies for compensating the population groups that were most adversely affected by rate increases. However, the distribution of the funds was riddled with problems. The local governments found it difficult to cope with the related administrative tasks, while the companies had trouble accepting the fact that their contributions were used outside their specific service areas. This experiment proved to be short-lived, and after 1999 the government indirectly provided subsidies to the public through energy rate increases below the inflation rate.

Curbing rate increases became an accepted practice of the Municipality of Budapest in its role as price authority. Under an agreement concluded in 2000, the rates charged for water services were reduced below the inflation rate. In the period between 1997 and 2000, the real value of rates only increased in the field of sewage services (1.19), while they remained practically unchanged in waste disposal services (1.01), and decreased in district heating (0.88). However, even the increase in sewage rates did not exceed the increase in the public's average income.[2]

In spite of all these restraints, the rate increases placed a heavy burden on a significant part of society. The Municipality of Budapest, through its rate compensation scheme, has always tried to directly subsidize adversely affected consumers. The recipients of social allowances automatically qualified for such compensation, the others got access depending on their income level – but in both cases compensation is strictly tied to the consumer's willingness to pay the rates.

Funding for this compensation – which is officially called the Housing Utility Subsidy – comes partly from public utilities (that are expected to make contributions), and partly from the Municipality of Budapest's budget. The public utilities account for these "contributions" as costs, or write them off against their profits (e.g., Főtáv). All in all, the companies' contributions had increased to over HUF 1 billion by 1998.

Table 1
SOURCES OF RATE COMPENSATION IN BUDAPEST 1995–2001 (HUF million)

CONTRIBUTORS	1995	1996	1997	1998	1999	2000	2001
Companies total	500	700	925	1055	1115	1207	1244
Főtáv	250	300	400	450	450	490	490
Vízművek	125	150	200	230	260	287	296
FCSM	125	150	200	230	260	260	283
FKF		100	125	145	145	170	185
Budapest Municipal Gov.				525	150	150	150

Sources: Documents of the General Assembly of the Municipality of Budapest, December 14, 2000, http://www.budapest.hu/2000/kozgy; Minutes of the General Assembly of the Municipality of Budapest's November 29, 2001, meeting.

Besides its regular monthly compensation scheme, the Municipality of Budapest also offers an additional annual compensation for the winter season. We must also make mention of the gas supplier's independent rate compensation fund. The independent rate compensation fund provides an example of a method that can address a series of welfare and other problems in a gradual manner on issues pertinent to the sensitive area between subsidies tied to willingness to pay and exclusion from services. Preliminary estimates indicated that in 2001, the capital city's compensation scheme was extended to 22,000 households in the field of district heating, 42,000 households in water services, 36,000 households in sewage services, and 42,000 households in waste disposal services.

---

[2] ÖKO, 2001

SOURCES AND LITERATURE

Cave, M. – Valentiny, P., 1994: *'Privatization and Regulation of Utilities in Economies in Transition', in Saul Estrin ed.: Privatization in Central & Eastern Europe. Longman, London, 1994.*

Central Office of Statistics, 1999: *'A kommunális ellátás fontosabb adatai – public utilities 1998.' (Prime Figures of Communal Services – Public Utilities 1998.) Budapest*

Decamp, A., 2000: *'The Financial Resources of Local Authorities'. Study prepared as part of the 4th General Report on Political Monitoring of the Implementation of the European Charter of Local Self-Government. Draft Memorandum, Volume I, March 2000, CPL/GT/ CEAL(6)18.*

Dunleavy, Patrick – O'Leary, Brendan, 1987: *Theories of the State: The Politics of Liberal Democracy. Houndmills: Macmillan.*

Enyedi, Gy., 1984: *Az urbanizációs ciklus és a magyar településhálózat átalakulása. (Urbanization Cycle and the Evolvement of the Hungarian Settlement Network.) Akadémiai Kiadó, Budapest.*

Eurostat, 1996: *Európa számokban. (Europe in Numbers.) Budapest*

Finance Research Co., 1991: *'Összefoglaló a tíz önkormányzati tulajdonban lévő közüzemi vállalat szervezeti és pénzügyi átvilágításáról.' (Summary of the Organizational and Financial Due Diligence of Ten Public Utility Companies Owned by the Municipality.) Budapest*

Hermann, Z., – Horváth, M.T., – Péteri, G., – Ungvári, G., 1999: *'Allocation of Local Government Functions: Criteria and Conditions – Analysis and Policy Proposals for Hungary.' Washington, DC: The Fiscal Decentralization Initiative for Central and Eastern Europe.*

IEA/OECD, 2000: *Energy Policies of Hungary – 1999 Review. Paris*

League of the Hungarian Professional District Heating Providers, 2000: *'Magyar Távhő Évkönyv 2000.' (Hungarian District Heating Yearbook 2000.) Budapes*

Ministry of Traffic, Transportation and Water Management, 1999: *'A közlekedés, hírközlés és a vízügy EU-csatlakozással összefüggő középtávú gazdaságstratégiai célkitűzései.' (Medium-term Strategic Goals of Traffic and Transportation, Telecommunication and Water Management in relation to EU-accession.) Budapest*

ÖKO, 2001: *'Az 1997-2000. évi csatorna-, távhő és hulladékkezelési közszolgáltatási díjmegállapítások értékelése.' (Evaluation of the Pricing System of the Public Utility Services in the Fields of Solid Waste and Waste Water Collection and District Heating in the years 1997-2000.) Budapest*

Pallai, Katalin, 1998a: *Közüzemi privatizáció Budapesten. (Public Utility Privatization in Budapest.) The Office of the Mayor of Budapest, Budapest.*

The Office of the Mayor of Budapest, 1998d: *'Legal and Financial Information.' Yearbook. Budapest*

The Office of the Mayor of Budapest, 2003: *'A Fővárosi Önkormányzat gazdálkodása az elmúlt 10 évben.' (The Economic Management of the Municipality of Budapest in the past 10 years.) Review on the homepage of the Municipality, http://www.fph.hu*

Valentiny, P., 2000a: *'Property Rights, Corporate Governance and Company Restructuring in Hungarian Energy Industries'. mimeo, January 2000, p. 25.*

Valentiny, P., 2000b: *'Az univerzális szolgáltatás és a közszolgáltatások értelmezéséről az Európai Unióban.' The Interpretation of Universal Services and Public Services in the European Union. Közgazdasági Szemle, April, 2000, pp. 341-360.*

Valentiny. P. 2000c: *'Economic Regulation of Public Utilities in Hungary'. mimeo, October 2000, p. 28.*

PUBLIC UTILITY ALLOWANCES IN BUDAPEST

Péter Győri

BACKGROUND

In Hungary, the transition to free market economy in the early 1990's entailed a series of fundamental changes which presented major challenges to the local governments. With regard to the subject of the present paper, these challenges included:

- an unusually high, two-digit annual inflation rate, which persisted for nearly a decade;

- the elimination of the system of central price subsidies, which also affected the maintenance costs of housing and the partial decentralization of the central pricing system to the level of the local governments;

- the privatization of the public utility companies and the inclusion of amortization in the cost and price calculation mechanisms;

- the accelerated decrease of the population's real income in the first half of the 1990's, coupled with a dramatic growth of unemployment, an accelerated rate of impoverishment and more marked inequalities in the population's incomes.

In the 1990's, energy price increases, public utility rate hikes and the ever higher costs of housing maintenance regularly went beyond the already high rate of inflation.

Food and housing maintenance represented the bulk of the Hungarian households' total expenditure. In 1989, households spent an average 32 percent of their total budget on food and 10 percent on housing maintenance. By the first half of the 1990's, the former figure had increased to an average 40 percent (1997) and the latter had almost doubled to 18 percent. In the lowest fifth of the income scale, the latter figure reached 20 percent, and it exceeded 40 percent among those who received social allowances.[1] By way of comparison, the costs of housing maintenance represented an average 22.7 percent of the population's total consumption spending in the 12 EU member states in 1988. The respective figures were 24.3 percent in Belgium, 29.2 percent in France, 20.6 percent in Germany, 24.1 percent in the United Kingdom, 20.2 percent in Greece, and 14.2 percent in Portugal.[2]

---

[1] Central Office of Statistics, 1998, p. 103

[2] Eurostat, 1996, p. 219

Table 1
PRICE INDEX CHANGES OF SOME BASIC HOUSEHOLD ITEMS (1990–1999)

YEAR	FOODSTUFFS	HOUSEHOLD ENERGY, HEATING	RATE OF INFLATION (1990=100)
1991	121,9	181,0	135,0
1992	145,6	259,2	166,1
1993	188,1	311,8	203,4
1994	232,1	348,3	241,6
1995	304,3	522,5	309,7
1996	356,9	692,3	382,8
1997	419,4	899,3	452,9
1998	479,8	1060,3	517,7
1999	493,7	1160,0	569,5

Source: Welfare Statistical Yearbook, KSH, Budapest, 2000

It was inevitable to continuously increase local public utility rates in Budapest (as we have discussed in the introductory part of the present chapter). However, this trend was pregnant with grave consequences, as it:

- elicited a drastic increase in the number of the households that could not cover the increased costs of housing maintenance;

- increased the number of households where indebtedness got out of control;

- reduced the households' willingness to pay simultaneously with their declining solvency, and the tendency involved more households than the ones who really could not afford paying. This occasionally manifested itself in latent or explicit acts of "civil disobedience."

As a result of all these developments:

- Certain social strata have lost their housing security to the extent that large numbers of people had to face losing their homes.

- The fast and cumulative increase in the costs of housing maintenance has drastically reduced the market value of the affected apartments (primarily those in housing estates that were inherited from the era of "state socialism"). This in turn has accelerated segregation, promoted the emergence of slums and produced a series of difficult-to-manage problems in the fields of urban policy and ecology.

- The public utility companies which could not (or were not supposed to) penalize non-payers by switching off their services (e.g., water, sewage, waste disposal, or district heating services – precisely the ones where the rates are set by the Municipality of Budapest) have had to reckon with a drastic increase in their receivables.

- All these induced further rate hikes and thus boosted insolvency threatening the public utility service providers' liquidity. The process may culminate in the imposition of partial restrictions on services, radical drops in the servicing standards, or even in service providers' bankruptcy.

Up to the present day, it is the central government that fixes the price of electric energy and natural gas. However, since the early 1990's, local governments have set the rates for district heating, water supply, sewage, and waste disposal services. These function as owners of the servicing companies (or as part-owners, in the case of the privatized companies).

It was for this reason that in 1994 – when the Municipality of Budapest, in its dual capacity as owner and pricing authority, had to confront the above-mentioned threats for the first time – the leaders of the capital city decided to accelerate the drafting of a system for subsidizing the population's housing utility payments.[3] Although the servicing companies' return from sales continued to increase (along with the consumer price index), the ratio of the arrears was also growing rather dynamically (6 percent in 1992, 10-12 percent in 1993, 14-19 percent in 1994). For example, arrears at the District Heating Company almost doubled between 1991 and 1993 (from HUF 460 million to HUF 915 million), foreshadowing the threats outlined above.

Table 2
RETURNS FROM SALES AND RECEIVABLES*

ITEMS		1993 FACT	1994 PROJECTION	1995 PLAN
District heating	Return from sales (HUF bn)	9,5	10,5	15,6
	Arrears (HUF mn)	915	1416	2817
	Arrears/return from sales (percent)	9,6	13,5	18,1
Water supply	Return from sales (HUF bn)	5,1	5,8	8,5
	Arrears (HUF mn)	600	907	1500
	Arrears/return from sales (percent)	11,8	15,6	17,6
Sewage	Return from sales (HUF bn)	3,9	4,3	7,2
	Arrears (HUF mn)	422	814	1316
	Arrears/return from sales (percent)	10,8	18,9	18,3

*The service providers' calculations, 1994

A prudent assessment of these immediate short- or medium-term risks prompted the city's leaders to attempt to devise a new method for solving these problems. The result of these efforts has become known as the system for Housing-related Cost Allowances in Budapest (Hungarian abbreviation: BLT). The name suggests a wider scope for the system than it actually has: this system exclusively includes utility charge allowances, the other types of support come from the district governments.

---

[3] Since these trends were already manifest in the preceding period, attempts had been made to introduce a so-called Municipal Uniform Supplemental Housing Maintenance Allowance. However, back in 1991, the Municipality of Budapest did not have sufficient scope of authority to manage such a program.

INTRODUCING THE BLT

Under the so-called Welfare Law of 1994, the local governments of the 23 completely independent Budapest districts are entitled to grant housing maintenance allowances to the needy. Hungary's welfare system is markedly decentralized: some districts have resorted to this tool, while others have not. The conditions were rather diverse (often verging on the incidental), and allowances were on average exceptionally low.[4]

Meanwhile, the Municipality of Budapest is not authorized to grant financial aid to households, even though this inability to pay raises the specter of the above-mentioned threats. At the same time, the affected servicing companies have been financially interested in maintaining the consumers' solvency, or at least in preventing a dramatic increase in arrears.

Based on these considerations, the Municipality of Budapest has set up a Foundation – its colloquial name is Compensation Fund. Its board of directors consists of delegates of the servicing companies, representatives from the city's General Assembly and members of certain civil organizations. Under its statutes, the servicing companies (i.e., the water supply, sewage, waste disposal, and district heating companies) transfer 1-2 percent of their sales returns to the Foundation (this contribution equals nearly 10 percent of the arrears). The companies are granted special tax exemptions based on these public utility transfers.

At first sight it may appear that the servicing companies' direct financial involvement in the BLT's funding runs counter to the liberal city leadership's basic principle according to which it is not expedient to confuse issues of economic efficiency with those of welfare security. This principle also calls for the separation of the systems that serve these goals. However, in this specific case there is a clear interdependence between the relevant economic and welfare issues.

In its capacity as a pricing authority, the Municipality of Budapest establishes cost-covering utility rates (the methods applied are described elsewhere in this volume) and it expects the city's public utility companies to finance their own operations. It is the public utility companies' basic business interest to keep arrears at a level that does not jeopardize their daily operations or the provision of their long-term services. These companies regard their contribution to the Foundation as a business technique aimed at reducing their losses and also as a guarantee for the smooth continuation of their services (as we will see, these contributions are directly linked to the companies' attempts to preserve their consumers' willingness to pay).[5]

---

[4] In 1999, Budapest's 23 local governments spent a total of HUF 872 million on local housing maintenance subsidies (the respective figures were lower in the preceding and the following years). A total of 31,000 households were involved in the program and the average subsidy per household was HUF 28,500.

[5] Let us take a simple example. An average apartment with district heating has an annual heating bill of HUF 100,000. If this exceeds the given household's solvency, the servicing company will likely not be able to collect this sum. If there are 20,000 such households, the servicing company's outstanding debt reaches HUF 2 billion. However, once these households receive HUF 20,000 each in subsidies through the BLT (the sum total would be HUF 400 million), even the families in the lower income brackets would be able to pay the rest of their bills, which would mean that the servicing company could then collect an additional HUF 1.6 billion.

A further economic argument behind the BLT's introduction was that external (explicit or implicit) subsidies may "soften" the management of the public utility companies with regard to economic efficiency and cut back their efforts toward increasing cost efficiency and reducing arrears.

The decree of the General Assembly regulates the BLT's target group, associated conditions and the amount of the allowance per household. Each year the Municipality of Budapest publishes (through various PR channels) the terms of eligibility for the allowances and also the amounts granted. The application forms are issued by – and can be submitted to – the local (district) mayor's offices. The forms are collected and checked by the Foundation's staff who then forward them to the servicing companies' billing departments. Each bill lists the amount to be paid based on actual consumption, the amount of the allowance and the difference between these two figures, which is to be paid by the consumer. Once the consumer pays his/her part, the Foundation transfers the other part, the individual amount of the allowance. Of course, technical solutions simplify the process which in practice entails only minimal bureaucratic burdens. Only those who have already paid their share of the bill can access the allowances. This way the companies can also make certain that their contributions are credited to the account of the servicing company in question.

Since the continuously increasing prices endanger the solvency of the households that fall into the lowest income brackets in the first place (as indicated by the statistics as well as by the empirical sociological surveys), these households became the target group for eligibility. Of course, the amount of available allowances also determines eligibility. Consequently, we decided to grant district heating allowances to households in the lowest tenth of the income scale (maximum 25,000 households) and water, sewage, and waste disposal allowances to 50 percent of the households in the lowest tenth of the income scale (40,000 households). We established the eligibility criteria accordingly. Meanwhile, we made every effort to keep the application, verification and control processes as simple and complaint-free as possible. Citizens in the upper margin of the lowest income tenth are eligible for district heating allowances (the limit value is adjusted to the calculated error of statistical estimations and income declarations). In the case of the other allowances, the circle of eligible citizens includes the recipients of regular – centrally regulated – allowances from the local (district) governments, as well as those who do not receive such aid for one reason or another, but whose income level is rather low. It tells a lot about the operability of this system that only one or two complaints have been filed each year regarding the allocation of allowances.

The per unit amounts of the allowance must not be too low (because then it fails to achieve its purpose), but at the same time it cannot exceed the average amount of the rate hike per household. Consequently, the allowances tend to cover around 15-20 percent of the utility bills per household.

The BLT is a uniform, normative, so-called open-ended allowance. This means that all citizens who meet the requirements are eligible for these allowances (and who submit proper data along with their applications). Their account will be automatically credited with the amount of the allowance for 12 months. During the preliminary calculations of our annual resources and the amount of allowance per household, we make allowance for a slightly higher number of households than what the actual number of applications would be (presuming a higher degree of efficiency on the part of the publicity work). As a result, the Foundation ends up with a surplus on its books each year (initially this surplus amounted to 20 percent, but this has since been reduced to around 5 percent today).

For example, while preparing our calculations for 2002, we knew that out of the 250,000 households with district heating around 25,000 would meet the eligibility criteria. Based on the experiences of the preceding years, we expected to receive applications from 20,000 households. Eventually, 18,000 applications were filed (and thus our conservative calculations had automatically generated a modest surplus). Out of Budapest's 820,000 households about 45,000-50,000 would meet the eligibility criteria for water supply, sewage, and waste disposal allowances. The experiences of the preceding years prompted us to expect 40,000 applications. Eventually, 38,000 formally acceptable applications were filed.

The BLT's reputation and recognition, and also its social context are revealed by the findings of a survey which was conducted two years after the program's introduction. The servicing companies conduct such surveys every year to monitor the changes in their consumers' status and preferences.

Table 3
SURVEY OF THE DISTRICT HEATING COMPANY'S CONSUMERS (1996)*

QUESTION	ANSWER	%
Have you heard of the utility allowances (BLT)?	Yes	63
Have you heard of... (among those with a per capita monthly income of HUF 12,000)	Yes	78
Do you know how to apply for the BLT? (among those who have already heard of the program)	Yes	86
Do you agree with the argument that those who cannot afford to pay should be subsidized rather than punished?	Yes	78
Do you agree with the argument that the servicing company should switch off district heating if 50 percent of the tenants do not pay their bills?	Yes	19
Would you become unable to pay in case of a district heating rate hike?	Yes	68
Has your/your family's financial status deteriorated over the past 5 years?	Yes	77
Is your/your family's financial status likely to deteriorate by the fall of next year?	Yes	67
What part of your family budget is represented by the utility bills?	Over 50%	40
What part of your family budget is represented by the district heating bills?	Over 20%	66

Selected questions and answers from a survey conducted by the Marketing Centrum.

Drawing on the above-mentioned surplus from the regular monthly allowances (and also from its interests and the Foundation's other revenues), we have created another allowance system for arrears balancing. Conditions for accessing this type of allowances are spelled out in the Foundation's statutes. The applicant must cooperate with the professional welfare workers of the local government or of other civil organizations with appropriate references and receive their letter of recommendation. An important condition is that the applicant must clear 50-80 percent of his or her arrears (the percentage depends on the duration of the unpaid debt). This payment may come from other social allowances as well. (The regular monthly allowances mentioned earlier are accessible to those whose arrears will likely not increase any further once they start paying the subsidized bills).

Besides the fact that this allowance relieves the housing-related burdens of several financially strained families, it also offers significant financial benefits to the servicing companies: the allowance ensures the continuous collection of the arrears that otherwise would not be collectible, or the collection of which would require expensive legal procedures.

A special type of arrears balancing allowance is called crisis allowance. This type of allowance aims to extend financial support to the families who face eviction from their home. The purpose of this aid is to prevent them from losing their homes. In these instances the conditions relating to the payment of the families' own share are considerably more lenient.

The various allowance types – organized in a gradual system – aim to provide direct support to the households that wrestle with difficulties in maintaining their homes. The system is supplemented by the following "modules":

–   In recent years, the Municipality of Budapest has invited targeted tenders to support civil organizations that are engaged in the development of a system whereby social apartments are exchanged. The aim is to offer free of charge "real estate agency services" and legal advice to those who do not expect to be able to maintain their apartments (not even with external help) and who themselves are inexperienced and defenseless on the real estate market.

–   Another type of supplementary subsidy aims to help local governments' family aid centers to employ debt management advisors and social workers and lawyers specialized in the field of allowance allocation.

LESSONS AND RESULTS

Having operated the BLT for a few years now, our experience is that the service provider companies manage their outstanding debts rather differently. Their "sensitivity" to this problem is determined by their ability to deny or switch off their particular service, and also by their market position, the effect of the arrears on their profits, and the level of preparedness of their management. Some of the service providers operate rather inaccurate billing systems and their records of arrears are likewise erratic. Other service providers reacted to the introduction of the BLT by completing serious technical development projects in the fields of billing and debt management and also try to regularly monitor the BLT's effects.

Based on these analyses we can conclude that while the efficiency of the monthly collection[6] of district heating utility rates decreased gradually from an average 95 percent in the late

---

[6]   I.e., what percentage of the sums billed in a given month are collected by the set deadline.

1980's to around 80-85 percent, the respective figure remained as high as 97 percent among households that benefited of the BLT. In other words, the system has enabled at least part of the most insolvent households to keep up with their monthly utility payments.

Over the past few years, the water supply, sewage, waste disposal and district heating allowances have managed to help preserve the housing security and solvency of some 60,000 households. Meanwhile, there are tens of thousands of households in Budapest (certain sources estimate their number at 40,000) with six months or longer utility payment arrears (these include the above-mentioned services as well as bills for electricity and gas supply, rent, and common costs of condominiums). To date, a total of 10,000 households benefited from the BLT's arrears balancing subsystem. In the period preceding the BLT's introduction – when the central pricing authority's decisions were still not coupled with a system of allowances – the servicing companies' arrears had reached critical heights. The efficiency analyses show that the BLT (together with other associated measures) has halted the dramatic decline of the servicing companies' "collection efficiency" (i.e., the ratio of billed and to actually paid amounts). The new system has had a stabilizing effect. Similarly, the servicing companies have managed to stabilize or slightly reduce the volume of their aggregated arrears.

Summing up: we believe that the BLT gave a timely and efficient response to the changes in the situation of service providers and consumers during the transition to the free market economy. It also responded well to the radical changes in the general economic, social, and administrative environment.

At the same time, we must note that, following a prolonged crisis period, Hungary's economy has stabilized over the past few years. The country is now on the path of sustainable development (the GDP has been increasing year-on-year). In this new situation it would be possible and necessary to introduce a uniform national system of allowances for housing maintenance. This system should be guaranteed and appropriately regulated. With its cost-efficient and complaint-free record, the BLT could serve as a model for this new system. At the same time, however, the introduction of this new system would require the reconsideration of the BLT's future prospects and sustainability.

DISTRICT HEATING – A NON-PRIVATIZED UTILITY

PÉTER VINCE

The Municipality of Budapest performs certain public utility services through non-privatized companies that it owns 100 percent. The practical management experiences of these companies show that the Municipality quite often has to operate amid conflicting requirements: it must simultaneously provide public utility services and adapt the servicing companies to market conditions. Although the problems facing the capital city's public utilities service providers differ according to area, these companies share several common management characteristics.

We shall now look at the example of the Budapest District Heating Company (Főtáv Rt.), which we consider to be typical in this respect.

PECULIARITIES OF DISTRICT HEATING IN BUDAPEST

In the capital city, district heating (as well as hot water supply) is provided for about a quarter of the total households (i.e., 240,000 apartments), and also to some 5,000 public institutions and industrial, servicing, and commercial ventures. About two thirds of the heat energy utilized by the district heating company comes from external sources (power stations), and so the main profile of the company is that it operates the district heating networks. Purchasing heat energy on the market is important since its costs are the largest expense of the service. Meanwhile, neither the capital city nor the company itself can influence energy rates since in this case the Hungarian State is the pricing authority.

This service functions as a natural monopoly, in that consumers do not have alternative services to choose from. Furthermore, due to the inherited technical setup of the district heating network, the service can only be provided only to communities, i.e., it is practically impossible to satisfy individual consumer demands. Under standing regulations an individual consumer can opt to disconnect from the system, but due to the high associated investment costs this has so far been a very rare occurrence.

Another peculiarity of this system is that about 80 percent of consumption originates from households, of which figure housing estates represent 85 percent. The poor technical quality of the buildings erected in the previous decades (i.e., outdated heating systems), as well as the arrears in the fees paid by housing estates' socially handicapped inhabitants, explain the problems associated with the housing estates.

This monopolistic status not only has a negative effect on consumers but also on the servicing company Főtáv itself. While these "forced" consumers cannot order services tailored to their individual needs, the service provider remains dependent on the consumers. The most striking sign of this dependence are the accumulated arrears of payments by consumers. Over the years, these arrears have become one of the heaviest burdens on the company's operations.

Servicing obligation, which is prescribed for the capital city and the servicing company by the Act on Local Governments[1] and the Act on District Heating[2], is another result of this monopolistic status. The Act says: "The local government – in the capital city, the municipal government – [...] is obliged to provide district heating to apartment buildings and other buildings connected to the district heating system through the licensed operation of the district heating public utility service company." Consequently, it falls on the local (municipal) governments to define the operating conditions of the public utility service provider. The Municipality of Budapest and the district heating company cooperate on the basis of the so-called Cooperation Agreement, which defines both sides' tasks in a normative manner and identifies the tools and methods of their implementation.

The first such comprehensive agreement dates from the year the privatization tender was issued. The reason behind its drafting was that foreign investors were seen to only regard an appropriately regulated system of relationships as understandable and attractive.

Furthermore, the capital city is also obliged to set up regulations for the supply process, i.e., it must regulate the relationships between the servicing company and the consumers. Under Paragraph 34, Section 1 of the Act on District Heating: "the district heating provider is obliged to conclude general public utility service contracts with the individual consumers." According to law, the Municipality of Budapest must issue a decree to specify the "detailed rules of the legal relationship between the district heating provider and the consumer."

EVOLUTION OF THE CAPITAL CITY'S FUNCTIONS

The Municipality of Budapest's tasks related to district heating have evolved through several steps. The capital city became the owner of the service in 1990-1991. The so called Act on the Capital[3] of 1991 defines district heating in Budapest as an obligation on the part of the Municipality. The assets required for the service were transferred to the Municipality's ownership under the Act on Assets[4] of 1991. The Act on Defining Prices[5] of 1990

---

[1] Acts and Decrees, 1

[2] Acts and Decrees, 11

[3] Acts and Decrees, 6

[4] Acts and Decrees, 5

[5] Acts and Decrees, 2

authorized the capital city to establish district heating rates and to spell out the conditions for their application. Consequently, the General Assembly of the Municipality of Budapest simultaneously became both the owner and the price authority. On the basis of the latter license, the Assembly may issue decrees to define standing public utility service rates.

The decision by the General Assembly of the Municipality of Budapest in 1994 to transform the service provider into a share holding company with well defined independence (deed of foundation, procedures) was the third fundamental step in determining the division of the decision-making competence between the owner and company management.

At the same time, the new legal form made explicit the conflict that had existed between the company's public service tasks on the one hand, and, on the other, its obligation as a corporation to operate profitably. The owner's possible claim for dividend, and its expectations related to efficiency and financial performance are now to be interpreted in the light of the public service nature of the company's activity, the justifiable costs, and actual market demand.

Since the capital city is not only the owner but also the subject of the servicing obligation, it may have certain considerations that it chooses to rank above its interests as an owner. Specifically, the municipal government's number one interest is for the Budapest District Heating Company to provide its services safely and in good quality, and to keep district heating rates at a socially acceptable level. Quality service requires investments, which the service provider wants to recover from the rate revenues. The capital city is interested in moderating the service provider's rate hike attempts, and in improving the operation's economic efficiency.

These diverse requirements are omnipresent in the local government-controlled district heating service, and they often clash with each other.

THE MUNICIPAL GOVERNMENT AS AN OWNER

The municipal government has a host of tools at its disposal to enforce its ownership rights. It enforces its rights as owner through the various local government bodies. The company is controlled by bodies made up of representatives, and not by organizations specialized in company management, asset management or profit management (This explains the rigidity and inflexibility of the "committee-type" corporate governance system of the district heating company.)

The General Assembly of the Municipality of Budapest transferred some of its ownership rights to its own Ownership Committee. The latter is in charge of some of the issues that require decisions from shareholders. As for the Budapest District Heating Company, certain issues regularly end up before the Ownership Committee, while others are occasionally discussed by this body.[6] As was the case with other public utility service companies, the capital city set up the supervisory board by electing representatives of the General Assembly. Their role is to exercise the owner's political control over the company's activity.

The Ownership Committee holds annual meetings to discuss and approve the company's balance statements and business plans. The Committee defines the main indices for the company's operations during these meetings, in addition to the meetings being legally necessary. The Committee decides on the use of the dividends during these meetings – in years when the financial performance of the company is such as to permit dividend yields. (Profits are by and large a function of the rate hike applied.)

In recent years, the municipality has usually decided to leave the profits with the company. This dividend policy is closely related to the owner's principle that the main task of a public utility service company is not to increase the municipal government's revenues. The municipality's dividend policy aimed instead to improve the company's financial status and to cover the costs beyond the company's daily operations.

In short, the expectations for profitability are subjected to the requirements relating to the maintenance of the company's financial stability. Stability is a complex issue, and in our case it means that the company is expected to maintain its financial liquidity, service its debts, pay its public payments, meet its financial obligations vis-à-vis its partners, and satisfy its other tasks as prescribed in the relevant regulations. If this type of stability is sustainable, the owner even accepts transitory losses. At the same time, the losses always send signals to the municipal government that it has to decide when and what type of measures are needed to prevent negative trends from expanding (such as the decline of the company's liquidity status).

On the topic of the owner's role, we must add that the municipal government not only relegates the requirement of profitability to the background, but also behaves unlike other owners that operate amid real market conditions, as it does not have capital to invest in order to reorganize the company's activities or to expand its markets. Anyway, the municipal government expects its company to finance its own operations, and does not intend to support its investments.

The Ownership Committee approves the business plan, which is important here in at least two respects. As part of this process, the Ownership Committee defines wage increases and investment expenditures. Regarding wages, the approval of the business plan only "codifies" them, as the wage issue is decided in a series of preliminary consultations between the municipal government, the other public utility service companies and the employees' unions. The wage increase approved at the municipal-level meetings and enjoying the

---

[6] The Ownership Committee exercises its rights through coordinating with the other committees of the municipal government. The decision-making mechanisms entail complex and intricate processes, and are slower than those employed at the privately owned share holding companies. This type of ownership control through a committee is rather difficult to manage and is often considered inefficient by both the municipal government and the company.

municipal government's consent is specified in the business plan, on the proviso that its implementation is possible concerning the company's projected financial status. To date, this method of wage regulation has not generated labor conflicts, notwithstanding the presence of a rather large employees' union at the company. One reason for the lack of conflicts is that the company has so far been able to recognize and honor the wage increase proposals. (Wage hike decisions are not only reached in a centralized manner as far as the companies owned by the municipal government are concerned: the Privatization and State Holding Company – APV Rt. – also follows this practice for the state-owned companies in its portfolio.)

Up to a certain value, the company decides on the investment projects laid down in the business plans, while the decision on more valuable projects belong to the competence of the Ownership Committee. The investment projects featured in the business plans are also preliminarily approved by the affected sides. These investments, which represent 8-9 percent of the company's revenues, also serve as points of reference for the company for rate bargaining when the scheduled hike of the district heating rates is suspected to be insufficient to cover investment costs. The service provider's main source of funding for its investment projects comes from depreciation allocations and not from profits. After all, profits are few and far between, and cannot serve as a basis for strategic investments. Above and beyond its moves described above, the capital city also secured funding for the investments associated with the stipulations of the Act on District Heating (i.e., metered charging, see below). For this end, the city temporarily incorporated a new cost element in the heating rates.

In a less thorough manner, the owner also gets involved in the strategic issues related to the company's management that have a direct impact on the customers. First among these are the long-term contracts under which the company obtains heat energy from the power stations. Since the value of purchased energy accounts for two thirds of Főtáv Co.'s budget, the prices set up in the contracts have a decisive effect on the consumer rates applied. These contracts also stipulate the pricing methods that are to be used during future heat energy purchases, and it falls on the owner's competence to approve these terms.

The long-term contracts' influence on the price of the input heat energy is limited, since they cover only those costs which are independent of the state-controlled natural gas and electric energy prices.[7] Costs (i.e., their increase) are predictable thanks to the contracts that also define the dates for their enforcement. Consequently, the municipal government can discuss rate hikes according to a previously agreed schedule.

Time and again the owner also has to deal with the issue of accumulated payment backlogs by the consumers. The fact that nearly 5 percent of the total heat consumption is unpaid for by the consumers is a cause for permanent financial tensions.

---

[7] The Municipality of Budapest has a rather limited role in determining the input price of energy. In the longer run, the owner could increase its say through its more marked involvement in Főtáv Rt.'s efforts to broaden its heat and electric energy resource-base. For the time being, this remains a hypothetical possibility, whose viability should be considered in the context of the gradually liberalized Hungarian energy market.

In the beginning, the owner used to approve financial transactions aimed at managing (selling) the payment backlogs. Though these transactions reduced the company's profits or even caused losses, at least they contributed to a more clear-cut picture of the company's real financial situation. The payment arrears were sold irregularly (yearly or biannually).

As a next step in managing the arrears, the District Heating Company – with the consent of the owner – established a factoring company to which it sold the arrears regularly (monthly) and under preset conditions.

As a conclusion of our review of the local government's tasks as owner, we shall concentrate on one of its decisions. This particular decision greatly influenced the future of district heating. Back in 1997, the Ownership Committee initiated the partial privatization of Főtáv Rt. as part of the drive to privatize public utility companies owned by the capital city. The Municipality invited tenders for the sale of two different share packages. The first offered a minority stake (25 percent plus one vote) with special management rights, while the second offered a majority stake (50 percent plus one vote). However, the tender was subsequently canceled due to the absence of appropriate purchase offers.

At the initiative of the Ownership Committee, a series of studies were completed on the causes of this fiasco. According to these analyses, the basic reason was that potential investors had no ground to expect reasonable returns on their investments. The company's revenue-generating potential was modest, and the conditions for competition were greatly restricted by the centrally regulated natural gas prices that disfavor industrial consumers. Furthermore, the expansion of the distance heating market was considered limited, and payment arrears were extremely difficult to collect. Last but not least, neither the company nor the Municipality had enough experience in managing their contractual ties.

The company's external operational (legal and institutional) conditions also contributed to the fiasco of the privatization tender. At the time, there was no law to regulate district heating, potential investors therefore considered the legal and economic conditions to be fluid and insecure.

Besides the privatization strategy applied in the above process, certain solutions have been proposed during the past few years from a different approach.[8]

CHANGES IN THE DETERMINATION OF THE RATES

The local government is authorized to set the rates for district heating and also to determine the conditions under which the rates should apply. In its capacity as a price authority, it can

---

[8] The alternative option tries to overcome the factors blocking privatization. It radically differs from the former constructions as it proposes to break down the monolithic company into smaller units and to contract out services. This approach is also referred to in other papers of this chapter: 'Infrastructure Policies', 'Utility Privatization', 'Infrastructure Development'. *(The editor)*

influence the revenues and profits of the company, and has the power to make decisions that affects the consumers' expenditures. The local government has to simultaneously keep an eye on maintaining the conditions for the company's financial stability and on the consumers' ability to foot the bills.

Since 1997, the Municipality of Budapest and the service provider have been jointly setting rates based on a contractually regulated procedure, which fits into their comprehensive institutionalized cooperation framework.

The past few years have witnessed significant changes in the methods applied to pricing district heating. These changes affected not only the "contents" of the rates (i.e., the methods and factors of their calculation), but also the pricing procedures applied.

Since 1994, when the company was transformed into a share holding company, the rates have been raised yearly (or even more frequently). The pricing procedure has been regulated since 1997. The local government chose to adopt the normative pricing principles that were established by the government during the privatization of the energy sector in 1996. According to the city of Budapest's interpretation of this principle: "… Similarly to licensed electric energy and natural gas providers, the district heating provider should also be entitled to cover its costs and investments from the rate revenues, and should be able to generate enough profits to ensure its sustainable operation."[9]

The establishment and introduction of the new rate calculation method (the so-called rate mechanism) was meant to serve this principle. Although the original and final (2002) versions of the rate mechanism differed in several important and less significant respects, it continued to refrain from defining a guaranteed limit for the profits attainable by the service provider. In this respect, it differed from the calculation methods applied in the case of the state-controlled gas and electric energy providers.

In the absence of competition and alternative services, the method of rate calculation could only be cost-based. Initially, in 1997, the pricing authority established what was identified as the starting rates, in which it incorporated the real market price of the heat energy input of the service provider. In addition, it approved a calculation method ("formula") for determining the company's accepted operational costs. Furthermore, this rate mechanism enabled the company to transfer the price hike effects of the input energy – primarily natural gas – in a regulated manner. Once a year, all the other cost elements were recalculated and their approved effects were enforced.

In 2002, the rate mechanism included the following cost elements:

– the prices of natural gas, miscellaneous energy and heat energy purchased by the service provider;

– the service provider's operational costs;

– the coverage for the investments prescribed by the Act on District Heating.

---

[9] Acts and Decrees, 17

Each year, the three-year rate mechanism also sets efficiency-related requirements for the company. On top of this, the rate also covers the amount of money which the company contributes to a fund set up by the Municipality of Budapest and the public utilities service providers to support the consumers with payments arrears (see later).

It is worth mentioning that the potential profits do not translate into capital gains. Instead, they are used by the service provider to cover its obligations and debits, thereby creating resources for further investments.

Due to the consumers' limited willingness to pay, the rate mechanism can only generate minimal profits. Losses occur in the years when the pricing authority does not allow the enforcement of the full rates calculated according to the rate mechanism. The involvement of certain cost elements are delayed and approved only at a later hike.

Between January 1, 1997, and October 2001, district heating rates charged to consumers increased by an average 38 percent. In the same period, the consumer price index (CPI) increased by 67 percent. The fact that the rate increase lagged behind that of the CPI resulted in the decrease of the share of these expenses from 8.3 percent to 6.5 percent of the consumers' (per capita average gross) income.

During the past few years, the service provider – induced by several circumstances – has always proposed alternative rate increase packages. On the one hand, despite the regulated calculation methods, both the Municipality and mainly the company have regularly come up with considerations for including new cost elements or for making the rate formula more sophisticated. On the other hand, the formula incorporated elements which should be determined by the Municipality.

In retrospect, we can establish that the municipal government's decisions on the rate hikes, and also its choices between alternative rate hike packages, were mostly based on case-by-case evaluations, i.e., its priorities varied from case to case. In some instances the municipal government even opted to postpone the planned hike, while at other times it approved favorable or less favorable packages for the service provider.

The company was not very successful in persuading the Municipality to accept its proposals to include the new elements of its own operational costs in the rate hikes, covering its losses and the modifications to the cost calculation methods. Whenever the bigger rate hike alternative was approved, the reason was to cover the investments prescribed by the 1998 Act on District Heating.

The increase in the price of the input energy (mostly natural gas) determined the rate hike's lower limit. The range above this limit was subject to bargaining between the municipal government and the service provider as the rate is determined by the authority and not by the market. The fact that the service provider was clearly better informed of its own situation determined the basis of the bargaining process. Meanwhile, the municipal government has the authority to decide if the company's rate hike claim is justified and socially and politically acceptable.[10]

Under the terms laid down in the Cooperation Agreement, the rates (except for natural gas prices) can be modified once a year only. The Agreement also stipulates that the service provider is entitled to implement subsequent corrections if the justified hikes are delayed or if the price authority deviates from the rate mechanism.

OTHER AUTHORITY LICENSES

The Municipality of Budapest also acts as authority in two other key areas: it regulates the legal relationship between the service company and the consumers, and it enforces the obligations laid down in the Act on District Heating. In these roles, the municipal government has to represent and enforce a series of often conflicting interests.

In its former capacity, the Municipality regulates every aspect and detail of the company's services (including the public service contracts between the company and the consumers, the contents of the service, the business regulations, the rate payment schemes, etc.). In other words, it defines the frameworks for the provision of the services and the company's operations. The public utility contracts approved by the municipal government define the ways the monopolistic service provider should provide for the needs of consumers.

A municipal decree associated with the Act on District Heating prescribed the way the company should create the conditions for the enforcement of the new rate collection method (charge by the meter). Charging by the meter is a departure from the decades-old method of charging average rates, and it enables the company to set up meters in every apartment block. The rates charged on these blocks are divided up by the apartment owners at their own discretion. For the time being, the introduction of meters in every apartment would require an enormous expenditure. The current "half-baked" solution is nevertheless expected to improve the service's efficiency.

The municipal decree prescribed the creation of the conditions needed for the introduction of a system in which the consumers are charged according to their actual consumption. Specifically, the decree obliged the service company to guarantee coverage for the required investments. The municipal government had to find a way to split costs between the service company and consumers. Under the decree, these expenditures are to be recovered from the heating rates over a period of several years.

---

[10] The method for rate determination applied by the Municipality is reviewed in the paper 'Infrastructure Policies'. Here we emphasize two features of the method. (1) The rate consists of two parts: one part is calculated by a strictly regulated price formula and is to cover the operation and depreciation expenses of the company, while the other part is annually determined by the Municipality and is to cover investment. The Municipality is free to deliberate and negotiate only this second, discretional part. (2) During the process of the annual determination of the rate – both in principle and practice – the individual factors within of the formula is strictly separated from the possible reconsideration and modification of the formula itself. The latter is connected to the improvement of the set of parameters to be taken into account, while the former is connected to the employment of the rules in practice. *(The editor)*

ECONOMIC STABILITY AND SOCIAL RESPONSIBILITY

The Municipality of Budapest has to consider the feedback from consumers who represent about 40 percent of the capital city's total population. Besides the quality of the service, consumers are primarily affected by rate hikes. Főtáv Co.'s average rates were doubled between 1995 and 2000.

As we have seen, the general political responsibilities toward consumers greatly determine the process of pricing and the drafting of the utility service contracts.

In terms of direct costs and profits, district heating is relatively expensive. Its financially balancing positive effects manifest themselves on the level of national economy, but its overall cost is incalculable since its positive environmental effects are practically impossible to quantify. The direct costs are borne by the public sphere and individual consumers. If we consider that 85 percent of apartments with district heating are situated in housing estates, and that the income level of the owners of these apartments is below the national average, we cannot but conclude that the (involuntary) use of the district heating service places a heavy financial burden on a significant number of individuals, and also presents a huge rate collection challenge to the service provider.

It would be economically untenable for the service provider to let rate arrears increase beyond a certain limit. It is likewise not an option for the company to cut off the service, as it would be technically impossible to manage and would also unjustly discriminate against certain groups of consumers (technically, it is not possible to turn district heating off only in apartments with rate arrears). Consequently, the service provider has no choice but to somehow protect the consumers' liquidity and their inclination to pay.

The Municipality of Budapest's plan to conditionally subsidize the consumers with rate arrears is a promising attempt to solve this economic and social problem.

Drawing on the contributions of the other affected public utility service providers as well as its own, the Municipality of Budapest has set up a foundation which offers subsidies to the families and individuals who commit(!) themselves to amortizing their rate arrears. Public utility providers expect this system to prevent their losses from increasing further, and to keep socially and financially handicapped consumers among their paying customers. In order to protect the affected companies' financial stability, the Municipality, in its role as owner, approves the transfer of funds to the foundation. The subsidies are granted in accordance with the terms laid down in a municipal decree.

Főtáv Rt. also contributes to this foundation. Its annual contribution amounts to 1-1.5 percent of its revenues. The actual amount is determined by the owner. Nearly 10 percent of Budapest apartments with district heating receive subsidies from this foundation every year.

CLOSING REMARKS

The study surveyed the roles played by the local governments in the management of a public utility sector in Budapest. These roles have evolved in the course of the social-economic transformation of Hungary as new institutions and regulations that could not rely on organic precedents were established. The novelty of the tasks was that the local governments responsible for the public utility sector had to behave as owners, authorities and political bodies – in market economy conditions and taking into consideration the social tensions accompanying transition. When providing public services they had to apply considerations different from those of the market economy, which often collided with their owner-type interests. This set-up has necessarily given birth to different types of collisions. The conflict between the above mentioned roles is obvious, and compromises between them characterize the state of public services. The Municipality of Budapest has developed an ever increasing set of means to control the problem of its conflicting roles, and seeks solutions to keep each of its roles intact and meet the requirements of each.

THE TRANSFORMATION OF THE BUDAPEST PUBLIC TRANSPORT COMPANY

ÉVA VOSZKA

> *It is a wonder that the trams run at all, a noted Hungarian economist is said to have commented in the 1950's when he grasped the logic of the socialist planned economy. Rather paradoxically, today, a decade into the free market economy, we still seem to have every reason to wonder what enables the public transport system to go on working in the Hungarian capital. Against the backdrop of ever-higher ticket prices, the performance of the Budapest Transport Company (BKV) has declined year after year, and its losses are mounting rapidly.*

All over the world, public transport systems in large cities cause headaches to travelers, politicians and transport engineers alike. The difficulties are not merely technical and logistical – as a public service, mass transport entails the distribution of financial resources, i.e., it is a political issue. What are the structural reasons behind the difficulties? How did the transport providers and their owners try to overcome these problems? What were their successes and failures and what obstacles did they have to overcome? My answers are built on publicly accessible information sources, as well as on the analyses of the companies' documents and in some cases on personal experiences gathered during the process of decision-making.[1]

STOCK CORPORATION – IN HYBRID MARKETS

For all the significant changes in recent years, the Budapest Transport Company has retained its old character in several fundamental respects.

As a single-owner stock corporation, the Budapest Municipal Government has run BKV since 1991. In essence, it has monopoly power[2] over the city's mass transport market, its

---

[1] The author has been a member of BKV's Board of Directors since 1996. The author does not provide detailed references for the company documents cited in this study, since these documents are not accessible to the public. However, the proposals and programs made public by the Budapest Municipal Government are referenced by title. Figures are taken form inner documents of BKV and do not necessarily coincide with documents found on the home page of the company. The figures go up until the end of 2000, while the analysis of events goes up to the autumn of 2001. The author expresses her gratitude to the staff of the Budapest Municipal Government, and especially to BKV's management, for providing access to the necessary documents and data, and for their critical remarks on the first draft of this study.

[2] Similar services are only provided by the state rail company MÁV and the bus company Volán. However, the passengers' right to choose is rather limited geographically.

only competitor being individual travel. However, the increase in the volume of car traffic results in unfavorable external effects such as congestion and environmental damages.

The exclusive nature of this public service necessitates central regulation and places the burden of responsibility on the transport provider. The Act on Local Governments has placed the municipal authorities in charge of mass transport. Accordingly, through an annually renewed performance contract with its owner, BKV is bound to fulfil this task at prices determined by the Budapest Local Government. Thus, the company's hands are tied as it has only limited chances to modify the dimensions and structure of its operations. As a buyer, BKV operates in a real market environment. However, its sales prices are not primarily a function of supply and demand.[3]

BKV generates revenues from two primary sources: fares (including the so called fare-compensation granted by the state to certain groups such as students or pensioners) and municipal subsidies. Under the legal regulations in force, the Budapest Municipal Government must secure the consent of the Ministry of Finance (PM) before modifying the fares chart. The reason behind this obligation is that the state granted subsidies to BKV between 1992 and 1996, and has been subsidizing fares through fare-compensation schemes in the subsequent years.[4]

The Ministry of Finance has no direct stake in either the operation of these services or BKV's performance as a business. It is up to the government in power how much its indirect stake is acknowledged in the approval of the fare charts as well as in the state subsidies granted to mass transport. In general, the ministry aims to keep fares low, as it wants to cut state expenditures and keep inflation at bay.

The Municipal Government's motives are more complex than that. In its capacity as a price authority and an elected public body, its interests lie in keeping costs at realistic levels and, wherever possible, reducing them. It also aims to at least maintain the volume and quality of its services and to moderate fare hikes.[5] At the same time, as owner, the Municipal Government should seek profits (or at least minimize losses and municipal subsidies).

---

[3] However, since in public transport the customers' right to choose is more marked than for other public services, the price flexibility of the demand is also larger.

[4] In 1992, the distribution of the population's personal income taxes was radically changed. Prior to that, 100 percent of taxes remained with the local government that had collected them. Under the new system, this figure was reduced to 50 percent (it was later cut further). In an effort to counter this admittedly radical move, the state decided to subsidize the capital city's public transport system. However, the real value of these subsidies was constantly decreasing. In 1997, even these subsidies were cancelled.

[5] The unfavorable external effects of the proliferation of individual forms of transport also appear to justify the efforts to maintain a relatively high role for public transport, and to halt the decline of the "modal split" ratio.

A simple model below explains the Municipal Government's contradictory goals and limited options:

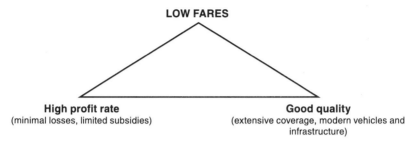

Of the three goals specified at the tips of the triangle, only two may be simultaneously satisfied. If tram tickets are cheap and subsidies are low, the quality of the service suffers. If the aim is to provide quality service at low fares, the company is bound to accumulate losses or draw on more subsidies. High ticket prices alone result in both quality service and a positive business balance.

Needless to say, in real life every decision boils down to measures. We are now entering the realm of the art of the impossible – i.e., that of politics. However, we must add right away that the daily operation of Budapest's mass transport system is permeated not only by politics in the general sense but also by politicking in the narrow sense of inter-party bickering.

The subsidies spent by the Budapest Municipal Government on BKV's operation and development represent a sizeable, although proportionately decreasing, entry in its annual budget.[6] Consequently, the issue is bound to be a focus of heated inter-party debates. To make matters worse, the state also wants a say in determining the fares chart and cannot be bypassed in decisions on large infrastructure investments (e.g., the construction of the Metro underground system). Several examples could be cited from recent years to prove that the decisions do not as a rule rest on professional considerations.

Inter-party clashes affect not only the operation of the elected bodies but also the work of the municipal administration. The contradictions inherent in the goals associated with public transport quite often manifest themselves in conflicting requirements and directives that various leaders, departments and committees present to BKV's management.

While the company has only limited powers to influence its results through formal channels, the non-unified internal structure of the owner gives it a fairly broad room for maneuver. Through officially submitted proposals and personal negotiations, BKV has a chance to influence practically every entry in its revenues column, most importantly the size of the municipal subsidies. In principle, BKV enjoys a rather strong bargaining position due to

---

[6] Between 1991 and 2000, the nominal value of the capital city's total subsidies increased twofold, from HUF 9 billion to HUF 18 billion. While in the first half of the decade these subsidies represented 12-17 percent of the city's annual budget, in the years up until 2000 this figure fluctuated between 6.6 and 8.8 percent. *(Table 1)*

its size, its monopoly, and the associated servicing responsibilities. Due to these structural traits, that gain extra importance in the current context, BKV has in many respects retained the characteristics of a large socialist enterprise: its day-to-day operation is determined by the authorities' regulatory decisions, it depends heavily on subsidies, it manifests the benefits and disadvantages of an "ownerless" public entity" and it is engaged in continuous bargaining on prices.

Of course, this does not mean that no changes have occurred at BKV. The company's managers, as well as owners, have attempted several changes in recent years. However, they never once managed to break through the "magic triangle" due to the company's structural set-up and the interest and power relations interwoven within it.

BKV's services hold up in international comparison in terms of both quality and volume. Compared with the mass transport services of eight other cities of similar size,[7] Budapest has a relatively large number of lines and stops and the system's utilization is also high.[8] In terms of modal split, i.e., the ratio of public transport for all personal transport to individual transport, Budapest still boasts a fairly favorable rate: around 60 percent. The Europe-wide average is 50 percent. However, the same index for Budapest was around 80 percent a decade ago, indicating a negative trend. In the period between 1990 and 2000, significant drops were recorded in the commonly used gauges of passenger kilometer and seat kilometer *(Table 2).*[9] And yet, Budapest's public transport system handles over 1,400 million passengers per year. Of the companies included in our survey, BKV has the smallest investment budget and its vehicle park is old and outdated. Services are decreasing, while fares are increasing. There were a few years when the fare hikes lagged behind inflation, but in other years, they exceeded it. Overall, the price of public transport in Budapest increased with inflation during the past ten years *(Table 3)*. Finally: the real value of the Municipal Government's current subsidies, concerning its share in the company's revenues, has decreased by more than half, representing today a mere 23 percent of them. By 1999, BKV's losses on the books had climbed to HUF 10 billion *(Table 4)*.[10]

The cardinal figures show that while none of the goals identified in the "magic triangle" have been fully met, none have been terminally damaged either. Throughout the company's recent history, the decision-makers have had to walk a very tight rope. In retrospect, we can establish that despite limited subsidies and relatively low fares, BKV has managed to keep its shrinking services afloat. Modest as this accomplishment may appear, it required significant efforts from both the company and its owner.

---

[7] Prague, Stockholm, Hamburg, Marseilles, Lisbon, Milan, Munich, Vienna. The benchmark analysis was conducted by the consulting firm Roland Berger & Partner, based on data from 1998 and 1999.

[8] In the second half of the 1990's, there were approximately 4,600 stops, and the utilization ratio stood around 28 percent.

[9] The decline in the number trips stopped in 1999, and the following year witnessed a modest increase. We will come back to the causes later.

[10] As we will see, the improvement registered in 2000 was the result of one-off factors.

ORGANIZATIONAL AND OPERATIONAL REFORMS

Public transport is a key element in the life and operation of the city of Budapest, and BKV is the Municipal Government's largest company in terms of both manpower and capital. Initially, BKV was a major entry in the city's books: in 1991, it accounted for nearly 17 percent of Budapest's annual budget, i.e., more money was spent on public transport than on culture as a whole. No wonder that, at least in principle, the owner always had to pay special attention to this company.

After 1990, the city's representatives were bound to realize that the institutions and operational structure that they had inherited (or had been granted) could no longer be financed at the expected level, what with inflating costs. They also found that the volume of centrally distributed resources fluctuated unpredictably. For these reasons, the city's leaders decided early on to strive to boost the Municipal Government's own revenues (with respect to public transport to increase rates above inflation), and simultaneously to reduce the current per unit expenditures and subsidies while trying to maintain the level and quality of its services. The additional, mostly one-time revenues (from the sale of real estate and equities) and the loans, were allocated primarily for strategic investment projects.[11]

It was in this vein that the owner, in the first half of the 1990's, decided to drastically reduce the real value of BKV's operational subsidies. Between 1991 and 1994, the subsidies amounted to HUF 9-11 billion per annum, while the rate of inflation topped 20 percent (Tables 1 and 3). According to the Municipal Government, BKV became chronically short of capital (i.e., underfinanced) in 1992, when the changes in the central distribution of tax revenues significantly reduced the city's incomes. Furthermore, in the same year, BKV found itself on the receiving end of other discriminatory measures.[12] Successive fare hikes – up to 50 percent in 1991, and again a year later – could cover only the company's current losses. In the absence of revenues, BKV had to forgo the replenishment and development of its vehicle park. As a result, the company has accumulated an ever-growing list of future investments, which it labeled as "internal debt." In 1993, and again in 1995, BKV received two rather sizeable development loans from international financial institutions.. Debt servicing was undertaken by the Municipality in the case of the 1993 loan, and by BKV in the case of the 1995 loan. Accordingly, the company's external debts also began to increase.

Although the company's goal to become profitable in the medium term was set as early as 1991, at that time the fare hike was only complemented by management changes. These early plans called for staff reduction, transparent accounting as well as cleaning up the portfolio and quickly privatizing certain services (boats, funicular services in Buda Castle and on János Hill) as part of a broader privatization/concession program.[13]

---

[11] The Office of the Mayor of Budapest, 1991 and 1992

[12] The Office of the Mayor of Budapest, 2001. For the discriminatory measures and the proposals to eliminate them see the subchapter on alternative financing.

[13] Foundation for a European Hungary, Local Government Experts' Office, 1991

During streamlining procedures in the following years, the number of employees was reduced by several thousand[14] yet there were hardly any other changes in the company's operational conditions. The first significant step forward took place in 1996 only. The development program for the city of Budapest that was drafted in the wake of the 1994 general elections envisaged the privatization of a number of companies, but BKV was not included in this list on account of the "critical state" of its basic services. At the same time, however, the program called for the transformation of BKV into a stock company in order to rationalize its operations, and it also projected the separation of those of its departments that performed services unrelated to the company's main business profile.[15] It was on the basis of these principles that BKV was transformed and reorganized between 1996 and 1998. As part of this process, the company became leaner and its internal operational and management structures were also modified. Reorganization was followed by a two-year stabilization program.

This short review alone shows that the Municipality made continuous efforts to reshape both the principles and the practice of the company's operation. The intentions of the owner are reflected in several documents of the period. The comprehensive, general goals are summarized by the urban development and transport system concepts. Programs for a full election period – e.g., the so-called Demszky-program from 1991 – and the annual budgetary concepts preparing the following years' budgets were the next series of more concrete proposals. Programs running over at least a few years are associated with these types of programs (e.g., the reorganization of the stabilization program). The parameter book spells out expectations regarding the volume of the services, while the annual budget determines the actual level of subsidies.[16] We may reconstruct the municipal drives, expectations towards the company and changing priorities in reshaping external conditions for the company on the basis of these documents. However, I have not met a single document that, for each decision-maker and for the government, summarized and made clear the long term, detailed strategy of the owner, including crucial points and the comprehensive, long-term financing plan. Lack of consensus between the parties of the municipal coalition and the ever varying governments concepts that follow each other render external conditions completely unstable and do not provide satisfactory grounds for elaborating a long term plan.[17]

---

[14] The company had 23,000 employees in 1991, about 15,000 in the mid-1990's, reduced to 12-13,000 by 2000.

[15] Alliance of Free Democrats (SZDSZ), 1994

[16] The financial leaders of the Municipality consider the agreements concluded with the great international financial institutions as documents revealing the strategy of the owner. Surely, these include some important indices prescribing the increase of the self-financing capacity of BKV (e.g., cost-covering rates), yet business agreements can hardly be considered as constituting a governmental concept.

[17] Up to the beginning of 2003, government policy has been steadfast in only one point: the state has allocated decreasing amounts to the financing of public transportation in the cities. In the opinion of municipal leaders, the precondition for working out any reasonable long term concept for public transport is either a state decision of binding force to take part in financing or the complete reform of the local government financing system. *(The editor)*

CHANGE IN THE FORM OF THE ENTERPRISE

The transformation of BKV into a stock corporation enabled the owners to separate roles and to set up the ownership and controlling bodies as stipulated in the Companies Act. It also enabled them to compile a relatively realistic assessment of the company's assets as well as to ensure the latter's divisibility and traceability.[18]

However, despite the change in the form of the enterprise, the company has remained underfinanced: BKV's revenues continued to lag behind its expenditures. The ownership structure as well as other structural aspects have also remained unchanged. The transformation did not eliminate "micromanagement." In a way, it even reinforced and formalized political attempts to influence the management. The balance of power among political parties in the Assembly of the capital determines the composition of the Directorate and the Supervisory Board. And yet, due to deficiencies in the system of institutional ties bounding delegates to their delegating bodies, disagreements within these bodies as well as inconsistencies in their goals, BKV's leading bodies are not characterized by perceptible political divisions.

This situation partly amplifies the ever-occurring phenomenon, well known to happen to such bodies whether state-owned or private: the Directorate and the Supervisory Body tend to represent the interests of the company rather than that of the owners. Asymmetric information channels significantly weaken the role of the supervisors, too. The management is better informed of all the details than the board members, who do not have such close ties to the organization and who rely primarily on the management's proposals and accounts.

Accordingly, we may deduce from this analysis that the share company form itself is not enough to alter the modes of operation and to improve results. This is due to the management problems of large organizations in general that are amplified by the characteristics of public ownership and by the peculiar nature of both the activity and its market.

At the same time as the share company form of the enterprise was changed, the owner and the company's management launched a program reorganizing the company's structure since both were clearly aware of the problematic situation. The 1994 urban policy program determined the main thrust of the changes. The company's management proposed concrete frameworks for change while the Directorate and the Supervisory Board oversaw the process. BKV's reorganization process that aimed at exploring company reserves took place between 1996 and 1998, and entailed a total of 37 projects. The process focused on two main areas: the reorganization of the company's capital and organizational structure and the reform of its internal organizational-management system.

---

[18] According to the starting balance, the company's registered capital was HUF 127 billion, as opposed to the previously specified HUF 6 billion. This was supplemented by capital reserves worth HUF 45 billion prior to January 1, 1996, and HUF 49 billion after that date. In the years that followed it became clear that certain assets were unrealistically valued. Several of the company's vehicles were worth more, while certain real estates could not be sold at book value.

STREAMLINING THE ORGANIZATION

In reorganizing its capital and organizational structure, BKV followed patterns well known in the free market economies. Practically all Hungarian state-owned companies had employed these patterns in the 1990's. However, BKV's move was rather belated. The three main elements of the process were the following: the company, as majority stakeholder, set up a number of limited liability ventures, it cleaned its portfolio by discontinuing certain services and reduced premises by selling off real estate.

BKV's aim with moving its non-core services into separate legal entities was to reduce costs and to boost efficiency. The managers expected to see positive results at both the newly formed LTD's and at the mother company. The new ventures were expected to yield better results because of: the distinct cost-revenue accounts of the now distinct profiles, the strengthened responsibilities and direct interest of the managers, the newly defined product structure, and the acquisition of new orders acquired not only from the mother company. BKV could expect a decrease in its current operating expenses thanks to the lower price of services purchased from its limited liability companies and from reducing staff and equipment at the mother company. Furthermore, BKV could even increase its revenues through the dividends from the profitable operation of the LTD's.

Under the reorganization process, BKV set up nine fully owned limited liability companies. Their core capital was approximately HUF 3 billion and they employed 1,570 people.[19] Compared with 1996, this represented 2.4 percent of the company's total registered capital and 8.3 percent of its workforce. The two largest spin-off ventures, each with a core capital of around HUF 1 billion, specialized in railcar and vehicle maintenance and repair. The spin-offs' (specialized in infrastructure maintenance, escalator repair, boat services, and transport health care) respective core capitals were set between HUF 100 million and 400 million. The companies specialized in construction and telecommunications, as well as the company operating the funicular, were launched with smaller core capital.

The subsidiaries were set up with distinct technological identities and goals, and were also clearly separable from an accounting point of view. Some of these companies were rather loosely affiliated with BKV's operational units, while others were specialized in services that the mother company could not obtain from outside partners.

Some other profiles, however, had to be cancelled due either to their marginal nature or to the negative price effects of excessive market supply. BKV stopped performing its own activity in printing, cloth supply, money moving, rail freight, security and defense, cleaning and provisions services, and it now purchases these services from outside contractors.

---

[19] Prior to the launch of the program, the company spinned off and privatized its travel bureau under the name of BKV Tours. During the reorganization process, BKV increased its stake to 100 percent in the advertising venture Peron Ltd., and it also set up DBR Metro Ltd. to coordinate the investments into the construction of the new South-Buda Metro line.

BKV's aim by selling off some of its buildings and other real estate was to reduce the company's current expenditure and to generate direct cash revenue. The real estate holdings were released thanks to the internal restructuring process, the reorganization and reduction of the company's welfare services and the rationalization of space utilization (All in all, some 1 million square meters of company real estate was released, representing nearly 15 percent of the total.). By the time the reorganization program was completed in mid-1998, 44 real estate units were sold. There are 29 such deals underway today, and a further 38 are expected to be sold in the coming years.[20]

REFORM OF INTERNAL STRUCTURE AND MANAGEMENT

The creation of a new divisional structure and the updating of the IT-system were the two most important elements of the internal restructuring of the "streamlined" company.

The goals defined by the management included separating the company's strategic and operative tasks, reducing the costs of coordination and clearly identifying tasks and responsibilities. By eliminating a "medium-level" management grade, the company created a two-tier organizational and management system. Each of the plant directorates that were organized earlier into three groups[21] became independent divisions. Altogether nine such divisions were set up: the five, regionally divided autobus divisions, plus the Metro, the HEV suburban train, the tram and the trolley services.[22] The operations of these new divisions were coordinated by BKV's restructured central "integrator" units.

This reorganization entailed decentralizing tasks and responsibilities. The executive units gained more independence to perform their tasks in such fields as material acquisition, shop maintenance, network technical operations and education. Each division drafted its own plan, and were individually answerable for the attainment of plan targets and the utilization of financial and economic resources. As a result of these measures, a new division of labor was introduced between the center and the divisions, which affected such key areas as accounting for traffic performance or the human resources, financial, accounting and administrative processes.

The above changes made it imperative to radically renew the company's IT-system. Under the TransIT project completed between 1997 and 1999, BKV gradually renewed its computer infrastructure and introduced a state-of-the-art digital management system. There are special modules in place now to manage all data associated with passenger traffic or fares revenues. BKV has considered it a priority to continuously debug and upgrade these applications, and the company has provided computer training to hundreds of its employees. Now, the integrated IT-system opens the way for the company to transfer and process data

---

[20] The sum total of the revenues is specified under the subhead 'Results and Limitations of Reorganization'

[21] Discounting river transport, which was spinned off into a separate limited liability company.

[22] The bus division was overseen by a Coordination Directorate until the final settlement of the new operational structure.

quickly and reliably, and thereby to improve the preparations for, and the monitoring of, the decision-making and execution process.

RESULTS AND LIMITATIONS OF REORGANIZATION

Both the company's management and the owner expected the reorganization process to generate cash revenues and result in a permanent reduction of costs. The one-off revenues were earmarked for financing the reorganization process itself, while the savings were expected to cover the current losses.

The financial plan that was compiled in 1996 projected the net income to total HUF 10 billion.[23] HUF 3.3 billion worth of cost reduction and about twice this amount in revenues from the utilization of assets. The expenditures, in net terms, were estimated at HUF 4.4 billion (this sum included the technical and logistical costs of the real estate sales, the relocations and company incorporations, as well as severance payments, miscellaneous personnel expenditures and the installation of the IT-system). As a result, the books showed a balance of HUF 5.6 billion.

However, the summary report that concluded the program in the summer of 1998 painted a considerably bleaker picture. While the cuts in expenditures turned out to be bigger than originally planned, the sale of the company's real estate generated only HUF 2.2 billion. Since the HUF 3.9 billion figure in the net expenditures column came rather close to the higher figure in the revenues column, the company found itself in the black by only HUF 1.8 billion.

In interpreting the results, we should heed a series of considerations. First, contrary to the original plans, the reorganization process failed to generate enough revenue to cover the costs of the IT development project. The bill turned out to be bigger than projected, and so the Budapest Municipal Government had to chip in with HUF 1.3 billion. If we include this entry in our revenue calculations, the short-term financial balance is reduced to a marginally small figure.

On the other hand, the revenues from the real estate sales lagged behind the planned figures not only as a result of the optimistic preliminary assessments of the sales prices and the sales officials' initial lack of experience, but also because of certain extraneous problems. Clarifying the ownership-rights of several real estates took too long. On many occasions, the company had no free resources to execute the preparatory tasks and to complete the relocation of the services and organizations. On top of all this, the Hungarian real estate market was down at the time. The expected one-off oversupply and the assumption that BKV was under pressure pushed prices further down, decision-makers therefore often postponed transactions. Later on, when these difficulties eased, the company's real estate sales accelerated again. Eventually, between 1996 and 2000, BKV chalked up a total of HUF 5.2 billion in revenues from the sales of its real estates. This figure was only HUF 1.5

---

[23] For the sake of comparison, this equaled the amortization that was accounted for a 12-month period.

billion short of the plan target – calculated at current prices. All in all, the direct revenues and expenditures associated with the reorganization process showed a positive balance.

It is a fact beyond dispute that shrinking infrastructure and decreasing personnel costs has reduced general operational expenditures. Between 1996 and 1998, BKV reduced its workforce by 15 percent. However, 1,570 of the 2,700 employees affected by the staff cuts were transferred to the newly established limited liability companies. By setting up its subsidiaries, BKV managed to reduce its direct expenditures in material, labor and utilities. However, it had to pay more for material services. Balance is far from being guaranteed – in fact, it can be negative for the mother company, depending on the prevailing pricing policies and the subsidiaries' bargaining positions.

According to BKV's calculations,[24] the company's losses between in 1996, 1997 and 1998 would have been HUF 2 (and 4 and 6) billion higher, respectively, without the reorganization process. However, these estimates are only applicable to an unchanged operational and servicing structure, and rest on assumptions that are rather difficult to verify. The measurement of the direct financial effects of the process rests on rather shaky foundations.

The developments of the past few years have revealed the structural problems associated with the establishment of subsidiary companies. If the mother company is simultaneously the majority stakeholder in, and the largest customer of, the smaller company, its goals are bound to contradict themselves. It is interested in keeping the prices low, but at the same time, it also wants its supplier to avoid accruing losses. Quite often, the subsidiaries get into trouble as a result of BKV's lagging orders (which in turn is the result of the mother company's shortage of funds). Under such conditions, it is rather difficult to enforce responsibility and interests. The underlying situation is similar to that of the public transport company and the Budapest Municipal Government. In its capacity as owner, now BKV – this time on the other side of the table – has to cope with the problems of information asymmetry and mutual dependence. The situation has not improved with the appointment of the Supervisory Board members, the establishment of the independent bureau for portfolio management and the transferring of the management and supervisory functions to the Economic Directorate – BKV has remained a weak owner throughout the process.

All in all, benefits were gained from the reorganization process: a new IT-system, a streamlined company, better cost effectiveness and the loosening of the old, ossified structures. It took a few years to get to a positive balance of cash revenues and direct expenditures, even then only at nominal value. It is difficult to quantify the indirect, long-term savings, but without the reorganization, BKV surely would have accumulated greater losses.

---

[24] These calculations and analyses are organic elements of a company's interest enforcement mechanism. Since the verification of these calculations would require the involvement of objective but sufficiently informed external experts (which would obviously be an expensive and time-consuming process), the owners tend to avoid resorting to this tool. For similar reasons, it is rather difficult (and therefore fairly rare) to compile thorough criticisms of, or alternative proposals to, a company's internal proposals. This is a manifestation of information asymmetry.

The program did not – and, due to its nature and scope, could not – produce a breakthrough in the company's economic and financial status. The one-off revenues were much too small to cover the costs of renewing the vehicle park and the infrastructure, and the operational savings could not counterbalance the losses. Many of the measures employed required subsequent corrections. Eventually, the company could not avoid putting the restructuring of its whole financing system on its agenda.

FINANCIAL STATUS, FINANCING

BKV has been continuously in the red since 1993. Initially, the company's losses were relatively small. By 1995, the balance losses had increased to HUF 4 billion. In 1999, the respective figure was close to HUF 10 billion. A year later – due primarily to a series of one-off effects – the losses dropped to below HUF 7 billion (Table 4). The accumulating losses are bound to slowly eat up the company's capital reserves, which were set rather high at the time of the incorporation. BKV has lost over 15 percent of its core capital during the past five years, while its debts have increased tenfold. The company's loan-to-capital ratio is still relatively low, and the proportion of long-term loans has successfully increased over the past few years. However, liquidity indices have been continuously declining.[25]

The company could not, however, execute all the required investments and modernization projects for all these loans. Considering actual depreciation and adjustment to inflation, BKV accumulated HUF 25 billion in losses in its development projects between 1993 and 2000. The company accounts for this as "internal indebtedness." For years, BKV has had to spend a significant part of its rather modest depreciation budget on financing its operations – i.e., on reducing losses. The vehicle park is growing older, the costs of repair and maintenance are increasing and service disruptions due to technical hitches have become everyday occurrences.[26] In recent years, the company has completed a few spectacular infrastructure renovations (the old underground, the tram terminus in Hűvösvölgy, several main tram lines), but other projects – such as the long-overdue overhaul of the oldest Metro line – had to be postponed for lack of funds.[27]

The situation described above is to a large extent the result of the restructuring of BKV's financing process.

---

[25] The period analyzed in this paper ends in November 2001. Since then, the company could not avoid financing debts from ever shorter-term loans. The situation where BKV verged on bankruptcy was temporarily relieved by a one-time interference by the central government, that repaid all of BKV's debt (HUF 38 billion). Still, it is important to note that this was a one-time intervention and that the long-term solution remains to be found. *(The editor)*

[26] The company's bus park is the youngest. The average age of the vehicles is less than 10 years. The respective figures are 21 for the Metro cars, 24 for the HÉV cars, and 29 for the trams.

[27] The reconstruction of the metro line will start in 2003. *(The editor)*

ATTEMPTS AT TIGHTENING BUDGETARY CONSTRAINTS

The main thrust of the changes in financing has been the government and the owner's efforts to tighten the company's budgetary constraints. In other words, the aim was to limit the amount of freely accessible external resources.

In 1997, the state cancelled the direct state subsidy extended to BKV since 1992 *(Table 1)*. Originally, this subsidy was meant to counter the adverse effects of the changes in the state funding of the Municipal Government. Although the amount of the fare-compensation increased in nominal value along with the fare hikes, the calculation index was steadily decreasing.[28] The state also failed to cover in full the costs associated with the free of charge travel right for senior citizens (aged 65 and above) that was approved in 1998.[29] While the share of central subsidies in BKV's total revenues (including fare-compensation) was on the increase in the first half of the 1990's, it dropped from 30 percent in 1996 to 23 percent *(Table 4)*. According to the company's calculations, the government's decisions dating from the period between 1996 and 2000 resulted in lost revenues to the tune of HUF 20 billion. This amount equals the company's current debt stock.

Meanwhile, as we have seen, in the first half of the decade, the owner was also successful in reducing operational subsidies. The efforts to this end were amplified by the introduction of a new financial strategy in 1996. The premise of the strategy was that, in a best-case scenario, the revenues of the city of Budapest could retain their real value, while other investment resources would likely dry up with the conclusion of the ongoing major privatization projects. The only way for the city to maintain the balance of the budget and to uphold the prospect of development was to keep the operational balance in the black by cutting expenditures and pursuing an active fiscal policy. To this end, the city launched a series of institutional reforms (zero-base budgeting, task financing instead of base financing, one-off subsidies to investments aimed at reducing per unit operational costs). Furthermore, the Municipal Government decided to spend the revenues from privatization (which in 1997 amounted to one fifth of the city's annual budget) on investments. The city drafted a four-year (and, subsequently, a seven-year) development plan, and decided to issue bonds while continuing to draw loans.[30]

Of all these developments, further cuts in owner subsidies were the most perceptible change for BKV.[31] Between 1996 and 2000, the increase in current subsidies again lagged behind

---

[28] The compensation index for student and senior passes has dropped from 300 percent in 1995 to 208 percent. Meanwhile, the respective figure still stands at 900 percent in suburban and regional transport. Consequently, the discounted price and subsidies together do not cover expenditures. However, in essence, the compensation for preferential student and senior passes does not help BKV but on the contrary, it helps socially preferred consumer groups (We shall return to this problem later.)

[29] In return, the government promised the Municipality to soon work out a proposal for the normative financing of public transport.

[30] Pallai, Katalin, 1999

the rate of inflation. The investment and targeted subsidies that were first extended in 1993 had stayed in the HUF 1.5-2.5 billion range (apart from a peak in 1995) until 2000, when they started to increase again *(Table 1)*.

From the beginning, the municipality was inclined to counter the disappearance of state subsidies (or the decline of their real value) with fare hikes targeted above the inflation rate. In 1996, and again a year later, the fares went way above the average price increase (Table 3). However, the Ministry of Finance repeatedly rejected the fare hike proposals. BKV has often complained about the Ministry's decisions to curtail the suggested hikes, and especially its most recent limitations (running counter an agreement between the Ministry and the Municipality) to keep the fare hike below the rate of inflation.[32] Anyway, the share of the fares in the revenues increased against that of the subsidies, from 30 percent in 1990 to 42 percent. In other words, the so-called cost coverage ratio has perceptibly improved.[33]

BKV's market revenues depend not only on the price of the tickets but also on the number of passengers and their inclination to pay for their ride. Public transport requires a flexible pricing policy and a constant awareness of the fact that fares are often difficult to collect (i.e., people appear to have an inclination to just skip fares). For these reasons, the quality of the service must be high and supervision must be efficient. Partly due to tightening supervision, the so-called realization ratio (the increase in the money collected versus fare hikes) has improved.[34]

---

[31] Figures are shown in Table 1 up to 2000. For the following two years the temporary (untenable in the long run) increase of municipality subsidies became inevitable due to the insensitive government policy at the time. *(The editor)*

[32] In 1998, as a result of preliminary consultations with the government, the Budapest Municipal Government was allowed to have annual price hikes at a rate of over 6% of the annual inflation rate. This right was to be used at the Municipality's discretion, and for a transitory but unspecified period of time.

[33] The World Bank was also in favor of this move: a condition of its loan was for the company to cut the cost coverage index (which in practical terms meant the reduction of the ratio of subsidies) and to improve the operational ratio, which was defined as the quotient of total revenues and total expenditures. The cost coverage index would be considerably higher if the state subsidies were not considered part of the company's subsidies. The rationale behind this argument is that the subsidies are extended not to BKV but to certain consumer groups instead. A weak point in the company's oft-heard argument is that, due to the price flexibility of the service, solvent demand for BKV's services (and thus the fare revenues total) would be lower without these discounts. The evaluation of fare-compensation is continuously debated by the international financial institutions.

[34] In 2000, the former increased by 12 percent, while the latter only by 6 percent. However, this example also clearly proves that, alongside price flexibility and the company's overall performance, certain other external factors (such as increasing fuel prices and parking fees) must also be taken into consideration here.

PROPOSALS FOR AN ALTERNATIVE FINANCING SYSTEM

During the 1990's, the owner municipality continuously pressed for cost reduction and, through this, for reorganization. The BKV management was seeking an increase in state and local government subsidies and for the modification of the relevant access procedures. Since 1996-1997, the company management itself has been reorganizing its structure, in parallel with insisting on reshaping the financing system. These efforts were incited by external conditions, which were adverse to the company and the company's worsening financial situation.

The "alternative financing system," which is a summary of the various proposals, focuses on the external conditions of operation. According to BKV's own analyses, the company has dried up its internal reserves. The reorganization process and the other related measures have reduced expenditures to a bare minimum. Any further cuts would have detrimental effects to traffic and technical safety, and would hurt the interests of the owners and customers alike. If revenues fail to increase, the company would be inoperable.[35]

The proposed solution argues for increased subsidies. The company expects the state to extend addressed or targeted subsidies for its development programs, and to remove all forms of negative discrimination of local transport versus regional transport. These include: the partial or full elimination of the consumption tax on diesel fuel[36] – similarly to rail and water transport –, the defraying of commuter costs for BKV employees on the same terms as is custom and practice at the state rail company MÁV and the bus company Volán, and the adjustment of the metropolitan fare-compensation index to that applied for regional transport. If this turns out to be impossible, the base subsidy taken into consideration should at least be brought on par with the actual costs – i.e., those that include the Municipal Government's subsidies and relative losses.

The elimination of these discriminative elements would result in the uniform, equalized treatment of the various branches of transport.

The concept of normative regulation also occurs in the proposals concerning the relationship between BKV and the Municipal Government. According to the company, the investment and operational subsidies should be set apart, and the latter should be determined according to a clear-cut and long-term fares calculation scheme. The Municipal Government's subsidies should cover all justified expenditure, but simultaneously the Municipal Government should maintain pressure on the company to improve its efficiency.[37]

---

[35] An external advisor's calculations in 1998 projected that the company's balance sheet losses would reach HUF 20-30 billion by 2002. In the calculations, the revenues and expenditures were adjusted to inflation but the company's structure was assumed to remain unchanged. The advisor said the projection would hold only if the company cut its capital investments further. A failure to do so would increase annual losses to double the projected minimum.

[36] Part of the consumption tax revenues went into the National Road Fund, which financed the development and maintenance of the country's road system. However, BKV hardly ever used these roads.

[37] Other proposals suggested increasing the revenues from local government sources by district contributions or by a transport tax. However, these proposals have been taken off the agenda out of theoretical and practical considerations.

One part of the alternative financing program (the so-called state part) can be reached through lobbying and advocacy with the top authorities. The main objective of the other part (that has to do with the Municipal Government) is to eliminate the need for endless bargaining. At the time of its incorporation, the company's management expected that the new organizational framework – making use of the professional and political influence of the members of the Directorate and the Supervisory Board – would boost its bargaining positions further. However, this expectation failed to materialize (if we use the volume of subsidies to measure bargaining power). To date, the management has not accomplished anything in the state turf. In the late 1990's, BKV was of the opinion that it would not make sense to ask the Municipality for increased subsidies, since the outcome of the annual budgetary debates was always dubious. For this reason, BKV's management aimed to shift the emphasis from the volume of subsidies to procedural aspects. The Municipality also welcomed the shift.

In principle, the decision-maker can also be interested in· replacing bargaining by predictability.[38] At the same time, however, the Municipal Government must be prudent. The lack or uncertainty about the size of the revenues is the basic problem. At a time when the capital city's revenues are unpredictable (primarily because of the fluctuations in centrally determined funding), it is rather risky to attempt to anchor the main entries in the expenditures column. This also explains the budgetary decision-makers' inclination to keep current subsidies at bay as part of their efforts to keep the operational balance in the black. In fact, they are more interested in controlling subsidies than the one-off and therefore more flexible capital expenditures.[39] Another major dubious question is the justifiable level of expenditures – a basic item in normative price regulation. In the absence of competition, it is very difficult to identify[40] the level below which subsidies cannot be replaced by further cuts in expenditure. Under these considerations the owner was reluctant to accept the proposal.

CLEANSWEEP: THE STABILIZATION PROGRAM

Considering BKV's increasing financial problems, the Municipal Government decided to go on the offensive in 1999-2000. However, rather than creating a normative system, it approved a two-year stabilization program, and as part of that program, urged the company to further explore its internal reserves.

---

[38] The elderly may remember that, even during the era of the planned economy, the move from individual subsidies toward equalized redistribution was considered an efficient, market conform measure.

[39] Investment and operation grants have sparked off heated political debates within the Municipal Government. However, both BKV and the Municipal Government eventually proved successful in cutting operational subsidies. While in 1991, the capital city spent 85 percent of its annual budget on operational purposes, in 2000 this figure was slightly more than 50 percent. Meanwhile, the expenditures on development and refurbishment increased from 14 percent in 1991 to nearly 30 percent in 2000. (Source: The Office of the Mayor of Budapest, 2000d:)

[40] BKV's cost efficiency is good in comparison with comparable large European transport companies. BKV's expenditures measured against vehicle kilometer and seat kilometer are the lowest among the eight companies

BKV was again screened, this time by a foreign consulting company. This company was directly interested in cutting BKV's expenditures. However, against the targeted saving of HUF 3 billion, the consulting company concluded that at best one third of that figure could be achieved in the short run through staff cuts, real estate sales and the reduction of sports-related subsidies. The consultants came up with two further packages, each promising to result in HUF 1.5 billion worth of savings. One of these proposed to curtail non-wage benefits, and the other to restructure the company's internal incentive system. BKV accepted the proposals with the exception of those that would have affected the Collective Contract, and started work on a more efficient motivation system.

In order to improve the quality of public transport, to keep modal split proportions up and to maintain the company's operability, the stabilization program envisaged a slight reduction of the traffic volumes and proposed that the capital city extend HUF 5 billion in targeted subsidies to help BKV replenish its assets. Furthermore, the program proposed a one-off revenue increase of HUF 12 billion, to be executed within two years. Fare hikes, the sale of further real estate and the privatization of certain subsidiaries and services, were identified as the sources for the extra revenues.

The program – unusually, laid down by the Municipal Government in detail – indirectly admits that with unchanged conditions, the services would have to be quantitatively reduced and the owner would have to reach deeper in its pockets to maintain the company's technical standards. The policy of reducing subsidies was not tenable. In 2000, the capital transfers earmarked for development purposes increased by almost 100 percent *(Table 1)*. Any further cuts beyond those entailed by the preceding reorganization process threatened to produce dubious results.

NEW EXPERIMENTS AND BREAKTHROUGHS

In the years following the launch of the stabilization program, the Municipality continued to attach high importance (at least in principle) to the efforts aimed at maintaining an integrated system of public transport that could outweigh individual transport on the market. Both the capital city's urban development concept and Budapest's transport system plan (completed in 2001) established that public transport was an important element for the city's operability and livability.[41] However, the subject of these documents provided no clues for curing BKV's ills.

The concrete elements of reform continued to be sought in the annual budgets. The owner – partly as a consequence of the debates among the ruling coalition – recently eased its tight grip not only on development subsidies but on current subsidies as well. In discussing the distribution of operational subsidies, the capital city's budgetary concept for 2001 declares that the Municipal Government must play an active role in "managing the underfinanced state" of the public transport system. However, it also adds that this is only a one-time solution that can only bring transitory ease to the tensions.

---

[41] The Office of the Mayor of Budapest, 1999b; Főmterv Co., 2001

During the internal debates at the Municipal Government, the leaders in charge of financing oppose the radical increase of BKV's subsidies – operational subsidies in particular – on the grounds that this would blur the government's responsibilities, and as a result, the Municipal Government would be obliged to spread the effects of the losses over the other public services in the capital. This would also accelerate their decline and would prompt the government to accuse the Municipal Government of mismanagement. This is why the Municipal Government wants to keep the problems focused on the specific area where they occurred and where the government's responsibilities are easy to identify.

According to these experts, the system of local government financing must be changed or else the system will inevitably collapse. The balance can be improved by the government's assuming further responsibilities. This can be done in several ways: the Ministry of Finance could approve a scheme that would allow for the increase of fares beyond the inflation rate over a period of several years (this at least would not limit the Municipal Government's responsibilities), and/or the central budget could significantly increase its normative subsidies for public transport. Identifying with this stance, the capital city's draft budget for 2002 declares that the central government must step in to solve BKV's problems.[42]

During the past two years, the company's management has been exploring other, longer-term solutions as well. BKV has drafted a comprehensive strategy, continued with the restructuring process, and come up with new proposals for modifying the system of financing. Certain departments and services have been privatized, and the company even considered the option of a major ownership change.

COMPANY STRATEGY

The strategy, presented in November 2000, outlined the company's strengths and weak-nesses, and summed up the management's views on BKV's mission, future goals, and operational principles. Based on the various aspects of the company's performance, the strategy established a balanced system of objectives. Having considered the probabilities and consequences of a series of external and internal changes, the drafters of the strategy drew up three scenarios and attached detailed action programs to them. The strategy favored the version ranked as "medium", considering the effects of the changes envisaged. This version promised to produce HUF 3 billion in extra revenues through internal changes, and a further HUF 10 billion through changes in the external conditions. The actions that were considered quickly executable were built into the company's business plan for 2001.

Since the implementation of these plans does not fully depend on the company's moves, the document should be considered more of a starting point for future action than a systemic summary of final decisions. It is not only the strategy itself but also its evolution process that deserves appreciation. The strategy was born through the intensive teamwork of several top

---

[42] The Office of the Mayor of Budapest, 2000b; The Office of the Mayor of Budapest, 2001.

and medium-level company leaders. The team employed new methods of analysis, while approaches, ideas and opinions were tested against each other. Drafting the strategy became an important element of the company's learning process.

The proposal to restructure BKV's financing system was a key part of the strategy but also appeared in independent motions. Alongside the proposals for actions by the company itself (further reductions in corporate grounds, reduction of stocks, continuing with the rationalization of the organization and operations, restructuring the system of incentives, cuts in welfare expenditure), the strategy has again brought the need for state and municipal participation to the fore.

In response to the continuous deterioration of the situation, the alternative financing program that was completed in the fall of 2000 proposed a faster increase of revenues than that prescribed in 1998. By this time, the company was fully convinced that it was inevitable to increase fares above inflation and to increase subsidies. Emphasis was laid on the goal of operation without losses and on the separation of the operational and investment-related financing schemes. In the operation scheme, subsidies should balance out the difference between fare revenues and current expenditures. According to the investment scheme the owner and the central budget would be responsible for financing the capital expenditures, including the amortization of the existing World Bank loans and the reorganization of the current asset loans.

The company continues to expect the restructuring of the decision-making mechanism and the establishing of a normative – i.e., uniform and predictable – financing system. BKV has drafted a proposal for the formula defining the capital city's long-term obligations in subsidizing (the operation of) public transport. The essential factor of the formula is efficiency measured by passenger kilometers. BKV now expects the Municipal Government to conclude a new operational contract, to simplify and speed up the owner's decision-making processes and to extend the company's independence in influencing the definition of network performance. A new element in the proposal is the attempt to limit the rights of the Ministry of Finance to determine the growth index for fare-compensation. Another new element is the proposition of a regional fare system that would be differentiated by zones and tied to performance.

CONTINUING AND ADJUSTING THE REORGANIZATION PROCESS

Simultaneously with the drafting of the strategies and the financing proposals, the company's management continued with the internal reorganization process.

The top-level management became more split in its views. The separation of the traffic and technical directorates resulted in the creation of the post of deputy general manager. The administrative tasks related to HR and organizational issues were raised to a higher hierarchical level. Meanwhile, BKV reduced the number of its executive units. The "further development" of the divisional organization means closure of one of the five recently established bus plants (the plant was closed down and was subsequently sold) and the amalgamation of the remaining four plants into two organizational units.

It is rather difficult to quantify the financial effects of these steps (except, perhaps, for the sale of real estate). Furthermore, the management's reorganization was not free from the age-old system whereby of changes are "tailored to the leader". In principle both amalgamation and separation may produce positive results.

The shrinking of the portfolio of the subsidiaries was a relatively more important event. As we have seen in Chapter 2, the privatization of certain services was proposed as early as in the 1991 program of the Mayor of Budapest. The privatization process was facilitated by the establishment of the smaller independent companies, some of which were put up for sale right after their incorporation in 1998. The principle of the company is that only those subsidiaries should be fully sold whose portfolios have little or no relationship with BKV's main business profile, where the services at issue are offered by many other ventures in the market, and if the selling of the stakes do not result in losses.

According to the first document, four out of the company's 11 subsidiaries were proposed to be privatized 100 percent. The document also proposed to privatize the majority stake of another two subsidiaries. However, due to the resistance of the affected organizations and the trade unions, and also because of the lagging demand in the market and the weak performance of some of the subsidiaries, the privatization process turned out to be slower than expected. BKV managed to sell two companies in 1999 and one each in 2000 and 2001.[43]

One of the aims of the privatization plan was to reduce current expenditure. Many of BKV's subsidiaries are up against permanent financial and market problems – often as a result of the inevitable cuts in the mother company's orders. BKV must finance their losses, either by modifying the prices or through owner's loans. Consequently, in some instances the management has also considered merging these subsidiaries into BKV or an affiliated corporation.[44]

The stabilization program amplified the other aim of privatization: to generate a one-off revenue for the company. Since its market value was estimated to be in the billion-forint range, BKV's telecommunications subsidiary appeared to be the obvious choice to be put on the block. A new element in the plan envisaged the spinning off of the recently established IT-department into an independent company, which would then be put up for sale. The debates over the fate of this company highlighted practically all the structural contradictions inherent in BKV's efforts when spinning off its vital services and especially when privatizing them.

Either spinning off or privatization surely changes the expenditure structure of the mother company, but the balance will remain questionable. Proceeds from the sales generate one-off revenue, but relinquishing ownership rights results in weaker influence. In the longer run, the mother company might have to pay considerably more for the services at issue. From

---

[43] These were: Peron Ltd. (75 percent sold), the Funicular and the construction and telecommunications subsidiaries.

[44] As was the case during the renewal of the infrastructure system.

BKV's point of view, privatization may also be considered an advance payment by the buyer to cover the projected expenditures. Consequently, beyond the appraisal of the expertise of the partner and the investment capacity it is worth to consider the balance of one-time revenue and current expenditure as the price of a loan – if taking up loans is considered to be a realistic alternative.

NEW LEVELS OF PRIVATIZATION

The other way of privatizing – when the rights of operation are privatized rather than the assets and organizational units themselves – turned out to be likewise controversial.[45]

As an experiment, BKV in 1999 subcontracted the operation of two bus lines for a period of five years. The subcontractor, a private firm, operates its own new buses, but its fares and company image do not differ from those of BKV. The company accounts for its expenses on the basis of gross expenditure as a percentage of bus mileage. Under the second stage of the plan, 14 bus lines involving 60 vehicles were contracted in September 2001.

Faced with World Bank's requirements and the owner's intentions, BKV procrastinated in implementing this program that planned to improve efficiency and create competition. The company did not want the subcontractor to present a discriminatory basis for comparison. Furthermore, BKV did not want to set a precedent for the disruption of the integrated unity of the public transport, which was one of the pillars of the company's business strategy. If it is possible to subcontract the operation of more and more bus lines, what would prevent decision-makers from wanting to operate all the bus lines – or, for that matter, all the divisions – along similar lines?

The threshold-price set for the bus lines at the first tender did not take into account the proportionate losses of the company, thus the bids were lower than BKV's actual expenses. Upon inviting public procurement tenders for the second phase, the owner insisted that BKV calculate the breakeven threshold price (the direct expenditure of the lines should include the proportional company loss).

However, there were no bidders at this price. The following tender with modified conditions was successful. Though the price did not fully cover the proportionate company loss, BKV could reckon with beneficial external effects as the subcontractor launched its operations with new vehicles, and thus offered higher quality service. BKV itself could not have financed such an investment. A total of 60 new buses were introduced, and this perceptibly reduced the company's investment and refurbishment obligations, as well as the calculated depreciation costs. Further savings were realized through the closure of a bus garage.

Disregarding the above-mentioned external effects, with unchanged fares, subcontracting the operation of the lines does not reduce BKV's losses – in fact these might slightly increase. If the company had sufficient resources (either from depreciation or from external sources) to continuously update its vehicles, subcontracting the lines would not result in savings

---

[45] Similarly to the sale of the subsidiaries, this idea also originated in the Mayor's program for 1991. However, the launch of the program was also delayed for almost a decade.

in the present conditions.[46] Under current conditions, the contractual operation benefits in providing a market gauge for BKV performance. Furthermore, it reduces the need for investment grants and improves the quality of the service at the same fare levels.

Besides the cautious privatization of its operations, BKV's strategy also proposed the reorganization of the company's ownership structure. The options considered included the company's transfer to state ownership; a mixed ownership structure with the state and the Municipal Government acting as predominant shareholders; the involvement of the management and the employees as shareholders; the involvement of other external owners through the Municipal Government (district, agglomeration); and the involvement of private capital. BKV's management expects the new shareholders[47] to bring in additional investment resources (This obviously explains the inclusion of the state and the Municipal Government in the list of potential shareholders.). Furthermore, the reduction of the Budapest Municipal Government's monolithic, 100 percent share package is expected to broaden the management's scope of activity and improve the interest enforcing power of the company. Having weighed the pros and cons of the various options, the drafters of the strategy opted for an ownership structure in which 51 percent of the shares would be held by the capital city and the remaining 49 percent by miscellaneous investors.

The modification of the context of the company's operation, primarily the modification of the financing system, is a prerequisite of the tightly interpreted privatization deal – now excluding the state and other local governments. At present conditions (fares set by authorities, uncertainty in state and local government grants), the shares of the company doomed to losses cannot be marketed. This circumstance is presumably taken into account by the municipal leaders who – as in the mid-1990's – argue for the primacy of solving the problems of the financing system and consider the change in ownership a secondary, irrelevant proposal. However, it is worth taking into consideration the fact that the improvement of the financing context and privatization can be combined both in principle and in practice, as has been shown by cases when state (even local government) companies in several sectors have been sold. We see this as a mutual connection. On the one hand, regulations guaranteeing predictable operation without losses are really a prerequisite of the change in the ownership structure. On the other hand, the preparation for privatization – as a consequence – exerts pressure upon the relevant actors, including the government, to develop a new financing system. Serious debates on this proposal could move negotiations away from the present deadlock – but this point had not been raised by the fall of 2001.

WHITHER NOW?

In recent years, the owner has made several attempts to restructure BKV's organization, operation and financing. The prime goal was to tighten the company's budgetary constraints

---

[46] With the improvement of the financing conditions this contracting out surely would result in further savings, as many examples in European cities show.

[47] With a natural exception of the employees. Employee and management ownership might strengthen personal interests in principle – but practice raises doubts concerning both the extent and the drive of this interest.

while maintaining the quality of its services. Faced with deteriorating technical and financial conditions, the management made significant efforts to keep the company afloat. The balance of these efforts may well be considered positive: the trams are still running, and are only a little bit more expensive and noisy than they used to be and the fare hikes have not been excessively steep despite the cuts in subsidies. The company's staff has been reduced by half, its cost effectiveness has increased and the number of passengers was up in 2001.

However, this situation does not seem tenable even in the short run. BKV's is about to dry up its reserves. In the absence of supplementary resources, the company is facing financial or technical collapse.

In other words, the attempts to solve the company's problems have not produced long-term solutions. The biggest of all accomplishments is that attempts have been made. There are two reasons for this. First, the owner's representatives and the company's management have analyzed the causes of the problems in detail and weighed short- and long-term consequences. This was a serious learning process which has elicited new approaches and methods and has also altered the old structures and routines. Second, limited as they are, the experiments have still produced certain results. It has become clear that the changes implemented to date cannot be expected to produce a breakthrough. If the owner and the company want to find long-term solutions to BKV's chronic problems, they will have to take steps that are more radical.

The documents drafted by the Municipality and the intentions of the company make us conclude that the sides are interested in maintaining and improving the (qualitative and quantitative) standards of the capital city's public transport system. Accordingly, based on the "magic triangle" described in subchapter "Stock Corporation – In Hybrid Markets", they appear to have several options.[48]

The first scenario would include the introduction of a fare system to cover the company's justified costs. This could be implemented either through a "big leap", or over a period of a few years, according to a strict schedule.[49] Once the relatively low current fares are increased, the revenues (which also include fare-compensation) should be enough to cover the company's operational and capital expenditures. However, while this method is fairly common in the public services sector, it remains only a theoretical possibility in the field of public transport. Political obstacles may perhaps be removed by extending discounts to a broader circle of people (although this will no doubt boost the volume of fare-compensation) but two economic obstacles are bound to remain.

First, BKV holds a monopoly position, hence the limits of comparison and information asymmetry make it difficult to define "justified costs" and "necessary investment" at any given moment. Non-market price bargaining would survive. Second, but more important is that as a result of radical fare hikes and due to the substitutability of the service and its

---

[48] The scenarios that follow reflect the private opinion of the author. She has not consulted with either the owner or the company on these options.

relatively high price flexibility, even those citizens who would otherwise be able to pay for the full fares would most likely be inclined to switch to using their cars. As a result, BKV's fares revenues would drop, while the proportion of its subsidized customers would increase. Since a significant part of the expenditures are permanent, sooner or later, either BKV itself would have to be subsidized again, or the company's performance would have to be reduced.

The second scenario is also based on a fare increase. However, since it aims to institutionally separate investment from operation, this scenario would earmark the fare revenues for covering current expenses (including regular maintenance[50]), and would leave infrastructure development and vehicle replacement (including annual depreciation) to the Municipal Government and/or to the state to finance. This scenario (similarly to the case of the highways) admits that the costs of major investments cannot be shifted on to consumers: prices can only cover operational costs, taken in a broader sense. Fares calculated this way would be significantly lower, since they would not cover investments, and thus would be competitive with individual transport.[51] Under this scenario, it is likewise difficult to define the "rational" level of costs and investments, to externally and separately manage and finance a part of the depreciation and to define the respective tasks for the Municipal Government and the state.

The third scenario proposes to relinquish the principle of low subsidies concerning both investments and operations. If BKV received normative, long-term operational subsidies tied to well defined performance indices, as it was proposed by the alternative financing program, this would amount to a significant departure from the current practice (here the central budget might also participate as co-financier.). For the owner, the deficiency of this scenario is that it limits the pressure for efficiency. For the company, it fails to provide long-term guarantees for the established conditions: political changes may override them at any moment.

Finally, the fourth scenario would break through the boundaries of the "magic triangle" by separating the roles of the customer, the regulator and the investor from each other. This could ease the confusion caused by the conflicting roles of the Municipality. It proposes to give a greater role to private capital in public transport in order to reduce the burdens on the community, and to boost efficiency. This would require the gradual and thorough reconsideration and restructuring of BKV's current operations and characteristics (publicly owned, monopoly, servicing responsibilities) and the reshaping of the whole financing system.

---

[49] A fare system reform, adjusting the fares to the quality and quantity of the actual services could either be carried out following this schedule or separately from it. This reform should specify different fares on a regional basis, and should introduce special fares for the express and "branded" services. We should keep in mind that the investment costs (e.g., the Metro gates) are enormous.

[50] During the planned economy era, this was known as "dynamic maintenance."

[51] Competitiveness depends on several other conditions, e.g., on the expenses of car maintenance, on the tariffs and physical difficulties of parking and on the quality of public transport.

There are two basic ways to eliminate public ownership: either the operation or the company must be privatized. In both cases, it is indispensable to create competition – to facilitate a series of service providers' entry to the market.

In view of the latter condition, it would be questionable to sell a minority or majority stake of BKV to new owners. Should the Municipal Government's monopoly be replaced by a monopolistic entity under mixed ownership, the consumer's freedom of choice would clearly not increase. Furthermore, this scenario would preserve bargaining as the main method of revenue and resource acquisition between the company and the part owner regulatory authority. It would not eliminate the conflict of roles on the level of the local government. The company might acquire additional capital from the new shareholders and its bargaining position might also be boosted by the appearance of a strong private investor or a number of small investors (i.e., district or suburban local governments). However, the company's structural characteristics – and thereby its future prospects – would remain unchanged.

One way of privatizing BKV would be to dissolve the company into smaller units, by establishing several smaller companies or making the present divisions independent. In either case, the infrastructure should also be divided up.[52] It is clear that the different activities would present different problems to tackle: it is fairly easy to privatize the bus lines and rather difficult to sell the more capital intensive tram services. The other way could be to keep the infrastructure and to guarantee free access (as is the case with landline telephones). This would amount to privatizing operation – expanding the system of subcontractors. All the services may be provided by private ventures, and the present BKV could become the operator of the infrastructure kept in municipal (or partly in state) ownership, financing maintenance from rental (concession) revenues.

The restructuring of public transport, the preservation of a certain level of integration within the system, the drafting of a new fare system and the division of the financing of investments are difficult tasks burdened with professional and political conflicts. However, all actors presumably agree that it is worth to begin exploring possibilities, discussing their pros and cons at public professional debates and defining the required conditions and frameworks as soon as possible – at least while the trams are still running.

---

[52] Certain laws would have to be amended for this to be possible. This would take time, but does not seem to be impossible.

Table 1

SHARE OF BKV IN THE BUDGET OF THE MUNICIPALITY (HUF million)

ITEM	1991	1992	1993	1994	1995	1996	1997	1998	1999	2000
Municipal budget total	54 922	65 798	74 581	92 087	115 409	137 424	191 566	217 426	239 206	260 198
of which: operation subsidy for BKV	9 279	9 279	9 063	9 250	11 800	10 600	11 416	12 375	13 905	13 905
bonus	-	-	-	-	-	-	-	300	300	300
investment subsidy for BKV *	-	-	336	1 828	5 460	1 434	1 240	2 154	2 570	4 677
BKV total	9 279	9 279	9 399	11 078	17 260	12 034	12 656	14 829	16 775	18 882
BKV/Municipality (%)	16,9	14,1	12,6	12,0	15,0	8,8	6,6	6,8	7,0	7,3
Subsidy form state	-	1 000	2 000	2 000	2 300	2 000	-	-	-	-

Different from actual drawing
*Source: BKV**

Table 2

SERVICE PERFORMANCE OF BKV, 1990–2000

YEAR	PASSENGER KILOMETERS ('000 000)	SEAT KILOMETERS ('000 000)
1990	7 448 100	26 506 304
1991	7 065 292	26 598 724
1992	6 440 446	26 549 578
1993	6 406 776	26 131 273
1994	6 667 832	24 773 716
1995	6 604 878	23 166 043
1996	6 235 327	21 845 086
1997	6 058 603	21 677 829
1998	5 918 001	21 421 740
1999	5 963 246	21 183 486
2000	6 089 254	20 812 498
2000/1990	**81,7%**	**78,5%**

Source: BKV

Table 3

CHANGES OF FARES AND INFLATION

YEAR	PASSENGER KILOMETERS ('000 000)	SEAT KILOMETERS ('000 000)
1991	47,1	35,0
1992	46,3	23,0
1993	18,9	22,5
1994	16,0	18,8
1995	27,5	28,2
1996	46,7	23,6
1997	30,9	18,3
1998	14,9	14,3
1999	18,7	10,0
2000	6,0	9,8

Source: BKV

Table 4
REVENUES AND EXPENSES OF BKV, 1990–2000 (HUF million)

ITEM	1990	1991	1992	1993	1994	1995	1996	1997	1998	1999	2000
REVENUE FROM PUBLIC TRANSPORT of which	15515	18341	22644	23548	25466	29387	35722	39391	44378	50191	53891
Fares	4318	5547	6741	7231	8381	10098	13460	16804	18753	22413	25057
Fare-compensation	2153	3214	4403	4940	5835	7485	9441	10995	12606	13550	14538
Maintenance subsidy	324										
Earmarked state subsidy			1000	2000	2000	2300	2000				
Municipal subsidy + bonus	8720	9580	10500	9377	9250	9504	10794	11567	12995	14204	14200
Suburban subsidy							27	25	24	24	96
OTHER REVENUES	1250	1186	630	846	1411	2193	1905	2241	2065	2031	3321
FINANCIAL REVENUES				10	56	13	82	32	34	11	263
SPECIAL REVENUES		160	190	457	975	318	310	2948	1877	1483	4138
GROSS REVENUE	16765	19687	23464	24861	27908	31911	38019	44612	48354	53716	61613
VAT		159									
NET REVENUE	16765	19528	23464	24861	27908	31911	38019	44612	48354	53716	61613
MATERIAL TYPE EXPENSES of which	5013	7949	9797	10078	11265	12466	13029	15736	16303	18848	21115
Material expenses	2339	2903	3637	4312	4922	5651	5607	5214	4956	5706	6166
Material type services		1331	2074	1828	2316	1757	1318	2483	3178	3990	4245
Energy costs	2674	3615	3944	3869	3909	5019	5998	7372	8111	9124	10679
Purchase value of goods sold		100	142	69	118	39	106	667	58	28	25
Wages	4498	6024	7241	8170	9926	11403	13015	13686	15370	17397	18763
Personal type services		366	711	701	775	800	1108	1655	1763	1965	2208
Public charges (health contribution)	1939	2595	3254	3662	4447	5114	5662	5997	6688	6669	7193
PERSONAL EXPENSES	6437	8985	11206	12533	15148	17317	19785	21338	23821	26031	28164
DEPRECIATION	1946	2153	3715	3717	4381	5405	8777	9580	9868	10150	10825
OTHER EXPENSES	2105	266	406	421	536	910	1298	1401	2578	3309	3428
OTHER ALLOCATAIONS	736	545	522	892	1149	1700	3877	2443	2009	3029	2304
FINANCIAL ALLOCATIONS				19	17	211	588	555	1582	1934	2206
EXTRA ALLOCATIONS			346	662	788	1691	530	2868	2289	1729	2226
GROSS ALLOCATIONS	16237	19898	25992	28322	33284	39700	47884	53921	58450	65030	70268
Activated own performances			2614	3203	4466	4047	3145	2450	1376	1551	1796
NET ALLOCATIONS	16237	19898	23378	25119	28818	35653	44739	51471	57074	63479	68472
RESULT	528	-370	86	-258	-910	-3742	-6720	-6859	-8720	-9763	-6859
State subsidy (including fare-compensation) (%)	12,8	16,3	23,0	27,9	28,1	30,7	30,1	24,6	26,1	25,2	23,6
Municipal operation subsidy (%)	53,9	48,7	44,7	37,7	33,1	29,8	28,4	25,9	26,9	26,4	23,0

Source: BKV

Table 5
INVESTMENTS, 1995–2000 (HUF million)

ITEM	1995	1996	1997	1998	1999	2000
Loans + State Environment Subsidy		1 033	1 158	946	3 208	5 082
Municipal investment /earmarked subsidy	5 887	726	1 205	2 184	2 746	4 233
Own investments	2 407	3 181	4 433	6 645	1 721	4 810
Value adding refurbishment	2 771	2 525	2 525	3 293	3 900	
Total	11 065	7 465	9 321	13 068	11 575	14 125
Municipal share in investment (%)	53,2	9,7	12,9	16,7	23,7	30,0

Source: BKV

299

UTILITY PRIVATIZATION[1]

Ferenc Szűcs

Few would argue today that privately owned companies are more efficient than companies in state or other types of public ownership. In addition to working with lower costs and a higher return on investment, they are more efficient, which means a better utilization of all available resources.

It is in the vital interest of countries, towns, lower administrative units and local communities to use available resources at maximum efficiency. If that is not the case, their position can weaken and opportunities remain unutilized. Viewed in that light, privatization can assume a meaning broader than selling companies to private investors.

In addition to calculating the economic use of a private company, it is interesting for the analyst to consider how private business can help better satisfy the welfare, cultural, health, etc. needs of the community. Outside the field of business, the operation of a private company is desirable in cases where additional profits are not exclusively channeled to the private investor but where the community is also a direct or indirect beneficiary. With the political changeover in 1990, a unique window of opportunity opened in Hungary: to reform the public service sector up to then built on an entirely state-owned and crisis-ridden institutional structure.

The present paper offers an insight into the privatization transactions made by the Municipality of Budapest.

INITIAL STEPS

As early as 1990-91 the Municipality of Budapest set out to examine the public utilities and other companies in its ownership so as to work out the best organizational and ownership patterns for long-term operation. (The organizational and financial due diligence covered 11 companies: Budapest Gas Works, Waterworks of Budapest, Municipal Sewerage Works, Budapest District Heating Company, Liquid Waste Management Company, City Park Maintenance Company, Budapest Cemetery Company, Fuel System Control Company, Public Space Maintenance Company, Budapest Public Bath and Spa Company and Budapest Film Company.)[2] Later on, the Pharmafontana Pharmaceutical Company and the Amusement Park Company[3] were also scrutinized for the same purpose.

---

[1] The author finalized the manuscript in March 2002. *(The editor)*

[2] Hungarian names: Fővárosi Gázművek, Fővárosi Vízművek, Fővárosi Csatornázási Művek, Budapesti Távhőszolgáltató Vállalat, Fővárosi Településtisztasági Vállalat, Fővárosi Kertészeti Vállalat, Budapesti Temetkezési Intézet, Fővárosi Kéményseprő és Tüzeléstechnikai Vállalat, Közterület-fenntartó Vállalat, Fürdőigazgatóság

[3] Hungarian names: Pharmafontana Gyógyszerészeti Vállalat, Fővárosi Vidámpark Vállalat

For each of the companies due diligence focused on:

- the scope of activity, including the relation between basic and complementary activities,
- the stock of assets,
- the financial status (pricing mechanism, operating and investment grants),
- relations between the various companies,
- potential obstacles (legal or economic) to streamlining the organizational set-up,
- unclarified aspects in separating the powers of central and local government.

Work done at that time served to get a picture of the state of affairs, prepare subsequent efforts towards organizational development, and define possible directions for progress. However, the scene was not yet set for privatization.

The conditions for organizational development and future privatization had also tangibly improved in the local government-controlled public services sector by 1993-94. Let us illustrate that point with some examples: the transfer of certain state-owned assets to local governments was completed, the financial system of the local government-controlled public services assumed its final shape (the state and the local governments agreed on how to divide the rights to set prices between themselves and the mechanism to ensure central budget funds for developing public services), and the conditions were ensured for converting state- and local government-owned enterprises into limited companies.

During 1993-95 the companies in the ownership of the Municipality of Budapest were transformed into limited or share companies. Because asset valuation always preceded conversion, the assets of the newly formed limited companies were posted at their real value (which in many cases exceeded their earlier registered book value by far). Conversion made it possible to separate equity in the physical sense from the transferable stakes and shares (which represented the ownership rights).

At the same time, or following conversion, organizational transformation occurred to a varying degree (as, for instance, decentralization) at the following companies: City Park Maintenance Co., Liquid Waste Management Co., Fuel System Control Co. and Budapest Public Bath and Spa Co. However, no noteworthy steps were taken towards privatization at those companies.

PREPARING PRIVATIZATION

The next step along the road to privatization at the Municipality of Budapest was to work out the concepts that would underpin privatization. Consulting firms selected on a competitive basis were commissioned for this purpose. Each concept had to address the following issues: a detailed description and assessment of the economic and financial situation of the company concerned, the enumeration of potential development requirements and, most importantly, a level-headed analysis of the expected benefits and potential risks inherent in privatization.

Ad hoc privatization teams were set up to do ground work and prepare decisions. The teams consisted of members of the General Assembly of the Municipality of Budapest (both from the ruling majority coalition and the opposition), privatization experts and members of the management of the companies concerned. The teams charged trusted to see through until the implementation of the decisions of the General Assembly of the Municipality of Budapest and of the Ownership Committee of the General Assembly, liaise with the consulting firm and the company concerned, discuss and assess interim working papers and put forward recommendations on privatization-related decisions to the decision-making bodies.

The privatization teams played an important role in keeping the several party groups (also called factions) of the General Assembly of the Municipality of Budapest informed on the recommendations and other developments. The teams were in charge of the professional preparation of privatization and submitting recommendations. They discussed economic, legal and technical aspects of the matters but were not tasked to give out judgments of merit. Still, as they were representatives of the majority and opposition parties in the General Assembly (note that opposition deputies headed some of the privatization teams), they managed to call the attention of the decision-making bodies to the relevant professional issues. As a consequence, politically motivated debates – that are unavoidable concomitants of privatization-related decisions – did not overshadow professionalism in the decision-making process.

Detailed privatization concepts were worked out and privatization teams operated at the following companies: Budapest Gas Works, Pharmafontana Co., Budapest District Heating Co., Waterworks of Budapest, Municipal Sewerage Works, Public Space Maintenance Co., Amusement Park Co. and Budapest Film Co.

PRIVATIZATION ATTEMPTS THAT FAILED

Privatization did not take place after all at the District Heating, Public Space Maintenance and Amusement Park companies. The causes for this differed in each case.

In the case of the Budapest District Heating Co. part of the problem was (and still is) that, for other than business considerations, the price of natural gas has been fixed at a low level, which radically weakens the competitive aspect of supplying district heating. The gas bill is the largest single item among the expenditures of the District Heating Co., because by far the greatest proportion of heat energy that the company buys (the bigger part) or itself generates (the minor part) is derived from natural gas.

The price of gas does not reflect (anywhere in the world, at least to our knowledge) the negative externalities of individual heating, which exceed those of district heating. Hence it follows that the price the population pays for gas does not realistically reflect the actual social cost of gas consumption. Still, where the forces of the market are freer to exert their strength, the free market allows large gas consumers to get discounts at such a rate (or alternatively the retail consumer price of gas is so high) that district heating tends to be competitive with individual heating. Hungary, however, has a long way to go before the ratio of prices becomes economically rational. Defining the price of gas is outside the local governments' competence. It is decided by state agencies, in fact, it is part of governmental policy.

Disadvantageous as the price system is for the District Heating Company's gas bill, the company should (if it were to become attractive for investors) generate enough revenues from the price margin of the wholesale and retail consumers to cover the costs of operation, capital expenditure and give out profits to investors.

After examining the situation, potential investors were partly justified in voicing the following concern: under the given conditions, it may prove difficult to make consumers accept district heating prices high enough to make the company efficient, generate revenues for capital expenditure and revenues for the investors. Potential investors claimed that this amounted to a considerable business risk.

Although a changeover to individual heating requires a one-off expenditure and although in some places technical obstacles all but make it impossible (hence the near monopoly position of district heating in some places), district heating cannot have an economically sound future as long as its prices remain uncompetitive.

In the case of the District Heating Co., the authors of the privatization concept recommended to sell the company's shares following a "revenue-centric" concept. (The authors of the concept supposed that capital investment in the company would equal the value of assets represented by the shares sold, and the investors' revenues would be proportional to their participating interest and not adjusted to the level of the improvement of corporate efficiency.) Eventually investors did not put forward any acceptable bids to buy the shares. The only bid that was submitted failed to satisfy formal requirements. The door was thus left open to future negotiations on the sale of the District Heating Co.

> In 1996, when efforts were made to privatize the District Heating Co., the company's gross domestic revenues stood at HUF 18,453 million, profit after taxation being a little over HUF 200 million. The company's equity on 31 December 1996 was HUF 33,313 million, of which subscribed capital was 28,359 million. The company had no long-term liabilities. Invitations to bids were issued in two versions: (a) the sale of shares granting 25%+1 of the votes, (b) 50%+1 of the votes. The nominal value of shares offered for sale was (a) HUF 7,090 million, (b) HUF 14,180 million.

Privatization could have followed another road by separating the maintenance of the service infrastructure from the service itself. This proposal included a proposal to set up a "thermo-ring" as well as plans for financing it – all these could have launched competition among the primary suppliers of heat energy. In this case the service suppliers would have been interested in savings on energy purchase with the condition that savings should be shared with the customers.

Privatizing operation would have improved efficiency in contrast to maximizing privatization revenue. However, the contractual interests of the consulting firm diverted it from that road, as its fee would have been proportional with the revenue to be derived from privatization. (The authors of the privatization concept claimed that capital investment was necessary for modernizing the district heating service. They disregarded the fact that capital is only invested if the investor is assured of a return, thus making it an expensive development source.) A few years later, in 1999-2000, further detailed proposals were elaborated for the Municipality of Budapest as regards privatization, taking into consideration the real characteristics of the district heating market and separating heat production from distribution, as well as focusing on operation. By that time however, governing coalition parties' approaches to privatization had become so different that the recommendation could not get off the paper.

The **Public Space Maintenance Co.** (henceforward **PSM**) consists of disparate divisions. Some of these divisions' services are delivered solely to the Municipality of Budapest (for instance, removing snow from streets, dusting streets with sand to avoid them being slippery, maintaining public roads, organizing urban traffic, etc.). Other divisions earned the right, on the basis of competitive tenders, to deliver other services (as for instance, the collection of communal refuse). A considerable part of the revenues of the company directly originate from the budget of the Municipality of Budapest. The privatization of the company could have occurred if due attention had been paid to the different business characteristics of the disparate activities and if various solutions had been applied. The coalition parties that ran the City could not agree on whether or not to decentralize the company. Consequently, the privatization process ground to a halt.

> In 1997, when PSM's privatization was on the agenda, PSM's domestic revenues amounted to HUF 9,745 million, profit after taxation being HUF 3.4 million. The company's equity on 31 December 1997 was HUF 22,055 million; of which subscribed capital was HUF 16,744 million. The company had HUF 102 million in long-term liabilities.

At first sight the privatization of the **Budapest Amusement Park Co.** seemed easy. Similar entertainment centers in other metropolises make massive profits. Unless justified by some special local consideration, local municipalities do not need to be involved in their operation. In Budapest, however, the amusement park is situated in a public park that is home to several structures of historic value. The land where the amusement park operates was not included in the assets of the Budapest Amusement Park Co. and was kept as the city's in-kind contri-bution to the operation so as to ensure that it would remain under special protection. When the Amusement Park was converted into a limited company, only the machines and the structures that housed them were posted as assets.

As it happened, the amusement park did not prove to be attractive for investors for the following reasons: the greater part of the machines are obsolete (and some of them are protected as having historical importance), the company is not the owner of the land it occupies, and the amusement arcades of Budapest's mushrooming shopping malls offer a tough competition.

Despite earnest efforts on the part of the consulting firm concerned, privatization failed at the first attempt. Heeding the recommendation of municipality bodies that were in charge of privatization, the General Assembly continued in its interest to privatize the company. Consequently, it initiated direct negotiations with interested potential investors the same year, in 1997. As the negotiations with the two eligible groups of investors were inconclusive, at the end of 1997 the General Assembly declared the directly negotiated privatization process unsuccessful. The company was instructed to work out and implement a medium-term development concept. Its privatization was for the time being removed from the agenda. The so-called "City park concept" that was still in force hindered the establishing of the conditions for successful privatization, as the concept froze the real estate market for the affected area.

> In 1996, the last full year before attempts at privatization began, the gross revenues of the Budapest Amusement Park Co. stood at HUF 254 million, profit after taxation being about HUF 8.6 million. On 31 December 1996 the company's equity was HUF 346 million, of which subscribed capital was HUF 168 million. No long-term liabilities burdened the company.

When work began on the privatization concept for the **Budapest Film Co.**, the Municipality of Budapest defined clear-cut preferences concerning the distribution of films and operating cinemas in Budapest. The Municipality of Budapest decided that a broad and colorful assortment of films, including art films, should be available in the city. The Budapest Film Co. should continue providing film distribution as a cultural mission, the way it had been doing ever since the early 1990's. That is why emphasis was laid on maintaining the network of prestigious art cinemas. The Municipality of Budapest was (and still is) unable to provide financial support for those cultural objectives. Consequently, those assets can be used a basis for attaining the above-mentioned cultural goals that the company received when it was converted from a municipal enterprise into a limited company.

Budapest's cinema market had undergone a radical transformation by the year 2000. The number of conventional cinemas is fast declining (only a handful of art cinemas are holding out), and there is fierce competition among the burgeoning multiplexes. Under such conditions, the privatization of the Budapest Film Co. could yield additional market share for the major US companies that distribute films and operate multiplexes, which would run contrary to the declared cultural aims of the Municipality.

With those considerations in mind the Municipality of Budapest retained exclusive ownership of the Budapest Film Co., and the entire assets transferred at conversion remained the property of the company. Taking into consideration the requirements of the company's different activities of (such as film distribution, the operation of cinemas, asset management, video rental, etc.), the Budapest Film Co. set up companies with a relatively low level of subscribed capital. The Budapest Film Cultural Service Ltd., in which (following the relevant decision of the Municipality of Budapest) the employees and the management became minority stakeholders, is the most important among them.[4] Using

---

[4] Hungarian name: Budapest Film Kulturális Szolgáltató Kft.

the funds of the Budapest Film Co., a foundation was set up to ensure across-the-board grants for "art cinemas." Thanks to the decentralization of the company's structure and the skillful management of the real estate at the company's disposal, the group of companies that are owned by the Budapest Film Co. managed to fulfile the cultural expectations of the Municipality of Budapest for some years.

During the last years, due to intensifying competition in the fields of film distribution and the operation of cinemas, the Budapest Film group has had to face more and more financial difficulties that have almost eliminated its capacity to finance the art cinema network.

PRIVATIZATION TRANSACTIONS
THAT SUCCEEDED

PRIVATIZATION OF THE BUDAPEST GAS WORKS CO.

As early as during the first due diligence of the Budapest Gas Works Company, the experts' opinion was that the company could be privatized. The Act on Local Governments obliges local governments to provide piped gas service for the population. However, the sectoral law governing the conditions, rules and related procedural routine of gas service does not refer to the local governments. Consequently, in the course of privatizing the Budapest Gas Works Co. no obligations other than the requirement to maintain and develop the service had to be reckoned with.

The most obvious form of privatization was to issue a tender invitation for a package of the company's shares. In 1995, two options were published: both the minority and the majority shareholdings were up for sale. Although the tenders submitted for majority shares were financially more favorable, the decision-making bodies gave preference to political rather than business considerations and decided to sell the minority of the shares. (As a consequence, the privatization revenue of the Municipality of Budapest was by far smaller than what it could have been, and no noteworthy advantage compensated for the unearned revenue.)

By late 1995 the company had been partially privatized: the Municipality of Budapest was the single majority shareholder, while VEW Energie AG-Ruhrgas AG consortium assumed control over 32% of the shares. A closed-ended capital increase then occurred, which led to a further 8% of the shares of the Municipality of Budapest being sold. In 1998, the Hungarian Energy Office approved the sale of the shares of VEW Energie AG to WGV AG und Co. KG and the sale of the shares of Ruhrgas AG to RGE Hungária Ltd. In 1999 WGV AG und Co. KG transferred its shares (which represented 32.67% of the share capital) to WGV Beteiligungs BmbH. Presently, the (directly and indirectly) German consortium holds 49% of the company's subscribed capital.

In compliance with the recommendations of the privatization concept, employees of the company could also buy shares. Presently, they own 1% of them. The Municipality of Budapest owns the remaining 50% of the shares. Calculated at the price valid at the time of the sale, the Municipality of Budapest had a one-off privatization revenue of HUF 17.4 billion and is entitled to dividends proportional to its ownership rate.

At the time of privatization, in 1996, Budapest Gas Works Co. had HUF 41,943 million gross domestic revenue from sales, the profit after taxation being HUF 930.5 million. On 31 December 1997 the company's equity amounted to 85,118 million, of which the subscribed capital was 68,396 million. (Part of that sum was the 8% capital increase in early 1996, wherefrom the company had a revenue of HUF 4.7 billion, calculated at the price valid when subscription occurred.) The company's long-term liabilities amounted to HUF 21 million.

The shares owned by the Municipality of Budapest are a type of preferential shares that ensure additional rights when voting future modifications independently from the owner of the shares' proportion of equity ownership. Thus, in order to enable the Municipality to fulfil its obligations that derive from the Act on Local Governments, the shareholders' meeting of the company may not pass a decision on certain essential issues, such as those enlisted below, without the approval of the Municipality:

a) formulation or amendment of the Articles of Association, except in case of equity increase;

b) modification of the rights attached to the different types of shares;

c) decision on the company's conversion or termination without a legal successor;

d) modification of the types of the company's shares;

e) issues that under the Companies Act require a three-fourth majority of the vote, except in case of an equity increase;

f) electing at least one member of the Board of Directors and one third of the members of the Supervisory Board;

g) any other issues in the competence of the shareholders' meeting that materially affect the obligation resting on the company, on the Municipality of Budapest and other competent district local governments and state companies to ensure Budapest's gas supply.

As can be seen from the above list, the Municipality of Budapest managed to retain control over the key issues in the course of the company's privatization, irrespective of the size of its shareholding.

The Municipality has retained control over key posts in the company. The Board of Directors consists of seven members. The investors nominate three of them. The Supervisory Board consists of nine members. Investors nominate two of them. The Municipality nominates the remaining members of the Board of Directors and the Supervisory Board.

The right to nominate the general manager of the company also belongs to the Municipality. The investors nominate the deputy general manager who may veto decision on certain issues (as, for instance, the approval of the annual business plan). The Shareholders' Agreement signed by the Municipality and the investors regulates those issues where, irrespective of the breakdown of shareholding, the Municipality and the investors need to agree in order for a decision to be made. (The list is similar to that detailed above in connection with the powers of the Shareholders' meeting.) As can be seen, the Municipality of Budapest and the consortium of German co-owners jointly operate the company. There are several areas where joint approval is indispensable for a decision.

The Municipality and the investors have signed two agreements: the Agreement on Share Purchase and the Shareholders' Agreement. The latter governs issues related to the management of the company, the ownership and sale of shares. Those agreements do not include formulae or commitments concerning the calculation of preferential dividend allocations (which would serve the return on the investment of the German partners) or concerning a so-called management fee. The investors, just as the Municipality and other shareholders (some employees), are entitled to the dividends generated from the company's profit after taxation. (Consequently, there is no need for additional settlement between the major co-owners.)

The Budapest Gas Works Co. is a close company, where the Municipality and the German consortium jointly decide the most important issues of the company's operation. The co-owners are entitled to revenue only in the form of dividends provided the company is profitable. As the Municipality has no control over the circumstances under which the company operates and the Municipality is not responsible to consumers for the company's prices, there does not seem to be any cause of conflict between the co-owners. Apart from the right to appoint the company's key officeholders and the entitlement to dividends, the powers accorded to the Municipality are likely to lose importance in the future.

PRIVATIZATION OF PHARMAFONTANA PHARMACEUTICAL CO.

The authors of Pharmafontana Pharmaceutical Co.'s privatization concept had to reckon with the decision of the Municipality of Budapest on separating the pharmacies – the retail network – from the company. The pharmacies would be privatized by the pharmacists under a separate concept and with preferential conditions. The remainder of the company consisted of wholesale activities and the manufacturing of pharmaceuticals.

No legally defined local government obligation or responsibility was attached to the company's activities. Originally the authors of the privatization concept recommended the sale of a simple majority of the company's shares (50% + 1 vote) in a public, single-round domestic competition. As the competition conducted in that form was unsuccessful, the General Assembly of the Municipality of Budapest modified the conditions of the shares offer: in addition to 50% + 1 vote, an option was also offered for the investors to buy all the shares owned by the Municipality. (At that time the precise number of the shares offered for sale was unknown. The Municipality had set aside a certain number of shares to be purchased by employees of the company while it had also expanded the offer to strategic investors to shares set aside for employees but as of yet unsubscribed.)

Two of the tenders submitted in the course of the second competition were found valid. Naturland Co.'s tender proved to fit the declared quality criteria best. When the contract was signed (in April 1996), Naturland Co. paid HUF 1,892 million for obtaining 66% of the shares. Later on – paying monthly installments – it bought all the shares that used to be owned by the Municipality. The entire price it paid by June 1997, including the fee for the right of pre-emption, had run to HUF 2,797 million. This made the privatization of the company complete.

> At the time of privatization, in 1996, the gross domestic sales of Pharmafontana Pharmaceutical Co. amounted to HUF 24,136 million. Profit after taxation amounting to HUF 405.8 million. The figures to some extent reflect the effects of the privatization of pharmacies because sales revenue naturally could not include the revenue of the pharmacies already privatized. The company's subscribed capital amounted to HUF 3,064 million. Disregarding the shares allocated for ESOP, the company's shares were sold at 103% of the shares' nominal value.

Privatization proved to be favorable to the Municipality's interests. The decision to separate the pharmacies and make them available to tender by the pharmacists was politically motivated. (In a few years' time the most valuable pharmacies were obtained, directly or indirectly, by foreign-owned wholesale companies. As a result of that process, the major part of the revenues from the retail network privatization went to the pharmacists, and a minor part to the Municipality, i.e., indirectly, to the population of Budapest.)

Having been stripped of its network of retail outlets, Pharmafontana Pharmaceutical Co. lost its hold over the market of pharmacies soon after privatization and its financial standing became weaker and weaker. If privatization had not taken place in 1996, it would probably have proved to be impossible to sell it, and it would have been wound up with a final settlement or liquidation.

PRIVATIZATION IN THE FIELD OF WATER AND WASTEWATER MANAGEMENT

Closing the survey of successful privatizations of the Municipality of Budapest's companies up to this day, let us now examine the rather untypical privatization of the Waterworks of Budapest Co. and the Municipal Sewerage Works Co. To begin with, local governments are legally obliged to supply the population with water and sewage service. The requirement to ensure uninterrupted public services does not depend in any way on the organizational set-up and ownership pattern of the public utilities concerned.

In the case of these services, highly sophisticated problems (i.e., issues more complicated than those faced by the previously discussed services) had to be solved in order to create the conditions for privatization and to work the practical ways by which privatization would be implemented. Since privatization techniques were more complex, we will need more space to describe them.

GENERAL CONSIDERATIONS OF WATER SUPPLY AND SEWAGE DISPOSAL

Some readers may find our approach to this question lopsided. However, our approach is guided by the focus of this paper: privatization. The analyst would probably apply another approach in case other aspects of those services were examined.

Below we are going to take a closer look at the following characteristics of water supply and wastewater management:

REQUIREMENTS RELATED TO UNINTERRUPTED SERVICE

The public services concerned must be ensured without interruption which necessitates requisite technical and economic conditions under any circumstances.

The facilities directly used for the provision of water and sewage service are qualified by law as part of the local government's core assets. In an economic branch characterized by relatively free competition, i.e., market conditions, it is only natural that the assets of a bankrupt company should be utilized in some other way in the same branch or elsewhere. If that is impossible, the assets are withdrawn from business.

This option cannot be chosen in water and sewage services for several reasons. Most of the facilities would be obviously useless in any other sector, and their withdrawal from operation would endanger the supply of services that the local governments are obliged to perform.

Uninterrupted services require severe protection guarantees for the facilities that therefore qualify as core assets. In recent years the legal approach to, and the for-profit utilization of the core assets, have not been consistent. Some legal practitioners claim that facilities classified as core assets are assets with limited transferability and, consequently, may not be transferred to privatized companies. According to the statement derived from this proposition core assets may only be registered in the books of local governments, and only non-infrastructure assets linked to the operation of the utilities can be taken into account when setting up a profit-oriented business organization.

Other legal experts say that the law authorizing local governments to provide water and sewage service by majority owned business organizations, opens the road to transferring core asset facilities to privatized companies. According to that legal interpretation, the requirement that local governments must have a majority ownership in business organizations set up for the purpose of public services provides sufficient guarantee for the special interest of protecting core assets. Privatization of a local government public utility may only involve the sale of the minority of shares.

As a matter of fact, the differences in the interpretation of core assets are not economic or legal in nature. (Adequate techniques have been developed for protecting the core assets from any danger.) Ambiguous regulation rather represents a hiatus in the process of legislation, and recent debates on the issue have been tinged with political motivations. To illustrate our point: none of the discussants have ever provided any examples of the Municipality of Budapest squandering assets. Another practical difficulty is that core assets and assets for operation cannot be exactly separated as technology makes it impossible to draw a borderline between them. Uncertainty over the interpretation of law has rather revealed general ideological differences on privatization.

NATURAL MONOPOLY

The pipe network for water and sewage service requires heavy investment. The character of the service hardly leaves any room for the emergence of rivals. Bringing about an alternative service infrastructure would make no sense and would be impossible in practice. It is next to impossible to imagine a situation where consumers could freely choose between rival service providers. Except among very special local conditions, it is impossible to look for alternative solutions. As a result of the monopoly position, the regulatory function of the market can hardly work. Business competition cannot regulate the prices of the services. Given these conditions, administrative price setting enforces cost-efficiency and keeps prices within reasonable limits.

Due to the imperative to ensure uninterrupted services, the extra protection guarantee for the related facilities and their monopoly position, the public utilities concerned have been cushioned from the "shocks" that companies in the competitive sector were exposed to while adjusting to the market economy. Because of the priority to ensure uninterrupted service, the public utilities concerned could delay the renewal of their organizational set-up and financial management and stall the conflicts that accompany all changes.

The efficiency of the financial management of a public utility company does not only depend on good market performance (anyway, there is no room for comparison because there are no noteworthy rivals and the conditions of operation are unique for each locality). It also depends on how effective the company's bargaining is with the supervising administrative authority. Due to a number of factors, such as the need for administrative interventions (which are occasionally problematic), the low rate of return on capital invested (and other important causes, such as the capital-intensity of the field), private investors have either been absent or appeared only recently in areas where public utilities enjoy a natural monopoly position. This holds true even for advanced market economies dominated by private investors.

THE COMPONENTS OF LOCAL GOVERNMENT PARTICIPATION

It follows from the above passages that local governments play a complex role in those areas. First, local governments are elected political representatives of the public interest. Second, they are public institutions legally obliged to provide public services. Third, they are the exclusive or majority owners of business organizations that fulfile public services. Fourth, they act as price authority and in that capacity may materially influence the financial management conditions of the companies that provide public services. As owners as well as public institutions responsible for public services they have a stake in the economic achievements of their public utilities. However, as elected political bodies and price authorities – understandably – they try to set prices as low as possible in order not to overburden voters and, in the interest of local communities, try to make public utilities work as efficiently as possible.

When passing important decisions on public services, politicians often have to bear conflicting considerations in mind. For instance, at times the public utility companies submitted recommendations that seemed to be beyond criticism in logic and professionalism, yet where the prices of services would have been intolerably raised should the recommendations have been approved. In such cases local government decision-makers find it difficult to realistically assess such recommendations and raise counter-arguments due to a lack of up-to-date insider information.As could be seen above, the local governments' aims and functions related to public utilities often form a strange mix. Moreover, their decision-making mechanism is structured to pass political decisions rather than for exercising the functions of an owner. As a consequence, local governments often find it difficult to goad public utilities to work more efficiently.

The Possibility and Criteria of Privatization

Even in the advanced market economies the water supply and sewage disposal companies have only been privatized relatively recently. Hungary could hardly benefit from the experiences of advanced countries for several reasons: the natural and legislative conditions as well as the level of the development of infrastructure are different. An extensive debate developed in Hungary among experts about the need for privatization, the goals to be attained, the results that could be achieved and the potential risks at stake.

The advocates of privatization said that, supposing legal conditions are established for the involvement of private business, privately owned companies are, as a rule, more efficient than those in state or local government ownership. The task, they claimed, was to make public utilities attractive for private investors, evolve strict institutional guarantees to ensure that water supply and sewage disposal would be safe and continuously developed even if public utilities are in mixed (private and local government) ownership, and allow consumers also to benefit from the increasing efficiency. (It was of utmost significance that the financing system of the services was transformed during the early 1990's. The fees were gradually but steeply raised, providing for substantial revenues for self-financing water supply and sewage disposal in Budapest.)

The advocates of privatization voiced the hope that technological development would accelerate, which would be likely to render the services safer and operation more efficient. They added that privatization would also be beneficial for the Municipality because the privatization revenues would generate a one-off source of funds.

The opponents of privatization expressed concern about the potential risks of the safety of the services. They added that, if the public utilities concerned become profit-oriented, fees would be raised unreasonably and conflicts would erupt between the private investors and the Municipality on strategic decisions about the development of the companies concerned.

Having weighed the pros and cons, the General Assembly of the Municipality of Budapest passed a decision on preparing the privatization of the Waterworks of Budapest Co. and the Municipal Sewerage Works Co.

THE IMPLEMENTATION OF PRIVATIZATION

To make privatization successful, goals and conditions need to be clarified and coordinated (and the legally prescribed requirements honored). In that case the goals and conditions were extremely complex and occasionally even contradicted one another, which rendered progress difficult. Let us supply some examples:

– To protect assets that ensure public services, it is required by law that the local government should retain majority ownership. However, sufficient scope needs to be provided for private investors so that they find the company attractive and have enough power to modify the company's operation and make it more efficient.

– Guarantees must be deployed to ensure uninterrupted service, yet the requirements of efficiency need also to be honored. Wherever it is possible, cost-benefit considerations should be allowed to reformulate decades-old organizational structures.

– Acting as a price authority, the Municipality defines the service fees in a decree. The fees should cover justified costs and expenditures (the financing of the service must not be endangered). However, the system should involve incentives to keep expenditures low.

– When determining the framework of conditions for private investment, the investors' risks should be set proportionate to their significant responsibilities in operation. Nevertheless, conditions must ensure that the investors' requirement on capital return are proportionate with efficiency reserves and do not overburden public services; in other words, the investors' pressure for raising service fees should not be unreasonably high.

At first sight privatization seems to be an ideal source of investment resource, especially in underdeveloped areas. Ostensibly capital investment does not incur direct debt servicing burden. But that is not the case. Experience gained from completed privatization transactions shows that the repayment requirements of capital invested are higher than money borrowed from commercial banks or elsewhere. (Note that investors themselves obtain their capital from the money market. The rate of return they expect from the capital they invest must be higher than the interest on their borrowed money.)

Capital investment is a justified source of investment funds only if a local government has no other option or if the rate of return investors expect can be balanced out with the savings their participation in the company generates. Disregarding other considerations, consequently, it is desirable to define the expected revenue from privatization in such a way that it should be proportionate to the responsibility the investor assumes in the company's operation, while financing development should be treated separately.

PRIVATIZATION CONCEPTION OF THE WATERWORKS AND THE SEWERAGE COMPANIES OF BUDAPEST

The consulting firms that elaborated the privatization conceptions of the Waterworks of Budapest Co. and the Municipal Sewerage Works Co. came to similar conclusions and put forward similar recommendations even though they worked separately. The conclusions were influenced by the preliminary considerations and guidance that the consulting firms received from the Municipality. Both teams put two options on the table. (Additional options, such as concessions and the leasing of facilities, may be seen as sub-categories of those options and may be aligned with the two main options.)

According to the first option, the original organizational structure would be all but retained and minority ownership offered for sale.

According to the second option, the core assets (that form the basis of public services) and the assets for the operation of the companies concerned (assets for operation, in short) would be separated organizationally and legally. A new company would be formed with the assets for operation and then the minority shareholding in that company would be privatized. In this case privatization would be confined to the assets for operation, while the core assets that are tied to public services would not be directly affected by the transaction. Thus, efficient operation – a marketable notion – could be institutionally separated from infrastructure assets and from the responsibility of the local government in upgrading and maintaining them. This does not eliminate the responsibility of the local government, but adjusts it to the characteristics of the specific sectors.

The liberal party faction of the Assembly took a stand for the privatization of operation but eventually, the competent bodies of the Municipality of Budapest opted for unitary privatization. (They also carried out certain preliminary organizational steps, like shedding some non-core activities: retail units and a civil engineering plant in the case of the Municipal Sewerage Works Co., and a pipe producing plant in the case of the Waterworks of Budapest Co.) Liberals accepted unitary privatization because had they refused it, the whole privatization process would have come to a halt.

Supposedly, one of the reasons why the Municipality decided not to break up the structure of those companies was that staff members of the companies concerned as well as those of the Municipality painted an overly gloomy picture of the uncertainties that the separation of the assets and the formation of new organizational units would entail. Once the decision was made, preparations for the practical implementation of privatization got under way, including the definition of the related economic, technical and legal assignments.

Characteristics of Partial Privatization under Unitary Organizational Structure

It became inevitable to identify what type of investors should be targeted so as to define the concrete form of privatization and the optimum percentage of the shareholding to be sold. The involvement of financial investors also had to be weighed. Apart from customary strategic shareholders' rights, financial investors would not participate in the direct management of the companies, but they would certainly focus on the appropriate rate of return of their investment.

Given Hungary's present capital market conditions, a financial investor is likely to be a foreign investor. In a similar manner to a strategic investor, a financial investor would make the following calculation when defining the sum to be paid for partial shareholding: a return on investment higher than the usual money market rate of interest, country risk, exchange rate risk, and the consideration that it is very difficult to resell public utilities. (Occasionally, even strategic investors insist on a repurchase option. Financial investors tend to be even keener on that requirement.)

Some privatization experts say that when a financial investor presses for higher efficiency as a tough (co-)owner and/or insists on making managerial work as professional as possible, he improves the company's efficiency and ultimately increases resources just as a strategic investor would. Acting as a "professional" (co-) owner, even a financial investor can bring about a tangible increase in the company's efficiency, much the same as if a strategic investor had been selected. In case there are problems in the exercise of the local government's classic functions as owner (we have pointed out that local governments fulfill functions that occasionally contradict one another), the involvement of a financial investor may be just as beneficial as that of a strategic investor. That also holds true if the operation of the company concerned does not require any extra expertise. The category in which the general managerial activity of venture capital is assigned, is really a question of definition. Venture capital is not sector-specific, and looks for investments with an aim to "buy cheap, improve and sell."

The City's finances were sound when the privatization bid was prepared. Consequently, decision-makers opted for involving strategic rather than financial investors.

The majority of decision-makers accepted the argument that privatization should go alongside the adoption of cutting-edge forms, techniques and methods of operation and the modernization of the technical base. If that is the case and the operation of the companies concerned becomes more efficient, service may become better and relatively less expensive. According to this argument, the source of the return of the money invested by the private investor may not only be the higher service fee, nor is improved efficiency, that could have been achieved without the involvement of the investor. The return on investment comes as the result of lower expenditure and the resultant revenue increase specifically due to the involvement of the investor. (A financial investor and a strategic investor are not supposed to differ in terms of the expected rate of return on their investment.)

After duly considering all – professional and other – aspects, the Municipality decided to offer the minority shareholdings of the water supply and sewage disposal companies for purchase to strategic investors that could satisfactorily prove that they had state-of-the-art techniques of operation and research bases of international reputation and know-how at their disposal. Thereby guaranteeing that the most efficient techniques and forms of operation would be adapted and utilized.

Experience has demonstrated that these were unfunded expectations. Practically no technological transfer happened and representatives of the investor delegated to the company management had no specific expertise of the field. They limited their role to representing the investor's direct financial interests, which led to conflicts with the municipal government, due to the variance in the understanding of certain elements of price calculation.

The Size of the Shares to be put up for Sale

According to relevant Hungarian legislation privatization may involve the sale of minority shareholding: 50% minus 1 vote. (That is also true if core assets are separated from assets for operation.) Taking into consideration that according to the arrangement that we are going to describe below, the payment the investors get does not depend on the size of their shareholding but on the revenue that is generated with their participation, the sale of 25% plus 1 vote seemed to be the most purposeful option.

Such an arrangement enables the potential investors to convene a shareholders' meeting. No resolution may be adopted without their approval during decision-making on the division of profits at the annual meeting. Under the Hungarian Companies Act, investors do not have greater powers than this even if they have a higher shareholding than 25% + 1 vote but are still minority shareholders. Hence it follows that nothing would have justified offering a higher shareholding for sale.

THE SALE OF SHARES

The General Assembly decided to organize an open, two-round international competitive bid for strategic investors to sell minority shareholding (25% + 1 vote) in the Waterworks of Budapest Co. and the Municipal Sewerage Works Co. Alongside those shares, the offer included certain operation-related extra rights, valid for 25 years. The Municipality committed itself to repurchase shareholding at the expiration of those rights for the amount it received at sale.

> Prequalification - i.e., the evaluation of the professional references of the applicants - took place in the first round. Strategic investors who cleared the first round were then invited to enter the second round. Both competitions attracted considerable attention, although by the time the second round had been reached, only two French-German consortia submitted valid bids for the two companies.

Eventually the consortium of Lyonnaise des Eaux S.A., R.E.W. and RWE Entsorgung Wasserwirtschaft GmbH bought minority shareholding in the Waterworks of Budapest

Co. (The name of the members of the consortium changed after privatization.) The sales agreement was signed and closing occurred in April 1997. The price paid was in excess of HUF 15.5 billion, calculated at the rate of exchange valid when the financial offer was submitted. As for the rights and duties related to the company's operation, the Municipality of Budapest and the consortium signed a Joint Venture and Management Agreement simultaneously with signing the Share Purchase Agreement.

> In the last full year before privatization, in 1996, the gross sales revenue of the Waterworks of Budapest Co. was HUF 10,188 million, and its balance sheet loss was about HUF 515 million. Despite that loss, the company's cash-flow position was satisfactory. It had considerable liquid assets (in excess of HUF 600 million). On 31 December 1996 the company's equity stood at HUF 69,629 million, of which subscribed capital amounted to 58,600 million. The company's long-term liabilities were HUF 21 million.

The Municipal Sewerage Works Co. was privatized about half a year later. The agreement on the sale of shareholding was signed and closing occurred in November 1997. The buyer was the consortium of Compagnie Générale des Eaux and Berliner Wasser Betriebe, which was runner-up in the competition for the Waterworks of Budapest Co. (Following privatization, the name of the buyers changed.) The shares sold were worth HUF 16.9 billion, as calculated on the rate of exchange valid on closing day. Alongside the Share Purchase Agreement, the parties signed a Shareholders' Agreement, in which they laid down the rights and duties of the co-owners.

> In the last full year prior to privatization, in 1996, the gross revenue of the Municipal Sewerage Works Co. was HUF 9,196 million, and its profit after taxation about HUF 1,972 million. (The considerable profit figure includes the investment fund ratio calculated in the sewage fee.) On 31 December the company's equity was HUF 85,118 million, in which subscribed capital amounted to HUF 68,396 million. The company's long-term liabilities stood at HUF 1,650 million. It was that high because it included investment fund ratio to be paid to the Municipality.

SPECIAL RIGHTS RELATED TO THE INVESTORS

It is reasonable to involve strategic investors if they get the opportunity to improve the company's efficiency. They should get powers beyond the size of their shareholding to have a say in the day-to-day running of the company's affairs, and it is desirable to ensure that their remuneration, the rate of return on their investment should be proportionate to the quantifiable increase in efficiency.

The investors may only exercise their right to direct the company's day-to-day matters if the majority owner, the Municipality of Budapest, ensures the requisite conditions. Hence it follows that the Municipality of Budapest and the investors had to divide the assignments and responsibilities among themselves. The institutional framework had to be elaborated in the economic, financial and technical fields. Legal safeguards had to be worked out to protect the identifiable interests of the contracting parties.

Measures had to be taken to ensure that under all conditions the Municipality would have access to the facilities indispensable for fulfilling its legal service commitments. Accordingly, the earlier public service contracts between the Municipality and the operators of water supply and sewage system were reformulated. The new contracts treated the various parameters of the services concerned, the technical and qualitative requirements, the techniques of and time limits for remedying disruptions, etc. in detail. The contracts include tough penalties for cases where uninterrupted service is endangered.

The Municipality retained the powers that it needed for ensuring the satisfactory technical state, value and development of the facilities that were contributed to the public-service companies and managed by the strategic investors. As for the standards of Budapest's water supply and sewage service, there is a striking difference between them.

As for the supply of drinking water, almost 100% of needs in Budapest are satisfied. The demand for drinking water is unlikely to grow in the foreseeable future since drinking tap water is less typical today than it was in the past and the number of industrial plants in Budapest has shrunk. Development efforts therefore focus on making the water supply more modern and raising the standards of the service. By contrast, in sewage service, especially in sewage treatment, Budapest lags considerably behind the desirable standard, which would need considerable future development. (Less than 90% of the consumers who have access to tap water are connected to the sewage network; and over half of sewage collected is not subjected to biological cleaning.)

Given those differences in the development requirements, different techniques were implemented to generate the necessary investment funds from the service fees. As for the upgrading of the drinking water service, the fee was defined in such a way so as to ensure investment funds for the Waterworks of Budapest Co. The resources are being used in compliance with the recommendation of the operator of the company, as part of the business plan and the investment plan, which is approved by the Municipality.

As far as the sewage service is concerned, it is inevitable to rely on funds from Hungary's central budget and investment grants obtainable from international finance institutions by competition. The facilities that are created in those investment projects are recognized as assets in the books of the Municipality. Accordingly, the Municipality has worked out a medium-term and a long-term development program, which are also to be financed from investment funds included in the sewage fee, collected by the company and paid to the Municipality.

Apart from the powers associated with ensuring the safety of service and the protection and development of the facilities, the Municipality conferred the rights related to the day-to-day management of the two companies onto the strategic investors. Accordingly, the investors are free to formulate the two companies' working schedules, procurement and sales policy, may decide to develop other activities, establish business relations, etc. The Municipality conferred onto the strategic investors the right to delegate a simple majority of the members of the Board of Directors to give them a free hand in day-to-day matters. However, the Municipality formulated the statutes of the Board in such a way that serious decisions in the Board's competence that go beyond day-to-day matters may not be passed without the approval of the majority of the Municipality Board members. The Management of the two companies may not withhold any information from the Board members, who must be given access to the companies' books and other documents. That is why the majority owner Municipality may, through Board members of its nomination, directly inspect the companies' operation and finances as well as the conditions and quality of the services provided.

The Municipality delegated the right to adopt strategic decisions to the shareholders' meetings of the companies, where in accordance with its majority shareholding it controls the majority of votes. The Supervisory Boards are appropriate instruments for inspecting the companies' finances. Half of the members of the Supervisory Boards are delegated by the Municipality. Under the Companies Act the Supervisory Boards enjoy broad powers, including the right to examine and evaluate specific cases, and come forward with recommendations at the shareholders' meeting.

Legally and organizationally speaking, such a division of labor ensures that the Municipality has sufficient powers to assert its interests concerning all those strategic matters that touch upon the maintenance of public services and the protection and future development of the facilities needed for them. As for passing day-to-day business decisions and solving daily tasks of operation, the strategic investors got a free hand and also the opportunity to improve the efficiency of the companies, which is the source of their revenues.

PRICE MECHANISM RELATED TO PRIVATIZATION AND THE ENTITLEMENT OF INVESTORS TO REVENUES

The Municipality of Budapest is authorized to determine the fees of water supply and sewage service in the territory of its jurisdiction by way of issuing municipal decrees. It was an important precondition for the success of privatization that the Municipality should exercise its price-setting authority in a predictable – one could say, self-disciplined – manner so that the potential investors could formulate a realistic business plan and, on the basis of a realistic calculation of the rate of return, could submit an appropriate offer for the shareholding concerned.

In addition to its stability and predictability, the price mechanism had to satisfy other key requirements. Throughout the privatization process it was a priority to keep the prices of the services at or below the level where they would have remained had the companies not been privatized.

The price mechanism – roughly the same for both water supply and sewage service – follows the following principle: the expenditures of the pre-privatization era are fixed (as basic expenditures) and thereafter year by year the consumer price is defined by revaluing those basic expenditures in view of the specific rate of inflation calculated for the specific expenditure item.

The price mechanism has a cash flow approach. In other words, it only reckons with those costs and expenditures that involve money transfers and revenues. (There is an exception though. The formula used for calculating the sewage fee includes a component that – in compliance with the relevant provision of the law on accounting – generates a resource for the company corresponding to the projected depreciation.) The company's results as posted in the company's accounting, which evidently includes expenditures and revenues that do not involve money transfer, may well be different from the profit that is calculated in the fee. In the course of preparing the price mechanism, experts also worked out a formula for the sewage fee based on the calculation of production costs. That approach also formulated what may be referred to as a "hypothetical value," which quantified the investors' savings. In addition, it would have taken into consideration those categories that were accounted for but did not involve money transfer. Because the privatization of the Waterworks of Budapest Co. was ahead of that of the other company, and the drinking water fee calculation had already been based on the cash flow approach, the Municipality came to the conclusion that the same formula should be used for the calculation of the sewage fee. (Even though the theoretical basis of the two formulae is identical, there are minor differences in detail.)

According to the privatization conditions of the Waterworks of Budapest Co., investors are entitled to a management fee recorded in the book under the heading of expenditures. The professional work of the investors is interpreted as a service contributed to the company, and this work is paid for in the form of the management fee that is calculated according to a certain formula based on quantifiable savings. Provided the formulae based on the cash flow approach are applied, the management fee is payable even if the company is loss-making by accounting standards. (That can happen if the water fee does not account for the entire depreciation that was posted. Alternatively, that can also happen if the management fee is paid after "savings" for which the financial cover is missing by accounting standards or, worse, even in cash.) The Joint Venture and Management Agreement includes a clause that is specifically meant to protect the company's equity, so that no investor decision could cause a loss that would squander the company's capital.

In the case of the Municipal Sewerage Works Co. the investors are not entitled to a management fee but instead to a dividend, which is posted under the heading of profits. Just as in the above case, savings derived from the improved efficiency of operation are the basis for the calculation of the dividend. A new preference share category had to be created for the investors to ensure that the size of dividend would be proportionate with savings. The Shareholders' Agreement includes the formula for the calculation of the dividend and the commitment referring to the approval of the dividend fund. As the dividend is generated under the heading of profits, under that arrangement there can be no loss by accounting standards. Thus, the protection of equity may be rephrased as the increase in capital that is realistically expected. (The clause on the protection of equity has introduced the notion of corrected equity. Its function – in connection with the liability of the investors – is to separate all items not related to the fulfillment of the service contract or clearly ascribable to decisions of the Municipality away from accounting. Expenditures due to flood prevention work carried out outside Budapest at the request of the Municipality of Budapest is a good example of the latter case.)

Involving corrective fee components in the calculation serves to save the price formulation from becoming unjustifiably rigid. Unforeseen expenditures that are independent from the day-to-day managerial activities of the investors may always be incorporated into the fees. Conversely, fee components that will not occur in the future – independently from the investors' activities – may be deducted from the fees through the corrective fee components.

The service fees as calculated according to the above principles may ensure coverage for justified costs and expenditures – at least at the efficiency level that was valid when basic expenditures were defined – and to objectively reflect changes in the economic context.

That way the (theoretical) service fees that have been revalued according to inflation and corrected in accordance with the expenditures of the time provide sufficient resources for the companies – at least at the efficiency level that was valid when basic expenditures were defined. A relationship may be established between, on the one hand, the quantifiable savings compared to the corrected basic expenditures and, on the other, the efficiency of the day-to-day managerial work of the investors. The savings (the size of which can be calculated with a formula based on the categories of the price mechanism) form the foundation of the investors' remuneration.

When discussing the aims of privatization above, we mentioned the priority that consumers should also benefit from privatization. A part (25%) of the savings that the investors report may be spent to reduce service fees.

All in all, the above-described arrangement enables the Municipality of Budapest to keep the powers that are needed to control strategic decisions on the services concerned. At the same time, it enables investors to utilize their expertise and experiences in passing decisions and taking measures to modernize the operation of those companies. The remuneration of the investors is proportionate to the revenue increase they achieve provided a part of the additional resources is used to reduce service fees.

PRACTICAL EXPERIENCES CONCERNING THE OPERATION OF THE PRIVATIZATION MODEL

The past few years enable us to assess the experience with privatization and evaluate the extent to which the expectations attached to privatization were fulfilled.

We may on the whole conclude that the strategic objectives of the partial privatization of water supply and sewage service were realized. Thanks to the efforts of the investors, the companies' management system was considerably modernized, its organizational set-up transformed and made more efficient. Certain aspects of the services were further improved in general, and customer service was improved in particular.

The technical state of the core assets related to public service satisfies the requirements, and the conditions necessary for uninterrupted service are in place.

Thanks to privatization the Municipality of Budapest received a sizeable one-off revenue, which could be used for a number of purposes.

Those preparing privatization often had to walk unbeaten paths. They had to respond to challenges for which they had no ready-made and tested techniques. It is a small wonder that some of the expectations proved incorrect.

The fact that the "cash flow" fee formulae could not in their original form keep the service fees within the expected limits was an important experience. The fact that the Municipality's business partners were multinational organizations with a strong lobbying potential was a challenge. They could keep the personnel of the companies concerned under control, and had access to almost unlimited intellectual and financial resources to exploit potential opportunities. The remuneration of the investors may be generated both by cutting actual expenditures and raising the "theoretical" expenditures (that form the basis for calculating the service fee). This is because the savings (that form the basis of the dividend) are defined as the difference between the "theoretical" costs and expenditures that appear in the fee's actual figures. As a consequence, the investors both strove to explore untapped reserves in operation and (fighting on two fronts) exerted considerable pressure on the Municipality (the pricing authority) to raise the service fees. When putting the Municipality under pressure, they took advantage of some vaguely defined components of the formulae or certain one-sided or unfounded interpretations of the Agreements and formulae.

Competition during the bidding process was so fierce that the price of the shares offered for sale ran rather high. This helps explain why the investors pressed for raising the fees. The two competing – French-German – consortia considered the Budapest "turf" as a reference achievement for further advance toward other countries in Eastern Europe. Outside observers had the impression that victory in the privatization competition was a question of prestige.

As the investment was high in comparison to the size and revenues of the companies, achieving an adequate rate of return was quite a challenge. Compared to the gross revenue of the companies at the time of privatization, the price paid for the shares was very high. (The ratio was about 160% in the case of both companies. The corresponding figure for the Budapest Gas Works Co. was 40%, even though a share package twice as big was sold there. In hindsight it is clear that the investors anticipated that by deploying "professional" arguments, they could exert pressure on the Municipality to raise service fees, which in turn would improve their rate of return conditions. It is hardly surprising therefore that the investors increasingly pressed for higher fees a few years after privatization. As the Municipality is not the pricing authority for gas services, the Gas Works could not press the Municipality for price increases.)

Keeping the fees within reasonable limits was also difficult because some one-off items were not eliminated when the basic expenditures were defined. As the years passed, those one-off items were also revalued according to the rate of inflation which put increasing an burden on the fee. It was also difficult to identify the costs and expenditures that would not occur in the future independently of the strategic investors' activities and that should have been weeded out from the fee.

When defining the fee from one year to the other the definitions of the fee's several components and the instructions for calculating them were based on the knowledge of the period when the Agreements were signed. As a consequence, some of the definitions could be interpreted in more than one way. This was a source of some problems. Time and again the recommended service fees as submitted by the companies were different from what the Municipality or its experts calculated and considered acceptable. As the same formulae were used both for efficiency-related savings and fee calculation, differences also emerged in connection to the investors' remuneration. Some of the items the investors reckoned with had nothing to do with improved efficiency and, in the case of the Waterworks of Budapest Co., were not even backed up by financial resources. The Waterworks of Budapest Co. amassed a considerable loss (by 2001), while the management fee grew steeply.

The management fee for the Waterworks of Budapest Co. (which was posted under the heading of expenditures) was understood to acknowledge the rendering of certain managerial services. In practice, however, it proved to be difficult to identify managerial services as invoices, and to divide the corporate tax payment obligation on the managerial fee between the co-owners.

The above-mentioned differences in approach and in the planned and actual processes knocked the companies' business and financial performance off from their desired course of equilibrium.

To remedy those problems, the contracting parties (withholding the validity of the original Agreements) agreed to enter into complementary agreements that closed the door to different interpretations, augmented the definitions of formulae and reflected whatever legislative changes had occurred in the meantime. (The Municipality signed those follow-up agreements with the investors of Waterworks of Budapest Co. in the summer 2000 and those of Municipal Sewerage Works Co. in the summer 2001.) As a consequence, debates on how to interpret the rules of fee calculations came to an end. The contracting parties agreed that in the future the fees could be raised only for reasons of adjustment to inflation, changes in volume and any change in the resource requirement for development. The contracting parties reconfirmed that 25% of the savings that the investors report about may be spent to reduce service fees.

In the wake of the follow-up agreements, the investors operating the two companies could focus their attention on exploring internal efficiency reserves, while pressure on the price authority to raise prices significantly decreased. The follow-up agreements brought anomalies down to a tolerable level, or even terminated them altogether. It opened the way for the Municipality to be able to better assert the benefits of privatization in the future.

The cash flow based formula for calculating fees proved feasible. (In 2002 the increase in both the sewage fee and the drinking water fee was lower than what independent experts estimated as the general impact of inflation.) In the case of both companies, the part of the fee financing operation[5] has decreased in its real value both in 2002 and 2003, while the accounting deficit of the Waterworks has also been eliminated.

We can see that it is imperative to give a detailed definition of the rules of internal accounting (down to the level of reference to the serial numbers of ledger accounts) and give a precise description of all the various activities that relate to the application of the fee formulae. A clear-cut definition must be given, for instance, for the method to differentiate

---

[5] Obviously only the formula calculating operational cost coverage is relevant for assessing the success of privatization from the angle of efficiency increase. The other part of the fee designated to cover investments is independent from the efficiency increase, as its amount only depends on the discretion of the Municipality.

maintenance from value-increasing investment; the qualifying principles for the so-called "other activities"; the rules related to the calculation of changes in the number of customers; the settlement of the co-owners' claims on the targeted reserves; a sufficiently detailed selection of indices for revaluation; the technique for calculating the fee-reducing influence of expenditures that cease independently from the investors' activities, etc. The follow-up agreements proved to be instrumental to attain those goals. It is indispensable that, acting through its senior officials delegated to leading bodies of the companies and relying on experts, the Municipality should continuously monitor the ebb and flow of the companies' finances and, if necessary, even check on the analytic correctness of the invoices.

The privatization of the water and sewage service of Budapest may, on the whole, be described as successful. New procedures were worked out and put into practice that have improved corporate efficiency. The agreements related to the privatization process have, on the whole, appropriately regulated the relations between investors and the Municipality of Budapest. The experiences of the City should serve as a warning: privatization needs careful preparation.

The community can enjoy privatization's justifiable and realistic benefits only if the tools used for the privatization as well as the guarantees for the distribution of profits are adequately elaborate, and are appropriately confirmed by relevant agreements. If those conditions are missing, society at large will hardly benefit from privatization at all.

INFRASTRUCTURE DEVELOPMENT

KATALIN PALLAI

INTRODUCTORY THOUGHTS

Urban infrastructure services are key determinants of the living conditions and the competitiveness of a city. For this reason, infrastructure policies (i.e., policies concerning the operation and development of the infrastructures) constitute an important part of urban policies. Their drafting requires substantial financial, social, and political expertise. At the same time, almost all the key elements of the related decisions depend on engineering expertise. Engineers, who may have only received technical training, are those who work out most of the conceptions, strategies, and projects of the infrastructure sectors. Meanwhile, the effects of their work reach far beyond the realm of engineering. The success of an urban policy conception hinges on the creators' ability to integrate engineering knowledge into the strategic process.

The first chapter of the present volume (which introduces the municipal reform process and analyzes the urban policy concepts and strategies) has already touched upon the question of how best to coordinate development and operation related issues. The chapter described the various different interpretations of strategic planning, and through the introduction of the concept of strategic real planning and process management it outlined the municipality's planning-related goals. It also included a detailed discussion of the comprehensive urban policy conceptions that have been drafted since the change of the political system. The present study ventures to offer further details on the evolution of the basic approach which guided Budapest's urban and infrastructure development conceptions in the direction of strategic real planning. We shall outline the successes of the various sectors, and shall also identify their weaknesses.

The introductory study of the present chapter summed up the goals and coherence of Budapest's infrastructure policies. The other studies of the chapter focus on utility rates, company management, and privatization. Those chapters detail – through a discussion of the financial, organizational, and political aspects of infrastructure services – the creation and reform of the tools thanks to which the above goals may be accomplished. Still, results remain the real issue here, i.e., the state and quality of the city's infrastructure networks and services. This closing study spells out the questions that hang on technical solutions. It summarizes how the developments of networks and services themselves have changed as a result of the financial and organizational measures. In other words, it describes the changes in the municipality's approach to infrastructure development, evaluates the evolution of the related engineering solutions, and assesses the changes in the services themselves.

If we seek answers to the above questions, we must take the state of the city's infrastructure services in 1990 (together with the development conceptions – with all their weaknesses – that prevailed at the time) as our starting point. We start from a situation where excellent teams of engineers and other experts came up with several professionally sound conceptions, which unfortunately neglected to pay sufficient attention to the conditions and constraints of their implementation. As they did not take feasibility into account, they were practically useless. It may seem that the professionals did not have an ear for the politicians' requirements and were not interested in harmonizing their views with external conditions, despite the fact that they were the ones who detained the necessary information and expertise. Their "culture", however, prevented them from adjusting to the "context." In such a situation, it was crucial to identify the chances for cooperation. It became very important to facilitate the emergence of economic and political cornerstones for planning, whereby harmony could occur in the fields of political, financial, and professional planning.

The present study seeks answers in two fundamental areas. First, it scrutinizes how much the leaders of the Municipality of Budapest managed to establish clear conditions for professional planning and to integrate the processes of financial, political, and professional planning. Second, it assesses the impact of extraneous processes on the planning of infrastructure development.

THE HERITAGE AND THE CHALLENGE

HERITAGE

Budapest evolved into a metropolis in the last quarter of the 19th century. At that time, amidst political conditions that were extremely favorable for the city,[1] a specific body – the Public Works Council – was set up with the mission to manage the planning and execution of Budapest's development. By the turn of the century, the Public Works Council had developed Budapest into a leading European city through its long-term plans implemented in close cooperation with the government and city leaders.

During the half century between the establishment of the Public Works Council and the outbreak of World War One, the quantity and quality of the infrastructure network improved to such an extent – spectacularly in what was then the heart of the city, also known as Little Budapest[2] – that even today these backbone networks constitute the base of everyday life in the city.[3] At the same time, the independent small settlements that surrounded Budapest

---

[1] After the Historical Compromise of 1867, which increased the political independence of Hungary within the Austro-Hungarian Monarchy and entailed an economic upswing, all parties agreed that Budapest, the Hungarian capital city, should be developed into a European metropolis. In this dynamic atmosphere, the necessary political and economic conditions were present and helped to accomplish this goal.

[2] Little Budapest represents the city area in 1870. It amounts to the core 194 square kilometer area of today's Large Budapest, which spreads over 525 square kilometers.

[3] The only exceptions are the gas and district heating networks. The district heating network was installed only after World War Two to supply the socialist housing estates, while the coal gas network for supplying kitchen and lighting demands, was rebuilt after the 1960s to accommodate the requirements of natural gas.

and constituted its agglomeration (extending over more than half of the area of today's Budapest), developed their own independent infrastructure networks with a village-like character.

In 1949, the agglomeration areas were attached to the city.[4] This marked the birth of the administrative area of today's Budapest (Large Budapest). The next few decades witnessed large-scale infrastructure developments primarily in connection with the construction of "socialist" housing estates on the outskirts of what used to be Little Budapest, and also the development of the industrial areas. These investments were full-blown networks with significant reserve potentials. Alongside these rather concentrated developments, the inevitable electricity and pipe water networks were installed in practically every built-up area. In the loosely inhabited areas, the development of the sewage network was seen as an issue that could be postponed by the environmentally insensitive decision-makers, while the development of the road network could be neglected due to the restricted number of private cars.

The absence and later the very slow increase of private car traffic was successfully balanced by the compact public transportation network. The high rate of modal split[5] has become a peculiarity of socialist cities. The other peculiarities – regrettably – were the housing estates and the district heating network, which were built with no attention whatsoever to operating costs. The district heating system which was installed in the poorly insulated housing estates is very hard to regulate and practically impossible to meter. As we shall see, it became a textbook example for "senseless frugality." In every post-socialist city this system is a ticking time bomb.

During the socialist era, besides the indifference towards environmental problems and costs, discretional central control decisively influenced infrastructure development policy. Due to the predominance of one-time decisions, the resources for individual services were greatly dependent on the political weight of the leaders of the individual public service companies. This contributes to explain that while the previous system has left behind top-notch water- and gas supply networks in Budapest, the sewage system dating from that period is very incomplete and cleaning capacities are exceptionally low.

When the political system changed in 1990, Budapest boasted a practically complete and good-quality water and gas supply network, an incomplete road and sewage network, extremely low wastewater cleaning potential and an exceptionally expensive district heating service.

Alongside physical aspects, the pool of engineers and company managers who had received their education and basic professional training during the previous era was another important element of the socialist heritage. Members of this generation boasted a remarkable

---

[4] This increased the city's area from around 200 square kilometers to 525 square kilometers.

[5] The modal split characterizes the ratio between public transport and individual transport (i.e., private cars). The modal split rate is high if the share of public transport is large.

engineering expertise, but their experiences in the field of planning were determined by the financial and political practices prevalent under the socialist system. Up until the 1950's, Western engineers were at least as supply-oriented in their outlook as their counterparts in the socialist block. Similarly to their Western colleagues, the socialist engineers were very good when it came to extrapolating trends or devising professionally flawless technical solutions to practically any kind of problems. The only difference was that socialist engineers kept this approach until the very end of the previous political-economic system. In addition, the typical socialist development approach had two peculiar features (which made it different from market economies): it almost exclusively identified development as permanent quantitative growth, and was completely insensitive to cost efficiency.

Another important characteristic of the socialists' practice was the (previously mentioned) "lobbying technique" used by sectoral leaders. Similarly to the council leaders of the day, the company managers went out of their way to improve their chances of getting support by keeping all-too-complete plans and long project lists on the table. The work of engineering itself seemed to consist of planning these complex systems. The engineers' professional principles could be fully implemented, since they were not bound by the findings of cost-benefit analysis and feasibility studies. No wonder perfect cooperation flourished between sectoral leaders and engineer-planners.

CHALLENGE

In the 1990's, Budapest's urban policy leaders faced a dual challenge in the field of public utility services. They had to maintain and improve the quality and standards of the services, while making up for the missing infrastructure elements. They also had to reduce municipality expenditure on public utilities, while maintaining universal services. The earlier supply-centered approach had no trouble to identify the elements missing for completing the networks in the different sectors. At the same time, it was also clear that the other objective – the provision of cost-covering services – was bound to remain a pie in the sky in such a context. The municipal leaders had to break through the stone wall created by the apparently unified front of engineers and sector leaders if they ever wanted the approach to infrastructure development to include respect for fundamental financial realities, for demand and for the market.

If we want to understand the change in the approach to infrastructure development, we need to take the traditional approach as our starting point. Traditionally, the responsibility for development planning fell on the engineers. For them, the easiest way to calculate the dimensions of the infrastructure investments that matched presumed requirements, was to extrapolate based on already existing trends of demand. (An example of the outcome of this simple extrapolation was the dream of a multi-level road for the Little Boulevard in Budapest's historic center.) This infrastructure development approach, fairly common throughout the world up until the 1960's, is called the "predict and provide" method. The impossibility of applying it in practice first became evident in the field of traffic planning. Large cities have had to learn from their permanent traffic crises that it is not possible to develop the road network in line with the ever-growing demand. This would be impossible to finance and would not solve the traffic problem either. Faster and more comfortable individual means of transportation induce urban sprawl, while new roads generate further traffic demand (along with increased utility expenditures). Consequently, we end up with an ever increasing crisis.[6]

Since supply-oriented planning could not offer a solution, there was a need to identify new methods. The path has led through a clearer understanding of demand and the quest for its satisfaction and through the devising of techniques for influencing it. The analysis of infrastructure demand has directed attention to the complex urban processes. It became obvious that the demand for transportation and other infrastructure was determined by developments in the real estate and apartment markets, and also by the geographical configuration of the residence of the labor force and the location of available jobs. Accordingly, the only way to rationalize infrastructure services was to coordinate their planning with the urban development goals. It became inevitable to tie infrastructure development to the urban development policies, and to consider infrastructure policy decisions in light of their effects on urban functions and development. Since then, urban and infrastructure development have been based on two fundamentally new approaches. The first is known as demand management,[7] which is linked to market-oriented planning, the other as integrated planning.

MARKET-ORIENTED PLANNING

The change in the municipality's approach to infrastructure development in the 1990's (which occurred within the conceptual framework of strategic real planning as described in the first chapter) can best be captured through the dichotomy represented by supply- and demand-oriented approaches. In this dichotomy, the typical supply-oriented approach is the central planning practice of the socialist era. In socialist planning, the definition of demand was based on ideological decisions rather than being determined by information on consumers' actual demand. This ideology assumed that a constant increase in demand in most fields was a reflection of "social progress" thus, the aim of planning was to satisfy this growing demand. In that system, "result" mostly equaled quantitative growth. The

---

[6] Although these sentences may remind the reader of the arguments of radical environmentalists who protest against the use of private cars, as we shall see, our proposed solution to this problem radically differs from theirs. We do not identify (not even in principle) with those who believe that private cars should be banned from the roads. We only concentrate on the competition between private and public transportation, and also on the possibilities of pushing their ratio towards a sustainable balance.

[7] The previously exclusive supply-oriented approach concentrated on how best to satisfy the assumed demand (which was generally planned to be constantly increasing), and what investments were required. In other words, the main goal was to generate sufficient supply to satisfy all assumed demand. This approach restricted economic analysis to the cost-efficiency analyses of individual projects. The market- or demand-oriented approach, and most recently the method of demand management, takes demand as its starting point. However, demand management does not aim exclusively to satisfy spontaneous demand. Instead, it strives to influence demand so that it generates sustainable services and processes. In this method, results are not measured by input, but by their contribution to the realization of the prevailing urban policy goals (See below for details).

engineer-planner could easily meet expectations by thinking in terms of complete networks and services. From an engineering point of view, this approach was attractively clear-cut and seemingly free of compromises. At the same time, it often produced excess capacities generating either wasteful systems, or demand that was out of sync with the universal urban objectives. Meanwhile, quantities and costs remained on a steady growth path.

Information on demand (usually defined by the consumers' willingness to pay) is the key to demand- or market-oriented planning, the objective of which is to achieve a balance between actual demand and supply generated by planning. This balance does not come about simply via satisfying demand. Balance is attained by conscious influence on demand by carefully planning supply. This means driving demand towards existing or sustainably developed supply, in harmony with the entire spectrum of urban interests. Unlike supply-oriented planning, demand-oriented planning uses the information on demand patterns for more than just defining the need for development. Instead, its goal is to identify the tools and methods (such as pricing, incentives, alternatives, etc.) that are conducive to the rationalization of both the demand itself and the method, timing, and system by which it will be satisfied. All this ultimately leads to rationalizing the functioning of the city. Demand-oriented policies are focused on influencing demand to a financially efficient and environmentally sustainable outcome. This approach judges results based on qualitative rather than quantitative criteria.

INTEGRATED PLANNING

It is relatively easy to evaluate the supply-oriented approach, since the immediate results of its services or investments (and especially their quantitative parameters) speak for themselves, and only the cost-efficiency analyses of the individual projects are to be carried out. At the same time, the effect and result as manifested in complex urban processes constitutes the essence of the market- or demand-oriented approach to planning. For this reason, the evaluation of this approach should focus on the complex urban processes themselves, and should also take the broader effects into consideration. All this points in the direction of integrated planning.

The need for integration makes it imperative for sectoral and urban planning approaches to change. It is not possible to subsequently coordinate investments that were justified and accepted on the basis of separate and independent sectoral plans (at least not up to the level of integrated planning as described above). For this reason, the planning process must also be altered. Process management could be the method applied (as described in the chapter entitled 'Strategic Planning and Management Reform'). Instead of attempting to define the investments and interventions themselves, planning should strive for a consensus in the goals that could guide the ensuing planning process.

This means that sectoral planning is not guided exclusively by its internal professional logic, and its aim is not to "prepare a plan." Urban development is the key issue in market- or demand-oriented planning. The strategies of the individual sectors are evaluated not simply on the basis of their particular professional logic, but also within the framework of their overall urban policy-related goals and their effects on the development of the city.

There is one more important argument for the use of the process management technique in planning. Cities tend to develop in an ever-changing context. This is why it makes no sense to draw up long-term, comprehensive physical development plans or program-lists. Instead, planners should strive to define a course for the required processes. The need is for a development strategy that rests on the understanding of the processes, lays down fundamental principles and directions, and creates consensus. Based on these, it remains possible to consider and coordinate the various measures taken amidst changing conditions. Process management means goal-oriented integration in the field of urban and infrastructure development.

Let us clarify what we mean by goal-oriented planning, and to what extent this represents a logical departure from the traditional approach. The term "goal-oriented planning" refers to a purely rational system that considers long-term principles and values as constant, and creates a consensus on the long-term goals on their basis. This approach chooses and ranks its tools exclusively according to their potential to promote the efficient accomplishment of the goals. Since at the time of planning we always have several options to choose from (and many of these depend on external factors), it is logically not possible to be definitive about future concrete decisions. Accordingly, the planning method which aims to "fix" an end-state in the future, fundamentally conflicts with the goal-oriented planning approach.

The above logic of the goal-oriented approach is in perfect harmony with a statement made by the deputy mayor of Budapest in connection with a political issue. We quote only the sentence relevant to our discussion: "Those who want to fix (i.e., to prescribe as the only option) today, how we shall decide 18 months from now (fixing it as the most rational way), in effect force their own will on reality and thereby are employing the most pure form of voluntarism."[8] If we translate this message to the field of urban policy, we can substitute "18 months" with ten or even 15 years.

In terms of its content, this interpretation of process management falls in line with the conclusions of the preceding chapters.[9] The need for process management is justified by the fact that – in the longer run – a city develops amidst unpredictable circumstances (economic and financial context, expectations, political balances, changes in value choices, etc.). The physical plan of the supply-oriented approach, that aims to "fix" the desired future end-state, is unable to adjust to the unpredictability of the future, and therefore cannot be used for integrating the development processes of the future. There is a need for a strategy that can define directions for the longer run, and upon its approval can become a tool for co-

---

[8]   Atkári, 2000: 2.

[9]   We use process management with the same meaning as in the previous chapters on strategic planning and financial management reform. "Process regulation is the technique of adapting to dynamically changing external conditions It starts not from individual decisions and the ensuing action plan fixed for the longer term, but from the clear-cut, principled definition of the goals and necessary conditions conducive to their realization. The clarification and approval of the principles and goals constitute the basis to rely on for the necessary subsequent adjustment processes. This way a single act of agreement can be the most effective guarantee for the evolvement of a clear-cut strategy." (Quoted from the paper on 'Financial Management Reform'.)

ordination. This strategy should remain open enough to accommodate and adopt short-term tactical decisions as well.[10]

Finally, it must also be stated that interference in complex urban processes is bound to entail uncertainties and doubts. For this reason, it is inevitable to keep track of the effects of a previously approved strategy. Thus the single-step "predict and provide" method of supply-oriented planning must be replaced by the "predictor-corrector" method (based on the tracking and evaluation of the effects) where planning is a continuous, iterative activity.

CHANGES IN ENVIRONMENTAL EXPECTATIONS

In the field of infrastructure planning, the third challenge that the post-socialist era had to face were changes in environmental expectations. These changes assumed key importance during the post-socialist transition, and especially during and due to accession to the European Union. Fundamental changes have occurred in the following two areas: emission regulation and regulation enforcement. The process of legal harmonization requires the reduction of pollution and contamination exports and also the enforcement of relevant regulations. All these represent a major improvement over the practices of the socialist era.

Considering the standards of the socialist period we find that, regarding most infrastructure services, the then National Construction Code prescribed quality requirements that are basically in line with the relevant regulations of the European Union. The key difference was in the enforcement of these regulations: during the previous era, pollution was an everyday occurrence. The country's accession to the European Union will once and for all make it difficult to bypass the regulations. In certain areas, this is seen as a potential cause for major problems. Making wastewater treatment universal is one such area that requires a remarkable one-time investment and significant and lasting rate hikes. Since the consequences of the changes are pertinent to specific sectors or areas, we refrain from discussing these in our general overview.

---

[10] Underlying this thought is the need to emphasize the separation between strategic and tactical levels of planning. It is important to underline the difference between these two levels. The strategic level focuses on long-term goals. Its gist is to accurately define targets and underlying principles and directions. Thereby it sets a long-term course for the associated political processes. This course, however, must be flexible enough to allow for the adjustment of the steps to changing circumstances. This brings us to the tactical level. The need for both direction and adjustment is a recurrent theme in the present volume. We consider it necessary to expand on it here because in the field of infrastructure and urban development – due to the decades-long practice of the physical planning approach – prevailing practices are still determined (more pronouncedly as in the field of financial planning) by the desire for a fixed ultimate state rather than by the implementation of process management.

THE TRANSFORMATION OF THE INFRASTRUCTURE POLICIES

In the paragraphs below we aim to single out a few key elements in the transformation of Budapest's infrastructure policies. (It would fall beyond the scope of the present volume to summarize the whole system of these policies.) The considerations referred to above – market- and goal-oriented and integrated planning, as well as sensitivity to the environment – were relevant to all areas, notwithstanding that their results differed according to sector. For this reason, we aim to highlight only the elements of policies that best show the shift in approach.

Although the scope of urban infrastructure services is rather broad, we focus on the areas where service provision is the responsibility of the Municipality of Budapest. The relevant areas and issues will be discussed at differing depth, depending on the given sectoral policy's relevance to the challenges outlined above.

While it may appear to fall beyond the scope of our study, we shall also venture to briefly assess how much urban development planning has become closer to market-oriented and integrated planning. We consider this digression important before discussing the infrastructure policies themselves because it is important for the evaluation of infrastructure development to know how much it is compatible with the broader context of urban development – with regard the above challenges. Another reason for this brief detour is that the urban policies of the post-socialist period have been strongly challenged to replace the supply-oriented approach of the preceding era. Rather than venturing to evaluate the urban development conceptions, we shall limit ourselves to highlighting a few key elements of these conceptions that demonstrate the conceptual changes in approaches.

URBAN DEVELOPMENT

The question of what exactly an urban development strategy is supposed to contain is a key and rather controversial issue among professional circles. The planners are inclined to believe that they can maximize their influence on the development process of a city by prescribing in minute detail the steps to be taken in the future. In this respect it is the same whether they do so within the framework of a hierarchical program structure or in a hierarchical system with all inclusive goals and objectives detailed in three or four level "subsystems." After all, the ultimate aim of both approaches is to precisely define the end-state, albeit the latter method might seem more "up to date." (This hierarchical system for goals and objectives was chosen by Prague and Warsaw for their urban strategies, and also by Budapest for the latest update to its urban development conception.[11]). The planners may perhaps entertain the hope that their conceptions (along with all the complex summary tables and explanations

---

[11] The Office of the Mayor of Budapest, 2002a

of programs and goals) will eventually become the decision-makers' "Bibles." However, we cannot but realize that these highly elaborate tables and documents carry almost no weight in influencing implementation. (At any rate, one merit is sure: they can protect municipal leaders from accusations that they work without an official strategy at hand.)

In practice, influences and powers of a different nature govern decisions, not such documents. The actual decisions are affected not so much by systemized planning documents put together following the previously criticized voluntaristic manner, as by well-understood and approved goals and the interests represented by the decision-makers. The ensuing definition for strategic planning strongly challenges the end-state definition-oriented approach and practice widely accepted in the transition region. Our concept of strategic planning is based on the belief that inter-disciplinary planning is useful and relevant only if it contributes to the adoption of a broad agreement on the directions and goals of urban development.

After the change of the political system in Budapest, the first redrafting of the urban development conceptions was the urban development chapter of the 1991 urban policy program (see the relevant part of the chapter "Strategic Planning and Management Reform"). The author of the urban development chapter (the deputy mayor in charge of this area) described a grand and comprehensive vision for the future, which aimed to "reorganize the city's spatial structure."[12] The "stretching" of the city along its north-south (Danube) axis, and in the southern parts of the city the replacement of the long-standing radio-concentric structure with a reticulated structure were the two key elements of this vision.[13] The stretching of the city along the Danube rested primarily on aesthetic and urban architectural considerations. This approach also defined the end-result to be attained and targeted accomplishment by employing conducive regulation and other tools typical of the supply-oriented approach (prescriptive development plan, detailed physical regulation, creation of infrastructure supply and investment project offers).

The planning and practice of urban development proceeded along several lines following this conception. On the one hand, in connection with the re-evaluation of the local regulations and the master plan, the urban planners and engineers drafted longer-term plans and attempted to coordinate their content. On the other hand, the concrete decisions of the local politicians sparked off a series of developments and restructuring processes in the capital city.

In 1994, the deputy mayor made another attempt to draft a comprehensive urban development conception that was never officially submitted. It also rested on the "physical planning" approach. Based on an imaginary end-state, this conception (still based on an admittedly supply-oriented approach) strove to define the necessary long-term interventions and investments for the entire city and all the sectors. The plans for the individual infrastructure

---

[12] Foundation for a European Hungary, Local Government Experts' Office, 1991: 11

[13] "...the transformation of this radio-concentric structure may serve as the basis for the urban development projects of the next decades. Rather than creating new rings within the city, we should envision urban development stretching along the river Danube." (Foundation for a European Hungary, Local Government Experts' Office, 1991: 19)

sectors were enlisted right next to the urban development programs. The plans were not prioritized, even though the total volume of the planned programs obviously far exceeded the municipality's potential resources.[14]

Although no alternative urban development conception was prepared at the time, the mere fact that the deputy mayor's conception never reached the desk of the decision-makers sufficiently proves that at that time the mayor and his cabinet already had a different approach to urban development.

In 1997, the municipality invited tenders for the conceptual summarization of the various urban development plans and for the drafting of an urban development conception. This happened more than a year after the financing reforms of 1996. By that time the general state of financing and the established methods of financial planning, along with the gradually reviewed sectoral plans, had provided sufficient ground for summarizing the urban development ideas and compiling a realistic set of associated tools. Budapest was already determined to pursue the path of strategic real planning. It was clear that planning should aim to create a realistic strategy[15] through the iteration of the relevant professional, political, and financial considerations. Another logical expectation was that the plans should also integrate ideas related to the sectors.

The tender was won by a multidisciplinary group, which included experts who had long been working for the municipality. From the beginning, they clearly strove to integrate sectoral ideas, and gradually managed to introduce the more advanced approach and some of the methods already applied in other fields of the Budapest urban policies to urban development planning.

The initial results of these efforts were already manifest in the document that was published for debate in 1998.[16] Rather than aiming to redefine the whole city, the group focused on a number of "strategic zones." However, within these zones the group continued to apply the supply-oriented approach, so in essence nothing much had changed. The conception listed all the tasks "to be accomplished" within these strategic zones. Consequently, the identification of the zones and naming them "strategic zones" did not in itself constitute a strategy. It was only the previously described financing projection[17] presented as part of the conception that sought the way that would lead to strategic real planning. The projection made it clear that there was no chance for the supply-oriented projects to materialize. The results of the first iterations between resources and ideas most probably pushed the group's conceptions towards the demand-oriented approach and towards strategic focusing. The

---

[14] The Office of the Mayor of Budapest, 1994b

[15] There was also reason to assume that – similarly to the financial management reform – this could lead to the creation of an integrated system of long-term goals, and by this to an agreement that could provide guidance for the definition of measures being able to adjust to the dynamically changing circumstances.

[16] The Office of the Mayor of Budapest, 1998c

[17] The financing projection is discussed in detail in the paper on 'Strategic Planning and Management'.

demand management techniques that had already been increasingly adopted on the field of transport planning also contributed to this development.

The requirement to prioritize among objectives prompted the planners to consider the effects of interference on the city as a whole and eventually to modify the underlying questions of planning. Previously, the predominantly supply-oriented approach concentrated on vision and interventions. The early conceptions aimed to describe what Budapest should be like in the future (1991-1994), or what should be accomplished in the "strategic zones" (1998). The new approach was different: it focused on the goals, processes, and effects.

> *"The aim of urban development is to improve competitiveness and the quality of life on the basis of a complex strategy of interference which regards the improvement of the spatial structures, the accessibility of the affected areas, and the general qualities of the city's districts as elements of a single coherent system. [...] The improvement of competitiveness and the quality of life requires the rehabilitation of the downtown areas as well as the development of the outskirts, and also the restructuring and re-evaluation of the transitional zone."[18]*

At the same time the focus of attention was also shifted from individual areas to improving the efficiency of the urban structure. European cities that may be labeled as efficient should have no drastically under-utilized enclaves that increase travel needs and infrastructure expenses. In addition, the city structure is efficient if – shaped by the real estate market – its density gradually decreases, measured from the center towards the outlying areas of the city. In cities where the real estate market could function relatively undisturbed, it could continuously settle diverse functions to real estate locations according to their added values produced. The socialists' economic policies paralyzed the real estate market, and thus hampered the efficient spread and relocation of the various functions. The end result was a distorted city structure.[19]

In Budapest, the industrial zones that were created on the city's perimeters in the 19th century (subsequently these became known as the socialist industrial ring) have by now become underutilized enclaves with perplexingly mixed profiles. These zones distort the city's structure, increase travel demand, under-utilize certain infrastructure potentials, and spoil the city's overall image. In short, their existence runs counter to the creation of an efficient city structure. The repositioning of these zones would restore the city's spatial and functional continuity and would balance the real estate market, and the utilization of the infrastructure systems and services.

Besides the quest for a more efficient city structure, the change in the approach to urban development is marked by the planners reformulating their questions: how could the

---

[18] The Office of the Mayor of Budapest, 1999b: 1 – 6. We quote from the 1999 version of the conception because these texts more appropriately show the change in approach. As described in the paper on 'Strategic Planning and Management Reform', the conception's 2002 version departed again from the goal of creating a strategy.

[19] Bertaud, 1995

brown fields be repositioned in order to upgrade its value, as this would contribute to the appreciation of other areas as well. Based on this question, it becomes possible to establish priorities among the long project lists on the table. For example, clearly one boulevard (the Körvasútsor Boulevard) is to be selected as a priority from the three perimeter boulevards envisaged earlier with similar weight by the planners. This infrastructure element should be highlighted not simply on account of its role in the city's transport network, but also because through this it becomes possible to create access to the most problematic areas of the underutilized brown fields. This promotes their redevelopment and the utilization of infrastructure networks and other urban services.

Since 1990, some development objectives pertinent to the downtown areas might appear to have undergone practically no change. The initial conceptions focused on the improvement of environmental conditions, and the preservation and rehabilitation of their historic character and structures. In a market-driven context, the goal is to enhance appreciating effects. Of course, environmental quality and rehabilitation are important aspects of this improvement process as well. Still, in the new approach, agreement on the goals is the crucial element. Its different phrasing is also important, as it can guide the strategy creation, the prioritization of interventions and the proper use of scarce resources. Traffic regulation, an efficient system of parking, and the rehabilitation of public areas are the activities or public roles that enable the public sector to exert optimal influence on the process of appreciation.

> *"Here, the strategy to follow is a development process driven by the rehabilitation of public spaces amidst improving environmental conditions due to traffic reductions. The measures to be associated with this process include the other elements of complex urban rehabilitation: rehabilitation of action areas, parking system improvement, demolition and cleaning, and new developments."* [20]

From the point of view of infrastructure policy, the key element here is the change in the approach to urban development.[21] The more detailed analysis of the urban development conceptions (i.e., beyond the implications of this change in approach) would fall beyond the scope of the present study, which aims to focus on the integration of infrastructure policies.

---

[20] The Office of the Mayor of Budapest, 1999b: 1–6. We quote from the 1999 version of the conception because these texts show more appropriately the change in approach. As described in the study on 'Strategic Planning and Management Reform, the conception's 2002 version again departed from the goal of creating a strategy.

[21] Of course, the visible change in approach is very important. Still, the real achievement would be, if on this basis, market-oriented planning should eventually produce an integrated urban development strategy (i.e. an agreement that can guide the ensuing policy process and at the same time is flexible enough to be adjusted to the dynamically changing circumstances.). However, rather regrettably, no such strategy and agreement have been completed during the first three municipal cycles in Budapest.

TRAFFIC AND TRANSPORTATION

The problems of Budapest's traffic and transportation system were already apparent at the time of the change of the political system. The public road network had practically not been developed since the beginning of the 20th century, and the city's roads became increasingly congested by the dramatically rising use of private cars. At the same time, the drastic drop in the resources of the public transportation system made it imperative for the municipality to rationalize (and also reduce) transportation services. Simultaneously, in the agglomeration urban sprawl was growing and settlement structures evolved that were increasingly disadvantageous for public transportation services. This process and the changes in life and work styles dramatically increased travel demand and individual transportation in particular (i.e., private cars).

About 80 percent of the municipality's car traffic uses the road network of the "Little Budapest" area and there are not enough transversal roads to connect the outlying areas with each other. The gravest consequence of this deficient network is that the decisive part of the city's car traffic has no choice but to cross the downtown areas. This puts a disproportionately large strain on the already heavily congested central parts of the city. Since the change of the political system it has been clear that the city's competitiveness and livability hinges on the solution to the ever greater traffic and transportation problems.

From a 21st century standpoint, we may well see that this complex problem cannot be solved on the basis of a supply-oriented approach. However, in the socialist era and in the first years of the new one no initiatives could exceed the limits of this approach. In the 1960's, the traffic planners of the day based their development conceptions on extrapolating on the increase in demand. In Budapest, they aimed to address the projected growth in traffic and transportation demand by increasing supply. They planned to do this via raised roads above the ground-level traffic of the Little Boulevard, and later also above the Hungária Boulevard. Although since the 1970's and 1980's this technicist solution has also been rejected by the transportation engineers themselves, the first development conceptions completed after the change of the political system could still not go beyond supply-oriented approaches. In a rather remarkable way, these conceptions merged traffic management (or occasionally reduction) techniques [22] with investment proposals that clearly rested on the supply-oriented approach.

The transportation development plan of 1994 was still fundamentally determined by the supply- and sector-oriented approach. It applied a network-logic to its comprehensive plan for the city's transportation services, and its deliberations were restricted to sectoral issues. This traffic conception that aimed at creating an optimal network was in full harmony with the (previously described) futuristic, supply-oriented urban development plans of the time.

---

[22] The supply-oriented approach is also open to solutions other than building further roads. It also recognizes the method of traffic management, which is aimed at facilitating the flow of traffic along existing roads through appropriate regulations. Accordingly, the traffic management component of such plans strives to increase the efficiency of the existing road network to accommodate the forecasted travel demand.

The change in the approach to traffic and transportation planning became perceptible in 1997-1998 in Budapest. Those years witnessed the birth of the first drafts of the subsequently approved transportation system development plan, which was already based on the method of integrated demand management (as defined in the literature and also above).[23]

We must add, however, that although the viability of the previous supply-oriented plans was greatly undermined by the unrealistic nature of its financing possibilities, limits in resources alone would not have been enough to elicit the shift in approach. The new approach has emerged side by side with recently developed financial management practices, but its advance was first of all the effect of the adaptation of the leading transportation planner approach in international practices. A single city's pool of experts could not draw the elaboration of a new integrated and sophisticated methodology and a complex set of tools for demand management exclusively on their own. Accordingly, the simultaneity of the changes in the approach to financial management and transportation planning cannot be directly ascribed to the clarification of the financing frameworks. Instead, the harmonious changes in approaches "only" indicate that the selection of the up-to-date professional approaches accessible in the given areas evolved along similar lines.

Here we must restrict ourselves to quote only a few examples from the Transportation System Development Plan for Budapest (in everyday usage: Transport System Plan), which was officially approved in 2001, that reflect on the adoption of the method of demand management. The conception states that:

> *"The transportation policies, which aim to provide the foundations for the operation and development of Budapest's transportation system, strive to satisfy the demands associated with the city's balanced operation, instead of trying to meet spontaneous transportation demand through quantitative solutions. This task requires the coordinated and differentiated management of the individual fields and methods of transportation (developments or restrictions, with a predominantly qualitative approach)."[24]*

> *"The practices, motivations, and decisions [on movement] are becoming increasingly more complex, and thus there can be no efficient and sustainable traffic and transportation policies without their integration in the complex set of objectives of the urban development and land use policies. It is also imperative to recognize the possibilities for influencing demand and to create an appropriate set of tools."[25]*

---

[23] In transportation planning, demand management maintains the efficiency of the existing road network (against an increasing demand) by influencing demand, either through restrictions or by redirecting traffic to other areas, periods, or means. The usual methods include influencing the modal split, regulating parking, or influencing demand through tools and fine-tuning parking rates.

[24] Főmterv Co., 2001: II/4

[25] Főmterv Co., 2001: II/5. It would fall far beyond the scope of this study to evaluate the specific proposals in the plan against these goals.

Another important point in demand-oriented transportation planning, besides its integration in urban and land use policy is that it is not guided by "network-logic" but focuses on the "behavior of the citizen who uses the transportation system."[26] Consequently, its strategy aims to make the citizens themselves interested in voluntarily changing their transportation-related habits. To this end, this approach analyzes the traffic flow along the network, and the "traffic chain" between the users' point of departure (e.g., place of residence) and their destination (e.g. workplace) because the competitiveness of a transportation system is determined by the speed of the traffic flow and the level of convenience of the "traffic chain". The main objective, again, is to exert goal-oriented influences.

Though the Transport System Plan was progressive in its "demand-management" approach and its general professional thrust, and it also had a remarkable influence on the approach to land use as well as the integration of the various development policies, it could not succeed in consistently drawing the conclusions. Thus, it is bound to be "only" a professional study of high quality with significant contributions to transportation policy. As the approval of the plan was not preceded by political decisions on the priorities among the diverse urban development goals, consequently the Transport System Plan could not build up a strategy either. In the absence of clear-cut decisions, the plan presented a 15-year and a longer-term development package. The project lists within the packages – just like in the "good old days" – are not prioritized, and the aggregate volume of the proposed investments are not adjusted to the financial possibilities. Due to these deficiencies the plan – though it is a very important factor in shaping the professional and political approaches, as it reveals the principles and inherences of modern traffic and transportation planning – fails to qualify as a strategy. In order to maintain professional and "political peace", the plan does not clarify the decisions that could be deduced from the relevant principles. Consequently, its approval could not either have the weight of a strategic agreement with the power to govern future choices.

The studies in the present volume discuss the ways in which financial management reform has influenced the transformation of individual fields and the whole of Budapest's urban policies. In connection with transportation policy, another important effect should also be mentioned: the increasingly prevalent demand management approach in transportation planning has accelerated similar changes in the approach to urban development. The effects were mutual: changing urban development approaches have also contributed to the clarification of the transportation-related ideas and the application of the demand management solutions. Accordingly, the case of transportation planning in the Budapest reforms clearly shows the complexity of influences that shape the evolution of urban policies.

WATER UTILITIES

In the field of water utility planning, the creation of a market-oriented strategy was also a big challenge. However, the changes in approach had to occur in a context markedly different from that of transportation policy. While the urban road network is traditionally a

---

[26] Főmterv Co., 2001: II/5.

local public good financed from public funds[27] and public transportation is, at least partially, also subsidized,[28] cost-covering rates are seen as desirable in the field of water utilities. The drive to establish cost-covering rates and to create a system of targeted welfare subsidies has been manifest since the publication of the city mayor's first election program in 1990.[29] It was also clear from the beginning that the rate hikes and the restructuring urban economy would result in a drop in water consumption. Consequently, in the field of water utilities the municipality's task was to establish market conditions for the services of a system that – albeit incompletely realized – had been developed for a use far larger than the forecasted future demand.

In principle, the introduction of cost-covering rates proportionate to usage can itself enforce the transition from supply- to demand-oriented planning approaches. When the companies are under increasing pressure to cover their operating costs from their rate revenues, it is not rational for them to calculate the rates according to a demand that exceeds future trends. If they do so, they cannot but charge the permanent cost elements (i.e., the ones that are not directly tied to actual use, such as the costs of network maintenance) based on higher calculated aggregate performance. As a result, the permanent costs charged on the rates for each cubic meter become lower. If the actual level of consumption turns out to be lower, these permanent cost elements cannot cover the actual permanent costs. Consequently, the rates calculated on the basis of unrealistic higher demand lead to lost revenues for the company. A company that operates amidst market conditions is not interested in installing and operating a network with a potential that exceeds the projected level of demand either, as this would entail higher investment expenditures. The markedly lower than optimal level of system utilization would also increase the per unit costs of maintenance.[30]

Accordingly, in the field of water utilities, the main question is not what the spark behind the change in approach was, but instead:

– the extent to which the policies of the local government could enforce efficient, market-based operation on the public utility companies;

– the cause and duration of the survival of the supply-oriented approach and the associated assumptions that demand would continuously increase (even against rate hikes);

– the extent to which the new conditions (i.e., pricing and privatization) set by the local government have changed the services provided and the planning of relevant investments.

---

[27] There are practical rather than principled considerations behind the public financing of the maintenance of the urban road network. The explanation is rather simple: with the exception of a few isolated urban systems (e.g., Singapore), the cities have not developed a proper method for calculating and collecting usage-proportionate tolls.

[28] The subsidization of public transportation from public funds is justified by its competitive handicap with its counterpart, the individual transportation. This handicap manifests itself in pricing. This issue is discussed in detail in the study on infrastructure policies.

[29] Alliance of Free Democrats (SZDSZ), 1990: 16 and 22

[30] The maintenance costs of the network increase as a result of the faster sedimentation of the pipes, as the level of the system's exploitation decreases, etc. Occasionally it can also happen that certain installations will have to be closed down completely.

Since two other studies in the present chapter discuss answers to the first question in detail,[31] here we only concentrate on the last two questions. In view of their diverse characteristics, we shall discuss water and sewage services separately.

WATER SUPPLY

In Budapest, the professionally and politically strong leaders of the Water Works had enough power during the socialist era to access sufficient resources for providing excellent services. As a strong, unconstrained, large socialist enterprise, the Water Works left a good quality system behind, which did not require any significant development or restructuring on the part of the local government.

The biggest of all challenges for the company was presented by the need to adjust to decreasing levels of water consumption. In the early 1990's, the city's inhabitants and businesses consumed 1-1.3 million cubic meters of water per day. By the end of the 1990's, this figure had dropped to 650,000-700,000 cubic meters. This drastic drop required the adjustment of the company's strategy. Remarkably, while the declining trend was already manifest at the beginning of the decade (4-6 percent drop annually), the company's leaders continued to apply the old socialist routine of planning for increasing demand, and came up with irrational proposals concerning both rate calculations and investment plans.

For certain projects, at the beginning of the 1990's, the municipality's freshly installed leaders accepted the false arguments of the company (which were duly echoed by the municipality's own departments) and made mistaken investment decisions. In each of the cases at issue seemingly logical arguments rested on unrealistic consumption prognoses.[32] As a result, false development objectives were identified and later fought for, applying the age old method of "hanging on the plan" as described earlier. By the time the alert members of the newly installed leadership perceived the mistakes, it was impossible to halt some of the projects.[33] The biggest of all these mistakes was the construction of the Csepel water management plant, which has a daily capacity of 150,000 cubic meters.[34]

---

[31] See the studies entitled 'User Charge Policy for Public Utilities' and 'Utility Privatization'.

[32] The false, supply-oriented arguments were buttressed by the possibility to access state grants for these investments. The grants were supposed to lead to savings by the municipality. However, in reality, due to the fact that projects were wrongly conceived, the grants triggered wasteful practices.

[33] These cases are a clear demonstration of the practice known as "hanging on the plan." Once a misconceived or plainly mistaken project is entered in the investment plans, it becomes politically very difficult to reject it. In all these instances, the projects at issue had already garnered enough support for disabling the critics from blocking their approval. Already in the realm of politics, vague political statements overcome clear professional arguments. (The only exceptions to this rule were the two major "project butcherings" described in detail in the study on financial management reform that in 1993 and 1994 were clearly forced on by external conditions.)

[34] The decision was reached in 1993, at a time when daily water consumption was only 88 percent of the 1990 level. By 1995 – date of the inauguration of the plant – the city's water consumption had dropped by an additional 10 percent (1990: 993,000 cubic meters per day; 1993: 876,000 cubic meters; 1995: 780,000 cubic meters). As a result of this drop in consumption, the plant remained idle. Finally, the company's 2003 business plan sanctioned the plant's liquidation and the sale of the plot.

Faced with these initial mistakes, the municipal leaders – who were interested in cutting expenditures – exercised an increasingly tough and ever more professional control on the investment proposals. This led finally, in 1994,[35] to the first such development plan that focused on the need to adjust to the decreasing demand rather than accept unrealistic projections for increasing consumption corresponding to the socialist-type slogan of "dynamic development."[36]

Chart 1
WATER CONSUMPTION AS A FUNCTION OF WATER RATES

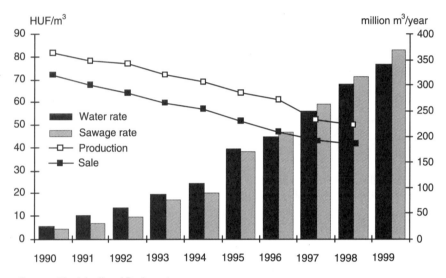

Source: Municipality of Budapest

The drop in water consumption prompted – besides the revision of the investment plans – both organizational and technical streamlining. In addition, the local government wanted to transform the large, unconstrained socialist enterprise into a cost-efficient business. However, the municipality did not find partners for its rationalization plans among the company's leaders. The breakthrough came with the privatization of the company, which is discussed in detail in the study on public utility privatization.

---

[35] By 1994 the average daily consumption had dropped by 15 percent below the 1990 level (from 992,000 to 840,000 cubic meters per day).

[36] Főmterv Co., 1994

WASTEWATER MANAGEMENT

The state of the municipality's sewage system and the related waste water management installations as inherited from the socialist era differed markedly from that of the water utilities. The bulk of the collecting mains was built by the Public Works Council in the 19th century. During the socialist era, this network was expanded only by the mains that served the large housing estates. The capacity of these mains is sufficient to satisfy the actual and foreseeable demands in the given collection areas. In other parts of the city, lower intensity development projects were approved without sewerage connection. As a result, the gap between the coverage of water and wastewater services was growing wider. The low percentage of treatment of the collected wastewater was another sign of lack of sensitivity for environmental implications.

At the time of the change of the political system, engineers and professionals considered the development of the sewage network and the related cleaning capacities a purely technical issue. In their opinion, the only issues that required decisions were the financing and the scheduling of the investments. A major dilemma for the city leaders was to work out who should pay for these developments. In principle, the investments filling up gaps could justifiably be financed from privatization revenues but these resources were obviously not sufficient. In the case of new, long-term investments, it is justified to charge a long-term loan on utility rates.[37]

In the middle of the 1990s, in the absence of sizeable subsidies either from the state or from the European Union, it appeared impossible to complete the Budapest wastewater treatment capacity by 2010 – to meet the accession terms of the European Union – even relying on loans. The costs would have required a 3-400 percent rate hike within a few years. By the second half of the 1990's, the municipality had gained access to important developmental subsidies (state, ISPA, etc.), and also to longer-term loans (with 20-25 year expiration). On that basis, it became possible for Budapest to draft a financing construction that did not require the accelerated increase of the public utility rates. According to the forecasted increase in real wages, the necessary rate hikes would remain acceptable.[38]

Similarly to the way wastewater treatment developed, the filling up of the gaps in the sewage network was a process that progressed in a gradual fashion (albeit relatively slower than for wastewater treatment). Although the development prospects of the areas are greatly determined by the availability of sewage network or investment plans, there are no tough deadlines for the completion of this network such as those that the EU accession conditions create for treatment capacity.

The local governments can apply for targeted state subsidies for their sewage system investments. However, these subsidies cover only parts of the associated expenditures.

---

[37] For an explanation of this statement, please see the subtitle 'Borrowing Policy' in the study on the 'Elements of the Financial Management Reform'.

[38] The spread of the real wages may present a problem in the paying capacity of some groups.

In Budapest the Municipality must provide the costs of the basic network that serves larger areas. The municipality complements the targeted state subsidies[39] with its own contributions (from the development brackets of the rate revenues and also from other budgetary resources). The costs of the local hubs and connections must be borne by local consumers' public utility development contributions,[40] and by the districts. To promote these investments, the municipality has created a fund in its budget from the development bracket of the sewage rate. The districts can annually tender for targeted sewage network subsidies, similarly to the case of targeted state subsidies.

It is clear from the foregoing that the tools for financing the gradual completion of the network and treatment capacity had (at least partly) been present prior to the change of the political system, while some important elements were only added in the 1990's. However, in this field, development planning was slower to adjust to the new conditions. Consequently it was hardly possible to use the development plans in force for decision making. And yet, due to the large investment need, it has always been possible to identify realistic development projects in this field and to draft detailed plans for their execution.[41]

In 1993, the municipality made an attempt to systematize the investment processes by commissioning new plans for the development of its wastewater system.[42] The attempt turned out to be a failure, however. Due to the professionals' old ingrained supply-based approach, the plans ignored drastically declining water consumption figures and – presuming a steady increase – planned a daily capacity of 1.5 million cubic meters for the new system. The plans rested on false assumptions, and the costs of their execution would have exceeded the citizens' burden-sharing potentials, so they proved to be useless. Consequently, the preparations of the subsequent investments continued in the old way of making individual decisions on the most urgent network and cleaning capacity investment projects.

Finally, the 1999 review of the sewage system development plan adjusted the technical proposals to the actual trends.[43] This document reduced the aggregate capacity of the proposed system to 600,000 cubic meters per day. For meeting this investment demand it was already possible to set up a financing scheme within the derogation period negotiated

---

[39] For details, please see the study on 'User Charge Policy for Public Utilities'.

[40] The system of public utility development contributions dates back to the socialist era. Since then, it has been re-regulated. The aim of this system is to provide a framework for the enforcement of local development needs. The local developers (district governments, citizens, businesses) establish public utility partnerships to cover expenses according to the proportions that sector-specific legal regulations determine for them.

[41] This last statement reveals the difference between the state of sewage and drinking water services. In the field of wastewater management systems development, owing to the markedly backward state of the sector, in spite of ill-conceived plans, it was possible to specify some investment projects to the extent of the available resources that were certain to be needed and realistic. At the same time, as we have seen, the wrong approach taken in the planning of drinking water services resulted in mistaken investment decisions.

[42] Főmterv Co., 1993

[43] Főmterv Co., 1999

with the European Union, as well as to save consumers and taxpayers from paying the huge financial burdens of wasteful investments and operation.

GAS

In Budapest, the coal gas network for supplying kitchen and lighting demands was rebuilt in the 1960's and 1970's to accommodate the requirements of natural gas also used for heating purposes. By the 1980's the gas network had practically reached all the areas where it could be economically installed. At the time of the change of the political system, the Municipality of Budapest took over a good quality gas system that could satisfy demands. In this field, the real issue was not development but questions concerning metering, rating, privatization, and rate compensation that have already been spelled out in the other studies of this chapter.

DISTRICT HEATING

The first units of district heating services in Budapest were installed in the 1930's. At the time, the thermal water wells of Margaret Island were used to supply heating to the new apartment blocs of a downtown district. Before World War Two, the small system was not enlarged any further. A major boost came with the construction of the large housing estates during the socialist era. These buildings were designed exclusively for district heating and central warm water supply, so they had no chimneys at all. The low energy rates and the socialists' public utility policies created a system with a very low cost efficiency rate. Costs were covered primarily from public funds, and to a lesser extent also from the flat rate payments of the consumers. In its 1990 state, the district heating system supplied 240,000 households (25 percent of the Budapest total) and some 5,000 institutions. Eighty-five percent of these households are in housing estates.

Following the change of the political system the energy market has remained in the ownership of the state (subsequently it was partly privatized). However, district heating has become a mandatory service for the Municipality of Budapest, and the ownership of the District Heating Company (subsequently renamed as District Heating Company of the Capital – Főtáv Co. in the Hungarian abbreviation) was transferred to the municipality.

Over half of the company's operating costs are associated with gas prices. Főtáv Co. can realize a 7-17 percent margin from the gas price gap between large and small consumers (the prices are set by the state). This is insufficient for making the service competitive as this margin should provide resources for balancing the fast depreciation of the system, the natural losses from heat transportation, the operation of a fundamentally wasteful[44] and

---

[44] Similarly to the other socialist countries, Hungary's district heating service was also built with a "single-pipe system." In this system it is practically impossible to meter consumption individually, thus hindering the rationalization of use. In Budapest, the past few years witnessed the introduction of the obligatory metering of consumption by apartment blocs, and there are also methods available for splitting up costs between individual consumers.

already highly amortized network, as well as the company's 25-30 percent overhead.[45] In other words, the company has to sell a very expensive service to a large number of relatively low income consumers (cf. housing estates).

It is clear that the service is kept alive by its inertia rather than by its viability as a business. In principle, the consumers could cancel the service and switch over to gas heating. However, this is only possible for houses that are equipped with chimneys. The number of homes in such houses is insignificant. It is also possible for a whole building to cancel its subscription to the district heating service. This requires the consent of every apartment owner in the given building, and also a sizeable investment on their part. In larger houses with several apartments, it is rather difficult to achieve 100 percent support for such an undertaking, and there are always people who simply cannot afford to shoulder such investments. (Needless to say, neither Főtáv Co. nor the municipality is interested in subsidizing the detachment of the households.)

Consumers living in housing estates – 85 percent of homes – have practically no chances to detach due to the social composition of the blocks, and to the high costs of switching services. Amidst such circumstances, Főtáv Co. judges the probability of losing customers en masse – and the entailing rise in per unit costs as well as the consequent rate hikes that would accelerate detachment and lead to an eventual collapse of the service – to be very low. Főtáv Co. rather faces the specter of collapse in connection with the accumulation of arrears[46] that is to be kept under control through the system of Housing Utility Allowances.[47]

A safe and long-term solution to the problem could only be presented by introducing a model thanks to which the service would become self-financing[48] and competitive with the other methods of heating.[49] Logically, the company's strategy could rest on three pillars: improving efficiency, reducing energy costs and rationalizing consumption. The company's attempts to improve its efficiency are discussed in another study of this chapter discussing the company's operation. The same study also looks into the questions relating to energy prices. The possibilities of privatization are tackled in the first study of this chapter. For this reason, we now focus on those – missing – issues that also have technical implications, or where the technical arguments are also relevant.

---

[45] This figure may seem to be very high. However, we must note that the service has to generate enough revenue during the five winter months to finance the company's operation throughout the year. The relatively mild climate of Budapest and the short heating season are disadvantages for the district heating service, since the consumers tend to prefer individual heating solutions. The situation is markedly different in cities in the northern parts of the region.

[46] See *Table 6* in the *Appendix*.

[47] The system is spelled out in the study entitled 'Public Utility Allowances in Budapest'.

[48] Self-financing here means the ability to cover the costs of operation, maintenance, and development.

[49] The question remains open whether Budapest's district heating service can at all be expected to become competitive, given the brief heating season. Nobody has attempted to answer this rather radical question yet, and the inertia of the transition period pushes the problem in the background, for the time being. This is why we also focus on the possibilities of boosting the service's efficiency.

Quite a number of important questions – not discussed in detail in the study on Főtáv Co.[50] – would fall into this category, as the possibilities of economic rationalization are always limited by technical limits. In the paragraphs below we shall look into two specific questions relating to the efforts to cut the costs of the district heating services. One has to do with the possibilities of reducing the price of purchased heat energy, and the other with the efforts to rationalize consumption.

Presumably, the price of the purchased heat energy[51] could be reduced if heat producers had to compete with each other.[52] A related benefit of more suppliers accessing the network would be that this system could eliminate the heating districts' dependence on their respective suppliers (which otherwise represents a serious price risk). In principle, the heat producers could be made to compete by allowing any heat supplier to connect to any local heating district of his choice.[53]

The ensuing competition, as an economic tool, may be damaged by the losses incurred in heat transportation as well as by the number of competing suppliers. After all, this scenario is beneficial only if the benefits from price competition exceed transportation losses and if there are enough suppliers to prevent the emergence of a price cartel type of agreement.

Főtáv Co.'s proposal for the creation of a "heating ring" seem to also rest on the idea of making suppliers compete with each other. Still, the heating ring would hook up all the heating districts with each other (i.e., it would cover the whole system.). In principle, the heating ring would connect the suppliers to a distribution system that would make them compete with all the other heat producers. The weakest point in this conception is its enormous investment cost, which can under no circumstances be offset by the potential cuts in expenditures. Of course, this huge network would also incur sizeable transportation losses. Another argument against the idea is that by creating uniformity between heat suppliers it would strengthen the monopolistic nature of the distribution service. Meanwhile, the other conception, which strives to strengthen the local heating district services, aims to structure the network in a reasonable way. For the owner, the last point is also important. Its significance can best be construed in the light of the alternative privatization model described in the 'Infrastructure Policy' paper.

Currently, the number of Budapest's heat suppliers is limited. The liberalization of the energy market may increase this number. A few associated heat producing private ventures have already entered the market in Budapest. New suppliers have already been connected to the network in certain areas, and some of the heating districts have also been linked.

---

[50] The study 'District Heating – a Non-Privatized Utility' in this chapter.

[51] Currently Főtáv Co. purchases 70 percent of its heat energy needs from external suppliers. Most of these supply heat to isolated heating districts, and are thus monopolies. There are only a few heating districts with two suppliers.

[52] In principle this requires technical conditions similar to the system of the electric energy suppliers. However, transportation losses are much higher in the case of heat energy, and thus the chances for competition are much more limited.

[53] Finance Research Co., 2000

The possibilities of further connections are still under investigation. Although Főtáv Co.'s official strategy rests on the heating ring conception, each new linkup is preceded by detailed cost-benefit analyses. The investments are agreed upon and executed only if they promise to produce direct financial gains. Consequently, most of the linkups occur on the local level. In view of this condition our previous effort to clarify the difference between the local connections and the heating ring conception was dictated only by our attempt to reach conceptual clarity.

The other way to cut costs is to rationalize the consumers' behavior. From an economic point of view it is clear that the introduction of consumption-based pricing in a service that used to be free or employed flat-rates would prompt the consumers to be more vigilant about their consumption. There are two basic conditions to the introduction of consumption-based pricing: the possibility for metering consumption, and the willingness to pay. As we shall see, in the field of district heating these two conditions are closely related, and both are difficult to achieve.

In retrospect, we have every reason to describe the socialists' district heating service as a "horrible creature." The service's sole aim was to maintain the centrally prescribed temperature in the apartments. To accomplish this goal the heat-flow in the badly insulated housing estates required apartments on the lower levels to have more heating units installed than the ones on the higher levels. The goal was to maintain uniform temperature and the price was also uniform and – compared to costs – symbolic. The system did not allow for customer choices, as there was no way to regulate the individual radiators.

In Budapest (similarly to the other socialist cities), the first housing estates were built with a so-called single-pipe heating system. This means that there was a single flow and a single reflow pipe. Heat output was gradual, could not be regulated by individual radiators and was impossible to meter. In these circumstances, the consumers (who paid a flat rate for the service) adjusted the temperature by opening their windows. Later on, housing estates were built with dual-pipe heating systems, which made it possible to adjust the heat on the individual radiators. However, a study completed by the Technical University of Budapest revealed that the regulation or switching off of the individual radiators created water flow problems and noise, and had the potential to damage the boilers. The only way to solve these problems was to refurbish the boilers.

Beside the regulation another problem was the difficulty of metering by consumers. Regulation does not make much sense if it is not tied to metering and consumption-based pricing. Metering is difficult because per unit heat loss is not uniform along the system. In this system, consumption-based pricing can not be based on simple calculations based on the quantity of water flowing through the pipes, but only on a complex calculation of heat loss. A rather common way to bypass this problem is to install heat sensors on the individual radiators. However, it is relatively easy to "fool" these sensors.

Still, the biggest of all problems with the apartments in housing estates is neither regulation nor heat metering. From a technical point of view, it is possible to produce a good approximation of consumption and thus, in principle, it could be made mandatory to meter consumption in each apartment individually. The big question is how to make people pay for the service. The housing estates in Budapest are known for their very poor insulation. Quite often there are gaping holes between the concrete panels. As result, the introduction of consumption-based pricing would require the owners of the apartments on the lower levels to pay maybe three or four times more than those living on the higher levels. Following this scenario, the owners of the lower-level apartments (who had bought their apartments on the same conditions as the upper floor owners) would often not be able to pay their bills. Furthermore, these apartments would completely lose their market value. Accordingly, a precondition to the introduction of consumption-based pricing would be to find a solution to this rather inequitable situation.[54]

The act on district heating[55] obliges the servicing company to meter consumption in each building individually. However, the law has no stipulations for metering consumption in individual apartments. Since in the existing system it is up to the joint will of the apartment-owners to install individual meters, in practice this does not happen. Thus metering has in practice little rationalizing effect on consumption.

The examples above, and the problems discussed in the introductory study of this chapter and also in the study on the evolution of the company's management, sufficiently reveal that the municipality has chalked up only modest successes in the field of district heating. District heating is considered a cause for major headaches all across the region. Budapest has yet to make its fundamental strategic decisions. A future strategy will have to resolve the dilemma outlined above, create competition among the heat energy suppliers, address the issues discussed in the introductory study and ultimately formulate coherent policies for this service.

SOLID WASTE

Budapest began to designate solid waste disposal areas in 1830. The same year also witnessed the launch of the municipal solid waste collection service. The municipality's solid waste incinerator was inaugurated in 1982. The plant treats 60 percent of the solid waste generated in Budapest.[56] Since the change of the political system, solid waste collection and disposal has been the local government's responsibility. To this end, the Municipality of Budapest operates the Public Space Maintenance Company (Hungarian abbreviation: FKF Rt.). The company began to charge for its services in 1996.

---

[54] It is important to emphasize that the liberal city leaders would have no problem accepting this situation if it applied only to the owners of newly purchased apartments. After all, in that case the difference would appear in the market price of the apartments. The moral dilemma is caused by the fact that a drastic reallocation of wealth would take place for people who had purchased their apartments earlier, under different conditions. There is a practical problem as well, since people cannot and do not want to cover the actual costs.

[55] Acts and Decrees, 11

[56] Each year, Budapest generates around 5 million cubic meters of solid waste. Sixty percent of this is communal waste. In addition, the city generates some 100,000 tons of hazardous waste.

Waste management is the term used for defining the activities related to waste collection and disposal. In Budapest, waste management includes collection, transportation, and disposal. Selective waste collection is still uncommon in Hungary, owing primarily to the absence of the required recycling infrastructure. The volume of energy generated by the waste incinerator is negligible, primarily due to the plant's outdated technology.

Following the change of the political system, the municipality had to face four major challenges in this field: it had to dispose of the city's waste, reduce associated environmental burdens, find financial coverage for the related activities and increase the cost efficiency of the service. The issues relating to cost coverage and cost efficiency have already been tackled in the introductory study, and thus we focus our attention here on the technical problems associated with waste disposal.

Since Hungary is on its way to become a full member of the European Union attention has focused on the environmental implications of waste disposal. Since the 1990's, the new waste disposal areas must have appropriate technical protection,[57] and the existing incinerator's emission levels are seriously sanctioned. To reduce emission, the municipality has begun upgrading the incinerator and a flue-gas treatment equipment is being built in it.

In the field of waste disposal, a long-debated issue has been whether the municipality should increase the capacity of the incinerator or should instead identify new waste disposal areas. The first plans for a second waste incinerator were completed prior to the change of the political system. It goes without saying that the decision hinged on the clarification of the municipality's financial potentials. Eventually, the second incinerator was taken off the agenda because of its excessive cost:

> *"The present program considers the 'modern' method of waste incineration as the expensive choice of countries that have no access to disposal areas. Until the municipality has access to such areas, it will refrain from choosing waste incineration, which is extremely expensive to install and operate. It is at least seven times cheaper to dispose of waste in technically protected areas than simply to operate a waste incinerator."*[58]

Eventually, the municipality decided to establish a new, large-capacity waste disposal area. It was built in 2000 outside the city borders, in Pusztazámor. The total cost of the project was around HUF 10 billion. The area's capacity exceeds 20 million cubic meters, which

---

[57] Technical protection means that the disposal area is first lined with plastic foil. Normally there are two layers of foil with drain pipes and monitoring wells to enable the authorities to check the status of the protection and prevent the contamination of the soil below. Once the pit is filled up with waste, it is covered with a top foil layer and soil. Then comes the planting of plants that tolerate this type of environment. The top layer protection is meant to isolate the biogas from the atmosphere. This gas is generated by rainfall and rotting, and is collected and either burnt or utilized. Biogas production starts to decline after about 20 years. It takes another 20-odd years for gas production to completely stop. This means that the area can be used again after 40-odd years. Under the current regulations, these areas can be used for all purposes except agricultural production.

[58] Alliance of Free Democrats (SZDSZ), 1994: 46

is expected to be sufficient for the next fifty years. The area is technically protected and applies the method of waste prism that is the most advance technique complying with the strictest environmental rules.[59] Besides the applied technology, there was also an important, new political element to this investment. Budapest had to pay 15 percent of the disposal area's total installation cost to neighboring settlements in compensation for accepting such an undesirable project.

CONCLUDING THOUGHTS

The present study focused on two fundamental questions. First, its aim was to evaluate the Municipality of Budapest's record in creating clear conditions for physical planning through financial reforms, and also through integrating the processes of financial, political, and professional planning. The other aim was to look at external influences on the municipality's infrastructure services.

The examples cited above sufficiently prove that urban policies are influenced by a wide variety of external and internal factors. They also demonstrate the significance of the two fundamental methodical components of Budapest's urban policies – strategic real planning and process regulation – in the field of infrastructure services. These two components – although they exert influence on each infrastructure services field – have differing consequences according to sector, and can be enforced by different factors.

In our discussion of the method of strategic real planning, we emphasized the need for iteration between the professional and the financial proposals. In the field of infrastructure services, it is likewise important to iterate between the diverse sectoral and urban development proposals. The infrastructure services discussed in this study clearly show that urban policies are influenced by exceptionally diverse effects. In an ideal case, the financial reforms influence policies in the same directions as the modern sectoral approaches. They can result in a gradual evolution of integrated conceptions and strategies and – in pace with the changing external conditions – associated implementation activities emerge only slowly and incrementally.

Local financial management reform – the focus of the present book – has affected the infrastructure sectors in three respects: it clarified the local government's potential resource-base, exerted a rationalizing influence through utility rates and strategic real planning and shaped the municipality's market-oriented approach. In certain fields the rate policies had a strong rationalizing effect. In the case of the privatized services, the investors' sensitivity

---

[59] This is considered the most advanced method of solid waste disposal. During the area's preparation, trapezoid holes (called prisms) are dug in the soil. These holes are lined with technical protection. The dumping of waste then begins. The 9-15-meter-high dumps of condensed waste are also prism-shaped. The dumps are covered with soil and plants. The precipitation is collected from the dumps and stored in special reservoirs. The water is used for watering the plants on the dumps. The vehicles used for transporting waste are washed before they leave the area, and the cleaning water is re-channeled to the reservoirs.

to costs was quite often decisive. Still, even those areas where the municipality has proved unable to create competition either on or for the market have experienced certain changes (e.g., district heating or solid waste disposal). Yet in these areas, the nature and conditions of the services have remained practically unchanged.

SOURCES AND LITERATURE

Alliance of Free Democrats (SZDSZ), 1990: *'A Szabad Demokraták programja Budapest számára.' (The Free Democrats' Program for Budapest. Election program.) Budapest*

Alliance of Free Democrats (SZDSZ), 2002: *'Fővárost Európának. Budapest európai fővárossá fejlesztésének programja.' (A Capital for Europe. Program for Developing Budapest into a European Capital. Campaign program of Gábor Demszky. Budapest*

Atkári, János, 2000: *'Mehr Licht'. Discussion Paper for the Conference of the Alliance of Free Democrats, manuscript.*

Bertaud, Alain, 1995: *'Cities Without Land Markets'. The World Bank Polic Research Working Papers 1477.*

Central Office of Statistics, 1991-2003: Statistical Yearbooks of Budapest. Budapest

Finance Research Co., 2000: *'A fővárosi távhőszolgáltatás egy lehetséges szervezeti modellje.' (A Possible Organization Model for District Heating in the Capital.) Budapest*

Foundation for a European Hungary, Local Government Experts' Office, 1991: *'Demszky Gábor programja a Főváros számára.' (Gábor Demszky's Program for the Capital City. Election program.) Budapest*

Főmterv Co., 1994: *'A Főváros Vízgazdálkodási Terve.' (The Municipality's Water Management Plan.) Budapest*

Főmterv Co., 1999: *'A főváros hosszú távú komplex csatornázási és szennyvízkezelési terve.' (The Long-Term Complex Sewage System and Waste Water Management Development Program of the Capital. Rewrite.) Budapest*

Főmterv Co., 2001: *'Budapest közlekedési rendszerének fejlesztési terve.' (Development Plan for Budapest's Traffic and Transportation System.) Budapest*

The Municipality of Budapest, 2002-2003: *Figures from Municipal Companies.*

The Office of the Mayor of Budapest, 1992b: *'Budapest kiemelt középtávú fejlesztési céljai.' (Budapest's Priority Medium-Term Development Goals.) Budapest*

The Office of the Mayor of Budapest, 1998c: *'Budapest Városfejlesztési Koncepciója.' (Budapest's Urban Development Conception. Coordination document.) Budapest*

The Office of the Mayor of Budapest, 1999b: *'Budapest Városfejlesztési Koncepciója.' (Budapest's Urban Development Conception. Draft submitted to professional and public dispute.) Budapest*

GENERAL CONTEXT OF THE HUNGARIAN LOCAL GOVERNMENT SYSTEM

GENERAL CONDITIONS OF A DECADE'S OPERATION

Tamás M. Horváth – Gábor Péteri

When discussing the „Budapest model", many types of condition would naturally have to be presented in order to obtain an accurate picture of the last decade. Political, public administration, service organization, economic, social, budgetary and other conditions have changed constantly and in parallel with each other. Of these we have chosen only a few factors. We have above all tried to describe those general conditions that determine the future development of the city and that have to be considered in the development of city policy in the long term.

Thus the following will be discussed:

1. The reorganization of the public administration system and the concept of the state in Europe. Both had an impact on the Eastern European region, where diverse local government solutions were devised to avoid crisis.

2. The Hungarian economic and budgetary cycles that created particular waves in decentralization policy: restraint went together with strengthening the local level, while growth accompanied centralization.

3. In Budapest's case this coincided with a turning point in urban development when the city went through a suburbanization phase. This had a fundamental effect on the institutional system of city development and operation, which only slowly and with delay adapted to the new circumstances.

4. Finally, an analysis of the local governments' and Budapest's scope for budgetary action may show the favorable and disadvantageous components of the new local government financial system introduced in 1990 for the city of Budapest. This will also give us a picture of how their effects changed over time.

The question that immediately arises is whether it is right to apply such a broad perspective to this topic. Local government financing, or the practice of current financial management in a broader sense is under normal circumstances only one of the areas of city development and not necessarily a priority area. Nevertheless, for various reasons, this particular policy area has been given a priority role in this case. We wish to examine the legitimacy of the creation of this priority. We will analyze relevant factors of city policy and within this regulatory policy, examining whether or not these have had an effect on the practices of the Municipality of Budapest, and if so, in what context and to what extent. If, however, we do not find sufficiently convincing links, we shall endeavor to discover the reasons behind this.

A metropolis is always exceptional – especially if it is the only large city in an otherwise small country. The introduction of the framework conditions for Budapest's financing and service-organizational model rests on three peculiar features of the city. Budapest is home to one-fifth of the country's total population, and thus benefits from a favorable economic and infrastructure status. This explains why the Budapest Municipal Government's legislative activities and budgetary decision-making processes depend fairly heavily on changes in the national (central) political scene. The existence of a two-tier (municipal and district-level) system of local governments in Budapest complicates matters further. During the period at issue, the development of the city was either riddled with controversies or progressed in a concerted manner, depending on the fluctuations of the political scene.

We sincerely hope that our outline of the most important general conditions will help the reader better understand the financial practice of the Municipality of Budapest[1] presented as the "Budapest model."

MUNICIPAL POLICIES OF STATE GOVERNMENTS IN AN INTERNATIONAL SETTING

Public administration began to undergo fundamental changes in the 1980's. In continental systems the traditional, Weberian operation of bureaucracy typified by predictability and rule following was confronted by the compulsion to renew the system. Perhaps the most important starting point in the process was the re-interpretation of the relation between public administration and society. The former rigid division between the public and private sectors gradually disappeared, closely connected with the desire to radically reduce its welfare and other community functions. Endeavors for a complete change of profile of state functions was concomitant with a compulsory, but nevertheless only partial, slimming down. Plans to reform and reorganize in Central Europe had to come face to face with the current level of state development in Western Europe.[2]

It is worthwhile to distinguish the more recent local government policy developments of "experienced" democracies from the programs and practices developed as part of the change of the political system. For the latter, the difficulties allied with their own development were also influential factors in addition to the environment in which they were being developed. The joint effect of these two forces produced individual results for each country, and thus in Hungary, as well.

TRENDS IN WESTERN EUROPE

The development of the current tasks of local governments is dependent on the state's general economic and social policy. In Western countries, by the 1980's the neo-conservative trend, which held up a striking concept regarding the role of the budgetary sector, gained clear ascendancy. Radical reorganizations were initiated as a consequence.

---

[1] Throughout this paper we use the terms Municipality (of Budapest) and Districts for the two tiers of government in the capital city.

[2] For details explained in the following see Horváth, 2000/a; Horváth P., 2000.

Apart from reducing public expenditures, the aim was to change the entire institutional system. Service provision was not seen as exclusively achievable through state-founded organizations. In the context of this endeavor the role of the state in the public sector was re-interpreted. In addition to applying new budgetary techniques, this meant rethinking the role of the market, market mechanisms and the private sector in organizing public functions.

The practical consequences of this neo-conservative philosophy proved to be relevant for the countries of Central Europe undergoing reorganization. One of the consequences of this logic was the announcement of the reorganization of the large state redistribution systems, such as education or pensions reform. In the former, in particular, creation of the conditions for a multi-sector system meant experimenting with introducing new resources, while in the pension system the revival of private insurers or the network of pension funds and numerous other structures led to a similar type of experiment.

These changes included the reorganization of all public services, and among these the reform of local public services, which perhaps accounted for the greatest part. The privatization of public services, contracting out and the simulation of market conditions in the human services (social care, education, etc.) are, to a significant extent, locally interpretable phenomena. Their individual characteristics can only be understood thus, although together they form a process on a national level.

The hegemony of the neo-conservative state, that rejected the classical welfare state, declined in the developed countries in the 1990's. The results regarding the rationalization and reorganization of the budgetary sector, however, were not denied anywhere.

By the mid-1990's the moderate Left ("the Left's right wing") succeeded the right-wing conservative governments. Some theorists characterized the essence of the new politics as the "opportunity-generating state." The essence of this is the use of neo-interventionalism, which is not aimed at increasing welfare consumption. Instead it is directed at areas that may be the motors of economic development, but where market mechanisms in themselves would not be enough to make development possible.

Using concepts borrowed from public sector economics, it may be added that the state is mainly justified to undertake a role in the areas of market failures, compensating for the limits of self-regulation. However, the basis of reference for this acknowledged yet minimized influence is no longer correction in the name of social justice, but maintaining the long-term viability of the system.

This new approach may be interpreted in at least two definitive ways. Emphasizing the opportunity-generating character is a position that is near to moderate Left, which from the local government point of view is expressed by the need for new partnerships between the various social sectors and players. Differing only marginally from this in emphasis, neo-conservative sympathizers talk of "enabling/facilitating", in so far as the state ought to acti-vate defined social players from the outside.

The process of decentralizing the public sector is closely and very substantially related to the change in the concept of the state. In this process there is a strong political dependence in so far as it was neo-conservative criticism that forced the unavoidable reorganization. At the same time this also left an impact on the leftist political forces.

So the new phase of development, it seems, spans the traditionally opposing left and right wings interpretations of the functions of the state. This is interesting because a kind of normative logic – that is classifying phenomena according to political attitudes – seems to be indispensable to understanding and accurately analyzing the trends discovered in the operation of the state. The value of decentralizing the public sector and the related changes in the local and regional governments' roles does not change. It seems to be built into the practice of modern state and social development, irrespective of the political leanings of the government.

The "opportunity-generating" and "enabling" state has also appeared locally and regionally. Indeed, it is perhaps exactly there that it manifests itself to the greatest extent. Thus a focused discussion on the subject is justified.

What has the change in local government policy in recent decades consisted of? In the conservative period, especially in Anglo-Saxon countries, a restricted state role in the assumption of public duties came to be central. Likewise, the role of local authorities as a consequence of this was not increased beyond all bounds nor was their influence broadened. On the contrary, governments forced them out of traditional areas of local functions through restrictive pressure. The reduction in the social housing sector, the lessening of general obligations in school management and the widespread privatization of public utilities are all examples of this.

In spite of this, conservative policy was not against local government. It cannot even be accused of disregarding the idea of local government. On the contrary, the outlines of a clear philosophy were defined. They believed that the activity of local authorities should be extended to enable every conceivable actor in society to organize and participate in community tasks in function of their interest. Enabling included, among other things, the private sector playing a role in public services through marketization, contracting out and other techniques; the incentive for society to organize the provision of public duties for itself; giving grants for voluntary activities in proportion with functions provided and guaranteeing equal operational conditions.

The saving of public assets and the mobilization of other social resources to replace them was the prime motivation behind all grants. Marketization by definition increased consumer burdens, but at the same time reduced high taxes. Subsidies for voluntary activity was based on the active participation of affected or motivated groups – as opposed to welfare, budgetary-based solidarity.

This political line doubly affected local governments. On the one hand, the forced savings in public expenditure affected them greatly. Reductions and restraint were permanent threats. On the other hand, directly turning to social players for the provision of public tasks demanded the renewal of public administration techniques, and indeed of the whole administrative approach. To cite but one example: contracted management did not just mean less in terms of quantity than if the local authority itself had organized the public task through its own organization, but it also meant that an entirely different form of public administration had to be performed as part of the local government's tasks.

This interestingly allowed local government operation to extricate itself from the hopelessness of restriction. The conservative philosophy tried to make savings appear as "healthy incentives" to constraint which would indirectly lead to innovation. This in the final analysis would produce advantageous social returns. Reality justified this train of thought and the entailing policies in as much as budgetary constraints really have become the motor of public administration management reform.

From the mid-1990's, increasingly strong criticism was expressed against this prevalent view that had acquired an official rigidity. This was related to the change of government and to the rise and coming to power of the social democratic parties. The correction of local government policy can again be derived from the underlying tenets of the new trend. In their opinion, improving the results of the new public administration management system became a goal in itself. Evaluating and managing social impacts was forced into the background. For local governments it was very forcefully put forward that every decision concerning service organization not merely entailed costs and profits, but most of all winners and losers in the local community. This had direct consequences on the local authority's activity.

In contrast with "enabling" that is today considered as shifting responsibility one-sidedly, the concept was embodied in the new partnership. Co-operation with the players in society took on a vital importance. Embedding local governments in their environment and the most efficient exploitation of relations possible played the main role.

Despite the greater stress laid on solidarity, this logic does not propound the return to the caring welfare state local government. Interestingly, it builds on the results of the new management rather than rejecting them. This means that its supporters do not wish to implement corrections at any price in the social redistribution system affected by public services, but strive to progress in exploiting socially accessible resources for the provision of public tasks.

The principal lessons of Western development processes for Hungary are as follows. Firstly, the budgetary restrictions typically resulted in the narrowing of the local governments' scope for action everywhere, and this condition did not change even with the passing of the conservative era. Secondly, the restrictions by definition meant that the amount of local tasks was not reduced to the same extent as the tightening of resources. Naturally, local governments were not pleased with this. Appropriately, innovative local politicians and experts could find and have indeed found ways out, i.e.,, good strategies to deal with the crises. In this way unified programs were created that went far beyond simple technical financial solutions.

TRANSFORMATION OF LOCAL GOVERNMENTS DURING THE CHANGE OF THE POLITICAL SYSTEM

While the process described above occurred in many developed countries, in Eastern Central Europe the change of political system influenced the process of local governments' transformation. In a political sense, an important and well-known outcome of this was the building of the institutional system of local democracy. There is, however, another factor that significantly determines the tasks of regional public administration. The change of political system is concomitant with the reinterpretation of state roles. This is partly a political constraint and partly an economic necessity. The socialist state's share in public expenditure, similar in size to that of the welfare state, became impossible to maintain at the current level of development, in the midst of a fallback in production due to the transformation. However, the program of reducing the expenditure of the state budget, fundamentally affected the local government sector and within this had a direct effect on local fiscal resources.

The local authorities, having just become democracy's front-line fighters, were immediately confronted by the endeavors of the likewise democratic, newly elected governments to, out of necessity, limit their room for maneuver. The seeds of a new conflict were sown this way.

The local government debates of the 1980's in the West started again in miniature, when conservative governments wanted to force their local governments to save and make reductions by any means. The difference is that the level of detail and depth of neither the development level of welfare services nor the labor organization and management techniques encouraged by savings matched those observable in countries which example was being followed. There was no possibility for this, if for no other reason due to the shortness of time and the development phases overlapping each other somewhat. Taking this as a starting point, the process of the new Hungarian local government development occurred in the following phases.

In the first stage, as a result of multi-party elections, new bodies were formed which started operating the new structure pursuant to the new law. In Hungary the phase of institution building was fundamentally closed in 1991. The reform of financial regulation at the end of the 1980s was an important predecessor of success, establishing the basis for future organizational changes. Hungary in this respect was more fortunate than its fellow states in Eastern Central Europe, which did not succeed in reaching the critical mass of changes by the same time with a similar swift stroke.

By the 1990's local authorities in Hungary had gained broad responsibility and relatively great independence. Quite a broad circle of guarantees were built into the system. The process seemed very promising from the point of view of the development of the political system.

However, other important trends in the change of political system seemed to cross the local governments' development path at certain points. The most significant of these was the program of lessening the role of the state in the various provision systems. The transformation of education, social services and, to some extent, health care gave certain solutions and institutions providing various public services and operated by the private sector or churches a role that was increasingly equal to that of the local governments. In the area of public utility services the advance of privatization resulted in the rearrangement of areas of responsibility.

The local government, in this situation, appeared on the same side as the national government. The provision of public services by the non-state sector naturally largely removed traditional tasks and assets and resources allocated to them away from the local government.

Budgetary restrictions constituted the other attack against the autonomy model. Hungary, like the other countries undergoing a change of political system, could not avoid their effect. Local governments, as the consumers of significant parts of public expenditure, became a natural and constant target for those chastising state extravagance. Thus in the midst of fiscal restraint, it gradually became impossible to exercise the formally and legally guaranteed broad area of responsibility.

Contradictory expectations led to frustration, but at the same time the local governments started to formulate elements of adequate answers to the challenges. The preconditions and certain elements of the models for interactive reactions were already provided by social and political conditions existent in the second half of the 1990's. The "responsive" local government is differentiated from the traditional model by being not so much against, but rather reacting to the factors motivating the above changes.

There is all the more need for openness as the local government is not itself civil local government but merely one of its forms. The development of human services provision in particular shows the need to expand the forms of multi-channeled self-activity and self-regulation. The provision of public tasks in market conditions is related to this, which the local government has to react to or in certain cases initiate.

It is practical to maintain the openness of relations and to extend it to relations with other local governments. In spite of – or more precisely for – the independence of the settlements, local governments have to associate closely to implement joint public tasks. Contrary to initial suppositions, this did not prove to be natural. Creating horizontal relations can be deepened by the appropriate development of the institutional system.

Sub-elements of the new model already exist in practice. Numerous legal institutions have been built, and many local governments comprehensively or in certain sectors seem to follow the new route in public policy. The initial motivation is often budgetary compulsion, but in fact a number of independent initiatives have been realized, often making their way towards regulation at a later stage.

Structural reforms have to be subordinated to government policy encouraging local government social interaction. That is, it is not practical to try to develop suitable public service management capacities primarily by making structural changes and by establishing new spheres of authority, as newer and newer concepts of reorganization suggest. It is much more expedient to think in terms of a social policy program and instrument system. If organizational questions arise, the development of operational conditions has first to be dealt with.

On the basis of this logic, it is practical to raise the question of the role of regional coordination while leaving local governmental levels untouched. This would be done in conjunction with the further expansion of the associative institutional system based on legal regulations, instead of large-scale local government mergers.

Apart from the government policy, the local governments' own policy practice may also contain guiding models. Such are certain city management reforms, local economic development programs, local changes in financing human services, experiments in consumer orientation, attempts to organize functional districts and local budget reforms.

The examples quoted so far are mainly urban, simply due to the necessary size of the capacities needed for making meaningful decisions in service management. At the same time, there are interactive "traditions" in small settlements as well, such as the success of the organization of small regions even prior to the regional development law.

Thus there are real living examples of interactive policy, whose development goes back to the establishment of the new local governments. These cases may become more widely known for practicing experts if they are disseminated and practically analyzed. One possible way is through education and training, the background material for which has been prepared by some institutions over several years. Another possibility is a channel of local government association through which "good practices" can be recorded in a database and information network.

Newer results of local government development fit into the whole of the change of the political system, so that after the phase of institution building and the introductory period, the development of mechanisms befitting the social function will come to the fore. Practicing local level functions form a large sub-type of tasks provided by the state. As in all subsystems, the re-interpretation of roles and revising the scale of responsibility arise here.

In part, reorganization covering the whole of public finance continuously "provokes" the local government system. Municipal and county budgets are affected, and often very deeply, by all reductions and restructuring. It should be noted that they not only have to face profound reorganizations but also simple restrictions.

Besides, accession to the European Union has strongly influenced changes in operation. The introduction of institutions harmonizing with the EU legal system is also a continuous challenge. Thus the obligation to apply public procurement procedures and rules of competition in public service areas becomes and will be in the near future the inducer of fundamental institutional changes.

The values and techniques of the public services' new management seem to have become instilled in the foundations of public administration organization across Europe. Surpassing does not mean returning to a previous era. It is clear to everybody that the welfare state will not come to the fore again. The notion of the state's role, contrary to that concept, is clearly understood in a limited manner.

The application of management techniques in close harmony with certain objectives of social policy, rigorous control of expenditure and the majority of alternative (i.e.,, not within direct government organizations) service delivery methods has not been questioned.

Even critics acknowledge that the conservative period's new management in many respects led to unintentional results. Such is the penetration of consumer mentality and language into the organization and provision system of public services. The role of the public has become equally important, by putting activities – that were considered insignificant formerly – and their implementation methods into the focus. Bureaucracy was exposed to new impulses as a result of which its role and working methods had to be revalued. A connection was created between social policy decisions and the systems of management instruments targeting their implementation, including the most thorough technical solutions.

The creation of institutional conditions for the application of all these instruments can also be useful in the reorganization of the Central European system. It enables the continuation of local government processes and promotes moving forward from the formal legal level towards solutions for organizing a plural society and management.

Demolishing the former practice of state organization does not necessarily create another viable system. Changes in the provision of public services in the last decade clearly show what serious hiatuses the collapse of still operating old systems can leave in forms of provision, not to mention the strengthening of conflicts which may be witnessed both socially and regionally.

Budgetary restrictions are often interpreted by local politicians and their advisers as the actions of an arrogant central power. In general it may be stated that there is always some element of truth in this. Governments are, to a lesser or greater degree, against local power. A noteworthy difference may only be in the extent and, naturally, in the efficiency of the local governments' resistance, which can change dependent on the times and individual regional conditions. In this subsection we intended to draw attention to the outcome of the existing optimal scenarios, that is to the fact that through appropriate governmental and local governmental policies innovative ways out may be found notwithstanding budgetary restrictions.

We take counter-effective tendencies into account next. As far as our topic is concerned, the possible and existing "correct model" carries the message that the contents of regulatory reforms should not be interpreted by themselves but in conjunction with the social policy aims to be followed. If this does not happen, local governmental strategy easily goes into the defensive.

COUNTER EFFECTS

The picture, however, is not so rosy. In fact, the processes which are clearly and continuously heading towards a defined positive objective in Central Eastern European countries are not linear. There are numerous circumstances that hinder, distract or even stop development. As regards the development of the local governmental system, four phenomena deserve highlighting:

a. stagnation in reorganization,
b. demolishing new institutions in a counter-reactive manner,
c. re-centralization,
d. the new spoils system.

a) In most transition countries the process of local government reform consists of "stop and go" stages. The institutionalization of new solutions demands a defined social interest and naturally political approval. Important structural decisions and the usually necessary amendment of the constitution cannot be made if any condition is missing. Because of the opposing interests of the political parties there was a reflux in the local reorganization in Poland in the mid-1990's.[3] In other countries there was trench warfare for a long time over the development of local basic units. Merging them became the source of various conflicting positions (Slovenia, Lithuania). In yet other countries there were long debates about local governmental levels (Slovakia, the Czech Republic). The question posed here was how restrictive the county or regional level should be as regards the newly developed, independent settlements. Similar trench warfare developed in the public administration of several capital cities (Budapest, Warsaw, Prague) as the possibility of a metropolis-level administration seemed to run counter the newly created autonomies of the districts.

It was not so much the debates themselves as their frequent autotelism and restraint up to a point of conflict of interest that threw the entire reorganization of regional public administration back somewhat. Plans that may have been more pressing were the victims of this further development. At the same time, testing and occasional rejecting alternative solutions is always an integral part of the seeking of new ways and means. Great concepts that are an end to themselves and serve as an alibi for simple (but eventful) reorganizations, entail just as many negative consequences as the risks of seeking new ways and means do.

b) There is no absolute guarantee to protect once accepted institutional or regulatory solutions. In Hungary, the Local Government Act requires a two-thirds majority, providing the basic structure with some protection. Here too, however, the inability to apply the principles and techniques of the financial regulation system in the long term is problematic. With regards to the legislative practice, that the budget acts contain fiscal regulatory details, changes are frequent and this has an effect on the methods of fundamental budgetary finance as well.

- The gradual melting away of the locally retained part of the personal income tax from 1991 onwards was particularly spectacular.

- Moreover, starting from the second free election cycle (1994–98) concepts were completely mixed up. A part, and later the overwhelming majority, of the personal income tax retained locally mixed up with the otherwise correct principle of taxing capacity, was ordered to be divided on a normative basis.

- The third cycle's (1998–2002) novelty with negative consequences was the allocation of addressed subsidies based on merit.

- In the struggle to win targeted subsidies corruption undoubtedly bloomed.

- The involvement of the regional development councils in the operation of the equalizing system (1998–) by bringing bodies of pro-government delegates into a decision-making position is also related.

---

[3] Regulska, 1996

For individual large investments not belonging to the area of local government finance, individual government decisions came to the fore at the end of the 1990's as regards both the allocation of grants and the system by which these grants were distributed. As a consequence of all these phenomena and processes, the municipality of Budapest clearly came into a losing position in the last cycle.

c) Recentralization is the counterbalance of every decentralizing reform. As the large reorganizations around 1990 were in some places fairly radical, rejecting the previous system, later the new authorities attempted to reinforce their own role, at least in part. Some authors believe[4] that, for example, in the Czech Republic, Poland and Hungary restrictive endeavors to continue decentralization of the central authority stood in the background of the much delayed regional reorganization. The development of the financial regulation systems, which in most countries did not follow the reorganization of structures, is even more typical of this. In this circle Hungary is an exception as regards the beginning of the process. However, in the course of operating the regulatory system, the restraining economic policies of the governments had a restricting effect also in Hungary.

Again it should be added that the tug-of-war between the national governments and the local authorities is typical for any decent public administration arrangement. It would be an illusion to believe that the interest-sensitive parties concerned would sportingly choose not to contest during a local government reform. Of course, the strength of intervention and the extent to which the independence of institutions is undermined do matter. The threat of damage is greater if newly germinating, not yet duly established mechanisms are exposed to powerful strains.

d) The heaviest burden on development is, however, the spoils system, which unequivocally promotes favoritism and corruption on the different levels of public administration. Connecting the circles of these two phenomena should not be so natural. The spoils system is imaginable within defined limits that would not particularly overburden the criminal investigation and the justice system. In any case with the passing of the first feverish period of the change of political system, signs of illegitimate penetration of private interests became decidedly stronger.

The institutional system reacted little, and then only with great delay to these problems. The reform had no way of really dealing with these problems, obviously because at the other end of the processes central decision-makers had (or could have had without any great difficulty) interest ties on many levels, leaving the status quo untouched. This inability directed by the system clearly had a counter effect on the reform processes.

Guarantees for the Hungarian local government system have not developed at the appropriate pace. Among others, suitable guarantees for decision making as a body are wanted. Only after much protraction and numerous unsuccessful attempts were conflict of interest rules for mayors and then councilors accepted in several phases. The institution of exclusion from decision making on the basis of personal interest however, is only built into the system in

---

[4] Illner, 1999

a very lax manner and is uncontrolled. Naturally, this affects the operation of bodies in the capital, including the districts. To which it may be added that as the distance from the electors is greater in the capital, the transparency of decision making is also more confused.

Thus these circumstances accompany and counteract the trend of local government development towards community interaction analyzed in the previous section. For each country and in each cycle the trends that seem stronger in a region's local government development processes may be judged differently. At the same time, the outlined double-edged contents are generally present in the Central-Eastern European region. This condition system for policy making greatly affects the actual successes in the establishment of a local government, as well as explains its potential failures.

Hungary's position is typical of the development and forming of local government policy in our region. Results here formed an effective, single process relatively early. At the same time, sources of danger and failures may accurately be defined. As regards the process itself, development prior to the turning point of 1990 was fortunate. After 1986 the contemporary soviet type council administration's management regulation system had to be reorganized. For this reason the new civil local government structure created after the democratic elections could at the same time be financed in a new manner. In most former socialist countries this could only be achieved in a system-like manner a long time after the political reorganization.

In the analysis prior to the preparation of the reform there are several similarities. Both contemporary Czechoslovakia and Poland attempted to apply "clear" solutions. Thus almost the same radicalism was applied in strengthening the local governments of settlements, the structural and administrative division of local government and state administration roles on the middle level, and emphasizing the role of local government lobbying. In the first zeal of reorganization, the "base local government" mentality was applied both in the capital and large cities quite similarly. These similarities in approach, however, did not mean that models were all uniform. For this reason it was natural that by the second half of the 1990's development paths differed more significantly.

As regards regulatory reform in the capital city, the message of the reorganization of the Hungarian local government system was that it would be right to continue the reorganization started in 1990, building on the results achieved then and those of the amendments of 1994. The capital city should be particularly interested in continuing the reforms as the system has found it hard to handle its special features until now. However, the inability to develop further, in addition to other local governmental aspects, also hinders the inclusion of the city's special features in the reform. Simultaneously, it hinders all "individual" endeavors. The regulatory reform in the capital, for instance, is obviously only able to react with difficulty to the needs of the population that are outside the capital city's administrative boundaries yet belong to its sphere of responsibility.

ECONOMIC AND URBANIZATION CONDITIONS

The economic, legal and fiscol environment fundamentally determined the Municipality of Budapest's operational options and development policy. The market economy conditions that came to the full during the 1990's created new possibilities for all Hungarian local governments. The change naturally ensured more favorable possibilities for settlements and regions that had had good economic and infrastructure features and human capital even prior to the reorganization. The capital and its environs belonged to these regions.

Budapest was not just an idle participant. Due to its weight in the country, it was also the shaper of this external condition system. As will be shown, it has a determining role in the entire country's economy. In developing the statutory conditions of local government, special attention was always given to the effects of the changes in the capital, which in a number of cases resulted in applying individual rules. Budgetary policy and regulatory techniques also contained a number of elements that adapted to the features of the capital. The political relation between the Municipality of Budapest and the central government determined in general how favorable these changes occurring in the system of external conditions were for Budapest.

As far as national local government policy is concerned, the two-tier local-government system made the application of specific conditions necessary in addition to the features arising from the size of the metropolis. The general local-government jurisdiction only defined the basic elements of the system in the capital city and a separate "Act on the Capital City" was passed for the development of special rules. This, following the basic concept of the two-tier local-government system, created a local government for the Municipality of Budapest ("regional") and for the settlement units ("District").

Naturally, for a metropolis, nationally applied general, electoral, task-sharing and financing methods could not be mechanically transferred but, nevertheless, the division of the two separate local government levels remained. In analyzing the general conditions of the Budapest model, it has to be borne in mind that the political trends and relations of the capital and districts determined the capital's judgment and the consequent regulatory and jurisdictional decision making.

In spite of this, the reorganization of the last ten years' economic and legal environment as regards the capital city is not restricted to four-year cycles. In fact, the turning points of the economic reorganization occurred at the beginning or in the middle of government terms (1992: deepest crisis, 1995/1996: „Bokros package", 1998/1999: normalization of inflation, stable growth). Besides, over the course of the decade the effect of the long-term urbanization cycle could be felt on the city's development. The paragraphs below will underline a few important elements of this external environment.

As the last ten years' economic events greatly influenced the reforms and managerial and service organizing innovations of the Municipality of Budapest, changes in this economic environment will be shown first. In addition to the short-term economic cycles, changes in the urbanization patterns were also fundamental in defining the development of the city. In analyzing the Municipality's results and operation, it is worth considering aspects of long-term urban development.

PHASES OF ECONOMIC POLICY

Budapest's weight within the country from an economic viewpoint is perhaps best characterized by the fact that its share of the new value produced in the country (34-35%) well exceeds the proportion of its population compared to the country as a whole.[5] Despite the uncertainties in calculating regional GDP, Budapest' one-third share of the economy well demonstrates the city's position within the country. Changes in economic policy thus also have a fundamental impact on the capital. The phases of short-term economic development in the 1990's come out clearly if one highlights three of the general features that describe the economy *(Table 1)*.

Table 1
THREE ECONOMIC INDICATORS

YEAR	RETAIL PRICE INDEX	UNEMPLOYMENT RATE OF THE ECONOMICALLY ACTIVE POPULATION (AGE 15–74 YEARS, %)	GDP IN % OF PREVIOUS YEAR
1990	128.9%	n. a.	
1991	135.0%	n. a.	88.1
1992	123.0%	13.9%	97.0
1993	122.5%	13.8%	99.2
1994	118.8%	11.7%	102.9
1995	128.2%	12.1%	101.5
1996	123.6%	11.8%	101.3
1997	118.3%	11.6%	104.6
1998	114.3%	10.1%	104.9
1999	110.0%	9.9%	104.4

Source: Magyar Statisztikai Évkönyv, 1990-1999, KSH (Hungarian Statistical Yearbook, 1990-1999) Central Office of Statistics

STRUCTURAL ADJUSTMENT

The first period began in the 1980's with economic structural adjustment and the development of market economy. The forced restructuring of foreign trade was one of the prime external driving factors. Exports had to be redirected from Eastern European markets to the developed countries. This switch of markets brought economic structural problems up to the surface. These problems thus appeared simultaneously in an explosive manner.

The first years of the decade saw a significant fall in production, causing a sudden jump in unemployment. Unemployment that had earlier been hidden suddenly became visible and in 1991 the unemployment rate of the economically active population rose to over 10%.

---

[5] Central Office of Statistics, 1999

In conjunction with this, inflation rose to a high level: the retail price index of the Central Statistical Office recorded an annual figure of 35%. The growing internal and external national debt lay behind this, having a decisive influence on the potential budgetary policy options.

The preparation for a turn in economic policy – which was labeled according to different catch phrases at the time – began in the second half of the eighties. Liberalizing imports, reducing state subsidy for economic organizations and permitting flexible operational forms for state property prepared ground for later privatization and the transition to a market-based economy.

Following the political changeover, the period between 1990-1992 witnessed accelerated legal and institutional change. The private economy created through diverse forms of privatization already accounted for half of the GDP in 1992. Following the tax reforms of 1988, the modification of the accounting system, restricting and decentralizing of the rights of price setting authorities and reducing consumer price subsidies helped to create the conditions for a modern market economy. The application of bankruptcy law was one of the necessary steps in the change. During those years bankruptcy proceedings affected approximately 10% of economic organizations (and production value). At the same time it became necessary to consolidate the banking system.

ECONOMIC DOWNTURN

As the market economy was gradually developing, experiments in economic policy adapting to the new environment were characteristic of the years between 1993 and 1995/1996. In Parallel with the aims of economic structural adjustment, economic stabilization became an equally important goal following the political changes. The need for this was especially great when the equilibrium deteriorated to a significant extent due to the incorrect assessment of certain favorable phenomena in the economy (e.g., growth in exports·in 1994, investment growth, foreign capital inflow). The German recession, with its determining influence on the European economy, strengthened this need.

The balance of payments deficit, the gross national debt accounting for 86% of GDP and the depletion of the necessary development resources for the economy gradually forced a new turn. The aim of this new turn was to guarantee the necessary revenues for business developments, complete started privatization and initiate a growth of equilibrium. Under these circumstances, following the structural transformation of the economy, there was already an opportunity for exploiting the advantages of market conditions.

For this obviously, it was necessary to implement swiftly and radically the series of measures announced in March 1995. The lowering of the rate of corporate income tax, the introduction of a crawling peg policy, together with the application of surtax on customs duties, as well as the forceful restrictions of budgetary policy based on a new concept all served the purpose of the later growth of a balanced economy. A new wave of bank consolidation in 1996 led to the final completion of privatization. In 1997, 70% of GDP was already produced by the private sector, one fifth of which came from enterprises with foreign majority ownership.

After the supplementary budget corrections regularly used in the period following 1992-1995, the reform of the fundamental elements of public finance commenced. The most important elements in this were as following: restructuring the relations between the social security system and the budget, introducing the three pillars of pension schemes, applying tuition fees in higher education, setting a limit to local government borrowing, and rapidly creating the treasury. The relation between the budget and the National Bank of Hungary was clarified once and for all in 1997 when the possibility for direct central bank finance disappeared and fiscal tasks were removed from the National Bank's tasks.

Chart 1
DEBT SERVICE AND DEFICIT AS A PERCENTAGE
OF THE STATEBUDGET 1991–2000

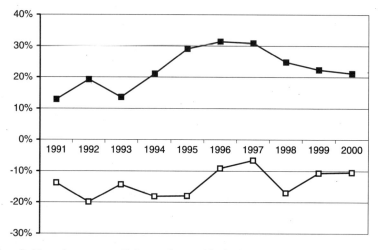

—■— Debt service   —□— Balance of current budget

Due to the jump in debt service payments, the budget deficit grew further, demanding budgetary restraint to be continued *(Chart 1)*. Newer tasks were extricated from public finance and as a consequence of other budgetary changes the current revenues and expenditure of general government budget decreased to a degree appropriate for developed countries (40-42% of GDP).

START OF GROWTH IN EQUILIBRIUM

All these changes created the conditions for the third large phase of economic policy. The aims of economic growth, maintaining equilibrium and modernization were typical of the period after 1997/1998. From this period up to the present, economic growth has stood at around 4% while the annual rate of inflation has slowed to 10-11%. Unemployment has also continued to fall and the national average has settled at 10%, thus falling below the average for European countries.

Achieving economic growth and stability allowed earlier economic policy goals to be revised. Moderating social differences in regional and infrastructure dimensions and incomes has become increasingly important. The methods by which these current processes can truly adapt to the market economy are developing now. Their results are mainly felt by the middle class, although the techniques for eradicating social backwardness can only be devised and efficiently operated in the long term. The degree and form of centralization and decentralization – irrespective of political direction – will be one of the key issues in achieving equilibrium.

PHASES OF FISCAL POLICY

Changes in the budgetary policy and the public sector more or less coincided with the above outlined three main phases of economic policy. These conditions directly determined the circumstances of operation for the local governments and the Municipality of Budapest.

INSTITUTION BUILDING

The first wave of legal and institutional changes lasted until about 1993. The base elements of the new local government and public finance system developed in the first two years of the period. As part of the local government jurisdiction process, a new division of tasks and spheres of authority, regulating the order of the transfer of property and the practice of capital transfers based on more or less normative rules developed. The institutional system of state and legal control was established.

By establishing the rules of the civil service and public employee system, not only the stabilization of the public service career structure began but an important regulatory and planning instrument was also created from the point-of-view of public finance. The application of the new rules of accounting, organizing the regional fiscal information system and the introduction of procedural rules and the budgetary planning schedule stipulated in the Public Finance Act were important for the practice of public finance.

In this period, the other main area of changes included devising the new sectoral order for local public services. The running of services based on the former system of revenue centralization, unified system of service provision and the practice of widespread subsidies had to be transformed for the multi-sectored economy. The privatization of social housing was very significant in comparison to other Eastern European countries. Concomitantly with this, the consumer price subsidies of public utility services practically disappeared.

The significant decentralization process made devising new rules for public education, training and social services necessary. All of these endeavored to give as much independence as possible in decision making to local governments with responsibility for providing and organizing services, while at the same time maintaining the content and financial conditions of unified and equal public services. In accordance with the sectors' features, this could be achieved by regulating the services' contents (e.g., curriculum, forms of social grants), by setting output conditions (e.g., exam), or ensuring a choice in the forms of organization (e.g., types of school, forms of contract). These legal frameworks gave Hungarian local governments, that already benefited from a broad responsibility, a great degree of independence in the Eastern European context.

BUDGETARY RESTRAINT

Following the structural changes, there was a need for developing local autonomy in the second large economic period. This time restriction was the primary objective of fiscal policy. Restriction was directed at restraining central budget and local government expenditures. In this period, with restricted resources, the level of services could only be guaranteed through making service and organizational methods more efficient. The best results in this were achieved in the areas of public utilities and communal services. Placing operating forms of organizations on a market basis afforded the opportunity to draw in external financial and professional investors. To this end it was necessary to regulate public procurement procedures and to introduce obligatory competitive bidding for certain services.

There were also vital changes in the public finance sector. Operating regulations for budgetary planning and state-financed institutions became increasingly directed towards separating revenue-oriented business and traditional community activities. Gradually, the independence of funds allocated within the state budget disappeared as they were transformed to targeted appropriations that can be more easily controlled and handled. The creation of the Hungarian State Treasury served a similar purpose which reduced the central budget's floating capital requirements and made the use of central budget appropriations more controlled. On the other hand, thanks to net financing, this removed potential revenues from local governments.

The budgetary regulation also wished to restrain the expenditure of local governments by prescribing a limit on borrowing, which defined the rate of loan repayment and undertaking guarantees in proportion to local revenues. Simultaneously, a new order for the debt management procedure for local governments was introduced, almost entirely excluding direct financial aid for local governments struggling with payment problems. All these rules created the general conditions for adapting to decentralization and autonomy.

Apart from the above, however, inflation was the most important instrument of budgetary restraint. The subsidization of real costs in the budget did not grow in practice and various techniques were introduced regarding the restraint of the real value of expenditure on wages. A dual public employee salary system was introduced, which required continuous and detailed negotiations. Faced with a lack of central subsidies, local governments were forced to borrow with a state guarantee in order to raise local wages and salaries.

During the three governments of the period examined a repeated argument was made on the different public sector salary agreements related to the inflation increasing effect of salary outflow and, as a consequence, the loss of value of the increment. At the same time, however, inflation remained the most important instrument for reorganizing the public sector. With a smaller degree of inflation the reduction of public sector wages could not have been achieved nor could the structure of public expenditures have been reorganized.[6] Consequently, the expected inflation and planned subsidies, the increase in own revenues, are still the most important issues regarding the allocation of general government funds.

---

[6] László, Cs., 1988

One of the main objectives of the restrictive measures was the reduction of the number of employees in the public sector. Between 1992 and 1997 the number of employees at state-financed institutions decreased by 8% (to 814,000). Lay-offs and the transfer of tasks were even more significant for central public organs (a reduction of 13%) although the number of employees here was less (280,000 people) than with the local governments. The reduction of staff at local government level was only 5% in this period[7].

ENDEAVORS TO CENTRALIZE

Following the strict restraint, a particular turn took place in the budgetary regulations applying to local governments in the third period lasting up to the present day. Earlier, in the period of budgetary restraints, decentralization had been a generally accepted aim. Through decentralization, several opportunities opened to devise more efficient solutions for service organization, while forced decisions with an unfavorable social impact were made at the local level. At the time when resources were slowly expanding, however, newer and newer anti-decentralization arguments arose.

Some of these related to efficiency aspects: the very fragmented local government system of settlements and the small service units would become more economical financially if they were larger. The regulation of local government associations (1997) and the seeking of operational forms of local governments for regions and small areas attempted to tackle this. For the time being, promoting cooperation remained voluntary and new regional organizations were only created to provide limited regional development or official, public administration tasks. The financial dependency between different types of local governments was reintroduced into the local government system, when the county local government became able to decide on targeted decentralized grants.

Another group of anti-decentralization arguments referred to the differentiation and increase of regional differences. A growing number of grants were allocated with the intention of creating a regional (horizontal) equalization among munnicipalities with less than average personal income tax revenue. The group of own revenues calculated in the equalization system was expanded with local business tax. At the same time, the vertical equalization method that applied to local governments with different tasks also changed. The distribution rate of personal income tax returned to the locality decreased to a minimal level of 5%. Parallel with this, the amount of state grants grew. This in any event proves the strengthening of dependence vis-á-vis the central budget.

Finally, the protection of sector positions strengthened as opposed to the local governments' independence in using funds. This started with the removal of public education from the general grant system when, alone among local government duties, the amount of the state grant was tied to the amount of the previous actual expenditure on education (80%, then 90%). Here the number of special indications of grant allocation grew and the amount of

---

[7] Ibid, p. 146

grants to be allocated according to the supplementary rules was expanded. These, however, are not included in the grants for non-state and non-local governmental institutions, and thus the previously equal non-profit institutions ("voluntary social organizations") gradually began to be forced into the background.

All these fiscal policy phases are well demonstrated in the development of the finances of the Municipality of Budapest and the districts. (The financial affairs of local governments and within this, Budapest's position, will be analyzed in the last section of this chapter.) In this section, we have had an opportunity to provide an outlined presentation of the phases and certain elements of the economy and fiscal policy in the 1990's.

The economic and budgetary processes described here briefly created changeable general conditions for the implementation of the city leaders' financing and service organization reforms. In the first two-three year phase of building the local government system, general decentralization rules were adapted to the particular conditions salient in the capital. In the strict restriction phase that followed, the Municipality introduced modern reforms based on its favorable property and own revenue position that were exemplary even for other urban local governments. At the time, the political and professional environment was still favorable for the city leadership.

However, the realization of the results of reform in the capital was most needed when economic growth started after 1998-1999. This period coincided with the strengthening of centralization affecting the local government system. This politically motivated process was decidedly hostile to the Municipality. Referring to aims of regional equalization, the unified, equal nature of the grant system decreased, and distribution mechanisms, increasing central dependency grew.

PROCESSES OF URBANIZATION

To objectively assess the changes of the last decade, these phases need to be fitted into the process of long-term urban development. However fast and fundamental the changes were, as regards Budapest's future, the issue must be addressed as to what extent these changes supported or hindered the urbanization trend measured over several decades.

Obviously, only a city development policy that recognizes these trends and supports them through their own means instead of being contrary to the development processes can be successful in the long term. Naturally, this question cannot be answered in every detail in this short analysis. Nevertheless, it provides us with an opportunity to outline a framework of interpretation regarding the changes in the 1990's based on the demographic, economic and service characteristics which describe the urbanization of Budapest and its environs.

On the basis of general experiences of the development of big cities, occurring both in Europe and North America, the growth of Budapest can be broken down into various urbanization

---

[8] Hörcher, 1981; Enyedi, 1984; Horváth–Péteri–Tosics, 1993

phases[8]. According to these the first period of concentration is typified by an accelerating rate of growth in population and production factors. This development, based mainly on industry, leads to the rapid and spectacular building up of the central area of the city. The growth is above all stimulated by the involvement of external resources and the exploitation of the advantages of its central position. This phase of development is observable in every large European city, although it occurred in different economic and historical periods. In Budapest this phase lasted from the middle of the 19th century to the 1920's.

The accelerating rate of growth is naturally only sustainable for a limited period of time. The "trap" of urbanization is that the favorable conditions, or difficulties, that appear in the city center can only be solved by further centralization. (See the problem of bridges in Budapest). Development directed at the center and its accompanying concentration means that city development policy must necessarily be restructured. The expansion of the service economy and the transportation infrastructure enables the start of the suburbanization stage.

This period is characterized by the slowing of the central city's growth and the building in of the hubs of suburban growth. As a consequence of the outflow coming from the city and its expansion, the center's residential function is transformed as the local sources of development change are transferred to the outskirts and suburbs. This in Europe and especially in Budapest does not lead to a typical American-type suburbia phenomenon, although the processes that lead to this development are similar. Following the unification of the public administration in 1950, this trend first occurred in Budapest within the public administration borders, in the outer districts. From the 1970's onwards it was observable within the narrow conurbation belt.

The end of the suburban period is marked by the start of a re-urbanization period as a consequence of the self-regulatory ability of organic urban development. The main feature of this phenomenon observable in the world's large cities is that the central part of the city area gains new functions and its population decline slows down. This process, currently taking place, is encouraged by the new settlement factors of the economy. In spite of the fact that the knowledge-based sectors of the economy do not require spatial centralization, the traditional city center's value increases. The advantage of the center is that it provides entertainment and supply functions, with environmental aspects coming to the fore, it is possible to expand better quality residential areas through reconstructing neglected city areas.[9] This re-urbanization process can only be perceived in its initial stage in Budapest. As it stands today, the central population is declining.

---

[9] Freire-Stren, 2001; Lloyd-Clark, 2000

Chart 2
NUMBER OF INHABITANTS OF BUDAPEST, 1869-1999 (head)

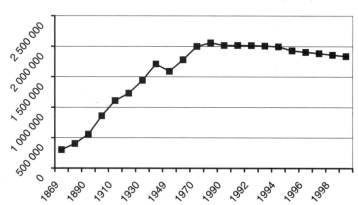

The long-term urbanization process is well demonstrated in *Chart 2* that presents the changes in the size of the city's population. Figures translated into the capital's present size show a period of fast growth and concentration, and then how the decelerating increase in the size of population turned into decline. Within this long-term process another, shorter cycle of a similar type took place after the Second World War. Following the creation of the Greater Budapest area, the population grew until the 1970's , then fell in the 1990's.

Typical of the suburban development phase, the size of population in settlements around the capital has continuously increased. Although the boundaries of the narrower conurbation belt were redefined a number of times, and thus the trend in the size of the population is not comparable, an increase in the size of the population can be observed in the whole of Pest county *(Table 2)*.

Table 2
TRENDS IN POPULATION RATES IN THE CONURBATION AND PEST COUNTY

YEAR	BUDAPEST	CONURBATION BELT	METROPOLITAN AREA (TOTAL)	PEST COUNTY
	PERCENTAGE OF NATIONAL POPULATION			
1980	19.2%	3.8%	23.1%	9.1%
1990	19.4%	6.0%	25.4%	9.2%
1996	18.7%	6.4%	25.1%	9.6%
1999	18.0%	6.4%	24.4%	10.3%

Conurbation: 1980: 44 settlements, 1991: 92 settlements/municipalities, 1999: 79 settlements/municipalities
Source: Területi Statisztikai Évkönyv (Regional Statistical Yearbook), 1980, 1990, 1999

The change in the size of the population is due to two factors. The balance of immigration was negative in Budapest after 1990, while in Pest county there was a sudden rise in migration into the county. In both areas there was a natural decline process (a higher number of deaths than births). As a result of the two factors the population of Budapest fell significantly while that of Pest county grew *(Table 3)*.

Table 3
DEMOGRAPHIC CHANGES IN BUDAPEST AND PEST COUNTY, 1985–1999

ITEMS/YEAR	BUDAPEST	PEST COUNTY
Balance of immigration difference		
1985	14837	1306
1990	11751	2842
1995	-11204	13726
1999	-14409	17888
Natural increase		
1985	-10553	-1198
1990	-10242	-1534
1995	-11832	-1940
1999	-12650	-3417
Population change		
1985	4284	108
1990	1509	1308
1995	-23036	11786
1999	-27059	14471

Source: Területi Statisztikai Évkönyv (Regional Statistical Yearbook), 1985, 1990, 1999

Demographic changes affect local government services through changes in the age composition of the population. The rate of dependency for the elderly population of Budapest is much higher (24.1% in 1999) than the national average (21.4%), or than the average for Pest county (18.1%). At the same time, by including the young population in calculating the full dependent population, the situation is more favorable here than in the country as a whole (Budapest: 44.4%, Pest county: 44.3%, while the national average is 46.4%).

The economy's tendency to be centered on the capital city is far stronger than the concentration of population in the capital. At the start of the decade almost half of all newly founded companies were located in Budapest. In 1991, 52% of joint-stock companies (Rt.-s) and 46% of limited liability companies (Kft.-s) were registered in Budapest, while in Pest county these proportions followed the population rates (Kft.-s: 9%, Rt.-s: 5%). Over the decade the concentration of the country's businesses in the capital city increased slightly from 27% to 30%, while their proportion within the country fell. As it did with the change in the number of inhabitants, Pest county here too demonstrates characteristics typical of the suburban development phase: the proportion of larger companies within the country grew (in 1999 Kft.-s: 10%, Rt.-s: 7%).

A similar trend is observable in the regional location of foreign companies – that are important for economic transformation. In 1991, 56% of foreign companies were based in Budapest (Pest County: 7%). This proportion decreased somewhat by the end of the decade (1999: 52%). At the same time, the regional breakdown of these companies' registered capital shows an unchanged weight in favor of the capital (56%). Larger companies moved into Pest county: in 1991 their share within the country was 6% and in 1999 it was 9%.

Despite these favorable features, the new value produced in the economy is concentrated in Budapest at only 34% (Pest county: 7%). Since 1994, when the calculation of regional GDP began, the capital's weight has fallen (although to an extent only measurable in tenths of a percent) and that of Pest County has slightly increased. Per capita GDP in the region has developed in parallel with this *(Chart 3)*. In Budapest, per-capita GDP is 186% of the national average while in Pest county it is 77%.

Chart 3
PER-CAPITA GDP

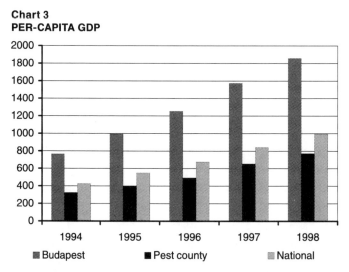

As a result of its advantageous economic features, the concentration of employees in the capital is also significant. There are no comparable figures for the whole of the decade, but the rate of employees in Budapest out of all employees throughout the country was 27% in 1991 and 35% in 1999. The proportion for Pest County did not change (6%). Unemployment is much lower in the capital; in 1997, the worst year for unemployment, only 18% of the nationally registered unemployed were in Budapest. Today this rate has dropped to 15%. The fall from 33% to 23% of those employed in industry and the building trade, together with the fact that 85% of people working in the country's financial sector are in Budapest, shows a change in the employment structure.

However there is no really striking difference in the earnings trend *(Chart 4)*. The differentiation began at the end of the 1980's. Compared to national average earnings, average earnings in Budapest were 29% higher at the start of the decade and 33% higher in 1999. In Pest County, except for a period at the beginning of the 1990's, average earnings followed the national average.

Chart 4
TRENDS OF EARNINGS, 1985–1999

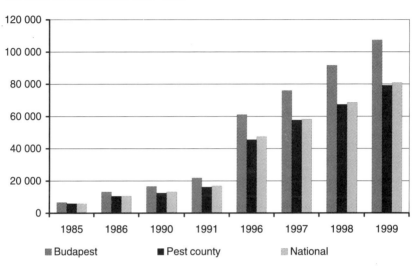

As a result of the concentration of the country's economy around the capital, the level of services in Budapest and its population's income position have exceeded the national average for decades. Via the establishment of the local government system, the goal of budgetary and regional development policy was to reduce the difference between Budapest and the provinces. The difference has lessened by today as a result of the rapid development of the countryside.

Without a detailed analysis of the degree of supply, two indicators demonstrate this equalization. As a consequence of the rapid development of networks, the supply of telephones in Budapest and Pest County increasingly approaches the national average. In 1999, there were 359 lines per 1,000 people (145% the national average) while in Pest county telephone lines stood at 96% of the national average. In 1990, the figures were 237% and 35% (96 lines), respectively. The supply of cars similarly reflects average incomes. Accordingly, in Budapest the supply is 32% higher than the national average (225 cars/ 1,000 people), while in Pest County it is 6% higher. The relation of the tendencies has changed since the mid-1990's as – despite the decline in the Budapest population – the per-unit supply is lower. In the country as a whole, and in Pest County, the percentage indicator has grown steadily.

The trend of incomes and consumption also indicates that the capital's earlier significant advantage is changing and new types of problems have arisen. As regards net annual income per capita in households, the figure for Budapest is only 18% higher than the national average *(Table 4)*. This is due to the income equalizing effect of taxation and contribution payments, as labor income is much higher than the national average (131%). Grants and social allowances that appear as social income are 10% higher than average.

Table 4
CONSUMPTION AND INCOMES, 1999

ITEM	BUDAPEST	WEST TRANSDANUBIA
Annual income per capita in households	IN PERCENT OF THE COUNTRY	
Labor income	131.2%	111.0%
Social income	109.5%	87.2%
Net income	118.6%	100.5%
Average expenditure per capita		
Total personal expenditure	116.8%	97.3%
Food	102.2%	100.6%
Service expenditures	153.3%	94.4%
Housing current expenditures	130.0%	95.7%

Despite the higher incomes, consumption also exceeds the national average. As Budapest is a large city, costs per capita for home maintenance (130%) and services (153%) are much higher than the national average, or Western Hungarian region, likewise considered rich. The cost of food for daily needs approaches the average (102%). These figures for consumption indicate that, projected onto the whole population of Budapest, its inhabitants' income is not outstanding. Indeed, the price of public utilities, transport and other services important from the viewpoint of the local government's operation is higher, fundamentally influences the structure of consumption.

All these outlined features of urbanization also affect the Municipality's service organizing and administrative endeavors. Above all, as a consequence of the decline of demographic and service performance indicators, there was a perceivable need to react swiftly to numerous problems in Budapest. The social service and health systems – in spite of the good average values for Budapest – had to struggle with poverty and tasks related to population aging.

The figures show well that, due to the economy's concentration in the capital, the city's economic position is favorable and employment indicators are good. However, we can also see that Budapest's advantage in average earnings did not change in the period under examination. Higher earnings are accompanied by the consumption structure's effect of increasing expenditure per capita, stemming from the nature of the metropolis.

Based on the urbanization pattern, we can see that administrative and planning solutions were only connected with the long-term city development trend to a limited extent. Mechanisms for regional cooperation, joint tasks and load sharing did not develop in the suburbanization period. The privatization of public services would demand unified regional local government intervention, yet only the first steps towards this can be seen.

Balanced and controlled development within its administrative boundaries was the Municipality's principal aim. Its results, which have promoted the development of the re-urbanization phase observable in Budapest today, can clearly be seen. In the meantime, however, no partnership has developed within the Metropolitan Area. This did not only depend on the Municipality and service organizing techniques, but on the lack of national sectoral policies (e.g., the unification of public transport). Party political considerations (e.g., in regional development issues) were also an obstacle. In the future, the Municipality must develop new relations with the outlying metropolitan region belt. The development of the central city, with its falling population, can only happen within the greater city via and thanks to the cooperation of partners from the conurbation belt.

REGULATORY CHANGES IN BUDAPEST'S LOCAL GOVERNMENT SYSTEM

Public administration matters in Budapest may be categorized into two sets of relations. One of them is the current internal local authority system of the city. Here the key issue is the number of administrative layers and their relation to each other as well as the boundaries of the districts and their division into parts. The other is the relation to the city's conurbation belt. In this approach not only are the various horizontal contacts interesting, but so are the institutional communication frameworks and solutions with historically changing regional and governmental levels.

LEGAL REGULATION

REPRESENTATION

The new local government system was established as part of the change of the political system in 1990. With regard to Budapest's distinctive position, as one fifth of the country's population lives in the city, the special features of the new structure relating to the capital were dealt with separately. Through Act XXIV of 1991, the capital again became the subject of self-regulation. The districts received fairly broad local government licenses. According to the Act, the district exercised essentially the same rights as any other individual settlement. Only for specifically named tasks did the Municipality of Budapest receive priority. This solution is mechanically based on the national system, which decentralized the majority of local roles to base units of the communities of settlements. Every larger regional unit was considered subsidiary to these. The Municipal level of the capital was in all respects built upon the districts' local governments. The electoral system also expressed this, ensuring a place for district representatives in the general assembly of the Municipality of Budapest. In this period there was neither time nor energy to institutionally handle the individual features of the whole of the greater city.

This approach has been decisive ever since. In Hungary there are over 3,100 local governments for a population of 10 million. In fact every settlement no matter how small has an independent local authority. Budapest is Hungary's only large city by international standards.

It has always been handled as a special case when forming local administration systems. However, the way in which the city was formed has never managed to creatively interpret – in the sense of adapt to – these individual features. One fifth of country's population lives there. Including its environs, over 3 million people are affected by the greater city in one way or another. The public administration system has never handled the overweight nature of Budapest, compared to the rest of Hungary, according to its true value. The change of political system opened the way for another series of experiments.

The new order was almost immediately amended in 1994. The general assembly of Budapest gained supremacy in important matters of regulation, and thus above all in the sharing of revenues and city planning. Sharing funds, which covered the sharing of certain revenues originating from the central budget as well as local revenues between the Municipality and the Districts, used to be bound to the consent of the Districts' mayors. The amendment reduced the Districts' influence to give their opinion. Previously, in city planning the compulsory power of the capital's general city plan for the districts could be questioned. In this respect, the general assembly of Budapest's primary regulatory authority was established in the course of this amendment.

The internal structure of the system of representation was also amended in as far as the districts' delegates were no longer members of the general assembly. The special regulations for Budapest were directly made part of the Local Government Act. As the local government law requires a two-thirds majority in Parliament, amending the provisions in respect of the capital is only possible with broad political consensus. Thanks to this, the political weight of the decentralized institutions of the city significantly grew compared not only to the districts but to the current governments, as well.

To strengthen the unity of the capital, other statutes gave licenses to the organs representing the whole of the city. Above all, Act LXXVIII of 1997 on the development and protection of the built environment, progressed in this direction in respect of regulations on city planning for the capital. A specific system of urban master plans and a hierarchical structure was established, which was to serve the unified management of the city.

REGIONAL DEVELOPMENT

In contrast with the efforts towards an institutional expression of city integration, the realization of a system of relations for cooperating and exchanging information with the belt was less successful. Act XXI of 1996 on regional development and regional planning dealt with the larger regional relation systems. As the county system was left untouched in respect of development, the metropolis' characteristics could only be asserted restrictively, and contradictorily. Of the so-called broader belt (an encircling ring with a radius of almost 60 km) and the narrower conurbation belt, the latter was affected by public administration, although in a limited form.

The operating area of the Budapest Conurbation Development Council (BCDC), as a regional development council, covered the capital and 78 settlements in the belt. These settlements are part of the local government public administration unit encircling Budapest, that is Pest

County. Not much later, based on a new, and to some extent independent viewpoint, the region of Central Hungary was created. The national regional development concept [Parliamentary resolution 35/1998. (III. 20.)] links Budapest and Pest County together as a planning and statistical region.

The definitions of the conurbation and the region were based on different points of view. The theory was that the system of relations with the conurbation would come about in a spontaneous manner, thus only a framework needed to be provided. Defining the region, however, followed requirements for European accession, at least in the form of a regional/ statistical unit, so as to be able to link up with the system of EU structural subsidies. This viewpoint sought to correspond with the existing public administration boundaries, thus respecting the integrity of Pest County.

After the amendment of the Act on regional development and regional planning in 1998, the operational area of the newly established regional development council adapted to this through the simultaneous abolition of the BCDC. There seemed no point in maintaining the parallel structures, although the roles were already quite restricted. This brought an end to the short and contradictory process that nevertheless wished to respect the coherence of the actual spatial structure in the organization of regional public administration.

REGIONAL RELATIONS

It should be added that the entire institutional system of regional development is much less thought through and emphasized in Hungary than the regional local government system is. The original aim was to avoid regional development being managed by the government and to adapt to European models. Compared to this, the framing of the law has only been successful in creating a relatively powerless coordination forum. The mechanism for implementing regional policy, however, was totally ruined by the 1998 amendment. At that time, the further development of the councils, run on a delegation principle, did not move towards the originally planned social partnership. Ministry representatives replaced the remaining non-state representatives. Instead of the originally intended agency structure, public administration and official roles came into the foreground.

Closely connected with the process, available funds did not increase. Actual regional development activity and campaigns could not be continued on this pattern. However, the reason why regional relations were not expressed was not only that the demarcations were unfortunate and rigidly followed the impractical regional public administration boundaries (principally the county borders) but also due to a complete lack of assets. Naturally, the significance of the latter was much greater than that of the boundaries. In this context the fact that Budapest's regional connections is a problem that has not yet been effectively dealt with, only highlights the essential weaknesses of institution building.

The law's consequence on the structure by which policies for the capital city are developed is that recognition of the capital's internal cohesion and external emanation is lacking both within the local government system and within the different forms of regional planning. As a result, local reforms are stuck within conventional limits. Does it therefore follow that the issue of regional connections and smaller local government formations is not a relevant problem? Hardly, as living conditions demonstrate many aspects of the connections. No doubt, each sectoral policy field has got the lesson to find out how ways across the rigid borders can be created in a not-especially-friendly legal environment.

THE DISTRICTS' ENDEAVORS

As a result of the introduction of the local government system, the fact that the local governments of the districts became a real local authority was perhaps the most spectacular development in the administration of the capital. Independence on the one hand meant the possibility of more efficient action in face of the capital's decision-making institutions. On the other hand, differences between the districts also became clearer. In the course of the first cycle, differences, partly due to subjective reasons and partly due to real disparities in living conditions, became strikingly obvious.

One of these phenomena was the quality difference in the districts' conflicts. Tension between bodies and office-holders are frequently characteristic of local governments on some level. In numerous cases debates in the inner districts often went to the point of, or even succeeded in, making them unable to function. Occasionally real stalemate developed between the factions, resulting in crippling the district leadership. The outer districts, however, usually handled conflicts better. More charismatic leaders emerged here for some reason. Although there were great differences and spectacular changes in party support for the mayor here, too, the leadership, however, was able to handle the debates better and on balance won or escaped without suffering serious losses.

The conflicts between the outer districts and the Municipality, and in particular its leadership, became increasingly strong. This statement is generally true, and surprisingly, the conflicts even proved to be independent of party support. In the first cycle, for instance, tensions appeared within the party that won the local elections. Even following later resignations from the parties, the disputes were not transformed into party political conflicts.

The outer districts made a relatively successful alliance to implement joint goals. The Alliance of Outer Districts became the most important lobby within the capital and successfully gave voice to their interests on several occasions, initiating several reform proposals concerning the whole of the capital. No comprehensive partnership developed to such a degree between inner districts.

There are a number of reasons for this difference, one being the organization of public administration. The difference between the tasks of outer and inner districts is worth noting. The functions of the outer districts rather resemble those of settlement (municipal) local governments. The provision of compulsory tasks can be better interpreted and the borders are more real. In spite of all the changes and development, the independent settlements attached to the capital in 1950 have preserved much of their independence. In terms of settlement structure, the separation is certainly valid. In the long term, the available resource types also differ.

In the outer districts the mayors' local support is more significont. A trace of local patriotism, revived after the political changeover, has appeared here, even if not to the same degree as in small provincial towns. It appeared as endeavors for independence in political programs. In the course of the decade, several districts' leadership proposed the idea of potential secession. As these were districts with a large population, they could have aspired to the status of a county town. Csepel's and Újpest's endeavors to secede were especially vocal. At the same time, the initiators soon came to realize that being part of the capital had many everyday advantages for the population that would be put at risk by such a radical step. The most important of these was the link to the capital's subsidized public transport system as well as to public utility systems and services.

There was also strivings for independence of another form within the districts of Budapest. Of these, the separation of Soroksár, formerly part of the 20th district, was successful, thus creating the capital's 23rd district. The direct effects of becoming a district within the city of Budapest, however, are less measurable than those of a secession.

Location differences had other consequences. Thus, since the change of political system there has been a perceivable difference between the inner and outer districts' stability in leadership and, in a certain sense, politics. This led to significant differences in interest. We may add, however, that these do not seem to be based on political colors. The reasons behind this difference can rather be traced back to differences in public administration features which, naturally, greatly build on the features of the structure and organization of the city's development and society.

The organization of the system of relations also became different. Districts with more independent profiles do not have a balanced relation with each other based on mutual linkages but rather they have unequal relations with each other. Everybody uses the inner city, yet the peripheries do not necessarily have intense daily contact with each other.

In connection with this, the strength of a given district's contacts do not all have the same intensity. Not all parts of a metropolis enter into constant, symbiotic relationships with each other. At the same time, there is a strong bond between the outer districts and a clearly definable and separate circle of neighboring or close settlements within the belt.

This has brought a stronger classification of interests, to which the outer districts' stronger level of organization can be attributed. Differences within the districts led to their expectations of the Municipality's public administration to appear more strikingly and more explicitly than before. The same resolution is similarly justified with regard to the relation to the metropolitan belt, or at least the so-called narrower ring.

Conflicts between the Districts and the Municipality were less manifest after the amendment of the Local Government Act in 1994 when the municipality's positions were strengthened. From then on the significance of the mayors' forum decreased as it had lost its former right of consent in the important issue of sharing funds. Other licenses were also restricted. Deviation in interests, however, lessened little.

Another step forward was that both parties became more open as regards the building of systems of relations in the first decade of the changes. At the beginning, the districts did not wish to form a too formal community beyond what was absolutely necessary both with each other and with the Municipality. After long debates, however, a certain measure of cooperation developed. The parking association targeting joint action in developing parking zones, and collecting and enforcing parking fees is an example of this. Today this is an operational and spreading system. On the whole, however, a model built on the provision of tasks in the capital continues to be applied for the solution of joint tasks. Financing mechanisms and regulators as well as task allocating licenses prefer this form.

TENSIONS BETWEEN BELTS

The entire public administration of the capital has become permanently embedded in a multi-layered field of conflicts. Although there are no signs of crisis as this is undoubtedly the country's most developed city public administration and, since the change of the political system, the most successfully developing and changing administration in the country, it is worthwhile to take stock of the unsolved problems. It is common that none of the various regulations knew what to do with these conflicts. They were special issues that did not fit into the system. The "special" classification, however, is contradictory when referring to the capital. Due to its size, a focused approach would be justified. Furthermore, ever since the end of the First World War, successive systems have not known what to do with this ever-growing central region.

Based on the above, a cyclical structure of conflicts and contradicting regulations can be outlined:

- between inner districts–outer districts in as much as their roles fall under a standardized regulation, allowing little opportunity for expressing special features;
- between Districts–Municipality, as a problem of acknowledging the unity of the city;
- between the Municipality–narrow belt, primarily referring to the indirectness of public administration relations with the conurbation belt, and secondarily to the relation with Pest County;
- between the Municipality–broad belt, that is the areas of the counties that more or less neighboring Pest County public administration boundaries. The Municipality has intense, but formal hard-to-define relations with these counties.

390

The first two conflicts appeared primarily as debates on local government regulation in the last decade. The other two arose while developing the regional development system, and tensions there were perhaps even sharper over city policy matters.

In the operating institutional system of regional development there is not really a place for Budapest and its conurbation. At present the following organizations are competent to comprehensively deal with the belt's problems:

- Central Hungary Regional Development Council
- Pest County Local Government
- Pest County Regional Development Council
- Municipality of Budapest.

The areas of competence of these organizations significantly overlap each other. It is a problem that at this time Budapest does not have a regional development council. The Central Hungary Regional Development Council cannot assume this role, neither could its predecessor the Budapest Conurbation Development Council. Their energies were largely tied down by the distrust of Pest County and the fact that they accepted the Municipality's desire for a limited partnership. The latter's reluctance — disregarding party political conflicts — is due to the Municipality's capacities being far more significant compared to the assets of the counties and regions, thus the conditions for partnership are simply lacking within the present institutional frameworks. Pest County above all seeks to protect its autonomy and integrity. The recognition of any form of unity between the city and the belt would be tantamount to questioning the existence of a "county with a hole in the middle." In the regional development council, based on the experience of the last one cycle, the interests of the county tend to be dominant. This is strange, as in fact a significant part of developments in the belt depend on the decision of the Municipality.

There is no longer any place in the system for the inner conurbation of Budapest. The regional development problems of the outer districts cannot win acceptance either from within or without, although the sub-centers of the narrower belt can all be found here. Thus these suburbs, from the point of view of settlement morphology, have great potentials for regional organization. Within the greater city, the outer districts' developments that have a greater impact can only happen if they benefit the interest of the whole city. There is no possibility of an independently led clash of interest through "official" channels.

Although the Local Government Act allows for the association and cooperation between the districts and local governments in the belt outside the city, there has been little of this. However, regarding living conditions, the systems of relations of urbanization are shaped like the "slices of a cake." The outer slices are in daily, intensive contact with their neighboring slices, both within and without the city.

The public administration structure, however, cannot accommodate these contacts very easily, although neither the local government system nor the regional development structure creates formal obstacles to this system of relations. Indeed, both encourage it verbally in their own way. The local government logic encourages the development of horizontal contacts mainly through associations. The regional development system puts spontaneous development contacts, channeled in non-state resources and partnership conforming with EU principles, to the foreground. However, these aims lack adequate institutions and guarantees, which is especially important in an environment where actors that are "condemned to cooperate" have a gut reaction against each other.

The issue was raised particularly sharply in relation to the regional development system. The problem is not that by becoming part of the institutional system there is an immediate hope of new funds. According to the present situation, the part of regional development induced by the state, which runs through specialized institutions, does not account for a very significant part of government expenditure. However, for Budapest and its environs, additional funds, which with a suitable institutional system would in themselves be capable of having a beneficial effect on regional development, are available. (In many parts of the country it is precisely the insufficiency of additional own assets that cripples otherwise developed structures.) Regulatory solutions in no way help the handling of the system of contacts outside the city.

The mechanism that operates today has made us become further removed from the possibility of establishing public administration based on real spatial connections. There are no decisions being made. In this way, the real belt loses its own individuality, and aspects of the inner conurbation continue to be dispersed into Greater Budapest, or, in the best case scenario, into a unifying community of districts. An example of the latter is that during the preparations of the most recent amendments of the regional development law, Budapest was only debated from the point of view of whether representation should be given to the Municipality and/or the Districts. There was no discussion of not giving Budapest its due weight or the need for various partial interests to have better representation. For political and other reasons there was no real readiness to make finer distinctions although, apart from blurring the features of the districts, the elimination of the capital's weight questions the future reality of operation in the long term.

The development of the institutional system of regional development did not help the problem either. The decisions turned solely on the acceptance of future EU funds, as if they were traditional subsidies. Tasks encouraging true spatial relations were forced into the background, despite the fact that these types of decisions are only able to successfully create the added own proportion of funds required for the application of structural funds. This type of problem handling from the viewpoint of Budapest and its regions, however, would be particularly effective.

The inability to deal with numerous matters of city policy shows the lack and insufficiency of institutions and interest reconciling mechanisms. One example of this is the long protracted issue of harmonizing public transport in the capital and its environs. It is in this framework that the connections between urban public transport and neighboring inter-town public transport should be resolved. The harmonization of joint tariffs, routes and timetables, and coordinating developments are proceeding with difficulty in spite of all the agreements. A new problem is preserving the green space in the capital and the region. As it is a prosperous region, it is equally in the interest of the municipality, the districts and the neighboring settlements to encourage property sales to businesses on the most favorable terms possible. Environmental impacts of those businesses may however be seen in other parts of the urbanized region.

The capital's drinking water supply – for which the not-directly-interested neighboring settlements should pay – is another example. Another problem is the capital's long-term waste disposal, which clearly cannot be solved within city limits (i.e., the area of competence of the local government). The transport burdens of shopping centers and industrial parks built in the belt affect the part of the city that is "on the way" to those centers, thus its development needs coordinating. Finally, the long wrangling over constructing an orbital motorway bypassing the city, which was caused by the resistance of neighboring settlements and the inability on the part of the Municipality to respond to their claims .

The lack of assets in the regional institutional system makes the normal management of these and many other similar city policy problems difficult. In the present situation the only possible direction for a solution lies in shifting development up to a sectoral level. Conflicts are sometimes handled this way, although this is not always a fortunate or a practical solution.

The rigidity of the local government and regional development systems has other consequences from the viewpoint of administering the capital. Very little attention is given to the tasks arising from the broader belt. Dealing with the need stemming from this can only be done on a national level through the indirect and informal participation of the regional representations. The maintenance of contacts is still quite intense, and even daily, with towns within a circle of 60 km around the capital. Those relations are moreover by no means one way. Managing the relations of transport and other service organization, however, today falls almost completely outside the sphere of authority and influence of public administration for Budapest and the region. State tasks in this respect have shifted up to the central level.

In summary, the following conclusions may be drawn about the reforms that occurred following the political system changeover and that were directed at the development of the institutional system of public administration in the city and its environs. In the pre-1990 period, the "impotence" of the whole of the system hindered radical changes to a great extent. Numerous studies and elements of studies made since the 1970's, in particular those which pertain to the real processes of the region, have proved to be true in many respects today.

After the change of the political system, the opportunity arose to rethink the whole concept of local administration. However, in the period available, there was no sufficient energy left to devise an individual system for the capital and its environs. For this reason, the conceptualization and legislation of the city's public administration system was imitative in nature. The administration of the city was a schematic derivative of the whole country's system for local and regional administration. The corrections of 1994 only managed to "tip" the existing system to one side. The results and effects of this only appeared in a restricted manner. Its inconsistencies sowed the seeds of further conflicts and contradictions.

393

The future individual development of the local/regional administration of the capital and its environs is undoubtedly justified. One fifth of the country's population lives within the current public administration boundaries of the city, and at least a further half a million live in neighboring settlements whose living standards and daily contact link them with the capital. This should be solved as an independent range of topics and not be dealt with as a local government and regional development systems problem that should be solved with the least possible disturbance to and with as little difference as possible from typically applied and operating forms.

FISCAL SCOPE FOR ACTION

When presenting the changes that have occurred in the economy in previous sections, we mentioned that fiscal policy was typically restrictive in the last decade. The elements of a modern system of public services adapting to market economy had to be developed in a way that expenditure could continuously and significantly be reduced. From the point-of-view of the whole of general government finances, this transformation was successful. Today the weight of the public sector within the economy is similar to the average of developed European countries.

Reduction of available funds and expenditure opportunities also affected the budgets of local governments. Over the decade local government expenditures have gradually been reduced. The weight of local governments with an extended range of tasks compared to GDP was 16-17% at the beginning of the 1990's. Today it is around 12%.[10] In spite of the fact that as a consequence of the economic growth the expenditure rate compared to GDP has since fallen, this is still indicative of the strong decentralization of the Hungarian local government system.

The budgetary restraint that occurred in several waves affected various sub-systems of public finance in a similar way. The share of expenditures on local governments within the national budget hardly changed in practice; it was around 23-25% during the decade. Parallel to central budget expenditures, the budgets of local governments also decreased. Changes within general government expenditures were only to the detriment of extra-budgetary funds, so that the share of the expenditure of social security funds grew.

This process of general restraint, in parallel with the building of the local government financial system, brought several changes in local expenditure and revenue options. In the following, the main characteristics of the changes within the whole of the local government financial system, as well as their effect on the budgetary position of the local governments operating in Budapest will be examined. We aim to give an exact picture of the budgetary

---

[10] Davey, K.–Péteri G., 1998

opportunities of the Municipality – advantageous from many aspects – thus contributing to the objective assessment of the implemented reforms.

CHANGES IN LOCAL GOVERNMENT FINANCE

The trend of local government expenditure was influenced in part by changes in economic policy and in part by political cycles.

Chart 5
EXPENDITURES OF LOCAL GOVERNMENTS, 1991–2001

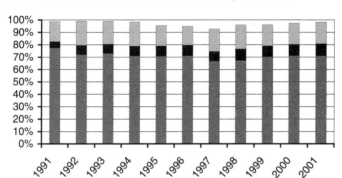

■ Current expenditures   ■ Transfers   ▦ Capital expenditures

At the start of the decade, as one of the first steps in the decentralization process, various grants and social provisions grew within local government expenditure to up to 7-8% of operating expenses. This change had little impact on development expenses that were on average around 19%. A change only occurred in 1995-96 at a time of severe restraints, when the burden of the repayment of loans appeared on the one hand, and on the other, existing funds had to be regrouped to finance the operation of the local governments due to the reduction in central subsidies.

Only in 1998, a year of elections, was there some measure of change, when development expenses again grew. After this the composition of local government expenditure became relatively stable. 81-82% of the budget was spent on current expenditures and within this the share of social allowances and other grants grew a little to 9-10%.

Exploiting local government property and the revenues therefrom helped to keep capital expenditures relatively stable. Within local government capital revenues, the growing rate of revenue from property sales and privatization were the main sources of development until 1997 *(Chart 6)*. Subsequently, capital revenues decreased significantly in the absence of saleable property, and investments had to be financed from other sources.

Chart 6
CAPITAL REVENUES AND EXPENDITURE, 1991–2001

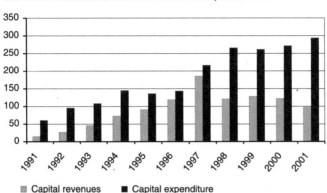

■ Capital revenues　■ Capital expenditure

These changes are well reflected by the transformation in the internal composition of the local governments' balance sheet. At the start of the decade, an overemphasis on tangible assets, i.e., mainly land and buildings, was typical in the balance sheet for fixed assets (1991: 77%, 1992: 56%[11]). After this, with the start of privatization and through to the restructuring of local government public utilities into business organizations, the proportion of financial assets and within this, share holdings, grew (1991: 2%, 1996: 35%). 1995-96 represented the peak of the sale of assets, a time that coincided with the period of strongest restraint, when the rate of tangible assets on the balance sheet fell down to 44%. Subsequently, it seems that this one-off source had exhausted itself and that the property situation of the local governments had stabilized.

Local government property and related income possibilities are novel elements but naturally only of little significance as local government resources *(Chart 7)*. In the nineties central grants

Chart 7
MAJOR CATEGORIES OF LOCAL GOVERNMENT REVENUES (1991–2002)

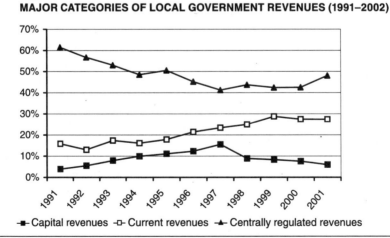

-■- Capital revenues　-□- Current revenues　-▲- Centrally regulated revenues

---

[11]　The home page of the Ministry of Home Affairs

– excluding transfers from the general government budget, primarily disbursements received from the Social Security Fund – were prominent features of the revenues of the local government budget.

These centrally regulated revenues were comprised of state grants and shared revenues. As will be discussed later, the regulations on generating and distributing the two types of funds have become more and more similar during the decade. Altogether these revenues are of increasingly small significance for local governments. As a consequence of decreasing local government transfers and the merging of the two fund allocation methods, the subsidization of local governments in the central budget has ever less weight (1991: 20%, 2000: 11%[12]).

One of the most important issues of intergovernmental finance regulation in the decade were the state grants and the share of personal income tax. The decision to transfer personal income tax was made when this budgetary source was not yet terribly important for the central budget. The local PIT with its indirect connection to local government operation was a good revenue to be a local source, even if tax policy and tax administration were not local government tasks. The centrally collected PIT transferred according to place of origin with a two-year delay proved to be a good regulatory instrument both economically and politically.

Chart 8
SHARED PIT AND PIT ON DERIVATION BASIS AS SHARE OF LOCAL GOVERNMENT REVENUES

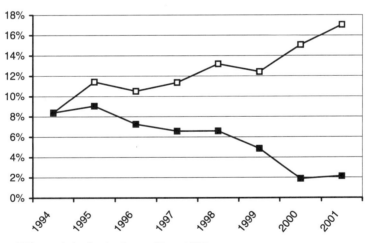

-■- PIT on a derivation basis   -□- Shared PIT

However, as soon as PIT revenues began to grow, the proportion of shared tax transferred to the local level fell. As the sharing ratio was fixed in the annual Budget Act, it was easy to change this local revenue from year to year. In 1991, local governments received half of the PIT revenue of the two preceding years. Then, from 1993 onwards, they received only 30%

---

[12] The home page of the Ministry of Home Affairs

of their original PIT revenues. In 1998 according to a schedule for steady growth announced in advance, the level of transfer grew to 40%.

In this period, however, the regulation on sharing was also amended. In spite of the fact that the local governments now only received a certain percentage of PIT, from 1994 only a part of this went back to the municipal government where it originated from. This shared fund had first to be used for equalizing purposes, and then to cover a part of the equalizing of state grants. As a result, the shared PIT fulfilled its original function to an ever lesser degree, as the role of local government decisions and delayed tax revenue was less and less significant. Today PIT transferred according to locality accounts for only 2% of local government revenues, while the proportion of all shared funds within the budget is increasingly large.

These two problems with the system of sharing PIT (i.e., the annually changing distribution rate and a decrease in the amount transferred according to its origin) are a crucial problem for cities and so for Budapest too. One third of the country's total PIT revenue is generated in Budapest, thus even small changes in regulations have a strong influence on the budgets of local governments operating there. The Municipality and Districts are equally sensitive to changes in transferred funds, as these are funds shared within the capital.

Finally, within the local government budget the third type of funds, the own current revenue of local governments, has shown steady growth. Institutional revenues and local taxes, as the two largest revenues within this type of funds, account today for 27-28% of local budgets. This fact shows the advantages of decentralization, as these two types of income depend almost entirely on local government decisions. The number of local governments imposing local taxes as well as the size of the rates applied rose steadily. It is true that the role of local business tax, accounting for four fifths of local taxes, was decisive and its growth was in keeping with the improved performance of the economy.

The three most important new elements of local government finances affected the economy of local governments in the capital city differently. Through the transfer of property, privatization revenues and the imposition of local business tax, the local governments of the capital city clearly did well as Budapest was in a favorable position.

The effect of the general grant system may be described as neutral. The uniform state grant, irrespective of local government revenue capacity, obviously favored local governments with higher own revenues. It is true, however, that per capita grants do not in general cover the operating costs of a given task, thus the total expenses of the "receiving" local government increases due to "commuters." In general the, "sender" settlement local government does not transfer the missing funds from its own sources. At the same time, these additional (municipal) expenses accompanying commuting, on a per capita basis, are typically less for the receiving local government than the average expenditure covered by the state grant.

Cities with a high income population, such as Budapest, are clearly the losers of the changed system of personal income tax sharing. The local PIT revenue transferred back to the locality has fallen steadily and is at a minimal level today. Neither own development nor current revenue, nor the state grant system compensate for this loss.

BUDAPEST'S FISCAL POSITION

Changes in the regulatory system and political cycles equally influenced Budapest's budgetary situation within the country. Budapest's weight prior to 1990 was 26-27% *(Chart 9)*, compared to local expenditure as regards both total expenditures and capital expenditures This level was achieved relatively soon, in 1992, as regards annual expenditure. With capital investment, however, the only opportunity for this was in 1995. This rate within the country remained the same for the rest of the cycle. From this time onwards Budapest's share of the budget of both types of expenditure within the country – exceeding only slightly its rate within the population – was about a quarter.

At the same time, this relatively constant proportion within the country means that the size of the local government investments realized in the capital was not exceptional. No matter how favorable the revenue and fund-acquiring possibilities were, the rate of capital investment within the local government budget followed the national average. When the new local government system was established, as a result of the operating debts of the large institutional network and the low capital revenues, the rate of investments was even below the national average. With the exception of 1995, the rate of capital investments only continued to move in line with the other local governments in the country.

In spite of impressive and in many cases nationally significant developments in Budapest, a kind of national regional equalizing policy was implemented: the pace of development in the provinces was higher than or similar to the rate of investments realized in the capital within the local budget.

Chart 9
EXPENDITURES OF THE MUNICIPALITY OF BUDAPEST
AS SHARE OF ALL LOCAL GOVERNMENT EXPENDITURES

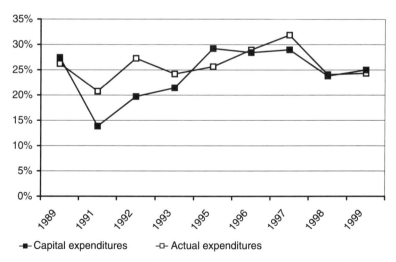

Over the last decade capital expenditure has been shared between the Municipality and the Districts in proportion with the weight of the local government budgets. While in the socialist council system, capital investments were typically realized from the Municipality's budget, since 1991 the rate of capital expenditure within the budget was in general similar for both the Municipality and the Districts. The rate of capital expenditure for both entities was 10-12% at the start of the decade, and 16-17% in 1993. The situation only altered at the end of the decade when in 1998 and 1999 the rate of developments for the Municipality within the budget was typically above 20% while that of the Districts was 4-5% less.

As for most local governments in the country, a significant source for capital investments was local government property. According to the figures of the real estate register dating back to 1994, one quarter of the property in the country is today owned by the Municipality and the Districts together.[13] This share – perhaps due to the uncertainty of valuation – varied significantly from year to year. Budapest's rate within the country moved between 12 and 26% in the period examined.

Naturally, high-value detached properties are a decisive part of real estate. A significant part of unbuilt up areas has not been valued. Thus they do not appear in the real estate register. As regards "space not for housing purposes", which is important from the viewpoint of revenues, only figures in kind are available. But even on this basis, Budapest is in a very favorable position compared to other local governments as 46-47% of properties important for the local budgets, including shops, offices, warehouses and garages, are located in the capital. Within this group, shops had the greatest weight from the point of view of revenues: in 1999 half the shops in local government ownership and 56% in terms of area were located in Budapest.

By the middle of the decade the proportion of tangible assets, and within that shore of land and buildings, in local government fixed assets had declined. As a consequence of privatization and the transfer of property as well as the changes in public utilities (before their privatization), Budapest local governments had significant shares in business organizations. According to one survey, 14% of business organizations with a local government share were located in Budapest, while the proportion calculated on the basis of proprietorial shares was 73%.

The position of the capital city is also favorable considering that in the course of privatization provincial local governments had mainly small ownership stakes. Shares under 5% afforded little power to influence. In contrast, business organizations with a majority (over 51%) local government ownership accounted for 90% of local government property in the capital city.

Of course, with public utility privatization this situation gradually changed. Starting from 1995, the privatization of the gas and water works, and the sewerage company altered these rates. At the same time the local governments obtained significant revenue from privatization (1995: HUF 13 billion, 1996: HUF 5 billion from gas, 1997: HUF 34 billion from water and sewerage privatization[14]).

---

[13] Ministry of Home Affairs–Regional Information Service for Public Finance, 2000a

[14] Pallai, 1998a

All this one-off and operating revenue originating from local government property was necessary in Budapest as state subsidies divided between the local governments were 10-15% less than the national average. The detailed figures for Budapest show that, corresponding to the changes in own revenue, state subsidy appearing in the Municipality's budget always remained 5-10% below grants for the Districts *(Chart 10)*.

Chart 10
CENTRAL GOVERNMENT SUBSIDIES AS SHARE OF TOTAL REVENUES

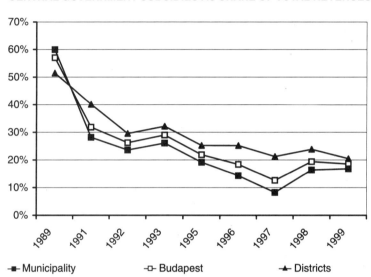

Considering the entire amount of local government revenue, the proportion of the budgets of the Municipality and Districts shows a similar trend. Within the whole of Budapest, the budget of the Municipality only grew to two thirds of local government expenditure in the period of larger developments. At other times, the expenditures of the Municipality and the Districts were approximately the same.

In summary, on the basis of the financial figures, we may state that Budapest's budgetary position altered together with that of the other local governments of the country. Changes in important elements of the regulatory system also affected the administration of the Municipality. Due to the higher proportion of own revenues and its favorable property situation, however, the uncertainty stemming from central dependence was less acute here. The capital's local governments had to react to these changes by constantly seeking ways to increase their own operating and development revenues.

One of the most important goals voiced since the establishment of the local government system, decreasing the capital's weight within the country, was achieved in this decade. In spite of the capital's development, an increasingly small amount of the central funds are used here. At the same time, as a counterbalance, the local governments of the capital have well exploited opportunities for independent management and fund generating that were afforded by the local government system. Although the features enabling this are unique, their relatively successful strategies have given other urban local governments of the country a positive example to follow.

CONCLUSIONS

In summary, the following statements and conclusions may be made concerning the restructuring of financing on the level of the capital as well as the quality of the reactions to budgetary policy.

1. The change in the European public service system and concept of the state also affected Eastern Europe where, in order to handle the crisis, various local government solutions were created. According to the neo-conservative stance, management instruments created through budgetary restraints generate innovations that later lead to further savings. On the contrary, in the moderate Left's local government concept of savings and management, means have a particular social purpose, that is best described by the concept of a new partnership. In accordance with the development processes in the West, as an effect of budgetary restrictions, local governments' scope of action typically narrowed across the board. The restraints meant that the amount of local tasks did not decrease to the same extent as funds were reduced. Innovative local governments, however, could find good strategies for handling crises. In Central-Eastern Europe, at the same time, demolishing the former practice of state organization was not accompanied by the simultaneous creation of another viable system. Changes in the public services during the last decade show how serious hiatuses the collapse of still operating old systems can leave in forms of service provision and in strengthening the social and regional conflicts. This undoubtedly acted against the spread of innovative solutions.

2. The Hungarian economic and fiscal cycles created particular waves in decentralization policy: restraint went together with strengthening the local level, while growth accompanied centralization. Budgetary and political institution building, strict fiscal restriction and today's centralization attempts created unstable general conditions for the implementation of the Municipality's own financing and service organization reforms. General decentralization rules were adapted to the particular conditions of the capital in the first two-or three-year period of building the local government system. In the phase of strict restraint that followed, the Municipality introduced modern reforms based on its favorable property and own revenue position that were exemplary for other urban local governments. At that time the political and professional environment was still favorable for the city leadership. The time for realizing the results of the capital's reforms came when economic growth started after 1998-1999. This was, however, accompanied by forceful centralization, which affected the local government system.

3. This for Budapest coincided with a turning point in urban development when the suburbanization phase was completed in city development. The urbanization indicators show that the administration and planning solutions were only linked to the long-term city development trend in a limited manner. In the suburbanization phase no mechanisms developed for

regional cooperation and the sharing of joint tasks and burdens. The privatization of public services would require a unified regional local government presence, yet only the first steps towards this are seen.

The reforms directed at changing the institutional system of the public administration of the city and its environs were greatly hindered in the period prior to 1990 by the "impotence" of the whole system. After the change of political system, the opportunity arose to rethink the whole concept of local administration. The conceptualization and legislation of an individual system for the capital and its environs was imitative in nature however. The administration of the city is still just a schematic copy of the national system of local and regional administration, although here special problems have to be dealt with that should normally form a separate area within public administration reform.

4. The introduction of the new system of local government financing in 1990 had different effects for local governments and Budapest's scope for action. An increasingly small part of the nationally available central funds was used in Budapest. Later, out of the transferred local funds, the method for sharing personal income tax was most disadvantageous for the budgets of the capital's local governments. Due to the higher rate of own revenue and the advantageous property position, however, the uncertainty stemming from central dependence could be reduced here. By increasing their own current and capital revenues, the capital city's local governments still managed to reduce the deficit that appeared due to the tightening central funds in the 1990's.

The new challenge is whether the capital city's local governments, and among them the Municipality of Budapest, are able to initiate innovative strategies in city policy, besides "complaining" about dependence on the government. The practices of Budapest's 24 local governments show different examples. Results may greatly differ and also change according to policy forming areas. Developing the Municipality's finance system is one of the reform areas. In the analysis of this local policy instrument, the extent to which those implementing it were sensitive to external (global, social and regional, etc.) challenges, and the extent to which they managed to create harmony with other important city policy program opportunities and strategies, remains to be shown.

SOURCES AND LITERATURE

Batley, Richard – Stoker, Gerry eds., 1991: Local Government in Europe: *Trends and Developments. Houndmills: Macmillan.*

Bennett, Robert J., 1998: *'Local Government in Postsocialist Cities', in: Enyedi, Gy. ed.: Social Change and Urban Restructuring in Central Europe. Budapest, Akadémiai Kiadó, pp. 9-34.*

Central Office of Statistics, 1991: *Területi Statisztikai Évkönyv, 1990. (Regional Statistical Yearbook, 1990.) Budapest*

Central Office of Statistics, 1999: *Területi Statisztikai Évkönyv, 1998. (Regional Statistical Yearbook, 1998.) Budapest*

Davey, K – Péteri G., 1998: *A helyi önkormányzati pénzügyi rendszer átalakítási lehetőségei. 'Helyi önkormányzati know-how program.' Transformation Possibilities of the*

Local Governments' Financing System. Program of Local Government Know-How. Pontes Kft., Nagykovácsi.

Dunleavy, Patrick – O'Leary, Brendan, 1987: *Theories of the State: The Politics of Liberal Democracy. Houndmills: Macmillan.*

Enyedi, Gy., 1984: *Az urbanizációs ciklus és a magyar településhálózat átalakulása. (Urbaniztion Cycle and the Evolvement of the Hungarian Settlement Network.) Akadémiai Kiadó, Budapest.*

Freire, M. – Stren, R. eds., 2001: *The Challenge of Urban Government. The World Bank Institute Development Studies.*

Goldsmith, Mike, 1992: *Local Governments' Urban Studies, Vol. 29, Nos. 3/4, pp. 393–410.*

Hesse, J. and Sharpe, L. J., 1991: *'Conclusions' in J. Hesse ed.: Local Government and Urban Affairs in International Perspective. Baden-Baden: Nomos Verlagsgesellschaft.*

Hörcher, F., 1981: *'Az urbanizáció Európában.' Urbanization in Europe. Területfejlesztési Közlemények, No. 12.*

Horváth M. Tamás, 1993: *'Towards the Enabling Authority in West and East: Hypothesis.' In: T. M. Horváth ed.: Public Administration in Hungary. Budapest: Hungarian Institute of Public Administration, pp. 130–147.*

Horváth M. Tamás, 1997: *'Decentralization in Public Administration and Provision of Services: an East-Central European View.' Environment and Planning C: Government and Policy, vol. 15, pp. 161-175.*

Horváth M. Tamás, 2000a: *'From Local Government to Civil Society.' East Central Europe, vol. 27, pp. 77—97.*

Horváth M. Tamás, 2000b: *'Tézisek. Helyi közszolgáltatások szervezése a modern államban. Elméleti alapok az önkormányzati feladatok menedzseléséhez.' (Theses. Organizing Public Utilities in the Modern States. Theoretical Foundations for the Management of Local Government Tasks.) Közpolitika, No. 3.*

Horváth M. Tamás ed., 2000c: *Decentralization: Experiments and Reforms. Local Governments in Central and Eastern Europe. Budapest: Local Government and Public Service Reform Initiative.*

Horváth M. T. – Péteri G. – Tosics I., 1993: *'Budapest és környéke új közigazgatási modellje.' (A New Public Administration Model for Budapest and its Agglomeration.) Városkutatás Kft., Budapest.*

Horváth, Péter, 2000: *'A közfeladatok ellátásának kihívásai.' Challenges in Managing Public Duties. Magyar Közigazgatás, No. 10..*

Illner, Michal, 1999: *Territorial Decentralization: An Obstacle to Democratic Reform in Central and Eastern Europe? in Kimball, Jonatan D. ed.: The Transfer Power: Decentralization in Central and Eastern Europe. Budapest: Local Government and Public Service Reform Initiative.*

Judge, D. – Stoker, G. – Wolman, H. eds., 1995: *Theories of Urban Politics. London: SAGE.*

King, Desmond, 1995: *'From Urban Left to the New Right: Normative Theory and Local Government' in: Stewart and Stoker, 1995.*

Ladányi. J. – Szelényi, I., 1996: *Vázlat az "esélyteremtő állam" elméletéhez: A jóléti államon és a neokonzervativizmuson túl. (A Draft-theory for the "Chance-generating State." Beyond the Welfare State and Neo-conservatism.) 2000, No. 12., Vol. VIII. pp. 9–15.*.

László, Cs., 1988: Twists and Turns: *The History of the Hungarian Public Finance Reform.* in: Bokros, L-Dethierm J-J. eds.: *Public Finance Reform during the Transition. The World Bank, Washington, D.C.*

Lloyd, R. – Clark T. N., 2000: *The City as an Entertainment Machine. Presentation at the American Sociological Association.*

Ministry of Home Affairs–Regional Information Service for Public Finance, 2000a: *'Ingatlanregiszter, 1994–1999.' (Real Estate Property Register, 1994–1999.), Budapest*

Ministry of Home Affairs–Regional Information Service for Public Finance, 2000b: *'Az önkormányzatok ellátottságának főbb pénzügyi és naturális mutatói, 1989-1999.' (The Main Financial and Natural Indicators for the Degree of Supply of the Local Governments, 1989-1999. National total, the Municipality of Budapest, the districts of the capital.) Budapest*

Montin, Stig, 2000: *A Conceptual Framework. In: Amna, Erik and Montin, eds.: Towards a New Concept of Local Self-government? Local Government Development in Comparative Perspective. Bergen: Fagbokforlaget.*

Official Gazette of the Republic of Hungary, 1991–2001: *Annual State Budget Acts. Budapest*

Pallai, Katalin, 1998: *'Financial Management and Reform of the Municipality of Budapest 1990-1998. Study prepared for The Office of the Mayor of Budapest.*

Pickvance, C., 1995a: *'Marxists Theories of Urban Politics', in: Judge et al. eds., 1995: pp. 253–275.*

Pickvance, C., 1995b: *'Decentalization and Democracy in Eastern Europe: C Sceptical Approach' Conference paper on the Conference on Democratization and Decentralization: From Years of Local Transformation in Central and Eastern Europe, 2–6 August 1995, Cracow, p. 27.*

Regulska, Johanna, 1996: *Decentralisation and Deconcentration: Sruggle for Political Power in Poland. Environment and Planning C: Government and Policy 14.*

Sharp, Elaine B., 1990: *Urban Politics and Administration: From Service Delivery to Economic Development. New York: Longman.*

Stoker, Gerry, 1991: *'Introduction: Trends in European Local Government', in Batley, R. and Stoker, G., eds.: Local Government in Europe: Trends and Developments. Basingstoke, Macmillan.*

Stoker, Gerry, 1997: *'From New Right to New Labour: Tensions and Hopes in the Reform of British Local Government.' Paper presented for International Seminar, Oslo, 12-13 December 1997.*

Stoker, Gerry, 1998: *'From New Management to New Labour: Tensions and Hopes in the Reform of British Local Government.' Paper for the Norwegian Research Council's Workshop in Copenhagen, Denmark. 16 – 18 April, 1988, p. 30.*

The home page of the Ministry of Home Affairs: http://www.b-m.hu/onkormanyzat/

APPENDIX

SOURCES AND LITERATURE

Albers, Rebecca, 2001: *'Participatory budgeting in Porto Alegre', in Freire-Stern, eds.: The Challenege of Urban Government, Policies and Practices. WBI, Washington DC, pp. 129-145.*

Alliance of Free Democrats (SZDSZ), 1990: *'A Szabad Demokraták programja Budapest számára.' (The Free Democrats' Program for Budapest. Election program.) Budapest*

Alliance of Free Democrats (SZDSZ), 1994: *'Budapest Jövője: Várospolitika 2000-ig.'*[1] *(The Future of Budapest: Urban Policy up to 2000. Eleciton program.) Budapest*

Alliance of Free Democrats (SZDSZ), 1998: *'Világvárost építünk.' (Building a Metropolis. The election program of Gábor Demszky.) Budapest*

Alliance of Free Democrats (SZDSZ), 2002: *'Fővárost Európának. Budapest európai fővárossá fejlesztésének programja.' (A Capital for Europe. Program for developing Budapest into a European Capital. Campaign program of Gábor Demszky.) Budapest*

Atkári, János, 2000: *'Mehr Licht'. Discussion paper for the conference of the Alliance of Free Democrats, manuscript.*

Batley, Richard – Stoker, Gerry eds., 1991: *Local Government in Europe: Trends and Developments. Houndmills: Macmillan.*

Bennett, Robert J., 1998: *'Local Government in Postsocialist Cities', in: Enyedi, Gy. ed.: Social Change and Urban Restructuring in Central Europe. Budapest, Akadémiai Kiadó, pp. 9-34.*

Bertaud, Alain, 1995: *'Cities Without Land Markets'. The World Bank Polic Research Working Papers 1477.*

Cave, M. – Valentiny, P., 1994: *'Privatization and regulation of Utilities in Economies in Transition', in Saul Estrin ed.: Privatization in Central & Eastern Europe. Longman, London, 1994.*

Central Office of Statistics, 1991: *Területi Statisztikai Évkönyv, 1990. (Regional Statistical Yearbook, 1990.) Budapest*

Central Office of Statistics, 1991-2003: *Statistical Yearbooks of Budapest. Budapest*

Central Office of Statistics, 1998: *'Az önkormányzati segélyezés és a segélyezett háztartások életkörülményei.' (Local Government Allowance System and the Living Conditions of the Supported Households.) Budapest*

Central Office of Statistics, 1999: *'A kommunális ellátás fontosabb adatai – public utilities 1998.' (Prime Figures of Communal Services – Public Utilities 1998.) Budapest*

---

[1] Project leaders: József Hegedüs, Katalin Pallai, Iván Tosics. Experts: Pál Baros, Györgyi Barta, Zoltán Erő, Zsuzsa Foltányi, Ferenc Gazsó, Iván Illés, Balázs Krémer, Gábor Locsmándi, Viktor Merker, Éva Orosz, Katalin Pikler, István Pólay, Péter Schneider, János Schulek, Ottó Szenczi, András Vígvári.

Central Office of Statistics, 1999: *Területi Statisztikai Évkönyv, 1998. (Regional Statistical Yearbook, 1998.) Budapest*

Central Office of Statistics, 2000: *Szociális statisztikai évkönyv. (Statistical Yearbook of Social Conditions.) Budapest*

Central Office of Statistics, 2002: *'Háztartás-statisztikai közlemények, 2001.' (Statistical Findings on Households, 20. 2001. Q1–Q4) Budapest*

Davey, K – Péteri G., 1998: *A helyi önkormányzati pénzügyi rendszer átalakítási lehetőségei. 'Helyi önkormányzati know-how program.' Transformation Possibilities of the Local Governments' Financing System. Program of Local Government Know-How. Pontes Kft., Nagykovácsi.*

Decamp, A., 2000: *'The Financial Resources of Local Authorities'. Study prepared as part of the 4th General Report on Political Monitoring of the Implementation of the European Charter of Local Self-Government. Draft Memorandum, Volume I, March 2000, CPL/GT/CEAL(6)18.*

Dunleavy, Patrick – O'Leary, Brendan, 1987: *Theories of the State: The Politics of Liberal Democracy. Houndmills: Macmillan.*

Enyedi, Gy., 1984: *Az urbanizációs ciklus és a magyar településhálózat átalakulása. (Urbaniztion Cycle and the Evolvement of the Hungarian Settlement Network.) Akadémiai Kiadó, Budapest.*

Eurostat, 1996: *Európa számokban. (Europe in Numbers.) Budapest*

Finance Research Co., 1991: *'Összefoglaló a tíz önkormányzati tulajdonban lévő közüzemi vállalat szervezeti és pénzügyi átvilágításáról.' (Summary of the Organizational and Financial Due Diligence of Ten Public Utility Companies Owned by the Municipality.) Budapest*

Finance Research Co., 2000: *'A fővárosi távhőszolgáltatás egy lehetséges szervezeti modellje.' (A Possible Organization Model for District Heating in the Capital.) Budapest*

Foundation for a European Hungary, Local Government Experts' Office, 1991: *'Demszky Gábor programja a Főváros számára.'*[2] *(Gábor Demszky's Program for the Capital City. Election program.) Budapest*

Főmterv Co., 1993: *'A főváros hosszú távú komplex csatornázási és szennyvízkezelési terve.' (The Long-term Complex Sewage System and Waste Water Management Development Program of the Capital.) Budapest*

Főmterv Co., 1994: *'A Főváros Vízgazdálkodási Terve.' (The Municipality's Water Management Plan.) Budapest*

Főmterv Co., 1999: *'A főváros hosszú távú komplex csatornázási és szennyvízkezelési terve.' (The Long-term Complex Sewage System and Waste Water Management Development Program of the Capital. Rewrite.) Budapest*

---

[2] Project leaders: János Atkári, István Kemény, Katalin Pallai, István Rév, István Teplán.

Főmterv Co., 2001: *'Budapest közlekedési rendszerének fejlesztési terve.'* *(Development Plan for Budapest's Traffic and Transportation System.)* Budapest

Freire, M. – Stren, R. eds., 2001: *The Challenge of Urban Government. The World Bank Institute Development Studies.*

Goldsmith, Mike, 1992: *Local Governments' Urban Studies, Vol. 29, Nos. 3/4, pp. 393–410.*

Hermann, Z., – Horváth, M.T., – Péteri, G., – Ungvári, G., 1999: 'Allocation of Local Government Functions: *Criteria and Conditions – Analysis and Policy Proposals for Hungary.'* *Washington, DC: The Fiscal Decentralization Initiative for Central and Eastern Europe.*

Hesse, J. and Sharpe, L. J., 1991: 'Conclusions' in J. Hesse ed.: Local Government and Urban Affairs in International Perspective. Baden-Baden: Nomos Verlagsgesellschaft.

Horváth M. Tamás, 1993: 'Towards the Enabling Authority in West and East: Hypothesis.' In: *T. M. Horváth ed.: Public Administration in Hungary. Budapest: Hungarian Institute of Public Administration, pp. 130–147.*

Horváth M. Tamás, 1997: *'Decentralization in Public Administration and Provision of Services: an East-Central European View.'* *Environment and Planning C: Government and Policy, vol. 15, pp. 161-175.*

Horváth M. Tamás, 2000a: *'From Local Government to Civil Society.'* *East Central Europe, vol. 27, pp. 77—97.*

Horváth M. Tamás, 2000b: *'Tézisek. Helyi közszolgáltatások szervezése a modern államban. Elméleti alapok az önkormányzati feladatok menedzseléséhez.'* *(Theses. Organizing Public Utilities in the Modern States. Theoretical Foundations for the Management of Local Government Tasks.)* *Közpolitika, No. 3.*

Horváth M. Tamás ed., 2000c: *Decentralization: Experiments and Reforms. Local Governments in Central and Eastern Europe. Budapest: Local Government and Public Service Reform Initiative.*

Horváth M. T. – Péteri G. – Tosics I., 1993: *'Budapest és környéke új közigazgatási modellje.'* *(A New Public Administration Model for Budapest and its Agglomeration.)* *Városkutatás Kft., Budapest.*

Horváth, Péter, 2000: *'A közfeladatok ellátásának kihívásai.'* *Challenges in Managing Public Duties. Magyar Közigazgatás, No. 10..*

Hörcher, F., 1981: *'Az urbanizáció Európában.'* *Urbanization in Europe. Területfejlesztési Közlemények, No. 12.*

IEA/OECD, 2000: *Energy Policies of Hungary – 1999 Review. Paris*

Illner, Michal, 1999: *Territorial Decentralization: An Obstacle to Democratic Reform in Central and Eastern Europe?* in Kimball, Jonatan D. ed.: *The Transfer Power: Decentralization in Central and Eastern Europe. Budapest: Local Government and Public Service Reform Initiative.*

411

Inter-party document of municipal party factions, 1992: *'Az összefogás programja.'* *(A Program for Joining Forces.) Budapest*

Judge, D. – Stoker, G. – Wolman, H. eds., 1995: Theories of Urban Politics. London: *SAGE.*

King, Desmond, 1995: *'From Urban Left to the New Right: Normative Theory and Local Government'* in: *Stewart and Stoker, 1995.*

Ladányi. J. – Szelényi, I., 1996: Vázlat az "esélyteremtő állam" elméletéhez: *A jóléti államon és a neokonzervativizmuson túl. (A Draft-theory for the "Chance-generating State". Beyond the Welfare State and Neo-conservatism.) 2000, No. 12., Vol. VIII. pp. 9–15..*

László, Cs., 1988: Twists and Turns: *The History of the Hungarian Public Finance Reform. in: Bokros, L-Dethierm J-J. eds.: Public Finance Reform during the Transition. The World Bank, Washington, D.C.*

League of the Hungarian Professional District Heating Providers, 2000: *'Magyar Távhő Évkönyv 2000.' (Hungarian District Heating Yearbook 2000.) Budapest*

Lloyd, R. – Clark T. N., 2000: *The City as an Entertainment Machine. Presentation at the American Sociological Association.*

Ministry of Home Affairs–Regional Information Service for State Finance, 2000: *'Az önkormányzatok ellátottságának főbb pénzügyi és naturális mutatói, 1989-1999.' (The Main Financial and Natural Indicators for the Degree of Supply of the Local Governments, 1989-1999. National total, the Municipality of Budapest, the districts of the capital.) Budapest*

Ministry of Traffic, Transportation and Water Management, 1999: *'A közlekedés, hírközlés és a vízügy EU-csatlakozással összefüggő középtávú gazdaságstratégiai célkitűzései.' (Medium-term Strategic Goals of Traffic and Transportation, Telecommunication and Water Management in relation to EU-accession.) Budapest*

Montin, Stig, 2000: A Conceptual Framework. In: Amna, Erik and Montin, eds.: *Towards a New Concept of Local Self-government? Local Government Development in Comparative Perspective. Bergen: Fagbokforlaget.*

Moody's Investor's Service, 2002: *'Moody's assigns A3 issuer ratings to the city of Budapest'. Fundamental Credit Research, Rating Action, Published 29 Aug 2002. London*

Official Gazette of the Republic of Hungary, 1991–2001: *Annual State Budget Acts. Budapest*

ÖKO, 2001: *'Az 1997-2000. évi csatorna-, távhő és hulladékkezelési közszolgáltatási díjmegállapítások értékelése.' (Evaluation of the Pricing System of the Public Utility Services in the Fields of Solid Waste and Waste Water Collection and District Heating in the years 1997-2000.) Budapest*

Pallai, Katalin, 1998a: *Közüzemi privatizáció Budapesten. (Public Utility Privatization in Budapest.) The Office of the Mayor of Budapest, Budapest*

Pallai, Katalin, 1998b: *'Dél-budapesti "közlekedési játék", avagy Dél-Budapest közlekedési problémájának stratégiai játék formájában való elemzése'. "Transportation Game" in South-Budapest, or the Analysis of the Trasportation Problems of South-Budapest in the Form of a Strategic Game. Tér és Társadalom, No 3-4, pp. 133-153.*

Pallai, Katalin, 1998c: '*Financial Management and reform of the Municipality of Budapest 1990-1998. Study prepared for The Office of the Mayor of Budapest.*

Pickvance, C., 1995a: '*Marxist Theories of Urban Politics*', in: *Judge et al. eds., 1995: pp. 253–275.*

Pickvance, C., 1995b: 'Decentalization and Democracy in Eastern Europe: *C Sceptical Approach*' *Conference paper on the Conference on Democratization and Decentralization: From Years of Local Transformation in Central and Eastern Europe, 2–6 August 1995, Cracow, p. 27.*

Regulska, Johanna, 1996: *Decentralisation and Deconcentration: Sruggle for Political Power in Poland. Environment and Planning C: Government and Policy 14.*

Sharp, Elaine B., 1990: Urban Politics and Administration: *From Service Delivery to Economic Development. New York: Longman.*

State Audit Office, 2001: '*0123 sz. Jelentés a nagyvárosi tömegközlekedés feladatellátásának és finanszírozásának ellenőrzéséről.*' (*Report No. 0123 on the Control of Metropolitan Public Transport concerning the Services and their Financing.) Budapest*

Stoker, Gerry, 1997: '*From New Right to New Labour: Tensions and Hopes in the Reform of British Local Government.*' *Paper presented for International Seminar, Oslo, 12-13 December 1997.*

Stoker, Gerry, 1998: '*From New Management to New Labour: Tensions and Hopes in the Reform of British Local Government.*' *Paper for the Norwegian Research Council's Workshop in Copenhagen, Denmark. 16 – 18 April, 1988, p. 30.*

Stoker, Gerry, 1991: '*Introduction: Trends in European Local Government*', in Batley, R. and Stoker, G., eds.: *Local Government in Europe: Trends and Developments. Basingstoke, Macmillan.*

The home page of the Ministry of Home Affairs: *http://www.b-m.hu/onkormányzat.hu/*

The home page of the State Audit Office: *www.asz.hu*

The Municipality of Budapest, 2002-2003: *Figures from municipal companies.*

The Office of the Mayor of Budapest, 1991: '*Budapest Főváros Önkormányzata 1991. évi költségvetése.*' (*Annual Budget of the Municipality of Budapest, 1991.) Budapest*

The Office of the Mayor of Budapest, 1992a: '*Budapest Főváros Önkormányzata 1992. évi költségvetése.*' (*Annual Budget of the Municipality of Budapest, 1992.) Budapest*

The Office of the Mayor of Budapest, 1992b: '*Budapest kiemelt középtávú fejlesztési céljai.*'[3] (*Budapest's Priority Medium-term Development Goals.) Budapest*

---

[3] Project leader: dr István Schneller, deputy mayor. Experts: dr. Balázs Arató, dr. Zoltán Csorba, Katalin Gyarmati, Aba Hadházy, Viktória Hegedűs, dr. Károly Oszkó, Katalin Pallai, Katalin Pongrácz, István Pólay, Zoltán Sági, János Schulek, Sándor Simonyi, László Sipos, István Soltész.

The Office of the Mayor of Budapest, 1993: *'Fejlesztési program 1993-94.' (Budapest's Capital Investment Program, 1993-94.) Budapest*

The Office of the Mayor of Budapest, 1994a: *'Privatizációs koncepció.' (Conception on Privatization. Presentation to the General Assembly, July 14, 1994.) Budapest*

The Office of the Mayor of Budapest, 1994b: *'Budapest Városfejlesztési Koncepciója, térszerkezet.'*[4] *(Budapest's Urban Development Conception, Spatial Structure. Discussion document.) Budapest*

The Office of the Mayor of Budapest, 1995a: *'A Főváros hitelpolitikája.' (The Borrowing Policy of the Municipality.) Memorandum of the deputy mayor. Budapest*

The Office of the Mayor of Budapest, 1995b: *'Fővárosi fenntartású intézmények gazdálkodási reformja.' (The Financial Management Reform of the Municipal Institutions. Presentation to the Cabinet of the Mayor.) Budapest*

The Office of the Mayor of Budapest, 1995c: *'Koncepcióvázlat az 1996. évi költségvetéshez.' (Draft Conception for the 1996 Budget. Memorandum of the deputy mayor.) Budapest*

The Office of the Mayor of Budapest, 1996a: *'Tervkoordinációs csoport létrehozásáról.' (On the Creation of a Group for Plan Coordination. Presentation to the Cabinet of the Mayor.) Budapest*

The Office of the Mayor of Budapest, 1996b: *'Irányelvek az intézményracionalizálási célú célkeretek felhasználására.' (Regulatory Guidelines for the Institution Rationalization Brackets. Memorandum of the deputy mayor.) Budapest*

The Office of the Mayor of Budapest, 1996c: *'Javaslat Budapest Főváros Önkormányzata 1997. évi költségvetési koncepciójára.' (Proposal for the 1997 Budget Conception of the Municipality of Budapest.) Budapest*

The Office of the Mayor of Budapest, 1998a: *'Hitel- és beruházáspolitika.' (Investment and Borrowing Policy. Memorandum of the deputy mayor.) Budapest*

The Office of the Mayor of Budapest, 1998b: *'Javaslat Budapest Főváros Önkormányzata 1999. évi költségvetési koncepciójára.' (Proposal for the 1999 Budget Conception of the Municipality of Budapest.) Budapest*

The Office of the Mayor of Budapest, 1998c: *'Budapest Városfejlesztési Koncepciója.'*[5] *(Budapest's Urban Development Conception. Coordination document.) Budapest*

The Office of the Mayor of Budapest, 1998d: *'Legal and Financial Information.' Yearbook. Budapest*

---

[4] Project leader: dr. István Schneller, deputy mayor. Experts: dr. Zoltán Csorba, Viktória Hegedűs, József Raab, Sándor Simonyi (from the Urban Development Department of the Office of the Mayor); Mihály Lelkes, Krisztina Liszkai, Ottó Szenczi (from BUVÁTI Co.).

[5] Project leaders: Katalin Pallai, Iván Tosics. Strategy-team: Pál Baros, Györgyi Barta, Judit Bányai, Zoltán Erő, Lajos Koszorú, Gábor Locsmándi, László Molnár, Katalin Pallai, Péter Schuchmann, János Schulek, Iván Tosics.

The Office of the Mayor of Budapest, 1999a: *'Tájékoztató a normatív feladatfinanszírozásról és a nullabázisú költségvetés-tervezésről.'* *(Information on Normative Task Financing and Zero Based Budgeting. The deputy mayor's report to the Financial Committee.) Budapest*

The Office of the Mayor of Budapest, 1999b: *'Budapest Városfejlesztési Koncepciója.'*[6] *(Budapest's Urban Development Conception. Draft submitted to professional and public dispute.) Budapest*

The Office of the Mayor of Budapest, 1999c: *'Javaslat Budapest Főváros Önkormányzata 2000. évi költségvetési koncepciójára. (Proposal for the 2000 Budget Conception of the Municipality of Budapest.) Budapest*

The Office of the Mayor of Budapest, 2000a: *'Alternatívák' (Alternatives. Presentation to the Cabinet of the Mayor) Budapest*

The Office of the Mayor of Budapest, 2000b: *'Javaslat Budapest Főváros Önkormányzatának 2001. évi költségvetési koncepciójára.'* *(Proposal for the 2001 Budget of the Municipality of Budapest.) Budapest*

The Office of the Mayor of Budapest, 2000c: *'Legal and Financial Information.' Yearbook. Budapest*

The Office of the Mayor of Budapest, 2000d: *'A Fővárosi Önkormányzat gazdálkodása az 1991-1999. évi tényleges teljesítések és a 2000. évi tervadatok tükrében.'* *(The Economic Management of the Municipality of Budapest on the basis of the 1991-1999 records and the planned figures for 2000.) City-hall Papers, Budapest*

The Office of the Mayor of Budapest, 2001: *'Javaslat a Budapest Fővárosi Önkormányzat 2002. évi költségvetési koncepciójára.'* *(Proposal for the 2002 Budget Conception of the Municipality of Budapest.) Budapest*

The Office of the Mayor of Budapest, 2002a: *'Budapest Városfejlesztési Koncepciója.'*[7] *(Budapest's Urban Development Conception.) Budapest*

The Office of the Mayor of Budapest, 2002b: *'A Fővárosi Önkormányzat gazdálkodása az 1991-2001. évi tényleges teljesítések és a 2002. évi tervadatok tükrében.'* *(The Economic Management of the Municipality of Budapest on the basis of the 1991-2001 records and the planned figures for 2002.) City-hall Papers, Budapest*

The Office of the Mayor of Budapest, 2002c: *'Budapest az első S&P által minősített magyar helyi önkormányzat.'* *(The Municipality of Budapest is the First Hungarian Local Government Rated by S&P. Press release, 29 Aug.) Budapest*

---

[6] Project leaders: Katalin Pallai, Iván Tosics. Strategy-team: Pál Baros, Györgyi Barta, Judit Bányai, Éva Beleznay, Zoltán Erő, Lajos Koszorú, Gábor Locsmándi, László Molnár, Katalin Pallai, Péter Schuchmann, János Schulek, Iván Tosics, András Török.

[7] Project leaders: Katalin Pallai (till the end of 2000), Iván Tosics. Strategy-team: Pál Baros, Györgyi Barta, Zoltán Erő, Lajos Koszorú, Gábor Locsmándi, Molnár László, Katalin Pallai (till the end of 2000), Péter Schuchmann, János Schulek, Iván Tosics.

The Office of the Mayor of Budapest, 2002d: *Figures from the Departments of the Office of the Mayor of Budapest – 2002-2003.*

The Office of the Mayor of Budapest, 2002e: *'Legal and Financial Information.'* Yearbook. Budapest

The Office of the Mayor of Budapest, 2003: *'A Fővárosi Önkormányzat gazdálkodása az elmúlt 10 évben.' (The Economic Management of the Municipality of Budapest in the past 10 years.) Review on the homepage of the Municipality, www.fph.hu*

The Office of the Mayor of Budapest, homepage: *www.budapest.hu*

The SZDSZ and MSZP party factions of the Municipality, 1995: *'Budapest várospolitikai feladatterve, 1995-98.' (Urban Policy Work Plan for Budapest, 1995-98. Attachment to the coalition agreement.)* Budapest

Valentiny, P., 2000a: *'Property Rights, Corporate Governance and Company Restructuring in Hungarian Energy Industries'. mimeo, January 2000, p. 25.*

Valentiny, P., 2000b: *'Az univerzális szolgáltatás és a közszolgáltatások értelmezéséről az Európai Unióban.' The Interpretation of Universal Services and Public Services in the European Union. Közgazdasági Szemle, April, 2000, pp. 341-360.*

Valentiny. P. 2000c: *'Economic Regulation of Public Utilities in Hungary.'. mimeo, October 2000, p. 28.*

ACTS AND DECREES

1. Act on Local Governments (Act No. LXV of 1990)
2. Act on Defining Prices (Act No. LXXXVII of 1990)
3. Act on Local Taxation (Act No. C of 1990)
4. Act on Accounting (Act No. XVIII of 1991)
5. Act on the Transfer of certain State Assetes to the Local Governments (Act No. XXXIII of 1991)
6. Act on the Local Governments of the Capital and the Districts of the Capital (Act No. XXIV of 1991)
7. Act on Public Finance (Act No. XXXVIII of 1992)
8. Act LXX., 1994 on the Cancellation of the "EXPO '96 Budapest" International Exhibition
9. Act on the Mandatory Resort to certain Local Public Utility Services (Act No. XLII of 1995)
10. Act on the Debt Settlement Procedure of the Local Governments (Act No. XXV of 1996)
11. Act on District Heating (Act No. XVIII of 1998)

12. Act on Social Management and on Social Benefits (Act No. III of 1993)

13. Act on Juvenile Care (Act No. XXXI of 1997)

14. Act on Public Education (Act No. CXXVIII of 1997

15. 1071/1994. (3 Aug.) Government Decree on the realization of certain outstanding investments of the municipality of the capital city through state financial means

16. 2067/1995 (6 March.) Government Decree on the effectuation of the Governmnet decree on concluding agreement to realize certain outstanding investments of the municipality of the captal city through state financial means

17. General Assembly Decree No. 49/1997. (13 Aug) on defining the prices employable for District Heating and on the amendment of the General Assembly Decree No. 13/1994 (31 March) on the employment of prices

18. General Assembly Decree No. 50/1998. (30 Oct.) on the regulation of the preparation, approval and execution of the investments and refurbishments at the Municipality of Budapest and at its intstitutions.

TABLE 1
REVENUES OF THE MUNICIPALITY OF BUDAPEST (thousand HUF)

Source: The Office of the Mayor

ITEM	1991 ACTUAL	%	1992 ACTUAL	%	1993 ACTUAL	%	1994 ACTUAL	%	1995 ACTUAL	%	1996 ACTUAL	%	1997 ACTUAL	%	1998 ACTUAL	%	1999 ACTUAL	%	2000 ACTUAL	%	2001 ACTUAL	%	2002 ACTUAL	%
a) State grant for operations	14,040,993	24.63	15,354,632	22.72	18,245,734	23.30	19,750,802	20.71	20,850,253	17.47	19,934,643	13.99	18,832,162	9.62	23,814,013	10.5	26,930,033	10.78	20,205,614	7.32	20,338,074	7.17	28,334,826	8.58
b) Targeted and specific purpose disbursements	1,635,000	2.87	1,949,484	2.88	1,772,615	2.26	2,007,987	2.11	2,380,030	1.99	2,291,090	1.61	2,170,057	1.11	4,005,438	1.77	4,773,602	1.91	4,665,219	1.69	5,695,614	2.01	721,864	0.22
Total budgetary grant	15,675,993	27.50	17,304,116	25.60	20,018,349	25.56	21,758,789	22.81	23,230,283	19.46	22,225,733	15.60	21,002,219	10.73	27,819,451	12.27	31,703,635	12.69	24,870,833	9.01	26,033,688	9.18	29,056,690	8.80
Personal income tax	9,403,148	16.49	12,139,737	17.96	9,338,667	11.93	11,682,912	12.25	13,720,264	11.49	16,142,973	11.33	18,914,371	9.66	16,819,340	7.42	13,417,355	5.37	11,812,695	4.28	14,100,570	4.97	15,592,979	4.72
Health care transfers from the Social Security Fund	15,525,133	27.23	17,526,178	25.93	17,246,957	22.03	21,692,513	22.74	24,096,673	20.19	28,351,523	19.90	30,671,877	15.67	33,360,342	14.71	37,520,852	15.01	40,829,649	14.77	43,829,964	15.45	53,320,787	16.15
Total centrally regulated funds	40,604,274	71.22	46,970,031	69.50	46,603,973	59.52	55,134,214	57.81	61,047,220	51.14	66,720,229	46.84	70,588,467	36.07	77,999,133	34.4	82,641,842	33.07	77,513,177	28.06	83,964,222	29.60	97,970,456	29.68
Own revenues in the reporting year	12,224,891	21.44	17,320,303	25.63	21,651,604	27.65	30,116,579	31.58	43,294,875	36.27	57,241,641	40.18	106,601,797	54.47	85,132,624	37.55	105,615,686	42.28	114,928,606	41.62	106,203,543	37.44	116,912,748	35.42
Current revenues	9,336,569	16.38	15,271,366	22.60	18,810,928	24.02	19,534,022	20.48	23,265,719	19.49	39,487,092	27.72	57,441,571	29.35	70,196,549	30.95	91,150,642	36.48	94,861,938	34.35	91,856,701	32.38	100,421,845	30.42
a) operating revenues of institutions (including VAT)	5,344,742	9.37	5,773,940	8.54	6,444,167	8.23	8,149,888	8.54	8,748,339	7.33	14,007,692	9.83	23,931,465	12.23	30,273,137	13.35	32,174,140	12.88	32,365,460	11.72	28,795,996	10.15	30,791,025	9.33
b) local taxes	281,194	0.49	3,930,131	5.82	6,527,347	8.34	7,425,780	7.79	9,897,501	8.29	18,255,210	12.82	24,709,641	12.63	29,357,121	12.94	46,955,005	18.79	46,737,270	16.92	50,243,383	17.71	56,919,012	17.24
- business tax	–	–	–	–	–	–	–	–	9,725,771	8.15	17,837,017	12.52	24,240,246	12.39	28,758,921	12.68	46,364,516	18.55	46,088,012	16.68	49,542,720	17.46	56,304,473	17.06
- tourism tax	–	–	–	–	–	–	–	–	171,730	0.14	418,193	0.29	469,571	0.24	598,200	0.26	590,489	0.24	649,258	0.24	700,663	0.25	614,539	0.19
c) stamp duties	2,894,892	5.08	2,850,908	4.22	2,708,010	3.46	1,897,676	1.99	2,972,929	2.49	4,270,369	3.00	5,723,662	2.92	6,729,971	2.97	7,765,517	3.11	10,020,899	3.63	6,405,417	2.26	6,698,324	2.03
d) environmental fine	–	–	30,267	0.04	15,466	0.02	19,529	0.02	32,863	0.03	39,550	0.03	46,902	0.02	30,603	0.01	294	0.00	–	–	–	–	–	–
e) other specific revenues	–	–	558,173	0.83	571,414	0.73	336,694	0.35	371,275	0.31	468,304	0.33	562,940	0.29	716,175	0.32	921,985	0.37	1,217,643	0.44	1,117,233	0.39	1,073,297	0.33
f) funds received for operating purposes	815,741	1.43	2,127,947	3.15	2,544,524	3.25	1,704,455	1.79	1,242,812	1.04	2,445,967	1.72	2,466,785	1.26	3,089,542	1.36	3,333,701	1.33	4,520,666	1.64	5,294,672	1.87	4,940,187	1.50
Accumulation and capital-type revenues	2,888,322	5.07	2,048,937	3.03	2,840,676	3.63	10,582,557	11.10	20,029,156	16.78	17,754,549	12.46	49,160,226	25.12	14,936,075	6.60	14,465,044	5.80	20,066,668	7.27	14,346,842	5.06	16,490,903	5.00
a) sale of tangible assets	–	–	231,701	0.34	524,417	0.67	1,270,518	1.33	1,042,150	0.87	1,040,780	0.73	2,369,914	1.21	1,512,151	0.67	2,231,204	0.89	3,148,570	1.14	970,673	0.34	1,348,258	0.41
b) sale of flats owned by the municipality	–	–	–	–	–	–	18,717	0.02	1,067,034	0.89	786,538	0.55	9,109,761	4.65	492,413	0.22	743,998	0.30	485,638	0.18	578,967	0.20	1,164,748	0.35
c) revenues from privatisation	–	–	1,141,077	1.69	923,739	1.18	654,980	0.69	28,166	0.02	35,859	0.03	51,764	0.03	2,331,440	1.03	27,062	0.01	23,145	0.01	35,842	0.01	20,855	0.01
d) revenues from the sale of companies	–	–	–	–	–	–	–	–	1,300,365	1.09	2,387,704	1.68	5,490,547	2.81	3,456,604	1.52	1,824,130	0.73	56,948	0.02	24,182	0.01	3,061,187	0.93
e) sale of other pecuniary rights	–	–	65,183	0.10	279,598	0.36	545,824	0.57	53,195	0.04	25,383	0.02	22,785	0.01	20,839	0.01	15,385	0.01	14,992	0.01	11,155	0.00	11,759	0.00
f) rent revenue on other assets	–	–	–	–	–	–	–	–	–	–	–	–	–	–	–	–	–	–	200,160	0.08	2,474,899	0.90	1,068,586	0.38	1,375,586	0.42
g) return on financial investments	–	–	–	–	188,000	0.24	1,146,355	1.20	14,312,229	11.99	7,656,848	5.38	35,533,641	18.16	1,530,022	0.68	4,785,364	1.92	9,767,501	3.53	2,977,049	1.05	3,236,465	0.98
- sale of shares and stakes	–	–	–	–	–	–	–	–	13,927,726	11.67	7,397,179	5.19	35,285,125	18.03	515,917	0.23	2,898,138	1.16	7,240,695	2.62	366,319	0.13	16,990	0.01
- dividends and yields received	–	–	–	–	–	–	–	–	384,503	0.32	259,669	0.18	248,516	0.13	1,014,105	0.45	1,887,226	0.76	2,526,806	0.91	2,610,730	0.92	3,219,475	0.98
h) funds received for accumulation	1,254,646	2.20	610,976	0.90	924,922	1.18	6,946,163	7.28	2,226,017	1.87	5,821,437	4.09	4,781,814	2.44	5,592,606	2.47	4,637,741	1.86	4,094,975	1.48	8,680,388	3.06	6,272,045	1.90
Total revenues in the reporting year	52,829,165	92.66	64,290,334	95.13	68,255,577	87.17	85,250,793	89.38	104,342,095	87.42	123,961,870	87.02	177,190,264	90.54	163,131,757	71.95	188,257,528	75.35	192,441,783	69.68	190,167,765	67.04	214,883,204	65.10
Residual funds	2,539,237	4.45	1,962,258	2.90	3,696,056	4.72	2,871,940	3.01	2,993,365	2.51	3,905,398	2.74	5,005,058	2.56	3,617,665	1.60	8,719,580	3.49	9,539,537	3.45	15,035,944	5.30	32,140,456	9.74
Redemption of Government securities	1,065,761	1.87	784,127	1.16	31,470	0.04	524,200	0.55	191,234	0.16	8,144,115	5.72	11,857,474	6.06	40,015,080	17.64	50,552,619	20.22	68,494,520	24.80	62,976,396	22.20	46,304,242	14.03
a) maturity within one year	–	–	–	–	–	–	–	–	–	–	8,144,115	5.72	11,292,174	5.77	34,727,694	15.31	35,374,235	14.15	43,427,971	15.72	41,208,642	14.53	29,929,965	9.07
of which: municipality	–	–	–	–	–	–	–	–	–	–	8,143,176	5.72	11,292,174	5.77	34,727,694	15.31	35,348,718	14.14	43,379,755	15.7	41,208,642	14.53	–	–
institutions	–	–	–	–	–	–	–	–	–	–	939	0.00	–	–	–	–	25,517	0.01	48,216	0.02	–	–	–	–
b) maturing over one year (municipality)	–	–	–	–	–	–	–	–	–	–	–	–	–	–	563,300	0.29	5,287,386	2.33	15,178,384	6.07	25,066,549	9.08	21,767,754	7.67	16,374,277	4.96
Total revenues	56,434,163	98.98	67,036,719	99.19	71,983,103	91.93	88,646,933	92.94	107,526,694	90.08	136,011,383	95.48	194,052,796	99.15	206,764,502	91.19	247,529,727	99.06	270,475,840	97.93	268,180,105	94.54	293,327,902	88.86
Loans	578,870	1.02	546,953	0.81	6,321,141	8.07	6,732,771	7.06	11,835,253	9.92	6,437,910	4.52	1,658,802	0.85	19,979,389	8.81	2,345,882	0.94	5,719,222	2.07	15,493,166	5.46	36,763,361	11.14
Grand total of revenues and loans	57,013,033	100.00	67,583,672	100.00	78,304,244	100.00	95,379,704	100.00	119,361,947	100.00	142,449,293	100.00	195,711,598	100.00	226,743,891	100.00	249,875,609	100.00	276,195,062	100.00	283,673,271	100.00	330,091,263	100.00

TABLE 1

REVENUES OF THE MUNICIPALITY OF BUDAPEST

DEFINITION OF REVENUE TITLE ITEMS[1]

- ### State grant for operations

  This item includes the equalised state grants linked to population and tasks, grants for theatres, central allocations, grants for the fire brigade, and complementary grants linked to individual tasks.

- ### Targeted and specific purpose disbursements

  This item includes specific purpose and targeted state grants earmarked for certain objectives of high social priority or large investment projects and developments allocated in the annual Budget Act.

- ### Personal income tax

  This item includes the portion of transferred personal income tax due to the City, the whole transfer to the capital having been allocated in the annual Budget Act and shared among the City and the Districts.

- ### Transfers from the Social Security Fund for health care

  Social security under state finance is a mandatory system of insurance derived from the common undertaking of risk by society, which operates in line with the principles of insurance and solidarity.

  Pursuant to law, the health care system comprises all health care service providers who have operating licenses for the provision of certain health care services on the basis of professional standards. For local governments owning and maintaining health care institutions and for the organisation responsible for the management of the National Health Insurance Fund (NHIF) providing health care is a mandatory duty. As part of this obligation, the owner provides the material and professional conditions required for the provision of the services, while NHIF directly finances the services provided by the institution; in short, it covers the operating costs. This amount is shown in the budget of the City under the title of "Transfers from the Social Security Fund for health care." This item accounts for about 90–95% of the operating expenses of the health care institutions affected. The annual projection is based on the data supplied by the institutions, generally taking actual performance of the previous years into consideration. No significant change in legislation — with an effect on the budgeting of the Municipality — can be envisaged in the years to come.

---

[1] From: The Office of the Mayor of Budapest, 2002e

– **Operating revenues of institutions**

Major categories of these revenues:

- revenues from core activities,
- other revenues related to core activities,
- other specific revenues of the institutions,
- VAT revenues and refunds,
- business revenues,
- interest income.

This item includes revenues of the budgetary units realised while performing the tasks set forth in their founding charters. The types of revenues are determined by legal provisions. In view of the fact that a given type of service is provided concurrently by a large number of institutions, fees are regulated on the basis of uniform principles. The first two categories include fees paid for services by recipients in residential institutions, the price of tickets and entrance tickets in cultural institutions and in museums, respectively. Specific revenues include the rental or the leasing fee of facilities and assets owned or managed by budgetary units. VAT revenues include amounts claimed back from the tax authority in relation to the institutions' taxable activities the input of which are charged by VAT as well as VAT paid by customers of their products, services and tangible assets sold. VAT received by the Mayor's Office relates to tax settlements for the individual investments in the sewage system. The interest revenues of the Mayor's Office are composed partly of interest from fixing temporarily free funds on the budgetary settlement accounts and partly interest from the fixing of funds managed on segregated accounts.

Local taxes (as a specific kind of operating revenue)

Authorised by legislation, the Municipality introduced local business tax and tourism tax over the administrative territory of the capital. Decree No. 21/1991. (IX. 5.) of the General Assembly (as amended) ordains the imposition of business tax payable from September 5, 1991, the rate of which changed over the years. Both types of taxes are shared between the Districts and the City.

– **Stamp duties (as a specific kind of operating revenues)**

This item includes the stamp duties due to the City by legislation, taking into consideration the provisions of the annual Budget Act on the local governments' share.

– **Environmental fine (as a specific kind of operating revenues)**

This item includes revenues from fines collected in the administrative territory of the Municipality in order to enforce the protection of the environment and historic monuments.

– **Other specific revenues**

This item includes the housing rents paid by tenants of flats owned by the City, revenues from the rentals of real property and other facilities, and charges for the use of public places.

- **Funds received for operating purposes**

  In the case of institutions, this item includes funds predominantly from competitive tendering as well as funds received from the Vocational Training Fund. In the Mayor's Office, this category includes, inter alia, funds directly related to specific tasks — benefits for the homeless unemployed and their employment for common good — as well as funds from BKV Rt. to cover World Bank interest payment obligations on loans, and funds from the Parking Association to operate the parking system.

- **Sale of tangible assets**

  In line with the accounting terminology this item includes revenues from the sale of pecuniary rights and intellectual property, real property and machinery owned, managed or used by the Municipality. These may include: buildings, land, real property, marketable plots and real property, all falling under the category of core assets, or revenues from the sale of land for housing development.

- **Sale of flats owned by the municipality (as a specific kind of accumulation and capital type revenues)**

  This item includes 50% of the revenues from the sale of flats in the ownership of the District Councils, revenues from the sale of flats in the ownership of the City and revenues from housing mobility and from the transfer of the right to assign tenants.

- **Revenues from privatisation (as a specific kind of accumulation and capital type revenues)**

  In case of the sale of non-public utility companies — operated earlier under Council control — by the Hungarian Privatisation and Holding Company (HPHC–ÁPV Rt.), 50% of revenues is due to the Municipality of Budapest as the legal successor of the company's founder. The revenue appears partly in cash, and partly in compensation notes. The above item includes revenues from this procedure.

- **Revenues from the sale of companies (as a specific kind of accumulation and capital type revenues)**

  This item includes revenues from the privatisation of companies sold by the City as well as 25% of the price of land due to be paid by HPHC to the City when selling state owned land with superstructure.

- **Sale of other pecuniary rights (as a specific kind of accumulation and capital type revenues)**

  This item includes revenues from the utilisation and sale of real property previously under Soviet control.

- **Return on financial investments are accounted for by the following categories:**
    - sale of shares and business stakes, which means revenues from the sale of public utility and portfolio shares (business stakes) and securities;
    - dividends and yields received, which includes revenues from shares.

- **Funds received for accumulation**

  This item includes funds received for the purposes of accumulation and to finance investment projects by the City and its institutions.

- **Residual funds**

  This item includes the amount of residual funds from the previous year and allocated for current year expenses in the annual budget. In the annual financial statement, this item includes residual funds consumed during the year.

- **Redemption of Government securities purchased in preceding years**

  This item includes the amount received when redeeming securities with maturity within and after one year, purchased — in line with legal provisions — in order to invest temporarily free funds.

- **Loans**

  This item includes loans that may be or have been obtained in line with legal provisions.

TABLE 2

EXPENDITURE OF THE MUNICIPALITY OF BUDAPEST

TABLE 2
EXPENDITURE OF THE MUNICIPALITY OF BUDAPEST (billion HUF)

Source: The Office of the Mayor

ITEM	1991 ACTUAL	%	1992 ACTUAL	%	1993 ACTUAL	%	1994 ACTUAL	%	1995 ACTUAL	%	1996 ACTUAL	%	1997 ACTUAL	%	1998 ACTUAL	%	1999 ACTUAL	%	2000 ACTUAL	%	2001 ACTUAL	%	2002 ACTUAL	%
Operating expenditure	46,5	84,6	53,4	81,2	58,7	78,7	66,2	71,9	75,9	65,8	88,2	64,2	102,3	53,5	115,2	53,0	130,0	54,4	138,0	53,1	147,3	59,0	188,1	68,2
Refurbishments	1,2	2,2	1,4	2,1	1,2	1,6	1,2	1,3	1,3	1,1	2,2	1,6	4,3	2,2	3,5	1,6	6,4	2,7	7,4	2,8	6,0	2,4	12,2	4,4
of which:																								
- road and bridge*	-	-	0,5	0,8	0,2	0,3	0,2	0,2	0,2	0,2	1,1	0,8	2,6	1,4	2,1	1,0	3,4	1,4	5,0	1,9	3,7	1,5	7,8	2,8
Capital and accumulation expenditures	7,0	12,8	10,6	16,1	14,3	19,2	21,8	23,7	24,8	21,5	24,9	18,1	44,3	23,1	50,7	23,3	58,2	24,3	73,1	28,1	64,1	25,7	59,7	21,6
of which:																								
- physical investments	7,0	12,8	10,6	16,1	14,3	19,2	21,8	23,7	24,8	21,5	20,6	15,0	26,4	13,8	35,8	16,5	37,2	15,6	44,3	17,0	42,2	16,9	55,5	20,1
- government securities	0,0	0,0	0,0	0,0	0,0	0,0	0,0	0,0	0,0	0,0	4,3	3,1	17,9	9,3	14,9	6,9	21,0	8,8	28,8	11,1	21,9	8,8	4,2	1,5
Debt service	0,0	0,0	0,0	0,0	0,1	0,1	2,5	2,7	5,3	4,6	10,8	7,9	5,8	3,0	12,6	5,8	1,2	0,5	0,5	0,2	2,4	1,0	2,7	1,0
Orther expenditure **	0,2	0,4	0,4	0,6	0,3	0,4	0,4	0,4	8,1	7,0	11,3	8,2	34,8	18,2	35,4	16,3	43,4	18,1	41,2	15,8	29,9	12,0	13,1	4,7
Total expenditure	54,9	100,0	65,8	100,0	74,6	100,0	92,1	100,0	115,4	100,0	137,4	100,0	191,5	100,0	217,4	100,0	239,2	100,0	260,2	100,0	249,7	100,0	275,9	100,0

* 1991 data is not available.

** Year-end balance of securities maturing within the year.

TABLE 3

BORROWING TRANSACTIONS OF THE MUNICIPALITY OF BUDAPEST

TABLE 3
BORROWING TRANSACTIONS OF THE MUNICIPALITY OF BUDAPEST

Source: The Office of the Mayor

TITLE	Type	CONTRACTED AMOUNT	YEAR OF LIABILITY	GRACE PERIOD	REMARK
Debt service taken over from obligations before 1992					
Budapest Congress Center	project	120000000 HUF	1986-2000		the part taken over
North-Pest Traffic Management Center	project	63100000 HUF	1995-2004		debt service from WB BKV loan
Borrowing in 1992					
Loan for vechicles for BKV	project	880000000 HUF	1992-1997	2 years	fully prepaid in 1996
Borrowing in 1993					
9 commercial bank contracts	general purpose	4937500000 HUF	1992-1998		prepaid in 1996, except for the 2 billion bond element that was repaid on schedule
	project	5 500 000 USD			
	project	8 000 000 DEM			
EBRD Public transportation loan	project	38 204 462 USD	1993-2008	3 years	fully prepaid in1998
	project	58 415 855 DEM			
Borrowing in1994					
5 commercial bank contract	general purpose	6000000000 HUF	1994-2000		prepaid in1996 and 1997
Borrowing in 1995					
3 commercial bank contracts	general purpose	3500000000 HUF	1995-2001		2,5 billion HUF draw down and prepaid in 1996
World Bank urban traffic loan	project	38 000 000 USD	1995-2010	5 years	in 2003 full prepayment
Borrowing from 1996					
Euro-bond	general purpose	150 000 000 DEM	1998-2003	5 years	will be paid at expiration date
World Bank, Waste Water loan	project	27 600 000 EUR	1999-2014	5 years	
EIB I, environment and Infrastructure project	project	110 000 000 EUR	1998-2003	6 years	started in 2001
EIB II: Infrastructure and Service development	project	370 000 000 EUR	2003-2028	7 years	
Syndicated loan	general purpose	130 000 000 EUR	2002-2009	2 years	

TABLE 4

REVENUES OF UTILITY COMPANIES

TABLE 4
REVENUES OF UTILITY COMPANIES (billion HUF)

Source: The Office of the Mayor

ITEM	1991	1992	1993	1994	1995	1996	1997	1998	1999	2000	2001	2002
Budapest Public Transport Co.												
User charge revenues	5,547	6,741	7,231	8,381	10,098	13,460	16,804	18,753	22,413	25,057	26,885	27,453
State user charge subsidy	3,214	4,403	4,940	5,835	7,485	9,441	10,995	12,606	13,550	14,538	15,779	16,798
Operating subsidy	9,580	11,500	11,377	11,250	11,804	12,794	11,567	12,995	14,204	14,200	14,205	16,202
Investment subsidy	0	547	261	1,801	6,904	4,585	1,948	2,748	5,999	8,039	14,948	12,844
Other reveneues	1,187	820	1,313	2,442	2,524	1,932	2,266	2,089	2,055	7,752	12,995	7,050
Total company revenues	19,528	24,011	25,122	29,709	38,815	42,212	43,580	49,191	58,221	69,586	84,812	80,347
Waterworks of Budapest Co.												
User charge revenues	3,451	4,289	5,686	6,697	8,869	10,188	12,069	13,836	14,789	17,684	20,419	20,986
Investment subsidy	140	64	26	2,090	2,499	1,033	104	103	60	37	0	42
Other reveneues	29	31	121	501	548	2,821	3,428	844	1,161	820	1,106	754
Total company revenues	3,636	4,339	5,890	7,390	9,792	13,222	16,549	16,768	17,198	19,386	21,971	22,253
Municipal Sewerage Works Co.												
User charge revenues	1,899	2,423	3,936	4,314	6,839	8,728	10,976	12,652	13,879	16,279	17,758	18,410
Other reveneues	644	677	1,166	870	849	1,199	3,940	4,725	6,007	7,247	9,582	8,825
Total company revenues	2,543	3,100	5,103	5,184	7,688	9,927	14,916	17,377	19,886	23,526	27,340	27,235
Budapest Gas Works Co.												
User charge revenues	25,692	23,916	25,702	24,035	31,525	41,943	54,194	59,224	61,151	63,189	76,722	81,723
Other reveneues			398	852	1,128	2,007	2,819	3,382	4,618	4,175	5,220	2,789
Total company revenues	25,692	23,916	26,100	24,886	32,653	43,950	57,013	62,606	65,769	67,364	81,942	84,512
Public Space Maintenance Co.												
User charge revenues												
Solid waste user charge						4,518	5,328	6,527	8,548	9,854	11,536	12,717
Municipal orders	2,587	3,966	4,310	4,874	5,190	2,222	2,706	3,321	3,534	3,911	4,485	6,723
- solid waste	1,970	2,165	2,444	2,601	3,184							
- public cleanliness	616	974	932	1,102	1,146	1,381	1,689	2,083	2,066	2,234	2,745	4,334
- road maintenece		827	934	1,171	861	841	1,017	1,238	1,468	1,677	1,740	2,389
Investment subsidy	70	48	94	213	268	832	670	440	3,161	1,864	161	777
Other reveneues	1,161	561	591	823	800	1,731	1,779	6,561	8,291	9,015	10,691	11,202
Total company revenuesn	3,747	4,527	4,901	5,698	5,990	8,470	9,813	16,409	20,372	22,780	26,712	30,642
Budapest District Heating Co.												
User charge revenues	7,100	8,702	10,254	11,521	16,488	20,201	26,138	28,324	28,210	29,280	32,584	34,931
Other reveneues	666	232	875	1,776	4,769	5,357	7,423	9,783	2,804	1,122	885	1,101
Operating subsidy	2,881											
Total company revenues	13,142	11,109	12,744	14,868	23,171	27,902	36,594	41,395	34,289	33,801	37,252	40,086
Budapest Public Bath and Spa Co.												
User charge revenues	683	761	670	850	1,202	1,464	1,747	2,093	2,357	2,848	3,656	3,940
Operating subsidy	80	0	113	120	252	282	282	282	232	182	152	164
Investment subsidy	0	0	5	0	0	0	26	216	1,125	1,294	1,604	2,477
Other reveneues	30	52	67	35	74	137	102	171	84	179	168	156
Total company revenues	793	812	854	1,005	1,527	1,883	2,157	2,762	3,797	4,503	5,581	6,737
Liquid Waste Management Co.												
User charge revenues	280	303	298	317	303	252	369	358	427	502	492	573
Operating subsidy	0	0	0	0	0	35	35	43	46	49	49	53
Investment subsidy	0	0	0	19	16	3	6	5	5	6	8	7
Other reveneues	20	15	17	8	15	25	20	16	28	71	33	48
Total company revenues	299	318	315	345	334	315	430	423	506	629	582	681
Total revenues of utility companies	69,380	72,133	81,029	89,084	119,970	147,882	181,051	206,929	220,037	241,575	286,190	292,493
Total of user charge revenues	47,866	51,539	58,717	61,950	82,809	110,195	138,619	154,374	165,324	179,232	205,831	217,530
Total of user charge + subsidy revenues	63,204	67,664	74,898	82,317	109,741	131,980	155,937	174,311	192,565	207,521	239,838	254,340
User charge in % of user charge + subsidy revenues	**76**	**76**	**78**	**75**	**75**	**83**	**89**	**89**	**86**	**86**	**86**	**86**
Revenues of the Municipality	52,829	64,290	68,256	85,251	104,342	123,962	177,190	163,132	188,258	192,442	190,168	214,883
Proportion of user charge and municipal revenues	**0.91**	**0.80**	**0.86**	**0.73**	**0.79**	**0.89**	**0.78**	**0.95**	**0.88**	**0.93**	**1.08**	**1.01**

TABLE 5

EXPENDITURES ON UTILITY SERVICES

TABLE 5
EXPENDITURES ON UTILITY SERVICES (billion HUF)

Source: The Office of the Mayor

ITEM	1991	1992	1993	1994	1995	1996	1997	1998	1999	2000	2001	2002
Budapest Public Transport Co.												
Operating expenditure of Co	19,898	23,378	25,118	28,818	35,653	44,739	51,471	57,074	63,479	68,472	76,978	79,860
Refurbishment expenditure of Co	0	1,791	1,741	2,309	2,812	2,267	2,550	4,783	3,903	5,302	5,526	6,387
Investmnet expenditure of Co	1,944	3,399	4,163	6,723	12,442	10,000	9,459	13,678	14,799	15,093	26,647	19,616
Total expenditure	21,842	28,568	31,022	37,850	50,907	57,006	63,480	75,535	82,181	88,867	109,151	105,863
Water supply												
Operating expenditure of Co		4,340	5,645	8,403	9,167	13,487	16,712	16,272	16,523	17,778	20,061	20,021
Refurbishment expenditure of Co	487	396	685	390	1,148	1,884	1,960	2,862	2,403	2,875	2,135	2,806
Investmnet expenditure of Co	167	163	248	218	366	1,101	350	278	1,564	581	413	1,223
Other investments*	0	40	415	271	694	237	106	239	550	955	879	1,005
Total expenditure	653	4,940	6,994	9,282	11,374	16,709	19,127	19,651	21,041	22,189	23,488	25,055
Waste water management												
Operating expenditure of Co	2,526	3,041	3,720	5,151	6,320	7,383	12,254	12,274	13,821	17,123	18,617	18,908
Refurbishment expenditure of Co	622	538	444	547	1,402	1,682	1,732	1,811	2,966	4,558	4,544	4,614
Investmnet expenditure of Co	335	899	1,648	2,904	3,150	2,494	1,655	910	410	2,424	805	1,236
Other investments*	83	96	112	125	116	141	693	610	780	1,755	1,632	1,870
Total expenditure	3,566	4,574	5,924	8,727	10,988	11,700	16,334	15,605	17,977	25,860	25,598	26,628
Budapest Gas Works Co												
Operating expenditure of Co	24,078	22,973	24,851	24,018	30,144	39,779	51,072	57,442	57,421	58,941	72,562	76,773
Refurbishment expenditure of Co	337	291	307	172	281	421	886	781	944	804	566	956
Investmnet expenditure of Co	523	968	1,464	2,534	2,061	1,726	3,083	3,032	4,061	3,887	4,590	4,668
Total expenditure	24,937	24,232	26,623	26,723	32,487	41,926	55,040	61,255	62,426	63,631	77,717	82,396
Public Space Maintenance Co												
Operating expenditure of Co	3,588	4,605	4,998	5,847	6,453	8,470	9,810	16,240	19,852	22,330	26,272	29,951
- solid waste	1,681	1,525	1,972	2,352	3,128	4,158	4,940	6,199	7,495	8,859	9,975	11,378
- public cleaniness	677	1,094	1,141	1,032	1,397	1,481	1,757	2,055	2,264	2,341	2,881	4,316
- road maintenace	0	0	103	1,244	959	1,468	1,141	1,299	1,734	1,900	2,045	2,807
- others	1,231	1,987	1,782	1,219	969	1,363	1,972	6,686	8,360	9,230	11,371	11,451
Refurbishment expenditure of Co	0	0	0	0	0	0	0	0	0	0	0	0
Investmnet expenditure of Co	1,003	571	544	957	313	971	2,282	1,364	2,162	7,144	3,605	3,846
Other Municipal expenditures*	1,323	1,644	1,742	469	1,235	2,338	1,576	1,179	1,472	1,186	1,412	1,115
Total expenditure	5,914	6,820	7,283	7,273	8,002	11,779	13,668	18,782	23,486	30,660	31,289	34,912
Budapest District Heating Co												
Operating expenditure of Co	10,313	8,847	9,022	10,230	13,895	18,512	23,727	25,748	25,687	25,460	29,195	29,411
Refurbishment expenditure of Co	736	289	418	787	1,287	2,012	1,562	1,907	2,139	2,122	1,382	2,004
Investmnet expenditure of Co	372	198	206	512	935	426	579	991	803	2,713	1,648	3,130
Total expenditure	11,421	9,334	9,645	11,529	16,118	20,950	25,868	28,647	28,628	30,296	32,225	34,545
Budapest Public Bath and Spa Cot												
Operating expenditure of Co	787	883	894	998	1,532	1,883	2,127	2,545	2,797	3,288	3,911	4,463
Refurbishment expenditure of Co	0	57	0	14	27	12	13	35	27	57	69	106
Investmnet expenditure of Co	98	116	87	76	125	190	124	416	1,228	1,309	1,759	2,704
Total expenditure	886	1,056	981	1,088	1,684	2,085	2,263	2,995	4,052	4,654	5,739	7,274
Liquid Waste Management Co												
Operating expenditure of Co	278	376	332	374	374	342	442	438	519	622	623	667
Refurbishment expenditure of Co	0	0	0	0	0	0	0	0	0	0	0	0
Investmnet expenditure of Co	23	9	6	30	17	14	24	35	30	131	129	41
Total expenditure	301	385	338	403	391	356	466	474	549	753	753	708
Total expenditure of utility companies	68,114	78,130	86,541	102,011	129,906	159,795	193,871	220,916	237,538	263,015	302,037	313,391
Total expenditure on utilities	69,520	79,910	88,809	102,876	131,951	162,511	196,246	222,944	240,339	266,912	305,961	317,381
Expenditures of the Municipal budget	54,700	65,400	74,200	89,200	102,000	115,300	150,900	169,400	194,600	218,500	217,400	260,000
Proportion of utilities' and municipal expenditure	1.25	1.19	1.17	1.14	1.27	1.39	1.28	1.30	1.22	1.20	1.39	1.21

TABLE 6

ARREARS OF USER CHARGES

TABLE 6
ARREARS OF USER CHARGES (billion HUF)

Source: Utility Companies

TITLE	1991	1992	1993	1994	1995	1996	1997	1998	1999	2000	2001	2002
Waterworks of Budapest Co												
Arrears within year*												
Cummulative arrears*	552	849	1,508	2,197	2,961	2,708	2,742	2,897	2,797	3,485	3,027	3,163
Charges for small users**				76	1,289	2,521	3,191	3,983	7,021	10,524	11,723	13,010
Revenues from small users**				70	1,110	2,295	2,904	3,625	6,370	9,546	10,725	12,139
Municipal Sewerage Works Co												
Arrears within year*	–48	97	382	444	907	363	340	83	215	198	2	60
Cummulative arrears*	379	476	858	1302	2209	2572	2912	2995	3211	3409	3411	3471
Charges for small users**						1664	2291	2955	3528	4542	5157	5935
Revenues from small users**						1523	2096	2718	3327	4296	4894	5639
Budapest Gas Works Co												
Arrears within year*	–	–	–	–	–	981	1265	1302	1998	1361	1449	1645
Cummulative arrears*	–	–	–	–	–	1433	1730	1782	2573	2015	2081	2164
Arrears sold in the given year	–	–	–	–	–	–	–	–	–	–	112	369
Sale price of arrears	–	–	–	–	–	–	–	–	–	–	31	125
Loss from factoring											81	244
Public Space Maintenance Co												
User charges *						3,280	4,160	4,926	5,898	6,739	8,004	8,983
Revenues form user charges *						2,985	3,785	4,482	5,497	6,294	7,492	8,427
Budapest District Heating Co												
Arrears within year*	120	320	141	431	456	961	718	1,254	1,233	2,227	1,325	1,363
Cummulative arrears*	467	787	915	723	484	1,445	2,163	1,461	407	1,828	1,806	1,734
Arrears sold in the given year	0	0	176	1,186	3,581	3,622	5,345	8,339	2,287	806	1,347	1,435
Sale price of arrears	0	0	158	913	3,119	3,368	4,971	6,875	1,098	182	380	402
Loss from factoring			18	273	463	254	374	1,464	1,189	624	967	1,033

* The figures refer to the charges billed for the large consumers by the company itself.

** Collection of the charges of the small users is managed by a utility charge collecting company.
· The collection rates to be achieved are fixed in the collection contracts each year.

DETAILED TABLE OF CONTENTS

438

G<small>RAPHIC DESIGN AND LAYOUT</small>
SmartWorks Ltd, Budapest

D<small>ESIGNER AND OPERATOR</small>
Viktor Baranyi

Printed in Hungary by Arktisz Design Studio